Forty Years of Innovation in Chinese Economic Theory

Zhuoyuan Zhang, Jiayong Hu, and Jun Wan
Translated by Yongbin Sun and Xiaobing Qu

Forty Years of Innovation in Chinese Economic Theory

PETER LANG

New York · Berlin · Bruxelles · Chennai · Lausanne · Oxford

Bibliographic information published by the Deutsche Nationalbibliothek
The Deutsche Nationalbibliothek lists this publication in the Deutsche Nationalbibliografie; detailed bibliographic data are available on the Internet at https://dnb.dnb.de.

Library of Congress Cataloging-in-Publication Data
A CIP catalog record for this book has been applied for at the Library of Congress.

This book's publication is subsidized by Chinese Fund for the Humanities and Social Sciences.
The original version was written by Zhang Zhuoyuan, Hu Jiayong, and Wan Jun.

ISBN 978-3-0343-5975-7 (Print)
ISBN 978-3-0343-5973-3 (ePDF)
ISBN 978-3-0343-5974-0 (ePUB)
DOI 10.3726/b23794

Published by Peter Lang Publishing Inc., New York, USA

info@peterlang.com

This is an authorized translation from the Chinese language edition.
Published by arrangement with China Renmin University Press Co., Ltd.

This publication has been peer reviewed.

www.peterlang.com

Contact for General Product Safety Regulation (GPSR): gpsr@peterlang.com.

Contents

Figure and Tables

Chapter 5: Theory of Income Distribution

Chapter 8: Theory of Economic Development

The Emergence and Evolution of Economic Theory of Socialism with Chinese Characteristics

With the launch of the reform and opening-up (hereafter R&O) policy in 1978, China began a remarkable journey of rapid economic growth. Society has changed with each passing day, creating one miracle after another that has amazed the world. Back in 1978, when the reforms were just beginning, China's per capita GDP amounted to a paltry 190 US dollars, and the issues of basic subsistence—such as adequate food and clothing—remained unresolved. However, after nearly four decades of sustained development, this figure had soared to around 9,000 US dollars by 2017, elevating China into a country categorized as upper-middle-income. The country then stands at a critical juncture—approaching the full realization of an all-round moderately prosperous society while progressing toward a modernized economy. These sweeping changes are firmly anchored in the course of socialism with Chinese characteristics. As General Secretary Xi Jinping emphasized in his speech delivered at the 19th National Congress of the Communist Party of China (hereafter the Congress): "Socialism with Chinese characteristics has been the focus of all of the Party's theories and practice since reform and opening up began. It is the fundamental achievement of our Party and our people made through countless hardships at enormous cost. The path of socialism with Chinese characteristics is the only path to socialist modernization and a better life for the people. The theory of socialism with Chinese characteristics is the right theory to guide the Party and people to realize national rejuvenation. The system of socialism with Chinese characteristics provides the fundamental institutional guarantee for progress and development in contemporary China. The culture of socialism with Chinese characteristics is a powerful source of strength that inspires all members of the Party and the people of all ethnic groups in China." As socialist practice in China has advanced, the theory of socialism with Chinese characteristics—economic theory included—has developed accordingly and now exerts a more significant influence on shaping practice.

1. Deng Xiaoping's Original Proposal for Building Socialism with Chinese Characteristics

As an essential element, the economic theory plays a central role within the theoretical system of socialism with Chinese characteristics. To study the formation and development of this economic theory, we must first understand the formation and development of socialism with Chinese characteristics.

Socialism with Chinese characteristics was first proposed by Deng Xiaoping. On September 1, 1982, Deng Xiaoping mentioned in the "Opening Speech at the 12th National Congress of the Communist Party of China": "We must integrate the universal truth of Marxism with the concrete realities of China, blaze a path of our own and build a socialism with Chinese characteristics—that is the basic conclusion we have reached after reviewing our long history."

The context in which Deng Xiaoping introduced the idea concerning socialism with Chinese characteristics can be discerned through several key historical factors.

First, it was essential to reflect on and draw lessons from the over 30 years of socialist progress since the People's Republic of China came into being, especially the overall mistakes of the "Cultural Revolution." The 11th Central Committee's Third Plenary Session, held in late 1978, abandoned "taking class struggle as the key link," shifting the Party's focus to economic construction while initiating the R&O process. This session fundamentally broke free from the long-existing shackles of "Leftist" mistakes, corrected the ideological orientation of the Party, and reaffirmed the Marxist line with regard to ideological, political, and organizational aspects. Since then, the Party has undertaken a comprehensive review of its historical experience from multiple dimensions, and scientifically expounded many theoretical and policy issues related to socialist construction raised from practice. Later in June 1981, the Sixth Plenary Session formally adopted the "Resolution on Certain Questions in the History of the Party since the Founding of the People's Republic of China," which marked the successful finalization of this correction to the Party's guiding ideology.

Second, the nascent stage of the R&O process showed that China's economy was full of vitality, and economic growth accelerated as market mechanisms began to take effect. By adopting the "Contract Responsibility System for Households," rural productive forces saw a significant release, leading to a swift recovery and rapid growth in agricultural output. The combined output value of agricultural, forestry, livestock, and fishery industries in 1982 increased by 29.2% compared with 1978, with an average yearly growth of 6.6%, over twice the historical average growth rate of 2% to 3%. After easing price restrictions on selected farm and sideline products as well as consumer commodities, there was a dramatic surge in market supply capacity, and the same went for other sectors. Pilot programs for special economic zones (SEZs) and efforts to seek foreign investment began to achieve preliminary results. These positive developments reflected the tremendous potential inherent in the country's R&O efforts, which was quickly recognized and supported by the Chinese people, simultaneously boosting their national confidence.

Third, some visionary people have questioned the traditional economic theory and system of socialism since the 1950s, and have suggested that the construction of socialism should respect objective economic laws, especially the law of value. In 1956, Sun Yefang published an article entitled "Placing planning and statistical work on the basis of the law of value" in the sixth issue of *Economic Research Journal*. Gu Zhun also published an article entitled "A tentative discussion on commodity production and the law of value under the socialist system" in the same journal (Issue 3, 1957), proposing a bold proposition that allows enterprises to adjust production according to price fluctuations. Yu Guangyuan argued that all types of products in circulation should be recognized as commodities.[1] Before the convening of the 11th CPC Central Committee's Third Plenary Session, an article "Act in accordance with economic laws and accelerate the realization of the Four Modernizations"—penned by Hu Qiaomu and published in the *People's Daily* on October 6, 1978—also highlighted the significance of respecting the law of value. All of these provided the ideological and theoretical framework for the commencement of R&O in late 1978 and Deng Xiaoping's initial proposal of socialism with Chinese characteristics soon after.

Socialism featuring Chinese characteristics is constantly enriched and refined in tandem with evolving practices, especially the R&O practice. The broader R&O initiative has advanced steadily, accompanied by notable economic growth and overall social progress. By 1997, the year of the 15th Congress, socialism with Chinese characteristics was deemed to have established a scientific system. Jiang Zemin elaborated in his congressional report: "To sum up, *Deng Xiaoping Theory* constitutes a new, scientific system of the theory of building socialism with Chinese characteristics. It has been gradually formed and developed under the historical conditions in which peace and development have become the main

1 Guangyuan Yu. Discussion on the problem of commodity production under the socialist system. *Economic Research Journal*, 1959 (7).

themes of the times, in the practice of China's reform, opening up and modernization drive, and on the basis of reviewing the historical experience of successes and setbacks of socialism in China and learning from the historical experience of the rise and fall of other socialist countries. For the first time, it has given preliminary but systematic answers to a series of basic questions concerning the road to socialism in China, the stages of development, the fundamental tasks, the motive force, the external conditions, the political guarantee, the strategic steps, Party leadership, the forces to be relied on, and the reunification of the motherland. It has guided our Party in formulating the basic line for the primary stage of socialism. It is a fairly complete scientific system which embraces philosophy, political economics and scientific socialism and covers, among other things, the economy, politics, science and technology, education, culture, ethnicity, military and foreign affairs, the united front and Party building. It is also a scientific system which needs to be further enriched and developed in all aspects."

The report to the 17th Congress advocated supporting and promoting the pivotal project of socialism with Chinese characteristics. It pointed out: "To sum up, the fundamental reason behind all our achievements and progress since the R&O policy was introduced is that we have blazed a path of socialism with Chinese characteristics and established a system of theories of socialism with Chinese characteristics. Essentially, to hold high the great banner of socialism with Chinese characteristics means to keep to this path and uphold this system." In his important address at the national ceremony commemorating the CPC's 90th anniversary in 2011, Hu Jintao added the notion of the socialist system with Chinese characteristics. Hu emphasized: "We have embarked on the path of socialism with Chinese characteristics, formed a system of theories of socialism with Chinese characteristics and established a socialist system with Chinese characteristics. These achievements made over 90 years of endeavors, innovation, and enrichment, should be valued, upheld on a long-term basis and continuously built upon by our Party and people."

"Xi Jinping Thought on Socialism with Chinese Characteristics for a New Era" reconstitutes the most recent theoretical innovation in adapting Marxism to China's realities as well as the latest realm of the theory of socialism with Chinese characteristics. General Secretary Xi Jinping, while making the report to the 19th Congress, highlighted: "With decades of hard work, socialism with Chinese characteristics has crossed the threshold into a new era. This is a new historic juncture in China's development." "The *Thought* makes the following things clear: It makes clear that the overarching goal of upholding and developing socialism with Chinese characteristics is to realize socialist modernization and national rejuvenation, and, that on the basis of finishing the building of a moderately prosperous society in all respects, a two-step approach should be taken to build China into a great modern socialist country that is prosperous, strong, democratic, culturally advanced, harmonious, and beautiful by the middle of the century. It makes clear that the principal contradiction facing Chinese society in the new era is that between unbalanced and inadequate development and the people's ever-growing needs for a better life. We must therefore continue commitment to our people-centered philosophy of development, and work to promote well-rounded human development and common prosperity for everyone. It makes clear that the overall plan for building socialism with Chinese characteristics is the five-sphere integrated plan, and the overall strategy is the four-pronged comprehensive strategy. It highlights the importance of fostering stronger confidence in the path, theory, system, and culture of socialism with Chinese characteristics. It makes clear that the overall goal of deepening reform in every field is to improve and develop the system of socialism with Chinese characteristics and modernize China's system and capacity for governance. It makes clear that the overall goal of comprehensively advancing law-based governance is to establish a system of socialist rule of law with Chinese characteristics and build a country of socialist rule of law. It makes clear that the Party's goal of building a strong military in the new era is to build the people's forces into world-class forces that obey the Party's command, can fight and win, and maintain excellent conduct. It makes clear that major country diplomacy with Chinese characteristics aims to foster a new type of international relations and build a community with a shared future for mankind. It makes clear that the defining feature of socialism with Chinese characteristics is the leadership of the Communist Party of China; the greatest strength of the system of socialism with Chinese characteristics is the leadership of the Communist Party of China; the Party is the highest force for political leadership. It sets forth the general requirements for Party building in the new era and underlines the importance of political work in Party building." "The *Thought* builds on and further enriches *Marxism-Leninism*, *Mao Zedong Thought*, *Deng Xiaoping Theory*, the *Theory of Three Represents*, and the *Scientific Outlook on Development*. It represents the latest achievement in adapting Marxism to the Chinese context and encapsulates the practical experience and collective wisdom of our Party and the people. It is an important component of the theory of socialism with Chinese characteristics, and a guide to action for all our members and all the Chinese people as we strive to achieve national rejuvenation. This *Thought* must be adhered to and steadily developed on a long-term basis." The report also lists the following 14 aspects of the essence of the *Thought*: (1) Upholding the Party's leadership across all sectors of society. (2) Staying committed to the people-oriented development philosophy. (3) Advancing comprehensive and in-depth reforms. (4) Embracing a new development vision. (5) Safeguarding the people's right to fully act as masters of the nation. (6) Advancing law-based governance across all areas of state affairs. (7) Adhering to core socialist values. (8) Enhancing and safeguarding people's livelihoods through development. (9) Promoting harmonious coexistence between humanity and nature. (10) Adopting a comprehensive strategy toward national security. (11) Maintaining the Party's unconditional leadership of the people's armed forces. (12) Remaining committed to the principle of "one country, two systems" while advancing the cause of national reunification. (13) Championing the idea of a common future community for all mankind. (14) Enforcing comprehensive and strict governance over the Party.

The economic theory is an integral part of the broader theory of socialism with Chinese characteristics. With the comprehensive theoretical system deepening, China's economic practice advances in tandem, given that China's R&O originated primarily within the economic sector. Therefore, the most dazzling highlights of socialism with Chinese characteristics include several key theoretical achievements. These encompass theories on socialist market economy, the primary stage of socialism, the fundamental economic system during this stage, the establishment of a modern market system, and macroeconomic management with indirect management as the mainstay. These also include the distribution theory that prioritizes work-based distribution while allowing multiple forms to coexist, the theory developing from *development as a top priority* and the *Scientific Outlook on Development* to the new development philosophy featuring innovative, coordinated, green (as in environmentalism), open and shared development, the theory of the coordinated advancement of new-type industrialization, IT application, urbanization and agricultural modernization, the theory of making full use of both domestic and international markets as well as both home and overseas resources, the theory of China's economic development entering a new normal phase and advancing supply-side structural reforms, the theory of building a modernized economy, etc.

2. Socialism With Chinese Characteristics: The Sole Path Conforming to China's Primary Stage Reality

Socialism with Chinese characteristics is a historic achievement that the Chinese Communists proposed to follow independently, following a period of arduous exploration after 1949. Why was this so difficult? The main reason is that during a certain period subsequent to the establishment of the People's Republic, as there was no successful precedent to follow, the Chinese had to explore on their own.

Especially regarding the accurate understanding of their national conditions, the Chinese had to proceed from the reality instead of replicating other models. To engage in socialist construction, it was entirely up to them to explore. However, the exploration turned out to be slow progress and often over-ambitious intentions. As a result, a great many detours have been taken: more haste, less speed.

Then, what are China's most fundamental national conditions? The most significant factor to take into account is not the large population, nor the large land area, nor yet the abundance of resources: it is rather that China remains in the primary phase of socialism, and this condition will persist for an extended period. This is the most far-reaching and fundamental element of its national conditions, viewed from the nature of economic society, as well as the stage of social progress. To build socialism, first of all, we must proceed from this biggest and most basic reality. The primary stage of socialism means that socialism in China is, as yet, in an underdeveloped stage. China embarked on socialism with very underdeveloped social productive forces and had to go through quite a long historical stage to realize the industrialization, urbanization, marketization, and modernization achieved by many developed nations within capitalist frameworks. Deng Xiaoping noted in April 1980: "We should research earnestly how to carry out socialist development. At this time, we are reviewing the experience gained in the past three decades since the founding of the People's Republic. To sum up, it is as follows. First, we should not adopt 'Leftist' policies by divorcing ourselves from reality or skipping over necessary stages. Otherwise, the task of building socialism will not be accomplished. We have suffered losses from 'Leftist' policies. Second, whatever we do must contribute to developing the productive forces."[2] The Sixth Plenary Session of the 11th CPC Central Committee (June 1981) first explicitly stated: "Our socialist system is still in the primary stage." In August 1987, Deng Xiaoping emphasized again: "The Thirteenth National Party Congress will explain what stage China is in: the primary stage of socialism. Socialism itself is the first stage of communism, and here in China we are still in the primary stage of socialism—that is, the underdeveloped stage. In everything we do we must proceed from this reality, and all planning must be consistent with it."[3]

The theory of the primary stage of socialism, notably, is not only a fundamental element of scientific socialism, but also that of the economic theory featuring socialism with Chinese characteristics. Efforts to develop and disseminate this

---

2 Xiaoping Deng. *Selected Works of Deng Xiaoping, Vol. 2*. Beijing: People's Publishing House, 1994, p. 312.

3 Xiaoping Deng. *Selected Works of Deng Xiaoping, Vol. 3*. Beijing: People's Publishing House, 1993, p. 252.

theory were also supported by Chinese economists. Su Shaozhi and Feng Lanrui (1979) took the lead in publishing an article, frankly admitting China had not truly finished building socialism and was "still in an underdeveloped socialist society and in a transitional period of socialism."[4] In 2008, Yu Guangyuan remarked: "In 1981, when I participated in drafting the 'Resolution on Certain Questions in the History of Our Party Since the Founding of the People's Republic of China,' I advocated that the judgment that our country was still in the 'primary stage of socialism' should be written down into the file so as to have a deeper understanding of the detours that had been taken. At that time, some comrades did not agree to do this, and there were disputes. But in the end, the concept of the 'primary stage of socialism' was written down."[5]

The 13th Congress presented the first systematic exposition of the primary stage of socialism. According to it, "China is now in the primary stage of socialism. There are two aspects to this thesis. First, the Chinese society is already a socialist society. We must persevere in socialism and never deviate from it. Second, China's socialist society is still in its primary stage. We must proceed from this reality and not jump over this stage. Under the specific historical conditions of contemporary China, to believe that the Chinese people cannot take the socialist road without going through the stage of fully developed capitalism is to take a mechanistic position on the question of the development of revolution, and that is the major cognitive root of 'Right' mistakes. On the other hand, to believe that it is possible to jump over the primary stage of socialism, in which the productive forces are not to be highly developed, is to take a utopian position on this question, and that is the major cognitive root of 'Left' mistakes." "Precisely because our socialism has emerged from the womb of a semi-colonial, semi-feudal society, with the productive forces lagging far behind those of the developed capitalist countries, we are destined to go through a very long primary stage. During this stage we shall accomplish industrialization and the commercialization, socialization and modernization of production, which many other countries have achieved under capitalist conditions." "How do things stand in China, now that socialism has been developing here for more than three decades? On the one hand, a socialist economic system based on public ownership of the means of production has been instituted, a socialist political system of people's democratic dictatorship has

---

4 Shaozhi Su & Feng Lanrui. The questions of the stage of social development after the proletariat taking power. *Economic Research Journal*, 1979 (5).

5 Guangyuan Yu. Background and topics: a review of discussions on several economic theoretical issues in the initial stage of reform and opening up. *Economic Science*, 2008 (6).

been established, and the guiding role of Marxism in the realm of ideology has been affirmed. The system of exploitation and the exploiting classes have been abolished. China's economic strength has grown enormously and educational, scientific, and cultural undertakings have considerably expanded. On the other hand, the country has a huge population and a poor foundation to start with, and its per capita GNP still ranks among the lowest in the world. The picture is very clear: Out of a population of more than one billion, 800 million people live in rural areas and, for the most part, still use hand tools to make a living. A certain number of modern industries coexist with many industries that are several decades or even a century behind present-day standards. Some areas that are fairly developed economically coexist with vast areas that are underdeveloped and impoverished. A small amount of science and technology is up to the highest world standards while the scientific and technological level as a whole is low, and nearly one-quarter of the population is still illiterate or semi-literate. The backwardness of the productive forces determines the following aspects of the relations of production: socialization of production, which is essential for expanded socialist public ownership, is still at a very low level; the commodity economy and domestic market are only beginning to develop; the natural economy and semi-natural economy constitute a considerable proportion of the whole; and the socialist economic system is not yet mature and well developed. In the realm of the superstructure, several economic and cultural conditions that are necessary if we are to promote a high degree of socialist democracy are far from ripe, and decadent feudal and capitalist ideologies and the small-producers' force of habit still have widespread influence in society and often corrode Party officials and public servants. All this shows that we still have a long way to go before we can advance beyond the primary stage of socialism." "It will be at least 100 years from the 1950s, when the socialist transformation of private ownership of the means of production was basically completed, to the time when socialist modernization will have been in the main accomplished, and all these years belong to the primary stage of socialism. This stage is different from both the transitional period, in which the socialist economic basis was not yet laid, and the stage in which socialist modernization will have been achieved. The principal contradiction we face during the present stage is the contradiction between the ever-growing material and cultural needs of the people and backward production. Class struggle will continue to exist within certain limits for a long time to come, but it is no longer the principal contradiction. To resolve the principal contradiction of the present stage, we must vigorously expand the commodity economy, raise labor productivity, gradually achieve the modernization of industry, agriculture, national defense, and science and technology and, to this end, reform such aspects of the relations of production and of the superstructure as are incompatible with the growth of the productive forces."

Since then, five consecutive CPC National Congresses, ranging from the 14th to the 18th, have all reiterated and emphasized that the country remains in the primary stage of socialism. This point was also reaffirmed by General Secretary Xi Jinping at the 19th Congress: "The basic dimension of the Chinese context – that our country is still and will long remain in the primary stage of socialism – has not changed. China's international status as the world's largest developing country has not changed. The whole Party must be completely clear about this fundamental dimension of our national context, and must base our work on this most important reality – the primary stage of socialism. We must remain fully committed to the Party's basic line as the source that keeps the Party and the country going and that brings happiness to the people. We must lead and unite the Chinese people of all ethnic groups in fulfilling the central task of economic development. We must uphold the Four Cardinal Principles, continue to reform and open up, be self-reliant, hardworking, and enterprising, and strive to build China into a great modern socialist country that is prosperous, strong, democratic, culturally advanced, harmonious, and beautiful."

Before the Third Plenary Session of the 11th CPC Central Committee, the fundamental reason for the serious mistakes in China's socialist construction was that the proposed goals, tasks, policies, and measures exceeded the most fundamental realities of the primary stage of socialism. For example, China's social productive forces were very underdeveloped, with the degree of socialized production proving insufficient to support the establishment of comprehensive public ownership over the means of production. However, in the pre-reform era, public ownership constituted the mainstay of the Chinese economy, with the private sector having been completely phased out, and there were only 100,000-some-odd self-employed enterprises in the country. This failed to inspire hundreds of millions of people to engage in production and operation. All kinds of products were in serious shortage; the issue of inadequate access to necessities like food and clothing for hundreds of millions of people had not been solved, and the superiority of socialism could not be manifested. With the advancement of technology, the variety and quality of products have continued to increase, and people have had more and more individual needs for products. Scale operation is often no longer an effective option, so we have not yet seen the prospect of comprehensive public ownership of the factors of production or the phasing out of individual production and operation. Another example is that the commodity market economy represents a necessary phase that social development cannot bypass. However, before R&O, when the commodity market economy remained very underdeveloped, China excluded the market and restricted commodity production and exchange. This practice, which was beyond the development stage, hindered the development of social productive forces and affected the growth and accumulation of wealth. In contrast, the rapid take-off of China's economy after R&O stems from the various principles and policies we have adopted, all proceeding from the national conditions that China is still in the initial stage of socialism and is expected to be positioned in this condition for an extended period. The people and all parties have been fully motivated, releasing all kinds of production potentials that were previously shackled. In other words, social productive forces have been fully liberated and advanced, so that the advantages of socialism could be brought into play.

The same is true of the economic theory of socialism with Chinese characteristics, which has evolved in the reforming process. It is similarly grounded in the understanding that China remains in, and will long remain in, the primary stage of socialism. As the core component of the socialist economic theory with Chinese characteristics, the theory on socialist market economy is grounded in the recognition that China's development remains at an initial phase where productive forces are at a relatively low level. It is essential to harness market mechanisms to stimulate economic vitality and to leverage the strengths of the market economy in enhancing resource deployment efficiency, narrowing the gap with developed economies, and establishing a robust groundwork for people's common prosperity. Additionally, its fundamental socialist economic system, taking public ownership as its foundation when encouraging the coexistence of various ownership forms, and the theories that support it, are established considering the same recognition. It is essential to maintain public ownership as the principal component while enabling individual, private, and foreign-funded sectors to survive and prosper, to open up employment opportunities, and advance the national economy with greater speed and higher quality. The first step is to address the basic needs of our people for sufficient food and clothing, the next step is to achieve a well-off status with surplus in these areas, and the third step is to enjoy a rich and fulfilling life.

3. Reform and Opening Up as the Most Distinctive Feature of Socialism with Chinese Characteristics

R&O stands as the defining feature of socialism with Chinese characteristics, which is the fundamental difference between socialism featuring Chinese characteristics and traditional socialism. This conclusion was made in the 17th Congress.

Therefore, R&O epitomizes the defining trait of the economic theory of socialism with Chinese characteristics, which has been shaped and refined through ongoing economic reforms and openness. The report of the 17th Congress pointed out: "In 1978, the Party held the historic Third Plenary Session of the 11th Central Committee, which ushered in the new historical period of reform and opening up." "Reform and opening up constitute the most salient feature of the new period. From the countryside to the cities and from the economic to other areas, the process of sweeping reform has unfolded with irresistible momentum. From the coastal areas to areas along the Yangtze River and the borders, and from the eastern to the central and western regions, the door has been resolutely opened to the outside world. This great undertaking of reform and opening up, never seen before in history, has greatly stimulated the enthusiasm of hundreds of millions of Chinese people and brought about China's historic transformation from a highly centralized planned economy to a robust socialist market economy, and from a closed or semi-closed state to all-round opening up."

The groundwork for socialism with Chinese characteristics was laid through a gradual process of reflecting on and learning from nearly thirty years of socialist construction. As highlighted in the 17th Congress report, "In a precarious situation left by the 'cultural revolution' (1966–76), the second generation of central collective leadership, persisting in emancipating the mind and seeking truth from facts and displaying immense political and theoretical courage, made a scientific appraisal of Comrade Mao Zedong and *Mao Zedong Thought*, thoroughly repudiated the erroneous theory and practice of 'taking class struggle as the key link,' and made the historic policy decision to shift the focus of the work of the Party and the state onto economic development and introduce reform and opening up. It established the basic line for the primary stage of socialism, sounded the clarion call of the times for taking our own road and building socialism with Chinese characteristics, founded *Deng Xiaoping Theory*, and led the whole Party and the people of all ethnic groups in striding forward on the great journey of reform and opening up."

Within a mere 40 years, the reforming practice has profoundly transformed the whole country's social and economic landscape. China's economy has surged from the eleventh largest to the second-largest in the world, emerging as the top manufacturing nation, the leading exporter of goods, and an important outbound investor. China's GDP constituted 15.3% of the global aggregate in 2017, marking a 13.5 percentage point increase since 1978. Between 2013 and 2017, China remained a major contributor to global growth, with its annual contribution staying above 30%. The world has hailed China's rapid economic rise as a "China Miracle" and has become a focal point of study for economists from all over the world. China's successful reforming practice proves indisputably that it is completely correct for China to embark upon the road of socialism with Chinese characteristics. Besides, the theory of socialism with Chinese characteristics, including the economic theory, has incomparable vitality.

This unique socialism evolves alongside the times and develops continuously. Along with the further deepening of R&O and the continued advancement of socialism with Chinese characteristics, the theory of socialism with Chinese characteristics has also been developing continuously. *Deng Xiaoping Theory*, the *Theory of Three Represents*, the *Scientific Outlook on Development*, and *Xi Jinping Thought on Socialism with Chinese Characteristics for a New Era* are the main symbols of the continuous development of this special socialism. Among them, *Xi Jinping Thought on Socialism with Chinese Characteristics for a New Era* represents the latest major theoretical innovation.

The economic theory of this distinctive socialism has also been shaped and progressively enriched in the tide of the reforming practice. Since China's reforms have consistently centered on economic reforms, the results of economic reform have been particularly dazzling, and the theoretical achievements of economic reform have also been relatively numerous and outstanding. For example, as China centers its economic reforms on fostering a socialist market economy, the corresponding theory has become the central pillar supporting the reforming initiative. Undoubtedly, it is not an overnight achievement for the socialist market economy theory to take shape and advance. During the early days of reform, it was necessary to introduce market mechanisms to revitalize the economy. The next step is to confirm that the socialist economy belongs by nature to the category of commodity economy, and that the high-level development of the commodity economy represents an inevitable stage that cannot be bypassed in social and economic advancement. Going a step further, it is under the condition of socialized production that the commodity economy essentially functions as a market economy. Within this framework, the socialist market economy enables the market to perform a fundamental function in resource distribution, and subsequently, it is acknowledged that the market should play a decisive role in this process. Meanwhile, it is necessary to better leverage government functions. Another example is the fundamental economic system where public ownership holds a leading position alongside diverse ownership forms, serving as the bedrock of our country's socio-economic development. The theoretical synthesis of this system—the theory regarding fundamental socialist economic arrangements—forms the cornerstone of socialist economic thought with distinct national characteristics. China has advanced reform and growth by embracing openness, with its economy rapidly expanding through greater engagement with the global market, leading to the establishment of a new openness-oriented theory that makes up an essential component of the economic theory within the Chinese-style socialism. At the outset of China's reform process, the setup of the four SEZs, namely Shenzhen, Zhuhai, Shantou, and Xiamen, represented a crucial advance in China's pursuit of international market engagement. It was a brand-new experiment in developing a socialist economy by using overseas capital, technology, and management skills, and had achieved great success. After that, China successively opened over a dozen coastal cities and created economic open zones in the Yangtze River Delta, Pearl River Delta, Southeast Fujian, and the Bohai Rim; Hainan was granted provincial status and designated as a special economic zone; Pudong New Area was then developed, etc. China's accession to the World Trade Organization (WTO) in 2001 signaled a new phase in the country's pursuit of opening up. After the 18th Congress, new steps have been taken in opening up to the outside world. Eleven pilot free trade zones (FTZs), including Shanghai, have been established; the establishment of free trade ports has been explored; the opening of inland borders has been expanded; the Belt and Road Initiative (BRI) has been advocated; outbound investment has been expanded; and a new open economic system has been built. We have advocated economic globalization, opposed de-globalization, facilitated the process of improving global economic governance through active engagement, and proposed establishing a community with a shared future for humanity. In the context of deepening opening up, the country's global standing has risen consistently, and new content has also been added in *Xi Jinping Thought on Economic Theory of Socialism with Chinese Characteristics for a New Era* during this process.

4. Marketization as the Central Line of Socialist Economic Theory with Chinese Characteristics

Marketization stands as the principal thread running through socialist economic theory marked by Chinese characteristics. The reason stems from the fact that China's R&O commenced by incorporating market mechanisms into economic practices, and the evolution and enrichment of the economic theory of socialism featuring Chinese characteristics have been grounded in the steady progression of reform toward a market-oriented system. Here comes a review of the history.

At the outset of the R&O period, China started to invigorate its economy gradually by introducing a market mechanism. First of all, the Household Contract Responsibility System was put into practice in the countryside, granting rural households greater autonomy in managing their own farming activities. This policy allowed them to bring their own agricultural and by-products to market for trade, which significantly enhanced their motivation and was conducive to the swift revitalization and progress of agricultural production. Secondly, the pricing structure of small commodities, agricultural and sideline products, as well as industrial consumer goods, was gradually deregulated with fruitful results. Although the price could rise to a certain extent once the price of any commodity was deregulated, the price could also be stable with the rapidly increasing supply. This could bring prosperity to the market, and the reform pioneer could be the first to know the benefits. Thirdly, state-owned enterprises started gaining greater independence. By granting them more decision-making authority and allowing a higher proportion of their earnings to be retained, these reforms injected new vitality into the corporate sector. Finally, China further embraced external engagement by establishing special economic zones, attracting foreign investments, and importing advanced technologies along with valuable experience in business management. Those initiatives were widely noticeable, and the people felt a sense of urgency to bridge the gap with developed countries and regions.

It is confirmed that the socialist economy belongs to a commodity economy, which gradually expands the market-oriented reform. In the early 1980s, with the penetration of the market mechanism into many socio-economic practices and the expansion of the regulatory scope of the law of value, some economists believed that the socialist economy belonged to the commodity economy as well, and enterprises were producers and managers of commodities, holding autonomous economic interests. Although this claim was questioned and opposed by other economists, the trend of reform was nevertheless irreversible due to the remarkable effect of the market-oriented reform. The Third Plenary Session of the 12th CPC Central Committee (1984) made the "Decision on Reform of the Economic Structure," affirming that the socialist economy was characterized as a planned commodity economy—an inevitable phase in the evolution of society and the economy. Moreover, it emphasized the need to build a new order and new system under the socialist planned commodity economy, thereby providing additional confirmation of market regulation's impact. Since then, the market-oriented reform has been further advanced in many aspects in the economic field. A framework highlighting "state regulating market, market guiding enterprise" has been put forward, emphasizing the market's function across all social domains. Therefore, regarding the law of value, its regulatory effect has been further clarified.

China did not stop its pace of reform. Some people questioned the market-oriented reform of previous years, and even proposed to go back to the "planned orientation" after the political turmoil in the late 1980s. However, this perspective did not prevail. On the contrary, some economists considered that it was necessary to persist in reforms geared toward market principles, and the socialist commodity economy was essentially a socialist market economy, or a market economy regulated through macro-level governance. Deng Xiaoping has explicitly demonstrated since 1990 that planning and the market are both economic tools. It was in the spring of 1992, on his trip to southern China, that Deng Xiaoping unequivocally stated: "The proportion of planning to market forces is not the essential difference between socialism and capitalism. A planned economy is not equivalent to socialism, because there is planning under capitalism too; a market economy is not capitalism, because there are markets under socialism too. Planning and market forces are both means of controlling economic activity." This has provided the firmest political support for formulating the reform objective of a socialist market economy.

Jiang Zemin, then General Secretary of the CPC Central Committee, also held expert symposia to solicit their opinions from October to December 1991. Nearly 20 experts from the Chinese Academy of Social Sciences, the Development Research Center of the State Council, the State Commission for Restructuring the Economic Systems (SCRES), the Institute of Macroeconomics of the State Planning Commission, and the Bank of China were invited to discuss how to determine the goals of economic reform at the 14th Congress that would be convened in 1992. The symposia were held 11 times in total, each for half a day, and were presided over by General Secretary Jiang Zemin. General Secretary Jiang Zemin expressed his views and comments from time to time. The main achievement of these eleven symposia was to formulate a tendentious proposal of "socialist market economic system." Two interpretations were given for this key articulation: First, the market acts as a basic regulator in distributing resources; Second, the market is subject to national macro-control rather than laissez-faire. All of these established an essential theoretical groundwork for the address delivered on June 9, 1992, by Jiang Zemin, then CPC General Secretary, at the Party School of the CPC Central Committee. They also paved the way for the 14th Congress (October 1992) to adopt the reform objective to establish a socialist market economic system.

In October 1992, then General Secretary Jiang Zemin emphasized at the 14th Congress: "The development of practice and the deepening of understanding require us to clearly state that the goal of China's economic reform is to establish a socialist market economy so as to further emancipate and develop the productive forces." "The socialist market economy we would like to establish is to make the market play a basic role in resource allocation under the macro-control of socialist countries."

Following the formulation of a socialist market economy as the reform objective, China's marketization reforms have made notable headway. To begin with, state-owned enterprise reform has seen a shift in focus from delegating managerial authority and transferring profits to promoting institutional innovation. The reform path clearly aimed at building a modern enterprise system, marked by clearly defined property rights, explicit authority-responsibility boundaries, separation of government from enterprise management, and scientific management, in order to align with the evolving market economy. The strategic realignment of the state-owned economy's structure and distribution, together with the corporatization of large and medium-sized state-owned enterprises (SOEs) into shareholding entities, enabled the state-owned sector to overcome its earlier hardships. Many such enterprises have changed their operating mechanisms, which has improved their vitality and market competitiveness. Consequently, the state-owned economy strengthened its functions. At the same time, township and village enterprises (TVEs) flourished and emerged as a significant driving force in economic growth for a time. Secondly, China's non-public economy, encompassing individually owned businesses as well as private enterprises, has developed dramatically. In 1993, 1994, and 1995, the private sector experienced growth rates exceeding 50%. The 15th Congress (1997) further affirmed that the non-public sector, comprising self-employed households and the private economy, constituted an integral part of China's socialist market economy. Given the rapid development of these sectors, by 2017, the non-public economy contributed over 60% to the national GDP and accounted for over 60% of the country's total fixed asset investment. Its contribution to national tax revenue has exceeded 50%, and that to new jobs has exceeded 80%. Thirdly, the fiscal system has undergone major reforms. The 1994 tax-sharing system reform was carried out to align with market economy development. The tax-sharing system was put in place between central and local fiscal levels, superseding the former local fiscal contracting regime. One notable outcome was the sharp increase in fiscal revenue brought about by the reform. The revenue in the national general public budget in 1993 was 434.895 billion yuan, and soared to 15.955208 trillion yuan in 2016, a nominal increase of more than 35 times. Another notable trend was that the share of fiscal revenue retained by the central government saw a gradual rise. By 1993, it represented 22% of the overall national fiscal revenue, and rose to more than 45% in 2016, which greatly enhanced the capacity at the central government level to implement transfers to local governments. The twenty-first century has seen a major transformation in the fiscal system, that is, from a system focusing on economic construction to one prioritizing public service, which entails achieving equal access to basic public services for all members of the public, stepping up financial inputs into poverty alleviation programs, and increasing proportions of expenditures for underdeveloped areas and lower-income populations. Finally, in November 2001, China formally joined the WTO, representing a new phase in its process of opening up to the international community. This major move aligns with the wave of economic globalization and marks a major milestone. Post-accession efforts have shown that the gains from China's WTO membership surpass the drawbacks. Since joining the WTO, China has accelerated its development of economic strength, foreign trade, foreign capital utilization, foreign exchange reserves, etc. Since 2013, China has accounted for more than 30% of global economic growth, reflecting its expanding role in the world economy. Joining the WTO signaled a new era in the country's opening-up efforts and served as a strong catalyst for deepening domestic market reforms. In the process of fulfilling WTO commitments, China has abolished and amended a range of legal and policy provisions that conflicted with the general norms in a market economy.

Following the 18th Congress, China has consistently deepened its market-driven reform agenda. The Third Plenary Session of the 18th CPC Central Committee (2013) adopted the "Decision of the Central Committee of the Communist Party of China on Some Major Issues Concerning Comprehensively Deepening the Reform," and decided to use the articulation that "the market plays a decisive role in resource allocation" instead of "the market plays a basic role in resource allocation" which had been used for 21 years. The word "decisive" enables a more precise and distinct articulation of the market mechanism's predominance in allocating resources, and more effectively captures the basic law of a market economy—namely, the inherent requirements of the law of value. The "Decision" also clearly stated: "We must deepen economic system reform by centering on the decisive role of the market in allocating resources." Since then, the market-oriented reform has developed in-depth in various sectors of the economy: 69 state-owned enterprises under the central government have been transformed into corporate systems in 2017; the mixed-ownership reform of SOEs has been rolled out one after another, providing an effective pathway for monopolistic sectors to open up avenues for competitive market entry; the pilot project of employee equity stakes in mixed-ownership enterprises has gained a lot of experience; the pilot program of investing and operating companies with state-held capital, and that of expanding powers of the company's board of directors have been carried out; business system reforms have promoted the rapid growth of market entities. The average daily increase of new enterprises reached more than 16,000 in 2017, while the figure was just more than 6,000 in 2013. The price reform continues to move forward. By the end of 2016, over 97% of goods and services had seen their prices deregulated and regulated by the market, with fewer than 3% still subject to government pricing—basically restricted to key public utilities, public welfare services, as well as natural monopolies based on networks. China has intensified its opening up by launching 11 pilot FTZs and cutting the foreign investment negative list by half, from 190 items in 2013 to 95 items in 2017, etc.

5. Continuous Advancement of Socialism with Chinese Characteristics via Incremental Reform

The economic reform in China has been progressively advanced, commonly known as "crossing the river by feeling the stones," and the economic theory of socialism featuring Chinese characteristics has been constantly developing through the incremental reform.

Shortly after the initiation of R&O, market mechanism introduction boosted economic dynamism and the gradual enrichment of the supply of materials. In particular, the reform of deregulating prices achieved remarkable results wherever it was implemented, so some economists proposed the idea of one-off price deregulation.[6] In 1987, when eight research groups commissioned by the SCRES were tasked with making the mid-term reform plan for 1988–1995, some groups also proposed achieving a transformation in China's economic operational framework within three to five years.[7] Some people considered these economists who held this view as radical reformers. However, China's actual situation required that China's reforms could only follow the path of incremental reform, and practice had also proved that incremental reform was the only correct choice for China's economic reform. Under actual circumstances, implementing radical reforms, including one-off price deregulation, would bring about major changes in group interests, easily trigger social turbulence, and affect social stability. Taking the one-off price deregulation as an example, owing to the long-term implementation of administrative pricing under the planned economy system, the price structure was seriously distorted, with some high and some low prices. If the price had been deregulated all at once, the producers and operators with low prices of products would have made a lot of profits, and the producers and operators with original high prices of products would have suffered losses. Such drastic changes in interests would affect the basic life of some people and hinder

6 Jiaxiang Wu, et al. The idea of controlling the currency and one-off price liberalization. *World Economic Herald*. Aug. 8th, 1988.

7 Department of Comprehensive Planning in the National Economic System Reform Commission. *China's Reform Ideas*. Shenyang: Shenyang Publishing House, 1988.

the smooth advancement of reform. From 1979 to 1984, China mainly adjusted prices and only lifted price controls on small commodities and select agricultural products. As a result, the average annual price increase rate was only about 3%. In contrast, after 1985, the price deregulation was the mainstay, followed by a sharp rise in prices for some time thereafter. For instance, in 1988 and 1989, prices rose by 18.8% and 18% respectively, and in 1994 they even rose by 24.1%. It was conceivable that if China had deregulated the prices from the very beginning instead of having focused on price adjustment in the first five years of the reform, the price increase rate would have been much higher. Under such circumstances, it would be very difficult to proceed with the reform smoothly. Over the four decades of R&O, China's consumer price index (CPI) has sustained an average annual increase within 5%. The reform has been carried out on the condition that prices are generally stable, and the reform has been steadily deepened. Such price stability has provided crucial support for the relatively smooth progress of China's reform endeavors.

Incremental reform was also prominently manifested in the fact that it started from economic reform and gradually developed into a five-sphere integrated plan. China launched its reform drive by reforming the economic system in late 1978. Initially, market mechanisms were introduced into economic activities to stimulate vitality. This was followed by pilot programs in SEZs as well as the utilization of foreign capital, which soon gave rise to robust economic expansion. Following the 1992 adoption of the socialist market economy goal, market-oriented reforms have been accelerated in an all-round way. Following its WTO accession in 2001, China's opening up has accelerated, with reforms advancing in tandem, each reinforcing the other. From the outset of the twenty-first century, as the socialist market economy has steadily improved and the economy has maintained rapid and steady growth, institutional reforms involving political, cultural, social, and ecological spheres have emerged as increasingly significant and urgent areas beyond economic system reform. In 2012, the 18th Congress proposed comprehensive reform advancement as a timely response to changing circumstances. Building upon the principles established at the 18th Congress, the Third Plenary Session of the 18th CPC Central Committee in 2013 advanced a comprehensive reform task covering the economic, political, cultural, social, and ecological systems—collectively known as the five-sphere integrated plan—thereby ushering in a new stage of reform. Firstly, the reform goal was higher and more comprehensive. In the past, the main objective of economic restructuring was establishing and improving a socialist market economic system, while this Session set the overall reform goal as refining the socialist system featuring Chinese characteristics, and modernizing structures and capabilities of national governance. It promoted the theoretical generalization to a higher level. Secondly, the holistic and deep-going reform referred to a five-sphere integrated strategy to promote coordinated advancement in five interrelated domains: the economy, politics, culture, society, and ecological civilization. Although the economic system reform was its focus, it was now confirmed that the comprehensive promotion of the five-sphere integrated plan is necessary. Thirdly, the proposition of comprehensively deepening reform was a necessary and logical extension of ongoing economic system reforms. In fact, the country's economic system reform had not been put into practice from the very beginning. In the course, China actively advanced institutional restructuring in political, cultural, social, and ecological domains to move in tandem with the evolving economic reforms, leading to significant accomplishments. While the reform sections of each CPC Congress report primarily focused on transforming the economic system, they also consistently addressed reforms involving political, cultural, and social arenas as distinct topics. The 15th Congress (1997), for instance, introduced the national strategy of governance according to law. Later, in 2004, the Fourth Plenary Session of the 16th Central Committee issued a dedicated resolution on strengthening the Party's strategic governance competence. Recognizing the need to further reform and pursue greater openness, the Fifth Plenary Session of the 16th CPC Central Committee emphasized accelerating administrative system reform and advocated for building a resource-efficient and environmentally sustainable society. Later in 2011, the Sixth Plenary Session of the 17th CPC Central Committee passed the "Decision of the CPC Central Committee on Major Issues Pertaining to Deepening Reform of the Cultural System and Promoting the Great Development and Flourishing of Socialist Culture." The report presented at the 17th Congress in 2007 marked a structural shift by treating the advancement of social development—centered on improving people's livelihood—as an independent section on par with economic, political, and cultural development. This framework was extended in the report of the 18th Congress, which incorporated ecological progress as a standalone focus. Together, these adjustments shaped the five-pronged overall reform structure covering economic, political, cultural, social, and ecological dimensions. This progression clearly demonstrates how China's reform theories, including those related to the economy, have been steadily enriched and expanded in tandem with the deepening of reform efforts.

Incremental reforms are not perfect either. The biggest problem with incremental reform is that different interest groups would emerge during the reform process, and some groups with vested interests would gradually become resistant to reform. The most prominent example was that after reforming the welfare housing system and implementing housing commercialization and marketization, some people who had made more profits in the reform would become opponents of the real estate tax reform because they owned more and larger houses. That was because the implementation of the real estate tax would make them pay more taxes and hurt their interests. A further illustration is the *Third Plenary Session Decision* (2013), which stressed the necessity to strengthen the multilevel capital market and implement the reform to introduce a system of registration for issuing stocks. However, if someone proposed to really push forward the reform to introduce a system of registration for issuing stocks, hundreds of millions of shareholders would scold him, because they would be worried that after the reform, there would be more stocks listed, which would cause the stock price to fall and harm their interests. Even officials from the China Securities Regulatory Commission are now avoiding talking about the reform to introduce a system of registration for issuing stocks. Reforming the government's review and approval mechanism also proved to be a formidable challenge. since officials who originally had the power would inevitably lose many interests after the abolition of the review and approval system. This was also a significant reason for excessive resources under the government's direct allocative governance.

In response to this situation, a stronger push from the top and well-conceived top-level planning were increasingly needed to effectively deepen market-oriented reform. A major highlight of the "Decision of the Central Committee of the Communist Party of China on Some Major Issues Concerning Comprehensively Deepening the Reform" issued by the Third Plenary Session of the 18th CPC Central Committee was: "The Party Central Committee has instituted the Leading Group for Deepening Reform Comprehensively to be in charge of designing reform on an overall basis, arranging and coordinating reforms of different sectors, driving forward overall reforms and supervising the implementation of reform plans." After the adoption of this "Decision," the subsequent years of reform practice have fully demonstrated that the Party Central Committee's establishment of this Leading Group was both timely and correct. This Leading Group has been vital to advancing reform efforts. It is through its top-level design and vigorous promotion that reform has been able to overcome entrenched interests and maintain continuous progress.

6. Report to the 19th CPC National Congress: Further Arrangements for Economic Reforms and Recapitulation on Theories of Economic Reforms

In the 19th Congress report, Xi Jinping emphasized that through decades of endeavor, socialism with Chinese characteristics had stepped into a new era, signifying a paradigm shift in China's historical development trajectory. This Congress formally adopted *Xi Jinping Thought on Socialism with Chinese Characteristics for a New Era* as the Party's overarching theoretical foundation, marking it as the most recent milestone in advancing socialism with Chinese characteristics and signaling the entry into a new phase. Economic reforms for this new era must be guided by the *Thought*. The Congress report provides a latest summary of this theoretical innovation, and sets the direction for further pushing forward economic reforms.

In this report, Xi Jinping also emphasized that China's economy is shifting from rapid expansion to quality-driven development. This transition marks a crucial juncture to restructure the growth paradigm, optimize economic institutions, and cultivate new development impetuses. Building a modernized economy is a vital necessity for navigating key transitions and a long-term strategic vision for China's future growth. More robust drivers have become one of the three major reform goals to promote economic development (the other two are the goals for better quality and higher quality). As we all know, the core objective of reforming the economic system is to fuel economic growth. In this context, exploring and understanding the new growth engines for the new era is of vital importance to advancing high-quality economic transformation. It shows that further arrangements for economic reform have been made in this new era, and the corresponding theory has been further generalized. According to our learning experience, at least the following areas can be identified as major growth drivers for the new era:

First, innovation stands as the foremost driver of development.

As emphasized in the 19th Congress document, innovation is not only the leading force in advancing development but also a strategic pillar in constructing a modernized economic system. This broad concept of innovation includes advancements in science and technology, institutional reforms, theoretical exploration, managerial practices, and cultural development, with scientific and technological innovation playing a pivotal and guiding role. This requires us to make China a country of innovators at a faster speed, ensuring that progress in social productivity and labor efficiency is increasingly driven by technological breakthroughs and creative solutions. A cohort of world-class research institutions, cutting-edge laboratories, top-tier research universities, and innovative enterprises should be established. The strategy of development powered by innovation should be earnestly implemented with a strong orientation toward the global scientific and technological frontiers, core areas of the national economy, as well as the country's critical strategic needs, so as to drive new breakthroughs in key fields of sci-tech innovation. For China's industrial upgrading to the medium-high end, sustained enhancement of total factor productivity (TFP), and realization of high-quality development, it is imperative to catalyze scientific and technological innovation from an innovation ecosystem perspective and strengthen the technological contribution to economic expansion. China has witnessed substantial achievements since the 18th Congress. The sci-tech progress contributed an increasing share to economic growth, rising from 52.2% in 2012 to 57.5% in 2017, significantly driving industrial transformation and upgrading. Despite the progress made, there is still room for improvement, as the contribution rate in many advanced economies has surpassed 70%, and we still need to catch up. We already have a number of technologies and industries with an international advanced level, but it is far from enough. We have not yet mastered many core technologies in the manufacturing industry. For example, China imports more than 220 billion US dollars of chips a year, mainly high-end chips that we do not have the capacity to produce. China's external dependence on core technologies and key technologies is 50%, highlighting a considerable gap compared to developed countries, where the ratio generally falls below 30%. To facilitate the upgrading of China's industrial sector toward the mid-to-high end of global value chains and to develop several globally competitive advanced manufacturing clusters, it is essential to consistently expand investment in research and development (R&D). A key objective is to gradually enhance the R&D intensity ratio (R&D expenditure/GDP)—from 2.12% in 2017 to over 3% by 2025. Achieving this goal requires strengthening the national innovation system, enhancing mechanisms for intellectual property protection and incentives, and fostering a pool of high-level talent in sci-tech innovation. Furthermore, promoting the logical, and efficient flow of diverse human resources will be crucial. It is vital to fully harness the function of science and technology as the fundamental driver of productivity.

At its 19th Congress, the CPC reached a pivotal decision of historic significance: ensuring a fully completed moderately prosperous society and launching a new construction phase for an all-round modern socialist country. The goal is to fully establish a moderately prosperous society by 2020, essentially complete the modernization process by 2035, and by 2050, transform China into a great modern socialist nation characterized by prosperity, strength, democracy, cultural sophistication, harmony, and environmental beauty. Achieving this grand goal entails upgrading China's industrial structure to the medium-high and high-end segments, with economic growth increasingly driven by enhancements in total factor productivity. Consequently, China is projected to enter the high-income country category and progressively attain the status of a middle-developed country. Looking ahead, there will be an even greater need to depend on sci-tech innovation and advancement to significantly enhance the economic quality and growth efficiency, enabling innovation to genuinely serve as the primary driving force behind development.

Second, tap and fully leverage diverse new growth engines.

As stipulated in the 19th Congress report: "Furthering supply-side structural reform. In developing a modernized economy, we must focus on the real economy, give priority to improving the quality of the supply system, and enhance our economy's strength in terms of quality. We will work faster to build China into a manufacturer of quality and develop advanced manufacturing, promote further integration of the internet, big data, and artificial intelligence with the real economy, and foster new growth areas and drivers of growth in medium-high end consumption, innovation-driven development, the green and low-carbon economy, the sharing economy, modern supply chains, and human capital services."

The economy, since the 18th Congress, has undergone upgrading and transformation, accompanied by a shift in development approaches and the progressively deepening supply-side structural reforms, leading to the continuous emergence of diverse new driving forces. The stage with traditional drivers as the mainstay has been gradually transformed into the rise of new drivers, with the accelerated development of entrepreneurship and innovation, the Internet economy, the digital economy, and the sharing economy. For example, the "China Sharing Economy Development Report 2017," jointly released by the Sharing Economy Research Center of the State Information Center and the Sharing Economy Working Committee of the Internet Society of China, highlighted that the transaction volume in China's sharing economy market reached approximately 3.5 trillion yuan, representing a 103% increase compared to 2016. Some experts estimate that by 2025, China's total information consumption is expected to approach US$2 trillion, while the volume of e-commerce transactions is projected to reach US$10 trillion. In 2016, high-tech sectors contributed 12.4% to the total added value of industries above a designated size, marking a three percentage point increase compared to 2012. On April 13, 2018, China's National Bureau of Statistics announced preliminary estimates indicating that in 2016, the "three new" economy—comprising new industries, business formats, and models—reached an added value of approximately 11,371.9 billion yuan, representing 15.3% of the country's GDP. Calculated at current prices, the "three new" economic added value growth rate was 11.8%, surpassing the GDP growth rate by 3.9 percentage points. New growth engines stemming from new industries, new business forms, and new models have fueled rapid employment growth. Premier Li Keqiang emphasized at the 2017 Summer Davos Forum that the contribution rate of new drivers accounted for about 70% of the new urban employment in

2016. Some reports pointed out: According to the estimates of relevant institutions, new drivers contributed to more than 30% of GDP growth.

Among all productive factors, the labor force remains the most active one. In the past, we relied on huge low-cost labor to expand production scale, which became a crucial contributor to fueling rapid economic progress. If we aim to shift toward high-quality development at this stage, we cannot continue to rely on migrant workers to do rough work, but rather provide professional and technical training for the labor force, encourage them to do fine work, be craftsmen, and let robots do some rough work. Accelerating high-tech emerging industries requires cultivating a contingent of world-class scientists, technological leaders, young tech talents, and high-performance innovation teams in strategic priority areas. To achieve this goal, we need to vigorously develop education, expedite educational modernization, develop vocational education, train on-the-job workers, comprehensively enhance educational quality, improve workforce quality at all stages of socio-economic advancement, and enhance the value leverage of human capital, including stimulating and protecting entrepreneurs spirit, so as to shift China's labor force advantage from a quantitative dividend to a quality-driven one, which constitutes a vital component of fostering stronger economic growth through reform.

As indicated in the 19th Congress report, the rural land contract system is to be maintained with long-term stability, and upon termination of the current contractual round, a 30-year extension will be granted to ensure continuity and security of land rights. This major decision has made the rural land contracting practices stable for 75 years from the first round of contracting, fully reflecting its commitment to safeguarding the rights and interests of farmers, while providing them with a strong sense of security. It is also conducive to protecting and mobilizing farmers' enthusiasm for production and operation, thereby generating new momentum for the growth of agricultural production. By late 2016, the central committee promulgated "Opinions on Improving the Measures for Separating Rural Land Ownership from Contracted Management Right," implementing the tripartite separation of rural land rights, namely ownership, contract, and management rights. This represents a milestone in China's continuum of rural reforms, which can effectively promote the process of agricultural modernization. After the 18th Congress, China's urbanization rate has averaged a 1.2% growth per year, with over 80 million rural migrants becoming urban residents. By 2017, the urbanization rate of the permanent population rose to 58.5%. Moving forward, this rate is expected to continue rising, which will, in turn, promote improvements in labor productivity.

Third, drawing on openness to advance reform and foster development has been a valuable lesson from China's four decades of R&O.

As outlined in the 19th Congress report, "Make new ground in pursuing opening up on all fronts. Openness brings progress, while self-seclusion leaves one behind. China will not close its door to the world; we will only become more and more open. We should pursue the *Belt and Road Initiative* as a priority, give equal emphasis to 'bringing in' and 'going global,' follow the principle of achieving shared growth through discussion and collaboration, and increase openness and cooperation in building innovation capacity. With these efforts, we hope to make new ground in opening China further through links running eastward and westward, across land and over sea. We will expand foreign trade, develop new models and new forms of trade, and turn China into a trader of quality." Since the 18th Congress, its opening up has picked up pace and achieved remarkable results. The *BRI* has been unveiled; 11 pilot FTZs including Shanghai have been built; the economic globalization has been upheld toward a more open, inclusive and balanced direction for mutual benefits; the vision of building a community with a shared future for mankind has been proposed; regional opening up has been optimized; trade and investment have been liberalized and facilitated; new models of outbound investment cooperation have been explore, etc. The strategic plans for broader opening up laid out at the 19th Congress are set to provide strong momentum for high-quality economic growth.

Fourth, the fundamental priority lies in expediting the improvement of the socialist market economy.

As stated in the 19th Congress, "In our economic reforms, we must concentrate on improving the property rights system and ensuring the market-based allocation of factors of production, so that property rights act as effective incentives. We should ensure free flows of factors, flexible prices, fair and orderly competition, and that business survival is determined by competition." As a foundational element of the socialist market economy, a modern property rights system is defined by clear ownership boundaries, explicit rights-responsibility alignment, robust protection, and efficient transfer mechanisms. The "Decision" adopted at the Third Plenary Session of the 18th CPC Central Committee on comprehensively deepening reform identified improving the property rights protection system as the top priority in economic system reform. The 19th Congress further stressed that improving the system of property rights should remain at the heart of economic reform. This focus is highly pertinent, as in recent years, the inadequate implementation of property rights protections has, at times, led to private capital flowing out of the market and a slowdown in the pace of fixed asset investment by private enterprises. (For example, the increase in fixed asset investment by private capital was only 3.2% in 2016, compared with 10.2% in the previous year). To this end, on November 27, 2016, the CPC Central Committee and the State Council jointly issued the "Opinions on Improving the Property Rights Protection System and Protecting Property Rights in Accordance with Law." Since then, the implementation of the document has been better, which has given various market entities, especially those in the non-public sector, reassurances for investing and starting businesses. The 19th Congress report identifies refining the property rights system as a central priority in the upcoming economic reforms, continuing and developing the Resolution adopted at the Third Plenary Session of the 18th CPC Central Committee. Regarding factor allocation through market mechanisms, it essentially signifies the decisive function of market forces in distributing resources. Echoing market-based allocation of factors, the 19th Congress specifically advocated to accelerate the market-oriented reform of factor prices, which is a bright spot and a major measure to let the market exercise its decisive influence over resource allocation, and to activate the market mechanism with real effectiveness.

A further top-level design has been made for pushing forward with deeper reforms in state-owned enterprises. It was highlighted in the 19th Congress report that "We will improve the systems for managing different types of state assets, and reform the system of authorized operation of state capital. In the state-owned sector, we will step up improved distribution, structural adjustment, and strategic reorganization. We will work to see that state assets maintain and increase their value; we will support state capital in becoming stronger, doing better, and growing bigger, and take effective measures to prevent the loss of state assets. We will further reform of state-owned enterprises, develop mixed-ownership economic entities, and turn Chinese enterprises into world-class, globally competitive firms." Of all the components in the economic reform, restructuring SOEs emerges as the toughest challenge. In the wake of the 18th Congress, SOE reform began to gain momentum and deliver notable progress, but the public continues to anticipate faster and more substantial progress. Many of the reform initiatives outlined in this report had already appeared in earlier Party documents. Since they had not been completed well, they needed to be reiterated. In addition, the report set forth new reform measures with higher requirements. For example, it urged accelerating efforts to boost the state capital's robustness, excellence, and size, and set a clear requirement for the regulatory body for state-owned assets to "focus primarily on capital management," as stipulated in the "Decision" of the Third Plenary Session of the 18th CPC Central Committee. Moreover, cultivating internationally competitive, top-tier enterprises demonstrates China's robust economic power and underscores its rigorous standards required for constructing a modernized economy.

It is essential to foster an equitable and competitive market setting, in turn unleashing the vitality of all types of market players. As outlined in the report of the 19th Congress, "We will introduce a negative list for market access nationwide, sort through and do away with regulations and practices that impede the development of a unified market and fair competition, support the growth of private businesses, and stimulate the vitality of various market entities. We will deepen reforms in the business sector, break administrative monopolies, preclude the forming of market monopolies, speed up the reform of market-based pricing of factors of production, relax control over market access in the service sector, and improve market oversight mechanisms." The negative list of foreign investment in China's pilot FTZs has been reduced from 190 items in 2013 to 95 items in 2017, a reduction of half. Based on the summary of previous pilot experiences, relevant departments proposed to continuously improve the supporting systems to guarantee the formal rollout of a unified national negative list system for market access starting in 2018. There are also some new formulations in the 19th Congress report, which are highly targeted, including boosting the growth of private businesses, preventing the emergence of market monopolies, accelerating market-oriented pricing reforms for production factors, etc. It seeks to enhance the modern market system, securing equal competitive opportunities for all kinds of enterprises and invigorating micro-level market entities.

It is necessary to pursue innovation and improvement in macro-regulation. In its report, the 19th Congress underscored that "We will develop new methods to improve macro-regulation, give full play to the strategic guidance of national development plans, and improve mechanisms for coordinating fiscal, monetary, industrial, regional, and other economic policies." Relative to the "Decision" adopted at the Third Plenary Session of the 18th CPC Central Committee, this report incorporates regional policy while leaving out price policy. This is practical. After the Decision was adopted, price reform has witnessed a series of new developments. As of 2016, over 97% of merchandise and service offerings had been deregulated, with market forces taking the lead, making it difficult for price policy to continue functioning as an effective economic lever. In contrast, China is a large nation characterized by a vast and expansive territory. Regional policies are crucial for optimizing the allocation of productive forces as well as advancing the synergistic growth of regional economies. Facilitating the alignment of major economic structures and the efficient distribution of productive resources stands as a key objective within macroeconomic regulation.

It is necessary to deepen fiscal and taxation reforms. As demonstrated in the 19th Congress report, "We will expedite the creation of a modern public finance system, and establish a fiscal relationship between the central and local governments built upon clearly defined powers and responsibilities, appropriate financial resource allocation, and greater balance between regions. We will put in place a comprehensive, procedure-based, transparent budget system that uses well-conceived standards and imposes effective constraints; and we will implement performance-based management nationwide. We will deepen reform of the taxation system, and improve the local tax system." Deepening fiscal and taxation reforms is very important and also requires determined efforts to overcome. Taking fiscal and tax reform as an example, raising the proportion of direct taxes, levying real estate taxes, establishing an individual income tax framework that integrates comprehensive and categorical approaches, and refining the local tax system all involve major adjustments of interests, which are really "hard nuts" to crack. And these reforms are crucial to modernizing the country's governance system and capabilities.

It is necessary to deepen the financial system reform. As stressed in the 19th Congress, "We will deepen institutional reform in the financial sector, make it better serve the real economy, increase the proportion of direct financing, and promote the healthy development of a multilevel capital market. We will improve the framework of regulation underpinned by monetary and macro-prudential policy, and see that interest rates and exchange rates become more market-based. We will improve the financial regulatory system to forestall systemic financial risks." It is worth noting that this time, the two-pillar regulatory framework of monetary and macro-prudential policy is specially proposed. This is very important because monetary policy mainly focuses on price stability and whether inflation occurs or not. There has long been debate over whether monetary policy should take asset price fluctuations into account. Before the 2008 global financial crisis erupted, price levels in America were steady, but financial asset prices rose sharply. After the outbreak of the crisis, there has been a reflection that to preserve financial system stability, just one monetary policy focusing on prices is not enough. A macro-prudential policy is also needed. A two-pillar regulatory framework was proposed at the National Financial Work Conference (July 14–15, 2017). The essence of macro-prudential policy lies in incorporating a wide range of financial activities, such as real estate finance, into the regulatory framework, with the purpose of avoiding systemic financial risks.

By accomplishing the above points, we will be capable of establishing an economic system marked by a functioning market mechanism, vibrant micro-level entities, as well as well-calibrated macro-regulation, thereby consistently enhancing China's capacity for innovation and competitiveness.

The deployment of new growth engines represents a major advance in economic reform theory. First, the expansion of economic reform is not limited to the market-driven reform efforts that have long been carried out previously. As China advances toward a development model that prioritizes quality over speed, innovation—particularly in frontier science and technology—has assumed a central position in driving progress, underscoring the growing emphasis on leveraging innovation as the core engine of economic transformation. Of course, effective scientific and technological innovation relies fundamentally on reforming the institutional mechanisms governing science and technology, with an emphasis on market orientation and responsiveness to market signals, which combines the driving force of innovation with market-oriented reform. Second, supply-side structural reform is also an important part of economic reform. Emerging sectors such as the new economy, new technologies, new business models, and new industries have become key drivers of high-quality economic development. They can also be regarded as the connotation of the structural reform. Since this change can replace the old driver with a new one, it can thus become a new driving force in the new era. Certainly, reforms centered on market mechanisms remain the primary focus of economic restructuring. Persisting in improving the socialist system with a market orientation remains a pivotal matter amid China's economic shift and serves as the main source of momentum for advancing high-quality development. So far, it has been observed that economically and technologically advanced countries have achieved development within the framework of a market economy. To build a modernized economy, we should progressively realize this goal through the ongoing advancement of the socialist system with market-oriented features.

7. Key Objectives of Economic Reform: Liberating and Boosting Productive Forces & Accomplishing Common Prosperity

At the heart of China's R&O lies the fundamental purpose of releasing and expanding productive forces, alongside advancing prosperity shared by all. This objective constitutes the core of the economic theory that grounds socialism with Chinese characteristics. R&O is a dual goal, not a single goal, and not limited to unleashing and developing productive forces; it also aims to guarantee that the gains from development will be shared by the entire population.

R&O is, first and foremost, about unleashing and expanding social productive forces. It involves not only adjusting production relations but also transforming the superstructure to align with the needs of productive force development. In reforming the original economic governance system, what matters most is to inspire enthusiasm and initiative of all economic entities, break down various systems, laws and regulations and policies that restrict the dynamism of economic entities, and mobilize all factors of production in the whole society, so that talents and energies of all people are bursting out, resource allocation is optimized, the technological progress is accelerated, and the economic efficiency is improved. With the rollout of R&O, China has experienced a dramatic economic takeoff, sustaining an average annual growth rate close to double digits for over three decades. In 2009, it outpaced many other economies to secure its position as the world's second-largest. By 2017, the per capita GDP had approached USD 9,000, placing it among the upper-middle-income countries. In the years spanning 2013 to 2017, China's average annual GDP growth reached 7.1%, and its contribution to global economic growth exceeded 30%. These remarkable achievements fully demonstrate the critical role of R&O in unleashing and advancing productive forces. It is a pivotal decision that has shaped the course of contemporary China. The facts speak for themselves: There is no other path but R&O for developing socialism featuring Chinese characteristics and bringing about the great rejuvenation of the entire nation. Only by continuing along this road can China advance, socialism thrive, and socialist modernization proceed in the right direction.

As a far-reaching new revolution, R&O is destined to encounter challenges along the way and cannot be completed overnight.

R&O signifies a profound shift in how economic governance is structured and a major adjustment of interests, which will definitely conflict with the ideology of maintaining the status quo and the traditional socialist economic theory. It can be seen that at the start of R&O, ideological and theoretical disputes often occurred, and sometimes they were quite fierce. For example, when the planned economy was denied, and the socialist commodity and market economy were affirmed, there was a serious ideological and theoretical confrontation. At that time, because Deng Xiaoping and other political leaders remained committed to R&O, they gradually unified their understanding relatively smoothly and made this initiative move forward steadily. R&O also entails a deep-seated restructuring of interest relationships. Those who have lost interests (there were not many cases during the early phase of China's R&O drive) will naturally try to obstruct or resist. This also depends on the promotion and persistence of the upper levels to open the channel. As China implements incremental reforms, new interest groups will inevitably emerge or even become vested during the reform. When the reform is about to hurt their interests, their power of obstruction and resistance should not be underestimated. To overcome the obstacles posed by vested interests, a well-conceived top-level design is essential. Reform must be driven from the top down by a strong and authoritative body—such as the Central Leading Group for Comprehensively Deepening Reform established at the Third Plenary Session of the 18th CPC Central Committee. Only through such institutional leadership can China sustain the momentum of deepening and broadening its reform agenda.

R&O is not an endeavor that yields results in a single day. China's remarkable journey of reform has shown that incremental reform is much more effective than the method of one-step rapid reform. The most important thing is that incremental reform is conducive to making the reform solid on the premise of maintaining social stability, and will not bring about major social turmoil and result in more haste, less speed. The incremental reform has continuously unleashed and developed productive capacity, invigorating both the national economy and micro-level entities. This is what has fueled China's rapid and sustained economic rise since R&O.

R&O also aims to gradually achieve common prosperity, ensuring that the benefits of development are shared by all. It is not solely about enhancing economic efficiency, but also about reforming the original distribution system of indiscriminate egalitarianism, taking pride in labor, encouraging people to pursue prosperity through diligent work, continuously improving labor productivity as well as total factor productivity, while encouraging certain regions and segments of the population to achieve prosperity ahead of others. Meanwhile, efforts should be made to regulate income distribution through a combination of fiscal transfers, taxation, social security programs, targeted poverty eradication, and the equitable supply of basic public services. Those who achieve prosperity first should support those still on the way, so as to steadily advance with common prosperity as the ultimate objective. The "Decision of the Central Committee of the Communist Party of China on Some Issues Concerning Building a Socialist Market Economy" adopted at the Third Plenary Session of the 14th CPC Central Committee (1993) put forward that efficiency should be prioritized and fairness should be taken into consideration, which was in response to the fact that the economy was relatively backward and the national economy required development as soon as possible, and was in accordance with the prevailing conditions of that period. Entering the twenty-first century, even as China's economy has hit new highs, the widening income gap has brought issues of fairness and equity increasingly to the forefront. Therefore, following the adoption of the "Decision of the CPC Central Committee on Enhancing the Leadership Competence of the Party" at the Fourth Plenary Session of the 16th CPC Central Committee in

2004, the Party Central Committee's documents no longer adopt the description that efficiency should be prioritized and fairness should be taken into consideration. It is proposed that efficiency and fairness are of equal importance, with increased attention given to fairness in distribution, especially redistribution. At the 19th Congress, General Secretary Xi Jinping emphasized: "Ensuring and improving living standards through development. The wellbeing of the people is the fundamental goal of development. We must do more to improve the lives and address the concerns of the people, and use development to strengthen areas of weakness and promote social fairness and justice. We should make steady progress in ensuring people's access to childcare, education, employment, medical services, elderly care, housing, and social assistance. We will intensify poverty alleviation, see that all our people have a greater sense of fulfillment as they contribute to and gain from development, and continue to promote well-rounded human development and common prosperity for everyone." This passage fully embodies the Party's unshakable devotion to serving the people, along with its people-centered philosophy. It also exemplifies the fundamental tenet of China's socialist political economy—taking people as the foremost priority.

References

Chen, Jun & Hong Nan. *Jiang Zemin and the Proposition of the Socialist Market Economic System—20 Years Review of the Socialist Market Economy.* Beijing: Central Party Literature Press, 2012.

Communist Party of China. *Moving forward along the road of socialism with Chinese characteristics—Report at the Thirteenth National Congress of the Communist Party of China.* Oct. 25, 1987.

Communist Party of China Central Committee. *Decision of the Central Committee of the Communist Party of China on Reform of the Economic Structure.* Oct. 20, 1984.

Communist Party of China Central Committee. *Decision of the Central Committee of the Communist Party of China on Some Issues Concerning Building a Socialist Market Economy.* Nov. 14, 1993.

Communist Party of China Central Committee. *Decision of the Central Committee of the Communist Party of China on Some Major Issues Concerning Comprehensively Deepening the Reform.* Nov. 12, 2013.

Deng, Xiaoping. *Selected Works of Deng Xiaoping, Vol. 3.* Beijing: People's Publishing House, 1993.

Department of Comprehensive Planning, National Economic System Reform Commission. *China's Reform Ideas.* Shenyang: Shenyang Press, 1988.

Hu, Jintao. "Hold High the Great Banner of Socialism with Chinese Characteristics and Strive for a New Victory in Building a Moderately Prosperous Society in All Respects." Report to the 17th National Congress of the Communist Party of China, Beijing, Oct. 15, 2007.

Jiang, Zemin. "Hold High the Great Banner of Deng Xiaoping Theory and Comprehensively Push the Cause of Building Socialism with Chinese Characteristics into the 21st Century." Report to the 15th National Congress of the Communist Party of China, Beijing, Sept. 12, 1997.

Peng, Sen, Chen Li, et al. *Major Events in China's Economic System Reform, Vol. I, II.* Beijing: Renmin University of China Press, 2008.

The Writing Team of This Book. *The Guidebook for the Report of the 19th National Congress of the Communist Party of China.* Beijing: People's Publishing House, 2017.

Xi, Jinping. "Secure a Decisive Victory in Building a Moderately Prosperous Society in All Respects and Strive for the Great Success of Socialism with Chinese Characteristics for a New Era." Report to the 19th National Congress of the Communist Party of China, Beijing, Oct. 18, 2017.

Zhang, Zhuoyuan, et al. *Outline of the History of Economics in New China (1949–2011).* Beijing: China Social Sciences Press, 2012.

Zhang, Zhuoyuan. *Economic Transformation and Reform.* Beijing: China Renmin University Press, 2017.

Theory of Socialist Market Economy: The Main Pillar of the Economic Theory of Socialism with Chinese Characteristics

The implementation of reform and opening up at the end of 1978 marked the beginning of China's journey of building socialism with Chinese characteristics. The brand-new socialist road pioneered by Deng Xiaoping has brought about tremendous changes in China's economy and society in just 40 years. China has transformed from a country once economically and technologically underdeveloped into the world's second-largest economy. Its per capita GDP has soared from US$190 in 1978, when reform and opening up began, to around US$9,000 in 2017, making China an upper-middle-income country. The Chinese people are full of confidence to build a moderately prosperous society in all respects by 2020, basically realize modernization by 2035, and build China into a great modern socialist country that is prosperous, strong, democratic, culturally advanced, harmonious, and beautiful by the middle of the twenty-first century, and realize the great rejuvenation of the Chinese nation. The key to China's journey toward national rejuvenation lies in the steadfast implementation of reform and opening up. This includes the gradual advancement of the five-sphere integrated plan, with a focus on establishing and improving the socialist market economy. China has remained committed to opening its door to the world and to building new institutions for an open economy. Amidst the groundbreaking evolution of forging socialist paradigms with Chinese stylistic attributes, China has accumulated a wealth of experience. Under the leadership of the Communist Party of China and guided by *Marxism*, the Chinese people have developed a series of significant theoretical achievements. In the economic realm, these achievements include the theory of the primary stage of socialism, the theory of the socialist market economy, the theory of the fundamental socialist economic system, and the theory of the fundamental socialist distribution system, the development theory from *development as a top priority* and the *Scientific Outlook on Development* to the new development philosophy featuring innovative, coordinated, green (as in environmentalism), open and shared development, the theory of opening to the outside world, the theory of China's economy entering a new normal, the theory of supply-side structural reform, the theory of promoting the coordination of new types of industrialization, IT application, urbanization, and agricultural modernization, the theory of building a modern economy, etc. Foremost among these is the conceptual framework for integrating market mechanisms within a socialist system, which serves not only as a central theoretical foundation for China's reform and opening up but also as a core pillar of the economic theory underpinning socialism with Chinese characteristics.

This is for the following reasons: First, China's reform and opening up started with the introduction of market mechanisms and respect for the law of value in social and economic activities, thereby continuously enhancing economic vitality. Second, the core issue of economic system reform is to properly handle the relationship between the government and the market, and the theory of the socialist market economy scientifically answers this important question. The authoritative 1992 Congress of the CPC's fourteenth national session affirmed: "The socialist market economic system we want to establish is to make the market play a fundamental role in resource allocation under the macro-control of socialist countries so that economic activities follow the requirements of the law of value and adapt to changes in supply and demand; through the function of price leverage and competition mechanism, resources are allocated to links with better benefits, and pressure and motivation are given to enterprises to realize the survival of the fittest; we should take the advantage that the market is more responsive to various economic signals to promote the timely coordination of production and demand. At the same time, we must also see that the market has its own weaknesses and negative aspects, and we must strengthen and improve the state's macro-control over the economy." In 2013, the "Decision" adopted at the 18th CPC Central Committee's Third Plenary Gathering further emphasized: "Economic system reform is the focus of deepening the reform comprehensively. The underlying issue is how to strike a balance between the role of the government and that of the market, and let the market play the decisive role in allocating resources and let the government play its functions better. It is a general rule of the market economy that the market decides the allocation of resources. We have to follow this rule when we improve the socialist market economy. We should work hard to address the problems of market imperfection, too much government interference, and poor oversight." Third, it is precisely because of the adherence to market-oriented reforms since reform and opening up that China's economy has taken off rapidly, with an average annual growth rate of 9.5% for four decades in a row. The country's economic prowess, global clout, and citizen welfare have surged at a remarkable speed. Today, China is making a determined transition from being a large economy to becoming a strong economic power on the world stage. Fourth, from the perspective of the history of economic thought, it is a remarkable innovation in human society that a populous nation of over one billion people has developed a market economy within a socialist framework. The successful integration of socialism with a market economy, and of public ownership with market mechanisms, long deemed incompatible by Western mainstream economics, represents a theoretical and practical breakthrough. China's successful practice of constructing an economic model integrating socialist principles with market mechanisms, along with the theoretical framework derived from it, challenges the long-standing assumptions of Western economic orthodoxy. This achievement stands as one of the most significant and transformative contributions of the Chinese Communists and Marxist economists to the development of scientific socialism and political economy!

1. Gradual Formation of the Theory of the Socialist Market Economy in the Tide of Reform

The theory of the socialist market economy has gradually been formed in the tide of China's reform and opening up. Its development process can be roughly segmented into four stages as follows: the theoretical groundwork laid prior to the "Cultural Revolution"; the initial phase of introducing market mechanisms in the early years of reform and opening up; the stage during which the theory of the socialist commodity economy was formulated; and finally, the phase in which the implementation of the socialist market economy was set as the strategic goal of reform.

I. Theoretical Preparations Before the "Cultural Revolution"

The first stage is the theoretical preparation stage before the "Cultural Revolution." Between the founding of the People's Republic of China in 1949 and the onset of the "Cultural Revolution," Chinese economists engaged in extensive debates on key issues such as the interactive mechanism between planning and market forces in socialist economic systems, the nature of commodity production under socialist economic systems, and the function of the law of value under socialism. Notable contributions during this period included:

In 1956, Sun Yefang put forth the notable argument that the law of value should underpin the framework of economic planning and statistical operations. As he contended, the fundamental content and function of the law of value, namely, that value is determined by average socially necessary labor (content), and the development of social productive forces is promoted, the social production is regulated, or the social productive forces are distributed on this basis (function), exist in both socialist and communist societal systems.[1] In 1964, he additionally put forth: the law of value always comes first, no matter how many laws there are. Sun Yefang also proposed in an internal research report in 1963: Profit serves as the most comprehensive indicator reflecting both an enterprise's technological level and the quality of its operational management. The average profit rate of social capital is the average level achieved by each enterprise. Those that exceed the average level are advanced enterprises, and those that do not reach this level are backward enterprises.[2]

In 1957, Gu Zhun released an article positing that the socialist economy represents a contradictory unity of planned economy and economic accounting, where the law of value regulates social production via the economic accounting mechanism. The highest level of this adjustment is to "make the material rewards of laborers closely related to the degree of profit and loss of enterprises, and make price the main tool for adjusting production. Because enterprises will spontaneously pursue production with favorable prices, and prices will also fluctuate spontaneously, this rise and fall actually regulates production. At the same time, the whole society also has a unified economic plan, but this plan is 'some forecasts, not the synthesis of individual plans,' so it is more flexible, and more inclined to stipulate some important economic indicators and less for enterprise economic activities."[3] Gu Zhun essentially advocated for comprehensively applying the regulatory function of the law of value in socialist production, managing production through the spontaneous fluctuations of prices, which is an essential element of the socialist market economy. In this regard, Gu Zhun can be regarded as the pioneer of the socialist market economy theory in China.

Of course, as the traditional socialist planned economic system was dominant before the "Cultural Revolution" and conventional socialist economic theories held mainstream status, the above views and propositions of Sun Yefang and Gu Zhun were severely criticized at that time.

---

1 Yefang Sun. Placing planning and statistical work on the basis of the law of value. *Economic Research Journal*, 1956 (6).

2 Yefang Sun. Profit Index in the Management System of Socialist Planned Economy, in *The Complete Works of Sun Yefang*, Vol. 2. Taiyuan: Shanxi Economic Publishing House, 1998.

3 Zhun Gu. A tentative discussion on commodity production and the law of value under the socialist system. *Economic Research Journal*, 1957 (3).

II. Market Mechanisms: Introduced into Social and Economic Activities in the Early Stage of Reform and Opening Up

In December 1978, the historic Third Plenary Session of the 11th CPC Central Committee marked the beginning of a new era of reform and opening up, ushering in the journey of cultivating socialism anchored in China's civilizational context. The plenary session rejected the wrong theory and practice of "taking class struggle as the key link," and instituted a pivotal realignment of national priorities toward economic modernization, concurrently activating systemic reforms and global integration. The "Communiqué" of the plenary meeting pointed out: "A serious shortcoming of our country's economic management system is that power is too concentrated, and there should be bold decentralization with leadership, so that localities and industrial and agricultural enterprises have more autonomy in operation and management under the guidance of the unified national plan." "We should resolutely implement the law of economics, attach great importance to the role of the law of value, pay attention to combining ideological and political work with economic means, and fully mobilize the enthusiasm of officials and workers for production."[4]

During the 1978–1984 institutional transition, China introduced a series of reform and opening-up measures that gradually brought in market mechanisms and revitalized the national economy. These included the implementation of the Household Contract Responsibility System across rural areas, which recognized farmers' autonomy and status as independent commodity producers; the deregulation of transactional value mechanisms for non-essential merchandise and designated agro-subsidiary commodities; the legalization and encouragement of individual economies; the creation of designated market reform pilot areas and the active attraction of foreign capital; as well as the expansion of operational autonomy for state-owned enterprises, etc. These reform and opening up measures that introduced the market mechanism have made China's national economy rapidly active. The output and wealth have grown rapidly, and the market has begun to prosper. The officials and the masses have personally experienced the magical effect of the market mechanism.

Economists have also been inspired into action by reform practice. In April 1979, the 2nd National Symposium on Economic Theory was held in Wuxi, Jiangsu Province, in alignment with the Party's guiding principle of liberating thought and pursuing truth based on facts. The discussion revolved around the function

---

4 Reference Office of the Institute of Economics, Chinese Academy of Social Sciences, et al. *The Relationship Between Planning and the Market in a Socialist Economy, 2 Vols.* Beijing: China Social Sciences Press, 1980.

of the value law in a socialist framework. Over 300 individuals participated in the seminar. Xue Muqiao and Sun Yefang, two of China's leading economists, were present at the event and delivered speeches. The conference attracted a large number of scholarly papers and presented many profound and forward-thinking theoretical perspectives. Included among these was the acknowledgment that a socialist economy can also be seen as a form of commodity-based economy, and the affirmation of the roles played by market regulation and competitive mechanisms within socialism. Certain scholars proposed that enterprises should be viewed as autonomous or semi-autonomous producers and distributors of commodities, and called for a gradual expansion of their operational autonomy. In January 1980, Jiang Yiwei introduced the well-known theory centered around enterprises.[5] Reforming the current inefficient pricing and management structures is crucial, as well as gradually narrowing the "scissors gap" between industrial and agricultural product prices.[6] It now appears that the Economic Theory Seminar in 1979 has played a leading role in China's reform practice.

III. Sharp Ideological Confrontation Occurring in the Process of Establishing the Theory of the Socialist Commodity Economy

The establishment of the theory of the socialist commodity economy was a key advancement in shaping the concept of the socialist market economy. In the late 1970s and early 1980s, particularly at the 1979 Second National Seminar on Economic Theory, many Chinese economists published works arguing that the socialist economy is fundamentally a commodity economy, with the law of value serving a crucial role in regulating social and economic processes. However, there were also some economists who opposed it, and it caused a heated debate for a time. A significant event took place in 1982, when five comrades, including Lin Jianqing and Yuan Mu, who had been involved in drafting the report for the 12th CPC National Congress, jointly sent a letter to Comrade Hu Qiaomu, who was then overseeing ideological work. In the letter, they criticized the mainstream proposition in the economic theory community in those years, which emphasized the role of the market mechanism and believed that the socialist economy is also a commodity economy. The letter said: "In our country, although there is still commodity production and commodity exchange, our economy must not be generalized as a commodity economy. If such a generalization is made, the

5 Yiwei Jiang. Enterprise-based theory. *Social Sciences in China*, 1980 (1).

6 Reference Office of the Institute of Economics, Chinese Academy of Social Sciences, et al. *The Problem of Price Formation under the Socialist System*. Beijing: China Social Sciences Press, 1980.

relationship of common possession and joint labor among people under socialist conditions will be described as the relationship of the exchange of equivalent commodities; it will be determined that our economic activities are dominated by the law of value, instead of the basic economic law and the law of planned development of socialism. This will inevitably blur the boundaries between a planned socialist economy and anarchic capitalism, and blur the essential difference between a socialist economy and a capitalist economy."[7] In August 1982, Hu Qiaomu forwarded the letter.

Since then, for about a year, numerous articles criticizing the notion of viewing the socialist economy as a commodity economy appeared in domestic forums, while writings advocating that the socialist economy is also a commodity economy had disappeared. Nonetheless, the opposition to the wave of reform is inevitably destined to fade away. As the economic system reform gradually progressed, the economic dynamism driven by the market mechanism profoundly challenged the foundations of conventional economic theories. Since 1983, the theory of socialist commodity economy, bolstered by a more solid practical foundation and comprehensive theoretical support, has reappeared in China's forums, gaining widespread attention and backing from various sectors of society. In particular, on October 20, 1984, the Third Plenary Meeting of the 12th CPC Central Committee adopted the "Decision on Reform of the Economic Structure," which established that China's socialist economy is a strategically organized commodity economy rooted in state or collective ownership. Through Party documents, it encapsulated the discussions within the economic community during those years. The Decision stated: "To reform the planning system, we must first break through the traditional concept of opposing the planned economy with the commodity economy, and clearly understand that the socialist planned economy must consciously base and apply the law of value, and is a planned commodity economy based on public ownership. The full development of the commodity economy is an insurmountable stage of social and economic development and a necessary condition for realizing China's economic modernization. Only by fully developing the commodity economy can the economy be truly invigorated, and enterprises can be urged to improve their efficiency, operate flexibly, and flexibly adapt to complex and changing social needs, which cannot be achieved simply by administrative means and mandatory planning." Since then, the shared comprehension of the economy at the initial stage of socialism in our country advanced to a new level.

---

[7] Sen Peng, Li Chen, et al. *Major Events in China's Economic System Reform, Vol. 1.* Beijing: Renmin University of China Press, 2008, p. 120.

Deng Xiaoping praised this "Decision" highly. On October 22, 1984, the third day after the "Decision" was approved, he said in the "Speech at the Third Plenary Session of the Central Advisory Committee": "When the decision was adopted by the Central Committee the day before yesterday, I made a few remarks. I said I thought it read like the draft of a textbook on political economy that integrated the fundamental tenets of Marxism with the practice of socialism in China. That was my assessment of it."[8] "The document on reform of the economic structure is a good one, because it explains what socialism is in terms never used by the founders of Marxism-Leninism. There are some new theories. I think it has clarified things. We could never have drawn up such a document without the experience of the last few years. And even if it had been produced, it would have been very hard to get it adopted—it would have been regarded as heresy. Our experience has enabled us to answer new questions that have arisen under new circumstances."[9]

The "Decision" of the Third Plenary Session of the 12th CPC Central Committee also has shortcomings in understanding. It proposed a point of view that has been surpassed by later reform practices: "Under the conditions of socialism in our country, the labor force is not a commodity, nor are all state-owned enterprises and resources such as land, mines, banks, railways, etc."

IV. All Roads Leading to the Theory of the Socialist Market Economy

Following the formation of the socialist commodity economy theory, market-oriented reforms have steadily progressed; the individual and private economy have developed rapidly; the transformation of state-owned enterprises to decentralize power and transfer profits has been further advanced; enterprises in towns and villages have flourished; economic operation mechanism reform, most notably price reforms, have led the way, promoting the thriving growth and advancement of commodity and service markets; factor markets have also begun to be established; macroeconomic governance has evolved from direct to indirect control; a wide-ranging approach to international openness has been put into action; we have actively participated in international market competition, etc.

In 1987, the State Commission for Economic System Restructuring coordinated with eight central and local departments to formulate medium-term (three-year, five-year, and eight-year) reform plans. Each plan shares a common consensus that the mid-term reform goal is to solidify the leading role of the emerging socialist

---

[8] Xiaoping Deng. *Selected Works of Deng Xiaoping, Vol. 3*. Beijing: People's Publishing House, 1993, p. 83.

[9] Ibid., p. 91.

commodity economy by transitioning from the previous system to the new one. The core framework of this novel system is characterized by "government regulation of the market alongside market guidance of enterprises," encompassing three interconnected elements: the "marketization of economic operations, the corporatization of enterprises, and the indirect approach to macro-economic control." Some research groups also explicitly stated that "a planned commodity economy system is a market economic system with macro-management."

In 1987, the document of the 13th Communist Party Congress emphasized that "the socialist planned commodity economy should be a system that originally combines planning and the market," stating that "both planning and the market function across the entire society. On the whole, under the new economic mechanism, the state regulates the market and the market guides enterprises. The state regulates the relation between supply and demand through economic, legal, and necessary administrative means and creates a favorable economic and social environment in which enterprises are guided towards correct management decisions."[10]

Subsequent to the 13th CPC National Congress, China's market-based reform has progressed even more extensively. In 1988, an attempt was made to carry out price reform and to deregulate prices in a large number, but it was unsuccessful due to the interference of inflation. On the forum, there were more and more articles promoting the idea that a socialist economy operates as a market economy, arguing that it is more efficient to distribute resources through the market mechanism than by planning. However, this momentum was disrupted by the political upheaval in 1989. During that period, some economists expressed doubts or denials about the market-oriented reforms in those years. For example, some people criticized, "They said that commodity economic relations are the basis of socialist production relations, and advocated that what we want to build is an economic system that is compatible with commodity economy." "They only emphasize the commodity economy, and use this invisible hand to regulate everything. Then the planned economy can be abandoned." They also listed "doubting the possibility and necessity of a socialist planned economy and advocating the role of market regulation" as "the eighth manifestation of bourgeois liberalization." Some people argued that a market economy "can only be a capitalist economy." Some people also said, "The market economy is the abolition of public ownership, which means that it negates the leadership of the Communist

---

10 Department of Comprehensive Planning, National Economic System Reform Commission. *China's Reform Ideas.* Shenyang: Shenyang Press, 1988, p. 2.

Party, negates the socialist system, and engages in capitalism." Others said that, in economic terms, "marketization" means "liberalization."[11]

Of course, there were also many scholars who insisted on market-driven reform and the concept of a socialist market economy. What should be specially mentioned here are several articles by the influential Huangfu Ping among the articles refuting the "planning-oriented school." Let's talk about the background first. Prior to the 1991 Spring Festival, Deng Xiaoping inspected Shanghai. He said earnestly to the person in charge of Shanghai, "Our Party should adhere to the policies of reform and opening to the outside world for decades to come ... If I am the only one to speak in favor of reform and opening up, it won't be enough. The entire Party membership should do so too, and for decades. Of course, we should not be too impatient; we have to use facts to demonstrate that our policies are correct. When we proposed instituting the Household Contract Responsibility System with remuneration linked to output, many people disagreed and doubted that the system was socialist. They didn't say anything, but in their hearts, they were not convinced, and they dragged their feet about applying it. Some people refused to apply it for two years, and we just waited." "Do not think that any planned economy is socialist and any market economy is capitalist. That's not the way things are. In fact, planning and regulation by the market are both means of controlling economic activity, and the market can also serve socialism." "I hope the people of Shanghai will further emancipate their minds, be more daring and move ahead faster."[12] After Zhu Rongji, the head of the Shanghai Municipal Committee of the Communist Party of China, summarized the main ideas of Deng Xiaoping's speech at a meeting of the Municipal standing Committee, Zhou Ruijin, Secretary of the Party Committee of *Jiefang Daily*, along with Ling He, head of the newspaper's Commentary Department, and Shi Zhihong from the Policy Advisory Office of the Shanghai Municipal Party, under the pseudonym "Huangfu Ping," authored a set of four opinion pieces, which were successively released in *Jiefang Daily* from February 15 to April 22, 1991. Among them, the second commentary published on March 2 titled "New ideas should be brought into reform and opening up" recommended preventing a "new ideological stalemate" and condemned "some comrades are always accustomed to equating planned economy with socialism, and the market economy with

---

11 Wu Jinglian's research group. Medium-term (1988–1995) Reform Planning Outline of the Economic System // Comprehensive Planning Division of the National Economic System Reform Commission. *China's Reform Ideas*. Shenyang: Shenyang Press, 1988. p. 199.

12 Xiaoping Deng. *Selected Works of Deng Xiaoping, Vol. 3*. Beijing: People's Publishing House, 1993, p. 367.

capitalism, believing that behind the market economy there must be the specter of capitalism." It was clearly stated that "capitalism has a plan and socialism has a market," and said, "The acquisition of this scientific understanding is another greater emancipation of our minds on the issue of the socialist commodity economy." The piece argued that advancing the socialist goods economy and market system should not be confused with capitalism; utilizing overseas investment does not conflict with the principle of self-reliance; advancing reform is not at odds with guaranteeing discipline and correction; and striving for consistent and stable economic growth without haste does not negate the importance of maintaining a sense of urgency. "In short, to further emancipate the mind is a necessary condition to ensure that we can achieve the strategic objectives of the second step." Huangfu Ping's third commentary, "The consciousness of expanding opening up should be stronger," was published in *Jiefang Daily* on March 22. It said: "If we are still constrained by the question of 'is it socialism or capitalism,' then we can only miss the opportunity." "If we still get caught in the confusion of 'new Shanghai or old Shanghai,' we can never step forward, and it is difficult to accomplish great things."

Huangfu Ping's articles were also criticized by some people. On April 20, 1991, *Present Ideological Trends* published the article "Can we not ask whether it belongs to socialism or capitalism?" The piece stated: "In the days when the liberal ideology was seriously rampant, there was a fashionable slogan called 'never ask it belongs to socialism or capitalism.'" "How about the results? Under the exclusion of asking whether it belongs to socialism or capitalism, some people have indeed led reform and opening up to the evil path of capitalism. If we don't figure it out, reform and opening up will inevitably be led to the road of capitalism and the cause of socialism will be ruined." The 7th issue of *Pursuing the Truth* in 1991 published an article "Reintroduction of the question of whether it is belonging to socialism or capitalism," arguing that "the so-called reform without asking whether it is belonging to socialism or capitalism was originally a smoke grenade cast by the 'elites' to pretend to advance along one path while secretly going along another." [13] Beijing's major newspapers and magazines carried similar criticism.

At a critical moment in the reform debate, Deng Xiaoping made a speech. In the early months of 1992, Deng Xiaoping said more bluntly in the famous Southern Talks: "The proportion of planning to market forces is not the essential difference between socialism and capitalism. A planned economy is not

13 Sen Peng, Li Chen, et al. *Major Events in China's Economic System Reform, Vol. 1.* Beijing: China Renmin University Press, 2008.

equivalent to socialism, because there is planning under capitalism too; a market economy is not capitalism, because there are markets under socialism too. Planning and market forces are both means of controlling economic activity." "Special economic zones are socialist, not capitalist." Deng Xiaoping's statements echoed the essence of China's reform efforts, and won the support and enthusiastic response of the broad officials and the masses, as well as many economic scholars. In March 1992, a meeting of the Politburo of the CPC Central Committee clearly stated: "Both planning and the market are economic means. We must be good at using these means to accelerate the development of the socialist commodity economy."[14]

Just prior to this, between October and December 1991, Comrade Jiang Zemin, then General Secretary of the CPC Central Committee, convened eleven expert symposia (each session spanning approximately half a day), most of which were attended by economists. Participants included Liu Guoguang, Jiang Yiwei, Li Cong, Zhang Zhuoyuan and Chen Dongqi from the Social Sciences Academy of China; Wu Jinglian, Wang Huijiong and Lin Yifu from the State Council's Development Research Institute; Yang Qixian, Fu Fengxiang and Jiang Chunze from the National Commission for Economic System Reform; Zhou Xiaochuan representing the Bank of China; Guo Shuqing from the National Planning Commission; as well as experts from the Ministry of External Affairs, the State Security Ministry, and the CPC Central Committee's Department of Liaison, altogether fewer than 20 people. The symposium focused on three key topics: first, an analysis of why capitalism "lingers and does not collapse"; second, an exploration of the upheavals in Eastern Europe; and third, a debate on the next steps for advancing China's opening to the outside world. The aim of these discussions was to set the stage for the restructuring of the economy and policy proposals to be presented at the upcoming 14th CPC National Congress. Each session was chaired by General Secretary Jiang Zemin. At the symposium, some experts suggested the implementation of a socialist market-oriented economic structure, because the economic development practice of various countries in the world at that time had demonstrated the market's superior efficiency in dispersing resources compared to centralized planning. This opinion was generally agreed upon by the participating experts. Therefore, the main achievement of the symposium was to formulate the tendentious proposal of "socialist market economic system," and meanwhile, two explanations were given for

---

[14] Jun Chen, Nan Hong. *Jiang Zemin and the Proposition of the Socialist Market Economic System—20 Year's Review of the Socialist Market Economy*. Beijing: Central Party Literature Press, 2012.

this important formulation: First, the market is essential in the distribution of resources; Second, the market is subject to national macro-control rather than laissez-faire. It provided important theoretical preparations for General Secretary Jiang Zemin's address at the Central Party School on June 9, 1992, and for defining the objective of creating a socialist market economy at the 14th CPC National Congress in October 1992.

It is now evident that Deng Xiaoping's Southern Talks in early 1992, along with the symposium chaired by General Secretary Jiang Zemin in late 1991, were instrumental in forming the foundation of the socialist market economy.

In October 1992, the 14th CPC National Congress officially announced: "The goal of China's economic system reform is to establish a socialist market economic system," and clearly pointed out: "The socialist market economic system is to make the market play a fundamental role in the allocation of resources under the macro-control of the socialist country." This means that the long-standing debate between planning and the market, as well as between a government-controlled economy and an economy based on market forces, has effectively come to an end, resulting in the formation of the economic theory.

In 1993, the Third Plenary Session of the 14th CPC Central Committee made the "Decision of the Central Committee of the Communist Party of China on Some Issues Concerning Building a Socialist Market Economy," which outlined the reform targets present at the 14th CPC National Congress. The "Decision" further clarified the essential structure of the economic system: "The establishment of the socialist market economic system is to make the market play a fundamental role in resource allocation under the state's macro-control. To achieve this goal, we must adhere to the policy of taking public ownership as the main body and developing various economic components side by side, further transform the management mechanism of state-owned enterprises, and establish a modern corporate system that meets the requirements of the market economy, with clear property rights, clear rights and responsibilities, separation of enterprises from government, and scientific management; establish a unified and open market system across the country, realize the close integration of urban and rural markets, as well as the interconnection between domestic and international markets, and promote the optimal allocation of resources; transform the government's function of managing the economy, establish a sound macro-control system based on indirect means, and ensure the healthy operation of the national economy; establish an income distribution system that focuses on distribution according to work, gives priority to efficiency, and takes into account fairness, encourage some areas and some people to become better-off first, and follow the path of common prosperity; establish a multi-level social security system to provide urban and rural residents with services that are suitable for China's national conditions, and promote economic development and social stability. These main links are an organic whole featuring mutual connection and restraint, and constitute the basic framework of the socialist market economic system." The points outlined above serve not only as the key pillars supporting China's economic system but also constitute the core elements of the economic model.

2. Reforms Promoted to Move Forward by the Establishment of the Theory of Socialist Market Economy

After the establishment of the specific reform goals in 1992, China's economic transformation has advanced significantly. By the close of the twentieth century, the economic system was first set up, which shifted the management from a plan-led type to a market-led type.

In 1994, through negotiation and coordination among various parties, the original outdated fiscal contracting system was replaced by the tax distribution system commonly used in market-economy countries, so that the revenue of the central government eventually comprised half of the national total, thus enhancing its control over fiscal resources. Under the tax-sharing regime, no other tax plays a more prominent financial role than the value-added tax. Fiscal revenues are predominantly centralized, with local administrations receiving just a quarter of total tax collections. All income generated from excise duties goes to the central fiscal authority. Additionally, The portion of value-added tax (VAT) and consumption tax revenues exceeding the previous year's level shall be rebated to local governments at a ratio of 1: 0.3. In one respect, this adjustment significantly boosted fiscal revenue, with national fiscal income reaching 434.895 billion yuan in 1993. By 2007, the national fiscal revenue had jumped to 5.13 trillion yuan, marking a growth more than tenfold compared to the base year (nominal growth). In the other respect, there was a rapid rise in the central authority's share of the nation's fiscal resources. Back in the early 1990s, the figure was 22%; it peaked at 54.1% in 2007 and has hovered close to the 50% threshold ever since.

With the continuous expansion of private and self-employed sectors, the monopoly of public ownership has been eroded, giving rise to a foundational economic structure that prioritizes public assets yet accommodates various types of ownership arrangements in parallel. In 1993, 1994, and 1995, the private sector experienced growth rates exceeding 50% each year, while from 1996 to 2002, it remained at an average annual growth rate of over 15%. Please refer to Table 1 and Table 2 for details.

Table 1: National Individual Economy Development from 1992 to 2012

Year	Quantity (10,000)	Figure of individuals (10,000 people)	Stated Capital (100 million yuan)
1992	1,534	2,468	601
2002	2,377	4,743	3,782
2012	4,059	8,000	19,800

Table 2: National Private Economy Development from 1992 to 2012

Year	Quantity (10,000)	Figure of individuals (10,000 people)	Stated Capital (100 million yuan)
1992	14	232	221
2002	243	3,409	24,756
2012	1,086	12,000	310,000

Source: The Editorial Contributors to This Book. Guidebook of "The Decision of the Central Committee of the Communist Party of China on Some Issues Concerning the Improvement of the Socialist Market Economic System." Beijing: People's Publishing House, 2003; The Writing Team of This Book. Guidebook of "The Decision of the Central Committee of the Communist Party of China on Some Major Issues Concerning Comprehensively Deepening the Reform." Beijing: People's Publishing House, 2013.

Following the opening of its markets, China began to integrate international capital. The 1992 establishment of a market-driven economic model, along with joining the WTO in 2001, propelled China toward a rapid increase in foreign investment. See Table 3 for details.

Table 3: Overview of China's Foreign Investment Inflow in Some Years Unit: US $100 million

Year	Total amount	Among them, cross-border direct funding	other funding
1991	115.54	43.66	3.00
1992	192.03	110.08	2.84
2002	550.11	527.43	22.68
2012	1,132.94	1,117.16	15.78

Source: China Statistical Yearbook over the years.

By the end of 2012, there were 440,609 foreign-invested enterprises nationwide, with a total investment of US$3,261 billion and a registered capital of US$1,881.4 billion, of which the foreign registered capital was US$1,490.3 billion. About 60% of the foreign investment in China went to manufacturing.

Due to the sustained growth of self-employed businesses, privately held firms, and foreign-funded enterprises, by 2012, China's non-public economy accounted for more than 60% of GDP, with these enterprises accounting for more than 80% of job opportunities. This sector has become an indispensable driver of national prosperity, economic revitalization, and addressing the varied demands of society.

The corporate and shareholding reform of publicly owned companies has progressed steadily. With the acceleration of economic liberalization, numerous government-owned companies have fallen into trouble due to the defects of their mechanisms and their inability to adapt to the market. In 1997, the administration introduced the mission of aiding government-run businesses to overcome their challenges. The goal was: Starting from 1998, most sizable and mid-scale public corporations could recover from their difficulties within roughly three years, and by the close of the twentieth century, most major and mid-tier key public-sector firms could aim to establish modern corporate frameworks. As of 2000's end, this goal had essentially been completed. As of 1997, the total number of major and mid-sized firms in the public domain reached 16,874, with 6,599 experiencing financial setbacks, which accounted for 39.1%. By 2000, the count of loss-making companies had dropped to 1,800, a reduction of nearly three-quarters. While assisting these enterprises to overcome difficulties, the state launched a pilot program to implement a contemporary business framework, progressively implementing corporate and shareholding structures. This reform aimed to convert state-run businesses into market-centric and legally compliant organizations that support the advancement of the socialist market model. As a result, public-sector firms gradually adapted to the evolving market environment. See Table 4.

In 2012, 54 state-owned enterprises in China were featured in the *Fortune* Global 500. The public sector economy maintains strong control over vital industries and key sectors essential to the country's economic well-being. By the close of 2012, 953 government-owned corporations were publicly traded, making up 38.5% of the total number of companies listed on China's stock exchanges, with a combined value of 13.71 trillion yuan, representing 51.4% of the entire market worth of these public offerings.[15]

The transformation of the economic operating mechanism accelerated, as the market increasingly took on a central role in the deployment of resources. After 1992, price reform increasingly focused on introducing market-based pricing for resource products and factors of production. By the end of the twentieth century,

---

[15] The Writing Team of This Book. "*The Decision of the Central Committee of the Communist Party of China on Some Major Issues Concerning Comprehensively Deepening the Reform*" *Guidebook*. Beijing: People's Publishing House, 2013.

Table 4: Several Economic Indicators of the Development of Publicly Owned Industrial and Commercial Companies from 1998 to 2012

Project	1998	2003	2012
Number of state-run firms (10,000)	23.8	14.6	14.5
Assets (trillion yuan)	14.87	19.78	85.37
Operating income (trillion yuan)		10.73	42.38
Total profit (100 million yuan)	213.7	3,202	16,100
Taxes paid (100 million yuan)		8,362	33,500
Number of central enterprises		196	116
Overall profits of state-affiliated firms (100 million yuan)		3,006	11,315
Total taxes of central enterprises (100 million yuan)		3,563	14,058

Source: Shao, Ning. Record of State-owned Enterprise Reform (1998–2008). Beijing: Economic Science Press, 2014; The Writing Team of This Book. Guidebook with Q&A for the "Decision" of the Third Plenary Session of the 18th Central Committee of the Communist Party of China. Beijing: Party Building Books Publishing House, Learning Publishing House, 2013; Chi, Fulin. The Market Decides. Beijing: Economic Press China, 2014. The total earnings and taxes of central SOEs in 2012 are based on the results from 2011.

prices for goods and services in China were largely deregulated and governed by market forces, culminating in the creation of a cohesive and accessible market where competition is conducted in an orderly manner. The overall marketization level of China's economy was estimated to have reached approximately 70%, accompanied by significant changes in the market structure. The shift to a buyer-dominated market replaced the seller-driven market that had held sway in China for almost five decades. A survey conducted by the Ministry of Internal Trade[16], later recognized as the State Bureau of Internal Trade in 1998 and subsequently abolished in 2001, on the production and consumption of over 600 significant commodities revealed that signs of oversupply had emerged as early as 1995. Grounded in the relationship between the availability and consumption of most commodities, the proportion of commodities in excess supply had begun

[16] In March 1998, after the Ministry of Internal Trade was abolished, the State Bureau of Internal Trade was established, managed by the State Economic and Trade Commission. The State Bureau of Internal Trade was abolished on February 19, 2001.

to exceed that of commodities in short supply. By mid-1998, China's goods retail market saw no shortage of products, with 25.8% of the inventory in excess.[17]

From the start of the twenty-first century, China has been proactive in advancing the overhaul of pricing models for resource-based products, adhering to the direction of marketization, and improving the degree of marketization. The first is to deregulate coal prices, which have been regulated by the market. The modification of petroleum product pricing has progressed. By 2012, China's refined oil prices had been indirectly in line with global petroleum prices. In March 2013, the pricing revision interval was reduced from 22 to 10 days, and the restriction on the range of adjustments was removed. However, upper and lower boundaries were introduced for refined oil price adjustments, with the ceiling capped at US$130 and the floor at $40. The further development of natural gas pricing policies has introduced an adaptive mechanism linking gas prices with those of competing energy sources. This reform achieved the unification of prices for both existing and newly added non-residential gas supplies. Following the deregulation of direct supply, natural gas prices for end users, market forces began to determine the prices at non-residential gas gate stations, representing 80% of the overall natural gas usage. The previously undervalued water price has been gradually increased, accompanied by changes in levies for water resources, effluent disposal, and wastewater processing. In addition, tiered pricing systems for residential water, electricity, and gas have been progressively implemented across various regions to promote resource conservation. These measures have yielded notable results.

The shift toward market-based pricing of production factors has been gradually advancing. In the labor market, the remuneration of migrant workers is governed by market principles. The process of aligning interest rates with market forces has progressed steadily. Loan interest rates are deregulated first, followed by deposit interest rates, including the rate of increase. The RMB's value has also been gradually deregulated. By the late 1990s, the current account exchange rate had already been shaped by market forces, and capital account convertibility had also gradually advancing. The land market and prices have also gradually increased the degree of marketization.

China's formal acceptance into the World Trade Organization marked a significant step toward embracing economic globalization and represented a milestone in the country's development. This step marked the onset of a new chapter in China's economic liberalization. In the course of China's WTO membership

[17] Guoguang Liu. *China's Ten Five-year Plan Research Report*. Beijing: People's Publishing House, 2006, p. 613.

talks, many expressed concerns that joining the organization might threaten national economic security and severely impact several key industries, including finance, commerce, agriculture, and the information sector, etc. However, the practice after China's accession to the WTO has proved that the advantages of China's accession to the WTO outweigh the disadvantages, and many of the original worries have not appeared. After China's accession to the WTO, China's foreign economic and trade relations have achieved great development, boosting the openness and global integration of China's economy. Figures from the WTO show that between 2002 and 2012, China's exports grew at an average of 21.3% per year, propelling it from sixth place to first globally. By 2012, China's merchandise shipments constituted 11.2% of the worldwide export total. The country's aggregate goods trade reached US $3.867 trillion, securing its place as the runner-up worldwide. China's services trade hit US $471 billion, ranking third globally, with service exports placing fifth. Regarding outbound investment, China's international capital outflows stood at US $87.8 billion in 2012, securing the third spot in global rankings.[18]

From 2003 to 2012, China's economic restructuring decelerated amidst its fast-paced development, but it continued to promote reform and achieved certain results. These efforts included a series of important policy changes. In 2005, China launched an overhaul of the split-share system for publicly traded firms. Shortly after, changes were introduced to the system that governs the value of the Chinese currency, aiming to enhance its adaptability to market fluctuations. That year also marked the complete listing of the four major government-owned financial institutions, signaling a major shift in the banking sector. By 2006, the agricultural tax was abolished, providing much-needed relief to farmers. At the same time, reforms were introduced to the rural land ownership system, offering residents more secure rights to their land. Besides, the pricing system for refined petroleum products was restructured, and the consumption tax framework was modified to better reflect economic conditions. Simultaneously, pilot projects for property tax reform were initiated, while other changes took place in the cultural and healthcare sectors, aiming to address broader societal needs. Additionally, significant progress has been made in building a social security system aimed at achieving universal coverage, etc. In addition, we must also admit that there is

---

[18] Hucheng Gao. Accelerating the cultivation of new competitive advantages to participate in and lead international economic cooperation, in The Writing Team of This Book. "*The Decision of the Central Committee of the Communist Party of China on Some Major Issues Concerning Comprehensively Deepening the Reform" Guidebook.* Beijing: People's Publishing House, 2013, pp. 197–198.

indeed no particularly important and critical link in the past few years to drive the overall reform. This also plays a role in enhancing the understanding of market-driven economic principles within a socialist framework.

3. Deepening and Development of the Theory of the Socialist Market Economy After the 18th CPC National Congress

I. "The Decision of the Central Committee of the Communist Party of China on Some Major Issues Concerning Comprehensively Deepening the Reform," issued by the CPC Central Committee, emphasized broadening the scope of market-oriented reform, both in thought and in implementation.

In 2013, the Third Plenary Session of the 18th CPC Central Committee made the "Decision of the Central Committee of the Communist Party of China on Some Major Issues Concerning Comprehensively Deepening the Reform" (hereinafter referred to as the "Decision" in this section), which marked a decisive call to fully accelerate reform efforts and ushered in a fresh phase of advancing all-encompassing structural changes. The reform section of the "Decision" highlights several key points. These changes not only drive further economic shifts but also play a crucial role in the development of socialist economic ideas. Additionally, they are essential for deepening our understanding of these concepts.

(1) A major shift in the "Decision" is the revision of a long-standing principle. The former expression, which highlighted the market's central role in factor deployment, has been replaced by the claim that the market now plays a decisive part in determining how resources are managed and utilized.

The "Decision" points out that "economic system reform is the focus of deepening the reform comprehensively. The underlying issue is how to strike a balance between the role of the government and that of the market, and let the market play the decisive role in allocating resources and let the government play its functions better." "We must deepen economic system reform by centering on the decisive role of the market in allocating resources." "Decisive" and "fundamental" are only one word apart, but the meanings are quite different. The word "decisive" more effectively captures the market's central influence over factor deployment, aligning more closely with the core logic of market-based operations and underscoring the essential function of value dynamics. The statement emphasizing the market's pivotal function in guiding how resources are managed includes three core aspects.

First, resolve the issue of excessive government intervention in resource allocation. Up to 2012, China's economy still faced the challenge of undue state control over the handling and flow of essential resources. Additionally, some local governments exhibited a strong corporatization tendency, prioritizing short-term regional GDP growth at the cost of resource depletion and environmental degradation. A considerable share of available materials was not effectively leveraged, giving rise to extensive wastage, as well as environmental pollution and ecological damage, deep in debt, and insufficient attention was paid to people's livelihood issues. The people complained a lot about it. Some central departments were keen to maintain the approval system and pursue departmental interests, and certain cadres were involved in trading political influence for monetary rewards. illegally seeking personal gain. At the same time, government performance lagged in offering core social support, safeguarding fair market conditions, monitoring the safety of consumer goods and medical products, and curbing ecological degradation. Therefore, this "Decision" pointed out: "We must actively and in an orderly manner promote market-oriented reform in width and in depth, greatly reducing the government's role in the direct allocation of resources, and promote resources allocation according to market rules, market prices and market competition, so as to maximize the benefits and optimize the efficiency." It is evident that government reform and the transformation of government functions are central to this round of deepening reform and crucial for realizing the market's decisive role in resource allocation. Since then, the State Council has continued to facilitate transformation in governance by cutting unnecessary procedures, expanding delegated authority, bolstering regulatory functions, and improving service. Premier Li Keqiang, while delivering "the Government Work Report" on March 5, 2017, made the following remarks: "My administration's goal of cutting the number of items requiring government review by a third had been achieved ahead of schedule. On that basis, last year we canceled the requirement on a further 165 items for review by State Council departments and authorized local governments. We also overhauled and standardized 192 items of intermediary services for government review as well as 220 items of approvals and accreditation for professional qualifications." In comparison, local governments must intensify their reform efforts. They need to provide more effective solutions for significantly reducing direct resource allocation, gradually eliminating dependence on land-based financing, tightening financial constraints to prevent disorderly debt expansion, and enhancing their responsibilities in welfare delivery, oversight of market activities, governance of social affairs, ecological conservation, etc.

Second, solve the problem of the market environment where the market system is not perfect, and a fair competition has not truly formed. In order for the market to effectively assume a decisive function in directing resource use, it is essential to establish a nationwide system that ensures consistency, transparency, and a level playing field for all participants. As the "Decision" states, "Establishing a unified, open, competitive and orderly market system is the basis for the market to play a decisive role in the allocation of resources. We must put in place a modern market system in which enterprises enjoy independent management and fair competition, consumers have free choice and make autonomous consumption decisions, products and factors of production flow freely and are exchanged on an equal basis, strive to remove market barriers, and raise the efficiency and fairness of resource allocation." Prior to 2012, the institutional foundations supporting China's market activity were still incomplete, primarily due to insufficient marketization of production factors and resource product prices, which led to varying degrees of distortions. This was related to excessive, improper government intervention and the immature market development. The environment for fair competition in the market was also not perfect. Some local governments implemented market barriers and practiced price discrimination against products and raw materials originating from other regions; they engaged in administrative monopoly and economic monopoly, abusing the dominant market position, hindering competition, and seeking illegitimate interests; in order to encourage the development of the production of high-energy-consuming products in the region, they implemented preferential electricity prices in disregard of the national ban, illegally carried out low land prices and zero land prices to attract investment, indulged in pollution discharge and tax incentives, etc. Fake and shoddy products also appeared from time to time, impacting the market and harming consumers. Since the "Decision" was promulgated, the process of building a modern market system has been significantly accelerated. The facilitation reform of the business system has promoted the development of market entities. For three years in a row, more than 10,000 new business entities have been created on average each day, and in 2017, there were as many as 16,600, which effectively promoted entrepreneurship and increased employment. Meaningful strides have been made in adjusting the nation's pricing mechanisms. By late 2016, more than 97% of prices for goods and various public offerings were set through market forces, with considerable progress made in liberalizing pricing across major industries, including power supply, petroleum products, gas utilities, and rail logistics. New breakthroughs have also been made in restructuring the nation's financial architecture. Once the cap on deposit returns in RMB was scrapped, interest rates began operating largely under market principles. A deposit insurance system has been established.

Financial regulation has been steadily reinforced and enhanced. In 2017, the Central Financial Work Conference established the State Council Financial Stability and Development Committee, primarily tasked with preventing systemic financial risks. Steps have also been taken to ease entry barriers and adopt a list-based approach that specifies prohibited sectors for overseas capital. On June 28, 2017, China's top economic planning authority, in collaboration with the national trade administration, issued an updated "Catalogue for the Guidance of Foreign Investment Industries (2017 Edition)." The new catalog further eases entry barriers for overseas capital in sectors such as services, manufacturing, and mining. China's economic regulatory officials emphasized that this round of revisions, which follows the substantial reduction of barriers in 2015, marks a further step in opening the domestic market to international participation. The 2017 edition of the catalog contains 63 restrictive measures, a decrease of 30 compared to the 93 measures listed in the 2015 edition.[19] As rural reform has progressed, the earlier model, which centered on collective control and household-use entitlements, was upgraded to a system featuring three distinct components: collective holding, contractual claims by farm families, and flexible land-use rights. By the end of 2017, more than 80% of the land ownership had been determined. A system has been put in place to facilitate the circulation of farmland-use entitlements, accompanied by the growth of diversified models of appropriately scaled agricultural production.

Third, eliminate biased rules targeting privately funded businesses by dismantling implicit barriers and resolving associated challenges. Prior to 2012, certain opinions within scholarly and economic communities still viewed privately driven sectors as obsolete, failing to fully recognize their importance and contribution to China's hybrid market structure. They overlooked the fact that privately operated and state-backed sectors are both essential components supporting the nation's development framework. As the first instance, it is clearly stated in the "Decision": "Both the public and non-public sectors are key components of the socialist market economy, and are important bases for the economic and social development of China." This is also a key feature of the "Decision." For a period of time, due to misunderstandings and the protection of vested interests, certain biased policies and measures were formulated and implemented against privately operated businesses. The existence of hidden entry barriers and selective approval mechanisms has hampered fair competition, while unequal access to credit has resulted in elevated financing costs for many non-state-owned firms. China's leadership and relevant

[19] Shaohua Sun. China's first national version of the negative list of foreign investment was released. *Economic Information Daily*, June 29, 2017.

authorities have actively introduced measures to address these issues. The "Decision" clearly states: "Supporting the healthy development of the non-public sector. The non-public sector plays an important role in sustaining growth, stimulating innovation, increasing employment, increasing tax revenues, and so on. We will persist in equality of rights, opportunities, and rules, abolish all forms of irrational regulations for the non-public economy, remove all hidden barriers, and adopt specific measures for non-public enterprises to enter franchising fields. We will encourage non-public enterprises to participate in SOE reform, foster mixed enterprises with non-public capital as the controlling shareholder, and encourage qualified private enterprises to establish the modern corporate system." Subsequently, initiatives were undertaken to improve conditions for enterprise growth, encourage the expansion of hybrid ownership structures, and support private-sector funding in public infrastructure development across multiple regions. According to data released by fiscal authorities, as of June 2017, 13,554 public-private partnership (PPP) projects were recorded, with a combined investment of 16 trillion yuan. Additionally, efforts have been made to both promote and regulate outbound capital flows, contributing to the stable advancement of privately operated businesses.

(2) The second major breakthrough in the "Decision" lies in redefining the role of oversight bodies for state-held assets, shifting their focus from directly overseeing companies to concentrating on managing state equity and financial interests.

The "Decision" says: "We will improve the state-owned assets management system, strengthen state-owned assets oversight with capital management at the core, reform the authorized operation mechanism for state-owned capital, establish a number of state-owned capital operating companies, and support qualified SOEs to reorganize themselves into state-owned capital investment companies. State-owned capital investment operations must serve the strategic goals of the state, invest more in key industries and areas that are vital to national security and are the lifeblood of the economy, focusing on offering public services, developing important and forward-looking strategic industries, protecting the ecological environment, supporting scientific and technological progress, and guaranteeing national security." On August 24, 2015, the "Guiding Opinions of the Central Committee of the Communist Party of China and the State Council on Deepening the Reform of State-owned Enterprises" pointed out: "The transformation of the functions of state-owned asset supervisory and management authorities shall be promoted with the focus on capital management. State-owned asset supervisory and management authorities shall accurately grasp the positioning of performing the duties of investors in accordance with the law, scientifically define the boundaries of supervision of state-owned assets investors, establish a list of supervision powers and responsibilities, and realize the transformation from focusing on management of enterprises to focusing on management of capital."

In 2002, during the 16th Party Congress, a governance model was introduced for public-sector wealth that combined financial supervision with human resources and administrative oversight. At the national, provincial, and municipal levels, dedicated regulatory bodies were created to oversee publicly owned assets, effectively addressing the long-standing issue of fragmented oversight. However, it was still difficult to solve the problem that the State-owned Assets Supervision and Administration Commission (SASAC) had to be both a "boss" and a "steward," so it was also difficult to achieve the separation of enterprises from government. Shifting the focus of public capital oversight bodies from direct involvement in enterprise operations to emphasizing equity-based control marked a major advancement in the transformation of state-affiliated businesses and also introduced a new conceptual breakthrough in the broader evolution of economic governance. It means:

First, the SASAC is no longer the direct boss that state-owned enterprises must ask for instructions on everything. Under the previous model of focusing on enterprise-level oversight, even when a publicly funded entity had undergone structural transformation and established a governing board, that board often lacked the authority to exercise the legal functions granted by China's corporate legislation. Decisions on major company issues cannot be made independently, as nearly all significant matters must be approved in consultation with the SASAC. In other words, the company does not even have the right to make decisions on its own operations, making it impossible to function as an autonomous market entity. As a result, the influence of market forces over how resources are distributed fails to take effect within specific organizational units, such as publicly funded firms. Under the "capital-centered" model, and with limited exceptions, SASAC essentially functions as the principal investor, assigning shareholder delegates and executive leadership to affiliated firms. This structure allows the top decision-making body of the company to exercise its duties and authority as outlined in the national corporate legislation. In July 2017, the central government released the "Implementation Plan for the Restructuring of Corporate System of Central SOEs," requiring that all central enterprises, excluding financial and cultural units, under SASAC's oversight and still operating under the 1988 law on wholly state-owned industrial firms, be transformed into either limited liability entities or shareholding corporations in line with *The Company Law*, with the transition to be completed before the close of that year. This restructuring effort involved the head offices of 69 centrally administered enterprises, out of a total of 101 such entities, and extended to more than 3,200 affiliated companies. The assets involved approached 8,000 billion yuan at the core level and approximately 5.66 trillion yuan across the subsidiaries.[20] After more than 20 years of delays, this reform finally took effect at the end of 2017. It represents not only an urgent need to deepen the reform of state-owned enterprises, but also a crucial prerequisite for implementing the "mainly managing capital" approach. Only after the above-mentioned 69 central SOEs and more than 3,000 subsidiaries are converted into corporations can it be possible for the SASAC not to directly manage these enterprises, and gradually turn to "mainly managing capital."

Second, dedicated entities for asset management and strategic equity deployment have been created or reshaped to function as key platforms for overseeing public capital under market-based principles. To enable the SASAC to "mainly manage capital," it is crucial to establish or revamp platforms responsible for managing public-sector assets and deploying equity investments. Authorities responsible for managing public-sector assets shall, under the law, fulfill ownership-related obligations toward capital operation units, investment arms, and select affiliated enterprises, and empower them to handle similar functions within their authorized scope. Accordingly, such publicly affiliated firms will, going forward, primarily coordinate with capital operation bodies and investment-focused institutions entrusted by SASAC to exercise ownership rights. Since 2014, the SASAC has initiated experimental projects for capital management platforms and investment firms. By 2017, 10 such firms had been selected, with notable participants such as COFCO, SDIC, Shenhua Group, China Minerals, Baowu Group, and others. According to the report, the pilot program focused on three main areas. The first objective was to enhance the professional management of public assets while exploring effective investment and operational strategies. The second focused on refining the relationship between SASAC and enterprises, as well as improving the public asset oversight system. The final goal was to drive reforms within public capital management and operating entities, fostering management models driven by market dynamics.[21]

Third, the central role of SASAC is to better support national strategic goals by improving the distribution of public assets, boosting their operational effectiveness, and increasing their flexibility. The "Decision" outlines that future

---

[20] Ye Yang, Kexin Huang. The restructuring of 8 trillion in assets of central SOEs will be completed by the end of the year. *Economic Information Daily*, July 27, 2017.

[21] Ye Yang. Relevant supporting documents are expected to be released within this year, and the pilot program of state-owned capital investment and operation companies will be accelerated. *Economic Information Daily*, August 9, 2017.

investments of government-held resources will be concentrated in five main sectors: enhancing public service provision, nurturing vital forward-thinking industries, safeguarding ecological health, supporting technological advancements, and fortifying national defense. This stipulation provides greater detail and clarity than the "Decision of the Central Committee of the Communist Party of China on Some Major Issues Concerning the Reform and Development of State-Owned Enterprises" made by the Fourth Plenary Session of the 15th CPC Central Committee in 1999. The "Decision of the Fourth Plenary Session of the 15th CPC Central Committee" specifies that the state-owned economy should maintain control over industries related to national security, natural monopolies, providers of essential public goods and services, as well as key backbone enterprises within pillar and high-tech sectors. The "Decision" no longer speaks broadly about controlling natural monopoly industries; instead, it specifies that in natural monopoly sectors where publicly held assets retain managerial authority and remain actively involved in operations, networks will be separated from operations, and competitive businesses will be deregulated according to the unique characteristics of each industry. The "Decision" also identifies environmental conservation as a major priority for the deployment of publicly owned financial resources, which also indicates the further expansion compared with the four major areas proposed in 1999. As of 2017, publicly held financial resources were still not sufficiently directed toward strategic fields and essential domains linked to national defense and the backbone of the country's economic framework. Instead, a considerable share of publicly controlled assets continued to be allocated to sectors characterized by widespread market rivalry, including the real estate sector, which attracted strong interest from many central enterprises (government-subsidized housing not included). Future efforts should involve strategic rebalancing, ensuring that by 2020, the vast majority of government-owned equity (exceeding 80%) is allocated to the five principal fields emphasized in the "Decision."

Fourth, the SASAC will concentrate on enhancing the performance of publicly held assets while ensuring their value is maintained and incrementally increased. Under the condition of "mainly managing enterprises," the SASAC oversees close to 100 centrally administered corporations, resulting in an overly extended supervisory chain, which is contrary to the more efficient requirements of direct management of about 30 enterprises in general principles of management, let alone the subsidiaries, second-tier subsidiaries, third-tier subsidiaries, and the subsidiaries with five or six tiers or even as many as ten tiers under the central SOEs, which are beyond the reach of the SASAC. This situation diverted the SASAC's attention from optimizing the utilization of national equity holdings, making it harder to maintain asset security and promote growth in returns. For a time, the internal governance of certain state-owned enterprises was disordered, leading to recurring losses of state assets resulting from embezzlement, corruption, related-party transactions, transfer of interests, and unlawful decision-making. For instance, in 2015, the central inspection team uncovered such issues in several central SOEs, including Sinopec, COSCO, CSSC, Shenhua, and Dongfeng Motor, etc. There were prominent problems such as engaging in the transmission and exchange of interests and making profits from related transactions to varying degrees.[22] There were many reasons for this drawback, but it had a certain relationship with the system and mechanism of "mainly managing enterprises." In the years ahead, the SASAC is expected to prioritize capital stewardship, directing its efforts toward the supervision of public funds and enhancing their performance and returns.

(3) It is proposed that the mixed-ownership economy is an important form of the fundamental economic system, which is another highlight of the "Decision."

The "Decision" says: "Vigorously developing a mixed economy. A mixed economy with cross holding by and mutual fusion between state-owned capital, collective capital and non-public capital is an important way to materialize the fundamental economic system of China. It is conducive to improving the amplification function of state-owned capital, ensuring the appreciation of its value, and raising its competitiveness, and it is conducive to enabling capital with all kinds of ownership to draw on one another's strong points to offset weaknesses, stimulate one another and develop together. We will allow more state-owned enterprises (SOEs) and enterprises of other types of ownership to develop into mixed enterprises. We will allow non-state-owned capital to hold shares in projects invested by state-owned capital. We will allow mixed enterprises to implement employee stock ownership plans (ESOP) to form communities of capital owners and laborers." This passage has important implications for reform theory and practice.

First, promoting diversified ownership structures is a key step toward enhancing the foundational economic framework, which emphasizes public-sector leadership alongside the coexistence of various types of property rights. Following the initiation of economic reforms, public-sector holdings, privately financed enterprises, and overseas investments have all seen remarkable expansion. By the close of 2016, assets overseen within the national public asset management framework amounted to approximately 144.1 trillion yuan. Meanwhile, privately

---

[22] Zhizhi Chen. Related party transactions are a chronic disease, and violations of discipline are still frequent. *China Discipline Inspection and Supervision News*, Feb. 7, 2015.

sourced funds had exceeded 30 trillion yuan. Since 2010, China's annual absorption of overseas corporate funding has consistently surpassed the US$100 billion mark. Moreover, over 60% of the nation's total expenditure on infrastructure and long-term physical assets came from privately mobilized financial resources. On a macro level, the current economic framework in China reflects a hybrid model that integrates various forms of ownership. According to the "Decision," strengthening ownership diversification at the firm level involves merging capital from public, communal, and private sectors through intertwined equity structures and strategic cooperation. On the one hand, this approach not only enhances the leverage and efficiency of state-owned capital but also helps secure its value appreciation. On the other hand, it facilitates mutual complementation among diverse ownership capital, allowing different types of investors to leverage their respective advantages, compensate for shortcomings, and pursue coordinated growth. What is more, employee equity participation is also allowed under this diversified ownership framework, creating an alternative approach to motivate the workforce. It was affirmed during the 15th National Party Congress that public ownership can be realized through the establishment of a shareholding framework. The Third Plenary Session held in 2003 emphasized that equity-based corporate structures would serve as the dominant model for implementing publicly owned assets. On this basis, the "Decision" points out that encouraging cross-ownership among different types of capital serves as a crucial tool for realizing the fundamental principles underpinning China's economic model. Sustained efforts in restructuring have revealed that corporate structures can take the form of wholly state-owned enterprises, or joint-stock companies where state-owned entities hold shares. In contrast, joint-stock companies in developed economies are typically dominated by private capital. Only the mixed-ownership economy can serve as a genuine economic entity characterized by a diversity of investment subjects, and broadening the range of investors is essential for transforming traditional state-run entities into modern corporations with diversified ownership, helping to address legacy inefficiencies and enhance operational effectiveness. In this regard, the blending of different ownership structures serves as an evolved form and an advanced stage of the shareholding system.

Second, actively advancing the expansion of blended ownership models entails several key directions. First, it is essential to fully activate the dynamism of different forms of capital and leverage their respective strengths. These advantages should not operate in isolation but should be integrated through equity interlocking and reciprocal integration. For example, to speed up the construction of public utility undertakings that generate significant spillover benefits, private investment can be brought in to improve performance, reduce the investment payback period, and align social benefits with economic returns. Second, this model can offer a new avenue for reforming sectors traditionally dominated by public monopolies. The "Decision" recommends that in sectors with inherent monopolistic features where government-held capital remains in a dominant position, efforts should be made to distinguish infrastructure management from service provision, and to liberalize segments that are open to market competition according to each industry's specifics. Numerous commercial operations embedded in traditionally monopolized fields are, in fact, competitive in nature and warrant liberalization. How can this be achieved? One of the most viable methods is to bring in capital from outside the state sector to broaden the equity base and reshape ownership patterns. This would enable the liberalization of competitive segments that have long been monopolized, thereby enhancing resource allocation and boosting operational efficiency. Simultaneously, state-owned enterprises in natural monopoly sectors can improve their core businesses by divesting shares in competitive operations, raising capital, and increasing investment in technological innovation. Before the "Decision" was issued, publicly funded companies operating in broadly contestable sectors had, for the most part, already experienced corporatization and shareholding reforms, achieving diversified ownership structures. By comparison, progress in overhauling sectors with monopolistic characteristics has been relatively slow. Hence, advancing hybrid capital models aims to address these persistent obstacles head-on and offers a viable path forward for advancing reform in natural monopoly sectors.

Third, following the promulgation of the "Decision," the mixed-ownership economy experienced rapid growth. Moreover, promoting hybrid ownership models was identified by several areas as the main pathway to deepen the transformation of publicly controlled enterprises. Premier Li Keqiang stressed in the 2014 "Government Work Report": We will craft tailored strategies that open the door for private and other non-state actors to invest in initiatives led by central government-backed enterprises and open up a number of sectors, such as banking, oil, electricity, railways, telecommunications, resources development, and public utilities, to such participation. On July 15, 2014, the SASAC launched a pilot program for the development of a mixed-ownership economy within central SOEs, selecting China National Pharmaceutical Group Corporation and China National Building Materials Group Corporation as initial pilot units. The pilot initiative focused on six major aspects. First, it sought to build a sound governance framework that ensures mutual oversight and safeguards the interests of all forms of ownership equally. Second, it tested the implementation of a system for professional executives, alongside a hiring model guided by market principles. The third one was to develop incentive and constraint mechanisms aligned with market principles. Fourth, the trial introduced shareholding schemes for employees in enterprises with diversified equity structures. Fifth, it explored viable oversight frameworks for these entities, along with strategies to safeguard public capital and avoid asset erosion. The last one was to explore an effective mechanism for implementing Party building within mixed-ownership enterprises.[23] In addition, several provinces and municipalities have rolled out their own policies and initiatives to promote the development of the mixed-ownership economy. Drawing from preliminary figures, over a span of three consecutive years, centrally administered enterprises saw the creation of close to 1,000 affiliated firms under diversified ownership structures. Notably, over 700 of these entities were established in 2017 alone. During the same period, approximately 338.6 billion yuan of private-sector funds entered via capital market channels. As 2017 drew to a close, more than two-thirds of enterprises under central administration had secured funding from diverse private-sector participants. Additionally, more than half of state-affiliated equity had been pooled into companies listed on the stock exchange. At the same time, three centrally managed corporate groups had undergone ownership diversification at the parent-company level. Among the enterprises below, second-tier subsidiaries of central government enterprises, those with mixed ownership accounted for more than 50%.[24] However, overall progress in mixed-ownership reform has remained relatively slow, and the experiences and outcomes of pilot enterprises have yet to be fully disclosed. In some central government enterprises, the reform progress is hindered by complex approval procedures and coordination mechanisms. In recent years, China Unicom has been designated by SASAC as a test case for reforms aimed at integrating diverse forms of ownership of funds, but until August 2017, there were still many issues to be coordinated, involving as many as ten central ministries and commissions. The core challenges of advancing mixed-ownership reform lie in determining equity share arrangements and accurately valuing state-owned assets, which also require gradual consensus, thoughtful coordination, and open and transparent operations.

(4) It is proposed to speed up the refinement of a well-functioning market framework, allowing market forces to fully shape the distribution and utilization of economic resources.

The "Decision" states that "Establishing a unified, open, competitive and orderly market system is the basis for the market to play a decisive role in the allocation

---

23 A new round of state-owned enterprise reform kicked off (Policy Interpretation; Reform Release Hall). *People's Daily*, July 16, 2014.

24 Central SOEs added more than 700 mixed-ownership enterprises last year. *People's Daily*, Feb. 1, 2018.

of resources. We must put in place a modern market system in which enterprises enjoy independent management and fair competition, consumers have free choice and make autonomous consumption decisions, products and factors of production flow freely and are exchanged on an equal basis, strive to remove market barriers, and raise the efficiency and fairness of resource allocation." In addition, the "Decision" outlines five directives for enhancing the structure of a contemporary market economy, with the following aspects being emphasized.

First, set up a rule-based environment that guarantees impartiality and openness in market transactions. Notably, the "Decision" was the inaugural Party document officially proposing adopting a negative list management model. It states: "We will implement a unified market access system; and on the basis of making a negative list, all kinds of market players may enter areas not on the negative list on an equal basis and according to law. We will explore a management model for foreign investors with pre-establishment national treatment plus the negative list." Previously, China's earlier regulatory framework was based on specifying allowable sectors, whereas in many high-income countries, only areas off-limits were identified. On June 28, 2017, following prolonged institutional reform, China's chief economic planning agency and commerce authority jointly released the "Catalogue for the Guidance of Foreign Investment Industries (Revised in 2017)." The updated version reduced the number of restricted and banned entries to 63, 30 fewer than in the 2015 edition. It also introduced a clearly defined framework outlining entry rules for overseas investors, signaling a shift toward a more transparent and rule-based model for regulating international capital inflows.[25]

The "Decision" puts forward: "We will make the business registration system more convenient by reducing the number of items that require qualification verification, turning certification before licensing into licensing before certification, and gradually changing the paid-in capital registration system into a subscribed capital registration system. We will propel reform of our domestic commodity distribution structure while building a business environment under the rule of law." Over the subsequent three years, China's business environment saw significant improvement. The optimization effectively unleashed market vitality and entrepreneurial creativity. Following the implementation of administrative streamlining in 2014, the pace of enterprise formation accelerated significantly. By 2017, the number of new companies had climbed to over 16,000, up from just over 6,000 per day in 2013, prior to the reform. The average number exceeded 10,000 daily during the reform's initial years. As reported in the "Doing Business

---

25 Shaohua Sun. China's first national version of the negative list of foreign investment was released. *Economic Information Daily*, June 29, 2017.

2017 Report" by the World Bank, China advanced in its overall standing for business-friendliness by 18 positions over the previous three years, averaging an increase of six places annually.[26]

Second, enhancing the mechanism through which market forces primarily determine prices. The "Decision" states: "Any price that can be determined by the market must be left to the market, and the government is not to carry out improper interventions. We will push ahead with pricing reforms of water, oil, natural gas, electricity, transportation, telecommunications, and some other sectors while relaxing price control in competitive areas. Prices which are determined by the government will be limited to important public utilities, public-welfare services and network-based natural monopolies while raising transparency and accepting social supervision. We will improve the pricing mechanism for agricultural products, and attach importance to the market's role in determining prices." After the "Decision" was made, the price reform has taken a big step and made obvious progress. First, government-priced items have been included in the list. A newly amended edition of the national-level pricing list was introduced by the country's macroeconomic regulator in late October 2015, significantly narrowing the pricing scope. The number of categories was cut from 13 to 7, a 46% reduction, while specific pricing items dropped from around 100 to 20, representing an 80% decrease. Simultaneously, local pricing catalogs were trimmed by approximately 50% on average. Regarding agricultural product pricing reforms, in 2014, the government deregulated the purchase prices of tobacco leaves and silkworm cocoons, marking the complete market determination of agricultural product prices. In 2016, reforms advanced in the corn purchase and storage system, accompanied by the establishment of a subsidy scheme for corn producers. The target price reform pilot programs for cotton in Xinjiang and soybeans in Northeast China and Inner Mongolia were generally smooth, and pricing within China moved closer to international benchmarks. In the area of energy price adjustment, pilot programs for electricity delivery pricing were first launched in the Shenzhen and Inner Mongolia power grids in late 2014. By mid-2017, this reform had extended to cover all provincial-level grids nationwide. In 2015, the inter-provincial electricity transaction prices were deregulated, allowing prices to be negotiated directly between the sender and receiver. In the same period, a new system linking coal and electricity prices was introduced. Responding to the ongoing decline in coal prices, the central pricing authority enacted a 3-fen-per-kWh cut for coal-powered generators in early 2016. Electricity tariffs for

26 Jing Ma. China's business environment ranking jumped 18 places in the world. *People's Daily*, Oct. 26, 2017.

typical business and industrial consumers were also lowered accordingly, resulting in an estimated annual reduction of about 22.5 billion yuan in corporate energy expenditures. In 2015, considerable progress was made in freeing up pricing for pipeline gas, with market determination applied to a substantial share of supply. Two years earlier, in 2013, fuel price policies were updated, shortening the review period from twenty-two to ten working days and discarding the requirement that international crude shifts exceed 4% before local prices could be modified. Meanwhile, tiered tariffs were gradually enforced for urban users in the areas of water supply, electricity, and gas provision. As of late 2015, all but two of China's 31 provincial-level regions, namely Qinghai and Tibet, had established a tiered water pricing system for urban residents; among 30 provinces (autonomous regions and municipalities) that had access to natural gas, 28 provinces (autonomous regions and municipalities) had established tiered natural gas pricing systems except Chongqing and Xinjiang. The tiered electricity pricing system has been running smoothly since its trial implementation in 2012. Except for Xinjiang and Tibet, all other provincial-level regions across the country have fully implemented the tiered electricity pricing system for residents.[27]

Third, establishing a harmonized mechanism for allocating land for construction that spans both metropolitan zones and outlying communities. The "Decision" proposes: "We will allow rural collectively owned profit-oriented construction land to be sold, leased and appraised as shares, on the premise that it conforms to planning and its use is under control, and ensure that it can enter the market with the same rights and at the same prices as state-owned land." Since that point, the initial system, involving group-held land and individual contracting, was refined into a three-rights framework, distinguishing between communal claims, household tenancy, and land-use management. In addition, efforts should focus on building institutional channels for reallocating rural land-use arrangements and fostering a variety of farming models suited to optimal operational size.

Fourth, enhancing the monetary market. The "Decision" states: "We will open the financial industry wider, and allow qualified non-governmental capital to set up, in accordance with law, financial institutions such as small or medium-sized banks on the precondition that this comes under stronger oversight." "We will improve the mechanism for market-based RMB exchange rate

[27] Guangjian Xu, Yuewei Ding. Deepening the promotion of price reform and striving to improve the level of "decentralization-control-service." *Price: Theory & Practice*, 2017 (5).

formation, accelerate interest-rate liberalization, and improve the national debt yield curve that reflects the relationship between market supply and demand." Since then, a number of private banks initiated and established by private capital have been operating one after another. Scrapping the cap previously imposed on interest rates for RMB savings deposits has essentially realized interest rate marketization. In February 2015, the State Council issued the "Regulations on Deposit Insurance," which took effect on May 1, 2015. These rules introduced a ceiling of 500,000 yuan for depositor compensation, signaling the launch of China's bank deposit protection framework.

Fifth, pushing forward changes in the governance framework for science and technology and facilitating the maturation of the technology sector. The "Decision" states: "We will set up and improve mechanisms and institutions that encourage original innovation, integrated innovation, and re-innovation based on introduction and absorption, improve the mechanism that encourages market-based technological innovation, and give free rein to the market's guiding role in technological research and development orientation, choice of paths, pricing of factors, and allocation of all innovation factors." Then, the "Recommendations for the 13th Five-Year Plan for Economic and Social Development" issued by the Fifth Plenary Session of the 18th CPC Central Committee in 2015 proposes to improve and firmly establish a new development philosophy featuring innovative, coordinated, green, open, and shared development. At the same time, it is pointed out that "innovation is the primary driving force for development. Innovation must be placed at the heart of China's development and advanced in every field, from theory to institutions, science, technology, and culture. Innovation should permeate the work of the Party and the country and become an inherent part of society." Guided by the nation's strategic emphasis on innovation-led growth, the market for technological applications and transfers has expanded rapidly. In 2015, approximately 307,000 agreements involving technological cooperation and transfer were concluded, resulting in a transaction volume of 983.5 billion yuan, an increase of 14.7% compared to the prior year. By 2016, the figure had risen to around 320,000 such agreements, with the total value climbing to 1.14 trillion yuan, reflecting a year-on-year growth rate of 16%.

II. The report of the 19th CPC National Congress: further proposing to accelerate the improvement of the socialist market economy and promote high-quality economic development.

At the conference in October 2017, General Secretary Xi Jinping delivered a report titled "Secure a decisive victory in building a moderately prosperous society in all respects and strive for the great success of socialism with Chinese characteristics for a new era." The report points out: "With decades of hard work, socialism with Chinese characteristics has crossed the threshold into a new era. This is a new historic juncture in China's development." "As socialism with Chinese characteristics has entered a new era, the principal contradiction facing Chinese society has evolved. What we now face is the contradiction between unbalanced and inadequate development and the people's ever-growing needs for a better life." "China's economy has been transitioning from a phase of rapid growth to a stage of high-quality development. This is a pivotal stage for transforming our growth model, improving our economic structure, and fostering new drivers of growth. It is imperative that we develop a modernized economy. This is both an urgent requirement for getting us smoothly through this critical transition and a strategic goal for China's development." During the significant assembly in 2017, policymakers offered systematic guidance on how to optimize national governance in economic affairs and advanced the conceptual basis underpinning China's distinctive development model.

First, it clearly emphasizes the need to push forward with efforts aimed at perfecting a system driven by market principles under public oversight, ensuring continued momentum in improving institutional arrangements. We must strive to shape an economic structure characterized by responsive allocation systems, robust enterprise activity at the grassroots level, and effective overarching oversight. Sound macro-regulation is used for the first time. It mainly refers to the role of macro-control to smooth out economic fluctuations. It can neither be left unchecked nor excessive. Timely and proper adjustments and controls are essential to foster a favorable macroeconomic environment that supports the healthy functioning of the economy.

Second, it is emphasized that our economic reforms should focus on enhancing the property rights system and guaranteeing that factors of production are allocated through market mechanisms, making property rights effective incentives. We must ensure the free movement of factors, flexible pricing, fair and orderly competition, and that business success depends on competitive performance. Compared with the previous policy document, which focused on strengthening protections for ownership claims, the statement from the 2013 Session places greater emphasis on refining the structures for property rights protection. The current proposal highlights the need to refine the legal and organizational framework surrounding asset control, so as to better stimulate initiative and ensure efficient utilization of resources. The proposal also highlights the need to accelerate adjustments in the pricing structure of core elements, laying the groundwork for improving how these elements are deployed across the economy through demand-supply dynamics.

Third, the proposal aims to further improve the scale, quality, and performance of public capital. This is a step further than the "Decision" of the 2013 Session, which proposes that the state-owned asset supervisory and management authorities "mainly manage capital." Departments responsible for overseeing public sector assets should shift their focus toward capital-related oversight, rather than managing the physical or financial components of public holdings, which include obligations and shareholder interests. If the debt-to-asset ratio exceeds 100%, the owner's equity is negative, as in some zombie companies. Compared with the directive issued in 1999 emphasizing the overall enhancement of publicly owned sectors, this proposal goes a step further by focusing on boosting the influence, efficiency, and scale of government-held resources. This is because the state-owned economy includes some public and welfare units whose primary mission is to enhance service quality, rather than simply becoming stronger, better, and larger.

Fourth, it is necessary to support the expansion of non-public sector entities, energize various types of business actors, break up government-imposed barriers, and guard against the concentration of market power. It is essential to foster and safeguard entrepreneurship, motivating more entities to innovate and start businesses. This marks the first time that "private enterprises" have been explicitly mentioned in a major Party document. The formulation in the "Decision" of the 2013 Session is "non-public enterprises." Private enterprises are more popular and straightforward, and everyone can understand them at a glance. It is suggested to foster privately funded businesses and safeguard entrepreneurial initiative, thereby unleashing their potential in boosting national output, advancing technological progress, expanding employment opportunities, and increasing fiscal contributions. The phrase "Precluding the forming of market monopolies" was newly included in a Party publication, signaling a clear stance on dismantling exclusive control and fostering a competitive environment.

Fifth, it is proposed to enhance the regulatory framework by integrating monetary policy with macro-prudential policy, and to further promote the market-based formation of interest rates and exchange rates. This regulatory framework requires financial regulators to go beyond maintaining price stability and also closely monitors fluctuations in asset values, property-related lending, shadow banking operations, and international capital flows.

Sixth, it is proposed to convert growth drivers and promote momentum changes during the transition toward more advanced and sustainable economic development. It includes at least four key dimensions. First, creative capabilities should be placed at the center of driving progress. Technological innovation, in particular, should lead comprehensive innovation efforts, functioning as a key component in building a new-style economy. Second, efforts should focus on upgrading the production system by enhancing the quality of manufacturing and fostering the growth of cutting-edge industrial segments. This involves deepening the application of digital technologies across traditional industries to foster new engines of expansion in areas like quality consumer demand, environmentally sustainable practices, collaborative business models, intelligent logistics networks, and talent-driven services. Third, high-quality development should be propelled through expanded opening up. Whether by promoting the Belt and Road Initiative or expanding global commerce, it is important to pursue greater openness in trade and investment practices, refine the spatial distribution of international engagement, pilot new types of special open zones, and explore creative models for overseas economic cooperation. All these measures can promote high-quality economic development. The fourth priority is to accelerate the refinement of the emerging institutional framework and steadily boost China's capacity for original breakthroughs and its overall economic strength. The transformation of growth dynamics represents a long-term objective that requires ongoing exploration and gradual refinement through practical application.

4. Some Laws of the Socialist Market Economy

Over the past four decades, China has undergone a sweeping transformation that unlocked vast productive potential and energized broad participation in economic growth. As market-oriented practices gradually took shape, various sectors of society became more engaged in driving development and innovation. Between 1979 and 2017, China's economy expanded at an impressive pace, with yearly output growth nearing double digits. Over the same period, per capita GDP surged from around US$190 in 1978 to approximately US$9,000 by 2017, reflecting China's transition into a more affluent developing economy. Since 2009, China has emerged as the world's second-largest economy and successfully attained its objective of fostering an all-encompassing standard of moderate prosperity across the nation by 2020. The take-off of China's economy from the 1980s to the first 20 years of the twenty-first century has been the most startling event in human history during this period, and has been called "China's miracle" by the world. Many economists are also constantly studying the "mystery of China's rapid economic growth." Indeed, the rapid growth of China's economy over the past 40 years has gradually shown some regularities, which are worthy of careful study and generalization by economists. Let's talk about our initial exploration of this issue.

I. The marketplace serves as the primary force in directing how assets are utilized, and the value principle acts as a guiding mechanism for the organization and flow of economic operations.

The essential contrast between a mixed economic system under socialism and a rigid, top-down model is reflected in their differing reliance on market dynamics to guide the distribution of key inputs. In a socialist market economy, the market serves as the primary and decisive force in regulating resource distribution, functioning as the principal mechanism of coordination. Conversely, in a centrally administered economic model, the influence of market interactions is either extremely limited or entirely suppressed, with resource allocation predominantly governed by administrative planning. Viewed through the lens of historical materialist economic theory, pricing dynamics rooted in labor value function as the chief coordinator of productive operations and material exchange. Yet in economies dominated by top-down planning, this law is largely suppressed, with state-mandated plans assuming the dominant role in directing economic activity.

So far, domestic and foreign economic practices have demonstrated that allocating and reallocating scarce social resources based on market signals, particularly price signals, is more efficient than relying on mandatory state or government planning. This is because: under the conditions of socialized mass production with continuous technological progress and the rapid development of individualized demands, not only are the variety of products and services in the hundreds of thousands or even millions, but also the needs of society and people are more complex, changeable, and constantly updated. Economic globalization and frequent economic exchanges between countries make the market demand change rapidly. Under such circumstances, any modern computing technology, including cloud computing, and strict administrative regulation adopted by the state planning department, cannot organically link and coordinate social supply and demand (including more and more individualized demands). The price fluctuations in the market provided signals of social demand that are far more timely, comprehensive, and accurate than directives issued by planning departments. These signals enable various economic actors to produce, operate, and deliver services in line with actual societal needs, thereby reducing resource waste and inefficiency. That is to say, when the law of value functions, societal inputs tend to shift away from less profitable or less efficient fields toward those offering greater economic returns, which typically align with areas of heightened public demand. However, within a given market segment, competition ensures that only the most competitive firms remain viable, which enables social resources to be effectively utilized and allocated. As Marx theorized in the concluding parts of his economic analysis, once the system based on private capital accumulation is abolished, the principle of value measurement will remain central to how resources are allocated across society. He said: "After the abolition of the capitalist mode of production, but still retaining social production, the determination of value continues to prevail in the sense that the regulation of labor-time and the distribution of social labor among the various production groups, ultimately the book-keeping encompassing all this, become more essential than ever."[28]

With the deepening of institutional restructuring and external engagement, China has gradually replaced its command-style economy with a more flexible model influenced by market forces and socialist ideals. It is because the drawbacks of the originally implemented planned economic system, which played a constructive role during the early years of the 1950s, had become increasingly prominent, such as low efficiency, lack of vitality, wrong goods, and lack of materials. Moreover, the economy experienced significant volatility with a noticeable slowdown in growth; disparities in productivity and innovation capacity compared to advanced economies became more pronounced, and improvements in household income and quality of life were sluggish. With the initiation of institutional transformation and integration into the global economy, the role of the market started to emerge, economic vitality has been reinvigorated, special economic zones have been established, foreign capital and technology have been introduced, individual and private economies have been allowed to develop, employment has been increased, and the national economy has risen rapidly. After 40 years of efforts, China, which was a poor and backward country, has become an important economy in the world, and is transforming into a strong economy. It demonstrates that moving away from a command-driven structure toward a market-regulated system with socialist characteristics can further unlock and advance the nation's capacity for material output, utilize, and allocate resources more effectively, and achieve fruitful development results.

Under the mixed economy characterized by both market coordination and public ownership, the principal rule governing economic operations is value-based pricing, whereby the cost of various products and services adjusts according to imbalances between market availability and consumer demand. Each firm modifies its operational strategies and output decisions in response to price movements

[28] Marx & Engels. *The Complete Works of Marx and Engels, Vol. 25*. Beijing: People's Publishing House, 1974, p. 963.

in the market, thereby promoting alignment between what society offers and what it requires. It embodies the essence of value determination as a central mechanism for shaping how goods are produced and distributed within the broader economy. When discussing this principle, Marx and Engels once echoed the phrasing of classical economist Adam Smith: "This kind of relationship is like the ancient god of destiny, who is free and easy on the world, and distributes the happiness and disasters of the world with an invisible hand."[29] Sun Yefang, a well-known Chinese economist, also proposed as early as the 1960s that the law of value always comes first, no matter how many laws there are.[30] This sentence basically applies to the current socialist market economy. Therefore, when we talk about respecting objective laws in economic work, we must begin with a respect for the law of value, along with other fundamental principles such as the laws of price, supply and demand, and competition, etc. Except for sectors involving network-bound monopolies, high externalities, or the delivery of non-excludable and non-rival outputs, all economic behavior in the marketplace ought to follow price signals shaped by market forces.

Within this economic model, interest relations are multifaceted, as is the structure of property rights, anchored by state participation, while other ownership mechanisms expand concurrently, and integrated ownership systems gain prominence. The market is open and fully competitive; the state's macroeconomic management is mainly indirect; employment modes, distribution methods, and social organization forms are diversified. In such a pluralistic and mixed economic system, various economic relations and interests are mainly regulated by the market mechanism, that is, regulated by the law of value. Here, advanced, and socially in-demand products and services can be rewarded handsomely, and backward and inferior products and services will be punished in different forms and to varying degrees, thereby continuously promoting technological progress and innovation, the enhancement of workforce efficiency, and the overall growth of productive capacity across society. The guiding influence of value principles in facilitating broad-based social transformation and economic expansion has been effectively harnessed.

---

29 Marx & Engels. *The Complete Works of Marx and Engels, Vol. 3*. Beijing: People's Publishing House, 1960, p. 39.

30 Yefang Sun. The law of value always comes first no matter how many laws there are. *Some Theoretical Issues of the Socialist Economy*. Beijing: People's Publishing House, 1979.

II. Enterprises: the core actors in economic operations under socialism, requiring institutional independence from administrative bodies and a clear boundary between public authority and asset ownership.

Under today's mixed economic structure, formerly government-controlled production units, whether publicly or collectively financed, are no longer subservient to administrative hierarchies as they were during the era of command-based economic governance. They now operate independently, assuming full financial accountability for their performance. In a system where public-sector participation forms the core and a variety of proprietary models are allowed to flourish concurrently, enterprises have become increasingly diverse, including state-affiliated, collectively operated, privately owned, internationally supported, mixed-equity, and shareholder-based organizations. These enterprises play a leading role in facilitating transactions and resource flows under market conditions. Non-public enterprises are independent market entities, which is not a problem. The main problem they face in their development lies in safeguarding property rights. In line with what is declared in the "Decision of the Central Committee of the Communist Party of China on Some Major Issues Concerning Comprehensively Deepening the Reform," "the property rights of the public sector are inviolable, as are those of the non-public sector." Enterprises held by the state must transition into fully operational business units with decision-making autonomy through organizational modernization and equity-based adjustment. In this hybrid model combining socialist oversight with market tools, the marketplace plays a pivotal role in shaping the distribution pattern of key developmental resources, which is realized through the most important micro-economic entities, that is, the activities of enterprises. According to market signals, mainly price signals, enterprises decide what and how much goods to produce and operate, and what and how many services to provide in order to maximize profits. It is the pursuit of economic benefits by each enterprise that enables social resources to be allocated to areas of social need. Under a system where market operations are integrated with socialist governance, the authorities also directly allocate a part of resources, but the government generally allocates only a small part of resources directly, and it is mainly limited to the field of market failure, and does not aim at maximizing profits. A large portion of economic factors is directed by firms according to signals emerging from competitive exchange environments.

To ensure that enterprises function autonomously within the marketplace and are accountable for their financial outcomes, the transformation of publicly owned firms is essential, which aims to build a contemporary corporate governance framework. It is defined by a transparent asset ownership system, a clear delineation of operational roles and duties, functional autonomy from state agencies, and the adoption of modern managerial approaches. Its concrete manifestation lies in modern business organizations, predominantly composed of liability-restricted enterprises and equity-financed corporations, the operation of which is regulated by the *Company Law*. As of 2017, more than 90% of government-backed firms had been restructured as incorporated companies, and even the most difficult 69 central state-owned group company headquarters and more than 3,200 central state-owned subsidiaries had all been converted into corporations by the late 2017. Organizations tasked with handling government-linked assets are gradually evolving, from operational oversight of firms to strategic supervision of capital flows, enabling company boards of directors to genuinely exercise their legally granted powers conferred by *The Company Law*, such as major decision-making, income distribution, the appointment or dismissal of staff, and the separation of enterprises from government can be achieved. Consequently, publicly controlled entities will acquire real operational autonomy and stand on level ground with firms under diverse ownership structures. Only the fittest will survive. In the context of ongoing pro-market restructuring, the original or newly-built collective units have been progressively reshaped into institutional formats suited to a market-oriented environment, including incorporation under modern enterprise systems.

To promote the autonomy of enterprises backed by public capital, we must ensure both administrative separation and the functional division between regulatory authority and asset-holding responsibilities, distinguishing governance from ownership. When public agencies perform their duties as a contributor to the state capital of wholly state-owned and shareholding enterprises, it is only a "boss" and a shareholder, not a "steward," and it cannot play the role of a board of directors or even a manager. Otherwise, it will become a "boss" plus a "steward," and there is no distinction between government and enterprise, and no division between government and capital. Therefore, it is very necessary for the state-owned asset supervisory and management authorities to change from primarily managing enterprises to primarily managing capital, which is in line with the requirements of the development law of the socialist market economy. It is evident that for the market to take a decisive role in allocating resources, we must first respect that enterprises, including state-owned enterprises, are independent market entities, truly operate autonomously, and are liable for their earnings, deficits, and market exposures. The government mainly performs the functions of public management. When the government performs the responsibility of the contributor to state-owned capital on behalf of the country, it should also be limited to the role of the contributor and shareholder, that is, it must respect the market entity status of the enterprise, respect the property rights of the enterprise, and shall abstain from unjustified meddling in the internal affairs of firms or any actions that undermine their lawful control over owned resources.

III. The main responsibilities of the government involve macro-level economic coordination, ensuring essential welfare infrastructure, regulating commercial activity, maintaining social order, and addressing ecological concerns.

In the context of a reform-era economy combining public control and market logic, although market activities determine the allocation of essential inputs, governance institutions should play an active part in ensuring that both systems reinforce each other effectively. The government's responsibilities mainly include macro-level economic coordination, ensuring essential welfare infrastructure, regulating commercial activity, maintaining social order, and addressing ecological concerns.

The core task of public administration lies in steering national economic trends, preserving the steady and sustainable functioning of the overall economy, and advancing development accordingly. Contemporary economic systems are not left entirely to unrestrained market forces; instead, they operate under overarching national policy guidance. The 16th National Party Congress, held in 2002, clearly articulated in its official document: "We must stimulate economic growth, create more jobs, stabilize prices and maintain balance of international payments as the main macroeconomic control objectives." It is a rational distillation of over two decades of macro-control experience gained during China's transition toward a more open and dynamic economy, and accords with the general logic of market development. Many market economies worldwide consider these four aspects as the primary objectives of country-level economic policy management. Both domestic and international practices confirm that, under market mechanisms, a sound approach must be taken to harmonize growth dynamics with overall economic resilience. Looking ahead over time, maintaining financial and structural stability proves to be the most effective means of supporting long-lasting economic progress. This is because a stable economy provides consistent and accurate market signals, enabling the market to allocate resources more efficiently. In contrast, if rapid economic growth is pursued unilaterally without regard for economic stability and without ensuring steady progress, it will be prone to big ups and downs, which will inevitably lead to waste and loss of productive forces. In the long run, the economic growth will be slower because of detours.

In 2013, the "Decision of the Central Committee of the Communist Party of China on Some Major Issues Concerning Comprehensively Deepening the

Reform" made by the Third Plenary Session of the 18th CPC Central Committee further pointed out: "The major tasks of macro control are to maintain balanced economic aggregates, coordinate major economic structures, optimize the distribution of the productive forces, mitigate the impact of periodic economic fluctuation, defuse regional and systematic risks, stabilize market expectations, and realize sustained and sound economic development." "We will establish a mechanism of participating in international macroeconomic policy coordination, and improve the overall global economic governance structure." The key advancement in the design of macro-level regulation in the "Decision of the Central Committee of the Communist Party of China on Some Major Issues Concerning Comprehensively Deepening the Reform" is reflected in: The first is to strengthen engagement in aligning global-level economic policy strategies, and the second is to promote the improvement of the international economic governance structure. This reveals that following four decades of dynamic policy reform and global integration, China has ascended to the position of the world's No. 2 economy, with its international status and influence constantly increasing. It reflects China's growing responsibility as a major global participant, requiring greater engagement in the joint formulation of international economic management agendas. Since 2016, China has vigorously promoted and led economic globalization, strengthened international mutually beneficial cooperation, and responded to various global challenges, resolutely opposed trade protectionism, and worked toward fostering long-term, balanced expansion of the world economy. This is a prominent example.

Under the current institutional arrangement, economic governance at the national level predominantly utilizes financial and statutory approaches, while administrative tools play a supportive role. This stands in sharp contrast to the mechanisms used in the era of centralized planning, when the state mainly used administrative means and mandatory plans to regulate social and economic activities. Specifically, it is mainly to use fiscal and monetary policies. When the economy is overheated or prone to overheating, we implement tight fiscal and monetary policies; on the contrary, when the economy is too cold, or deflation occurs, we implement loose fiscal and monetary policies. We can also pursue expansionary budgetary measures in tandem with a moderate stance on money supply, or apply a neutral fiscal approach paired with relaxed credit and interest rate policies. Its purpose is to maintain economic stability, forestall the development of economy-wide vulnerabilities (mainly financial risks), strive to smooth the volatility of economic changes, and prevent major ups and downs. This can also be called counter-cyclical measures, so that when the economy rises, it will not rise too high in a short period of time, and strive to make the rising period longer, and when it comes to economic depression, it will not shrink or fall sharply, and the period will not last too long. It can be seen that macroeconomic regulation and control are generally short-term (such as one or two years) policies, and it is not appropriate to make short-term policies long-term.

Macroeconomic control is mainly the aggregate control, that is, to fine-tune the alignment between the economy's overall productive capacity and demand levels to make them basically coordinated. The monitoring indicators are mainly GDP growth rate, investment growth rate, inflation rate, unemployment rate, balance of payments, fiscal deficit ratio, etc. Because macroeconomic regulation primarily involves managing overall aggregates, the authority for such regulation must fall within the jurisdiction of central institutions to ensure consistency and oversight. National economic governance in China additionally aims to ensure structural coherence across major industries and to refine the layout of the country's development resources. Therefore, industrial policy is also a tool for macroeconomic control. This calls for improved synergy between public finance tools and monetary instruments, as well as alignment between sectoral and territorial development strategies, while advancing the predictive capacity, precision, and consistency of macro-level regulation.

The "Decision of the Central Committee of the Communist Party of China on Some Major Issues Concerning Comprehensively Deepening the Reform" also points out: "We will improve the development progress evaluation system, correct the bias of evaluating political achievements merely by the economic growth rate. We will increase the weight of other evaluation indicators such as resources consumption, environmental damage, ecological benefits, excess production capacity, sci-tech innovation, production safety and new debts, while more emphasis will be put on employment, residents' income, social security and public health." Over the course of its decades-long economic transformation, China's swift development has come at the cost of overexploiting natural reserves, worsening environmental quality, and accelerating ecological degradation. The important reason is that in the previous period of China, success or failure was often judged by GDP growth. After the Party and the government discovered this problem, they have been working hard to correct it. As set forth in the "Decision of the Central Committee of the Communist Party of China on Some Major Issues Concerning Comprehensively Deepening the Reform," the foremost objective is to refine the system by which public administrators are appraised for their governance outcomes. Simultaneously, it is essential to reshape the mindset that has taken root during the country's industrial development phase, that the creation of more and more material wealth can fully respond to the needs of citizens. In fact, with today's rapid development of economy and technology, notably for states that are either classified as high-income or are progressing toward that economic bracket, people are prioritizing well-being and comfort, and are increasingly pursuing cultural entertainment, a beautiful environment, good ecology, healthy life, food safety, democratic systems, the supremacy of law, and spiritual enjoyment. Therefore, our development concept should also have a new change. In 2015, the Fifth Plenary Session of the 18th CPC Central Committee proposed the five development concepts of innovation, coordination, greenness, openness, and sharing, reflecting the new requirements of the times, and meeting the objective requirements of the new stage of China's economic development.

In addition to macroeconomic regulation, the government also bears significant responsibilities in providing public services, overseeing market operations, managing social affairs, and protecting the environment. Judging from the practice of China's four decades of economic restructuring, these aspects are exactly where the government is not doing enough, and the weakness of the government, and it is urgent to make up for it and strengthen them. This is also a crucial prerequisite for maintaining the healthy functioning of the socialist market economy.

IV. The overarching objective behind China's economic activities and progress: to share the fruits of development and move toward common prosperity.

The core goal of advancing the socialist market economy is fundamentally different from the goal of capitalist production, which is that capital pursues surplus value and maximizes profits. The result of capitalist economic development is that wealth is concentrated in the hands of a very limited number of capital predators, and poverty is accumulated on the other hand, causing polarization. The socialist market economy differs in that its entities also aim to pursue and increase profits. However, given that the foundational economic framework adheres to a system where publicly held assets play a leading role while encouraging the parallel advancement of various ownership forms, and considering that the nation operates under the leadership of the Communist Party, government policy focuses on persistently narrowing disparities in wealth and asset distribution. This is achieved through mechanisms such as fiscal tools, redistribution policies, the delivery of essential public services, the enhancement of social welfare programs, and other supportive measures. In addition, various economic actors, nonprofit bodies, and citizens are encouraged to be enthusiastic about charitable donations and relief causes, so as to avoid polarization, progressively reduce wealth and income disparities, and work toward ensuring equal access to the outcomes of national development, advancing together toward a more equitable and harmonious society.

Within the framework of the socialist market economy, it is understandable for enterprises to operate in accordance with the law to obtain profits. As we all know, after the human society has gone through the long primitive commune stage, the surplus product exists in every society. As Engels said: "The surplus of the product of labor over the cost of maintaining labor, and the formation and accumulation of social production and reserve funds from this surplus, have been and are the basis of all social, political and intellectual continual development."[31] In a socialist society, since there are always unproductive but necessary departments and institutions whose expenses are to be paid from the produced fund, and since the society has to have the accumulation fund and reserve fund for the expansion of reproduction, the labor of laborers in the production sector should be divided into necessary labor and surplus labor, and the products they create should be divided into necessary products and surplus products. The value form of surplus products is the profit of the enterprise.

It is evident that profit orientation is not a valid marker for identifying the essential differences between socialist-influenced and capitalist-oriented market structures. So, what exactly distinguishes socialist production from capitalist production? Let us recall Lenin's review of one of Bukharin's books. In his book *Economy in Transition*, Bukharin said: "Under the rule of capital, production is the production of surplus value, and production for profit. Under the rule of the proletariat, it is the production to offset the needs of society." In this regard, Lenin wrote this comment: No success. Profits also meet "social needs." It should be said: under these conditions, the surplus product does not belong to the class of the proprietors, but to all the working people, and only to them.[32] Lenin's comments above illustrate that who owns the surplus product (profit is its value expression) is what distinguishes socialist production from capitalist production.

The more complicated problem is that in the market economy in the primary stage of socialism, some of the profits produced by the private economy and foreign-funded economy are owned by the capital, rather than directly owned by all workers. However, it must be noted that the bulk, and in many cases almost the entirety, of China's surplus products are under the control of the government. For a long stretch, China's macro tax burden has always accounted for

[31] Marx & Engels. *The Complete Works of Marx and Engels, Vol. 20*. Beijing: People's Publishing House, 1971, p. 211.

[32] Lenin. *Commentary on Bukharin's "The Economy of Transition."* Beijing: People's Publishing House, 1958, p. 40.

more than 30% of the GDP, which constitutes the main source of the country's fiscal revenue. A small part of the fiscal spending is used to guarantee national security and infrastructure construction, support technical progress, and improve the ecological environment, while the larger part is mainly used for livelihood projects to ensure and promote greater prosperity and cultural vitality among the general public. The state motivates capital income to be channeled back into the economy to maintain development, drive technological transformation, support labor market expansion, and reinforce public finance. In essence, through policy, legal frameworks, and economic instruments, the state can guide the operation of market-driven and overseas-invested enterprises to ensure their development contributes to expanding economic efficiency, reinforcing national resilience, and enhancing people's livelihoods. In addition, authorities have rolled out supportive frameworks and incentives to motivate and encourage private entrepreneurs to improve their social responsibility, be enthusiastic about public welfare undertakings, and actively participate in donations and charitable activities to repay the society. With the progress of society and the improvement of civilization, this third adjustment, which can be called the distribution of national income, is poised to assume a greater strategic position moving forward. This clearly helps to make development fruits shared by all.

The "Recommendations" proposed in the Fifth Plenary Session of the 18th CPC Central Committee emphasize that sharing is a fundamental requirement of socialism with Chinese characteristics. We must ensure that development is for the people, that it is reliant on the people, and that its fruits are shared by the people. Efforts will be made to optimize relevant systems so that individuals experience stronger benefits while engaging in collective advancement and accessing its achievements, which in turn will boost motivation for growth, enhance societal solidarity, and promote steady movement toward inclusive prosperity.

This suggests that under a hybrid model where socialist principles guide market operations, economic modernization must respond to the mission of fostering equality and moving society as a whole toward greater shared well-being.

V. Implementing rule-based supervision of market practices and promoting the robust and balanced operation of the socialist economic model.

A contemporary economic system driven by market principles relies on legal norms for its proper functioning. Both domestic and international economic development experiences have demonstrated that the market economy can only function effectively and mitigate the negative consequences of its spontaneous adjustments when it runs within a legal framework. The market economy is a competitive economy, which implements fair and orderly competition to continuously improve efficiency. This necessitates oversight of competitive behavior to establish a fair and orderly framework for market interactions. This demonstrates that sustained growth and proper functioning of the socialist-aligned market structure are only possible through law-based governance.

The Party has gained profound insights into the inherent rules governing contemporary economic systems. Shortly after defining the blueprint for overhauling China's economic structure, it emphasized the necessity of legal governance in economic activities and explicitly stated that such an economy must fundamentally operate within a legal framework.

In 1997, the 15th CPC National Congress established the strategy of law-based governance. At that time, there was a discussion about governing by law or using law to govern, but a consensus on law-based governance was soon formed, marking a major transition in China from personalist rule toward a system grounded in legal norms and procedures. In that spirit, the Party's 2002 policy agenda proposed strengthening lawmaking and improving legislative quality to meet the demands of an era defined by economic system reform, advancing social modernization, and China's formal participation in multilateral trade mechanisms, aiming to establish a legal framework compatible with national realities and socialist governance by 2010. This legal system must reflect the dynamics of competitive economies, be robust in design and execution, and act as a cornerstone for sustaining the functioning of a socialist-aligned market structure. The 2003 conference further proposed to comprehensively promote the construction of the economic legal system, that is, in accordance with the basic strategy of law-based governance, focusing on establishing systems, regulating powers and responsibilities, protecting rights and interests, and strengthening economic legislation. It mainly includes: perfecting the legal system of market entities and intermediary organizations, so that all kinds of market entities truly have full capacity for conduct and responsibility; refining the property rights legal regime, promoting transparency and coherence in rights allocation, and protecting various property rights and interests; guaranteeing the freedom of contracts and transaction security, and maintaining fair competition; enhancing the legal framework governing budgeting, taxation, finance and investment, and standardizing economic regulation and market supervision; reinforcing institutional frameworks governing labor relations, job opportunities, and social protection to better uphold the lawful entitlements of individuals; advancing policy mechanisms in public welfare and green transformation to support economic growth and comprehensive social advancement.

In 2014, the Fourth Plenary Session of the 18th CPC Central Committee further issued the "Decision of the Central Committee of the Communist Party of China on Major Issues Concerning the Enhancement of all-round Law-based Governance." According to the "Decision," the hybrid economic structure rooted in socialism requires legal governance at its core. To strengthen the market's primary role in guiding the flow of production factors and improve public sector oversight, the construction of a comprehensive legal architecture for such an economic arrangement must be accelerated. This framework should primarily aim to safeguard ownership entitlements, ensure the credibility of transactional agreements, promote an integrated national marketplace, and encourage equitable transactions, orderly competition, and robust oversight mechanisms. Efforts must focus on optimizing the structure that ensures equitable ownership security, ensuring all types of business entities and individuals enjoy equal treatment under the law, while removing institutional barriers and outdated statutes that contradict the principle of fairness. It is crucial to reshape the institutional safeguards that correspond to the multiple models of public asset ownership, reinforce the secure management and utilization rights of assets under state or community stewardship, and guarantee the legal claims of all categories of incorporated organizations. The state upholds the principle that enterprises may operate under statutory guidelines with managerial discretion, assume fiscal responsibility for their performance, and possess asset entitlements recognized under the legal status of corporate persons, and enterprises have the right to refuse any organization or individual's request without legal basis. Efforts should be made to advance legislation on enterprise duties, fortify innovation-oriented property regimes, including those safeguarding proprietary knowledge, and design actionable procedures to support the real-world deployment of science and tech innovations. It is also important to improve the legal infrastructure that underpins market operations and to advance the codification of civil laws into a unified legal framework, formulate and improve the laws and regulations on development planning, investment management, land management, energy and mineral resources, agriculture, finance and taxation, finance, etc., and promote the free flow, fair trade and equality use of commodities and factors. We must strengthen and improve macro-control and market supervision, oppose monopoly, promote reasonable competition, and maintain the market order with fair competition in accordance with the law. It is also necessary to strengthen the legal guarantee for the in-depth development of military-civilian integration, etc.

As overconcentration of resources under public authority and frequent disruptions to enterprise autonomy remain common challenges, the assembly held in

2014 called for deepening rule-based administration and expediting the establishment of a legally regulated public sector. It involves giving full play to the proper roles of public institutions. The process of formulating government decisions needs to be more legally grounded and transparent. In addition, reforms should also advance the overhaul of law enforcement practices in the administrative sector. Not only that, it is essential to uphold the law application that is disciplined and conducted with due respect for citizens. Meanwhile, stronger checks and oversight must be placed on the use of executive power. Furthermore, efforts should be made to broaden access to official information and improve the transparency of public governance.

Ultimately, what matters in economic governance is striking the right balance between state functions, market operations, and corporate participation. Generally speaking, the government should not take care of anything that can be solved efficiently by the market; the government also should not take care of anything that can be solved independently and effectively by citizens, enterprises, and social organizations, including intermediary organizations, unless it is stipulated by law. An essential task of the government is to lay the groundwork for market vitality and enterprise growth, which includes managing overall economic policy, offering critical non-market services, ensuring consistent market governance and social stability, and ensuring consistent market governance and social stability. When the government uses taxpayers' money, it must be thrifty, efficient, transparent, and honest. Take it from the people, use it for the people, and serve the people. These must be determined by law.

References

Chen, Jun & Hong Nan. *Jiang Zemin and the Proposition of the Socialist Market Economic System—20 Years Review of the Socialist Market Economy.* Beijing: Central Party Literature Press, 2012.

Cheng, Zhiping. *Thirty Years of Price Reform (1977–2006)*. Beijing: China Market Press, 2006.

Communiqué of the Third Plenary Session of the Eleventh Central Committee of the Communist Party of China, Dec. 22, 1978.

Communist Party of China Central Committee. *Decision of the Central Committee of the Communist Party of China on Major Issues Concerning the Enhancement of all-round Law-based Governance*. Oct. 23, 2014.

Communist Party of China Central Committee. *Decision of the Central Committee of the Communist Party of China on Reform of the Economic Structure*. Oct. 20, 1984.

Communist Party of China Central Committee. *Decision of the Central Committee of the Communist Party of China on Several Issues Concerning Building a Socialist Market Economy*. Nov. 14, 1993.

Communist Party of China Central Committee. *Decision of the Central Committee of the Communist Party of China on Several Major Issues Concerning Comprehensively Deepening the Reform*. Nov. 12, 2013.
Deng, Xiaoping. *Selected Works of Deng Xiaoping, Vol. 3.* Beijing: People's Publishing House, 1993.
Department of Comprehensive Planning, National Economic System Reform Commission. *China's Reform Ideas*. Shenyang: Shenyang Press, 1988.
Hu, Jintao. Speech at the 30th Anniversary of the Third Plenary Session of the 11th Central Committee of the Communist Party of China. *People's Daily*, Dec. 19, 2008.
Jiang, Zemin. Accelerating the pace of reform, opening up and modernization, and achieving greater success in the cause of Socialism with Chinese characteristics, Oct. 12, 1992.
Marx & Engels. *The Complete Works of Marx and Engels, Vol. 25*. Beijing: People's Publishing House, 1974.
Marx & Engels. *The Complete Works of Marx and Engels, Vol. 3.* Beijing: People's Publishing House, 1960.
National Bureau of Statistics of the People's Republic of China. *2017 China Statistical Abstract.* Beijing: China Statistics Press, 2017.
Peng, Sen & Chen Li, et al. *Major Events in China's Economic System Reform, Vol. I, II.* Beijing: China Renmin University Press, 2008.
Sun, Yefang. *Some Theoretical Issues of the Socialist Economy*. Beijing: People's Publishing House, 1979.
The Literature Research Office of the Central Committee of the Communist Party of China. *An Excerpt of Xi Jinping's Discussion on Socialist Economic Construction*. Beijing: Central Party Literature Press, 2017.
The Writing Team of This Book. *The Guidebook for the Report of the 19th National Congress of the Communist Party of China*. Beijing: People's Publishing House, 2017.
Wu, Jinglian. *A Market Economy that Calls for the Rule of Law*. Beijing: SDX Joint Publishing Company, 2007.
Xi, Jinping. Decisive victory to build a moderately prosperous society in all respects and win the great victory of Socialism with Chinese characteristics in the new era, Oct. 18, 2017.
Zhang, Zhuoyuan, et al. *Outline of the History of Economics in New China (1949–2011)*. Beijing: China Social Sciences Press, 2012.
Zhang, Zhuoyuan. *A New Journey of Economic Reform.* Beijing: Social Sciences Academic Press, 2014.
Zhang, Zhuoyuan. *Economic Transformation and Reform*. Beijing: China Renmin University Press, 2017.

Theory of Socialism's Primary Stage

Since the Third Plenary Session of the 11th Central Committee of the Communist Party of China, China has made remarkable strides in its socialist development. Productive forces have surged ahead, economic output has kept expanding, and people's living standards have been on a steady upward trajectory. China's weight in the global economic framework and its clout in the international political arena have been growing consistently. Under the leadership of the Communist Party of China, the rollout of reform and opening-up policies, coupled with economic growth strategies tailored to the nation's distinct circumstances, ranks among the most acclaimed accomplishments recognized across the globe. By reviewing the ups and downs of China's socialist building process, drawing lessons from the historical fortunes of socialism in other countries, the Party has gradually crafted and polished the theory of socialism's primary stage. This theory offers a precise grasp of China's national conditions and acts as a foundational compass for advancing socialism with Chinese characteristics. Throughout the evolution of the theory of socialism's primary stage, economic scholars have made notable contributions. This theory defines the institutional structure and foundational conditions that form the basis for economic research in China. With the primary stage of socialism as its cornerstone, Chinese economists have carried out in-depth analyses of the socialist economic system and its operational mechanisms, yielding valuable theoretical findings. A series of pivotal theoretical advancements has expanded the theory's scope and played a vital role in the development of an economic system tailored to China's specific context.

1. The Emergence and Evolution of the Theory on Socialism's Primary Stage

The theory of socialism's primary stage took shape and advanced amid the new historical backdrop of reform and opening up. Since the Third Plenary Session of the 11th CPC Central Committee, the Party has revived the ideological line of emancipating the mind and seeking truth from facts. This shift has steadily broken free from the shackles of dogmatism and "Left" ideological tendencies. By re-examining socialism and accurately analyzing the country's basic conditions, a scientific judgment was reached—that China remains in the primary stage of socialism. It was on this foundation that the theory of socialism's primary stage gradually took form.

I. Deng Xiaoping's major contribution to the theory of the primary stage of socialism

Deng Xiaoping played a vital role in shaping the theory of the primary stage of socialism. Following the conclusion of the "Cultural Revolution," he keenly recognized the changing dynamics of the era and conducted profound contemplation on the essence of socialism and China's distinctive national circumstances. As far back as 1980, he noted that: "We must emancipate our minds and we should do so even in answering the question as to what socialism is. If the economy remains stagnant and the people's living standards remain at a very low level for a long period of time, we cannot say that we are building socialism."[1] He later pointed out: "What is socialism, and what is Marxism? We were not quite clear about this in the past."[2] These insights demonstrated Deng's remarkable political courage to forge a new path for socialist development, as well as his theoretical boldness in expanding the boundaries of Marxism.

By deeply reflecting on the historical experiences of China's socialist construction in the years following the founding of the People's Republic, Deng Xiaoping came to understand that building socialism in China must be rooted in national conditions and cannot skip developmental stages. He once proposed that: "We should research earnestly how to carry out socialist development. At this time, we are reviewing the experience gained in the past three decades since the founding of the People's Republic. To sum up, it is as follows. First, we should not adopt 'Leftist' policies by divorcing ourselves from reality or skipping over necessary

---

1 Xiaoping Deng. *Selected Works of Deng Xiaoping*, Vol. 2. Beijing: People's Publishing House, 1994, p. 312.

2 Xiaoping Deng. *Selected Works of Deng Xiaoping*, Vol. 3. Beijing: People's Publishing House, 1993, p. 63.

stages. Otherwise, the task of building socialism will not be accomplished. We have suffered losses from 'Leftist' policies. Second, whatever we do must contribute to developing the productive forces."[3] Under the guidance of this thinking, the Sixth Plenary Session of the 11th CPC Central Committee put forward, for the first time, the fundamental conclusion that China was in the primary stage of socialism. This conclusion was reaffirmed at the 12th CPC National Congress and the Sixth Plenary Session of the 12th CPC Central Committee. In order to better guide reform, opening up, and modernization drives, the drafting group for the report of the 13th CPC National Congress anchored their reasoning on the scientific assertion that "China is in the primary stage of socialism." When the overall blueprint of the proposal was submitted to Deng Xiaoping, he commended it, stating, "This blueprint is good." Prior to the 13th CPC National Congress, during a meeting with foreign visitors, Deng Xiaoping remarked: "The Thirteenth National Party Congress will explain what stage China is in: the primary stage of socialism. Socialism itself is the first stage of communism, and here in China we are still in the primary stage of socialism—that is, the underdeveloped stage. In everything we do we must proceed from this reality, and all planning must be consistent with it."[4] His ideas were comprehensively elaborated and served as the foundational rationale for the arguments in the report of the 13th CPC National Congress. After this Congress, when commenting on the report, he pointed out that a significant characteristic of the report was its elaboration on the theory of the primary stage of socialism, and under the guidance of this theory, we have steadfastly carried out the guidelines and policies adopted since the Third Plenary Session of the 11th CPC Central Committee.[5] During his "Southern Talks" in 1992, Deng Xiaoping reiterated the concept of the primary stage of socialism, stating: "We have been building socialism for only a few decades and are still in the primary stage. It will take a very long historical period to consolidate and develop the socialist system, requiring persistent effort from many generations—perhaps a dozen or even several dozen. We can never afford to rest on our laurels."[6] In these remarks, he underscored the protracted nature of the primary stage and called on the whole Party to keep striving steadfastly along the path of socialist construction.

In the new historical era of reform, opening up, and socialist advancement, Deng Xiaoping put forward a range of innovative viewpoints and perspectives

---

3 Ibid., p. 312.
4 Ibid., p. 252.
5 Ibid., p. 258.
6 Ibid., pp. 379–380.

on socialism and its developmental phases. These ideas not only carried forward the insights of earlier leaders but also broke away from traditional modes of thinking, thereby making a notable contribution to the establishment of the theory of socialism's primary stage.

II. Evolution phases of the theory of socialism's primary stage

The evolution of the theory on socialism's primary stage can roughly be categorized into three phases:

(1) The gestation phase of the theory (spanning from the Third Plenary Session of the 11th CPC Central Committee to the Sixth Plenary Session of the 12th CPC Central Committee).

In 1981, the Sixth Plenary Session of the 11th CPC Central Committee adopted the "Resolution on Certain Questions in the History of Our Party since the Founding of the People's Republic of China," marking the first time the claim that China was in "the primary stage of socialism" was put forward. The "Resolution" stated: "Although our socialist system is still in the primary stage, there is no doubt that our country has established a socialist system and entered a socialist society. Any point of view that denies this basic fact is wrong." Although the document recognized that China's socialist system was in its primary stage, the primary focus of this section was to counter doubts about the validity of China's socialist system. It firmly confirmed that socialism had been established in China and that the nation had already entered a socialist society. However, it did not offer a detailed account of the specific implications of the primary stage of socialism. At the 12th CPC National Congress, Comrade Hu Yaobang noted in his report that: "China's socialist society is still in the primary stage of development, and material wellbeing has not yet developed." This remark highlighted a defining feature of socialism's primary stage—underdeveloped material conditions. However, it remained a preliminary observation, and the concept had yet to be fully elaborated or systematically discussed. The "Resolution of the CPC Central Committee on the Guiding Principles for Building a Socialist Society with an Advanced Level of Culture and Ideology," adopted at the Sixth Plenary Session of the 12th CPC Central Committee in 1986, reaffirmed that China was in the primary stage of socialism. The document briefly outlined the economic traits of this stage and expounded on its cultural and ideological attributes, indicating that the Party had gained a deeper comprehension of the primary stage's essence. Nevertheless, the "Resolution" still failed to offer a thorough explanation of its complete meaning.

During this period, although the Party had repeatedly emphasized the concept of socialism's primary stage in several pivotal Party documents, and had developed a basic understanding—especially regarding its economic aspects—these views had not yet matured into a coherent, systematic theory. Thus, this phase is best understood as the gestation phase in the evolution of the theory of socialism's primary stage.

(2) The formation phase of a systematic theory (spanning from the Sixth Plenary Session of the 12th CPC Central Committee to the 13th CPC National Congress)

While the Party had already developed the foundational concept of socialism's primary stage by reflecting on historical experience, this crucial issue had not yet received adequate attention within academic and theoretical circles. In-depth exploration and debate on this subject remained relatively scarce. The drafting of the 13th CPC National Congress report marked a notable leap forward in the theoretical evolution of this concept. It brought the issue to the forefront, encouraging scholars and economists to engage more actively with the subject. As a result, theoretical debates surrounding socialism's primary stage grew more robust, gradually yielding substantial insights and laying the groundwork for a more systematic and well-defined theoretical framework.

The report of the 13th CPC National Congress stands as a key landmark in advancing the theory of socialism with Chinese characteristics. Leveraging the pooled wisdom of the entire Party and integrating the research outcomes of the academic community, this report for the first time comprehensively expounds on the theory of socialism's primary stage. Grounded in the reality that China remained in the primary stage of socialism, it systematically elaborated the core implications, overall features, main contradictions, and historical missions of this stage. It characterized socialism's primary stage as a unique historical period that China must necessarily undergo in the process of building socialism, due to its underdeveloped productive forces and underdeveloped commodity economy. The report pinpointed the main contradiction of this stage as the gap between the people's growing material and cultural demands and backward social production. To resolve this contradiction, it emphasized the urgent need to vigorously develop the commodity economy, enhance labor productivity, and progressively achieve the modernization of industry, agriculture, national defense, and science and technology. At the same time, it called for reforming aspects of the relations of production and superstructure that clashed with the demands of developing productive forces. Building on this, the report defined the Party's basic line and objectives for socialism's primary stage: "To unite with and lead the people of all ethnic groups, take economic development as the central task, uphold the Four Cardinal Principles, uphold the policy of reform and opening up, be self-reliant, hard-working and enterprising, and build China into a prosperous, strong, democratic, culturally advanced and modern socialist country." The report also put forward a "three-step" strategy for China's economic and social progress. The development of the theory on socialism's primary stage stands as an innovative, original contribution by the Communist Party of China to Marxist doctrine. For the first time in Marxist history, the scientific notion of socialism's primary stage was clearly set forth in the Party's official program.

(3) The phase of development and refinement of the theory (spanning from the 13th CPC National Congress to the present)

Since the 13th CPC National Congress officially laid the groundwork for the theory of socialism's primary stage, the Party has, through the sustained practice of advancing socialism with Chinese characteristics, kept summarizing new lessons learned, incorporating emerging theoretical gains, and enriching this theory with groundbreaking concepts and viewpoints. At the 14th CPC National Congress, drawing on the realities of socialism's primary stage, a major step forward was achieved in comprehending the relationship between planning and the market. The report explicitly defined the objective of China's economic reform as establishing a socialist market economy system. Subsequently, the 15th CPC National Congress revisited the theory of the primary stage of socialism and, for the first time, put forward the Party's basic program for this stage. It asserted that: "China is now and will remain in the primary stage of socialism for a long time," highlighting the extended and enduring nature of this historical period. This emphasis underscored the need for a deep awareness of the protracted and arduous character of this phase, fostering a mindset geared toward sustained effort. Furthermore, the report delineated the fundamental economic system appropriate for socialism's primary stage, and delineated the core targets and strategies for pushing forward socialism with Chinese characteristics in the economic, political, and cultural domains. These fundamental goals and measures form the Party's basic program for socialism's primary stage. This basic program represents a further extension of the Party's basic line in economic, political, and cultural realms, and this era stood as a pivotal distillation of the most critical lessons gleaned since the initiation of reform and opening up. The report of the 16th CPC National Congress provided an objective assessment of the progress made, reaffirming that China remained—and would continue to remain—in the primary stage of socialism for an extended period. While the general standard of living had reached a moderately prosperous level, it was still characterized by low quality, incompleteness, and significant regional disparities. Drawing on this understanding, the report systematically set forth the target of building a moderately prosperous society in all respects. In the wake of this, the report of the 17th CPC National Congress placed special emphasis on the Scientific Outlook on Development, pointing out that "in light of the fundamental reality of China's position in the primary stage of socialism, the *Scientific Outlook on Development* had been developed to address emerging development challenges. This framework was grounded in China's own practical experience while drawing on valuable lessons from other countries' development paths.." It functioned as a vital guiding ideology for China's economic and social progress, and a core strategic principle that must be adhered to and carried out in pushing forward socialism with Chinese characteristics. The report also laid out new targets for building a moderately prosperous society in all respects, seeking to turn China into a thriving, powerful, democratic, culturally refined, and harmonious modern socialist country. Maintaining and advancing socialism with Chinese characteristics stayed the central theme running through the report of the 18th CPC National Congress. The report emphasized that: "In building socialism with Chinese characteristics, we base ourselves on the basic reality that China is in the primary stage of socialism. Our overall approach is to promote economic, political, cultural, social, and ecological progress, and our general task is to achieve socialist modernization and the great rejuvenation of the Chinese nation." Rooted in a profound grasp of China's national conditions, the report confirmed the notable accomplishments achieved since the initiation of reform and opening up. Meanwhile, it openly recognized the ongoing difficulties in economic and social progress, reasserting that China is still in socialism's primary stage. Only by examining China's development through this lens can we precisely evaluate its achievements, identify its challenges, and map out a clear course for future advancement. This viewpoint helps fend off both overconfidence and excessive pessimism, securing a balanced stance that facilitates the continued progress of socialism with Chinese characteristics.

In the wake of the global financial crisis, the world economy has entered an era of profound transformation and realignment, while four decades of sustained growth have also brought China's development to a new historical juncture. Against this backdrop, the 19th CPC National Congress, factoring in changes in international, domestic, and Party conditions, laid out a comprehensive roadmap for building a modern socialist country in all aspects. It also formulated strategic arrangements to push forward the goal of achieving moderate prosperity for all. The report emphasized that as socialism with Chinese characteristics has entered a new era, the principal contradiction in Chinese society has undergone a transformation. The long-standing contradiction between the people's ever-growing material and cultural needs and backward social production had evolved into one between the people's ever-growing needs for a better life and unbalanced and inadequate development. This was a historic change related to the overall situation and would have a profound impact on the comprehensive advancement of socialism with Chinese characteristics. Meanwhile, the report emphasized that "we must recognize that the evolution of the principal contradiction facing Chinese society does not change our assessment of the present stage of socialism in China. The basic dimension of the Chinese context—that our country is still and will long remain in the primary stage of socialism—has not changed. China's international status as the world's largest developing country has not changed." Then the report made the requirement that "the whole Party must be completely clear about this fundamental dimension of our national context, and must base our work on this most important reality—the primary stage of socialism. We must remain fully committed to the Party's basic line as the source that keeps the Party and the country going and that brings happiness to the people," endeavoring to develop China into a great modern socialist nation that is thriving, powerful, democratic, culturally advanced, harmonious, and beautiful.

The emergence and evolution of the theory on socialism's primary stage reflect the Party's increasingly thorough and insightful grasp of China's national conditions and the essence of socialism. This continuous exploration into the development path of socialism with Chinese characteristics has advanced steadily in depth. The enduring great practice of reform and opening up, along with socialist development, will continue to imbue the theory of the primary stage of socialism with fresh connotations and understandings.

2. The Scientific Connotation of the Theory of Socialism's Primary Stage

I. The theory of socialism's primary stage as an accurate reflection of China's national conditions

A sound grasp of China's fundamental national conditions and its current historical phase stands as the core issue in advancing socialism with Chinese characteristics. This comprehension serves as the vital foundation for the CPC to formulate and carry out its guiding principles and policies. The report of the 13th CPC National Congress explicitly noted, "China is now in the primary stage of socialism. There are two aspects to this thesis. First, the Chinese society is already a socialist society. We must uphold in socialism and never waver from it. Second, China's socialist society is still in its primary stage." The notion of socialism's primary stage is not merely the initial phase that any nation might go through when first setting out on a socialist road. Instead, it specifically denotes the phase that China must traverse in constructing socialism amid the specific circumstances of low-grade productive forces and an underdeveloped commodity economy. This assertion represents a comprehensive and fundamental judgment of China's national conditions and serves as a critical prerequisite for advancing socialism with Chinese characteristics. Only by accurately grasping this fundamental national condition can we understand why we must follow the current path and policies instead of other ones. We must base our thoughts and work on this reality, and cannot go beyond this stage. Thus, in the process of advancing and developing socialism with Chinese characteristics, we must likewise proceed from this most critical context.

The Party underwent a difficult and winding journey before arriving at a full and accurate comprehension of China's fundamental national circumstances. During the period of the New Democratic Revolution, the CPC correctly recognized that China was a society that was both semi-colonial and semi-feudal. Building on this foundation, the Party innovatively integrated the universal principles of Marxism with China's revolutionary realities. Through in-depth analysis of the principal contradictions in Chinese society, it formulated sound guidelines, principles, and policies, ultimately achieving revolutionary success. Nevertheless, after the establishment of the People's Republic of China—especially once the socialist transformation of private ownership of the means of production was completed—the Party, in its quest to explore the path of socialist construction, occasionally strayed from China's actual circumstances. It overlooked the fundamental national realities of underdeveloped productive forces, a nascent market economy, and lopsided social progress. As a result, a series of policies and approaches were adopted that exceeded the country's historical stage of development, leading to significant setbacks. The overemphasis on "large in size, public in nature, socialist in purity (known as First Large, Second Public, and Third Pure)" seriously disconnected the relations of production and the superstructure from the productive conditions at that time, and severely hindered economic growth. Moreover, due to misjudgments about society's principal contradiction, the theory of class struggle became prevalent, ultimately culminating in the "Cultural Revolution." Prior to the reform and opening-up era, China's productive forces grew at a sluggish rate, the people's living standards showed little significant improvement, and socialism's advantages remained incompletely manifested. Since the Third Plenary Session of the 11th CPC Central Committee, the Party has conducted a pragmatic assessment of China's national conditions, reaching the scientific conclusion that China is in, and will long remain in, socialism's primary stage. This proposition not only clarifies the nature of Chinese society but also precisely pinpoints the specific phase of social development the nation is currently experiencing. It stands as the most succinct and accurate distillation of China's fundamental national conditions.

As reform and opening up have advanced further, and as the practice of developing socialism with Chinese characteristics has pressed forward, the Party's comprehension of socialism's primary stage has become ever more thorough and insightful. This deepened understanding is reflected in three key aspects.

(1) Understanding of the basic characteristics of the primary stage of socialism

The report of the 13th CPC National Congress summarized the fundamental characteristics of the primary stage of socialism in five aspects,

To put it specifically, this stage involves gradually shaking off poverty and underdevelopment; transforming an agrarian nation step by step into an industrialized one; shifting from a society dominated by natural and semi-natural economies to a highly developed commodity economy; establishing and evolving socialist economic, political, and cultural systems; and uniting the entire nation in the pursuit of national rejuvenation. The report of the 15th CPC National Congress expanded this framework to eight dimensions: a process where an agricultural country gradually evolves into an industrialized one; a transition from a society with a vast proportion of natural and semi-natural economies to a market-driven economic system; a shift from a nation with a large illiterate and semi-illiterate population to one with well-developed science, technology, education, and culture; a move from a society with a significant proportion of impoverished people to universal prosperity; a reduction in the uneven economic and cultural development across regions; the establishment and refinement of a socialist market economy, a socialist democratic political system, and other mature, vibrant institutions; the advancement of both material and cultural-ethical progress; and efforts to narrow the development gap with advanced nations. This expansion signifies a notable broadening of the Party's understanding of the primary stage's fundamental features. What was once centered on economic growth, institutional building, and national rejuvenation now encompasses a broader spectrum, including scientific and technological progress, education, public health, regional balance, income distribution, and the enhancement of cultural and ethical norms. This extension reflects the Party's increasingly comprehensive, detailed, and multifaceted grasp of the primary stage, spanning economic, political, social, and cultural realms.

(2) A recognition of the protracted nature of socialism's primary stage

The primary stage of socialism is not a fleeting transitional period that can be wrapped up in a short time. Instead, it constitutes an extended historical phase.

As noted in the report of the 13th CPC National Congress: "It will be at least 100 years from the 1950s, when the socialist transformation of private ownership of the means of production was basically completed, to the time when socialist modernization will have been in the main accomplished, and all these years belong to the primary stage of socialism." However, in the report of the 13th CPC National Congress, the basic assertion on China's basic national conditions and the stage of social development is: "Our country is in the primary stage of socialism." Starting with the 15th CPC National Congress, the Party refined its assessment to state that "our country is and will remain in the primary stage of socialism for a long time." This judgment has been repeatedly confirmed in the reports of subsequent Party congresses, starting from the 16th CPC National Congress. It embodies the Party's increasingly distinct and rational awareness of the protracted and arduous characteristics of this historical phase.

Since the launch of reform and opening up, China's productive forces have undergone tremendous growth. The nation's overall national strength has been significantly boosted, people's living standards have improved noticeably, and a historic shift has taken place—from prioritizing the resolution of basic subsistence problems to achieving a moderately prosperous life in general. Yet we must also plainly recognize that the current state of moderate prosperity remains low-level, incomplete, and highly unbalanced. As productive forces shape the relations of production, and the economic base underpins the superstructure, the underdevelopment of productive forces inevitably leads to an immature socialist market economic system. Moreover, the array of economic and social prerequisites needed to build a highly developed socialist democratic politics and a harmonious society remains insufficient, while issues like social inequity and corruption persist. All these realities indicate that we are still a long way from stepping beyond socialism's primary stage. Therefore, Comrade Xi Jinping pointed out, "Not only should we always base ourselves on the primary stage in economic construction, but we should also always keep the primary stage in mind in political, cultural, social, and ecological development; Not only should we base ourselves on the primary stage when the economic aggregate is low, but also keep in mind the primary stage after the economic aggregate has increased; It is necessary to keep the primary stage in mind not only when planning for long-term development, but also in daily work."[7] In socialism's primary stage, through the long-term and arduous efforts of the entire Party and the people

7 Jinping Xi. Closely focus on upholding and developing socialism with Chinese characteristics, study, publicize and implement the spirit of the 18th National Congress of the Communist Party of China. *People's Daily Online*, Nov. 19, 2012.

nationwide, China will gradually overcome its underdeveloped status and essentially achieve socialist modernization. This course of development will trigger far-reaching and revolutionary shifts in the economy, politics, culture, society, ecological advancement, and other domains.

(3) Recognition of how China's fundamental national conditions find concrete expression in the new century

Though the primary stage of socialism constitutes an extended historical era, it contains a number of distinct developmental phases within it. Each of the phases is characterized by unique features that reflect the evolving conditions and challenges faced by the country at different points in its modernization journey. The 17th CPC National Congress report outlines eight dimensions of China's developmental features in the new phase of the new century, summarizing its new-stage characteristics as follows: (a) Economic power has grown significantly, yet overall productive capacity remains low, indigenous innovation capability is insufficient, and long-standing structural issues, along with the extensive growth model, have not been fundamentally resolved. (b) The socialist market economy is largely established, but structural and systemic barriers that impede development persist; advancing reform in tough sectors confronts deep-rooted problems. (c) Moderate prosperity has been generally achieved for the people, yet the rising trend of income disparity has not been fully reversed. A sizable number of poor and low-income individuals remain in both urban and rural areas, making it harder to balance the interests of all parties. (d) Progress in balancing development has been notable, but agriculture's foundation remains frail, rural development lags behind, and the task of narrowing urban-rural and interregional gaps—while promoting balanced economic and social growth—remains arduous. (e) Socialist democracy has advanced steadily, with steady headway in governing by law, yet efforts to enhance democracy and the legal system still lag behind the need to expand people's democracy and drive economic and social progress, requiring deeper political structural reform. (f) Socialist culture is flourishing as never before, but people's cultural demands are rising, with thinking becoming more independent, selective, fluid, and diverse—placing stiffer demands on developing advanced socialist culture. (g) Society has grown significantly more vibrant, yet major shifts have occurred in social structure, organization, and interest patterns, bringing fresh challenges to social development and governance. (h) China is further opening up to the world, but global competition is growing fiercer. Developed countries' economic and technological edge will persist, both foreseen and unforeseen risks are on the rise, and coordinating domestic development with opening up is more crucial than ever. These phase characteristics reflect the specific expressions of China's fundamental national conditions within socialism's primary stage in the new century. As China's economy enters a "new normal," the context, conditions, tasks, and requirements for development are undergoing major shifts. Addressing the emerging challenges and contradictions of this era demands a more deliberate commitment to the new development concept and steadfast dedication to the path of scientific development. The report of the 19th CPC National Congress emphasized: "Development is the underpinning and the key for solving all our country's problems; our development must be sound development. We must pursue with firmness of purpose the vision of innovative, coordinated, green, and open development that is for everyone." The new development philosophy encapsulates China's strategic mindset, key focuses, and value orientations in the new era. It also marks a more profound grasp of the developmental principles that govern socialism's primary stage.

II. The doctrine of socialism's primary stage broadens our comprehension of socialism

For a long time, traditional and rigid conceptions of socialism significantly constrained people's thinking. After the October Revolution in Russia, some countries, including China has successively achieved victory in the socialist revolution and founded a socialist country. However, unlike the assumptions of the classic Marxist writers, these countries did not transition from a capitalist society with highly developed productive forces to a socialist society, but, without exception, entered a socialist society from a society with underdeveloped productive forces. Since the leaders of these socialist states lacked a clear grasp of socialism's essential features and development laws, the economic system of the Soviet Union—the world's first socialist nation—became the archetypal model of a socialist society, which other socialist countries sought to follow. The Soviet system, a highly centralized central planning economic system formed under special international environment and historical conditions, had a huge negative impact on other socialist countries in both theoretical and practical terms. For these socialist nations, due to the limitations of knowledge and the ideological influence of eagerness for success, many things that did not have the essential attributes of socialism, or things that were only suitable for certain special historical circumstances, were regarded as "socialist principles" to be upheld; and numerous practices that actually contributed to advancing productive forces—along with the commercialization, socialization, and modernization of production under socialist conditions—were wrongly categorized as "capitalist elements" and thus rejected. This way of thinking resulted in the formation of a rigid planned economic system and an excessively centralized political structure, both of which severely stifled the vitality and growth of the socialist economy. As early as the 1960s, the Soviet Union and some Eastern European socialist countries launched reforms and explored alternative socialist economic models, yet these endeavors failed to achieve significant breakthroughs. A critical factor was their persistent attachment to outdated, dogmatic conceptions of socialism, which prevented bold and essential transformations. Long-term stagnation in development ultimately led to the upheavals in Eastern Europe and the collapse of the Soviet Union during the 1980s and 1990s.

By reviewing both domestic and international experiences and lessons, the Party has come to a profound realization that, in the course of building socialism in China, the foremost question to clarify is "what socialism is and how to build it." To this end, we must figure out "what is socialism in the primary stage and how to build socialism in the primary stage." When building socialism in a country such as China—one with a huge population and underdeveloped productive forces—the circumstances we encounter are neither the construction of socialism on the foundation of highly developed capitalism as envisaged by the founders of Marxism, nor entirely identical to those of other socialist nations. For this reason, we must never depend on the models of other countries or the writings of theorists; instead, we must ground ourselves in reality. Proceeding from China's unique national conditions, we must integrate the fundamental tenets of Marxism with China's actual situation and, through practice, blaze a path of socialism with Chinese characteristics.

Beginning from the fundamental premise that China is in socialism's primary stage, the Communist Party of China has led the nation in a major exploration of building socialism with Chinese characteristics. In this endeavor, Comrade Deng Xiaoping—driven by the courage of Marxist theory, a dedication to seeking truth from facts, extensive practical experience, and strategic vision—engaged in deep reflections on socialism's essence. He explicitly pointed out that socialism's essence lies in liberating and developing productive forces, eliminating exploitation and polarization, and ultimately achieving common prosperity. Considering the context of socialism's primary stage, Deng Xiaoping stressed that overcoming poverty and underdevelopment necessitated making the development of productive forces the core focus of all work. Back then, China's actual situation was grim: not only were productive forces severely underdeveloped, but the long-entrenched rigid economic and institutional systems significantly constrained their further growth. The traditional understanding of socialism placed excessive emphasis on the "large-scale and public nature" of ownership, promoted egalitarianism in distribution, and rejected the growth of a commodity-based economy. This perspective denied the function of the law of value and held that the planned economy was an inherent and defining feature of socialism, while viewing the market economy as inherently capitalist and fundamentally incompatible with socialist principles. These wrong traditional concepts were deeply ingrained in the minds of some people. Whenever China's reforms faced a turning point, there would always be someone who would debate whether the reform belonged to "capitalism" or "socialism." Through the practice of reform and opening up, the Party's perception of how socialism relates to the market economy has undergone a fundamental shift. In his Southern Talks, Deng Xiaoping noted: "A planned economy is not equivalent to socialism, because there is planning under capitalism too; a market economy is not capitalism, because there are markets under socialism too. Planning and market forces are both means of controlling economic activity." "The proportion of planning to market forces is not the essential difference between socialism and capitalism."[8] This incisive assertion fundamentally lifted the ideological shackles of considering planned economy and market economy as belonging to the category of fundamental social systems. In order to further unleash and develop productive forces, it was necessary to reform the traditional centralized planned economic system and establish a socialist market economic system. The 14th National Congress of the Communist Party of China explicitly proposed the significant historical mission of building a socialist market economic system, marking a major leap in the understanding of socialism.

As China's economic system shifted toward a socialist market economy, a series of far-reaching changes unfolded in its economy: Unlike the swift economic overhauls in the Soviet Union and Eastern European nations—characterized by shock therapy and large-scale privatization—China's economic transition has gradually nurtured a competitive market environment through incremental reforms. Under state macro-regulation, the market has come to play a pivotal role in resource allocation. In terms of ownership structure, the fundamental economic system of the primary stage has essentially taken shape, with public ownership as the mainstay. It is supplemented by individual, private, and foreign-invested economies, where various economic sectors coexist and develop over the long term. In the realm of distribution, China has established the principle that diverse production factors—including labor, capital, technology, and management—participate in income distribution according to their respective contributions. A distribution system centered on distribution according to work, while allowing multiple forms of distribution to coexist, has been steadily refined. Meanwhile,

---

8 Xiaoping Deng. *Selected Works of Deng Xiaoping, Vol. 3*. Beijing: People's Publishing House, 1993, p. 373.

the state encourages the public to boost their property-based income. China's market-driven reforms have notably improved the allocation of production factors and raised enterprise efficiency, which in turn has spurred industrial growth and overall economic progress. Since the late 1970s, China has undergone a striking transformation, moving from a state of near-economic collapse to become the world's second-largest economy. This shift has been defined by an unparalleled four-decade period of sustained, rapid economic growth, frequently hailed as a "miracle" in modern economic history. In the great practice of building socialism with Chinese characteristics, the Party's comprehension of socialist construction has been continuously deepened. The primary stage of socialism is an underdeveloped phase of socialism, where economic development stands as the focus of all efforts. Nevertheless, as economic growth improves steadily, the comprehensive advancement of development in other areas like politics and culture has grown increasingly significant. The goals set at the 16th National Congress of the Communist Party of China for building an all-round moderately prosperous society are targets for the comprehensive development of the economy, politics, and culture under socialism with Chinese characteristics. The 17th National Congress of the Communist Party of China puts forward the initiative to promote all-round economic, political, cultural, and social development in line with the overall layout of the cause of socialism with Chinese characteristics. The report of the 18th CPC National Congress makes a five-sphere overall layout for promoting the construction of socialism with Chinese characteristics. "Taking the path of socialism with Chinese characteristics means we must, under the leadership of the Communist Party of China and basing ourselves on China's realities, take economic development as the central task and adhere to the Four Cardinal Principles and the policy of reform and opening up. It means we must release and develop the productive forces, develop the socialist market economy, socialist democracy, an advanced socialist culture and a harmonious socialist society, and promote socialist ecological progress." The report of the 19th National Congress of the Communist Party of China further defined the "five-sphere integrated plan" and the "four-pronged comprehensive strategy" for the cause of socialism with Chinese characteristics. This indicates that in the primary stage of socialism, merely expanding material wealth and enhancing living standards through economic growth is insufficient. It is equally crucial to advance political progress, cultural enrichment, social development, and ecological preservation to underpin the all-around development of individuals. Only by promoting coordinated progress across all these aspects can China steadily advance toward the goal of common prosperity for all people and eventually build a modern socialist country that is prosperous, strong, democratic, culturally advanced, harmonious, and beautiful.

These theoretical perspectives reflect the deepening of the Party's understanding of the primary stage of socialism, continuously enriching and developing this theory in both scope and depth.

III. The doctrine of socialism's primary stage profoundly uncovers the principal contradiction inherent in this stage

Mao Zedong once pointed out that: In the development process of complex things, there are many contradictions, and one of them must be the principal contradiction. Its existence and development determine or influence the existence and development of other contradictions. Therefore, when examining any issue, if it involves a complex process containing more than two contradictions, we must strive to identify the principal one. Once this principal contradiction is caught, all problems will be solved easily. The primary stage of socialism is a relatively long historical period, during which economic and social contradictions are particularly complex and multifaceted. To navigate this stage effectively, it is essential to look beyond the surface of these varied contradictions and gain a deep understanding of the principal contradiction. Only by accurately identifying and correctly addressing this central contradiction can we clarify the main problems facing society and define the core tasks to be undertaken during socialism's primary stage.

The Party's comprehension of the principal contradiction in socialism's primary stage has gone through multiple phases of refinement and adjustment. In the mid-1950s, after the socialist transformation of agriculture, handicrafts, and capitalist industry and commerce was completed, China's socialist system took shape in its basic form. At that time, the Party carefully analyzed the actual situation at that time and made an analysis of the principal contradictions in the country. The Eighth CPC National Congress pointed out in its "Resolution" on the political report:

Following the decisive triumph of socialist transformation, the contradiction between the proletariat and the bourgeoisie in China had been largely resolved, and the millennia-old history of class exploitation systems had largely come to an end. By this point, China's principal contradiction had already become the conflict between the people's desire to build an advanced industrial nation and the reality of a backward agricultural one, as well as the tension between the people's need for rapid economic and cultural advancement and the fact that the economy and culture failed to satisfy their needs. The core of this conflict, given that China's socialist system had taken shape, lay in the contradiction between the advanced socialist system and backward social productive forces. The primary mission of the Party and the entire nation was to focus on addressing this conflict, transforming China from a backward agricultural nation into an advanced industrial one as quickly as possible. Even from today's viewpoint, the analysis of the main domestic contradictions put forward at the Eighth National Congress of the Communist Party of China—after the socialist system was established—remains fairly objective and in line with China's actual national conditions back then. Yet, this important assessment of Chinese society's principal contradiction was not upheld or put into practice; instead, it was replaced by the notion that "the contradiction between the proletariat and the bourgeoisie, and between the socialist road and the capitalist road, remain the mainstay of our society today." The theory of continuing the revolution under the dictatorship of the proletariat, formulated based on this earlier understanding, resulted in major misalignments in the Party's priorities. It eventually culminated in the "Cultural Revolution," an era that caused severe and far-reaching harm to China's economic growth and socialist development.

After the Third Plenary Session of the 11th Central Committee of the Communist Party of China, the Party's perception of the country's principal contradiction got back on the right track. At the Fourth Plenary Session of the 12th Central Committee of the Communist Party of China, Deng Xiaoping made a preliminary review of the Party's past experiences and lessons, stating: "For many years we suffered badly from one major error: after the socialist transformation of the ownership of the means of production had been basically accomplished, we still took class struggle as the key link and neglected to develop the productive forces. The 'cultural revolution' carried this tendency to the extreme. Since the Third Plenary Session of the Eleventh Central Committee, the Party has shifted the focus of all its work to the drive for socialist modernization and, while adhering to the Four Cardinal Principles, has concentrated on developing the productive forces. That was the most important thing we did to set things right. The good situation we have today would not have come about if we had not thoroughly corrected the "Left" mistakes and resolutely shifted the focus of our work."[9]

The report of the 13th CPC National Congress made a clear statement for the first time on the principal contradiction in the primary stage of socialism. It pointed out: "The principal contradiction we face during the present stage is the contradiction between the ever-growing material and cultural needs of the people and backward production. Class struggle will continue to exist within certain limits for a long time to come, but it is no longer the principal contradiction.

---

[9] Xiaoping Deng. *Selected Works of Deng Xiaoping, Vol. 3*. Beijing: People's Publishing House, 1993, p. 141.

To resolve the principal contradiction of the present stage, we must vigorously expand the commodity economy, raise labor productivity, gradually achieve the modernization of industry, agriculture, national defense and science and technology and, to this end, reform such aspects of the relations of production and of the superstructure as are incompatible with the growth of the productive forces." Yet, not long after the 13th National Congress of the Communist Party of China drew to a close, China found itself facing new and intricate developments both at home and abroad. The upheavals in Eastern Europe, the dissolution of the Soviet Union, and domestic political disturbances gave rise to urgent questions—above all, whether the Party's assessment of the principal contradiction should be revised in response to these changing circumstances. Following meticulous study and analysis of the evolving situation, the Party determined that there was no need to modify its fundamental judgment on the principal contradiction in socialism's primary stage. The report of the 14th National Congress of the Communist Party of China reaffirmed this core assessment, stressing that it remained applicable. The report of the 15th National Congress of the Communist Party of China went on to provide an even more thorough and profound discussion, further cementing the Party's grasp of the principal contradiction and its guiding function in China's development strategy: "Different contradictions exist in China's economy, politics, culture, social activities and other areas, and class contradictions, due to international and domestic factors, will still exist within a certain scope for a long time to come. But the principal contradiction in society is the one between the ever-growing material and cultural needs of the people and the backward production. This principal contradiction will remain throughout the process of China's primary stage of socialism and in all activities of society. Hence we are destined to make economic development the central task of the entire Party and the whole country and make sure that all other work is subordinated to and serves this task." From the report of the 16th National Congress of the Communist Party of China to that of the 18th, the principal contradiction was analyzed within the broader historical backdrop of socialism's entire primary stage. The fundamental national reality that China is still in and will long remain in the primary stage of socialism has not altered, nor has the major social contradiction between the people's growing material and cultural demands and backward social production.

Four decades of reform and opening up have brought sweeping changes to China, and the country's development has stepped into a new historical phase. The report of the 19th CPC National Congress made a new important judgment on the changes of the principal contradiction in our society: "As socialism with Chinese characteristics has entered a new era, the principal contradiction facing Chinese society has evolved. What we now face is the contradiction between unbalanced and inadequate development and the people's ever-growing needs for a better life." As China's economy has grown, its social productive forces have advanced significantly, elevating the nation to the status of the world's second-largest economy with a comprehensive industrial system. Currently, China's existing industrial sectors span 39 major categories, 191 medium categories, and 525 subcategories. It stands as the sole country globally to encompass all industrial classifications outlined in the United Nations Industrial Classification, thereby earning the undisputed title of "World Factory." China has not only formed strong international competitiveness in labor-intensive industries, but has also begun to occupy a place in the international market in complex manufacturing sectors such as automobiles, shipbuilding, and aerospace, which is indicative of a nation's industrialization degree and high-end manufacturing capacity. China's productive forces have advanced significantly, greatly enhancing the capacity to satisfy the people's basic material and cultural needs. Sustained economic expansion has spurred a steady increase in household earnings, bringing about profound shifts in the structure of social demands. Today, people not only hold higher hopes for material and cultural fulfillment but also have growing aspirations for democracy, the rule of law, fairness, justice, security, and environmental quality. Despite impressive economic gains, issues like regional inequalities, urban-rural divides, and other types of unbalanced development remain, hindering the people's quest for a better life. As socialism with Chinese characteristics entered a new era, the long-standing description of the principal contradiction—"between the people's ever-growing material and cultural needs and backward social production"—no longer fully reflected China's social reality. In response, the principal contradiction was redefined as the conflict between the people's ever-growing desire for a better life and unbalanced, inadequate development. This redefinition represents a historic turning point, with extensive and far-reaching effects on China's overall development strategy.

Given this change in the principal contradiction and the significant progress in developing productive forces, a key question arises: Does this mean that China has already moved beyond socialism's primary stage? On this point, the report of the 19th CPC National Congress clearly emphasized that: "The evolution of the principal contradiction facing Chinese society does not change our assessment of the present stage of socialism in China. The basic dimension of the Chinese context—that our country is still and will long remain in the primary stage of socialism—has not changed. China's international status as the world's largest developing country has not changed. The whole Party must be completely clear about this fundamental dimension of our national context, and must base our work on this most important reality—the primary stage of socialism. We must remain fully committed to the Party's basic line as the source that keeps the Party and the country going and that brings happiness to the people. We must lead and unite the Chinese people of all ethnic groups in fulfilling the central task of economic development. We must uphold the Four Cardinal Principles, continue to reform and open up, be self-reliant, hardworking, and enterprising, and strive to build China into a great modern socialist country that is prosperous, strong, democratic, culturally advanced, harmonious, and beautiful." The question of the principal contradiction in the primary stage stands at the core of the theory of socialism's primary stage. Building on the experiences and lessons gleaned from over seven decades of socialist practice, the Party has precisely pinpointed and steadfastly stuck to its analysis of this stage's principal contradiction. By firmly focusing on both the principal contradiction and the central task of development, the Party has kept a clear and rational grasp of the overall picture of social contradictions. On this basis, the basic line and basic program for the primary stage of socialism have been progressively worked out and refined. This has guaranteed the deepening of China's reform and opening up, and enabled the cause of socialist construction to press forward with remarkable and lasting dynamism.

3. The Doctrine of Socialism's Primary Stage, Along With Associated Research Within China's Economic Academic Community

Since the Third Plenary Session of the 11th Central Committee of the Communist Party of China, the vigorous and profound practice of reform and opening up has kept giving rise to new phenomena and presenting new challenges. This has made it imperative for China's theoretical circle to develop new perspectives and theoretical frameworks to interpret the evolving realities and guide reform initiatives. Along with the adoption of the ideological line of emancipating the mind and seeking truth from facts, the long-standing restrictions imposed by "Leftist" ideological rigidities on academic discussions have been gradually removed. In this new intellectual environment, China's economic theorists engaged with great enthusiasm in studying the unprecedented institutional transformations and patterns of economic development. This surge of scholarly activity led to a wealth of theoretical achievements. Notably, studies on matters concerning socialism's primary stage have substantially enriched China's economic theory system. A great many of these significant academic achievements were acknowledged and adopted by the Central Committee of the Communist Party of China and the State Council, thus becoming key elements in formulating national economic policies and strategies.

As far back as the late 1970s, Su Shaozhi and Feng Lanrui put forward questions about the stage of social development following the proletariat's seizure of power.[10] They believed that from the capitalist society to the advanced stage of communism, it could be divided into three stages.

The initial phase was the transitional period from capitalism to socialism, which fell into two stages. The first stage stretched from the triumph of the proletarian revolution to the basic conclusion of the socialist transformation of ownership of the means of production. During this phase, multiple economic sectors and their corresponding social classes coexisted, rendering it an era of intense and acute class struggle. After the socialist transformation of ownership was largely completed, society would move into the second stage—underdeveloped socialism. This was followed by the third stage of developed socialism, and ultimately the final stage of communism. Scholars stressed that failing to differentiate between these stages or conflating them would result in severe theoretical and practical repercussions. For instance, if the transition from capitalism to underdeveloped socialism and that from underdeveloped socialism to developed socialism were regarded as a single period, the contradictions between the proletariat and the bourgeoisie, and between the socialist and capitalist roads, which existed in the first transitional stage, would be erroneously considered to persist throughout the entire historical process. This could lead to unnecessary escalation of class struggle. Another example is that applying policies appropriate for developed socialism prematurely to the underdeveloped socialist stage could cause harmful results, such as the early elimination of individual economies, the abolition of private landholdings and family sideline businesses, the abandonment of distribution based on labor input, and the neglect of commodity production and exchange—ultimately rushing the society toward communism before conditions were ripe.

Su Shaozhi and Feng Lanrui concluded in their article that China remained an underdeveloped socialist society, still in the transitional phase of socialism. They warned against viewing China's economic system as fully mature or entirely socialist. In comparison, Zhu Shuxian put forward a somewhat different division of stages following the proletariat's seizure of power. He identified three stages: first, the transition from capitalism to socialism; second, the initial phase of communism—also referred to as socialism—which he further split into

[10] Shaozhi Su, Lanrui Feng. The question of the stage of social development after the proletariat takes power. *Economic Research Journal*, 1979 (5).

underdeveloped and developed socialism; and third, communism's advanced phase.[11]

While Zhu shared Su and Feng's view that China was in an underdeveloped socialist period, he diverged from their assertion that it remained in a transitional stage. Instead, he argued that China was in the proper stage of underdeveloped socialism. The consensus among these economic theorists—that socialist society should be divided into distinct stages and that China was in the underdeveloped socialist stage—exerted considerable influence on both academic discussions and public understanding. Starting in 1981, the claim that "our socialist system is still in its primary stage" began to appear in documents released by the Central Committee of the Communist Party of China. This concept was later systematically expounded at the 13th National Congress of the Communist Party of China, where it was formally established as a foundational theoretical judgment and gained acceptance across the entire Party.

The exploration of the theory of the primary stage of socialism within China's economic community has, in essence, been a process of reinterpreting socialism through an economic lens. Since the initiation of reform and opening up, economists have carried out extensive studies on the economic challenges and realities unique to socialism's primary stage. Rooted in the actual state of economic development at that time, their research continuously broke free from the constraints of traditional theoretical frameworks—especially regarding the fundamental economic system of this stage. These endeavors yielded a variety of new viewpoints and creative concepts, which not only deepened the understanding of socialism's primary stage but also made substantial contributions to the formation, evolution, and refinement of the theory itself. In this way, the economics community played a crucial role in establishing a theoretical basis that still guides China's socialist economic practices to this day.

The first is the breakthrough in the structure of socialist ownership. Traditionally, it was once held that socialist ownership must be purely public, with purity regarded as the paramount virtue. The individual economy, meanwhile, was viewed as a persistent hotbed of capitalist inclinations, while the private economy was viewed as inherently capitalist and something that must ultimately be eliminated. However, this rigid interpretation began to shift after the reform era. A growing number of economists advocated for a more pluralistic understanding of ownership under socialism. They put forward the idea

11 Shuxian Zhu. Also talk about the stage of social development after the proletariat takes power—discussing with comrades Su Shaozhi and Feng Lanrui. *Economic Research Journal*, 1979 (8).

that a variety of non-public ownership forms—such as individual and private economies—could be developed, on the condition that public ownership retained its leading role. Xue Muqiao was one of the earliest economists to advocate for this diversified model. As far back as 1979, he argued that allowing a small remnant of the individual economy and capitalism to remain might actually do more good than harm.[12] His view marked a major departure from orthodox thinking and opened the door to broader theoretical innovation. As China's non-public economy expanded rapidly, Economic theorists went on to further deepen their insights into the ownership structure suited to socialism's primary stage. Chen Zongsheng put forward a "mixed economy" model as the target framework for China's ownership reform. Within this model, public ownership maintains a relatively dominant role, while private, individual, and state-capitalist sectors coexist and develop in tandem. Chen drew a distinction between two key dimensions of this model: "coexistence" denotes the presence of diverse ownership types—both public and non-public—across the national economy; "integrated growth" refers to the dynamic interaction and intermingling of these forms, even within individual enterprises. He also emphasized that this was not a mixed economy with private ownership in a dominant position, as seen in Western capitalist systems, but one where public ownership continued to play the leading role.[13] At the 15th CPC National Congress, the economic system with public ownership playing the leading role and all forms of ownership growing side by side was officially recognized as the fundamental economic system in the primary stage of socialism. As noted in the "Resolution" adopted at the Third Plenary Session of the 18th Central Committee of the Communist Party of China, the basic economic system serves as a crucial pillar of socialism with Chinese characteristics and forms the cornerstone of the socialist market economy system.

The second breakthrough lies in the form of socialist public ownership. Historically, socialist public ownership was perceived as being achieved exclusively through ownership by the whole people and collective ownership. Among these, ownership by the whole people was considered the superior form, while collective ownership was viewed as an inferior form that would ultimately evolve into ownership by the whole people. Nevertheless, in the early 1980s, He Wei noticed the emergence of new forms of public ownership in practice and contended that, in the context of these actual economic developments, the theory of

---

[12] Muqiao Xue. *Xue Muqiao's Memoirs*. Tianjin: Tianjin People's Publishing House, 1996.

[13] Zongsheng Chen. On the target mode of ownership reform. *Nankai Economic Studies*, 1987 (3).

socialist ownership of the means of production required re-evaluation.[14] Liu Shibai further advanced this view by emphasizing that, In an underdeveloped socialist society, public ownership forms a complex structure where ownership by the whole people holds a dominant position, while also incorporating collective ownership, joint ownership, and other types of public ownership.[15] Yu Guangyuan's landmark book *Economy in the Primary Stage of Socialism in China* was among the earliest systematic studies exploring economic issues specific to this stage, and it was recognized as "one of the 10 economic works that have influenced New China's economic construction." In his analysis, Yu Guangyuan identified the appearance of a range of new, non-conventional forms of socialist ownership in China[16], and predicted that over time, these complex forms of ownership would become more significant than the traditional, simpler forms. Regarding reform strategies, scholars like Li Yining promoted the shareholding system as a more efficient means of materializing public ownership, offering thorough justifications for this approach. Mirroring these evolving perspectives, the report of the 15th National Congress of the Communist Party of China formally recognized that public ownership could take on diverse realization. This perspective was further reinforced by the "Decision of the Central Committee of the Communist Party of China on Some Issues Concerning the Improvement of the Socialist Market Economic System" issued by the Third Plenary Session of the 16th CPC Central Committee, which pointed out "making the joint-stock system the major form for realizing public ownership." It also called for "vigorously developing a mixed economy involving state-owned capital, collective capital, and non-public capital, thereby promoting diversified sources of investment." The "Decision of the Central Committee of the Communist Party of China on Some Major Issues Concerning Comprehensively Deepening Reforms" issued by the Third Plenary Session of the 18th CPC Central Committee clearly put forward that "A mixed economy with cross holding by and mutual fusion between state-owned capital, collective capital and non-public capital is an important way to materialize

[14] Wei He. Socialist public ownership should take many forms. *People's Daily*, Dec. 31, 1984.

[15] Shibai Liu. Socialist Ownership Structure. Economic Research Journal Editorial Office. *Review and Prospect of China's Socialist Economic Theory*. Beijing: The Economic Daily Press, 1986.

[16] In the book, the basic form or non-complex form of socialist ownership refers to the traditional form of public ownership, and the non-basic form or complex forms of socialist ownership refer to public-owned enterprises with multiple shareholdings formed through horizontal alliance or fund-raising among public enterprises. Guangyuan Yu. *The Economy of the Primary Stage of Chinese Socialism*. Beijing: China Financial & Economic Publishing House, 1988.

the fundamental economic system of China. It is conducive to improving the amplification function of state-owned capital, ensuring the appreciation of its value, raising its competitiveness, and it is conducive to enabling capital with all kinds of ownership to draw on one another's strong points to offset weaknesses, stimulate one another and develop together." Therefore, it was necessary to "vigorously develop a mixed economy."

The third breakthrough relates to the form of ownership by the whole people. Historically, there was a consensus that ownership by the whole people could only exist in the form of state ownership, and that this was the only viable model. According to this view, the means of production owned by the socialist state were held solely by the state, acting on behalf of all working people. The state exercised direct control over state-owned enterprises by appointing their leaders through government agencies, which in turn oversaw the centralized planning of all production activities within these enterprises. At the start of reform and opening up, Dong Fureng questioned this long-standing perspective. He contended that the core of economic system reform was to transform the state-owned form through which ownership by the whole people was realized. He put forward a clear distinction between the state's administrative powers and the functions of economic organizations. He advocated that those economic activities should be carried out by various economic entities with independent decision-making power, operating under unified state guidance. These entities should implement comprehensive and independent economic accounting, have their own economic interests, and assume legal economic responsibilities.[17] Dong Fureng's article sparked the initial debates on reforming state ownership. From the 1990s onward, particularly following Deng Xiaoping's Southern Talks, discussions on reforming state ownership within economic theory circles became more vigorous and widespread than ever before. Zhou Shulian put forward that "ownership is an economic means."[18] He held that ownership, much like planning, constitutes an economic tool. The institution of state ownership is intended to drive the development of productive forces—this development being the ultimate objective—whereas state ownership itself serves merely as an economic means. He criticized those who treated state ownership as a goal of socialism and fell into blind faith in it. These individuals maintained that acknowledging the property rights of state-owned enterprises would alter the nature of state ownership and undermine socialism's

---

[17] Fuzheng Dong. On the form of socialist ownership in our country. *Economic Research Journal*, 1979 (1).

[18] Wenquan Yin. Ownership is an economic tool—interview with Professor Zhou Shulian. *Comparative Economic & Social Systems*, 1993 (5).

economic foundation. Such blind faith, in essence, clung to the state ownership model under the traditional socialist economic system, fundamentally regarding ownership as an end rather than a tool. The Third Plenary Session of the 16th CPC Central Committee underscored the critical importance of clarifying the property rights of state-owned enterprises. It stressed that building a modern property rights system featuring "clear ownership, distinct rights and responsibilities, robust protection, and unimpeded transferability" is crucial for safeguarding public assets and enhancing the leading role of the public economy. The Third Plenary Session of the 18th Central Committee of the Communist Party of China reaffirmed the nature and significance of state-owned enterprises, noting that "as entities owned by the whole people, state-owned enterprises constitute a key force in advancing national modernization and safeguarding the people's common interests." Consequently, it called for further efforts to promote the improvement of the modern enterprise system in state-owned enterprises.

The fourth breakthrough pertains to the socialist distribution system. The conventional perspective held that public ownership of the means of production dictated that distribution according to work was the sole socialist distribution principle, while the inclusion of factors like land and capital in distribution was dismissed as a relic of bourgeois vulgar economics. Gu Shutang and Cai Jiming contended that this viewpoint was inapplicable to socialism's primary stage. Their argument was as follows: Given the coexistence of diverse ownership systems during socialism's primary stage, the state, enterprises, and individuals each maintained relatively independent economic interests. Enterprises and individuals also enjoyed varying degrees of autonomy in income distribution and accumulation, rendering it unfeasible to implement a distribution system based solely on labor. Instead, they put forward that the guiding principle for distribution in the primary stage should be distribution according to contribution—that is, income should be allocated based on the actual contributions of different production factors to the creation of social wealth. The worth of these contributions would be determined by each factor's marginal revenue. They underscored that only by upholding the principle of distribution according to contribution could equal opportunities be guaranteed, efficiency enhanced, resources allocated optimally, and social productive forces developed effectively.[19] While their views sparked considerable debate, the ongoing reforms have since demonstrated the validity and practicality of this approach. The 16th CPC National Congress clearly stated that "We should establish the principle that labor, capital, technology, managerial

19 Shutang Gu, Jiming Cai. Distribution according to contribution is the distribution principle in the primary stage of socialism. *Economist*, 1989 (2).

expertise and other production factors participate in the distribution of income in accordance with their respective contributions, thereby improving the system under which distribution according to work is dominant and a variety of modes of distribution coexist" and ultimately acknowledged the validity of income distribution grounded in the contribution of production factors. The report of the 19th CPC National Congress continued to emphasize "We will continue to follow the principle of distribution according to one's work while improving our institutions and mechanisms for distribution based on factors of production, so as to make income distribution fairer and more orderly."

Clearly, economic theorists have played a crucial role in the formation and development of the theory of socialism's primary stage, making significant and lasting contributions throughout its evolution. "The theory of the primary stage of socialism and the theory of the socialist market economy together have become the most important and outstanding achievements in economic theory research since China's reform and opening up, and are the two pillars of contemporary Chinese socialist political economics. At this stage, the research on all economic issues in China and the formulation of various economic policies must be based on and guided by these two theories."[20] The identification and formulation of the theory on socialism's primary stage stand as a major contribution by China's economic scholars to Marxist economics and scientific socialist theory in the era of reform and opening up. As insights into the economic challenges specific to this stage grow deeper, the theory itself will keep evolving and being enriched.

References

Bo, Yibo. *A Review of Some Major Decisions and Events*. Beijing: Party School of the Central Committee of CPC Press, 1991.

Chen, Zongsheng. On the target mode of ownership reform. *Nankai Economic Studies*, 1987 (3).

Deng, Xiaoping. *Selected Works of Deng Xiaoping, Vol. 2*. Beijing: People's Publishing House, 1994.

Deng, Xiaoping. *Selected Works of Deng Xiaoping, Vol. 3*. Beijing: People's Publishing House, 1993.

---

[20] Zhuoyuan Zhang. Review and prospect of China's economic theory research since reform and opening up. *Collected Works of Zhang Zhuoyuan*. Shanghai: Shanghai Lexicographical Publishing House, 2005, p. 53.

Dong, Fuzheng. On the form of socialist ownership in our country. *Economic Research Journal*, 1979 (1).
Gong, Yuzhi, et al. *Mao Zedong's Reading Life*. Beijing: Central Party Literature Press, 2003.
Gong, Yuzhi. The theory, line and program of the primary stage of Chinese socialism. *Journal of the Party School of the Central Committee of the CPC*, 1998 (1).
Gu, Shutang, Cai Jiming. Distribution according to contribution is the distribution principle in the primary stage of socialism. *Economist*, 1989 (2).
He, Wei. Socialist public ownership should take many forms. *People's Daily*, Dec. 31, 1984.
Lenin. *Selected Works of Lenin, Vol. 4*. Beijing: People's Publishing House, 1995.
Liu, Shibai. Socialist ownership structure. *Review and Prospect of China's Socialist Economic Theory*. Beijing: The Economic Daily Press, 1986.
Mao, Tianqi. Fifty years of great changes: from a planned economy to a market economy. *Journal of Lanzhou University (Social Science Edition)*, 1999 (3).
Mao, Tianqi. *Theory of the Primary Stage of Socialism*. Zhang Zhuoyuan. *Controversy and Development: 50 Years of Chinese Economic Theory*. Kunming: Yunnan People's Publishing House, 1999.
Mao, Zedong. *Selected Readings of Mao Zedong's Works*. Beijing: People's Publishing House, 1986.
Marx & Engels. *Selected Works of Marx and Engels, Vol. 1, Vol. 3*. Beijing: People's Publishing House, 2012.
Shen, Baoxiang. *Mao Zedong and Chinese Socialism*. Nanchang: Jiangxi People's Publishing House, 1996.
Stalin. *Socialist Economic Problems in the Soviet Union*. Beijing: People's Publishing House, 1961.
Su, Shaozhi, Feng Lanrui. The question of the stage of social development after the proletariat takes power. *Economic Research Journal*, 1979 (5).
The Writing Team of This Book. *The Guidebook for the Report of the 19th National Congress of the Communist Party of China*. Beijing: People's Publishing House, 2017.
Wen, Jiabao. A few questions about the historical tasks of the primary stage of socialism and China's foreign policy. *The Bulletin of the State Council of the People's Republic of China*, 2007 (10).
Xi, Jinping. Closely focus on upholding and developing socialism with Chinese characteristics, study, publicize and implement the spirit of the 18th National Congress of the Communist Party of China. *People's Daily Online*, Nov. 19, 2012.
Xue, Hanwei. The primary stage of socialism and similar expressions in history. *Theory Front*, 1987 (4).

Xue, Muqiao. *Xue Muqiao's Memoirs*. Tianjin: Tianjin People's Publishing House, 1996.
Yin, Wenquan. Ownership is an economic tool—Interview with Professor Zhou Shulian. *Comparative Economic & Social Systems*, 1993 (5).
Yu, Guangyuan. *The Economy of the Primary Stage of Chinese Socialism*. Beijing: China Financial & Economic Publishing House, 1988.
Zhang, Zhuoyuan. Retrospect and prospect of China's economic theory research since reform and opening up. *Collected Works of Zhang Zhuoyuan*. Shanghai: Shanghai Lexicographical Publishing House, 2005.
Zhu, Shuxian. Also talk about the stage of social development after the proletariat takes power—discussing with comrades Su Shaozhi and Feng Lanrui. *Economic Research Journal*, 1979 (8).

Theoretical Framework of the Fundamental Socialist Economic System

Ownership remains a core theoretical focus in both Marxist political economy and the socialist political economy with Chinese characteristics. Marx and Engels explicitly emphasized in the *Manifesto of the Communist Party* that "in all these movements they bring to the front, as the leading question in each, the property question, no matter what its degree of development at the time."[1] Over the past four decades of reform and opening up, China has achieved remarkable progress in addressing ownership issues. The most notable theoretical advancement is the formulation of a fundamental economic system in which public ownership plays a dominant role, while multiple forms of ownership coexist and develop together. This theoretical framework has provided a crucial foundation for both the economic system during the primary stage of socialism and the functioning of the socialist market economy. Given its vital theoretical and practical implications for enhancing the socialist market economy and establishing a robust institutional basis for economic development in the new era, it is essential to review the evolution of this theory and explore its future development paths.

1. Structural Diversification of Ownership in the Early Phase of Reform and Opening Up

China's economic system reform began against the backdrop of a highly centralized planned economy, characterized by an ownership structure that was both large in scale and overwhelmingly public, with the state sector dominating the national economy. This historical context has profoundly shaped the

1 Marx & Engels. *Collected Works of Marx and Engels, Vol. 2*. Beijing: People's Publishing House, 2009, p. 66.

development, evolution, and continuous refinement of the theory of the fundamental socialist economic system. It also provides an essential foundation for analyzing the transformation of China's ownership structure and understanding the broader trajectory of ownership-related reforms. From the perspective of classical Marxist theorists, future society would be based on public or collective ownership of the means of production.[2] In the initial years following the success of the October Revolution in Russia, Lenin envisioned the abolition of private property, the nationalization of banks, railways, and major industries, and the establishment of socialism grounded in unified public ownership. However, these efforts did not yield the anticipated results. Then the "New Economic Policy" was implemented, allowing private industrial and commercial activities, and developing state capitalism in the industrial field, which achieved good results. After Lenin, Stalin diverged from the path of the "New Economic Policy" by establishing a strongly centralized economic planning system. He implemented an economic system dominated by a single public economy, elevating the state-owned enterprises as the superior type of public ownership, while viewing the collective economy as a lower tier of public ownership. In China, following the founding of the People's Republic of China in 1949, multiple economic sectors were allowed to exist. The "Common Program of the Chinese People's Political Consultative Conference" in 1949 stipulated: "The People's Republic of China ... protects the economic interests and private property of workers, peasants, the petty bourgeoisie, and the national bourgeoisie"; "shall encourage the active operation of all private economic enterprises beneficial to the national welfare and to the people's livelihood and shall assist in their development." In 1949, Mao Zedong stated at the Second Plenary Session of the Seventh Central Committee of the CPC: China's economy during the New Democratic stage comprised five distinct forms: the state-owned economy, cooperative economy, private capitalist economy, individual economy, and state capitalist economy. However, beginning in 1955, following the agricultural co-operative movement and the socialist transformation of handicrafts, as well as private industry and commerce, non-public sectors—including individual and private economies—began to diminish and were eventually phased out entirely. Until 1978, when the curtain of reform and opening up was opened, there were only about 150,000 self-employed individuals in China. These workers relied on their own labor and possessed their own means of production, with their goods or services generally owned by themselves

---

2 "Imagine an association of free men who work with public means of production and consciously use many of their individual labor forces as a social labor force." Marx & Engels. *Collected Works of Marx and Engels, Vol. 5*. Beijing: People's Publishing House, 2009, p. 96.

or their families, primarily operating in fields such as handicrafts, construction, transportation, and commercial catering. Compared with 1952, the number of self-employed individuals had dropped by 8.68 million. The fortunes of the private economy were more torturous because of the employment relationship. Following the fundamental accomplishment of socialist transformation, the private sector was effectively eliminated as an economic entity, and statistical records related to private enterprises were subsequently removed from official reports.

The change of China's ownership structure started with the recognition and gradual development of the individual economy. Once this opening was established, the ownership structure would gain the endogenous power of self-evolution and become the realistic basis for the continuous development of China's ownership theories. In 1978, at the Third Plenary Session of the 11th CPC Central Committee, it was stated that "Small plots of land for private use by commune members, their domestic side-occupations, and village fairs are necessary adjuncts of the socialist economy, and must not be interfered with."[3] In 1979, the "Decision of the Central Committee of the Communist Party of China on Several Issues Concerning Accelerating Agricultural Development" adopted by the Fourth Plenary Session of the 11th CPC Central Committee pointed out: "Small plots of land for private use by commune members, private livestock, their domestic side-occupations and village fairs are the appendages and supplements of the socialist economy. They must never be criticized and banned as capitalist economies."[4] In 1982, the *Constitution of the People's Republic of China* formally incorporated provisions recognizing and safeguarding the development of the individual economy: "The individual economy of urban and rural working people, operating within the limits prescribed by law, is a complement to the socialist public economy. The state protects the lawful rights and interests of the individual economy."

During the initial phase of China's reform and opening up, the development of the individual economy sparked intense debate within academic and theoretical circles, with the views of renowned economist Xue Muqiao standing out as particularly influential. He gave an example: "Practice has raised a question for us. We have always regarded long-distance trafficking as speculation and profiteering. Is this right? Mountain goods and local products have no legs, so how can they come to the city by themselves if no one does long-distance trafficking?

---

3 The Literature Research Office of the Central Committee of the Communist Party of China. *Selection of Important Documents since the Third Plenary Session, Vol. I.* Beijing: Central Party Literature Press, 2011, p. 7.

4 Ibid., p. 158.

Leaving the goods rotten on the mountain is called 'socialism,' and selling them to the city to enrich the market supply is called 'capitalism.' Can this be called Marxism? I don't think long-distance transport of goods can be equated with speculation and profiteering, and long-distance trafficking should be allowed." He further pointed out: "As for manual labor, I think that the collective economy and even the self-employed may be more superior than the ownership by the whole people, and the production relations must be suitable for the nature of productive forces. The idea that under any conditions (such as manual labor conditions) ownership by the whole people must be superior to collective and individual ownership is not Marxism." He advocated: "It is necessary for China's economic theorists to frankly discuss the existing ownership structure in our country. Why does it restrict the development of productive forces so seriously?"[5]

It can be argued that the growth of the individual economy aligned with the prevailing economic and social conditions of that period. First, a significant portion of the labor force remained unemployed, as the state-owned sector was unable to absorb all job seekers. In 1979, the number of unemployed "returning cities" educated youth reached 1.4066 million; in 1980, there were 5.415 million unemployed people in urban areas, of which 3.825 million were young people, accounting for 70.6%. Unemployed people needed a source of livelihood, it would affect social stability. One of the main reasons for introducing policies to support the growth of the individual economy during the early reform period was the serious employment pressure at that time. The individual economy was viewed as a crucial means to absorb the unemployed and ease the labor market strain. The second was a series of problems that urban residents encountered in their daily life at that time, such as difficulty in traveling on public transport, difficulty in having a house, difficulty in sourcing food, difficulty in finding basic services such as haircuts, difficulty in shopping or repairing goods, difficulty even in being able to take a bath, etc. These had always plagued residents, and the individual economy had a natural advantage in solving these problems. Third, the development of the individual economy did not require a large amount of capital, and the technical threshold and operating risks were relatively low, which was adapted to the economic development level at that time. Stimulated by various encouraging and guiding policies, the individual economy had developed rapidly. In 1980, shortly after the initiation of reform and opening-up policies, the first individual business license was granted to Zhang Huamei, a 19-year-old from Wenzhou. By 1992, the number of registered individual industrial and commercial enterprises

5 Mengfu Huang. *History of China's Private Economy • Memorabilia*. Beijing: Social Sciences Academic Press, 2009, pp. 148–149.

across the country had reached 15.339 million, employing 24.677 million people. These enterprises reported a registered capital of 60.09 billion yuan, generated an output value of 92.62 billion yuan, recorded a turnover of 223.89 billion yuan, and achieved retail sales totaling 186.13 billion yuan.

During the early period of reform and opening up, explicit policies were established to define the role of the individual economy within the socialist economic framework. The "Resolution on Certain Questions in the History of Our Party Since the Founding of the People's Republic of China," adopted at the Sixth Plenary Session of the 11th CPC Central Committee, affirmed that: "A certain scope of laborer's individual economy is a necessary supplement to the public economy"; Furthermore, the "Decision of the Central Committee of the Communist Party of China on Reform of the Economic Structure" adopted by the Third Plenary Session of the 12th CPC Central Committee pointed out: "Our current individual economy is associated with socialist public ownership, which is different from the individual economy associated with capitalist private ownership ... It is a necessary and beneficial supplement to the socialist economy, and is subordinate to the socialist economy."

The growth of the individual economy fostered the emergence of the private economy, which naturally evolved from the individual sector. The fundamental distinction between the private and individual economies lies in the presence of wage labor. As the individual economy expanded, the demand for wage labor inevitably arose. Within just a few years of opening the door to individual economic development, the scale of operations had grown sufficiently to create an objective need for employing wage laborers. In 1981, to promote the growth of the individual economy, the State Council released the Several Policy Provisions on the Non-Agricultural Individual Economy in Urban Areas. These regulations defined the policy boundaries for the employment of hired labor—referred to at that time as "helpers" or "apprentices." According to the guidelines, self-employed individuals were permitted to hire one or two helpers with the approval of the local industry and commerce administration. Those possessing advanced technical expertise or specialized skills were allowed to engage two or three apprentices, but the total number could not exceed five. By 1987, these restrictions on the employment of wage labor were further relaxed. In that year, the CPC Central Committee issued the circular "Driving the Rural Reforms in Depth." In addition to reiterating the provisions on the "helper" of the individual economy, it also proposed that, for some private enterprises that employed more than five employees in order to expand their business scale, it was also emphasized that policies should permit their existence, strengthen regulation, encourage their positive aspects while mitigating negative effects, and gradually guide their development. In practice, there were no strict limits on the number of employees hired by private enterprises, which provided ample policy flexibility for the integration of private capital and wage labor.

Of course, compared with the individual economy, during the initial phase of reform and opening up, the growth of the private sector encountered far more twists and hardships. The keynote of the government's policy was "it is not advisable to promote it, do not publicize it, and do not rush to ban it"[6], but the private economy grew secretly with its own tenacious vitality. On April 13, 1984, the first private business license following the reform and opening-up policy was granted through an exceptional approval from the State Council, awarded to Jiang Wei, an individual photographer in Dalian, Liaoning Province. On August 10, 1984, Jiang Wei's enterprise, as the first private enterprise in China, established Dalian Guangcai Industrial Co., Ltd. as a joint venture with Hong Kong Huayuan Investment Co., Ltd. In 1987, the developmental course of the private sector witnessed a substantial turning point, as the 13th National Congress of the Communist Party of China (CPC) furnished it with a definitive policy framework. The Congress report stipulated: "Developing an economy with different types of ownership, with public ownership remaining predominant." "The private sector of the economy is a sector which involves wage labor. But in socialist society, the private sector is bound up with the public sector, which remains predominant and strongly influences it. Practice has proved that a certain degree of development of the private sector promotes production, stimulates the market, provides employment, and helps in many ways to meet people's needs. It is thus a necessary and useful supplement to the public sector."[7] The *Revision to the Constitution of the People's Republic of China* in 1988 pointed out: "The state permits the private sector of the economy to exist and develop within the limits prescribed by law. The private sector of the economy is a complement to the socialist public economy. The state protects the lawful rights and interests of the private sector of the economy, and exercises guidance, supervision and control over the private sector of the economy." So far, the juridical standing of the private sector in China has been confirmed for the first time in the *Constitution of the*

---

6 When talking about the controversial employment issue at the time, Deng Xiaoping pointed out: "There are still other matters that need not be resolved in a hurry. The employment issue a while ago was quite shocking, and everyone was very worried. My opinion is to let it go for two years." See. Xiaoping Deng. *Selected Works of Deng Xiaoping, Vol. 3*. Beijing: People's Publishing House, 1993, p. 91.

7 The Literature Research Office of the Central Committee of the Communist Party of China. *Selection of important literature since the 13th National Congress of the Communist Party of China, Vol.I*. Beijing: Central Party Literature Press, 2011, p. 27.

People's Republic of China. In the same year, the State Council promulgated the "Interim Regulations on Private Enterprises of the People's Republic of China," which made qualitative provisions on private enterprises: "A private enterprise refers to a for-profit economic organization whose enterprise assets are privately owned, with more than 8 employees." It reiterated that the private sector served as a complement to the socialist public economy, with the state safeguarding the legitimate rights of private enterprises; within the scope of state laws, regulations, and policies, they were authorized to conduct production and business activities in sectors including industry, construction, transportation, commerce, catering, services, repair services, technical consulting, etc. In 1988, all parts of the country began to register private enterprises, and private economic activities began to be included in national economic statistics. By the conclusion of 1989, the nationwide registration records indicated 90,581 private enterprises had been lawfully incorporated, employing 1,640,051 people. The output value of industry, construction, and transportation was 9,740.05 million yuan, the turnover of catering, service, repair service, and other industries was 3,880.55 million yuan, and the retail merchandise sales were 3,374.34 million yuan.

During the initial phase of reform, economic theorists conducted substantial and invaluable research into the private sector's development, with a focus on the private economy's nature and orientation, as well as the issue of employment. Some scholars had spoken of the compatibility of the private economy with socialism. Shan Dong and Wang Zhengting believed: "In the private economy, the means of production are owned by the owners, and the employers obtain surplus value and exploit workers. This is the generality of the private economy. However, China's private economy exists in the context of socialist economy, and the public economy influences and dominates the private economy, which makes it different in nature and status from capitalist society. For China's private economy, its generality and particularity coexist, and its duality should be unified and compatible."[8] Xiao Liang believed that China's current private economy "depends on the socialist public economy and the socialist superstructure, and is also subject to the socialist public economy and the socialist superstructure," and "they have certain characteristics of state capitalism."[9] Wang Yong pointed out: "The private economy is an inevitable part of China's economy at this stage. Because under the conditions of the commodity economy, there is an inherent

8 Dong Shan, Zhengting Wang. Discussion on some theoretical issues of individual economy, private economy, and revitalizing public-owned enterprises. *Economic Perspectives*, 1990 (5).

9 Xiao Liang. Several theoretical issues about the private economy. *Tianjin Social Sciences*, 1988 (4).

economic connection between the private economy and the public economy, and it is this connection that constitutes the national economic system. In the market, all economic components of ownership are equal, and a relationship of interdependence is established among them. It is not only the private economy that depends on the public economy. In this system, the lack of any part is not conducive to the development of productive forces."[10]

Wage labor posed both theoretical and practical challenges to the development of the private economy, sparking intense ideological debate. The perspective on wage labor fundamentally influenced the private economy's developmental trajectory. Liu Juqi interpreted the emergence of wage labor as a reallocation of productive elements following the implementation of the Household Contract Responsibility System. He said: "The Household Contract Responsibility System has changed the original combination of production factors, which is embodied in the three surpluses of rural labor, capital and 'intelligence,' providing an opportunity for the flow and recombination of factors. The recombination and flow of production factors have led to various forms of management, so that wage labor management has also appeared in various rural areas." Regarding the nature of wage labor management, Jiang Zhenmin believed that the current wage labor management "not only creates value (taxes, collective retention, bank loan interest, etc.) that workers need in common for the society or the community, but also creates surplus value for private employers. Therefore, this kind of wage labor has both the character of the socialist united labor and the capitalist element."[11] Zhang Musheng and Bai Ruobing believed: "Under socialist conditions, the nature of rural wage labor management cannot be determined by itself, but depends on the conditions and tracks prepared by the country of people's democracy for it."[12]

At the time, discussions surrounding both the nature and function of the private economy—alongside the issue of wage labor within it—were generally framed within the overarching framework of China's economic system, which upheld public ownership as the predominant structure. The dominant viewpoint eschewed exclusive focus on private ownership of the means of production, instead emphasizing conformity to the core tenets of Marxist political economy. This approach not only offered theoretical validation but also cultivated a more

---

10 Yong Wang. Putting the private economy in the general environment of the commodity economy to study. *Economic Perspective*, 1988 (5).

11 Zhenmin Jiang. General and special of labor-hiring. *China Rural Survey*, 1986 (1).

12 Musheng Zhang, Ruobing Bai. The practice and theory of the current rural "labor-hiring" management. *China Rural Survey*, 1984 (2).

conducive ideological and public milieu for private sector development. Data on the evolution of China's individual and private sectors between 1978 and 1991 are presented in Table 1.

In the early stage of reform and opening up, the diversification of China's ownership structure was also manifested in its earlier opening to foreign capital. In January 1982, the CPC Central Committee, together with the State Council, formally approved the "Minutes of the Forum on Foreign Economic and Trade Work in Nine Coastal Provinces, Cities and Autonomous Regions," which put forward: seizing the current favorable opportunity, making bold use of foreign capital, and strengthening global economic collaboration and technological exchanges. In December of that very year, the "Minutes of Several Issues in the Current Pilot Operation of Special Economic Zones" was approved and circulated. The document emphasized that the primary sources of funding toward the construction and advancement of special economic zones would come from attracting funding from investors in Hong Kong, Macao, the overseas Chinese, and foreign regions. In 1983, the State Council issued the "Regulations for the Implementation of the Law of the People's Republic of China on Sino-Foreign Equity Joint Ventures," which provided clear policy frameworks for foreign capital utilization. Between 1979 and 1982, China's practical utilization of foreign investment totaled US $12.457 billion. By 1991, annual utilization had reached US $11.554 billion. The inflow of foreign capital not only helped alleviate the capital shortage that hindered early economic development, but also brought in advanced technology and modern management practices from abroad. Concurrently, the inflow of foreign capital, especially foreign direct investment, together with the individual and private economies, revolutionized China's economic ownership landscape. This process not only restructured property rights configurations but also laid the institutional and material foundation for the subsequent reform of the state-owned sector.

As the individual, private, and foreign-invested economies expanded, alongside the diversification of entities in the public economic sector, production factors such as capital within China's economy became increasingly multifaceted, with their quantities steadily accumulating. The nature of production factors like capital requires constant circulation and dynamic reallocation in order to maximize value creation and generate the highest possible income. Therefore, the shareholding system, which was an organizational form that integrated diverse production elements, including capital and had complementary functions, had arisen in practice. The concept of the shareholding system was first referenced in official documents of the CPC Central Committee and the State Council in 1986, when the State Council released the "Several Regulations on Deepening

Table 1: The advancement of China's individual and private economy from 1978 to 1991

Year	Individual economy				Private economy			
	Quantity (10,000)	Employees (10,000 people)	Registered capital (100 million yuan)	Turnover (100 million yuan)	Quantity (10,000)	Employees (10,000 people)	Registered capital (100 million yuan)	Output value (100 million yuan)
1978	Na.	14.0	Na.	Na.				
1979		31.1						
1980		80.6						
1981	182.9	227.5	4.9	21.1				
1982	263.7	319.9	8.3	100.7				
1983	590.1	746.5	30.7	210.9				
1984	930.4	1,303.1	100.1	457.7				
1985	1,171.4	1,766.2	164.2	750.6				
1986	1,211.2	1,845.9	179.7	914.2				
1987	1,372.5	2,158.3	236.0	1,034.4				
1988	1,452.7	2,304.9	311.9	2,731.2[1]	4.1[2]	72.4[2]	32.9[2]	
1989	1,247.1	1,941.4	347.4	3,055.4[3]	9.1	164.0	84.5	169.9[4]
1990	1,328.3	2,092.8	397.4	3,409.9[5]	9.8	170.2	95.2	216.3[6]

Table 1: (*Continued*)

	Individual economy				Private economy			
Year	Quantity (10,000)	Employees (10,000 people)	Registered capital (100 million yuan)	Turnover (100 million yuan)	Quantity (10,000)	Employees (10,000 people)	Registered capital (100 million yuan)	Output value (100 million yuan)
1991	1,416.8	2,258	488.2	4,105.9[7]	10.8	183.9	123.2	272.2[8]

Note: 1. Including 51.62 billion yuan of the output value of the individual industry, construction industry, and transportation industry, 119.07 billion yuan of the turnover of individual businesses, catering industry, service industry, repair industry, and other industries, and 102.43 billion yuan of the retail sales of commodities.

2. Excluding data from Shanxi, Heilongjiang, and Tibet.
3. Including 56.94 billion yuan of the output value of the individual industry, construction industry, and transportation industry, 133.92 billion yuan of the turnover of individual businesses, catering industry, service industry, repair industry, and other industries, and 114.68 billion yuan of the retail sales of commodities.
4. Including 9,740.05 million yuan of the output value of private industry, construction industry, and transportation industry, 3,880.55 million yuan of the turnover of private commerce, catering industry, service industry, repair industry, and other industries, and 3,374.34 million yuan of the retail sales of commodities.
5. Including 64.24 billion yuan of the output value of the individual industry, construction industry, and transportation industry, 149.75 billion yuan of the turnover of individual businesses, catering industry, service industry, repair industry, and other industries, and 127 billion yuan of the retail sales of commodities.
6. Including 12.18 billion yuan of the output value of the private industry, construction industry, and transportation industry, 5.15 billion yuan of the turnover of private commerce, catering industry, service industry, repair industry, and other industries, and 4.3 billion yuan of the retail sales of commodities.
7. Including 78.22 billion yuan of the output value of the individual industry, construction industry, and transportation industry, 179.82 billion yuan of the turnover of individual businesses, catering industry, service industry, repair industry, and other industries, and 152.55 billion yuan of the retail sales of commodities.
8. Including 14.66 billion yuan of the output value of private industry, construction industry, and transportation industry, 6.8 billion yuan of the turnover of private commerce, catering industry, service industry, repair industry, and other industries, and 5.76 billion yuan of the retail sales of commodities.

Enterprise Reform and Enhancing the Vitality of Enterprises." It pointed out: "All localities can choose a small number of qualified large and medium-sized enterprises owned by the whole people to carry out the pilot shareholding system." In 1987, the State Council-issued "Several Regulations on Further Promoting the Reform of the Science and Technology System" stipulated that scientific and technical personnel could hold shares with technological contributions and earn dividends proportionally. The report of the 13th CPC National Congress, convened that same year, endorsed the shareholding system, stating: "Various forms of a system of shares in enterprises have appeared during the reform. These include purchase of shares by the state, collective purchase by departments, localities and other enterprises and purchase by individuals. This system is one means of raising money for socialist enterprises."[13]

In the initial years of the 1980s and 1990s, the shareholding system was a hot topic of debate in the field of economic theory, and different viewpoints were intertwined. In 1985, the National Economic Reform Seminar for Young and Middle-aged Youth, jointly sponsored by the State Council's Economic Research Center, China Association for Economic System Reform, and the CPC Central Committee's Publicity Department Theoretical Bureau, Hongqi Magazine, and *Economic Daily*, was held in Tianjin. Most of the participants believed that: "The form of ownership with the state as the main body must be changed and replaced by a shareholding economy."[14] In 1988, the "Seminar on the Theory and Practice of Shareholding System" was held in Zigong, Sichuan Province. Most of the participants believed that: "The independence and differentiation of the economic interests of different property entities determines that they can only realize the centralized utilization of funds through the property organization form of the shareholding system, and realize the flow of funds by means of the transfer of stocks and the reinvestment of share capital."[15] Jiang Xuemo believed: "The shareholding system is a form of fund-raising that is compatible with the socialization and commercialization of production. It can be used by both capitalist enterprises and socialist enterprises. The horizontal economic union between socialist enterprises can take the shareholding system as the form of

---

13 Literature Research Office of the Central Committee of the Communist Party of China. *Selection of Important Literature since the 13th National Congress of the Communist Party of China, Vol. I.* Beijing: Central Party Literature Press, 2011, p. 25.

14 Yali Yu. A summary of the National Youth and Middle-aged Economic Reform Symposium. *Economic Perspective*. 1985(7).

15 Gang Yang. Introduction to the viewpoints of the seminar on the theory and practice of joint-stock system. *Economic Perspective*. 1988(5).

property organization, and the union of various economic components can also take the form of a joint-stock company. In addition, enterprises can also use the form of shareholding system to attract employees to buy shares or absorb social idle funds."[16] Li Yining believed: "In a socialist society, the establishment and development of joint-stock enterprises is not only necessary, but also feasible." He believed that the shareholding had the following advantages: First, it fundamentally changed the situation that the government and enterprises were not separated, and made the enterprise into a completely economic entity; second, it effectively addressed the issue of the optimal distribution of productive elements through steering capital flow to high-yield industries, so that funds and labor could be allocated more reasonably; third, it was conducive to the pooling of idle funds in the society to achieve financial integration.[17] For the nature of the shareholding economy, most scholars believed that it depended on the overall institutional environment and the proportion of public shares. Liu Guoguang believed that as long as the "state share as the main body" was maintained, the socialist nature of ownership by the whole people in the shareholding economy could be guaranteed.[18] Li Yining believed: "The nature of an enterprise funded by these shareholders is different from a joint-stock enterprise in a capitalist society. The operation and management of a joint-stock enterprise under socialist conditions must be constrained by the laws and supervised by administrative departments of the socialist country, so the socialist character of the enterprise can be guaranteed."[19] There were also experts who had reservations or even objections to the shareholding model. For example, some argued that "The idea and practice to implement shareholding and privatization by the shareholding system, and enable workers to be motivated to hold shares and develop the capital market in the form of shareholding, together with the idea and practice that shareholders may not work and the labor market determines the supply and demand of labor and the level of wages when workers do not hold shares are obviously the book worship of Western capitalism."[20]

---

16 Xuemo Jiang. Comment on the theory of "absence of the owner." *Economic Research Journal*, 1988 (3).

17 Yining Li. An exploration of the socialist ownership system. *Hebei Academic Journal*, 1987 (1).

18 Guoguang Liu. Several issues on the reform of ownership relations. *Economic Daily*, Janu. 4, 1986.

19 Yining Li. Ownership reform and management of joint-stock enterprises. *Reform of Economic System*, 1986 (12).

20 Bin Ma. The driving force of the enterprises owned by the whole people cannot be the shareholding system that turns the public into the private. *Economic Perspectives*, 1986 (10).

During the early 1980s, joint-stock enterprises started to emerge and gradually take hold. The initial joint-stock enterprises were mainly small urban cooperative enterprises established by means of fundraising. The period from 1984 to 1986 was the first climax of the development of joint-stock enterprises. Some enterprises began to transcend regional, departmental, and ownership boundaries, various economic coalitions were successively established, and steadily developed from single cooperation in production technology to investment in shares based on capital, technology, equipment, etc. Some enterprises had begun to explicitly adopt the form of shareholding to transform old enterprises and organize new joint-stock companies. In June 1984, Foshan Trust and Investment Company of Guangdong Province began to issue stock shares. In the same year July, Beijing Tianqiao Department Store Co., Ltd. was set up and issued 300,000 yuan of shares. It was the first joint-stock enterprise owned by the whole people in China. During September 1986, the Jing'an Securities Business Department of Shanghai Trust and Investment Company of Industrial and Commercial Bank of China started stock agency and trading business. By the end of 1986, a total of 11 billion yuan of stocks (not including countless intra-enterprise fundraising) had been issued. The year 1988 represented a new high point in the expansion of China's joint-stock enterprises. According to statistics, there were more than 6,000 joint-stock enterprises in the country at that time, and the amount of share capital raised was more than 6 billion yuan. By the end of 1989, a total of 4.2 billion yuan of Chinese stocks had been issued. According to incomplete statistics, about 65% of the stocks were publicly issued to the public, and about 35% were issued to corporate internal staff. According to the statistics of some provinces and cities, among all the shares, state shares accounted for about 35%, enterprise shares about 45%, and individual shares about 20%. From 1989 to 1991, due to national governance and rectification of the economic order, the shareholding system changed from "hot" to "cold," and many joint-stock enterprises returned to the original way. Most joint-stock enterprises ended the shareholding system by repaying the capital and interest. After 1991, a series of Party and government documents affirmed the shareholding system and highlighted the importance of pilot programs. China had set off another climax of the shareholding system. By the conclusion of 1991, China's cumulative share issuance had reached 4.6 billion yuan. Among publicly listed share-issuing enterprises, the equity structure showed that state-owned shares constituted 59.9% of total equity, the public corporate shares 26%, and the individual shares 14.1%.

During the initial phase of reform and opening up, the diversification of China's ownership structure was not only manifested in the growth of individual, private, foreign-funded, and shareholding economies, but also in the diversified forms of the public economy. In response to the "large in scale and public in nature" in the classic planned economy period, in the initial stage of reform and opening up, the Party Central Committee stressed the significance of the collective economy as a public economy. The Third Plenary Session of the 11th CPC Central Committee explicitly pointed out that "diversified management of communes and brigades is a socialist economy." In 1981, the State Council issued the "Several Regulations on the Implementation of the National Economic Adjustment Policy by Commune and Brigade Enterprises," pointing out that people's communes and production brigade enterprises had become an important part of the rural economy. Community and brigade enterprises were the prototype of China's township and village enterprises. As an indigenous form of collective economy in early reform China, township and village enterprises exerted significant influence on China's reform trajectory and economic development. The 1980s (especially the mid-to-late 1980s) witnessed a boom in China's township and village enterprises. In 1978, there were 1.52 million township and village enterprises (then known as commune and brigade enterprises) employing 28.27 million workers with a total output value of 51.5 billion yuan and profits of 9.5 billion yuan. By 1990, the number of township and village enterprises had surged to 18.72 million, with employment rising to 92.62 million, total output value reaching 958.1 billion yuan, and profits climbing to 60.8 billion yuan. When commenting on the rapid growth of township and village enterprises, Deng Xiaoping noted that: "In the rural reform our greatest success—and it is one we had by no means anticipated—has been the emergence of many enterprises run by villages and townships. They were like a new force that just came into being spontaneously. These small enterprises engage in the most diverse endeavors."[21]

Academia had carried out theoretical analysis on the nature and operation mechanism of township and village enterprises. Some scholars believed that township and village enterprises better reflected the fundamental tenets of socialism, that is, public ownership and work-based distribution continued to serve as the foundation. Li Bingkun believed: "Of the total output value of township and village enterprises, rural enterprises which clearly belonged to the collective ownership accounted for 66.6% in 1992. In addition, since a considerable part of the joint household enterprises was still collectively owned by villagers' groups, it could be confirmed that township and village enterprises were mainly of collective ownership. Township and village enterprises used piece-rate wages as the main form of distribution, which was directly linked to product quality and

[21] Xiaoping Deng. *Selected Works of Deng Xiaoping, Vol. 3*. Beijing: People's Publishing House, 1993, p. 238.

economic benefits. The implementation of more work, more pay, and less work, less pay, also better reflected the principle of distribution according to work."[22] Some scholars also analyzed why township and village enterprises could rise rapidly. Cai Fang analyzed the differing principal-agent relationships between township and village enterprises and state-owned enterprises, arguing that in township and village enterprises, community members had a more direct stake in the enterprise. It was easier for them to observe the business performance of the enterprise, and they could also supervise the operation of collective assets through various formal and informal channels.[23] Hong Yinxing and Yuan Guoliang also attributed the efficiency of township and village enterprises to differences in the principal-agent relationships compared to state-owned enterprises. They argued that the original principles of township and village enterprises were community residents, and the relatively small scale of these communities fostered stronger supervision motivation and greater oversight capacity among residents. The expected supervision risk was also small.[24] Some scholars had identified flaws in the property rights structure of township and village enterprises, particularly, the "fuzzy property rights" characteristic of collective ownership. Tian Guoqiang believed that township and village enterprises were operated under collective ownership, and "there is no clearly defined share, and no specific person assigned to it. In this sense, its property rights are unclear."[25] Unclear property rights would cause owners, operators, and workers to be unable to clarify their own interests through property rights, and would ultimately lead to the loss of motivation for enterprises and workers. Concurrently, due to the low divisibility, separability, and transferability of property rights in township and village enterprises, factors of production failed to flow efficiently across economic entities, thereby impeding optimal resource allocation. In the early 1990s, township and village enterprises initiated property rights reforms, primarily through asset sales, auctions, and the establishment of joint-stock cooperative and shareholding systems, with the objective of clarifying ownership. As a result of these reforms, some enterprises transformed into private enterprises, others into joint-stock cooperatives, and the rest into shareholding corporations.

---

22 Bingkun Li. Review and prospect of the fifteen years of reform and opening up of township enterprises. *Management World*, 1993 (5).

23 Fang Cai. The logic and successful conditions of the reform of the property rights system of township enterprises. *Economic Research Journal*, 1995 (10).

24 Yinxing Hong, Guoliang Yuan. High-efficiency property rights interpretation of township enterprises. *Management World*, 1997 (4).

25 Guoqiang Tian. The property rights structure and reform of Chinese township enterprises. *Economic Research Journal*, 1995 (3).

2. The Evolutionary Formation of the Theory of the Fundamental Socialist Economic System

From 1978 to the early 1990s, China's ownership structure underwent profound diversification, marking a critical transition from the planned economy's unitary public ownership. This structural transformation—contrasting sharply with the initial reform period—laid the practical foundation for the theoretical framework of the fundamental socialist economic system. The 1990s emerged as a pivotal era for ownership theory innovation and reform practice, during which the Communist Party formally proposed the fundamental socialist economic system theory, punctuated by landmark events such as Deng Xiaoping's Southern Talks and the 14th and 15th CPC National Congresses.

In early 1992, Deng Xiaoping embarked on an inspection tour of Wuchang, Shenzhen, Zhuhai, Shanghai, and other cities, where he delivered his iconic "Southern Talks." These addresses tackled a range of critical theoretical and practical questions surrounding the socialist market economy, articulating several core principles: socialism's essence lies in emancipating and developing productive forces, eradicating exploitation and polarization, and ultimately achieving common prosperity for all; both planning and market mechanisms serve as tools for economic regulation, applicable to both socialist and capitalist systems; the primary yardstick for evaluation should be whether a measure boosts socialist productive forces, enhances the nation's overall strength, and improves people's living standards; and there should be no reluctance to absorb the achievements of global civilizations, including adopting advanced operational methods and management techniques from developed capitalist countries that align with the laws of modern socialized production. This offered the basic theoretical guidance for us to grasp the ownership problem scientifically. Deng Xiaoping also specifically talked about some issues related to ownership. He said: "In the case of Shenzhen, the publicly owned sector is the mainstay of the economy, while the foreign-invested sector accounts for only a quarter. And even in that sector, we benefit from taxes and employment opportunities. We should have more of the three kinds of foreign-invested ventures [joint, cooperative and foreign-owned]. There is no reason to be afraid of them."[26] "Are securities and the stock market good or bad? Do they entail any dangers? Are they peculiar to capitalism? Can socialism make use of them? We allow people to reserve their judgment, but we must try these things out."[27] Deng Xiaoping also mentioned the "Fool's Sunflower

---

[26] Xiaoping Deng. *Selected Works of Deng Xiaoping, Vol. 3.* Beijing: People's Publishing House, 1993, pp. 372–373.

[27] Ibid., p. 373.

Seeds" of that year, a typical case of the self-employed business. Deng Xiaoping's Southern Talks exerted a far-reaching influence on defining the objectives of China's economic system reform and played a pivotal role in advancing the theory of the fundamental socialist economic system.

October 1992 saw the convening of the 14th National Congress of the Communist Party of China (CPC). One of the most important theoretical contributions was the formal establishment of the reform objective: "to build a socialist market economy," and define the connotation of the socialist market economy, that was, "to make the market play a fundamental role in the allocation of resources under the macro-control of socialist countries, so that economic activities follow the requirements of the law of value." According to the inherent logic of the socialist market economy, the report of the 14th CPC National Congress pointed out the ownership basis of the socialist market economy: "In terms of ownership structure, the public ownership including ownership by the whole people and collective ownership is the main body, supplemented by individual economy, private economy, and foreign-funded economy. Various economic components will develop side by side for a long time, and different economic components can also voluntarily implement various forms of joint operation. State-owned enterprises, collective enterprises and other enterprises have all entered the market and played the leading role of state-owned enterprises through equal competition."[28] The 14th CPC National Congress advanced the recognition of the shareholding system, pointing out that the shareholding system helped promote the decoupling of enterprises from government administration, transform enterprise operating mechanism, and facilitate the accumulation of social capital, and should be actively piloted; regarding the reform of small state-owned enterprises, it was explicitly stated that "some may be leased out or transferred to collectives or individual operators."

In 1993, the Third Plenary Session of the 14th CPC Central Committee was held, adopting the "Decision of the Central Committee of the Communist Party of China on Some Issues Concerning Building a Socialist Market Economy." This document laid out the fundamental framework for the socialist market economic system and represented a significant advancement in the theory of ownership. The progress was mainly reflected in: First, a departure from the traditional view that the "non-public economy" served merely as a "beneficial supplement" to the public economy, along with the formulation of a new policy stance: "adhering

---

[28] The Literature Research Office of the Central Committee of the Communist Party of China. *Selection of Important Documents since the 14th National Congress of the Communist Party of China, Vol. I.* Beijing: Central Party Literature Press, 2011, p. 17.

to the principle of public ownership as the main body and various economic components developing side by side. While actively promoting the development of the state-owned economy and collective economy, we must encourage the development of individual economy, private economy, and foreign-funded economy, and strengthen the management in accordance with the law." "The state should create conditions for all types of ownership economies to participate in market competition on an equal footing, and treat all types of enterprises equally." Second, it articulated for the first time the dominant role of public ownership. "The dominant position of public ownership is mainly reflected in the fact that assets owned by the state and collectives are dominant in the total social assets, the state-owned economy controls the lifeline of the national economy, and it plays the leading role in economic development, etc." Moreover, the dominant role of public ownership applied to the nation, with the understanding that "there may be differences in some places and some industries."[29] Third, it proposed the concept of a mixed-ownership economy, pointing out that "with the flow and reorganization of property rights, more and more economic units are mixed with property, and a new property ownership structure will be formed." This marked the first time in the reform and opening-up era that the mixed-ownership economy was elaborated on in Party documents. Fourth, it was suggested that the share of state-owned equity in enterprises should be determined according to specific conditions, rather than being applied uniformly or following a one-size-fits-all approach. "The appropriate proportion of state-owned equity in the company can be handled differently according to different industries and the degree of equity dispersion. Companies and military enterprises that produce some special products should be wholly owned by the state, and backbone enterprises in pillar industries and basic industries should be managed by the state. It is necessary for the state to hold shares and absorb non-state-owned funds to expand the leading role and scope of influence of the state-owned economy."[30] It is evident that the "Decision of the Central Committee of the Communist Party of China on Some Issues Concerning Building a Socialist Market Economy"—adopted at the Third Plenary Session of the 14th CPC Central Committee—laid out the fundamental socialist economic system, thereby providing a robust groundwork for the eventual development of its theoretical framework.

---

29 The Literature Research Office of the Central Committee of the Communist Party of China. *Selection of Important Documents since the 14th National Congress of the Communist Party of China, Vol. I.* Beijing: Central Party Literature Press, 2011, p. 458.

30 Ibid., pp. 456–457.

In 1997, the 15th CPC National Congress was convened. Its major theoretical contribution was the formal introduction and systematic articulation of the fundamental socialist economic system. The Congress declared that "the system with public ownership as the main body and multiple forms of ownership developing side by side is a fundamental economic system in the primary stage of socialism in China." This marked a significant leap in the theory of socialist ownership with Chinese characteristics. The concept of the fundamental socialist economic system encapsulated the theoretical and practical innovations achieved in the first two decades of reform and opening up, and opened up a huge space for the subsequent economic system reform. Its innovation was primarily manifested in the following:

First, it adapted to the reality of the diversification of the structure of ownership and expanded the scope of the publicly owned economy. It was also proposed that the publicly owned economy included not merely the state-owned economy and the collective economy, but also the state-owned and collective components in the mixed-ownership economy. The state-owned and collective components in the mixed-ownership economic entities (including shareholding enterprises, joint ventures, etc.) were brought into the category of public economy, reflecting profound theoretical and practical insight. According to statistics, in the year when the 15th CPC National Congress was held, in the industrial field, there were 13,100 joint-stock enterprises whose ownership structure was the main form of mixed economy, with a total industrial output value reaching 497.6 billion yuan. By 2016, in the industrial field, there had been nearly 110,000 mixed-ownership enterprises, including shareholding companies, limited liability corporations, jointly operated enterprises, and shareholding cooperative enterprises, with assets reaching 56 trillion yuan, main operating income 45 trillion yuan, and profit 2.6 trillion yuan. It could be seen from these data that China's mixed-ownership economy and its strength had developed rapidly, and so had the public economy and its strength.

Second, the report clarified the connotation of the dominant status of public ownership and the leading function of the state-owned economy. The document "Decision of the Central Committee of the Communist Party of China on Some Issues Concerning Building a Socialist Market Economy," adopted at the Third Plenary Session of the 14th CPC Central Committee, provided a preliminary definition of public ownership's dominant position. However, the expression in the report delivered at the 15th CPC National Congress was much clearer, emphasizing two main aspects: First, public ownership's dominant position was primarily reflected in the fact that public assets constituted most of the total social assets. The state-owned economy dominated the national economy's lifeline and exerted leadership through its command over systemic economic dynamics. Second, it was introduced that the quantitative scope of public ownership's dominant role should be understood dialectically. While public assets must maintain a quantitative predominance at the national level, this proportion may vary across different regions and industries. Public ownership should possess both quantitative and qualitative advantages. If the state maintained control over the lifeline of the national economy, a modest decline in the proportion of the state-owned economy would not compromise the socialist nature of China.

Third, it put forward a strategic restructuring of the state-owned economy, representing a notable theoretical breakthrough. The state-owned economy is required to retain a dominant position in critical industries and key sectors that are vital to the national economy's lifeline. In other domains, the emphasis should be placed on enhancing its strength through asset reorganization and structural reforms, thereby improving the overall quality of state-owned assets. The "Decision of the Central Committee of the Communist Party of China on Some Major Issues Concerning the Reform and Development of State-Owned Enterprises," adopted by the Fourth Plenary Session of the 15th CPC Central Committee, provided clearer guidelines on the distribution of the state-owned economy. Specifically, it identified four primary sectors: industries related to national security, natural monopoly, the provision of important public goods and services, and key backbone enterprises in pillar and high-tech industries.

Fourth, it emphasized that the forms of public ownership was realized could and should be diversified, fully affirming the practical significance of the shareholding system as a valid form of realizing public ownership. It was emphasized that efforts should be directed toward identifying a realistic form of public ownership capable of strongly driving the development of productive forces. As a capital organization model for modern enterprises, the shareholding system could equally be employed under socialism. Whether a shareholding economy was public or private depended on who held the controlling stake.

Fifth, it further challenged the notion that the non-public economy was merely a "supplement" to the socialist public economy, arguing instead that it constitutes an integral component of China's socialist market economy. The individual, private, and other non-public economic sectors should be encouraged and guided to achieve sound development, thereby elevating the status of the non-public economy to a new height both theoretically and practically.

During the 16th and 17th CPC National Congresses, the theory of the fundamental socialist economic system was further advanced. The report of the 16th CPC National Congress, for the first time, put forward the concept of "two necessaries" policy, namely "necessary to consolidate and develop unswervingly the public sector of the economy" and "necessary to encourage, support and guide the development of the non-public sectors of the economy," and pointed out that "we must stimulate the development of the non-public sectors while keeping the public sector as the dominant player, incorporating both into the process of the socialist modernization drive instead of setting them against each other." The "two necessaries" policy had been repeatedly reaffirmed in important documents of the CPC Central Committee and the State Council, evolving into the foundational theoretical and practical framework for balancing public and non-public economies. The Third Plenary Session of the 16th CPC Central Committee elevated the mixed-ownership economy to the status of the primary form of public ownership, marking a historic leap in socialist economic theory. It pointed out that what was required was to: "vigorously develop a mix sector of the economy shared by state-owned capital, collective capital, non-public capital, etc., realize the diversification of investment sources and make the joint-stock system as the major form for realizing public ownership." Meanwhile, it proposed to establish a modern property rights system characterized by clear ownership attribution, well-defined rights and responsibilities, strict protection, and unimpeded transfer. The 17th CPC National Congress pioneered the inclusion of "equal protection of property rights" in the theory of the fundamental economic system, placing "public property rights" and "private property rights" on an equal footing in terms of protection, forming a pattern of equal competition and mutual promotion of various forms of ownership. The Fifth Plenary Session of the 17th CPC Central Committee further clarified "to create an institutional environment in which various forms of ownership equally use production factors in accordance with the law, participate in market competition fairly, and are equally protected by law" and proposed "to deepen the reform of monopoly industries, introduce competition mechanisms, and strengthen government supervision and social supervision." This marked the start of the reform of monopoly industries such as water, electricity, gas, coal, oil, banking, insurance, etc., to gradually eliminate the monopoly of resources, prices, and profits in these industries, and the behavior of harming the interests of other industries, the interests of the public, and those of residents.

Over the two decades spanning from Deng Xiaoping's Southern Talks in 1992 to the 18th CPC National Congress in 2012, the economists and scholars engaged in extensive and in-depth discussions on the theory of the socialist fundamental economic system. They proposed numerous important theoretical perspectives, which significantly contributed to the formulation and evolution of this theory. Dong Fureng was one of the early economists who proposed the idea of a mixed economy. As early as the early 1980s, he said: A socialist economy cannot only have a public economy without private ownership, as this cannot drive the growth of production. The socialist economic system should be "developing a variety of non-public ownership (individual, private, mixed private ownership, etc.) under the conditions that the public ownership plays the dominant role," so that "the strengths and weaknesses of various ownerships can complement each other, and the issues of fairness and efficiency can be better resolved."[31] In the early 1990s, he used "eight-treasure rice pudding" to vividly compare and describe the ownership structure of the socialist economic system. He said: "The socialist economy is like a pot of eight-treasure rice pudding, which is mainly composed of glutinous rice, but also consists of bean paste, red dates, lotus seeds and other foods. Although glutinous rice is the main ingredient, glutinous rice itself is not eight-treasure rice pudding. Similarly, bean paste, red dates, lotus seeds and other foods, individually, are not the eight-treasure rice pudding as well ... Only the combination of glutinous rice, red bean paste, red dates, lotus seeds, etc., with glutinous rice as the main ingredient is the eight-treasure rice pudding."[32]

In the mid-to-late 1990s, the structural adjustment of China's state-owned economy became a pivotal focus of economic theory and policy, driven by systemic challenges and external shocks. An important work in this regard was *Strategic Restructuring of the State-Owned Economy*, published in 1998 by Wu Jinglian, Zhang Junkuo, Liu Shijin, etc. They believed that the overall lack of competitiveness of the state capital was owing to the fact that state-owned capital was too scattered among enterprises and industries, and the battle lines were too long. "Limited state-owned capital could not support such a huge state-owned economy."[33] Therefore, it was essential to implement a strategic reorganization of the state-owned economy, that was, "through the flow and reorganization of state-owned assets, on the premise of appropriately shrinking the state-owned economy front, we should improve the allocation structure of state-owned assets and the organizational structure of state-owned enterprises, and concentrate on strengthening the industries and enterprises the state must safeguard, so that the state-owned economy can play a better role in the socialist market economy."[34] As for the distribution scope of the state-owned economy, they believed that, "It should mainly focus on those undertakings that affect the overall development

---

[31] Zhuoyuan Zhang. *Controversy and Development: 50 Years of Chinese Economic Theory*. Kunming: Yunnan People's Publishing House, 1999, p. 159.

[32] Fuzheng Dong. *Research on Economic System Reform, Vol. 1*. Beijing: Economic Science Press, 1994, pp. 343–344.

[33] Jinglian Wu, Junkuo Zhang, Shijin Liu, et al. *Strategic Reorganization of State-owned Economy*. Beijing: China Development Press, 1998, p. 32.

[34] Ibid., p. 9.

of the national economy, control the lifeline of the national economy, cannot be conducted or done well by the non-state-owned economy and can only be completed by the state." The first was the national security industries, such as military and aerospace industries; the second was the large-scale infrastructure construction, including urban infrastructure, transportation backbone facilities, river management, major agricultural commodity foundations, and key shelter forest projects; the third was the super-large non-renewable resources, such as oilfields, coal mines and other development projects; the fourth was the development of high-tech that was of strategic significance to the nation's long-term development, such as the development of large-scale integrated circuits, the localization of major technical equipment, etc.

3. The Evolution of the Theory of the Fundamental Socialist Economic System in the New Era

Since the convening of the 18th CPC National Congress, the CPC Central Committee, with Comrade Xi Jinping at its core, has led China into a new era of reform, opening up, and economic development. In November 2013, the Third Plenary Session of the 18th CPC Central Committee adopted the "Decision of the Central Committee of the Communist Party of China on Some Major Issues Concerning Comprehensively Deepening the Reform" (hereinafter referred to as the "Decision" within this context). In October 2015, the Fifth Plenary Session of the 18th CPC Central Committee passed the "Recommendations of the Central Committee of the Communist Party of China for the 13th Five-Year Plan for Economic and Social Development." At the 19th CPC National Congress in October 2017, General Secretary Xi Jinping delivered the report "Secure a Decisive Victory in Building a Moderately Prosperous Society in All Respects and Strive for the Great Success of Socialism with Chinese Characteristics for a New Era." Since the 18th CPC National Congress, General Secretary Xi Jinping has delivered a series of important speeches on national governance. The practice and theoretical innovations since the 18th CPC National Congress have culminated in Xi Jinping *Thought on Socialism with Chinese Characteristics for a New Era*, which encompasses the innovation and development of the theory of the socialist fundamental economic system.

I. Raising the fundamental socialist economic system to a new theoretical and practical level

In 1997, the 15th CPC National Congress proposed the socialist fundamental economic system. Based on this, the "Decision" of the Third Plenary Session of the 18th CPC Central Committee in 2013 emphasized: "The fundamental economic system with public ownership playing a dominant role and different economic sectors developing side by side is an important pillar of the socialist system with Chinese characteristics and is the foundation of the socialist market economy."[35] This has raised the socialist fundamental economic system to a new level. The "important pillar" and "foundation" status of the fundamental economic system is a scientific distillation of the experiences garnered from four decades of reform and opening up—specifically, in building socialism with Chinese characteristics and a socialist market economy. This theoretical positioning has underpinned the steady enhancement of China's economic vitality and comprehensive national strength. With regard to capital formation, in 1998, the total amount of investment in fixed assets of the entire society was 2,840.617 billion yuan, including 1,536.930 billion yuan in the realm of the state-owned economy, 419.224 billion yuan in the collective economy, 200.75 billion yuan in the mixed-ownership economy, and 374.437 billion yuan in the individual economy, 297.381 billion yuan in the foreign-funded and Hong Kong, Macao and Taiwan-funded economy, and 11.895 billion yuan in other economies. In 2016, total fixed asset investment across society reached 60,646.57 billion yuan, including 12,903.85 billion yuan in the state-owned economy, 892.85 billion yuan in the collective economy, 22,084.98 billion yuan in the mixed-ownership economy, 1,211.05 billion yuan in the individual economy, 18,721.41 billion yuan in the private economy, 2,606.95 billion yuan in the foreign-invested and Hong Kong, Macao, and Taiwan-invested economies, and 2,225.47 billion yuan in the other economies. From the perspective of capital formation alone, there has been a situation of common development of various economic forms. This demonstrates, from a significant standpoint, that China's fundamental economic system is well-suited to the advancement of the social productive capacities. This foundational system arrangement helps stimulate the vitality and innovativeness of diverse ownership forms, laying a solid foundation and providing ample space for the sustainable and sound development of China's economy.

II. New development of the theory of mixed-ownership economy

Since the 18th CPC National Congress, one of the pivotal developments in the theory of the fundamental economic system has been a marked deepening of insights into the mixed-ownership economy. The "Decision" of the Third Plenary Session of the 18th CPC Central Committee stated: "A mixed economy with cross holding by and mutual fusion between state-owned capital, collective capital and

[35] Communist Party of China Central Committee. *Decision of the Central Committee of the Communist Party of China on Some Major Issues Concerning Comprehensively Deepening the Reform*. Nov. 12, 2013.

non-public capital is an important way to materialize the fundamental economic system of China. It is conducive to improving the amplification function of state-owned capital, ensuring the appreciation of its value, and raising its competitiveness, and it is conducive to enabling capital with all kinds of ownership to draw on one another's strong points to offset weaknesses, stimulate one another and develop together."[36] In 1993, the Third Plenary Session of the 14th CPC Central Committee proposed the idea of a mixed-ownership economy. After 20 years of theoretical exploration and practical advancement, the "Decision" elevated the mixed-ownership economy to a new plateau by defining it as "a crucial means of implementing the fundamental economic system." This designation signified a substantial deepening of insights into socialism with Chinese characteristics and the socialist market economy. The 19th CPC National Congress further emphasized the importance of developing a mixed-ownership economy as part of efforts to improve the modern enterprise system and facilitate the integration of diverse ownership forms. This emphasis aimed to boost the vitality and competitiveness of the state-owned sector while fostering the development of the non-public sector: "we will further reform of state-owned enterprises, develop mixed-ownership economic entities, and turn Chinese enterprises into world-class, globally competitive firms," treating the development of a mixed-ownership economy as a key approach to fostering world-class enterprises. Regarding how to advance such a mixed-ownership economy, there were many specific formulations in the "Decision," such as encouraging more state-owned enterprises (SOEs) and other ownership-type enterprises to restructure into mixed-ownership entities, allowing non-state capital to take equity stakes in state-funded projects, and enabling mixed-ownership enterprises to adopt employee stock ownership plans (ESOP)—these measures collectively foster shared-interest communities between capital owners and workers. The "Decision" explicitly stated that: "We will encourage non-public enterprises to participate in SOE reform, foster mixed enterprises with non-public capital as the controlling shareholder, and encourage qualified private enterprises to establish the modern corporate system." The concepts of "Cross holding by and mutual fusion," along with the growth of mixed enterprises with non-public capital holding a controlling stake, signified a major step toward integrating diverse ownership forms in a fair and competitive market environment. They could hold shares in two-way or multi-way, and their status was completely equal.

---

[36] Communist Party of China Central Committee. *Decision of the Central Committee of the Communist Party of China on Some Major Issues Concerning Comprehensively Deepening the Reform.* Nov. 12, 2013.

The mixed-ownership economy takes shape through the formation of a modern enterprise system, founded on a robust legal entity framework. This system is marked by well-defined property entitlements, clear delineation of entitlements and obligations, the separation of enterprise operations from government functions, coupled with the application of scientific management. At its core lies an effective corporate governance structure. Empirical evidence has demonstrated that the modern corporate system can form a more effective incentive and restraint mechanism, and can give full play to the entrepreneurial spirit. Therefore, this approach can lay a solid micro-foundation for macroeconomic operations and economic development.

Since the 18th CPC National Congress, the reform of the mixed-ownership economy has moved forward. In September 2013, the executive meeting of the State Council proposed opening a range of projects in sectors including finance, petroleum, electricity, railways, telecommunications, resource development and utilization, and public services and utilities to private capital. These projects were selected for their alignment with industry trends and their potential to advance transformation and upgrading. The aim was to create demonstration effects and advance the advancement of the mixed-ownership economy. The reform of central SOEs has seen significant outcomes. In July 2014, the State-owned Assets Supervision and Administration Commission (SASAC) chose two well-established entities—China National Building Materials Group and China National Pharmaceutical Group—as pilot enterprises for this reform. By the end of 2017, over 85% and 90% of the subsidiaries under these two groups, respectively, had implemented mixed-ownership reforms, with their operational revenue accounting for more than 70% and 90% of the group's total income. In 2015, after the release of the "Opinions of the State Council on the Development of a Mixed-Ownership Economy by State-owned Enterprises," the SASAC and the National Development and Reform Commission jointly implemented mixed-ownership economic reforms across seven strategic sectors (electricity, petroleum, natural gas, railways, commercial aviation, telecom sectors, and defense industries). By the close of 2017, three batches totaling 50 pilot enterprises had been selected. Of the first two batches, which included 19 enterprises, seven had completed introducing strategic investors, restructuring, listing, and setting up new companies. More than 40 investors of various types had been introduced, with capital exceeding 90 billion yuan. According to Gao Zhiyu, Deputy Director of the SASAC Property Rights Bureau, as of the end of 2017, subsidiaries of central SOEs at all levels, including 98 central SOE group companies, had basically completed corporate restructuring, and more than two-thirds of them had introduced various types of social capital to achieve mixed ownership. Property rights registration data for central SOEs indicated that between 2013 and 2016, the share of mixed-ownership enterprises among central SOEs and their subsidiaries at all levels rose from 65.7% to 68.9%. In 2017 alone, over 700 new mixed-ownership entities were founded under central SOEs, drawing more than 338.6 billion yuan in social capital via capital markets.

III. New ideas for state-owned economy reform initiatives

Reform of the state-owned economy has long held a pivotal role in China's economic system reform process, as it bears on the advancement and improvement of the fundamental socialist economic system and the socialist market economy. Since the 18th CPC National Congress, new ideas have emerged in the theory and practice of state-owned economic reform.

It is necessary to emphasize the rational distribution of state-owned capital, which has its own specific functions. State-owned capital can play a better role only when it is distributed in its own functional areas. The "Decision" proposed: "state-owned capital investment operations must serve the strategic goals of the state, invest more in key industries and areas that are vital to national security and are the lifeblood of the economy, focusing on offering public services, developing important and forward-looking strategic industries, protecting the ecological environment, supporting scientific and technological progress, and guaranteeing national security," which identified five functional areas of state-owned capital, offering a more specific and explicit framework compared to earlier expositions in the "Decision of the Central Committee of the Communist Party of China on Some Major Issues Concerning the Reform and Development of State-owned Enterprises" issued at the Fourth Plenary Session of the 15th CPC Central Committee in 1999. For example, the "Decision of the Central Committee of the Communist Party of China on Some Major Issues Concerning the Reform and Development of State-owned Enterprises" issued at the Fourth Plenary Session of the 15th CPC Central Committee proposed four major fields and industries that fall under state-owned economic control, including natural monopoly industries, while the "Decision" adopted at the Third Plenary Session of the 18th CPC Central Committee clearly stated that state-owned capital should retain its presence in natural monopoly industries, advance the separation of network infrastructure from operational services, and open up competitive segments in line with the unique features of each sector. It also identified ecological and environmental protection as a key area for state-owned capital investment, reflecting the shift in China's economic development to a new stage, along with the evolution of the principal social contradiction. The functional domains of state-owned capital were explicitly defined, thereby clarifying the overall direction of state-owned economic reform. Specifically, state-owned capital would be focused on five functional domains, establishing a foundational framework to underpin economic and social advancement alongside public well-being—enhancing its capacity for influence and control.

To correspond to the delineation of state-owned capital's functional domains, existing state-owned enterprises need to be categorized accordingly. In 2015, the "Guiding Opinions of the Central Committee of the Communist Party of China and the State Council on Deepening the Reform of State-owned Enterprises" classified state-owned enterprises into commercial and public welfare types. State-owned enterprises of varying operated under distinct operational mechanisms, assessment indicators, and regulatory principles. Public welfare state-owned enterprises primarily focused on protecting people's livelihoods, serving the public, and delivering public goods and services. They were mainly engaged in sectors such as education, healthcare, culture, infrastructure, and other public service fields. Their performance assessment emphasized cost control, service quality, and reliability. These enterprises may be wholly state-owned or involve diversified investment structures. Additionally, they encouraged participation from non-state-owned enterprises through service procurement, franchising, and entrusted management. In contrast, commercial state-owned enterprises were mainly concentrated in key competitive industries and areas of technological innovation. They implemented commercial operations in accordance with market rules, followed the law of value and competition as well as survival of the fittest, and took profits, asset value preservation and appreciation, and market competitiveness as the assessment objectives. Most commercial state-owned entities implemented the corporate governance system and introduced other state-owned or non-state-owned capital to achieve equity diversification. State-owned capital could have absolute holding, relative holding, or shareholding.

IV. Establishing a new system for the administration of state-owned assets

State-owned assets were owned by the entire people, yet the public could not directly manage them. Instead, an institution or entity must act as the representative of all people to exercise ownership duties, ensuring state-owned assets are managed and utilized effectively to serve public and overall interests. Thus, establishing a robust state-owned assets management system became particularly crucial. In October 1988, China established the State-owned Assets Administration, marking the fledgling phase of the state-owned assets management system. The Third Plenary Session of the 14th CPC Central Committee in 1993 emphasized that state-owned assets should be governed under a framework featuring unified state ownership, hierarchical government supervision, and independent enterprise operation. Building on this, the report of the 16th CPC National Congress in 2002 clearly proposed to "establish a state property management system under which the Central Government and local governments perform the responsibilities of investor on behalf of the state respectively, enjoying owner's equity, combining rights with obligations and duties and administering assets, personnel and other affairs." It was required that "the Central Government and the provincial and municipal (prefectural) governments should set up state property management organizations." In March 2003, the State-owned Assets Supervision and Administration Commission ("SASAC" for short) of the State Council was founded, with local SASACs subsequently established across provinces. This move addressed the long-standing issues where state-owned assets were primarily "controlled by insiders" of industrial and commercial enterprises, and where unclear division of responsibilities among government ministries led to a lack of accountability for state-owned assets." However, challenges remained in the governance and operation of state-owned assets, notably reflected in the dual role of the supervisory authority, which acted as both the "boss" and the "steward" of state-owned entities, and enterprises could not truly become economic entities that competed on an equal standing in the market. The SASAC was also happy to be the "steward" of the enterprise since it could have power and interests. This also affected the SASAC to better focus on how to optimize the allocation of state-owned capital in general, improve the flow of state-owned assets, advance and retreat, and better serve national strategic goals.

After the 18th CPC National Congress, a new approach emerged for reforming the state-owned assets management system. The Third Plenary Session of the 18th CPC Central Committee put forward the innovative notion of "strengthening state-owned asset supervision with capital management at its core," and pointed out: "We will improve the state-owned assets management system, strengthen state-owned assets oversight with capital management at the core, reform the authorized operation mechanism for state-owned capital, establish a number of state-owned capital operating companies, support qualified SOEs to reorganize themselves into state-owned capital investment companies." The "Guiding Opinions of the Central Committee of the Communist Party of China and the State Council on Deepening the Reform of State-owned Enterprises" promulgated in 2015 pointed out that the state-owned asset supervision and administration authorities must clearly understand their role as investors in line with legal provisions, precisely define the ambit of their supervisory responsibilities, establish a clear list of rights and obligations, and shift their focus from enterprise management to capital management. This signified a pivotal shift in the functions and focus of SASACs at all levels. In the past, the focus was on managing and controlling each state-owned enterprise, including selecting managers for them, determining the remuneration and total wages of managers, determining the investment, mergers, and acquisitions, etc. Now it is shifted to focusing on capital management and managing a limited number of companies invested in and operated under state-owned capital oversight, and the latter will send shareholder representatives and directors to holding and shareholding companies. The allocation of state-owned capital has been continuously optimized.

It is of great theoretical and practical significance for state-owned asset supervision and administration authorities to shift their functions from "primarily managing enterprises" to "primarily managing capital."

First, this transformation helps promote the separation of ownership rights and management rights in state-owned capital. Under the previous model of "mainly managing enterprises," the daily operation activities of holding and shareholding enterprises by state-owned capital will be interfered with by administrative actions. In reality, the disposal and sale of enterprise assets must go through the Equity Exchange designated by the state-owned assets supervisory and management authorities; financing mergers and acquisitions as well as equity transfers involving changes in the company's equity structure must be reviewed and approved by the SASAC and other departments; major investments and business development of enterprises are likely to require the approval and consent of the SASAC and other institutions; enterprises must accept the inspection and supervision of the SASAC and other departments; etc. This kind of regulation broke the modern corporate governance logic that only the direct shareholders could intervene.[37] After turning to the "capital management as the core" model, the "supervision" of state-owned capital should be "de-administrative," and companies invested in or operated by state-owned capital will shift to exercising shareholder rights. Shareholder rights are not the powers of review, license issuance and inspection, punishment, approval, etc., but the rights for shareholders to influence corporate behavior or make exit decisions through the shareholder meeting, the mechanism of the board of directors, and the recommended executives. The day-to-day operations of the enterprise are overseen by the managers appointed by the board of directors. This achieves the separation of ownership and management rights under the principle of "de-administration," enabling state-owned capital-holding enterprises to truly become independent market competitors that

---

[37] Wenkui Zhang. The choice of strategies for the reform of the state-owned assets supervision system: Observation from the intervention of mixed ownership. *Reform*, 2017 (1).

operate autonomously, assume sole responsibility for profits and losses, bear their own risks, and pursue self-development.

Second, it also facilitates the improved circulation of state-owned capital, enabling its optimal allocation and concentration in key strategic areas. At present, the state-owned capital still has prominent problems such as too wide distribution, too long front, and insufficient concentration, which seriously restrict the leading function of the state-owned economy. “Mainly managing capital” enables a stronger focus on national objectives by facilitating the adjusting the structure of state-owned capital promoting its concentration in critical industries, key sectors, and essential infrastructure involved in national security, the backbone of the national economy, and public welfare, as well as in competitive enterprises with strategic advantage.[38] The approach of “mainly managing capital” can enhance the mobility of state-owned capital, enabling its efficient movement across various sectors, regions, enterprises, and projects. This approach helps optimal allocation while simultaneously mitigating risks.

In addition, after the 18th CPC National Congress, the social sharing of state-owned capital gains has been lifted to a prominent position. State-owned capital belongs to the entire people, and the whole people should obtain tangible benefits from the use and income of state-owned capital to enhance their sense of gain. In the past, the earnings of state-owned enterprises were basically kept in the enterprise for adjustment and use, which did not fully reflect the ownership nature of state-owned capital. Meanwhile, a large portion of state-owned capital gains were inefficiently used or even wasted and embezzled. It was also one of the causes of repeated investment and a rigid industrial structure in state-owned enterprises. The “Decision” of the Third Plenary Session of the 18th CPC Central Committee proposed to improve the budgeting system for state-owned capital operations and increase the proportion of state-owned capital gains allocated to public finance. These funds were primarily used to supplement the social security fund and mitigate its historical liabilities. Additionally, the decision called for transferring part of the state-owned capital to further enrich the social security fund. In 2011, the operating income of central state-owned capital totaled 80.061 billion yuan, and the expenditure was 76.954 billion yuan, of which 72.36 billion yuan was returned to central SOEs in various names, while only 4 billion yuan was transferred to the public financial budget for social security expenditures,

---

[38] Zhuoyuan Zhang. From “mainly managing enterprises” to “mainly managing capital”: a major theoretical innovation in the reform of state-owned enterprises. *Expanding Horizons*, 2016 (3).

which was too little.[39] In 2014, the Ministry of Finance issued a pivotal notice to restructure the state-owned capital income remitted by central SOEs into five tiers based on industry characteristics: the first category was tobacco enterprises, and the payment standard was 25% of after-tax profits; the second category comprised 14 resource monopoly enterprises—such as those in petrochemicals, electric power, telecommunications, and coal with their turnover ratio increased to 20%; the third category included 69 companies in general competitive fields such as China Aluminum Industry, China National Building Materials, etc., and the turnover ratio was increased to 15%; the fourth category included 34 enterprises in the military industry and transformed scientific research institutes, and the turnover ratio was increased to 10%; the fifth category included two enterprises of China Grain Reserves Corporation and China National Cotton Reserves Corporation, which were exempted from paying the profits that should be paid for the year. According to the "Decision" of the Third Plenary Session of the 18th CPC Central Committee, the proportion of state-owned capital gains transferred to the general public budget is set to reach 30% by 2030.

V. The new orientation of the non-state-owned economy

In the early days of reform and opening up, the non-public economy was positioned as a "supplement" to the public economy. The 15th CPC National Congress elevated its status to "an important part of China's socialist market economy." Since the 18th CPC National Congress, there has been a further understanding regarding the role of the non-public economy in the socialist economy with Chinese characteristics. First, it was not only repeatedly reiterated that "both the public and non-public economy are important components of the socialist market economy," but further clarified that they were "an important foundation for China's economic and social development," and affirmed that the non-state-owned sector played a vital role in boosting economic growth, spurring innovation, creating more jobs, and raising tax revenues. On March 4, 2016, General Secretary Xi Jinping pointed out when participating in the joint group meeting of the China National Democratic Construction Association and the Federation of Industry and Commerce at the Fourth Session of the 12th National Committee of the Chinese People's Political Consultative Conference: "We emphasize that consolidating and developing the public economy is not opposed to encouraging, supporting and guiding the development of the non-public economy, but an organic unity." The second point was to underscore the equal standing of

39 Zhuoyuan Zhang. The management system of state-owned assets shall be improved mainly by managing capital. *Internal Reference for Reform*, 2014 (37).

different economic entities. It was proposed to adhere to the competition rules of "equal rights, equal opportunities, and equal rules" in the modern market economy, abolish all forms of discriminatory provisions on the non-public economy, ensure that all types of ownership economies use production factors equally in accordance with the law, equally abide by government regulations, and enhance the protection of property rights within the non-public sector. It was put forward that "the property rights of the public economy are inviolable, and the property rights of the non-public economy are also inviolable." The third was to eliminate unreasonable restrictions on various forms of the non-state-owned economy and create a more extensive scope for its development. Traditional state-owned monopoly sectors such as petroleum, natural gas, power, rail transport, telecommunications, resource exploitation, and public utilities were gradually opened to non-public economies. Additionally, non-state-owned enterprises were urged to take part in the reform of state-owned enterprises. It was proposed to promote the growth of mixed-ownership enterprises dominated by non-public capital and to ensure that all market entities have equal access—according to law—to sectors not included on the negative list, such as, enabling more state-owned economic entities and other ownership-based economies to evolve into mixed-ownership economies, allowing non-public capital to participate in state-owned capital investment projects, allowing qualified private capital to legally initiate the establishment of small and medium-sized banks and other financial institutions; allowing social capital to participate in the investment and operation of urban infrastructure via franchising and other approaches, encouraging social capital to invest in rural development, and allowing enterprises and social organizations to establish various undertakings in rural areas, among other measures. The fourth measure was to establish a new model of government-business relations. During the "NPC and CPPCC Sessions" in 2016, General Secretary Xi Jinping proposed the theoretical and practical proposition of establishing a new model of government-business relations, using the words "cordial" and "clean" to summarize the normal relationship between government officials and non-public enterprises. In China, government officials have control over many economic resources, and have many administrative powers such as licensing, prohibition, inspection, and punishment. They have a lot of room for discretion when implementing specific administrative actions. Therefore, to some degree, officials hold sway over the development scope of the enterprise, the difficulty of operation, the level of profitability, and even life and death. Some officials may seize benefits from enterprises by virtue of their power, while some companies transmit benefits to officials in order to cater to them, which distorts the ties between officials and enterprises, particularly non-public ones. The words "cordial" and "clean" proposed by General Secretary Xi Jinping provide scientific guidelines for handling the relationship between government and business. In 2015, the All-China Federation of Industry and Commerce conducted a questionnaire survey on the relationship between government and business across the country. The results showed that the main causes of unhealthy government-business relationships were: excessive government intervention in the market; excessive concentration of public power, especially the power of the top leaders; excessive discretionary power in administrative law enforcement and judicial affairs; and the inadequacy of the rule of law. Most public officials and entrepreneurs believed that "the government's excessive power to direct resource allocation" was the main reason for the collusion between officials and businessmen.[40] Therefore, some experts and scholars believed that to build a new model of government-business relations, it was essential to define the scope of the government's powers and responsibilities, and insisted that it could not be done without the authorization of the law, and the statutory responsibilities must be performed.

4. Further Improvements in the Theory of the Fundamental Socialist Economic System

After China stepped into the new era, the fundamental conditions for its economic and social development have experienced profound shifts. In terms of development stages, the Chinese economy has transitioned from a period of high-speed growth to a stage of high-quality development. Correspondingly, the primary social contradiction has evolved into the tension between the people's escalating need for a better life and the existence of unbalanced and inadequate development. From the perspective of economic complexity, China's economic relationships have become increasingly intricate, with a more refined division of labor, broader and deeper economic linkages, and a geometric expansion in the volume and diversity of economic information. Judging from the resource and environmental conditions of economic development, the extensive growth model characterized by high investment, high emissions, and high pollution has reached its end, while resource and environmental constraints are becoming ever more stringent. A World Bank research report pointed out: "China's current growth model has produced great pressure on environmental factors such as land, air and

---

40 Qinmin Wang. The direction of the new government-business relationship. *Study Times*, June, 30, 2016.

water, and the pressure on the supply of natural resources is also increasing."[41] From the perspective of economic growth drivers, the momentum once fueled by factor input and scale expansion has largely been exhausted. As a result, economic growth now relies increasingly on innovation and improvements in total factor productivity. From the demand perspective, consumption modes are growing increasingly diverse and personalized. Consumers are placing greater emphasis on product quality, consumption safety, and the availability of ecological goods. These emerging trends are crucial—they will profoundly affect the roles and positioning of different ownership types within China's economy. They also provide an important foundation for reassessing the ownership structure and advancing the fundamental socialist economic system.

In the context of this new era, refining and developing the theoretical framework of the fundamental socialist economic system requires in-depth exploration and resolution of several key theoretical and practical issues.

I. Scientific understanding and accurate positioning of the dominant position of public ownership and the leading role of the state-owned economy

Compared with the initial period of reform and opening up, the theoretical and practical problems faced by China at present in the ownership structure are completely different. In the initial phase of reform and opening up, the public economic sector "dominated the whole country." The important task of reform was to overcome both theoretical and practical constraints on the non-state-owned sector and to promote its growth, thereby harnessing its positive position in driving economic growth and supporting people's livelihoods. At that time, the dominant status of public ownership was not in question. As reform progressed steadily, the proportion of the non-public economy rose gradually. Over the years, some indicators have surpassed the public economy. The dominant status of public ownership and the leading role of the state-owned economy are no longer as self-evident or unchallenged as they were in the initial phase of reform and opening up. It has evolved into a theoretical and practical issue of great concern. Viewed from the data, in 2016, there were a total of 14.6184 million enterprise legal entities in China, of which only 2.13% were state-owned holding enterprises, 1.66% were collectively held, 85.76% were privately held, 0.71% were held by Hong Kong, Macao and Taiwan businessmen, 0.68% were held by

[41] A Joint Research Group of the World Bank and the Development Research Center of the State Council. *China in 2030: Building a Modern, Harmonious and Creative Society*. Beijing: China Financial and Economic Publishing House, 2013, p. 9.

foreign investors, and the others accounted for 9.06%. It can be seen from a little calculation that enterprise legal entities held by public capital accounted for only 3.79%, and 87.15% were non-public capital holding companies. Most enterprise legal entities were controlled by non-public capital. If China's current ownership forms are divided into state-ownership economy, mixed-ownership economy, and non-public economy, then, by 2016, the non-public economic sector had overtaken the traditional public sector in several key areas, including fixed asset investment across society, the total assets, and profits of industrial enterprises above a designated scale, urban employment, and tax payments.

As the non-public sector came to dominate many important indicators, public doubts began to emerge regarding the continued dominant status of public ownership and the guiding role of the state-owned economy. For instance, some pointed out that the non-public sector of the economy made up over 65% of China's GDP, leading to questions about whether the traditional ownership structure still reflected economic realities.[42] Before and after the 2008 global financial crisis, there was even a heated discussion in the economics circle about "state sector advancing and private sector retreating" or "state sector retreating and private sector advancing." Therefore, it is necessary to further clarify what is meant by public ownership and how to maintain the dominant position of public ownership.

The 15th National Congress of the Communist Party of China provided a scientific interpretation of the dominant status of public ownership, and this explanation remains relevant to this day. Its core content is as follows: The dominant status of public ownership is mainly manifested in two aspects: public assets hold a dominant position in the total social assets; meanwhile, the state-owned economy controls the lifeline of the national economy and plays a leading role in economic development. While public assets are dominant, there must be quantitative advantages, and more attention must be paid to the improvement of quality. Different industries and different regions may have differences. It is evident that the 15th CPC National Congress began to define the dominant position of public ownership in terms of its "quality" rather than merely its "quantity." Today, our doubts about the dominant status of public ownership are rooted in two aspects: one is to pay too much attention to economic indicators other than "assets"; the other is to pay too much attention to the indicators of "quantity" and ignore the indicators of "quality." Marx put forward the theory of "universal light" when discussing how one production was in a decisive position relative

---

[42] Zhanyang Wang. The field of ownership still needs great emancipation of the mind. *Exploration and Free Views*, 2012 (4).

to other productions. Marx pointed out: "In all social forms there is a definite production which determines the position and influence of all other productions, and therefore its relations also determine the position and influence of all other relations. This is a universal light with which all other colors are tinged and are modified."[43] Within the framework of the socialist market economy, the dominant status of public ownership and the leading role of the state-owned economy ought to be comprehended and expounded from the perspective of their extensive and foundational impact—what can be described as their "universal light," rather than simply relying on and applying certain quantitative proportions. As a kind of "universal light," the public ownership economy emits its own light and heat, illuminating various economic components and market entities, and allowing them to change their colors and reflect the rays of the sun. It is worth emphasizing that this "universal light" is naturally radiated through the operation of the market mechanism and the role of economic laws, rather than through administrative mechanisms. The dominant status of the public-ownership economy can also be likened to the function of the bone marrow in the human body—often unseen, but essential for sustaining life, providing the foundation and vitality for the entire system. The bone marrow forms the basic structure of the human body, which carries the entire weight of the human body, and supports people to walk upright and hold their heads high, while the weight of bones only accounts for 1/5 to 2/5 of the total body weight. Of course, the dominant status of public ownership needs to be guaranteed by a certain "quantity." Without a certain "quantity," a certain "quality" cannot be guaranteed. This is the dialectics of quality and quantity.

Judging from the above analysis, it can be concluded that, although the proportion of the public sector of the economy has dropped significantly over the past 40 years of reform and opening up, the dominant status of the state-owned sector and the leading position of the state-owned economy have not changed.

First, public assets still maintain the quantitative advantage. Public assets include operating public assets in the competitive field, network-based public assets in the infrastructure field (such as road networks, communication networks, pipeline networks, canal networks, etc.), public financial assets in the financial field, non-profit public assets in the public service field (such as schools, hospitals, nursing homes, etc.), resource-based public assets in the field of natural resources (land, minerals, water, rivers, forests, grasslands, oceans, etc.). At present, when estimating the "quantity" of public assets, a narrow caliber method is generally

---

[43] Marx & Engels. *Collected Works of Marx and Engels, Vol. 8*. Beijing: People's Publishing House, 2009, p. 31.

used. Most estimates only include operating public assets, some network-based public assets, and some public financial assets, while most non-profit public assets and resource-based public assets are generally not included. Some scholars also advocate using a narrower caliber to count public assets. For example, Zhao Huaquan believes that: To judge whether public ownership is the main body should mainly depend on the proportion of the operating public assets to the total social operating assets, excluding resource-based assets and administrative assets.[44] However, the narrow caliber cannot accurately reflect the actual scale of public assets. Except for operating public assets, the other four types of public assets have profound and extensive impacts on economic and social life, which are the fundamental prerequisites for the stable functioning of the economy and society. Therefore, from a theoretical standpoint, all public assets should be included in the statistical scope in order to accurately assess the proportion of public assets within total social assets. This comprehensive accounting would more accurately reflect the status, role, and influence of public ownership in economic and social life, as well as its capacity for control. However, current statistics on public assets remain incomplete—particularly in the quantification of certain resource-based public assets, which continues to pose significant challenges. Judging from the existing calculation data, it is certain that public-owned assets hold a predominant position in the total social assets. According to the calculation by researcher Pei Changhong, as of 2012, the total operational assets of China's three industries stood at approximately 487.53 trillion yuan, among which the assets of the public ownership economy amounted to 258.39 trillion yuan, making up 53%.[45] This estimate used a narrow caliber, and even so, the predominance of public assets in total assets was still valid. Zheng Zhiguo included natural resource-based assets in the calculation. Based on relevant data, he estimated that at the end of 2011, the value of national agricultural land was 61.4 trillion yuan, the national construction land value was 486.66 trillion yuan, and the economic value of 18 basic mineral reserves was 189.25 trillion yuan. The total value of these three resource-based public assets was 737.31 trillion yuan. When assets from industries such as industrial production, construction, wholesale, and retail (above a designated size), as well as accommodation and catering, were combined with natural resource-based assets, public assets amounted to 96.15% of the total, while

44 Huaquan Zhao. Quantitative analysis and evaluation of the main status of public ownership. *Contemporary Economic Research*, 2012 (3).

45 Changhong Pei. Quantitative estimation and development trend of the main status of public ownership in China. *Social Sciences in China*, 2014 (1).

non-public assets made up only 3.85%. This highlights the even more pronounced dominance of public assets.[46]

Second, public assets not only have the advantage of "quantity," but also have the advantage of "quality." Network-based assets, financial assets, public welfare assets, resource-based assets, and high-quality assets in competitive fields are mostly public assets. These assets are concentrated in critical sectors and vital sectors in economic and social activities, playing a foundational, controlling, and leading role in driving economic and social progress. Network-based assets, including road networks, communication networks, pipeline networks, and canal networks, support the flow of people, logistics, and information in the whole society. Financial assets are the infrastructure for capital flow and resource allocation, and the basis for preventing and resolving systemic financial risks. Public welfare assets such as schools, hospitals, and basic scientific research institutions provide basic guarantees for residents' living and scientific and technological progress. Resource-based assets are the basic conditions for the operation of the entire economy. In Marx's *Criticism of the Gotha Program*, natural resources are regarded as the first source of all labor materials and labor objects. Resource-based assets will become an increasingly important form of public assets. In the industrial field, although the shares of state-owned assets in fully competitive industries have been reduced to a very low level, in important industries such as resource, monopoly, and public service sectors, state-owned assets still have a clear advantage.

In 2020, China was on the verge of establishing a socialist market economy system characterized by a comprehensive framework, scientific standards, and efficient operations. This marked the beginning of a new chapter in forging a modern socialist country in an all-round way. This historical context provides the foundation for understanding the dominant status of public ownership and the guiding role of the state-owned economy. The Third Plenary Session of the 18th CPC Central Committee articulated a basic principle for managing the relationship between the government and the market: "let the market play the decisive role in allocating resources and let the government play its functions better." The report of the 19th CPC National Congress reiterated this principle, which is the fundamental theoretical thinking that we must adhere to in order to grasp the dominant status of public ownership and the leading role of the state-owned sectors. Therefore, to maintain and strengthen the dominant position of state ownership and the guiding role of the state-owned economy in the new era, we can start from the following aspects.

---

[46] Zhiguo Zheng. Public ownership as the main body covers resource assets. *Jianghan Tribune*, 2012 (12).

First, we must further clarify the functions of state-owned capital. State-owned capital is the foundation of the Communist Party's governance and one of the important means for the government to realize its own functions. This constitutes the fundamental rationale for the existence of state-owned capital. The "Decision" of the Third Plenary Session of the 18th CPC Central Committee systematically summarizes the roles and responsibilities of the government. Among them, "strengthening and improving public services, promoting sustainable development and common prosperity, and intervening in situations where market failure occurs" are the functions that the government must utilize state-owned capital to carry out. In order to strengthen the governance foundation of the Communist Party and effectively perform government functions, state-owned capital must firmly control the lifeblood of the national economy and key sectors related to people's livelihoods, undertake the responsibility of providing basic public goods and large-scale infrastructure, and effectively make up for the functional deficiencies of non-public capital and market mechanisms. The dominant status of public ownership and the guiding role of the state-owned economy ought to be manifested through the effective performance of state-owned capital's functions.

Secondly, for this purpose, it is crucial to expedite the optimization of its layout. In the report of the 19th CPC National Congress, General Secretary Xi Jinping highlighted the necessity of "speeding up better distribution, making structural adjustments, and carrying out strategic reorganizations." This calls for a systematic adjustment and optimization of the deployment of state-owned capital in line with its specific functions, with the goal of making it stronger, more efficient, and more competitive. Specifically, state-owned capital should accelerate its concentration in five areas: "public services, key forward-looking strategic industries, ecological environment protection, scientific and technological progress, and national security." Following four decades of reform and opening up, along with rapid economic growth, the conditions are now ripe to expedite the restructuring of public capital. First, a significant amount of non-public capital has been accumulated, which can swiftly enter and fill the space left by the exit of state-owned capital. This creates favorable conditions for state-owned capital to exit from non-essential sectors. To take industrial enterprises above the designated size as a case in point, non-public assets have accounted for 41.7% of the total, which has sufficient capacity to fill the economic space vacated by the withdrawal of public capital. Second, the reform of the public assets management system that "mainly manages capital" and the continuous advancement of the multi-level capital market have improved the flow of public capital and provided convenient conditions for the concentration of public capital in its own functional fields.

Third, we must foster a mixed-ownership economy and enhance the functions and influence of state-owned capital. The "Decision" of the Third Plenary Session of the 18th CPC Central Committee elevated the status of the mixed-ownership economy to "an important way to materialize the fundamental economic system of China." The report of the 19th CPC National Congress identified the development of a mixed-ownership economy as a key strategy for "transforming Chinese enterprises into world-class, globally competitive firms." Whether under the control of public or non-public capital, mixed-ownership enterprises can enhance the role and effectiveness of public capital, extending its influence. This, in turn, reinforces the dominant status of public ownership and the guiding role of the public economy. We need to further raise awareness of the mixed-ownership sector. An important form of mixed ownership is the shareholding system, and Marx's and Engels' discussions on share capital in those years can provide us with significant theoretical inspiration. According to Karl Marx, the capital of the joint-stock company "here directly takes the form of social capital (that is, the capital of those directly united individuals), as opposed to private capital";[47] Engels pointed out: "Capitalist production run by joint-stock companies, is no longer a private production, but a production jointly managed by many people."[48] Marx and Engels also held that share capital in capitalist society bears the attributes of "social capital" and "joint production." In a socialist market economy, public ownership plays a dominant role; therefore, share capital will inevitably embody the nature of "social capital" and "joint production" to an even greater degree. As a result, it can either serve as a form of realizing the dominant status of public ownership or integrate with this dominant position. Therefore, it can be considered that mixed ownership will be the microscopic mechanism for the emission of "universal light."

Fourth, it is essential to further advance the establishment of a modern corporate governance framework and transform public and state-controlled enterprises into efficient and competitive market players. The dominant status of public ownership and the guiding role of the state-owned sectors ultimately rely on the efficiency and competitiveness of public capital within entities—something that must be continually validated by the market and society. To achieve this, a governance structure must be established that ensures standardized, well-coordinated operations with effective mutual supervision and restraints. The board of directors

---

[47] Marx & Engels. *Collected Works of Marx and Engels, Vol. 7*. Beijing: People's Publishing House, 2009, p. 494.

[48] Marx & Engels. *Collected Works of Marx and Engels, Vol. 4*. Beijing: People's Publishing House, 2009, p. 410.

should be responsible for setting the company's strategic direction and objectives, while professional managers should be appointed to handle daily operations and management. This approach enables entrepreneurs to fully exercise their strengths in managing uncertainty, identifying future growth opportunities, and taking calculated risks.

II. Enhancing the property rights regime

Property rights form the core of the ownership regime, and the property rights framework serves as a key institutional underpinning for the market economy. It bears on people's enthusiasm for wealth accumulation, the allocation of resources, and the mobility of production factors, thus determining the endogenous power of economic development and the lasting vitality of the economy and society, and ultimately determining the development level of social productive forces and people's welfare. The "Decision" of the Third Plenary Session of the 18th CPC Central Committee proposes to put in place a contemporary property rights regime with "clear ownership, clear-cut rights and obligations, strict protection and smooth flow." The report of the 19th National Congress of the Communist Party of China identifies enhancing the property rights regime as a focal point of future economic system reforms. Another key aspect is the market-driven allocation of factors, which is also closely linked to the refinement of the property rights system.

A sound property rights system includes four interrelated components: first, clarifying the boundaries of property rights; second, effectively protect property rights through laws and other systems; third, enabling holders of property rights to freely use property rights according to their own will, thereby ensuring the unimpeded flow of production factors; fourth, acknowledging and protecting the various benefits derived from the property rights. Its protection system is the basic element of the modern property rights system. The reason why it is important is that it can provide legitimate incentives for various economic entities, encourage people to amass and efficiently deploy the resources at their disposal, and develop sufficient and effective competition.

Regarding the importance of the property rights system, the ancient Chinese thinker Mencius put forward the idea that "those who have permanent property have perseverance, and those who do not have permanent property have no perseverance," which had far-reaching influence. Modern economics also emphasizes the importance of protecting property rights. William J. Baumol, Robert E. Litan, and Carl J. Schramm pointed out that without effective protection of people's property rights, "the individual cannot be expected to risk losing his own money and time by investing in ill-fated ventures. Here, the rule of law — especially property and contract rights — is particularly important."[49] However, risk-taking was at the heart of innovation. Raghuram Rajan and Luigi Zingales argued: "The first step in the development of competitive markets requires governments to respect and protect the property rights of citizens, including those who are the most vulnerable and helpless."[50]

Compared with the traditional economy, the modern economic system has a much more complex structure. Compared with simple market exchanges such as clothes and food, the market for durable consumer goods such as automobiles, technology, knowledge, human capital, finance, and other modern services and natural resources is highly complex and uncertain. Future earnings will assume an increasingly significant role in people's income composition. Under such circumstances, the clear delineation and effective safeguarding of property rights become particularly crucial. John McMillan argued: "One of the fundamental tasks of government in market design is to determine property rights, because the easiest way to destroy the market is to destroy people's belief in the safety of their own property."[51] William J. Baumol, Robert E. Litan, and Carl J. Schramm argued that for a successful entrepreneurial economy, the following institutions were important: "(effectively enforced) rule of law, intellectual property protection (but not excessive), not overly burdensome taxation, and the rewards and mechanisms that facilitate imitation in a given environment,"[52] all of which involved the modern property rights system, including effective property rights protection. It is worth emphasizing that a modern property rights system can only be provided by the government. This is mainly because the government has the coercive power that other organizations do not have, and this coercive

49 This article has been submitted to the 2014 Annual Meeting of China Political Economics Forum. Quotes and reprints require the author's consent. Email: jyh@ucass.org.cn William J. Baumol, Robert E. Litan and Carl J. Schramm. *Good Capitalism, Bad Capitalism, and the Economics of Growth and Prosperity*. Beijing: CITIC Press, 2008, p. 6.

50 Raghuram Rajan and Luigi Zingales. *Saving Capitalism from the Capitalists: Unleashing the Power of Financial Markets to Create Wealth and Spread Opportunity*. Beijing: CITIC Press, 2004, Introduction.

51 John McMillan. *Reinventing the Bazaar: A Natural History of Markets*. Beijing: CITIC Press, 2004, p. 11.

52 Baumol, Litan, and Schramm argue that successful entrepreneurial economies are the most innovative and efficient: one in which "a large number of players in the economy not only have infinite drive forces and incentives to innovate, but also engage in cutting-edge or breakthrough innovations and commercialize them." William J. Baumol, Robert E. Litan and Carl J. Schramm. *Good Capitalism, Bad Capitalism, and the Economics of Growth and Prosperity*. Beijing: CITIC Press, 2008, p. 78.

power is necessary to define and protect property rights[53]; the government can set up judicial institutions to arbitrate economic disputes and enforce them.[54]

At present, the effective protection of property rights has become very important and urgent in China. There are two important reasons.

First, following four decades of market-oriented economic development, both the categories of property and the volume of each category have surged significantly. Not only has the volume of public property grown significantly, but non-public property—including individual and private enterprise assets, family-owned property, as well as assets of enterprises financed by investors from Hong Kong, Macao, Taiwan, and foreign countries—has also expanded substantially. From the perspective of the industrial economy alone, the quantity of various types of assets is huge. In 2016, the total assets of industrial-scale enterprises hit 108.6 trillion yuan, including 41.8 trillion yuan for public and state-owned enterprises, 24.0 trillion yuan for private enterprises, 8.8 trillion yuan for Hong Kong, Macao, and Taiwan enterprises, and 12.4 trillion yuan for foreign-funded enterprises. Among the state-owned assets, a vast number of natural resources, including mineral, land, and water resources, are owned by the state collectively. As the economy grows and the marketization drive progresses, the value of these natural resources is increasing rapidly, and the degree of capitalization is deepening. Various financing instruments have emerged in large numbers, and the scale of financing has grown rapidly. In 2002, the financing scale of the whole society was 14.9 trillion yuan, and in 2016 it reached 156.0 trillion yuan, at an average annual growth rate of 18.3%. The growth of household property is very rapid, and the household property of residents, including bank deposits, various types of securities, and real estate, has grown substantially. As per the statistics of China Merchants Bank and Bain & Company, in 2010, the total investable assets held by Chinese individuals (cash, deposits, stocks, bonds, funds, insurance, financial products issued by banks, overseas investments, and other types of financial assets and investment properties) reached 62 trillion yuan.[55] In order to make the capital and other production factors controlled by these properties

53 William J. Baumol, Robert E. Litan and Carl J. Schramm. *Good Capitalism, Bad Capitalism, and the Economics of Growth and Prosperity*. Beijing: CITIC Press, 2008, p. 96.

54 The coercive power of the government can effectively protect property rights. Of course, if this coercive force is not effectively checked and balanced, it can also evolve into a "predatory hand" that violates private property rights.

55 See "2011 China Private Wealth Report" jointly issued by China Merchants Bank and Bain & Company.

continuously put into the production process, flow fully, and get a reasonable allocation, an effective property rights protection system is the basic condition.

Second, the increased importance of innovation in economic development also highlights the urgency of property rights protection. The previous phase of rapid economic growth was largely dependent on large-scale factor input, government investment, and technology imitation. Most investments were concentrated at the low end of the value chain and within the infrastructure field. The role of innovation in economic growth was not obvious, which was unsustainable. The driving force of economic advancement should turn to depend more on innovation, the private sector, and entrepreneurial spirit, and it is essential to galvanize the wisdom and strength of millions of people, which requires a sound property rights protection system to safeguard people's interests. On the importance of the rule of law, property rights, and contractual rights to an innovative economy, William J. Baumol, Robert E. Litan, and Carl J. Schramm noted: "Innovative entrepreneurial behavior is a risky activity, and the individuals who take those risks must be properly compensated. That is, when they succeed in their efforts, they must have property rights to the resulting outcomes—money, land, products, or all three properties. In addition, entrepreneurs (and all businesses) must trust that their contracts signed with other parties are recognized."[56]

Over the four decades of reform and opening up, China's economy has maintained steady and rapid expansion. An important reason is that China's property rights protection has been continuously improved. William J. Baumol, Robert E. Litan, and Carl J. Schramm believed that one of the reasons for the success of the Chinese model was that it had made progress on two elements. "These two elements are effectively enforced property rights and contractual rights that provide entrepreneurs with the financial system in which capital can be used to support their businesses."[57] However, safeguarding property rights in China, particularly those of non-public property, remains a significant challenge. The survey results of the Entrepreneur Forum in 2010 showed that 28.6% of entrepreneurs said that their property was not safe, 44.2% of entrepreneurs believed that corporate regulations could not safeguard the interests of businesses, and half of the entrepreneurs believed that intellectual property protection was not in place. According to "China's Business Environment 2012," the research report of the World Bank and the International Finance Corporation, in 2011 and 2012, among 182 countries and regions, China's investor protection ranked 93rd and

---

[56] William J. Baumol, Robert E. Litan and Carl J. Schramm. *Good Capitalism, Bad Capitalism, and the Economics of Growth and Prosperity*. Beijing: CITIC Press, 2008, p. 96.

[57] Ibid., p. 132.

97th, respectively. The Investor Protection Intensity Index (1 to 10) was 5, indicating moderate protection.[58]

Owing to the weak protection of private property rights, a third wave of emigration has emerged since 2006.[59] According to the "2011 China Private Wealth Report" jointly released by China Merchants Bank and Bain & Company,

China's personal overseas assets expanded swiftly, boasting a compound annual growth rate of nearly 100% between 2008 and 2010. Meanwhile, the number of Chinese investment immigrants abroad rose sharply. Almost 60% of the surveyed high-net-worth individuals (HNWIs) had either completed investment immigration or harbored related plans. In the five years preceding the 2011 survey, the compound annual growth rate of cumulative Chinese investment emigrants to the U.S. hit 73%. The Bank of China and Hurun Research Institute carried out a survey on affluent individuals with assets exceeding 10 million yuan in 18 key cities nationwide. The findings revealed that one-third of these wealthy individuals held overseas assets, which accounted for 19% of their total assets on average. Additionally, 60% of the rich either intended to emigrate or had already applied for immigration—primarily through investment immigration—while billionaires allocated over 50% of their investments overseas. According to conservative statistics from Zhejiang Xintong Entry-Exit Service Co., Ltd., and other institutions, at least 1,500 people in Zhejiang Province had successfully achieved investment immigration every year, and the annual growth rate was 10% to 20%. Among the emigrants, the majority wielded influence over wealth, knowledge, and technology, with many being private entrepreneurs. Their exodus would exert a notable impact on China's economic and social progress.

A primary factor driving investment emigration is the absence of a stable, fair, and predictable judicial system, coupled with insufficient and ineffective protection of private property rights. Based on a survey conducted by China Merchants Bank and Bain & Company, the share of emigrants who left to safeguard their wealth stood at a high 43%.[60] Some scholars believe that protecting one's

---

58 Xingyuan Feng, Guangwen He, et al. R*eport on Living Environment of Private Enterprises in China 2012*. Beijing: Economic Press China, 2013.

59 Some scholars believe that there have been three waves of immigration in China: the first wave was after the end of the "Cultural Revolution," the second wave was in the late 1980s and early 1990s, and the third wave started in 2006 and has not yet ended. Xingyuan Feng, Xiaosong Su. The third wave of immigration: legal security as a major reason. *China Civil Entrepreneur*, 2013 (3).

60 According to research conducted by China Merchants Bank and Bain & Company, the three main reasons for HNWIs to invest and emigrate are: facilitating their children's education, accounting for 58%; ensuring wealth security, accounting for 43%; and preparing for future

property safety or the personal safety of family members, including bleaching the gray "first pot of gold," is a source of motivation for many private entrepreneurs to emigrate overseas.[61]

Therefore, establishing a contemporary property rights system that provides effective and equal legal protection for all types of property is fundamental. Such a system must ensure that, in the case of a contract conflict—whether between private parties or between private parties and the government—all involved can not only access legal aid but also benefit from a transparent, impartial, and effective judicial system that enforces the law without fear or favor."[62] Addressing this core issue is essential to improve China's property rights protection framework.

In November 2016, the Central Committee of the CPC and the State Council indeed issued the "Opinions on Improving the Property Rights Protection System and Lawfully Protecting Property Rights." The document put forward five guiding principles—equal protection, comprehensive protection, law-based protection, joint participation, and tackling both the symptoms and root causes—which signaled a major stride toward strengthening China's property rights system. To build a modern property rights system, the following three points are important: First, we must effectively protect public capital and its income, and prevent the loss of public capital. The adjustment of the public economic layout and the reform of mixed ownership entail the transfer, circulation, and reorganization of public assets. Without an effective public asset protection system, it is easy to cause the loss of public assets, especially the erosion of public assets by "insiders." The main ways for the loss of public assets include: deliberate underestimation of the value of public assets; behind-the-scenes transactions by the management team and transfer of interests; the concealed transfer of state-owned assets by state-owned enterprise leaders, etc. To effectively safeguard public assets, it is essential to accelerate the development of relevant legal frameworks and clearly define the legal responsibilities and consequences associated with the loss of such assets. At the same time, it is essential to improve the public asset transfer and transaction system, such as the marketization of public asset evaluation, the transparency of public asset transfer and transactions, and the standardization of transfer and

---

retirement, accounting for 32%. See the "2011 China Private Wealth Report" jointly issued by China Merchants Bank and Bain & Company.

61 Xingyuan Feng, Xiaosong Su. The third wave of immigration: legal security as a major reason. *China Civil Entrepreneur*, 2013, (3).

62 A Joint Research Group of the World Bank and the Development Research Center of the State Council. *China in 2030: Building a Modern, Harmonious and Creative Society*. Beijing: China Financial and Economic Publishing House, 2013, p. 22.

transaction procedures. Second, it is crucial to protect all forms of property rights effectively and equally, with particular emphasis on safeguarding the property rights of the non-public economy. The Third Plenary Session of the 18th CPC Central Committee has clearly stated: "The property rights of the public sector are inviolable, as are those of the non-public sector." However, from the perspective of judicial practice, sometimes a fair ruling on the non-public ownership sector is not achieved. When the property of a non-public enterprise is infringed, it faces many difficulties in filing a case, making a judgment, and executing it, and various transaction costs are high. When non-public enterprises and state-owned enterprises have economic disputes, such as property and contract disputes, the ruling and enforcement will sometimes favor state-owned enterprises. Third, we must restrain administrative power from infringing on non-public assets. Unrestricted executive power can sometimes become a source of infringement of the property rights of non-public economic entities. "In some places, personal property rights have been violated very brutally. Various trumped-up charges are used to infringe and occupy personal property rights, and even make some entrepreneurs bankrupt and send them to prison."[63] In this case, some local government agencies not only failed to act as protectors of legitimate private property, but even played the role of "plundering hands." The current situation of "new officials ignoring old accounts" is a clear example of this.[64]

III. Building a system and mechanism for equal competition and common development of economies of various ownerships

China's economy has transitioned from a phase of rapid growth to one of high-quality development. Priority should be placed on fostering an economic system featuring an efficient market mechanism and dynamic micro-level governance, with a view to steadily enhancing the innovation capability and

---

[63] Jiange Li. The two main lines of the next reform: market orientation and common development of various economic components. *China Reform*, 2013 (1).

[64] In early 2017, Ming Huang, chairman of Shandong Dezhou Huangming Solar Energy Group, reported "new officials ignoring old accounts," which is a vivid case. According to the report, the 2010 ISCI Congress was held in Dezhou, and Huangming Group implemented the instructions of Dezhou Municipal Party Committee and Municipal Government to build the main venue, supporting facilities, main scenic spots, old village renovation and model projects to highlight the theme of the congress with a total cost of about 3 billion yuan. From 1 billion yuan in cash on the account to about 2 billion yuan in debt. To this end, the government promised to compensate for the removal of the old village of Diaoligui and the surrounding land. Now 10 years have passed, and the villagers have already lived and worked in peace and contentment, but the current Party secretary does not accept the old promises. see http://finance. ifeng. com/a/20180221/15991258_0.html.

competitiveness of the nation's economy. A crucial element in this process is establishing a system and mechanism that enables diverse ownership-based economies to compete on an equal footing and develop in tandem. To establish a system and mechanism enabling diverse ownership-based economies to compete equitably and develop collectively, it is essential first to grasp scientifically that the non-public sector constitutes a vital component of modern productive forces. With the rapid advancement of science and technology, it is no longer feasible to equate the non-public economy and small—and medium-sized enterprises with backward productive forces.[65]

In the era of large-scale machinery-based industry, expanding production scale often served as the foundation for advancing productive forces. However, the development trend of modern productive forces is no longer confined to the single path of large-scale production; instead, it has evolved into a multi-faceted model encompassing large, medium, and small-scale production. Thanks to the flexible application of modern technologies, small and medium-sized enterprises (SMEs) and even micro-enterprises are fully capable of becoming organizational forms that accommodate and leverage modern productive forces. Moreover, SMEs have emerged as a crucial source of innovation. The existence of the non-public economy should be understood through the lens of "diversity." Diversity constitutes a fundamental prerequisite for adapting to economic complexity, mitigating uncertainty, spurring innovation, and satisfying individual demands. As noted, "Modern economies depend on societal diversity to attain prosperity ... economic vitality is also contingent on the diversity of entrepreneurs."[66] Given that a society's innovation willingness and capacity are closely tied to diversity, the variety of financiers, entrepreneurs, producers, and consumers—along with diverse enterprise organizational forms and social property structures—shapes a society's vitality and creativity.

It is necessary to build the institutional conditions for equal competition and common development of various ownership economies from three aspects: first, to build a fair law-based environment that effectively protects various property rights; second, to build a free entry mechanism for non-public economies; third, to build an institutional environment in which all types of ownership economies

---

[65] When analyzing the reasons for the existence of non-public economy and small and medium-sized enterprises, political economics textbooks and some related papers generally associate them with backward productivity and unbalanced economic development. This view needs to be changed with the development of modern productive forces.

[66] Edmund Phelps. *Mass Flourishing: How Grassroots Innovation Created Jobs, Challenge, and Change*. Beijing: CITIC Press, 2013, p. 41.

use production factors equally. The construction of a fair law-based environment that effectively protects various property rights has been discussed above. Below is an examination of the unrestricted market access for the non-public sector and the equitable utilization of production factors.

(1) Building a free entry mechanism for the non-public economy

The free movement of production factors and the freedom of enterprise investment constitute the foundational prerequisites for enabling the law of value and market mechanisms to exert a decisive influence on resource allocation. Consequently, relaxing constraints on the investment scope of the non-public sector and permitting its unimpeded entry into and exit from specific industries are critical to cultivating a fair, competitive market environment and advancing the socialist market economic system. Since the start of the twenty-first century, the State Council has issued a sequence of important policy documents aimed at expanding investment opportunities for the non-public economy. In February 2005, it released the "Several Opinions on Encouraging, Supporting and Guiding the Development of Private and Other Non-public Economy," widely known as the "Old 36 Articles" for the non-public economy. This document took the relaxation of market access as a fundamental policy measure to boost the growth of the non-public economy, putting forward such initiatives as "implementing the principle of equal access and fair treatment," and "allowing non-public capital to enter industries and fields that are not prohibited by laws and regulations." It also specified the fields that the non-public economy could enter, including electricity, telecommunications, railways, civil aviation, petroleum and other energy, transportation and communication fields, municipal water provision, gas supply, heating, public transportation, sewage and garbage disposal and other public utilities and infrastructure fields, education, scientific research, health, culture, sports and other social undertakings, banking, securities, insurance and other financial fields, and defense-related technology and industry construction; Meanwhile, the non-public economy was encouraged to take part in the restructuring of the state-owned economy and the reorganization of state-owned enterprises, as well as in key national initiatives like the development of western China, the revitalization of northeast China's old industrial bases, and the rise of central China.

In order to further promote the advancement of private investment and expand the growth space of the non-public economy, in May 2010, the State Council promulgated "Several Opinions on Encouraging and Guiding the Healthy Development of Private Investment," widely referred to as the "New 36 Articles" of the non-public economy. Compared with the "Old 36 Articles," the "New 36 Articles" opened fields to the non-public sector in a wider, clearer, and more specific manner. The document outlined the following principles to further broaden the areas and scope of private investment: the first was to encourage and guide private capital to flow into industries and fields that were not explicitly forbidden by laws and regulations, treat all types of investment entities equally, and not to attach additional conditions to private capital alone; second, government investment was mainly used in economic and social domains linked to national security and where the market could not effectively allocate resources. For infrastructure, municipal engineering, and other public services that could realize market-oriented operation, private capital should be encouraged and supported; third, the core domains of state-owned capital encompass vital industries and critical sectors closely linked to the national economy's lifeline. In competitive fields, a broader market space should be created to encourage private capital participation; the fourth was to take private social undertakings as an important complement to the public social service system, primarily supported by government investment and supplemented by private investment.

The State Council's "Old 36 Articles" and "New 36 Articles" of the non-public sector have opened almost all fields that can be opened for the non-public sector, including not only the general competitive field, but also the competitive links in the monopoly field, the parts that can be opened up in the realm of infrastructure and social undertakings, as well as the domain of national defense technology and industrial development.

The opening-up policies of governments at each level to the non-public economy have achieved practical results. The investment space of private capital has expanded, and it has begun to move toward the fields of infrastructure, modern services, and social services. However, market access for the non-public economy is still very difficult. Many fields that have been opened to the non-public economy or even encouraged the non-public sector to enter in terms of policies are still blocked by a "glass door" or "spring door," which is out of reach.

In the field of general competition, the non-public economy has been able to enter and exit relatively freely, but the government's macro-control policies, industrial policies, and credit policies often constitute barriers to the entry of the non-public economy. In times of macroeconomic austerity, the private sector often bears the brunt, with investment projects often in a failure of approval and bank credit. In the field of industrial policy, the government often restricts private enterprises from entering certain industries due to the consideration of "duplicate construction" and "overcapacity."

To break the entry barriers for the non-public sector and build a just competition environment, we can proceed from the following dimensions:

First, we must break down ideological barriers. The ideological entry barriers for the non-public economy involve almost all industries. In the subconscious of the public and policy makers, wherever possible, it is better to let the public ownership economy engage in corresponding investments and provide corresponding products and services. In those fields involving cultural promotion, national economy, people's livelihood, and high profitability, such as education, press and publication, public utilities, infrastructure, medical care, finance, and other fields, the ideological entry barriers are more prominent and serious. Therefore, eliminating ideological barriers, especially the ideological prejudice of officials with approval authorities, is essential for breaking the entry "glass door" of the non-public economy.

Second, it is imperative to address the imbalance in market power between the state-owned and non-public sectors. Since the turn of the twenty-first century, the number of non-public enterprises has grown swiftly, and their strength has expanded notably. As of September 2017, China was home to 26.0729 million private enterprises, with a registered capital of 165.38 trillion yuan and an average registered capital of 6.343 million yuan—representing a 1.38-fold increase from 2.665 million yuan in 2011, reflecting an impressive growth pace. That said, private enterprises still lag relatively behind state-owned and state-controlled enterprises in terms of strength. In September 2017, the average registered capital of state-owned and state-holding enterprises stood at 34.542 million yuan, 5.4 times that of private enterprises. Leveraging both its own capital strength and the advantages of government administrative power, the state-owned economy holds unique market advantages that the non-public sector cannot rival. In terms of economic clout and market influence, the non-public economy trails the state-owned economy by a significant margin, resulting in uneven competitiveness and unequal standing in the market.

Third, we must break the monopoly market structure. The monopoly market structure is an important obstacle for a non-state-owned economy to enter some important fields. Natural monopoly fields like electricity, telecoms, railways, commercial aviation, and postal services have been opened to the non-state-owned economy in terms of government policies, but the current monopoly vertically integrated market structure has blocked the non-state-owned economy from these fields. In the field of natural monopoly, there are both natural monopoly businesses and competitive businesses, and they often present a vertically integrated structure. Due to the large-scale economy and huge sunk costs, monopoly businesses need to be run by one or a few companies, while competitive businesses can be released and entered freely. At present, monopoly-related operations are authorized by the government to state-owned and state-controlled enterprises, which also engage in competitive businesses within these domains. As a result, state-owned enterprises hold an absolute dominant position in natural monopoly sectors, and they can block potential competitors from providing competitive services by controlling monopoly links to serve their own interests.

Fourth, we must greatly reduce administrative approval procedures. Why does the non-public economy face difficulties entering many industries and sectors, even when policies permit it? It has a lot to do with excessive government approval links, high approval standards, strict requirements for private enterprises, ideological biases of approval officials, and avoidance of political risks. Therefore, administrative examination and approval often block the non-public economy from certain fields, and vigorously simplifying the administrative review and approval procedures is an essential measure to break the "glass door" and "spring door."

(2) Constructing an institutional environment in which various ownership economies use production factors equally

Land, capital, and labor constitute the three fundamental factors of production, and equitable access to and utilization of these production factors form the basic prerequisites for fair competition and the common development of economies under various ownership structures, as well as the basic premise for the market mechanism to allocate resources.

Since the launch of reform and opening up, China's factor markets—particularly the labor market—have advanced rapidly, providing diverse market participants with greater access to production factors. However, the rights of different ownership economies to obtain production factors, especially important production factors, are still unequal, and the state-owned sector holds a privileged position and priority relative to other ownership-based economies. This is evident in financial markets. Research showed that the proportion of individual and private economies in bank credit and their contribution to economic growth and employment were significantly asymmetric. For example, from 2006 to 2011, the ratio of individual and private sector loans to all bank loans was 14.12% on average, 11.38 percentage points lower than their share in fixed asset investment in the whole society, and 5.27 percentage points lower than their proportion in the employment of the whole society.

The private economy not only has "financing difficulties" but also has "land use difficulties." According to the survey on the land use of private enterprises in Jiangsu Province, the right of private enterprises to use land fairly cannot be guaranteed at present. The cumbersome land use and construction procedures, insufficient land use indicators, and high land prices were important factors restricting the development of private enterprises. They accounted for 54.9%, 54.6% and 52.5% of the total sample, respectively, and 17.2% of the enterprises believed that the land transfer process was not transparent (see Table 2).

Table 2: Survey on the Difficulty of Land Use by Private Enterprises in Jiangsu Province

Survey subject	Options	Proportion of total surveyed enterprises (%)
Problems of land use policies	Cumbersome land use and construction procedures	54.9
	Insufficient land use indicators	54.6
	High land prices	52.5
	Non-transparent land transfer process	17.2
	other	1.8

Source: Zhiming Xu, Shan Gao, Mingxia Cao. The game of interests and the dilemma of private economic policy implementation: an empirical analysis based on 1087 enterprises in Jiangsu Province. Jianghai Academic Journal, 2013 (1).

The foremost priority is to advance further reforms in China's financial market (particularly the banking system and capital markets) and land market, ensuring that economies of all ownership types have equitable rights to utilize production factors. Setting aside ideological biases in the loan approval process, China's financial market structure is inherently ill-suited to meet the financing needs of the non-public economy. The non-public economy is primarily made up of small, medium, and micro enterprises (SMEs and micro-enterprises), whose credit demands are marked by small loan amounts, short terms, strong timeliness and flexibility, and a lack of collateral needs that local private banks are better equipped to satisfy. However, China's banking sector is dominated by large state-owned banks. Driven by considerations of information and operational costs, these large banks often favor large-scale credit operations and wholesale financial services for major enterprises, making lending to small, medium, and micro enterprises economically inefficient. While large state-owned banks like the Industrial and Commercial Bank of China have set up SME credit divisions to tackle the financing challenges faced by small, medium, and micro enterprises, the issue remains unaddressed.

Therefore, relaxing banking industry access for private capital is particularly important for the non-public economy to equitably obtain factors of production, especially credit capital. In a broader sense, easing access for private capital into the banking sector will advance the deepening of China's financial reform.

Promoting private capital's entry into the banking industry requires practical and effective measures to break down the "glass door" barriers. The first is to expand the shareholding ratio of private capital in large commercial banks to enhance the governance frameworks, credit behavior, and information and reputation transmission mechanism between various economic entities and financial institutions; the second is to scientifically formulate the access standards for private capital to enter the banking sector and advance the setup of private banks, which is particularly important at present. The establishment criteria for small and medium-sized private financial institutions need not be overly high or stringent. Private capital should be allowed to identify opportunities and take risks on its own, and the role of market mechanisms in identifying risks should be maximized. At the same time, it is essential to further strengthen financial supervision and promptly establish a deposit insurance system to diversify depositor risks, safeguard depositors' funds, control systemic financial risks, and maintain overall financial stability.

Once private banks start to develop, the problem of "financing difficulties" in the non-public economy can be fundamentally resolved. At the same time, private banks and large commercial banks dominated by state-owned capital can also form a benign division of labor and cooperation: Large state-owned commercial banks focus on providing loans and wholesale financial services to large enterprises (including major state-owned and non-state-owned enterprises), while private banks specialize in offering loans and retail financial services to small, medium, and micro enterprises. This division allows both to fully leverage their strengths in information, location, and personnel.

In addition to promoting the establishment of private banks, it is also essential to speed up the reform of interest rate liberalization, raise the share of bond financing, advance the reform of the stock market, and create more financing channels for the non-public economy.

Reforms to the land system and the growth of the land market are vital for ensuring that the non-public economy has equal access to land—a critical factor of production. It is essential to overhaul the government's monopoly on land expropriation and its dominant role in the primary land market, enabling the land market to take a decisive role in allocating land resources. Speeding up the development of the secondary land market and reallocating existing land resources will help boost both the supply and turnover of land, thereby expanding opportunities for non-public economic entities to acquire land and reducing land costs. Additionally, streamlining land use procedures for the non-public sector, enhancing market transparency, and eliminating preferential privileges enjoyed by public economic entities in land acquisition are essential steps toward a fairer land market.

References

A Joint Research Group of the World Bank and the Development Research Center of the State Council. *China in 2030: Building a Modern, Harmonious and Creative Society*. Beijing: China Financial and Economic Publishing House, 2013.

Baumol, William J., Robert E. Litan and Carl J. Schramm. *Good Capitalism, Bad Capitalism, and the Economics of Growth and Prosperity*. Beijing: CITIC Press, 2008.

Deng, Xiaoping. *Selected Works of Deng Xiaoping, Vol. 3.* Beijing: People's Publishing House, 2005.

Dong, Fuzheng. *Research on Economic System Reform, Vol. 1.* Beijing: Economic Science Press, 1994.

Jiang, Xuemo. Comment on the theory of "absence of the owner." *Economic Research Journal*, 1988 (3).

Li, Yining. An exploration of the socialist ownership system. *Hebei Academic Journal*, 1987 (1).

Liu, Guoguang. Several issues on the reform of ownership relations. *Economic Daily*, Jan. 4, 1986.

Shan, Dong, Zhengting Wang. Discussion on some theoretical issues of individual economy, private economy and revitalizing public-owned enterprises. *Economic Perspectives*, 1990 (5).

Wu, Jinglian, Junkuo Zhang, Shijin Liu, et al. *Strategic Reorganization of State-owned Economy*. Beijing: China Development Press, 1998

Yong Wang. Putting the private economy in the general environment of the commodity economy to study. *Economic Perspective*, 1988 (5).

Zhang, Zhuoyuan. *60 Years of Chinese Economics (1949–2009).* Beijing: Social Sciences Academic Press (China), 2009.

Zhang, Zhuoyuan. *A New Journey of Economic Reform*. Beijing: Social Sciences Academic Press (China), 2014.

Zhang, Zhuoyuan. *Economic Transformation and Reform.* Beijing: China Renmin University Press, 2017.

Theory of Income Distribution

Over the course of its transformation toward a more open and dynamic economy, China has continuously refined its principles and methods related to the sharing of economic gains. At the initial phase of China's economic transformation, in order to address the problem of uniformity in income, priority was given to material rewards, and a compensation model tied to personal input and effort was established. With the deepening of economic restructuring, alternative modes of earnings allocation, beyond compensation based solely on labor, began to emerge in daily economic life. Notably, various contributors to economic output have played an increasingly prominent role in shaping the way earnings are allocated. People's income now comes from a variety of sources, reflecting a trend of rapid growth. The 13th National Congress of the Communist Party of China (CPC) introduced the concept of "an income distribution system where distribution according to work is the primary form, supplemented by other forms of income distribution." Subsequently, during the 14th congress in 1993, a new foundational framework for allocating national earnings was introduced, where "distribution according to work is dominant, with various other distribution modes coexisting," signaling a notable leap forward in the theoretical framework concerning the sharing of national income. In the ongoing exploration of how earnings and wealth are distributed, the tension between justice and performance, as well as the challenge of narrowing income inequality while aiming for inclusive growth, has been a key issue in both academic research and policy-making. Since the 18th CPC National Congress, the theory of income distribution has seen further development, placing greater emphasis on fairness and justice, common prosperity, and the people's "sense of fulfillment." Additionally, "sharing" has been recognized as one of the five key development concepts of the new era.

1. Resurgence of Remuneration Linked to Personal Labor Input at the Outset of Nationwide Economic Liberalization

Revisions in the structuring and distribution of earnings signal significant shifts in the way societal interests are arranged, reflecting a deep and broad transformation of the nation's economic base. To comprehend how China's system for sharing economic gains has evolved, especially since the transition toward a market-responsive model, it is essential to examine the underlying principles and initial conditions that led to the formation of a new framework for dividing economic returns.

The theoretical foundation of the evolution of China's income distribution theory lies in the classic concept of distributing personal consumer goods in the future. In *Capital*, Marx described the distribution of personal consumer goods as "an association of free men": "the share of each individual producer in the means of subsistence is determined by his labor-time." And labor-time served as "a measure of the share in the part of the total product destined for individual consumption."[1] In his work, Marx provided a comprehensive account of how rewards and entitlements would be arranged in an advanced communal society, free from capitalist constraint: accordingly, the individual producer receives back from society —after the deductions have been made — exactly what he gives to it. What he has given to it is his individual quantum of labor. The same amount of labor which he has given to society in one form, he receives back in another."[2] Marx acknowledged that in a future society, there would be variations in the income and consumption of individual workers, due to differences in each person's labor capacity and family circumstances. Later, Lenin encapsulated Marx's approach to wealth allocation based on labor as "receiving equal products in exchange for an equal amount of labor." He also explored how labor-based remuneration mechanisms could be implemented in practice, adjusting them to fit the realities of Soviet socialist economic construction. For example, structured payment approaches involving time-based or output-based salaries served to realize compensation aligned with individual work contribution, alongside bonus and profit commission systems to ensure "more work for more, less work for less," etc. Lenin's theoretical and practical exploration of distribution according to labor had an important influence on China.

---

1 Karl Marx and Frederick Engels. *Marx & Engels Collected Works, Volume 5*. Beijing: People's Publishing House, 2009, p. 96.

2 Karl Marx and Frederick Engels. *Marx & Engels Collected Works, Volume 3*. Beijing: People's Publishing House, 2009, p. 434.

In the stage characterized by state-directed production and allocation, the notion of linking income to one's labor input was accepted as a guiding principle in both theoretical frameworks and policy design. The prevailing idea maintained that, given the communal ownership of key economic assets, wages should align with the intensity and quality of each worker's effort, meaning "more pay for more work, less pay for less work and no pay for no work." In actual operation, agricultural production teams in the countryside applied a "work points mechanism" to allocate earnings, whereas administrative bodies, publicly funded organizations, state-run firms, and city-based cooperatives employed a standardized wage structure to reward labor efforts. Since the 1950s, the "eight-level wage system" has been introduced for employees in enterprises. The "eight-level wage system" attempted to formulate different wage standards according to workers' technical level, labor target, and labor intensity, with the aim of adhering to labor-based compensation norms. Some scholars at the time argued that "the eight-level wage system is one of the specific manifestations of the socialist pay-for-work law,"[3] because it made it possible to differentiate earnings according to the amount and effectiveness of one's effort, the difficulty and significance of the work, rather than irrelevant factors like age, gender, or personal habits. However, both the salary structure and the labor credit system ultimately became dominated by egalitarian principles, where "everybody eating from the same big pot." The core reason was the complexity of labor measurement, and in an economy where planning governed all aspects, there were no practical methods to assess the actual amount and quality of work done by individuals. Labor was quantified solely by working hours, predetermined wage grades, and administrative ranks, which inevitably resulted in mere physical presence without genuine effort. It was neither fair nor efficient, and the result could only be equalitarianism. Some researchers computed the income inequality index for Chinese citizens in the initial phase of reforms, which clearly highlighted the tendency toward equal distribution during the era of centralized economic planning. According to Yang Xiaokai's calculations, the Gini index in the six cities directly governed by Hubei Province was 0.128, and it was 0.1545 and 0.1473 in rural areas and county-owned towns, respectively. After applying weighted calculations, the Gini ratio for Hubei Province in 1981 was determined to be 0.1332.[4] Scholars Tang Guoxing and Zheng Shaoyong from Fudan University calculated the Gini

3 Jirong Luo. On Eight-tier Wage Scale. *Journal of Xiamen University (Finance and Economics Edition)*, 1952 (3).

4 Xiaokai Yang. An Important Indicator of Social and Economic Development—Gini coefficient. *Journal of Wuhan University*, 1982 (6).

coefficient before and after the wage adjustment in 1979 based on a survey of 50 households in Shanghai. It was 0.142 before the adjustment and 0.139 after the adjustment. Based on Zhao Xuezeng's calculations, the Gini coefficient for 23 counties in Baoding, Hebei Province, in 1978 was as low as 0.029.[5] As per the World Bank's calculations, the income inequality index for urban households in China in 1980 was recorded at 0.16.[6] These studies and calculations showed that the income distribution across city dwellers and rural inhabitants in China during that period was remarkably consistent.

In response to the work complacency and inefficiencies brought about by enforced income equality during the period of planned governance, the Party reaffirmed policies centered on rewarding labor in proportion to effort and performance when initiating comprehensive economic changes. In December 1978, the Central Committee of the CPC convened a Central Working Conference, laying the groundwork for the forthcoming critical gathering focused on economic restructuring. At the closing ceremony, in his famous address "Emancipate the Mind, Seek Truth from Facts, and Unite as One in Looking to the Future," Comrade Deng underscored the role of reward-based motivation as a key element in advancing socialist practices. He said, "As far as the relatively small number of advanced people is concerned, it will not matter too much if we neglect the principle of more pay for more work and fail to stress individual material benefits. But when it comes to the masses, that approach can only be used for a short time — it will not work in the long run. The revolutionary spirit is a treasure beyond price. Without it there would be no revolutionary action. But revolution takes place on the basis of the need for material benefit. It would be idealism to emphasize the spirit of sacrifice to the neglect of material benefit."[7] Leader Deng also put forward the statement of "getting rich first," and at the same time explained the inner relationship between "rich first" and "rich together." He said, "We should allow some regions and enterprises and some workers and peasants to earn more and enjoy more benefits sooner than others, in accordance with their hard work and greater contributions to society. If the standard of living of some people is raised first, this will inevitably be an impressive example to

5 Xuezeng Zhao. Investigation on the Lorenz Curve and Gini Coefficient of the Distribution of Workers' Wages (Work Points) in China. *Journal of Tianjin Institute of Finance and Economics*, 1982 (4).

6 Word Bank. *China: Socialist Economic Development, vol. 1. (English Version)*, Washington: 1983, p. 83.

7 Xiaoping Deng. *Selected Works of De Xiaoping, vol. 2.* Beijing: People's Publishing House, 1994, p. 146.

their 'neighbors,' and people in other regions and units will want to learn from them. This will help the whole national economy to advance wave upon wave and help the people of all our nationalities to become prosperous in a comparatively short period."[8] Related to this, on the fourth anniversary of the October Revolution, Lenin gave an insightful elaboration on how material incentives could serve as a driving force within a socialist framework. He said, "We were inspired by a wave of enthusiasm. We first aroused the people's general political enthusiasm, and then their military enthusiasm, on which we once planned to rely to directly accomplish the economic tasks that were as great as the general political and military tasks ... But it showed that we were wrong in reality ... We cannot count on people's enthusiasm alone, but with the enthusiasm generated by the great revolution, relying on people's personal interests, the combination of personal interests, and business accounting."[9] In late 1978, the critical gathering focused on economic restructuring was convened. It highlighted that awakening the collective drive of the country's farming population required a sincere focus on their everyday well-being and long-term economic participation ... It was required that various production units implement compensation systems reflective of individual contribution, ensuring that both the intensity and effectiveness of labor were properly valued, and that tendencies toward indiscriminate leveling were systematically addressed.[10] Following that, the conference held in September 1979 approved the "Decision of the Central Committee of the CPC on Several Issues Concerning Accelerating Agricultural Development." It was pointed out that "distribution according to work, with more work, more gain, is the socialist principle of distribution, which is never allowed to be opposed as a capitalist principle"; "we should pay remuneration in accordance with the quantity and quality of labor, establish a necessary reward and punishment system, and resolutely correct egalitarianism"[11]. Afterwards, the 1984-held meeting approved the "Decision of the Central Committee of the CPC on Reform of the Economic Structure," which encouraged flexible responsibility arrangements and a compensation approach based on the effort and results delivered by each worker, specifically including: Firstly, enterprises funded and managed by the state should adopt a graded wage structure. "It is necessary to widen the wage gap and

---

8 Ibid., p. 152.

9 Lenin. *Lenin Monographs (Socialism)*. Beijing: People's Publishing House, 2009, p. 247.

10 Party Literature Research Center of the CPC Central Committee. *Selections of Important Documents since the Third Plenary Session of the 11th National Congress of the Communist Party of China: Part I*. Beijing: People's Publishing House, 2011, pp. 6–7.

11 Ibid., p. 158.

tiers in enterprises to fully embody rewards for the diligence and punishment for laziness, rewards for the good and punishment for the bad, fully embody more work more gain, less work less gain, and fully embody the differences between mental work and manual work, complex work and simple work, skilled work and unskilled work, heavy work and non-heavy work."[12] Secondly, egalitarianism must be overcome. "The ideology of egalitarianism is completely incompatible with the Marxist scientific view of socialism. The lessons of history tell us that the idea of egalitarianism is a serious obstacle to the implementation of the principle of distribution according to work, and that the proliferation of egalitarianism will inevitably destroy socially productive forces."[13] Thirdly, allowing some individuals to become wealthy first was regarded as the sole path to achieving common prosperity. "The socialist society must ensure the gradual improvement of the material and cultural living standards of the members of the society, and achieve the goal of common prosperity ... Only by allowing and encouraging some regions, some enterprises, and some people to get rich first through hard work can it have a strong attraction and inspiration for most people, and drive more and more people to become rich one after another ... The difference caused by some people getting rich first is that on the road to common prosperity, members of society would get rich earlier or later, and fast or slowly, but it is definitely not the kind of polarization, where only a small number of people become exploiters and the majority are trapped in poverty."[14]

In the early stages of China's economic transformation, intense debates unfolded within the ideological and academic circles about how earnings should be allocated, with many influential economists contributing to the discourse. Just from the spring of 1977 to the winter of 1978, four major seminars on distribution according to work were conducted, playing a significant role in the ideological emancipation movement of that period. It can be said that the process of restoring order in the economic field began with the debates surrounding the distribution structure. The majority of scholars held the view that implementing distribution according to work was an objective necessity within a socialist economy. Yu Guangyuan argued that the method of assigning rewards based on labor was a natural economic law, stating that "if distribution according to work is not implemented in the long run, the socialist system cannot exist. Distribution

---

12 Ibid., p. 162.

13 Party Literature Research Center of the CPC Central Committee. *Selections of Important Documents since the 12th National Congress of the Communist Party of China: Part II*. Beijing: People's Publishing House, 2011, p. 63.

14 Ibid., p. 64.

according to work is determined by the nature of socialism"; "No matter how people act and regardless of their will, the law of distribution according to work still works. It really does not depend on the will of people, and it plays a role in the economic life of socialist society all the time."[15] Most researchers approached the necessity of linking compensation to labor effort from the standpoint of public ownership. Xu He argued that within the framework of ownership by the entire people, "it already has sufficient conditions to function distribution according to work," and "from the perspective of each collective economic unit, the means of production are owned by the collective, and individual consumer goods are distributed according to the amount of labor contributed by the members."[16] Some scholars also explored the contrasts and commonalities between the real-world application of the economic system and Marx's proposed model for distributing goods to individuals in a future society. Marx's theory centers on the allocation of consumer items in relation to the amount of labor contributed. Upholding this point means insisting on distribution according to work. However, Marx outlined stringent prerequisites for the practical application of resource allocation based on labor. The two most critical requirements are: first, the establishment of collective control over the means of production throughout society; and second, the elimination of commodity-money relationships, where the labor of workers becomes direct social labor. Since these conditions are not met in reality, the actual practice of labor-based distribution deviates significantly from Marx's original conception. For example, in the real world, compensation for work is inevitably tied to monetary transactions. Instead of receiving "labor vouchers," workers are paid in wages and use this income to purchase the goods they need. Additionally, a nationwide system of equitable distribution based on labor is not feasible, as enterprises continue to operate under independent financial systems. Another example is that a unified distribution according to work across the entire society is unfeasible, as enterprises still operate with an independent accounting system. They continue to function as economic entities with their own distinct interests. In this light, Jiang Yiwei introduced the concept of "two-level distribution according to work,"[17] whereby society first applies the principle to enterprises, which then further applies it to individuals.

---

15 Guangyuan Yu. Several Questions about the In-depth Study of the Theory of Distribution According to Work. *Economic Research Journal*, 1979 (1).

16 He Xu. The Basic Economic Laws of Socialism, Distribution According to Work, Bonuses. *Academic Forum*, 1979 (1).

17 Yiwei Jiang. Several Questions about Distribution According to Work. *Workers' Daily*, 1980-03-21.

It is noteworthy that early reform-era discussions on the concept of "work" under the principle of rewarding based on labor input were rich in theoretical insight. The effective implementation of distribution according to work hinges on the scientific and precise assessment of "labor." The labor actually contributed by a worker is influenced by their skills, work intensity, and labor attitude. It refers to the true exertion of an individual's physical and cognitive effort, which is often challenging to observe directly. What is even more significant is that in practice, since the work carried out by employees is not inherently collective in nature, it becomes equally crucial to consider whether their efforts are directed toward socially beneficial objectives. Only the labor that contributes positively to society can serve as a basis for individual income distribution, whereas ineffective labor that fails to generate social wealth or use-values cannot be used as a measure for distribution. Before reform and opening up, some scholars proposed that the "work" used for distribution according to work was not individual labor, but the typical labor required by society to produce commodities of value.[18] During the early phase of reform, Hong Yuanpeng provided a thorough analysis of labor assessment. He believed that "to correctly implement the principle of distribution according to work, we need to figure out the important issue of how to accurately measure the work in distribution according to work," and he advanced the proposition that "the measurement of the work in distribution according to work must be in accordance with socially necessary labor time."[19] The amount of labor required by society is shaped by key factors such as the overall level of technological advancement, typical worker skills, the intensity of labor, and how well products meet societal needs. Therefore, using the concept of socially essential work time rather than natural work time to measure the actual labor input aligns with the objective principles of the value law in a commodity-based economy. From a contemporary standpoint, this view is notably prescient.

China's economic transition began with a system that allowed families to manage agricultural plots independently under contractual obligations. It fundamentally transformed the original "work-point system" of income distribution by adopting the approach of "fulfilling obligations to the state, retaining a portion for the collective, and allowing households to keep the remaining surplus for themselves." Scholars vigorously debated whether the rural contract-based production model aligned with the notion of labor-linked remuneration, though

[18] Xuezhong Hua. The Inevitability of Commodity Production under the Socialist System is Determined by the Economic Law of Remuneration for Work. *Study*, 1957 (8).

[19] Yuanpeng Hong. Discussion on Labor Measurement in Distribution According to Work. *Fudan University Journal*, 1979 (3).

the dominant view ultimately prevailed. According to Li Jiapeng's analysis, under the collective farming model, compensation was largely based on two categories of labor input: the latent form (the laborer's capacity to work) and the flow form (the amount of labor actually expended). Both approaches tended to incline toward egalitarianism. Compared to the earlier model, the land contract approach linked payment to the end products delivered by each household's labor. This method established a direct link between effort and output, enabling accurate evaluation of individual input and reflecting the practical essence of rewarding work proportionally.[20]

Central policy directives have persistently upheld the practice of linking remuneration to actual work performed. In 1985, when the central government summarized the experience of the wage system reform, it stated, "The focus of the wage reform in 1985 was to reform the current unreasonable wage system, gradually eliminate the entrenched shortcomings of egalitarianism in wage distribution, and initially establish a new wage system that can better reflect the principle of distribution according to work ... In the future, the wages of employees in China will grow constantly and steadily with the development of production and the growth of national income. This will fundamentally change the situation in the past in which wage was either left unmoved for a long time or the same increase for everyone. This will be a major step forward in implementing the socialist principle of distribution according to work."[21]

2. Creation of a Core Mechanism for Distributing Earnings Within a Socialist Framework

(1) Multiple channels and types of earnings available to individuals

In the course of four decades of economic reform, China has seen ongoing shifts in property relations and institutional arrangements, which have naturally led to adjustments in how income is distributed. The once-unified public ownership model from the era of central planning has been dismantled, with the swift expansion of private enterprises and foreign investments contributing to a more complex and heterogeneous ownership framework. The market now plays a larger role in how resources are distributed, requiring labor, capital, and land to

[20] JIapeng Li. The Contract to the Household is a Progressive Change in Production Relations. *Economic Research Journal*, 1983 (11).

[21] Party Literature Research Center of the CPC Central Committee. *Selections of Important Documents since the 12th National Congress of the Communist Party of China: Part II*. Beijing: People's Publishing House, 2011, p. 167.

be circulated through market systems. As a result, labor power and the means of generating output can no longer be simply and directly combined, often needing intermediaries such as capital. These shifts in ownership and economic mechanisms have driven a corresponding evolution in income distribution: non-labor factors have gradually been incorporated, and income from areas not tied to work-based distribution has grown steadily.

At the very beginning of the reform era, when the land-use contracts were established, the principles and patterns of income distribution had already begun to shift subtly. From that moment on, material factors began impacting household earnings and economic status. Xu He pointed this out when discussing the challenges of applying labor-based distribution in the collective economy. He said, "Each collective economic unit possesses different means of production and production capital, of which the fact leads to the disparity of production and income level among units, even at the premise of paying the same amount of labor. Under the condition of paying the same amount of labor, those units with good production conditions will earn more total income, and so will the personal income of each member; conversely, the total and personal income in those units with relatively poor production conditions will be less."[22] It is evident that since land-use rights were allocated to households, farming income has been shaped not only by work but also by variables such as soil conditions, planting inputs, support facilities, and local climate, etc. Those farmers who invest more money are equipped with a top level of operating management and have good natural conditions, showing their great advantages immediately. This fact, in turn, motivates other farmers to boost capital investment, update equipment, and enhance management and production conditions in order to achieve higher yields and increased income. This, in turn, enhances farming efficiency and boosts the earnings of rural producers. In theory, this reflects the initial formation of an input-driven distribution model alongside the launch of decentralized land responsibility arrangements.

One major adjustment in income patterns following the adoption of this economic system was the broadening of household income sources beyond just basic consumer goods. This contrasts sharply with the classic theorists' assumption that future social income distribution would be confined to individual consumer goods. With the shift to the new system, rural families could not only sustain their livelihoods but also accumulate surplus income for further development

---

22 He Xu. Socialist Basic Economic Laws· Distribution According to Work Bonus. *Academic Forum*, 1979 (1).

and input purchases.[23] Put differently, a portion of personal income could be redirected toward asset acquisition and productive input, signaling a structural transformation in China's mechanisms of accumulation and capital formation. This development also indicates the emergence and growth of non-public property and a diversification of the property structure. In this respect, the reform laid the groundwork for a new analytical framework concerning the distribution of economic returns.

A significant shift occurred as private entities gained ground, altering the foundational rules of economic reward and changing the makeup of household financial resources. The early proliferation of individually operated businesses marked the sector's initial formation. By endorsing individually managed farming, domestic by-production, and local market activities, reform-era policies provided rural residents with new opportunities to increase their economic returns. On December 11, 1980, a girl named Zhang Huamei in Wenzhou received the first self-employed business license after reform and opening up from the Wenzhou Administrative Bureau for Industry and Commerce, and became the first self-employed individual after reform and opening up. At the end of 1981, there were 1.82 million self-employed individuals registered nationwide, with 2.27 million employees, of which the total registered capital reached 458.4 million yuan, with a turnover of 2,113.99 million yuan. Under individual production systems, the worker keeps both the results of their labor and the income derived from using their own tools and resources. Although the income of the self-employed people belongs to labor income due to their hard work, it does not arise under the standard framework of compensation based on collective labor norms. Essentially, this income represents a form of market-based operating revenue, affected by different aspects like the level of work involved and the surrounding production environment, technological capabilities, and managerial competence of self-employed individuals, while also being constrained by the law of value.

China's non-public corporate sector appeared after individual businesses gained traction and were officially accepted in 1987. A year later, a constitutional revision confirmed this recognition, stating: "The state protects the lawful rights and interests of the private sector of the economy." Since then, the privately owned sector has undergone rapid expansion and has served as a crucial pillar supporting national economic growth and social progress. A defining characteristic of the private economy is its reliance on wage labor, marking its distribution model

---

[23] Zuyao Yu. The Household-based Contract System in Agriculture is the Prelude to China's Economic System Restructuring. *Economic Research Journal*, 1983(3).

fundamentally dissimilar to publicly owned economic units. Employers, on the other hand, derive income from multiple sources: as business operators, they earn labor income for their mental and physical contributions to decision-making and management; as capital owners, they receive capital income based on their investment and take part in the overall trend of return balancing; simultaneously, in managing enterprises, they extract the value added through the work of their employees; in addition, they also receive compensation for assuming business and property-related risks, surplus value, and risk premiums. The income distribution model in foreign-invested enterprises follows the same principle as that of the private sector.

With rising earnings and greater spending capacity in the early years of China's economic transition, residents' wealth expanded both in volume and in variety, with property income also rising and diversifying accordingly. Key elements of personal asset accumulation and unearned income consisted of bank deposits and the interest they generated. The combined savings of rural and urban populations grew from 21.06 billion yuan in 1978 to 2,966.23 billion yuan by 1995, multiplying almost 140 times. At that point, deposit rates ranged from 6.65% for six months to 13.86% for five years. Returns from deposit accounts constituted a major portion of financial gains. The second is the bonds issued by enterprises and governments, along with the interest earned. The bonds held by residents include corporate bonds, government securities, state investment bonds, state investment corporate bonds, and financial institution bonds. In 1995, the balance of corporate bonds was 67.987billion yuan, government securities amounted to 228.64 billion yuan, financial institution bonds totaled 87.629 billion yuan, state investment bonds stood at 13.939 billion yuan, and state investment corporate bonds reached 15.181 billion yuan. These financial instruments collectively constituted the stable-return assets held by households and businesses. Another major category was equity assets, including both profit-sharing returns and price appreciation. In the early 1980s, shareholding companies began to appear, with some opting to distribute shares to employees or the public to secure capital. By the close of 1989, China had issued a cumulative total of 4.2 billion yuan in shares, about 65% of which were issued to the public and the rest 35% were issued to internal employees. The income from stocks to holders consists of two parts: dividends and capitalized gains from the sale of stocks. The fourth is real estate, including the rental income and capital gains it generates. As reforms in the residential sector advanced, housing began to take on dual functions, as both a tradable good and a financial asset, thereby becoming a major component of household wealth. At present, the housing ownership rate in China has reached 70%. The holders' income brought by housing is composed of two parts: one is the rent from leasing, and the other is the capital gains from selling. Real estate brings generous capital gains for its owners.

Starting in the 1980s' second phase, more researchers began examining the transformation of income allocation norms and how personal earnings were structured across the population. In their 1988 work, "The Contradiction between the Theory of Distribution According to Work and the Reality," Gu Shutang and Cai Jiming analyzed the mismatch between theoretical distribution models and the evolving realities of income practices. Due to the ongoing diversity in property relations and the continued role of commodity-based production and trade in the early socialist context, it was pointed out that the government could not entirely dictate how income was allocated between reinvestment and use, nor fully align individual needs with broader societal priorities. Given that both organizations and workers held partial control over how revenue was distributed and saved, it became impractical to enforce the conventional model of remuneration strictly tied to labor contribution. The view was put forward that the early distribution practices followed a model based on each factor's input, with returns reflecting the degree to which labor, capital, and other elements contributed to overall economic output.[24] In practice, income is categorized to include returns generated through work alongside those obtained from non-working channels. Labor income is derived solely from mental and physical work, including wages of laborers, payment of labor in the income of self-employed people, employers, and entrepreneurs, while non-labor income is derived from the objective conditions of labor, such as natural conditions, means of production, etc., including interest, profit, and land rent. Zhang Wenmin believed that the labor contract system implemented in 1986 marked the establishment of the commodity nature of labor. Since then, the income of laborers has no longer been distributed according to work, but according to factors of production, which depend on the contribution of labor as a factor of production in the production process.[25] The notion of assigning income shares based on various productive elements has been met with skepticism by some academics. One prominent argument claims

---

[24] Shutang Gu, Jiming Cai. The Contradiction between the Theory of Distribution According to work and the Reality. Social Sciences in China, 1988 (3); Shutang Gu, Jiming Cai. Distribution according to contribution is the principle of distribution in the primary stage of socialism. *Economist*, 1989 (2).

[25] Wenmin Zhang. Thoughts on the Theory of Distribution According to Work. *Economic Research Journal*, 1987 (2).

that such a framework replicates Say's "Trinity Formula" and deviates from core socialist ideology.[26]

(2) Establishment of the Basic Socialist Distribution System

The foundational framework for income allocation under early socialism in China gradually took shape amid ongoing economic transformation. As the preceding discussion has shown, the initial reform era witnessed a diversification in both income distribution mechanisms and the composition of household earnings, laying a solid empirical basis for the system's evolution. In 1987, the 13th CPC National Congress formally proposed "to carry out diverse distribution forms with 'to each according to his work' as the main form," and pointed out that "there cannot be a single mode of distribution in the primary stage of socialism. We must adhere to the principle in which distribution according to work is dominant and supplemented with other modes of distribution. In addition to distribution according to work and individual labor income, there are several other types of income. When enterprises issue bonds to raise funds, there will be interest which people can get by creditor's rights; With the emergence of shareholding economy, there will be share dividends; The income of business operators includes part of risk compensation; Private enterprises employ a certain number of laborers which will bring some non-labor income to the owners. Such income should be allowed as long as it is legal."[27] While the Congress in 1987 did not specifically advocate for income allocation based on production factors, it did support the recognition of various forms of income unrelated to labor, effectively offering an indirect affirmation of the practice of distribution based on production factors.

At the 14th Party Congress, the strategic aim of transforming China's economic structure into a market-based model with socialist characteristics was officially articulated. Later, the Third Plenary Session in the same year issued a formal decision that, initially proposed the notion that "individual capital and other factors of production should be allowed to participate in the distribution of income," and the original "distribution according to work as the principal form, other modes of distribution as the supplement" was changed to "distribution

26 Zhongfan Guo. Axiology: On the Foundation and Starting Point of Political economy—and On the Theoretical Source of the Theory of Distribution According to Factors. *Journal of Hubei Normal University (Philosophy and Social Sciences Edition)*, 1992 (5).

27 Party Literature Research Center of the CPC Central Committee. *Selections of Important Documents since the 13th National Congress of the Communist Party of China: Part I*. Beijing: Party Literature Publishing House, 2011, p. 28.

according to work as the principal form, other modes of distribution coexist"[28]. The shift from "supplement" to "coexistence" signifies the increasing prominence of multiple distribution modes (particularly referring to "distribution according to production factors"). In the "Ninth Five-Year Plan" report, there are some changes in the expression of other modes of distribution, namely, "standardize and improve other modes of distribution. Land, capital, intellectual property rights and other factors of production shall participate in the distribution of income in a fair way in accordance with relevant regulations."[29] The 15th CPC National Congress put forward the fundamental socialist economic system, and clearly proposed "distribution according to factors of production." The Congress further made it clear that returns tied to the contribution of various economic elements should be both recognized and actively promoted: "We shall keep to the system in which distribution according to work is primary and in which a variety of modes of distribution coexist. Combining remuneration according to work and remuneration according to factors of production ... allowing and encouraging the use of capital, technology and other factors of production to participate in the distribution of gains."[30] The 16th CPC National Congress further upgraded "distribution according to factors" to a "principle" and proposed "we should establish the principle that labor, capital, technology, managerial expertise and other production factors participate in the distribution of income in accordance with their respective contributions, thereby improving the system under which distribution according to work is dominant and a variety of modes of distribution coexist." It was also pointed out that "all legitimate income, from work or not, should be protected,"[31] indicating that both wages and legally obtained non-wage income were granted the same status. The report of the 17th CPC National Congress reiterated that "we will adhere to and improve the system whereby distribution according to work remains the predominant mode and coexists with

---

28 Party Literature Research Center of the CPC Central Committee. *Selections of Important Documents since the 14th National Congress of the Communist Party of China: Part I.* Beijing: Party Literature Publishing House, 2011, p. 465.

29 Party Literature Research Center of the CPC Central Committee. *Selections of Important Documents since the 14th National Congress of the Communist Party of China: Part I.* Beijing: Party Literature Publishing House, 2011, p. 814.

30 Party Literature Research Center of the CPC Central Committee. *Selections of Important Documents since the 15th National Congress of the Communist Party of China: Part I.* Beijing: People's Publishing House, 2000, p. 42.

31 Party Literature Research Center of the CPC Central Committee. *Selections of Important Documents since the 16th National Congress of the Communist Party of China: Part I.* Beijing: Party Literature Publishing House, 2005, pp. 21,12.

various other modes. We will improve the distribution system to allow factors of production such as labor, capital, technology and managerial expertise to have a rightful share according to their respective contribution." It proposed that "conditions will be created to enable more citizens to have property income."[32] Between the 13th and 17th Party Congresses, the key components of China's socialist income system were progressively developed and institutionalized.

Theoretically speaking, the core model of income under socialism reflects the distribution ideas advocated by foundational Marxist scholars. On the topic of how income should be allocated, Marx articulated two foundational viewpoints that have become widely referenced. One is the exposition in the *Critique of the Gotha Programme*, that is, "any distribution whatever of the means of consumption is only a consequence of the distribution of the conditions of production themselves. The latter distribution, however, is a feature of the mode of production itself."[33] In this context, the phrase "distribution of the conditions of production" may be understood as referring to how the ownership of productive assets is organized. The second is the argument in the *Grundrisse (Foundations of a Critique of Political Economy)*, that is, "The relations and modes of distribution thus appear merely as the obverse of the agents of production ... The structure [Gliederung] of distribution is completely determined by the structure of production. Distribution is itself a product of production, not only in its object, in that only the results of production can be distributed, but also in its form, in that the specific kind of participation in production determines the specific forms of distribution, i.e., the pattern of participation in distribution."[34] The discussions above highlight that a society's income allocation framework is closely tied to how ownership is structured. As reforms unfolded, the formerly uniform public ownership system under central planning began to give way to a more heterogeneous configuration of asset rights, an evolution shaped by institutional change rather than personal will. The year 1997 marked the institutionalization of a foundational socialist market system, as endorsed by the Party's major congress held that year, which emphasizes "developing diverse forms of ownership, with public ownership as the dominant force." Share-holding companies, privately

---

32 Party Literature Research Center of the CPC Central Committee. *Selections of Important Documents since the 17th National Congress of the Communist Party of China: Part I.* Beijing: Party Literature Publishing House, 2009, p. 30.

33 Karl Marx, Friedrich Engels. *Collected Works of Marx and Engels: Volume 3*. Beijing: People's Publishing House, 2009, p. 436.

34 Karl Marx, Friedrich Engels. *Collected Works of Marx and Engels: Volume 8*. Beijing: People's Publishing House, 2009, p. 19.

run firms, and enterprises with blended ownership have all grown swiftly, now exerting ever-greater influence on China's economy and society. Accordingly, the core income-sharing framework, reflecting this diversified ownership pattern, should feature earnings tied mainly to individual effort while allowing several other distribution methods to operate alongside it. "The dominant role of public ownership" ensures the central role of distribution according to work, while the "diverse forms of ownership" facilitate the coexistence of multiple distribution methods. The primary form within these "multiple forms of distribution" is distribution according to production factors.

A major advancement in the structure of income allocation under socialism lies in recognizing the role of various productive elements in determining returns. This shift raises key theoretical questions, particularly concerning how generated value is shared and how income derived from ownership should be understood. Such a model evokes comparisons with Jean-Baptiste Say's well-known "Trinity Formula." He argued that the three production factors of labor, capital, and land are not only the elements responsible for creating the use value of commodities, but also the factors that generate the value of commodities. Therefore, these three elements should receive corresponding income, that is, labor gets wages, capital gets interest, and land gets rent; in other words, labor — wages, capital — profit, and land — ground-rent. In the third volume of *Capital*, Marx set up a special chapter to deeply criticize "the Trinity Formula,"[35] which is sometimes mistaken for Marx's denial of the income of factors of production. The fundamental flaw in Say's "Trinity Formula" lies in its assumption that the generation of value naturally justifies its distribution pattern. This perspective contradicts Marx's theory, which posits labor as the exclusive creator of value, asserting that material inputs alone cannot produce it. Therefore, using production as the basis for determining how value is divided would, paradoxically, exclude capital, land, and similar inputs from the actual distribution process. This, of course, cannot adequately explain real-world income distribution. Alternatively, if it is acknowledged that production factors contribute to value creation, it provides a justification for their inclusion in value distribution. This perspective runs counter to Marx's theory that labor alone is the origin of value. He rejected the premise of the "Trinity Formula," which placed capital, land, and labor on the same footing as contributors to value. Nonetheless, Marx acknowledged that both capital and land could yield monetary returns. As he states, "The means of labor, as such, which are by nature capital, thus become the source of profit, much as land, as

---

[35] Karl Marx, Friedrich Engels. *Collected Works of Marx and Engels: Volume 7*. Beijing: People's Publishing House, 2009, pp. 921–942.

such, becomes the source of rent."[36] In Marx's view, the processes of creating and distributing value are not the same. A prerequisite for claiming a share of the value produced lies in possessing the means of production. Moreover, within the Marxist paradigm, property ownership is viewed as a concrete social relation, not just an abstract notion. It is, at its core, an economic relationship, one that entitles individuals to claim the benefits derived from owning production factors. In his analysis of land ownership, Marx emphasized that "If we consider the cases in a country with capitalist production, where the investment of capital in the land can take place without payment of rent, we shall find that they are all based on a de facto abolition of landed property, if not also the legal abolition; this, however, can only take place under very specific circumstances which are by their very nature accidental."[37] By investigating land as a specific form of property, Marx illustrated the interplay between the generation of value and its redistribution. This examination helped clarify what ownership fundamentally entails, that is, "According to this theory then, the private ownership of objects of nature such as the land, water, mines, etc., the ownership of these conditions of production, this essential ingredient of production emanating from nature, is not a source from which flows value, since value is only materialized labor. Neither is it the source from which excess surplus-value flows ... This ownership is, however, a source of revenue."[38]

While control over economic resources is a key prerequisite for engaging in the distribution of returns, it is not the sole criterion for owners of production factors to take part in this distribution. While ownership grants individuals the right to participate in income distribution, this is widely accepted by society not merely because of the ownership itself, but because the production factors they own play a critical role in the generation of social wealth. Even if a production factor, in itself, does not directly create any "atom" of value, it still contributes to the overall creation of social wealth. In Marxian analysis, the theory of labor-derived value differentiates between the formation of value and the accumulation of material wealth. The act of producing value does not, by itself, equate to the generation of overall societal wealth, which encompasses both utility and exchange value. By drawing a clear line between these two processes, Marx aimed to expose the underlying mechanism of surplus extraction, emphasizing the structural features of value production. Therefore, "when applying the Labor Theory of Value, we

---

[36] Karl Marx, Friedrich Engels. *Collected Works of Marx and Engels: Volume 7*. Beijing: People's Publishing House, 2009, p. 934.

[37] Ibid., p. 849.

[38] Karl Marx. *Theory of Surplus Value: Book 2*. Beijing: People's Publishing House, p. 36.

should not replace the actual wealth creation process with that of value creation, which is abstracted from the former."[39] In *Critique of the Gotha Programme*, Marx and Engels examined the theory put forward in the draft program of the United Workers' Party of Germany—"Labor is the source of all wealth and all culture," pointing out that: "Labor is not the source of all wealth. Nature is just as much the source of use values (and it is surely of such that material wealth consists!) as labor, which itself is only the manifestation of a force of nature, human labor power. The above phrase ...is correct insofar as it is implied that labor is performed with the appurtenant subjects and instruments. But a socialist program cannot allow such bourgeois phrases to pass over in silence the conditions that lone give them meaning."[40]

The above analysis reveals that even though non-labor factors of production, including capital, land, technology, management, etc., do not contribute to creating value, they are factors for wealth creation. Marx elaborated on their functions in the wealth creation process. When discussing elements like land and mineral wealth, Marx saw that: "The bodies of commodities are combinations of two elements— matter and labor ... Man can work only as nature does, that is by changing the form of matter. Nay more, in this work of changing the form he is constantly helped by natural forces. We see, then, that labor is not the only source of material wealth, of use-values produced by labor. As William Petty puts it, labor is its father and the earth its mother."[41] He then illustrated this point with an example, stating that "With richer mines, the same quantity of labor would embody itself in more diamonds."[42] Thus, capital is a crucial factor of production, and we should pay special attention to its function in creating wealth and forming value. According to Marx, the primary function of capital is to bring together various factors of production, such as labor and land, etc., into the production process.[43] "By incorporating with itself the two primary creators of wealth, labor-power and land, capital acquires a power of expansion."[44] Furthermore, the utilization of technological advancements in production depends on the coordinating role

---

39 Yinxing Hong. Advanced Social Productivity and Scientific Labor Theory of Value. *Academic Monthly*, 2001(10).

40 Karl Marx and Frederick Engels. *Marx & Engels Collected Works, Volume 3*. Beijing: People's Publishing House, 2009, p. 428.

41 Karl Marx and Frederick Engels. *Marx & Engels Collected Works, Volume 5*. Beijing: People's Publishing House, 2009, pp. 56–57.

42 Ibid., p. 53.

43 Ibid., p. 53.

44 Karl Marx and Frederick Engels. *Marx & Engels Collected Works, Volume 5*. Beijing: People's Publishing House, 2009, p. 697.

played by capital. Without capital, it would be impossible to transform scientific advancements into actual productive forces; even the most advanced technologies would remain nothing more than abstract concepts.

Capital not only takes part in creating wealth but also influences value creation. The parts "v+m" in the value equation "c+v+m" denote the extra value generated by labor, and "c" refers to the transferred value from "things" or "capital," and "in creating wealth, such value is not involved passively, but rather playing an active role." Specifically, as the quality of capital improves, more advanced machinery and equipment will be used, leading to increased production. As a result, the amount of value is likely to be influenced.[45] As Marx pointed out, "An immense difference exists between the value of the weekly product of the Englishman, who works with a mighty automatic machine, and that of a Chinese, who only has a spinning-wheel."[46] "In addition, labor is not homogeneous, and it is also incorporated in the process of value creation by capital. By hiring live labor with higher quality, the capital can create higher value."[47]

At the 16th CPC National Congress, it was pointed out that "we should establish the principle that labor, capital, technology, managerial expertise and other production factors participate in the distribution of income in accordance with their respective contributions," and the 17th CPC National Congress reiterated that "we will improve the distribution system to allow factors of production such as labor, capital, technology and managerial expertise to have a rightful share according to their respective contribution." Both mentioned the "contributions" of production factors. The academic circles have had a heated debate on how to interpret "contributions of production factors." Based on the analysis above, this concept does not claim that resources generate value independently. Instead, it points to their contribution to creating wealth and shaping value. Therefore, it does not conflict with Marx's view that labor is the source of value.

In actual economic settings, capital and other inputs influence the allocation of new value through spontaneous market forces. The distribution is initially shaped by those who own these inputs, guided by the principles of market value, competition, and the interaction of supply with demand. In *Capital*, Marx explained this process scientifically with the theory of equalization of the rate of profit, that is, with the underlying rule of "capitals of equal magnitude yield equal profits,"

---

45 Yinxing Hong. Advanced Social Productive Forces and Scientific Labor Theory of Value. *Academic Monthly*, 2001(10).

46 Karl Marx and Frederick Engels. *Marx & Engels Collected Works, Volume 5*. Beijing: People's Publishing House, 2009, p. 699.

47 Ibid., p. 699.

production factors constantly flow among various products, departments, and regions, and as a result change their supply and demand as well as prices, and such changes in turn affect their profitability. This process continues until the profits yielded by an equal amount of production factors become equal in magnitude. Therefore, the profits earned by companies already reflect the outcome of the distribution of newly created value, in which production factors like capital play a role. Therefore, payments made by businesses to resource owners reflect the way value is distributed under market conditions.

With the implementation of the primary socialist framework for income allocation, discussions surrounding the rationale of distributing income via production inputs have intensified. Some experts analyzing its consistency with the Labor Theory of Value have proposed extensions of the theory to underpin this model. For instance, some scholars propose that the notion in the traditional Labor Theory of Value that "materialized labor only transfers value instead of creating value" should be modified, and only by affirming the role of both accumulated and active labor in the value creation process can the system of allocating income by production inputs be supported theoretically.[48] For some others, though they still use the term "Labor Theory of Value," they emphasize the contribution of "capital" to creating value. Wei Xinghua indicates that the denial of the Labor Theory of Value is, in fact confusion of concepts of "wealth" (use-value) and "value." "Wealth" consists of labor and other factors of production, while value only stems from labor. The theoretical foundation for distribution based on factors of production rests on the idea that these factors contribute to the creation of social wealth, rather than directly to value creation.[49] Some scholars study the relations between the distribution according to factors of production and exploitation. While some argue that the income derived from distribution based on factors of production represents exploitation, the majority contend that there is no direct connection between those two. Hu Peizhao argues that the rationality behind non-labor factors' participation in value distribution lies in their essential role in assisting value creation. Therefore, as long as their income is proportional to their contributions to production, it should not be seen as exploitation. Yang Jirui suggests that the duality of capital income must be clarified, which refers to distinguishing the income from exploitation and that from production factors. The former, a sign of an exploitative relation, is

48 Bohai Qian. Theoretical Discussion on Deepening Understanding of Labor Value. *Fujian Tribune*, 2001 (9).

49 Xinghua Wei. Do Not Misunderstand and Mislead the Spirit of the 16th National Congress of the CPC—A Discussion with Professor Yan Zhijie. *Theory Front*, 2003 (13).

associated with capitalism, whereas the latter only embodies the relations of distribution of factors, and it is in line with the market economy system. In the socialist market economy, the capital income is from production factors instead of exploitation.[50] Researchers have likewise explored how labor-based allocation relates to factor-based distribution. One viewpoint holds that, because labor itself functions as an input in a market economy, paying people according to their work is essentially a subset of allocating returns by productive factors. Wei Xinghua, however, asserts that workers play distinct roles in each distribution model. In the distribution based on production factors, workers participate solely as a production factor, while in the distribution based on labor, they take a leading role. In socialism, the primacy of workers should be emphasized, so it is inappropriate to categorize labor-derived remuneration within the overarching framework of returns to productive factors.[51]

As a continuation and expansion of Marxist ideas on how income is shared, the basic socialist distribution model supports the incentive framework in a market economy.

Firstly, the principle reinforces labor's leading role in income allocation, which is consistent with the essence of socialism and its commitment to distributive fairness. Marx envisioned a society where labor alone determined individual earnings. Although this standard has not yet been fully implemented, labor should continue to serve as the dominant benchmark. Adhering to this principle means staying faithful to the core ideas of classical theorists regarding individual distribution in the future.

Secondly, it acknowledges the existence of multiple forms of distribution, particularly emphasizing the recognition and encouragement of labor, capital, land, technology, management, and other production factors participating in distribution. The introduction of distribution based on production factors marks a significant breakthrough in adapting and modernizing the Marxist Political Economy theory of income distribution to Chinese realities and contemporary times. Traditional theories of individual income distribution overlook other types of labor income, and even more so, non-labor incomes derived from production factors. Such a restricted viewpoint contradicts the actual growth of productive capabilities in the initial stage of socialism and the core tenets of the socialist market system. By embracing distribution mechanisms that include production

---

50 Jirui Yang. Reanalysis of Capital-Income Property. *Journal of Sichuan University (Philosophy and Social Sciences Edition)*, 2008 (1).

51 Xinghua Wei. The Structure and Theoretical Conception of the Revised Edition of *Marxist Principles of Political Economy. Teaching and Research*, 2003 (7).

factors and non-labor earnings, a broader range of income-generating opportunities has been established, facilitating greater wealth accumulation.

Thirdly, it has introduced an incentive structure that is closely attuned to the principles of the socialist market economy, with personal interest functioning as the primary catalyst for economic actions. A sound system of income distribution must enable individuals' reasonable needs to be addressed, transforming these into a continuous force for both economic growth and social progress. The benefit framework established by the fundamental socialist distribution system aligns closely with the intrinsic incentive mechanisms of the socialist market economy. On one side, the principle of "distribution primarily based on work" motivates millions of workers to dedicate effort and build labor capital, fostering diligence and wealth creation. Conversely, allowing and promoting the allocation of resources based on production inputs stimulates individuals' desire to build wealth, enhances the efficiency of resource distribution, fosters the growth of social capital, boosts the flexibility of production elements, and provides the incentives needed at the ground level for the market to allocate resources effectively. In short, the basic socialist distribution system can "unleash all the vitality contained in work, knowledge, technology, management and capital, and give full play to all sources of social wealth."

3. Latest Developments of the Theory of Income Distribution in China in the New Era

Since the 18th CPC National Congress, under Xi Jinping's leadership, China has entered a new era characterized by sweeping reforms and accelerated economic progress. The 19th CPC National Congress report underscored the importance of strengthening both the socialist economic framework and the distribution system, positioning them as equally critical. During this period, significant strides have been made in the theory and practice of income distribution, resulting in notable advancements in the country's foundational allocation mechanisms.

(1) The focus on people in development: the central approach driving income distribution reforms and their execution in this phase of change

At the heart of China's reform and growth lies the people-centered approach, which propels the development of income distribution theory and its practical application in this transformative phase. On November 15, 2012, after being elected General Secretary of the Communist Party, Xi Jinping made a profound statement, "Our people love life. They want to have better education, more stable jobs, higher income, more reliable social security, higher-level medical and health services, more comfortable accommodation, and more beautiful environment, and they hope their children grow up better, work better and live better. The people's yearning for a better life is our goal." At the Fifth Plenary Session of the 18th CPC Central Committee in 2015, the "people-centered" approach was formally introduced, with "sharing" designated as one of the five key development principles. During the collective study session of the Political Bureau of the 18th CPC Central Committee on November 23, 2015, Xi Jinping pointed out, "We must adhere to the people-centered philosophy of development. To develop for the people is the fundamental position of Marxist Political Economy." At the 19th CPC National Congress, General Secretary Xi Jinping placed renewed emphasis on the people-centered approach to development.

The adoption of the people-oriented development philosophy has led to the emergence of two unique aspects in the income distribution framework for the current era. First, it pays greater attention to equity and justice, and emphasizes that we should distribute the "cake" properly while making it bigger. General Secretary Xi Jinping pointed out that "The growing 'cake' should be divided properly so that the advantages of the socialist system can be fully demonstrated and the people can have a greater sense of fulfillment." Second, it puts more emphasis on common prosperity. We will reform the system of income allocation through various policy interventions, strengthen the redistribution mechanism primarily through taxes, social benefits, and direct payments, and tackle disparities in earnings, ensuring that the fruits of development are more equitably distributed among the population.

(2) Strengthening the primary role of labor-based allocation, while prioritizing the increase in the share of compensation for work and the income of workers

At the outset of economic restructuring, income from labor, particularly derived from work-based distribution, was the major component of residents' earnings, which clearly highlighted the dominance of labor-based allocation. As multiple forms of income distribution emerged, including those linked to production factors, the contribution of labor income to overall earnings diminished, while the share of non-labor income, such as returns from production factors, increased. This transformation altered the national income distribution structure. The portion of labor compensation in primary income distribution dropped, and residents' income relative to total national income also declined. Data shows that labor compensation comprised 49.4% of GDP in 1992, fell to 42.14% in 2004, and rose slightly to 44.93% in 2011. Similarly, as labor's share of GDP shrank, the proportion of residents' income in GDP decreased from around 65% in 1992 to 41.6% in 2012. This reduction in both ratios weakened the dominance of labor-based income allocation. The report of the 18th CPC National Congress pointedly proposed the ideas of "two synchronizations" and "two improvements," that is, "increase individual income in step with economic development and work remuneration in step with improvement in labor productivity, and we should raise the share of individual income in the distribution of national income and increase the share of work remuneration in primary distribution"[52]. In 2013, the State Council formally endorsed the "Several Opinions on Deepening the Reform of the Income Distribution System," which detailed actions to increase the proportion of compensation for labor. These measures included implementing an employment priority strategy and more proactive employment policies, encouraging job creation and entrepreneurship, fostering an equal employment environment, enhancing workers' income-earning capacity, and promoting higher-quality employment. Additionally, the restructuring of the pay system was to be intensified, improving the mechanism for wage determination and growth within enterprises, public institutions, and government-affiliated organizations. The Third Plenary Session of the 18th CPC Central Committee also emphasized the circle importance of increasing labor remuneration: "We will place emphasis on protecting labor income, strive to synchronize the increase of remuneration for labor with the growth of labor productivity, and raise the proportion of labor remuneration in primary distribution."[53] The report of the 19th CPC National Congress reiterated that the "two proportions" should be increased.[54]

From 2011 to 2016, significant progress was made in the "two synchronizations" and "two improvements." Initial calculations reveal that labor compensation's contribution to local GDP grew from 44.9% in 2011 to 47.9% in 2015, representing a 3 percentage point rise with an average yearly increase of 0.75 percentage points (see Table 1).[55] From 2012 to 2016, the percentage of Chinese residents' income in GDP grew from 41.6% to 45.6%, a rise of 4 percentage points and an

52 The Party Literature Research Center of the CPC Central Committee. *Selections of Important Documents since the 18th National Congress of the CPC: Part I*. Beijing: People's Publishing House, 2014, p. 28.

53 *Decision of the Central Committee of the Communist Party of China on Some Major Issues Concerning Comprehensively Deepening the Reform*. (2013-11-12)

54 Jinping Xie. *Secure a Decisive Victory in Building a Moderately Prosperous Society in All Respects and Strive for the Great Success of Socialism with Chinese Characteristics for a New Era*. (2017-10-18)

55 Ying Hu, Lixiao Zheng. New Experience and Achievements of China's Income Distribution System Reform since the 18th National Congress of the CPC. *Studies on Marxism*, 2018 (2).

average annual increase of 1 percentage point (see Table 2). Both compensation for work and household income saw steady growth. In parallel, GDP and per capita income for both urban and rural residents expanded rapidly, with productivity gains aligning with rising compensation.

Table 1: Proportion of Labor Remuneration in Local GDP in China from 2011 to 2015

Year	Total Local GDP (100 million yuan)	Labor Remuneration (100 million yuan)	Proportion of Labor Remuneration in Local GDP (%)
2011	521 441.1	234 310.3	44.9
2012	576 551.8	262 864.1	45.6
2013	634 345.3	290 943.5	45.9
2014	684 349. 4	318 258.1	46.5
2015	722 767.9	346 159. 5	47.9

Source: Ying Hu, Lixiao Zheng. New Experience and Achievements of China's Income Distribution System Reform since the 18th National Congress of the CPC. Studies on Marxism, 2018 (2).

Table 2: Proportion of Chinese Residents' Income in GDP from 2012 to 2016

Year	Total Income of Urban and Rural Residents (100 million yuan)	GDP (100 million yuan)	Proportion of Residents' Income in GDP (%)
2012	225 061	540 367	41.6
2013	253 081	595 244	42.5
2014	281 339	643 974	43.7
2015	310 156	689 052	45.0
2016	339 476	744 127	45.6

Source: Ying Hu, Lixiao Zheng. New Experience and Achievements of China's Income Distribution System Reform since the 18th National Congress of the CPC. Studies on Marxism, 2018 (2).

(3) Enhancing the allocation based on production elements and boosting residents' asset-based earnings through various means

After the concept of "distribution according to factors of production" was presented at the 15th CPC Congress, income derived from production factors has played an increasingly significant role. Although strides have been made, significant obstacles remain in the advancement of China's market economy. In response, the 18th CPC National Congress proposed "we should improve the primary distribution system to allow factors of production such as labor, capital, technology and managerial expertise to have their due share of income according to their respective contribution"; the Third Plenary Session of the 18th CPC Central Committee proposed "to improve the system in which the returns for capital, knowledge, technology, managerial expertise and other production factors are determined by the market"; the 19th CPC National Congress proposed "to improve our institutions and mechanisms for distribution based on factors of production." The core of improving distribution based on production factors lies in building a well-functioning factor market. In such a market, production factors can flow freely, and their prices will precisely mirror both their role in generating social wealth and their relative availability. It is only within this framework that an equitable and efficient income distribution system can be realized, blending the allocation based on production factors with the prevailing system of income distribution according to labor.

With the introduction of distribution according to factors of production, people's property income has increased. Property income has a self-cumulating effect, which often quickly widens the income gap among members of society. In order to increase the income level of residents, and meanwhile alleviate the effect of property income widening the income gap, it is necessary to allow more people to obtain more property and get more property income. Both the report of the 18th CPC National Congress and the "Decision" of the Third Plenary Session of the 18th CPC Central Committee put forward "we should increase proprietary individual income through multiple channels." The 19th CPC National Congress proposed to "expand the channels for people to make work-based earnings and property income." The "Several Opinions on Deepening the Reform of the Income Distribution System" explicitly called for expanding channels for increasing residents' property income. The primary actions involve enhancing the development of a tiered capital market, creating a system for dividend distribution by listed firms, and safeguarding the rights of investors, particularly those from smaller enterprises. It further promotes the liberalization of interest rates, allowing a moderate expansion in the fluctuation of both deposit and loan rates to protect the interests of depositors, while also broadening the range of financial products, such as bond and money market funds. Further measures include supporting qualified enterprises in launching employee stock ownership plans, broadening residents' income sources, such as rents, dividends, and bonuses, and enhancing intellectual property protection. The policy emphasizes the refinement of income distribution systems linked to the commercialization of technological innovations and the exploration of various models, such as equity incentives and position-based dividends, to ensure fair rewards for innovation. Furthermore, the Third Plenary Session of the 18th CPC Central Committee's

"Decision" underlined the expansion of farmers' property rights. It proposed ensuring their rights within collective economic organizations, promoting rural joint-stock partnerships, and empowering rural residents to possess, gain returns from, transfer for compensation, mortgage, pledge, and inherit their shares in collective assets. The policy also aimed to protect the rights of rural households to utilize homesteads, reformed the homestead system, and encouraged the gradual promotion of the use as collateral, security provision, and compensated transfer of rural residential property rights. The establishment of a rural property rights transfer market was envisioned to facilitate fair, transparent, and regulated transactions. The "separation of three rights" system for rural land, introduced at the 19th CPC National Congress, provided the institutional basis for farmers to profit from the transfer of land management rights.

In summary, laborers are encouraged to gain not only higher labor income but also increased income from production factors. As additional elements of production contribute to the income distribution process, the proportion of labor compensation within overall earnings may reduce; however, this does not indicate a decrease in workers' total income. On the contrary, as laborers acquire and utilize more production factors, their total income is expected to grow accordingly.

(4) Cultivating and Strengthening Focus: The middle strata of earners

In October 2010, the concept of "middle-income group" was put forward in "Recommendations of the CPC Central Committee on Formulating the 12th Five Year Plan for National Economic and Social Development." The "Decision" of the Third Plenary Session of the 18th CPC Central Committee explicitly highlighted the importance of increasing the incomes of low-income populations, growing the size of the middle class, and reducing income gaps across urban and rural areas, regions, and industries. The aim is to gradually form an income distribution structure resembling an olive shape. The Fifth Plenary Session of the 18th CPC Central Committee further identified "expanding the middle-income group" as a crucial factor in realizing the full establishment of a moderately well-off society. This objective was also incorporated into "The Outline of the 13th Five Year Plan for National Economic and Social Development." Following the establishment of a moderately prosperous society, the 19th CPC National Congress report set a broader vision for the period from 2020 to 2035, aiming to increase the share of the middle class and lay the groundwork for the full realization of socialist modernization.

The middle-income group is characterized by distinct economic traits. Members of this group typically enjoy a relatively stable and sufficient income, enabling discretionary spending on durable goods, quality education, healthcare, accommodation, vacations, and other leisure pastimes. As China has now become a middle-income nation, the growth of this demographic is crucial for the country's sustained economic and social progress. Drawing on international experience, "a prosperous middle class is a necessary condition to promote consumer demand, maintain economic growth and get rid of the middle-income trap."[56] A major factor contributing to the failure of certain middle-income countries to escape the middle-income trap is their challenge in developing and growing a sustainable middle-income population. Because "without such groups, it is difficult to create the huge market, investment in education, institutionalized savings and social mobilization needed to support growth."[57] For example, in 1986, South Korea's income per capita was similar to Brazil's in 1979. Yet, South Korea managed to break free from the middle-income trap, whereas Brazil did not. A key factor in South Korea's success was the development of a sizable middle class, which made up about 55% of its population, roughly double the proportion of Brazil's at the time.

Since the 18th CPC National Congress, China has witnessed a significant expansion of its middle-income population. During the China-US Entrepreneurs Investment Forum in Seattle in 2015, General Secretary Xi Jinping highlighted that the number of middle-income individuals in China had reached approximately 300 million, with projections to double in the next decade. Some studies suggest that the share of middle-income earners in China's total population grew from 38.1% in 2012 to 47.6% in 2014. However, when compared to high-income nations, China's middle-income group remains relatively small. For instance, the middle class in the United States comprises about 230 million people, making up roughly three-quarters of the total population. In countries such as South Korea, Japan, and those within the EU, middle-income groups account for over 90% of the total population.[58] In comparison, China's middle-income groups still have significant potential for expansion. In the new era, it is crucial to speed up the expansion of these groups and aim to create an income distribution model that resembles an olive shape at the earliest opportunity.

---

56 Edwin Lim, Michael Spence. *Medium and Long Term Development and Transformation of the Chinese Economy*. Beijing: CITIC Press, 2011, p. 40.

57 Ibid., p. 42.

58 Ibid., p. 42.

(5) Targeted Poverty Alleviation and Finishing Building a Moderately Prosperous Society

Since the onset of economic restructuring, China has experienced substantial economic growth, which has been instrumental in lifting a significant portion of its population out of poverty. The "Annual Report on Poverty Reduction of China (2016)," published by the Chinese Academy of Social Sciences and the Poverty Alleviation Office of the State Council, reveals that between 1981 and 2012, nearly 790 million people were lifted out of poverty in China, representing 71.82% of the global poverty reduction in that period. The report of the Congress in 2013 outlined the goal of completing the creation of a moderately prosperous society by 2020, with the eradication of poverty as a top priority. General Secretary Xi has consistently highlighted poverty elimination as a critical milestone in reaching this national objective. From 1988 to 1990, during his work in Ningde, Fujian Province, he systematically thought about how to get rid of poverty. In December 2012, during an inspection tour centered on poverty relief and development in Fuping County, Hebei Province, he proposed: "By 2020, we will steadily realize the goal of assuring the target poor population that their food and clothing needs will be met and guaranteeing that they have access to compulsory education, basic medical services and safe housing." On November 3, 2013, General Secretary Xi Jinping visited Shibadong Village in the Xiangxi Tujia and Miao Autonomous Prefecture of Hunan Province to conduct a field investigation on poverty alleviation and development efforts. On this occasion, he initially presented the concept of "Targeted Poverty Alleviation." Then, in November 2015, the Central Conference on Poverty Alleviation and Development took place in Beijing. General Secretary Xi highlighted: "We should achieve the target that rural poor people have no worry about food and clothing and have access to compulsory education, basic medical services, and safe housing by 2020. At the same time, the growth of per-capita disposable income of farmers in poor areas should be higher than that of the whole country on average, and the indicators in the main areas of basic public services should be close to the national average." To date, China's poverty alleviation and development initiatives have transitioned into a new phase, prioritizing precise and long-lasting solutions to poverty reduction.

In 2012, China had a poverty-stricken population of 98.99 million, which decreased to 70.17 million by 2014. A target was established to eradicate poverty among all rural residents currently below the poverty line by 2020, and regional poverty would be eradicated in a comprehensive manner. According to the poverty alleviation plan, from 2014 to 2020, 30 million people should be lifted out of poverty through industrial support; 10 million people were to be lifted out of poverty through employment transfer; 10 million people through relocation;

while the remaining 20 million individuals, who had either fully or partially lost their ability to work, were incorporated into the subsistence allowance system, with social security measures put in place to guarantee their basic living needs. Since the Congress in 2013, China has made substantial strides in poverty alleviation. Between 2012 and 2017, the poverty-stricken population fell by 68.53 million, averaging a reduction of 13.7 million annually. Over this period, the national poverty rate dropped from 10.2% to 3.1%. By 2017, 28 impoverished counties, such as Jinggang Mountains and Lankao County, successfully emerged from poverty, marking the first historical decrease in the total number of poor counties. Table 3 shows poverty reduction in 2012–2017.

Table 3: Poverty Reduction in 2012–2017

Year	Poverty-stricken* Population (million)	Poverty-eradicated Population (million)	Rate of Poverty (%)
2012	98.99	23.39	10.2
2013	82.49	16.50	8.5
2014	70.17	12.32	7.2
2015	55.75	14.42	5.7
2016	43.35	12.40	4.5
2017	30.46	12.89	3.1

Source: National Bureau of Statistics of the People's Republic of China. China Statistical Yearbook 2017. Beijing: China Statistics Press, 2017.

4. The Focus of the Reform of the Income Distribution System in the New Era

Following four decades of economic reform, the main challenge in our society has transformed into a conflict between the public's rising expectations for an improved life and the nation's uneven and insufficient progress. China's economic trajectory has moved from rapid expansion to one emphasizing high-quality growth. The priority now lies in fostering development that is not only quicker but also of superior quality, more effective, equitable, and long-lasting. In line with the strategic blueprint set forth at the 19th CPC National Congress, on the basis of building a moderately prosperous society in all respects by 2020, socialist modernization will be basically realized by 2035. By that time, people's lives will

* The current poverty standard in rural areas is below 2,300 yuan per person per year (constant price in 2010).

be more prosperous; the proportion of middle-income groups will be significantly increased; the development gap between urban and rural areas and the gap in living standards of residents will be significantly narrowed. By 2050, we aim to establish a prosperous, powerful, democratic, culturally advanced, harmonious, and beautiful modern socialist nation. At that point, common prosperity will have largely been achieved for all citizens, as people enjoy more rewarding and wholesome lifestyles. The lessons from 40 years of economic restructuring have shown that the foundational distribution system, centered on rewarding work while incorporating various other methods, has been crucial in boosting citizens' earnings and the buildup of national wealth. This approach must remain central in the new era. However, given the evolving nature of social contradictions, the current phase of economic development, and changes in key factors influencing income distribution, it is necessary to polish the socialist distribution system to better address public concerns and promote more inclusive progress.

I. Reducing disparities in income and striving for shared prosperity

"Common prosperity" represents both a defining characteristic and the ultimate objective of socialism, as well as one of its greatest institutional strengths. Marx once explicitly stated that in the new social system, "the development of social productive forces will be so rapid ... production will be aimed at the enrichment of all."[59] Deng Xiaoping regarded "universal prosperity" as a core attribute of socialism, noting that "the essence of socialism is liberation and development of the productive forces, elimination of exploitation and polarization, and the ultimate achievement of prosperity for all."[60] General Secretary Xi Jinping has consistently highlighted the importance of reducing income inequality and pushing forward shared prosperity, ensuring that development benefits are more fairly distributed among the population. In the four decades of economic reform, significant advancements have been made in the financial well-being and quality of life for Chinese citizens. Nevertheless, the growing disparity in wealth has become a central issue, fueling social and economic tensions. Within the current era, addressing income disparity and striving for common prosperity has become a central theme in both the theoretical exploration and practical advancement of income distribution policies.

---

[59] Karl Marx and Engels. *The Complete Works of Marx and Engels, Vol. 46, III*. Beijing: People's Publishing House, 1980, p. 221.

[60] Xiaoping Deng. *Selected Works of Deng Xiaoping, Vol. 3*. Beijing: People's Publishing House, 1993, p. 373.

(1) Recognizing the gap between affluence and poverty in China from a vertical and horizontal perspective

Following 40 years of rapid economic development, China has risen to the status of an upper-middle-income country and successfully achieved the strategic objective of "getting rich first," thereby establishing a strong material foundation for the pursuit of "shared prosperity." At the same time, the gap between the rich and the poor has rapidly widened in the process, reaching a high level. We can specifically grasp this issue from the vertical time series comparison and the horizontal international comparison.

Firstly, since the onset of economic reform, the income disparity among Chinese citizens has expanded rapidly. In the initial stage, the Gini coefficient of China's residents' income was basically maintained at a low level of around 0.3. After entering the 1990s, it experienced rapid growth and, for the first time in 1994, surpassed the warning threshold of 0.4. Afterward, although there was a brief fall, the overall trend was upward. In 2012, China's Gini coefficient was 0.474, then dropped slightly, and was still as high as 0.467 in 2017.

Secondly, wealth inequality is more severe than income inequality. The richer the group is, the stronger the ability it has to save and invest. Therefore, the wealth gap has a rapid accumulation effect, and the inequality of wealth is usually much greater than the inequality of income. According to the "Chinese Household Finance Survey Report," the average value of the total assets of Chinese urban households was 2.476 million yuan, and the median value was 405,000 yuan. This means that the wealth of urban households in China is severely skewed to the right, and social wealth is highly uneven. Drawing on the 2013 data from the Chinese Household Income Project (CHIP) and the 2016 data from the China Family Panel Studies (CFPS), certain scholars computed the Gini coefficients for the total net worth of Chinese households using survey data, obtaining figures of 0.619 and 0.736, respectively. If the missing property of the high-end population was added, the Gini coefficient of residents' property would reach 0.747 and 0.796, respectively.[61]

Thirdly, China has already ranked among the countries with large income gaps. In accordance with the figures of the "Human Development Report 2007/2008" of the United Nations, China's income inequality, as measured by the Gini coefficient, stood at 0.469, placing it 93rd out of 126 countries surveyed. This positions China among the nations with significant income disparities. It should be noted that, in contrast, many of China's neighboring countries have managed

61 Chuliang Luo. Missing high-end population and income (wealth) inequality. *Journal of Translation from Foreign Literature of Economics*, 2017 (4).

to maintain a relatively equitable income distribution during their economic development. In Japan and South Korea in particular, in the process of growing into developed economies, the income gap has been maintained at a low level, achieving both fairness and efficiency to some extent.

(2) Exploring the correlation between economic advancement and income differences from international experience

In 1955, Kuznets introduced the "inverted U-shaped" hypothesis, which argues that income inequality initially rises during early economic development, especially when shifting from an agricultural to an industrial economy. Over time, however, inequality tends to stabilize and eventually decrease as development advances. After more than half a century, we re-examine the relationship between the two based on the data released by the United Nations and the World Bank, and obtain the following empirical facts.

Firstly, economic growth in developing countries does not always coincide with a widening of the income gap. Although income disparities typically grow as a country progresses from the least developed to the middle-income stage, several developing nations have kept their income gaps relatively narrow while achieving fast-paced economic development. For example, the Gini coefficient of India, Vietnam, Indonesia, and other countries with rapid economic development recently is mostly maintained below the warning line of 0.4. Historically, Japan and South Korea also maintained a small income gap over an extended period in the era of creating the "East Asian Economic Miracle" until they entered the ranks of rich economies. In this sense, the miracles created by these economies are not limited to the long-term growth of GDP, but also to maintain a win-win situation that benefits the whole society.

Secondly, in order for developing countries to successfully enter the ranks of developed countries, they must achieve a steady reduction in the income gap. Data show that almost all the developed countries have relatively equal income distribution. Even excluding those countries that pursue welfare, only the US has a Gini coefficient slightly above the alert threshold of 0.4. It means that relatively equal income is an essential feature of developed countries. Conversely, there were many rich countries in history that had regressed to middle-income countries, which tended to have higher income disparities. For example, Argentina's per capita income ranked ninth in the world in 1936, but today, its per capita income has declined to a level comparable to that of lower-middle-income countries, with a Gini coefficient reaching as high as 0.51, indicating significant income inequality.

Thirdly, historical developments since World War II reveal that numerous once-promising nations have fallen into the "middle-income trap," largely due to persistent income inequality. Countries or regions such as the "Four Asian Tigers" and Israel are among the few cases in which developing economies have successfully moved into developed economies since World War II. For the vast majority of developing countries or regions, poverty has become an almost persistent condition. Especially in the past 20 years or so, almost no developing economies have shown the trend of entering developed economies. Nearly every developing nation that has remained in the upper-middle-income range for prolonged periods faces a major obstacle in the form of persistent income inequality. In these nations, the widening chasm between the rich and those in need has gradually become a chronic issue, deeply embedded and resistant to resolution despite repeated efforts.

Based on the above empirical facts, China needs to work hard to narrow the income gap to avoid falling into the "middle-income trap" due to the excessive income gap.

(3) Excessive income gap: damaging the foundation of economic and social development

An overly wide income gap stands as a striking characteristic of nations caught in the "middle-income trap." Excessive income disparity will bring negative impacts on the economy and society in all aspects, and some potential impacts have already begun to appear in our country.

First, a significant gap in income is likely to cause social unrest and deterioration of public safety, increasing by extension the costs associated with securing property entitlements and social "stability maintenance." The United Nations' "Survey on Crime Trends and the Operation of the Criminal Justice System" shows that the homicide rate is significantly related to income inequality. Under conditions of similar prosperity, the homicide rate in the United States, which has higher income inequality, is more than four times higher than that in the United Kingdom and 12 times higher than that in Japan. Research indicates that in China, a 1% rise in income inequality corresponds to a notable increase of 0.37% in the crime rate.

Secondly, a widening income gap restricts social mobility, perpetuates inequality across generations, limits individual opportunities for free development, and undermines the principles of social fairness and justice. Social resources are mainly composed of economic resources, organizational resources, and cultural resources. The income, power, and prestige corresponding to these three resources are often in the hands of minority groups. Using these resources and networks, groups with social advantages can use various ways and means to achieve inter-generational transmission of dominant status. To date, China has not yet developed a stable olive-shaped social structure. The middle class as a whole is still relatively limited in scale, and signs of class rigidity are emerging, characterized by reduced opportunities for upward social mobility and a slower pace of social structural adjustment.

Thirdly, the excessive income gap has fostered an impetuous mentality and radical sentiment in modern society, creating numerous underlying risks for the continued progress of China's economy and society. A UNICEF report on child well-being shows the relationship between income inequality and the ideals of 15-year-olds: The more unequal the income is, the less willing children are to work in low-skilled jobs when they grow up. However, in societies marked by significant income disparities, there is frequently a wide divide between aspirations and the opportunities actually available. On the one hand, people generally have the mentality of "getting rich," but they lack the down-to-earth, hard-working spirit and corresponding outstanding skills. On the other hand, in a society that blindly pursues wealth, people are more focused on how to quickly realize their own demands, and less consideration is given to the corresponding social responsibilities and moral obligations.

Fourthly, the social instability caused by the large income gap makes the wealthy lack a sense of security, so they are keen to invest in immigration which weakens the wealth foundation for national development. This problem has been exposed in our country. The "2011 China Private Wealth Report" released by China Merchants Bank showed that multimillionaires had a strong willingness to invest in immigration. Of the billionaires surveyed, roughly 27% had finalized investment immigration, while 47% were contemplating it, together making up 74%. Data released by the USCIS in June 2012 showed that 70% of those who obtained U.S. investment immigration status in 2011 were Chinese nationals. As the primary beneficiaries of economic reform, the wealthy's wealth transfer activities will erode the financial foundation underpinning China's future economic growth.

(4) Narrowing the income gap and making steady progress toward common prosperity

Throughout the 40 years of economic progress, China has achieved fast economic expansion and established a fairly solid material base. Meanwhile, public aspirations for common prosperity have continued to intensify. The country now stands at a historical juncture, shifting its focus from the principle of "getting rich first" to the pursuit of "common prosperity." In his later years, Deng Xiaoping proposed the arrival of a historical turning point from "getting rich first" to "common prosperity." He said, "When China develops to a certain level, it must consider the issue of distribution." "How to distribute wealth after it becomes rich is a big problem. The problem has already come out, and it is more difficult to solve this problem than to solve the problem of development." "We talk about preventing polarization, but in fact polarization occurs naturally."[62] "A small number of people have obtained so much wealth, but most people do not. If things continue to develop like this, there will be problems one day. Unfair distribution will lead to polarization, and problems will arise at a certain time. This problem must be solved."[63] "When the economy has developed to a certain extent, we must achieve common prosperity."[64] General Secretary Xi has clearly articulated "The 'cake' of China's economic development continues to grow, but the problem of unfair distribution is relatively prominent. The income gap, and the gap between urban and rural areas of public services are relatively large ... To make steady progress towards common prosperity for all the people, there must be no phenomenon of 'the rich accumulate millions, and the poor eat the crumbs.'"[65]

In order to narrow the gap in earnings and make progress toward shared prosperity, it is necessary to maintain and refine the basic socialist distribution system rather than reject it or revert to outdated egalitarian practices and a single-income model. First, the principle of work-based distribution must hold a central position. This entails adopting a variety of policy measures to enhance the share of labor compensation in initial distribution and increase the ratio of household income to GDP, ensuring that wage growth keeps pace with improvements in labor productivity. Second, the system of factor-based distribution must be further developed. This requires improving factor markets, enhancing factor mobility, and ensuring that prices and returns more accurately reflect each factor's contribution. On this basis, channels for earning property income should be expanded so that more people can share in the benefits of asset appreciation, thereby making property income a significant driver of household income growth and a key pillar of common prosperity. Third, the effectiveness of income redistribution mechanisms must be enhanced. This includes augmenting the earnings of low-income individuals through social security, curbing excessive incomes through taxation, and eliminating illicit incomes through legal and regulatory means.

---

62 The Literature Research Office of the Central Committee of the Communist Party of China. *Chronicle of Deng Xiaoping (1975–1997), vol. iii*. Beijing: Central Party Literature Press, 2004, p. 1357.

63 Ibid., p. 1364.

64 Ibid., p. 1312.

65 Jinping Xi. Speech at the Second Plenary Session of the Fifth Plenary Session of the 18th Central Committee of the Communist Party of China. *Qiushi*, 2016 (1).

II. Properly handling the correlation between equity and efficiency

Throughout the economic shift, our understanding of the relationship between fairness and efficiency has continuously evolved alongside practical experience. In examining this relationship, it is crucial to first identify the historical origin. At the outset of reform, China faced severe economic inefficiency, low labor motivation, entrenched egalitarianism, widespread poverty, and a near-collapse of productive forces. The urgent task at that time was to prioritize the progress of social productivity, enhance economic efficiency, and lift the population out of poverty. Fairness, as a social right, must be contextualized within the prevailing stage of economic and cultural development. As Marx observed, "Rights must never go beyond the economic structure of society and the cultural development of society constrained by it."[66] This insight provides critical theoretical guidance for understanding the dynamic and historically conditioned relationship between fairness and efficiency.

In the initial phase of economic restructuring, overcoming egalitarianism and motivating productivity required an explicit theoretical and practical emphasis on "efficiency." The prioritization of efficiency gradually took hold and gained broad social acceptance. At that time, the principle of socialist material incentives was affirmed, along with the notion that some individuals could become prosperous through hard work and initiative. The 13th CPC National Congress in 1987 proposed the idea of "realizing social justice on the premise of promoting efficiency,"[67] acknowledging efficiency as the precondition for achieving social justice, though without clarifying their priority relationship. The 14th CPC National Congress was the first to articulate the need to "balance efficiency and fairness." Afterwards, in 1993, the Third Plenary Session of the 14th CPC Central Committee adopted the "Decision of the Central Committee of the Communist Party of China on Several Issues Concerning Building a Socialist Market Economy," which formally introduced the principle of "giving priority to efficiency with due consideration to fairness" and concurrently proposed "pursuing the path of common prosperity." This principle was reaffirmed at the 15th CPC National Congress. In 2002, the 16th CPC National Congress introduced nuanced adjustments to the expression of the fairness-efficiency relationship, reflecting a maturing understanding of the two principles within China's evolving economic setup. In addition to reiterating

---

66 Marx & Engels. *Collected Works of Marx and Engels, Vol. 3*. Beijing: People's Publishing House, 2009, p. 435.

67 The Literature Research Office of the Central Committee of the Communist Party of China. *Selection of Key Documents since the 13th National Congress of the Communist Party of China, Vol. I*. Beijing: Central Party Literature Press, 2011, p. 28.

the doctrine of "giving priority to efficiency with due consideration to fairness," it also made a specific statement on how to deal with interplay between the two: "In primary distribution, we should pay more attention to efficiency, bringing the market forces into play and encouraging part of the people to become rich first through honest labor and lawful operations. In redistribution, we should pay more attention to fairness and strengthen the function of the government in regulating income distribution to narrow the gap if it is too wide."[68] Since the 16th CPC National Congress, as income disparities have continued to widen, Party and government decisions and policy texts have given increasing prominence to the importance of fairness and the pursuit of common prosperity. Notably, beginning with the Fourth Plenary Session of the 16th CPC Central Committee in 2004, the phrase "giving priority to efficiency with due consideration to fairness" has no longer appeared in official discourse, marking a significant shift in the policy emphasis. The 17th CPC National Congress changed the original "primary distribution pays attention to efficiency, and redistribution pays attention to fairness" to "a proper balance will be struck between efficiency and equity in both primary distribution and redistribution, with particular emphasis on equity in redistribution."[69] This change signifies a wider perspective on balancing fairness and efficiency throughout the entire production and distribution process.

Since the 18th CPC National Congress, under the leadership of Comrade Xi, the CPC Central Committee has actively pursued extensive reforms in the economic system and development strategies. The introduction and implementation of the people-centered development philosophy has led to fresh perspectives on the balance between fairness and efficiency, with a growing focus on fairness. The 18th CPC National Congress clearly stated: "A proper balance should be struck between efficiency and fairness in both primary and secondary distribution, with particular emphasis on fairness in secondary distribution."[70] This formulation transcends the earlier notion that confined fairness mainly to redistribution, expanding the understanding of "fairness" to its core essence, centered on "equal rights, equal opportunities and equal rules" as fundamental components of social

68 The Literature Research Office of the Central Committee of the Communist Party of China. *Selection of Key Documents since the 16th National Congress of the Communist Party of China, Vol. I*. Beijing: Central Party Literature Press, 2005, p. 21.

69 The Literature Research Office of the Central Committee of the Communist Party of China. *Selection of Key Documents since the Seventeenth National Congress of the Communist Party of China, Vol. I*. Beijing: Central Party Literature Press, 2009, p. 30.

70 The Literature Research Office of the Central Committee of the Communist Party of China. *Selection of Key Documents since the 18th National Congress of the Communist Party of China, Vol. I*. Beijing: Central Party Literature Press, 2014, p. 28.

justice. This idea not only reflects the core principles of socialism but also aligns with the fundamental laws of a modern market economy, creating a strong basis for achieving a balanced approach between fairness and efficiency. In 2013, the "Decision" outlined the importance of further reforming social and income distribution systems. Key priorities included improving the well-being of the population, promoting fairness, achieving shared prosperity, and guaranteeing equal access to fundamental public services.[71] The "Recommendations for the 13th Five-Year Plan for Economic and Social Development" proposed to "adjust the distribution pattern of national income, standardize the primary distribution, and increase the adjustment of redistribution." As for the oversight of the distribution sequence, the proposal was to "protect legitimate income, regulate hidden income, curb the use of power, administrative monopoly and other non-market factors to obtain income, and outlaw illegal income."[72] During the 19th CPC National Congress report, General Secretary Xi underscored: "The well-being of the people is the fundamental goal of development … Use development to strengthen areas of weakness and promote social fairness and justice … To ensure that all our people have a greater sense of fulfillment as they contribute to and gain from development, and continue to promote well-rounded human development and common prosperity for everyone."[73]

In light of the changing historical backdrop, it is vital to refine both the theory and the system of income distribution, with an emphasis on achieving a balanced relationship between social equity and economic effectiveness. From the perspective of the whole process of fairness realization, it includes starting point fairness, process fairness, and result fairness, which follow one another and affect each other. In a modern market economy, if both the starting point and the process are fair, then the outcome of competition can generally be regarded as consistent with the principle of fairness, leading to broad social recognition and acceptance. As Bu Chanan observed, "if a general fairness of the distribution of initial endowments and abilities can be guaranteed, in this sense of actual expectations and normative preferences, I am relatively comfortable with the distributional

---

71 Communist Party of China Central Committee. *Decision of the Central Committee of the Communist Party of China on Several Major Issues Concerning Comprehensively Deepening the Reform*. Nov. 12, 2013.

72 The Literature Research Office of the Central Committee of the Communist Party of China. *Selection of Key Documents since the 18th National Congress of the Communist Party of China, Vol. II*. Beijing: Central Party Literature Press, 2016, pp. 814–815.

73 Jinping Xi. Win a decisive victory in building a moderately prosperous society in an all-round way and win the great victory of socialism with Chinese characteristics in the new era. Oct. 18, 2017.

outcomes of the competitive market process."[74] Therefore, ensuring fairness at the starting point and throughout the process is fundamental to building a just society. Nevertheless, the resulting disparities in income and wealth generated by fair competition are an inherent driver of economic development. Fairness in outcomes must be considered from two perspectives: on the one hand, the fairness of the initial conditions and the process that produces those outcomes must be guaranteed, since outcomes arising from unfair beginnings or procedures will not gain societal acceptance; on the other hand, the income and wealth gaps brought about by such outcomes cannot be too disparate and polarized. In addition, the fairness of the outcome also has its own independent value. This is because: First, unfair outcomes will undermine the equality of subsequent starting points and processes. Second, a reasonably equitable distribution of earnings and assets is essential for the stable and smooth functioning of social reproduction. However, there are limits to how much the results of fair competition can be adjusted; such corrections must not weaken the driving forces behind economic development and the smooth functioning of the market. Therefore, in the pursuit of fairness, the primary focus should be on creating conditions and an environment that ensures fair competition, fully harnesses people's potential to generate wealth, makes appropriate adjustments to competition outcomes, and keeps income and wealth disparities within socially acceptable bounds.

"Equal rights, equal opportunities, and equal rules" are fundamental to ensuring fairness in starting points, processes, and outcomes. To promote economic efficiency while simultaneously attaining social equity, priority must be given to guaranteeing a fair starting point and a fair process. Specifically, a fair starting point requires that all social groups, especially children from low-income families, have equal access to educational opportunities. "For the government, education policy is the most reliable way to make the country embark on a path of more equal distribution"; "Education is and will always be the primary way out for children from poor families to escape poverty."[75] The nutritional status of children from low-income families, the health of the labor force, and the living conditions of households significantly influence the equity of the initial point. For a fair

---

[74] Buchanan said: "If a general fairness of the distribution of initial endowments and abilities can be guaranteed, in the sense of actual expectations and normative preferences, I am relatively comfortable with the distributional outcomes of the competitive market process." James M. Buchanan. *Liberty, Market and State*. Shanghai: SDX Joint Publishing Company, 1989, p. 197.

[75] Gerald M. Meier, Joseph E. Stiglitz. *Frontiers of Development Economics: The Future in Perspective*. Beijing: China Financial and Economic Publishing House, 2003, p. 390.

process, the rules of competition must be impartial and clear, ensuring equal opportunities for everyone, and individuals should enjoy freedom of movement, job choice, investment, and trade, along with equal rights to access and utilize production factors. To foster a fair process, key reforms are necessary, including relaxing household registration policies, eliminating barriers to mobility, advancing financial markets, and enhancing information infrastructure. When both the starting point and process are fair, we can achieve socially acceptable fairness of the outcome to a greater extent. Building on this foundation, market competition results can be effectively balanced using tools like social protection systems, targeted financial assistance for disadvantaged groups, and poverty reduction initiatives, aiming to enhance distributive equity. At the same time, to mitigate the consumption gap stemming from disparities in income and wealth, it is essential to encourage affluent groups to channel a significant portion of their income and assets into reinvestment. This can be supported by strengthening property rights protections and developing robust financial markets. While expanding employment and income-generating opportunities for low-income groups, efforts should also focus on narrowing the actual consumption gap across society, thereby promoting greater equity in consumption and overall welfare.

References

Communist Party of China Central Committee. *Decision of the Central Committee of the Communist Party of China on Several Major Issues Concerning Comprehensively Deepening the Reform*. Nov. 12, 2013.

Deng, Xiaoping. *Selected Works of Deng Xiaoping, Vol. 2*. Beijing: People's Publishing House, 1994.

Deng, Xiaoping. *Selected Works of Deng Xiaoping, Vol. 3*. Beijing: People's Publishing House, 1993.

Gu, Shutang, Cai Jiming. The contradiction between the theory of distribution according to work and reality. *Social Sciences in China*, 1988 (3).

Hong, Yinxing. Advanced social productive forces and scientific labor theory of value. *Academic Monthly*, 2001(10).

Hong, Yuanpeng. A discussion on labor measurement in distribution according to labor. *Fudan University Journal*, 1979(3).

Lenin. *Collected Works of Lenin (Socialism)*. Beijing: People's Publishing House, 2009.

Lin, Chonggeng, Michael Spencer. *Medium- and Long-term Development and Transformation of China's Economy: Reflections and Suggestions from an International Perspective*. Beijing: CITIC Press, 2011.

Marx & Engels. *Collected Works of Marx and Engels, Vol. 3.* Beijing: People's Publishing House, 2009.

The Literature Research Office of the Central Committee of the Communist Party of China. *An excerpt of Xi Jinping's discussion on socialist economic construction.* Beijing: Central Party Literature Press, 2017.

Xi, Jinping. Win a decisive victory in building a moderately prosperous society in an all-round way and win the great victory of socialism with Chinese characteristics in the new era. Oct. 18, 2017.

Xu, He. Basic economic laws of socialism, distribution according to work, bonuses. *Academic Forum*, 1979 (1).

Yang, Xiaokai. An important indicator of social and economic development—the Gini coefficient. *Journal of Wuhan University*, 1982(6).

Yu, Guangyuan. Several questions about in-depth study of the theory of distribution according to work. *Economic Research Journal*, 1979(1).

Theoretical Framework for Macroeconomic Control in a Socialist Market-Oriented Economy

In economic operations, gaps between overall supply (AS) and overall demand (AD) often give rise to ups and downs at the macroeconomic scale. This situation inherently demands that governments put in place macroeconomic regulation measures to foster a rebalancing of the supply-demand framework and ease economic swings. During the planned economy period prior to reform and opening up, the government leaned on mandatory planning systems to attain an all-round equilibrium throughout the national economy. This macroeconomic management method had great drawbacks. Given the government's direct involvement in microeconomic operations under planned management, excessive intervention often stifled the dynamism and initiative of enterprises. Once the government relaxed its control, however, the soft budget constraints would give rise to the "investment hunger" of enterprises, leading to overheating in fixed asset investment and further aggravating supply-demand imbalances. As China embraced the socialist market economy as its development model, it progressively built a macro-control framework compatible with market-oriented mechanisms. Within the new macroeconomic regulation framework, direct interference has been overtaken by indirect adjustment, and management centered on planning has been substituted by sensible coordination between fiscal and monetary policies. And the strategic integration of industrial, pricing, and regional policies has further strengthened the effectiveness of macroeconomic regulation. Since the initiation of reform and opening up, China's economy has gone through several instances of macroeconomic ups and downs. Nevertheless, these swings have been mostly kept in check, owing to the continuous improvement of the macro-regulation system, the growing adaptability of regulatory instruments, and the buildup of precious experience in macroeconomic management.

Consequently, the national economy has sustained a generally fast, steady, and healthy growth trajectory.

In the process of building and enhancing the macroeconomic regulation system within the socialist market economy, China's economic researchers have exerted a crucial influence. They have not only provided intellectual support for the structural design of the macro-control framework but have also actively contributed insights and recommendations in response to past economic fluctuations, making significant contributions to the stable progress of China's economy.

1. Profound Impact of "Bashan" Cruise Conference on the Reform of Macroeconomic Management Methods

In October 1984, the Third Plenary Session of the 12th Central Committee of the Communist Party of China passed the "Decision of the Central Committee of the CPC on the Reform of the Economic Structure," advocating the acceleration of comprehensive reform of the economic system, with special focus on urban regions. While formulating a comprehensive strategy for advancing economic system reform, the report also explicitly stated that "the more the economy is invigorated, the more emphasis must be placed on macro-adjustment, and the more adept the government should be at comprehensively utilizing prices, taxes, credit and other economic levers on the basis of a timely command of economic dynamics. The purpose is to help adjust major proportional relationships such as social aggregate supply and aggregate demand, accumulation, and consumption, and adjust the flow of financial, material, and human resources, the industrial structure and the layout of productive forces, market supply and demand, foreign economic exchanges, etc. We used to be accustomed to using administrative means to drive the economy, but for a long time neglected to use economic levers to adjust. It should become an important task for economic management departments at all levels, especially the integrated economic management departments, to have a good command of economic levers and focus on this aspect in the leadership."[1] Therefore, for policymakers and theorists, how to better learn from foreign experience and build a theoretical framework and policy system of macroeconomic management with Chinese characteristics became a major problem to be solved at that time.

In order to draw on the macroeconomic governance experiences of developed countries and Eastern European socialist states more effectively during

1 Communist Party of China Central Committee. *Decision of the Central Committee of the Communist Party of China on Reform of the Economic Structure.* Oct. 20, 1984.

China's transitional phase, and with the authorization of the State Council, the China Society of Economic Reform, the Chinese Academy of Social Sciences, and the World Bank's Beijing Representative Office co-hosted an "International Symposium on Macroeconomic Governance" from September 2 to 7, 1985. Participants engaged in detailed discussions on the macroeconomic-management issues facing China's ongoing reforms. As the symposium took place aboard the cruise ship "Bashan" traveling down the Yangtze River, it became popularly known as the "'Bashan' Cruise Conference." More than 30 scholars and officials from home and abroad attended the conference. Experts from abroad include James Tobin, a Nobel Laureate in economics and professor of Yale University in the United States, Sir Alec Cairncross, ex-president of the Royal Economic Society and a faculty member at the University of Cambridge, János Kornai, a renowned Hungarian economist, Wlodzimierz Brus, a senior researcher of Oxford University, Edwin R. Lim, who was then the Head of Mission at the World Bank's Beijing Representative Office, etc. The domestic leaders and scholars attending the conference include Xue Muqiao, Ma Hong, An Zhiwen, Gao Shangquan, Hong Hu, Tong Dalin, Yang Qixian, Liu Guoguang, Wu Jinglian, Zhao Renwei, Zhang Zhuoyuan, Zhou Shulian, Dai Yuanchen, Xiang Huaicheng, Lou Jiwei, Guo Shuqing, etc.

The "Bashan" Cruise Meeting involved thorough exchanges on the target model for economic system reform and the shift of the economic system, and approaches to macroeconomic management, significantly enriching the understanding of key theoretical and policy-related issues. The discussion on macroeconomic management mainly focuses on the following five aspects.[2]

The initial topic revolved around the proposed framework for reforming the economic system. By that point, it had been settled that the socialist economy would operate as a planned commodity economy. However, how to achieve a harmonious integration of planning mechanisms with the dynamics of a commodity economy remained a key theoretical challenge and a practical problem that required thorough research and active exploration. At the conference, Hungarian economist János Kornai categorized economic systems based on their coordination mechanisms. He put forward the idea that the mechanisms steering economic activities could be roughly categorized into two types: administrative coordination (I) and market coordination (II). Each of these comprises two distinct

---

[2] Guoguang Liu, et al. Economic system reform and macroeconomic management—review of "International Symposium on Macroeconomic Management." *Economic Research Journal*, 1985 (12); Renwei Zhao. Retrospect and reflection on the "Bashan" Cruise Conference in 1985. *Economic Research Journal*, 2008 (12).

forms: direct administrative coordination (IA) and indirect administrative coordination (IB); unregulated market coordination (IIA) and market coordination under macro-level control (IIB). In the market coordination system with macro control, the macroeconomic management authority conducts regulation and management by means of unified and standardized macro-restraint means, or economic parameter means, rather than through direct administrative means or through a large number of frequent indirect administrative interventions in microeconomic activities to control economic operation. Some Chinese and foreign economists attending the meeting were generally interested in the market coordination system with macro-control, and believed that this system provided a new way of thinking for advancing economic system reform. Nevertheless, the theoretical foundations and institutional design of a market-coordination system with macro-level oversight presented numerous challenges. After deliberation, Chinese scholars argued that, so long as socialist principles were upheld, public ownership remained predominant, and national macro-decision-making and planning guidance were preserved, the valid core of this approach could usefully inform analysis of the intended framework for reforming the economic system and help identify how to combine micro-level dynamism with effective macro-level control.

The second topic centers on the move from direct regulation to indirect regulation. In the course of China's economic reform, the government's involvement in the economy has slowly shifted from direct administrative regulation to greater dependence on indirect approaches, with a growing use of economic tools instead of administrative means to guide and adjust economic activities. Whether the direct control of the government was still needed under the new system and how to successfully realize the transformation of macroeconomic management became the key issue. Foreign experts introduced the ways and policy tools Western governments adopted to intervene in economic activities, and believed that appropriate administrative intervention in macroeconomic management was necessary, and sometimes even more effective than traditional fiscal and monetary measures. Therefore, fiscal and monetary policies should be complemented by appropriate administrative interventions to enhance the overall effectiveness of macroeconomic management. Although administrative control is implemented by means of planning, planning does not equal administrative control. Planning can be divided into two categories. The first is the direct administrative control under the traditional system, which is incompatible with market coordination. The second is to explore the potential for economic development, lay the groundwork for informed decision-making, and coordinate the diverse interests across society, functions that can effectively complete and coexist with market-based coordination mechanisms. Chinese experts believed that as a competitive market system was gradually established and macroeconomic management methods evolved, the government should learn to regulate economic activities through economic levers such as prices, tax rates, and administrative tools, and planning mechanisms should not be abandoned, as these instruments could offset market deficiencies and help avert the effects inherent in market operations.

The third point relates to the use of fiscal policies and fiscal tools. James Tobin condensed the goals of macroeconomic administration into three primary aspects: securing a balance between total supply and demand, keeping the overall price level steady, and protecting the stability of a nation's external economic ties. Among these, he identified maintaining the equilibrium between aggregate supply and demand as the foremost priority. With the increasing diversification of economic participants, it is difficult for the government to exert centralized control on the supply side, so more emphasis was placed on achieving macroeconomic management goals through aggregate demand management. Fiscal and monetary policies serve as the primary instruments through which the government indirectly manages aggregate demand. Fiscal policies mainly based on government expenditure, taxes, and subsidies are the basis for controlling demand and stabilizing the economy. Under the objective framework of functional fiscal policy, the government can achieve the goal of adjusting aggregate demand by the direct adjustment of government revenue and expenditure. Compared with monetary policies, fiscal policies take effect quickly and directly. Both Chinese and international experts concurred that for fiscal policy to effectively fulfill its role in macroeconomic regulation, the government should prioritize the improvement of the taxation system, fully leverage the function of taxation, and issue public bonds when appropriate. Under no circumstances should "money creation" be used to raise money.

The fourth is about the application of monetary policies and credit leverage. Monetary policy is an important macroeconomic management tool, and its core is to control the total supply of money. At that time, China took the amount of cash in circulation as the only indicator of money supply. Foreign experts believed that China's financial environment still faced numerous challenges and unresolved issues. Complex influencing factors led to the lack of stability of money circulation speed, and also the lack of a financial mechanism necessary for the central bank to play its role in the total money supply. Therefore, it might be more realistic for China to use the total credit instead of the total money supply as a macro-control index. China also faced many challenges in effectively implementing monetary policies. The widespread existence of soft budget restrictions in state-owned enterprises notably reduced the efficiency of interest rates as a tool for economic regulation. Additionally, the deposit reserve system lacked a strong impact; the financial market remained underdeveloped, and market information was not readily accessible to the public. Experts generally believed that under China's financial system at that time, it was still necessary to maintain the total credit index set by the central bank and issue direct control layer by layer through professional banks to achieve macro management by means of financial instruments. However, it was imperative to progressively build and enhance the banking sector and financial arenas, address the issue of soft budget constraints step by step via enterprise reforms, and ultimately implement macroeconomic regulation primarily through indirect instruments like monetary policies.

The fifth point concerns the coordination between fiscal policies and monetary policies. Both serve as essential elements of macroeconomic management, operating primarily through indirect regulation. Only a reasonable combination of the two can achieve better policy effects. From the standpoint of policy coordination, fiscal and monetary policies typically fall into four combinations: tight fiscal policy with tight monetary policy; loose fiscal policy with loose monetary policy; A strict fiscal policy paired with an accommodative monetary policy; and an accommodative fiscal policy combined with a strict monetary policy. Back then, as the emphasis of economic restructuring shifted from rural regions to urban hubs, the economy saw a swift boom, which, before long, gave rise to indications of overheating. The surge in bank credit led to an oversupply of money, triggering inflation. Considering the demand-driven inflation triggered by the combined effects of "investment hunger," "import hunger," and "consumption hunger" in China's economy at that time, both domestic and international scholars broadly recommended the adoption of tight fiscal and monetary policies. Their aim was to restrain excessive aggregate demand and foster an economic environment where supply slightly exceeded demand-thereby creating more favorable conditions for advancing reforms.

Participants also discussed macroeconomic management issues such as wage control and personal income distribution policies, foreign trade management, and balance of payments. The scholars believed that macroeconomic management was inseparable from microeconomic activities. In order to realize the objectives of macroeconomic management more effectively, it was essential for macroeconomic policies to be formulated in a scientific and rational manner. Whether the microeconomic entities could make timely responses to relevant policies also made sense to a large extent. Therefore, China should not only build a macroeconomic management system that is aligned with the aims of economic system reform, but also establish a corresponding micro foundation. This necessitated strengthening budget constraints on enterprises, accelerating the development and refinement of the market system, especially in commodity and capital markets, pushing forward price reform in a proactive and resolute manner, and establishing robust systems for economic information and oversight as priorities for the next stage of reform.

The "Bashan" Cruise Meeting stood as a pivotal academic forum during China's shift from a planned economy to a planned commodity economy. "It is actually a high-level seminar for exploring economic system reform and strengthening macroeconomic management." "The participants of the conference basically consist of three groups: economists from China, including economic policy makers and theorists; economists from Eastern Europe or experienced in the economic reform of Eastern Europe; Western economists, especially those experienced in the macro management of market economy and economic transformation. From the composition of the participants, it can be seen that by the mid-1980s, China's economic reforms should not only learn from the experience of Eastern Europe and reset on the introduction of market mechanisms under the framework of the centrally planned economy, but also should further draw on experience in macro management of market economy and the way of transition from a planned economy to a market economy."[3] After nearly a week of exchanges and discussions on the "Bashan" Cruise, Chinese economists had a full understanding of the theoretical framework and policy practice of Western macroeconomic regulation and control. Scholars from China and abroad also developed a more profound grasp of the orientation of institutional reform and the challenges in economic operations. The conference has a positive and far-reaching impact, both then and now. "'Bashan' Cruise Conference has provided a basic framework for China's transition from direct to indirect macroeconomic management."[4]

2. Several Pressing Issues Regarding the Study of Macroeconomic Control Since the Formation of the Intended Framework for the Socialist Market Economic System

The 1992 14th National Congress of the Communist Party of China was a crucial occasion. Its report clearly defined the objective of China's economic system

3 Renwei Zhao. Retrospect and reflection on the "Bashan Cruise Conference" in 1985. *Economic Research Journal*, 2008 (12).

4 Zhuoyuan Zhang. Research and innovation of macroeconomic management theory with Chinese characteristics. *30 Years of Chinese Economics (1978–2008)*. Beijing: China Social Sciences Press, 2008: 167.

reform as building a socialist market economy. This represented a major advance in the Party's comprehension of the reform's target framework following over ten years of exploration—especially regarding how to properly handle and balance the connection between "planning" and "the market." The report also offered a thorough account of macroeconomic regulation within the socialist market economic system. It stressed that in a socialist market economy, the market would play a basic role in resource allocation under the state's macro-control guidance. On one side, the market's function should be fully utilized via pricing systems and competition to boost efficient resource distribution, guarantee that enterprises thrive based on their performance, and strengthen the alignment between production and demand. On the other hand, government macro-control must be strengthened and refined to address market deficiencies and mitigate potential negative outcomes. To attain the goals of macroeconomic regulation, China ought to vigorously advance the growth of a unified national marketplace, further strengthen the market's function, and make effective use of economic policies, regulatory tools, planning guidance, and necessary administrative steps to guide market development more effectively in accordance with the rules governing economic operations. The Third Plenary Session of the 14th CPC Central Committee later set forth four main missions of macroeconomic regulation: keeping the basic balance between total supply and demand, improving the economic structure, guiding the national economy to develop in a sustained, rapid, and healthy manner, and advancing all-around social progress. Additionally, the session laid out more specific and systematic blueprints for building and perfecting the macro-control system under the socialist market economic system. It was emphasized that economic measures should be taken as the main method of macro-control, including establishing a coordination and restriction mechanism among planning, finance, and public finance. Monetary, fiscal, and industrial policies should be employed to enhance the balanced growth of the national economy and society.

Since the convening of the 14th CPC National Congress, China has achieved notable headway in reforming its planning, fiscal, and taxation systems, as well as its financial system. The aim behind these efforts is to build a macro-control structure that dovetails with the socialist market economy. Mandatory planning has been replaced by indicative planning, and the emphasis of planning work has shifted toward the formulation and implementation of medium—and long-term plans aimed at comprehensively coordinating macroeconomic policies and economic instruments. A comprehensive fiscal reform was implemented, featuring a system known as "serving meals to different diners from different pots" — a figure of speech denoting the allocation of revenue and expenditure duties between the central and local governments, with each level held accountable for balancing its own budget under a "fiscal contract" arrangement. Following the reform, the local fiscal contracting system was replaced by the tax-sharing system, leading to the initial establishment of a central—local tax framework based on a more rational division of fiscal authority and responsibilities. The tax system had been reformed and improved following the principles of a unified tax code, equitable tax liability, a streamlined tax system, and rational decentralization. The mechanism of central government refund and transfer payments to local governments has been put into effect. The central government had tightened its control over its fiscal deficit, issuing short—and long-term treasury bonds instead of borrowing money from banks to cover its deficit. Under the direction of the State Council, the People's Bank of China autonomously carried out monetary policy and preserved currency stability through the management of money supply. Monetary policy tools had also changed from relying mainly on credit scale management to the application of deposit reserve ratios, central bank lending rates, and open market operations. The successive founding of the money market, foreign exchange market, bond market, stock market, insurance market, and futures market offered institutional backing for the foreign exchange system.

Since the start of the 1990s, China's economy has experienced several marked ups and downs. However, as insights into macroeconomic principles have grown deeper and the macro-control mechanism has been steadily refined, the nation has achieved considerable headway in easing these fluctuations. In dealing with earlier macroeconomic swings, Chinese economists carried out thorough analyses and lively debates on the domestic and foreign elements causing macroeconomic imbalances. They put forward numerous key countermeasures and suggestions, which contributed constructively to promoting the steady and sustained growth of China's economy.

I. Discussions on the inflation in the early 1990s

After Deng Xiaoping's Southern Talks and the successful holding of the 14th CPC National Congress in 1992, China's reform, opening up, and economic growth stepped into a new stage. The economy experienced rapid growth, with GDP increasing by 13.4% in 1993 and 11.8% in 1994. The excessive economic growth, however, also aggravated the long-standing economic imbalance, which was mainly manifested in the rapid rise in the price level. In 1993, the consumer price index increased by 14.7%, and the figure was as high as 24.1% in 1994, far exceeding the 18.5% in 1988, marking the highest increase since reform and opening up. This showed that in the era of rapid economic expansion and systemic transition, inflationary pressures stayed substantial.

Scholars discussed the causes of this round of inflation from different perspectives, and generally, there were four opinions: demand-driven inflation, cost-induced inflation, institutional-change inflation, and combined inflation. However, most scholars believed that the reasons for this inflation were more complicated, and it was difficult to simply attribute it to a certain type of factor. With the help of the extended Phillips Curve,[5] the Macroeconomic Research Center of the Comprehensive Development Institute (Shenzhen, China) expressed its opinion that the high inflation level back then arose from the interplay of demand-driven elements and supply-induced factors, and the general trend showed that the supply factor was the main factor of China's high inflation rate. Bai Qinxian identified[6] four interrelated factors contributing to this spell of inflation: demand-driven inflation, cost-induced and profit-induced inflation, external influences stemming from international economic and financial relations, and a decline in the overall supply of agricultural products due to continued erosion of the agricultural foundation. Many scholars also studied the relationship between economic transition and inflation from the backdrop that China was establishing the socialist market economy. Li Xiaoxi believed that the inflation at that time could not be simply attributed to aggregate demand inflation, because the supply capacity of many products was already greater than the demand, and some commodity markets even showed weakness, which was significantly different from the inflation caused by excessive consumer demand in the late 1980s. He characterized this round of inflation as structural inflation occurring during a period of economic transition, arguing that the primary cause lay in the structural imbalance between supply and demand, especially when key transmission mechanisms, such as interest rates, failed to function effectively.[7] Wang Yijiang employed a model to depict and analyze the inflationary trend emerging during China's reform process.[8] He contended that as the central government relaxed its control over resource distribution, local governments and enterprises acquired

---

5 Macroeconomic Research Center, Comprehensive Development Research Institute (Shenzhen, China). The Phillips model and China's inflation: a theoretical analysis of the causes, trends and policy choices of China's comprehensive inflation. *Economic Research Journal*, 1996 (2).

6 Qinxian Bai. A comparison of inflation between China and foreign countries and the characteristics, causes and countermeasures of current inflation in China. *Studies of International Finance*, 1995 (1).

7 Xiaoxi Li. Structural inflation in the transition process. *Economic Research Journal*, 1994 (10).

8 Yijiang Wang. The behavioral mechanism of investment expansion and inflation in economic reform. *Economic Research Journal*, 1994 (6).

greater command over both financial and material resources. This shift, in turn, fueled a strong incentive among enterprises to expand their fixed asset investments. Since enterprises invested a large amount of resources in fixed assets, it was bound to occupy the working capital for the normal production and operation of enterprises. With the help of local governments, however, enterprises were able to turn to banks for money, and banks would ask the central government for help. Consequently, the production and investment could still be carried out smoothly. Nevertheless, this expansion process of fixed assets, working capital loans, and production scale eventually led to inflation. Han Wenxiu conducted an empirical study on the connection between China's economic expansion and inflation in the era of reform and opening up,[9] and found that whenever China's economic growth exceeded 10% for two consecutive years, significant inflation was bound to follow. There were mainly six mechanisms through which high economic growth led to high inflation. First, high growth was inseparable from credit expansion and currency growth, while high currency growth was the direct cause of high inflation. Second, the excessive growth of fixed asset investment was an important driving force of high economic growth. High investment often causes the cost increase of fundamental goods, eventually influencing the price of other products. Third, high growth requires high investment. Excessive investment demand often drove up aggregate social demand. If aggregate supply could not meet aggregate demand, it would inevitably lead to price increases; Fourth, high growth tended to result in faster growth of personal income, which created cost-push pressure for inflation; Fifth, due to the imbalance of regional development, high growth would widen the regional economic gap and the inflation would eventually be transferred from developed regions to relatively backward regions; Sixth, economic overheating, when combined with systemic chaos, could artificially fuel an excessive rise in the overall price level.

The economists also offered suggestions to curb inflation. Most scholars believed that aggregate demand, especially investment demand, should be restrained moderately. Since the formation of inflation at that time was closely tied to the context of "dual-track regulation." This approach advocates applying different regulatory measures to microeconomic entities based on their ownership types. Specifically, it called for the continued use of direct administrative controls over state-owned sectors—particularly to curb excessive investment and "public-funded consumption"— while implementing various indirect regulatory

[9] Wenxiu Han. Research on the relationship between economic growth and inflation. *Management World*, 1996 (6).

tools for the non-state-owned economy.[10] Some scholars also put forward specific suggestions from the aspect of financial regulation.[11] They believed that the fundamental measures to control inflation were to establish and improve the commercial and credit principles of loans, and to establish a hard loan constraint mechanism for enterprises. Interest rates should be raised to increase the cost of loans, curbing excessive demand for loans from all sides. The central bank's independence and self-determination in formulating monetary policy should be enhanced, allowing it to resist lending demands and pressures from local governments and other state institutions. Reforming the central bank's organizational structure and monetary policy framework was urgently needed, including the complete elimination of the capital financing role of its provincial branches, in order to eliminate local government interference. The open market should be promoted as soon as possible, and strict control over the issuance of central bank loans should be imposed. Some scholars also believed that this round of inflation was related to the imperfect enterprise property rights system and market mechanism. To effectively curb inflation, it was crucial to further advance economic reforms, particularly by stepping up the reform of state-owned enterprises and tackling the soft budget constraints associated with lending and internal income distribution.[12]

To better manage inflation, the government implemented a moderately tight macro-control policy. This included adopting a "making-ends-meet" fiscal approach, tightening control over the money supply and credit expansion, regulating the magnitude of fixed asset investment, and curbing the excessive growth of consumer spending. These policies had achieved significant results, with the price increase dropping from 24.1% in 1994 to 2.8% in 1997. While the 1997 economic growth rate was below the 12.8% registered in 1992, it stayed strong at a high level of 8.8%. The implementation of macro-control policies not only significantly reduced the price increase but also achieved moderate and rapid economic growth and successfully realized a soft landing of the economy.

II. Discussions of deflation

Despite the success of tackling inflation, new challenges were soon to hit China's economy. The commodity shortages that had plagued China's economy for a long

---

[10] Gang Fan. "Soft Constraint Competition" and China's Inflation in Recent Years. *Journal of Financial Research*, 1994 (9).

[11] Ping Xie. Inflation and currency control in China's transition economy. *Journal of Financial Research*, 1994 (10).

[12] See the literature of Xiaoxi Li and Gang Fan cited above.

time were fading away, but overcapacity was creeping back. The Third National Industrial Census conducted in 1996 revealed that, in 1995, over half of more than 900 major industrial products had a capacity utilization rate below 60%. Notable examples included photographic film at just 13.3%, film footage at 25.5%, telephone at 51.4%, color TV set at 46.1%, household washing machines at 43.4%, bicycles at 54.5%, and internal combustion engines at 43.9%. In the late 1980s, key commodities such as large and medium-sized tractors, small tractors, and steel were still in short supply. However, by the mid-1990s, they encountered the reverse issue: underutilized production capacity.[13] China had been suffering from its first widespread overcapacity since 1949. At that time, domestic consumer demand was relatively weak, while external demand also began to contract as a result of the Asian financial crisis's influence. Moreover, a new round of supply and demand imbalance led to a continuous decline in price levels. Since April 1998, the increase of the consumer price index had been in negative territory for 24 months, while the factory price index of industrial products had been in a state of negative growth from June 1997 to January 2000, and the negative growth rate was much larger than that of the consumer price index.

Although the price level in China continued to decline at that time, there were different views in the academic circles on whether there was deflation in China. Deflation, as the name suggests, refers to a sustained decline in the price level. Some scholars believed that there was no deflation in China, because, in addition to the decline in price indicators, other macroeconomic indicators were on the rise. In reality, the idle production capacity and the increase in unemployment were not caused by insufficient demand and tight money, but due to repeated construction and corporate restructuring and downsizing.[14] Some scholars believed that there were only signs of deflation in China at that time, and it was not enough to predict the arrival of deflation only from the continuous decline of the price level. Deflation should have "two characteristics, one accompanying," namely, a continuous decline in the price level and a continuous decline in the money supply, usually accompanied by an economic recession.[15] The decline in the price level did not necessarily mean that deflation

---

13 National Bureau of Statistics. *Bulletin of the main data of the third national industrial census.* National Bureau of Statistics website.

14 Zuyao Yu. The assertion that "China is currently in a deflationary predicament" is groundless. *Journal of Shenyang Party Institute of CPC*, 1999 (2).

15 Macroeconomic Group, China Economic Research Center, Peking University. Facing up to the pressure of deflation, and speeding up the reform of micro-mechanism. *Economic Research Journal*, 1999 (7).

would inevitably occur. Only when the price level declined, and there was also an economic recession and a decline in currency circulation, would it mean the advent of deflation. At that time, while both China's economic growth rate and M2 growth rate stayed positive, some scholars maintained that the nation was already undergoing deflation.[16] Since the conclusion of World War II, economic recessions in Western nations have been less characterized by an absolute drop in economic aggregate and more by a slowdown in growth rates. Viewed from this angle, although China had experienced an outright economic recession or a contraction in the money supply during the years of continued price declines, the steadily slowing economic growth indicated the emergence of a "growth recession." Because the velocity of money circulation in China had slowed, it became necessary to expand the money supply to keep pace with the growth of the economic aggregate. As a result, China's deflation occurred alongside an increase in the money supply rather than a contraction. Some scholars admitted that deflation had already occurred, but believed that this was only a short-term, corrective, and comprehensive mild deflation, and the current deflation situation could neither be underestimated nor overestimated.[17] Some scholars contended that China had undergone a widespread and severe deflation, which had emerged as a significant barrier to the sustainable, rapid, and sound development of China's economy. They warned that without the implementation of monetary and related policies designed to counteract deflation, China risked falling into a deflationary spiral [18]

What factors contributed to the emergence of deflation in China? Many scholars attributed this to a lack of effective demand. Some argued that it stemmed from declines in consumer spending, investment, and exports, with the overall drop in aggregate demand being linked to systemic, policy-related, and structural factors within the economy.[19] Others examined the long-standing policy of high accumulation and contended that it had suppressed improvements in household income and consumption levels. However, because high accumulation had been transformed into high investment, the contradiction of insufficient consumption demand had been overshadowed by excessive investment demand. Insufficient

16 Tongsan Wang, Tao Li. The deep-seated causes of China's deflation. *Social Sciences in China*, 2001 (6).

17 Shucheng Liu. Deflation: neither underestimation nor overestimation. *Economic Research Journal*, 1999 (10).

18 Angang Hu. The characteristics, causes and countermeasures of China's deflation. *Management World*, 1999 (3).

19 Guoan Zeng. The causes of China's deflation in the 1990s and anti-deflation policies. *Contemporary Economic Research*, 2001 (2).

consumption had caused China to experience excess production prematurely, dragging down corporate profits, leading to shrinking investment, exposing the contradiction of insufficient effective demand in the whole society, and triggering deflation.[20] Some scholars also examined the role of weak external demand in contributing to deflation, linking it to the global austerity environment at the time and the harmful impacts of the Asian financial crisis.[21] Although many scholars focused on exploring the factors leading to deflation through demand-side analysis, there were also some scholars looking for the reasons from the supply side. Some scholars argued that the appropriate starting point for analyzing China's deflation at that time was not the lack of effective demand, but rather the losses incurred by businesses as a result of increasing manufacturing expenses. The fundamental cause of deflation in China was the decline in the economic benefits of enterprises. Due to the rising production costs, the issue of corporate losses became increasingly severe, compelling enterprises to adopt measures aimed at improving production efficiency and reducing costs. This, in turn, caused the aggregate supply curve to shift rightward, playing a role in pushing down the general price level.[22] Some scholars took a more comprehensive view, considering both supply-side and demand-side factors. They argued that the causes of China's deflation evolved over time. The sustained decline in prices in the late 1990s was attributed to a "credit contraction" alongside weakening demand and investment growth—characteristics of typical deflation. In contrast, the price decline in the early 2000s could not be explained by insufficient effective demand, but was instead the result of productivity gains and cost reductions.[23]

On the basis of discussing the causes of deflation, scholars put forward many countermeasures and suggestions to curb deflation. The first measure was the adoption of a proactive fiscal policy. In addition to increasing fiscal expenditure, the government needed to optimize the structure of that spending—continuing to boost investment in infrastructure, as well as in agricultural, forestry, and water conservancy projects—while also enhancing support for the development

---

20 Tongsan Wang, Tao Li. The deep-seated causes of China's deflation. *Social Sciences in China*, 2001 (6).

21 Ibid.

22 Yongding Yu. Breaking the vicious circle of deflation: a new challenge for China's economic development. *Economic Research Journal*, 1999 (7).

23 Gang Fan. Deflation, effective price reduction and economic fluctuation: an analysis of several characteristics of China's current macro-economy. *Economic Research Journal*, 2003 (7).

of "small towns."[24] Tax policies and spending policies should have their own priorities. Alongside deeper fiscal and tax-system reforms-and with the total tax burden remaining unchanged or even higher-partial adjustments to the current regime were needed. The long-standing tax structure, designed for a shortage economy and prone to curbing investment and consumption, had to be transformed into one that stimulates both. At the same time, any goal of reducing the effective tax load should be pursued within the shift from administrative fees to formal taxes, accomplished through measures that regularize and better govern the state's revenue system.[25] The second measure was to adopt an expansionary monetary policy and moderately expand the money supply. In the short term, the government should further expand the money supply, with a primary focus on boosting the nominal incomes of both urban and rural residents. This would help stimulate final consumption demand and support a recovery in the overall price level. Under the premise of preventing financial risks, some outdated controls would be removed, and the scale of credit issuance would be expanded; interest rate controls would be relaxed, and interest rate market-oriented reforms would be accelerated.[26] The third was to coordinate short-term policies with medium—and long-term policies, combine macroeconomic policies with institutional reforms, and resolve the deep-seated contradictions of deflation. In the short term, it is essential to implement proactive macroeconomic policies. In the medium term, reforms ought to center on the property rights regime, operational systems, investment and financing structures, and the unreasonable income distribution within state-owned enterprises. Over the long term, a fundamental transformation in the pattern of economic growth is necessary, alongside improving the quality and sustainability of such growth.[27]

When formulating the "Ninth Five-Year Plan," the Chinese government remained cautious, recognizing that factors driving price increases-both

---

[24] Xiaoan Qian. The causes, hazards and countermeasures of deflation. *Journal of Financial Research*, 1999 (9).

[25] Peiyong Gao. Tax policy choices under deflation—a discussion on current tax cut propositions. *Economic Research Journal*, 2000 (1).

[26] Conglai Fan. On the effectiveness of monetary policy in the period of deflation. *Economic Research Journal*, 2000 (7); Angang Hu. The characteristics, causes and countermeasures of China's deflation. *Management World*, 1999 (3); Ping Xie, Bingxi Shen. Deflation and monetary policy. *Economic Research Journal*, 1999 (8).

[27] Tongsan Wang, Tao Li. The deep-seated causes of China's deflation. *Social Sciences in China*, 2001 (6); Gang Fan. Deflation, effective price reduction and economic fluctuation: an analysis of several characteristics of China's current macro-economy. *Economic Research Journal*, 2003 (7).

demand-driven and cost-driven-were still present. Therefore, during the "Ninth Five-Year Plan" period, it kept emphasizing the necessity of adopting moderately tight fiscal and monetary policies, with the goals of securing moderate growth in overall demand and maintaining a balanced, reasonable demand structure. However, as the problem of insufficient demand at home and abroad had become more and more prominent, the trend of deflation had become more and more obvious, and macro-control policies had also undergone major adjustments. The control objectives of macro-economic policies had changed from striving for stability to active easing. Fiscal expenditures continued to rise, the scale of national debt issuance steadily expanded, and the central bank implemented multiple consecutive interest rate cuts. These targeted macroeconomic regulation measures played a role in enhancing China's economic performance. The economic growth rate climbed from 7.8% in 1998 to 9.1% in 2003, and the consumer price index went up from 0.8% in 1998 to 1.2% in 2003. As a result, China gradually emerged from the shadow of deflation and entered a new cycle of economic growth.

III. Discussions on the economic overheating

Since 2003, China entered a new phase of rapid economic growth, with GDP growth rates exceeding 10% annually from 2003 to 2005. Although the overall price level remained relatively stable during this period, the pace of investment expansion was notably high. Specifically, total social fixed asset investment expanded at an average yearly rate of more than 26%, reaching a peak of 27.7% in 2003 alone. These developments had also raised concerns about an overheating economy. Some scholars believed that China's macro economy had shown overall overheating, and even started the overheating of an inflationary economy. The root cause of overheating was poor growth quality and low efficiency.[28] Some scholars noted that the hallmark of this round of economic growth was not inflation, but rather an excessive surge in investment, particularly in fixed assets. Although the growth process did not lead to significant capital expansion or inflation, it was accompanied by disorderly development and over-exploitation of resources. This included the blind expansion of certain industries, overcapacity, excessive exports, unsustainable consumption of energy and resources, and worsening environmental degradation. If this situation were not stopped in

---

28 Jinglian Wu. China's economic "soft landing" is possible. *Chinese Cadres Tribune*, 2004 (6); Dapei Zuo. Macroeconomic overheating essentially stems from the economic predicament. *China Opening Journal*, 2004 (5).

time, there might be a large area of overcapacity in a few years, leading to a new round of bank bad debts.[29]

However, many scholars argued that China's economy was not experiencing overall overheating at that time. Zhao Xiao, for instance, emphasized that the key criterion for determining economic overheating was not the absolute levels of investment or GDP growth, but whether supply and demand remained in balance.[30] Although the economic growth rate was indeed high, China's economy had not entered an overheated state from the perspective of price movements driven by supply and demand. China's return on investment was also high, which meant that China's economic growth, driven by low inflation and high investment rates, was sustainable. The China National Accounting and Economic Growth Research Center of Peking University believed that China was experiencing its most favorable period since 1992. Notable headway had been made in the reform of state-owned enterprises, while macroeconomic policies suited to national conditions had effectively enhanced the overall economic climate. Meanwhile, new growth drivers were emerging within the national economy, the benefits of globalization were fueling further development, and the market-oriented economic model was functioning smoothly. Together, these elements played a part in speeding up China's economic growth. While certain industries and regions did experience signs of overheating, this rapid economic expansion should not be mistaken for overall economic overheating. Although there was an upward trend in prices at the time, suggesting the potential for inflation, deeper analysis revealed that the situation was more nuanced. While rising investment demand did push up the prices of certain production inputs, the overall pace of investment growth remained within a normal range. Moreover, it was unlikely that this whole led to a broad-based surge in consumption across society. Therefore, the possibility of demand-driven inflation was very low. The main challenge for China's economic development back then was employment, which made generating jobs and enhancing employment conditions a more pressing priority than controlling possible inflation.[31]

---

29 Weizhong Fang. Some views on the current economic situation and macro-control. *Shanghai Enterprise*, 2006 (10); Dong Tao. Be wary of economic overheating without inflation. *Development Herald*, 3rd Edition, August 12, 2003.

30 Xiao Zhao. China's high return on investment does not mean that the economy is overheating. *China Logistics & Purchasing*, 2006 (21).

31 China National Accounting and Economic Growth Research Center, Peking University. Analysis of China's economic trend from 2003 to 2004—has China's economy overheated? *Economic Science Journal*, 2003 (6).

Given the economic conditions at that time, the necessity of macro-control became a topic of debate. Some scholars argued that macro-control was essential for smoothing out economic fluctuations and promoting stable and coordinated development.[32] They maintained that as long as fluctuations existed within a market economy, macro-control remained a necessary policy tool. As for whether the macro-control policy was mainly based on tightening or expansion, it mainly depended on the changes in the macroeconomic situation. At present, there is not only local overheating, especially excessive investment in some sectors, but also the problem of oversupply and insufficient effective demand in general. Therefore, in terms of macroeconomic policies, it was neither possible to adopt the contractionary macro-control policies once used to control the overall economic overheating and severe inflation in the early 1990s, nor to adopt the expansionary macro-control policies used to control the cold economy and economic contraction in the late 1990s. A "sound" macro-control policy should be adopted, and the overall policy tone has changed from the expansionary "relaxed" in previous years to the appropriately tightened "sound." In terms of fiscal policy, it was crucial to lower the fiscal deficit and reduce the issuance of long-term construction-focused national bonds. Meanwhile, steps should be taken to refine the structure of national debt and enhance the makeup of fiscal spending. As for the monetary policy, it was also necessary to implement a sound policy of "a combination of protection and restriction, together with moderate tightening measures." Some scholars also believed that since the imbalance of the macro economy consisted of both aggregate and structural problems, it was far from enough to adjust the total amount from the perspective of demand management, and more consideration should be given to the combination of demand management and supply management. Special attention should be given to the function of fiscal policy.[33] It was essential to boost consumption and rein in investment by means of a moderately tight monetary policy and a moderately expansionary fiscal policy, thereby addressing the structural imbalance in aggregate demand.

Given the robust economic growth momentum and vigorous social investment at that time, the Chinese government made a prudent fiscal policy and a cautious monetary policy the centerpiece of its macroeconomic regulation strategy. To avoid significant economic fluctuations and address issues such as the excessive growth of fixed asset investment, overexpansion of money and credit supply, and

32 Guoguang Liu. Miscellaneous talks about macro-control. *Economic Perspectives*, 2004 (10); Guoguang Liu. Double prudent macro-control policies. *Chinese Cadres Tribune*, 2005 (1).

33 Wei Liu, Zhizhou Cai. China's macro-control mode faces challenges and reforms. *Economic Herald*, 2006 (6).

an overly large trade surplus, the government implemented timely adjustments to its fiscal and monetary measures. These measures included several adjustments to the reserve requirement ratio and the benchmark deposit and lending rates of financial institutions, along with the reduction or abolition of export tax rebates for energy-intensive, high-emission, and resource-reliant products. These efforts collectively contributed to maintaining stable and rapid overall economic growth.

IV. Macro-control policies to deal with the impact of the global financial crisis

The financial crisis that began in the United States and rapidly spread worldwide set off a global economic downturn. As China's economy grew more closely intertwined with the international economic system, it was unavoidably impacted by the far-reaching effects of this global financial upheaval. Chinese economists closely tracked the evolution of the crisis and its global ripple effects, promptly assessed its impact on China's economic performance, and actively put forward policy suggestions to alleviate its negative consequences.

The global financial crisis exerted a notable impact on China's economic growth. In the first quarter of 2008, the economy sustained a strong growth rate of 10.6%, but by the first quarter of 2009, this figure had plunged to 6.1%, marking a sharp slowdown in response to the global downturn. Some scholars pointed out that the domestic economy itself was in an unfavorable period of "double-factor superposition" of economic structural transformation and cyclical adjustment. The international financial crisis impacted China through several channels, including fluctuations in the RMB exchange rate, volatility in international market prices, and a sharp decline in external demand. As a result, China's three major drivers of economic growth—exports, investment, and consumption—were all affected to varying degrees, intensifying the challenges of economic adjustment and potentially prolonging its duration.[34] The effect of the global financial crisis on China's export sector was especially striking. As the global economic situation deteriorated rapidly, China's foreign trade growth in 2008 exhibited a clear downward trend. Although trade maintained relatively strong growth for most of the year, a notable decline began in November, when total import and export volume dropped by 9% year-on-year. Exports decreased by 2.2%, the first contraction since July 2001, while imports plunged by 17.9%. The downward trend deepened in December, with the total trade volume falling by 11.1%, including a 2.8% drop in exports and 21.3% decline in imports. In

34 Huiqing Gao, Yizhi Xiong, Shaowei Hu. The world financial crisis and its impact on China's economy. *Studies of International Finance*, 2008 (11).

particular, the growth in exports of mechanical and electrical goods decelerated markedly, and processing trade exports saw a sharp downturn.[35] At that time, China's exports were relatively concentrated, with shipments to the top ten export destinations accounting for 70% of China's total exports. Empirical studies by some scholars revealed that the financial crisis had severely affected the economic growth, financial markets, and employment conditions in these key trading partners, thereby applying the adverse impact on China's export sector. The downturn in the real economies of China's major trading partners significantly curtailed their import demand, triggering a sustained decline in China's export trade.[36] The international financial crisis also profoundly affected China's labor market, especially the job placement of migrant workers. Based on calculations by certain academics, approximately 34.81 million migrant workers faced the threat of structural unemployment, plunging China into its most acute employment challenge since the beginning of the twenty-first century.[37]

In response to the sudden external economic shock, the Chinese government promptly reassessed the evolving situation and adjusted the focus of its macro-control policies accordingly. The policy stance of "double prevention" (preventing the economy from shifting from rapid growth to overheating and from structural price increase to significant inflation) policy in early 2008 shifted to the "one maintaining and one controlling" (Keeping economic growth steady and fast while checking excessive price hikes) policy in the mid-year. By year-end, the government stepped up its response further by rolling out ten key measures to "boost domestic demand and drive economic growth." To ward off an overly sharp slowdown in economic growth, China implemented an active fiscal policy together with a moderately loose monetary policy. Specific steps included increasing the export tax rebate rate three times, slashing financial institutions' benchmark deposit and lending rates five times, reducing the reserve requirement ratio four times, cutting taxes and fees linked to housing transactions, and

35 Institute of International Trade and Economic Cooperation, Comprehensive Department of the Ministry of Commerce. Report on China's Foreign Trade Situation (Spring 2009). *Website of the Ministry of Commerce*, May 4, 2009.

36 Ping Pei, Qian Zhang, Zhifeng Hu. The impact of the international financial crisis on China's export trade: an empirical study based on monthly data from 2007 to 2008. *Journal of Financial Research*, 2009 (8).

37 Chewei Zhang. The impact of the global financial crisis on the employment of migrant workers: impact analysis and countermeasures. *Chinese Journal of Population Science*, 2009 (2).

strengthening credit support for small and medium-sized enterprises.[38] Notably, in November 2008, the Chinese government unveiled ten initiatives to further boost domestic demand, with a planned total investment of 4 trillion yuan over the subsequent two years. These funds were intended to speed up the building of affordable housing, rural infrastructure, and key transportation projects, including railways, highways, and airports. Additionally, the plan prioritized the development of healthcare, education, and cultural sectors; enhancement of ecological and environmental protection; promotion of independent innovation and industrial restructuring; advancement of post-disaster reconstruction in earthquake-affected areas; increases in urban and rural incomes; and the rollout of a nationwide value-added tax reform across all regions and sectors. All these measures were taken to encourage technological transformation of enterprises, increase financial support for economic growth, resist the international economic crisis, accelerate national construction, increase national income, and promote stable and rapid economic growth.

Economists broadly backed the use of macroeconomic regulation policies to counteract the financial crisis's effects. To boost the efficacy of these policy steps, numerous academics put forward helpful suggestions. Among them, some emphasized that priority should be given to stabilizing and promoting employment, considering it a fundamental factor in ensuring social stability and sustaining economic recovery.[39] Some scholars believed that expanding consumer demand was the focus of China's current expansion of domestic demand. It was essential to raise household incomes, with a focus on promoting employment as the primary means for residents to improve their earnings and enhancing their property income. At the same time, efforts needed to be made to narrow income disparities by addressing the unreasonable income gaps between employees in monopoly sectors and those in other industries. This required strengthening secondary income distribution through measures such as tax reform and other measures; we need to build a social security system that covers everyone, basic guarantees, narrowing gaps, and sustainability. It was also necessary to activate demand potential through supply-side reforms and continuously improve the convenience of consumption.[40] Certain scholars suggested that in the course

---

38 Wen Jiabao's government work report at the 2nd Session of the 11th National People's Congress. *Chinese Government Website*, March 5, 2009.

39 The research group of the Development Research Center of the State Council. China: Seeking new breakthroughs in responding to the crisis. *Management World*, 2009 (6).

40 Shijie Yin. Several issues of China's current expansion of consumer demand. *China Business and Market*, 2009 (7); Bin Yu, Changsheng Chen. Expanding consumer demand and

of carrying out the 4-trillion-yuan stimulus package, close heed should be paid to balancing economic growth. They emphasized that short-term investment expansion should be aligned with long-term development goals, ensuring that resources are directed toward promoting structural upgrades and fostering sustainable, innovation-driven growth.[41] Under the extensive growth model marked by large-scale expansion, issues such as irrational economic structure, imbalanced industrial development, low enterprise productivity, resource waste, and severe environmental pollution became increasingly prominent. For a long time, these deep-seated structural problems had been masked by the rapid pace of economic growth. The investment of 4 trillion yuan would certainly help to stimulate economic recovery. When the policy was implemented, however, if there were more plans to save existing enterprises and existing production capacity, but fewer plans to eliminate backward enterprises and reduce production capacity, and concrete measures to protect traditional industries, but slick measures to cultivate new industries, it might instead bring about the risk of rigidifying the existing, unreasonable economic structure. Therefore, it is vital to let the market take a decisive role in eliminating obsolete production capacity, while leveraging macro-control to actively support enterprises and industries engaged in independent innovation. At the same time, steps should be taken to upgrade traditional industries, encourage the growth of emerging sectors, and steadily advance the optimization and upgrading of the industrial structure. For the 4-trillion-yuan plan, some scholars believed that the negative impact it brought was too great.

China's macroeconomic regulation policies aimed at countering the crisis yielded noticeable outcomes in the short run.[42] China's GDP growth rate fell sharply quarter by quarter in 2008, but under the stimulus of the 4-trillion-yuan plan, from 2009, the quarterly GDP growth rate began to bottom out and rebounded, reaching a recent high of 11.9% in the first quarter of 2010. Various other macroeconomic indicators had also improved to varying degrees. In the context of the first contraction and steep drop in international trade from the conclusion of World War II onward, China's economic performance stood out as remarkably strong. Between 2009 and 2011, China contributed to more than

---

promoting substantial transformation of development mode. *Journal of the Party School of the Central Committee of the CPC*, 2010 (6).

41 Macroeconomic Research Group of Chinese Academy of Governance. Research on the impact of the international financial crisis on China's economy and its countermeasures. *Review of Economic Research*, 2009 (13).

42 Xi Jinping made four latest judgments on the world economic situation. *People's Daily Online*, Nov. 16, 2015.

half of global economic growth.[43] In this phase, China grew into a major engine for global economic recovery. Its GDP overtook Japan's in 2010, making it the world's second-largest economy.

V. The new normal of economy and supply-side structural reforms

As the boosting impacts of an active fiscal policy and accommodative monetary policy gradually faded, China's economy stepped into a new phase characterized by overlapping transitions of various kinds. There included the "shift of economic growth bracket," "throes of economic structural adjustment" and "digestion period of stimulant policies earlier" are superimposed. Structural problems overshadowed by long-term high growth began to emerge, and economic operation faced new challenges. Constraints such as rising wages, scarcity of land, energy shortages, and environmental degradation have become increasingly prominent, making it unsustainable for the extensive growth model with high factor input in exchange for rapid growth. As the rate of economic growth started to decelerate, fresh shifts emerged in China's economic structure and growth drivers. In response to these shifting dynamics, Chinese policymakers made a key strategic assessment, recognizing that "China's economy is entering a new normal." In his keynote address at the 2014 Asia-Pacific Economic Cooperation (APEC) Business Leaders' Summit, General Secretary Xi Jinping provided a comprehensive explanation of the concept of the "new normal" in China's economic development.[44] According to Xi, the "new normal" is characterized by several key features: "First, it has shifted from high-speed growth to medium-high rate of growth. Second, the economic structure has been continuously optimized and upgraded, the consumption demand of the tertiary industry has gradually become the main body, the gap between urban and rural areas has gradually narrowed, and the proportion of residents' income has increased. The achievements of development benefit more people. Third, it has shifted from factor-driven and investment-driven development to innovation-driven development." The "new normal" ushers in fresh avenues for progress. Although the pace of economic expansion has moderated, China's absolute growth remained substantial. Growth is now stable and powered by a broader array of drivers, while the nation's industrial structure continues to upgrade, lending greater resilience to long-term prospects. At the

---

43 National Bureau of Statistics. Reform and opening up creates a new chapter of brilliant economic development—the great changes in China's economic and social development since 1978. *Website of the National Bureau of Statistics*, Nob. 6, 2013.

44 Jinping Xi. Seeking sustainable development and building the Asia-Pacific dream together. *People's Daily Online*, Nov. 10, 2014.

same time, vigorous efforts to streamline administration and devolve power have further unleashed market dynamism. Understanding, adjusting to, and guiding these new normal forms the fundamental logic behind China's present and future economic strategies. Accordingly, the government has been reshaping its macro-management approach-refining the policy framework to keep the economy operating within a reasonable range, with a lower bound that safeguards growth and employment and an upper bound that guards against inflationary pressures. It is emphasized that the macro policy must be stable, and the micro policy must be active and determined, so as to avoid the practice of implementing strong stimulus when the economy fluctuates slightly.[45] These innovative ideas and measures have contributed positively to preserving overall macroeconomic stability, helping to cushion fluctuations and sustain steady development amid complex internal and external challenges.

In the early stage of addressing the global financial crisis, China's macroeconomic strategy gave priority to demand-side regulation, seeking to lift overall social demand by coordinating the use of fiscal and monetary policy instruments. While the macro-control measures centered on demand management did exert a positive effect, it cannot be denied that the policy's efficacy has diminished notably over time. Despite the continued implementation of stimulus measures, such as ramping up investment and repeatedly lowering interest rates and reserve requirements, China's economy continued to face significant structural challenges. Between 2010 and 2015, China's quarterly GDP growth rate showed a sustained downward trend. During this period, the consumer price index (CPI) remained sluggish, while the producer price index (PPI) underwent a sustained decline, dropping for 54 months in a row. The deceleration of economic expansion had also made the problem of structural overcapacity increasingly prominent, and sales at lower prices had become a competitive strategy that companies had to adopt to survive, resulting in a sharp drop in sales revenue and profit levels in the real economy, especially the manufacturing sector. These issues indicated that the challenges facing China's economy were not limited to insufficient aggregate demand but also stemmed from deeper structural imbalances within the economic system. Merely focusing macro-control policies on the demand side was insufficient; they should also turn their attention to the supply side. Some economists pointed out that aggregate regulation was not enough to "conquer the whole world." Given the pronounced structural issues

[45] Jiantang Ma, Haiping Mu, Xiaoguang Wang. Major innovations in China's macro-control ideas and methods under the new normal. *Journal of Chinese Academy of Governance*, 2015 (5).

within China's economy, it became objectively essential to focus on structural remedies. As a result, macroeconomic regulation needed to place greater emphasis on "supply management."[46] Macro-control should focus on supply management, supplemented by demand management. Demand management was used to maintain growth and employment, while supply management was used both to maintain growth and employment, and to adjust the structure. Through the adjustment of the supply structure, it was necessary to stimulate effective supply and reduce ineffective supply.

In November 2015, General Secretary Xi Jinping proposed at the 11th Meeting of the Central Financial and Economic Leading Group that supply-side structural reforms should be intensified, which signified a remarkable shift in macro-control thinking at the top level. In the latter part of that year, the Central Economic Work Conference emphasized that starting from 2016, while moderately expanding aggregate demand, priority should be given to strengthening supply-side structural reforms. By means of steps like slashing overcapacity, reducing excess stock, deleveraging, cutting costs, and shoring up weak links, China needs to tackle problems of industrial overcapacity and real estate surpluses, prevent and defuse financial risks, lighten the cost burden on enterprises, and reinforce both soft and hard infrastructure proactively and steadily. These efforts are intended to boost the quality and efficiency of the supply system, enhance the returns on investment, speed up the development of new growth engines, upgrade and transform traditional comparative advantages, and strengthen the impetus for sustainable development. Pushing forward supply-side structural reform represents a significant strategic innovation to adapt to and steer the new normal of economic development. It embodies a proactive response to the shifting global landscape of national competitiveness in the wake of the international financial crisis, and aligns with the internal demands of China's economic transformation amid the new normal.

Supply-side structural reform yielded remarkable outcomes. The downward trajectory of the economic growth rate was successfully checked. In 2016 and 2017, China's GDP grew by 6.7% and 6.9% respectively, reflecting a steady recovery. At the same time, industrial production experienced a marked rebound, signaling renewed vitality in the real economy. In 2016, the profits of industrial enterprises changed from a decrease of 2.3% in the previous year to an increase of 8.5%, and in 2017 it increased significantly by 21%. Since September 2016, PPI had ended

---

46 Kang Jia. Macro-control with Chinese characteristics: we must pay attention to rational "supply management." *Contemporary Finance & Economics*, 2010 (1); Wei Liu. China's macro-control under the "new normal." *Economic Science*, 2014 (4).

the 54-month decline in a row; fiscal revenue increased by 7.4% in 2017, reversing the slowdown in growth. Residents' income and newly added urban employment continued to grow.[47] Economic development presented a good situation in which growth and quality, structure, and benefits complemented each other.

3. The Industrial Policy in the Macroeconomic Control System

In China, industrial policy holds a vital position within the broader macro-control framework. The "Resolution" adopted at the Third Plenary Session of the 14th CPC Central Committee explicitly stressed that a socialist market economy requires a sound macro-control system. This system should utilize monetary and fiscal policies to regulate the fundamental balance between total social demand and supply, and work in close coordination with industrial policies to guarantee the balanced and harmonious development of the national economy and society. The report of the 17th CPC National Congress highlighted the need to give full play to the guiding role of national development plans, programming, and industrial policies in macro-control, and to comprehensively apply fiscal and monetary policies to enhance the standard of macro-control. The Third Plenary Session of the 18th CPC Central Committee underscored the necessity of improving the macro-control system under the guidance of national development strategies and plans. This enhancement should mainly depend on fiscal and monetary policies, while also strengthening the coordination and synergy between fiscal, monetary, industrial, and pricing policies. Such an all-round and coordinated approach is intended to better align macroeconomic regulation with long-term development objectives and boost the overall efficiency of economic governance.

In the course of reform and opening up, the role and positioning of the Chinese government in economic matters underwent a fundamental shift. Under the planned economy, the government functioned as an all-encompassing administrator, wielding broad control over enterprise operations. During the shift toward a market-oriented economy, the government persisted in utilizing industrial policies as a major instrument to steer economic restructuring. The experiences of East Asian economies like Japan and South Korea, as well as the government's experience in guiding economic development and industrial upgrading through industrial policies, have given China great inspiration. The effectiveness of industrial policies in facilitating rapid growth and structural transformation in these

---

[47] See the 2017 and 2018 Government Work Reports.

regions left a lasting impression on Chinese policymakers and scholars. At that stage, industrial policy was widely seen as a flexible and powerful instrument for government intervention in the economy. It could not only become a tool to enhance market mechanisms through indirect intervention, but also compulsorily reflect the government's will through project approval and price control. The government adjusted the economic structure through the implementation of industrial policies, particularly by formulating development plans and providing directional guidance for key industries. This approach allowed the government to maintain a certain level of influence over the allocation of resources while avoiding the pitfalls of rigid administrative control. Unlike mandatory planning under the planned economy, this form of guidance did not suppress the autonomy and vitality of enterprises, but rather aimed to create a supportive environment in which market forces could operate more effectively within a framework of strategic national priorities. Therefore, no matter what attitude people had on the value judgment of reform, they could agree with the industrial policy as the new form of government intervention.[48] Since the 1980s, the Chinese government has frequently formulated and implemented industrial policies. The government not only formulated national industrial policy frameworks at the macro level, but also developed more targeted sector-specific policies for key industries such as the automobile sector, and enhanced the competitiveness of strategic industries. Consequently, these experiences exerted a significant influence on China's macroeconomic regulation and the overall expansion of its industrial sector.

I. Domestic research on industrial policy since the 1980s

Beginning in the late 1980s, industrial policy gradually evolved into one of the most vibrant and widely discussed areas within China's economic academia. The relevant research at that time mainly revolved around the meaning, composition, and theoretical basis of industrial policy, the selection criteria of leading industries, and the experience and lessons of foreign industrial policies.[49] Building

---

48 Xiaojuan Jiang. *Industrial Policy in the Period of Economic Transition*. Shanghai: Shanghai SDX Joint Publishing Company, 1996.

49 Zhi Yang. *Introduction to Industrial Economics*. Beijing: China Renmin University Press, 1985; Shulian Zhou, et al. *Exploration of industrial policy issues*. Beijing: Economy & Management Publishing House, 1987; Mu Yang. *Industrial Policy Research*. Shanghai: Shanghai SDX Joint Publishing Company, 1989; Boxi Li, Zhishen Qian. *Industrial Policy and National Economies*. Shanghai: Shanghai Scientific and Technological Literature Press, 1990; Zhenhua Zhou. *A Systematic Analysis of the Economic Theory of Industrial Policy*. Beijing: China Renmin University Press, 1991; Huai Chen. *Research on Japanese Industrial Policy*. Beijing: China Renmin University Press, 1991.

upon comprehensive analyses of theoretical developments and policy practices in foreign industrial policy research, Chinese scholars explore the applicability of industrial policy within the domestic context. These studies examined the feasibility of implementing such policies in China, while also identifying key considerations and challenges in light of the country's unique economic and developmental stage. Although some scholars had recognized that industrial policy could not be too deified, the mainstream research at that time widely held that industrial policy was a crucial tool for achieving the modernization of the country's economic system, and formed the central element of the comprehensive economic policy system. The use of industrial policy by the government as a tool for macroeconomic regulation and intervention was viewed as extremely important, given that this method could effectively advance the coordinated, healthy, and stable development of both industry and the wider economy. Scholars generally agreed that the essence of industrial policy lay in facilitating the rational restructuring and transformation of the industrial structure.

As China's implementation of industrial policy gave rise to various problems, its practical results failed to live up to projections. Notably, the far-reaching effects of the Asian financial crisis on Japan and South Korea spurred more in-depth contemplation within the economic sphere regarding the prerequisites, procedures, and mechanisms required for the successful execution of industrial policy. Since the 1990s, the emergence and utilization of various new economic analysis tools have also enabled scholars to examine diverse issues in the formulation and execution of industrial policies from a fresh angle. Some scholars argued that the underlying assumption for the effectiveness of industrial policy was: first, the government's decision-making authorities possessed both the willingness and the capability to design sound and rational industrial policies; second, the government's administrative execution system had the desire and ability to effectively promote the industrial policies; third, solving problems through industrial policies cost less than through market mechanisms. However, the premise that the government was regarded as the representative of the "overall interests" and that the government could formulate policies "fairly and objectively" had some shortcomings. Industrial policies could not only solve industrial structure problems, but also cause industrial structure problems. When industrial policies were adopted in some competitive industries that would obviously interfere with the normal functioning of the market mechanism, the costs might exceed the scope of structural changes, and special caution was required.[50]

---

[50] Xiaojuan Jiang. The problem of public choice in the implementation of industrial policy in China. *Economic Research Journal*, 1993 (6).

Empirical research has been the main feature of domestic industrial policy research since the twenty-first century, and the research perspective has gradually shifted from macro-level industrial structure research to more specific industry research. Compared with general research at the level of industrial structure, research on industry-specific industrial policies is more conducive to identifying the performance of industrial policies, analyzing the mechanism and institutional basis of industrial policies, summarizing the experience and lessons in the formulation and implementation of industrial policies, and having a deeper understanding of the applicability and application areas of industrial policies. Some scholars evaluated the performance of China's industrial policy implementation through research on representative industries such as automobiles, textiles, electronics, and electrical appliances.[51] Building on the scholarly research outcomes, industrial policies had indeed exerted a notable impact in rapidly boosting the supply capacity of specific short-term products demanding large-scale investment, as well as in easing long-standing shortages in infrastructure. However, considerable evidence also suggests that actual outcomes of these policies often fell short of their intended goals. To adjust the irrational economic structure, the government employed a range of policy tools to support the development of what it identified as dominant or pillar industries. However, aside from the infrastructure sector, industrial policies did not appear to play a significant position in driving the development of competitive industries. There was insufficient evidence to demonstrate that the industries targeted by these policies had achieved substantial or sustained development. Many facts showed people from another aspect that, thanks to relatively sufficient market competition, some industrial sectors that had not been included in the scope of industrial policy support had grown rapidly. Against the original purpose of government industrial policies, in industries where government intervention was limited, regulation was relatively relaxed, and the state-owned sector held no absolute advantage, such as household appliances and washing products, the market forces steadily broke through the limitations set by those policies. Following the initial phase of repeated investments and intense competition,

---

[51] Xiaojuan Jiang, et al. *Growth, Performance and Industrial Organization Changes in Institutional Transition—An Empirical Study on Several Industries in China*. Shanghai: Shanghai SDX Joint Publishing Company, 1999; Ying Zhao. *Empirical Analysis of China's Industrial Policy*. Beijing: Social Sciences Academic Press, 2000; Yang Yu, Wei Lu, Xingzhi Xiao, et al. *China's Economic Reform and Development: Policy and Performance.* Dalian: Dongbei University of Finance and Economics Press, 2005; Xianpei Li, Lijun Hu. *China's Industrial Policy in the Early 21st Century*. Beijing: Economy & Management Publishing House, 2005.

the market structure underwent a cyclical process characterized by a phase of "centralization-decentralization-recentralization,"[52] and the industrial organization structure had been optimized through competition. A group of enterprises with mass production capacity and advanced production technology had been selected by the market mechanism. Conversely, in some competitive industries with deepest government involvement and the greatest intervention, although it was regarded as a key strategic industry and had long benefited from protective industrial policies and preferential resource allocation, the negative effects of these policies were evident, chiefly in how administrative intervention suppressed market competition mechanisms. Some enterprises regarded by the government as the "national team" had enjoyed high profits granted by industrial policies for a long time in a market environment with no impact from multinational corporations outside and no competition from private enterprises inside, and their core competitiveness had not been substantively improved. Therefore, some scholars believed: "The process of rapid development of many industries since the reform is a process of breaking through the predictions of relevant government departments, breaking away from their plans, and getting rid of their interference. If most of the government's intervention is realized, the development of these industries will be much delayed."[53]

II. Research on the performance of industrial policy implementation

Practical outcomes in most industrial sectors indicate a significant gap between the intended objectives of China's industrial policies and their actual implementation effects. What causes this divergence? This issue has emerged as a central focus in academic discussions on industrial policy. Some scholars have contended that the power dynamics between central and local governments constituted a critical factor behind the ineffective implementation of industrial policies.[54] They pointed out that during the economic transition, the system of administrative decentralization markedly enhanced local governments' capacity to distribute resources.

---

52 Houkai Wei. *From Repetitive Construction to Orderly Competition*. Beijing: People's Publishing House, 2001; Houkai Wei. *Market Competition, Economic Performance, and Industrial Concentration: An Empirical Analysis of China's Manufacturing Concentration and Market Structure*. Beijing: Economy & Management Publishing House, 2003.

53 Feng Lu, Kaidong Feng. *Policy Choices for Developing China's Auto Industry with Independent Intellectual Property Rights*. Major National Science and Technology Innovation Policy Commissioned Research Project, February 2004.

54 Xiaojuan Jiang, et al. *Growth, Performance and Industrial Organization Changes in Institutional Transition—An Empirical Study on Several Industries in China*. Shanghai: Shanghai SDX Joint Publishing Company, 1999, p. 51.

As local economic interests expanded, the central government's capability for macroeconomic management was relatively weakened, creating considerable leeway for local governments to pursue their own agendas.[55] Industrial policies were policy frameworks devised by the central government to advance the development of particular industries and regions, in line with the overall interests of the national economy. Due to the inherently biased nature of industrial policy, equitable resource distribution across industries and regions was unachievable. Therefore, industrial policy would inevitably conflict with the economic interests of certain regions to a certain extent. Drawing on game theory, some scholars have analyzed the strategic interactions and policy choices made between the local government and the central government, as well as among various local governments. It was believed that under the premise of a lack of an interest coordination mechanism in industrial development, regional interest obstacles were the fundamental reasons for the failure of industrial policy.[56] A research report from the Development Research Center of the State Council also stressed that the persistent problems of fragmentation and inefficiency—commonly characterized as "small, scattered, and disorderly" in China's automotive industry—were largely rooted in the frictions between central and local governments.[57] The power dynamics and competition for authority in industrial policy implementation significantly undermined the overall effectiveness of such policies.

Some studies have explored the micro-foundations underlying the implementation of industrial policies in China. Scholars have pointed out that China's approach differs fundamentally from that of countries like Japan and South Korea. While governments in those countries primarily interact with private enterprises when executing industrial policies, in China, the government has historically dealt predominantly with state-owned enterprises. In China, except for the light industry sector, most industrial policies in China, either deliberately or inadvertently, were designed with state-owned enterprises as the main beneficiaries or implementation targets.[58] Some scholars argued that both central and local governments extended a wide range of preferential policies to key sectors

---

[55] Peihua Huang, Deepak Bhattasali. *China: National Development and Sub-National Finance.* Beijing: CITIC Press, 2003; He Gao. Fiscal decentralization, economic structure and local government behavior. *The Journal of World Economy*, 2006 (10).

[56] Xuying Zhang. Game analysis of the reasons for the failure of industrial policy. *Economic Survey*, 2004 (1).

[57] Qingtai Chen, Shijin Liu, Fei Feng, et al. *Meeting the Chinese Automobile Society: Prospects, Problems, and Policies.* Beijing: China Development Press, 2004.

[58] Ying Zhao. *Empirical Analysis of China's Industrial Policy.* Beijing: Social Science Academic Press, 2000.

and state-owned enterprises favored by the national industrial policies, while non-priority sectors and non-state-owned enterprises were largely excluded from such benefits. This unequal policy treatment created an imbalanced competitive environment, limiting the development opportunities for private enterprises and emerging industries outside the focus of state support. "Policy rent" was given directly to the state-owned sector, rather than through an open competition for winners.[59] Certain scholars noted that during the 1980s and 1990s, a period when China was carrying out industrial policies extensively, the state-owned sector occupied a prominent place in the industrial landscape. The heavy policy burdens imposed on state-owned enterprises meant that they could only remain viable within a sheltered environment, protected from the pressures of full market competition.[60] Once the government decided to distribute camera-type rent through competition, state-owned enterprises with heavy social burden would undoubtedly be at a disadvantage in the fierce competition. The tight ties between state-owned enterprises and the government inherently hindered the state's ability to reach its established efficiency targets through competition. This delicate relationship distorted the incentive mechanism of industrial policy to a large extent, so that the rules of the game for industrial policy formulation and implementation ultimately chose to protect and support state-owned enterprises, rather than open and fair competition among all enterprises. Excessive implementation of targeted industrial policies with specific preferences ended up reinforcing entrenched interest groups and distorting the proper functioning of market mechanisms.

What types of industrial policy could genuinely deliver a positive role? Justin Yifu Lin had systematically provided an analysis of this question under the framework of New Structural Economics. In his view, industrial policy still held promise. The reason why the industrial policies of most developing nations had been unsuccessful in the past was that the governments of these countries were too ambitious, and when they chose industries to support, they deviated from their own resource base and development level, and preferred those industries that deviated from their own resource endowments and competitive advantages and were too advanced. He aimed to create a growth screening and contextualization framework designed to assist policymakers in developing nations to

59 Shaohong Zhu, Yi Quan. The conditions for effective implementation of industrial policy and the practice of industrial policy in China. *Asia-Pacific Journal of Economics*, 2002 (4).

60 Yifu Lin, Fang Cai, Zhou Li. The connotation of modern corporate system and the reform direction of state-owned enterprises. *Economic Research Journal*, 1997 (3).

pinpoint emerging industries that match their countries' comparative advantages.[61] Some scholars compared the research on industrial policy under two different theoretical paradigms: Evolutionary Economics and Neoclassical Economics. They believed that the New Structural Economics had serious defects and was not suitable for China. A technology catch-up strategy, rather than a pure comparative advantage strategy, was considered more suitable for China's national conditions.[62] Some scholars carefully combed the theoretical literature on industrial policy research at home and abroad in recent years and found that most of the so-called "market failures" in developing and transitioning countries were actually "government failures" or "system failures," and the implementation of industrial policies that directly intervened in the market would only exacerbate the problem. Therefore, the fundamental orientation of industrial policy should be to preserve and foster market competition, boost the efficiency of market mechanisms, and expand the range of market activities. Rather than replacing the market, industrial policy ought to function as a supportive tool, facilitating the healthy development of industry and national economy by continuously improving market-based institutions and expanding the position of the market in resource distribution.[63]

III. Research on industrial policy and emerging industry development

Despite the profound repercussions of the international financial crisis, many developed and emerging economies continued to prioritize the development of emerging industries, aiming to secure a competitive edge in the evolving landscape of global economic competition. In response, the Chinese government raised the development of new industries to the status of a national strategic priority. In 2010, it promulgated the "Decision of the State Council on Accelerating the Cultivation and Development of Strategic Emerging Industries," and in 2015, it formulated and implemented the "Made in China 2025" plan. The Chinese government proposed to enhance fundamental industrial capabilities, vigorously advance intelligent manufacturing, accelerate the deep integration

61 Justin Yifu Lin. *New Structural Economics*. Beijing: Peking University Press, 2012.

62 Genliang Jia. Evolutionary development economics and new structural economics—which theoretical paradigm of industrial policy is more suitable for China's national conditions. *South China Journal of Economics*, 2018 (1).

63 Xiaoping Li, Feitao Jiang. To intervene the market or to enhance and expand the market: issues, debates and theoretical reconstructions in industrial policy. *Comparative Studies*, 2012 (3).

of next-generation information technology with the manufacturing sector, and continuously achieve new breakthroughs in the path of industrialization with Chinese characteristics.

Chinese academic communities have actively participated in debates about the government's role in promoting the growth of strategic emerging industries. A number of scholars proposed that, considering the features and developmental patterns of strategic emerging industries, the government ought to adopt industrial policy mechanisms such as scientific and technological management systems, incentive policies and measures, and market environment construction, and appropriately use fiscal, tax, financial and even import and export policy tools at various stages of industrial development to drive the expansion and maturation of new industries.[64] Some scholars believed that when the government encouraged and guided enterprises to enter strategic emerging industries, it should formulate targeted policies and measures based on the inherent characteristics, developmental patterns, and the unique nature of strategic emerging industries, ensuring that the support provided aligns with their specific needs and stages of growth. Through differentiated policy guidance, targeted resource allocation, and effective organization and coordination, the government could help reduce uncertainties in the development of strategic emerging industries, thereby encouraging more capable enterprises to enter these sectors at an early stage.[65]

Numerous scholars acknowledged that when supporting the development of new industries, the government should abide by the laws of industrial growth and meticulously pinpoint key fields and links where support can be most impactful. Some maintained that in the initial phases of emerging industries—when technologies, products, and business models are still evolving—the scale of industrialization ought to stay moderate. Premature large-scale expansion could easily result in severe overcapacity and significant investment risks. At this stage, the government not only needed to provide supply-side support policies such as financial subsidies and discounted loans, but also needed to stimulate market demand for new products and new technologies through demand-side subsidies such as product application demonstration subsidies and new product purchase subsidies.[66] Some scholars analyzed the root causes of the severe overcapacity

64 Jinwen Ju. "Variables" in the development of strategic emerging industries: the division of labor between the government and the market. *Reform*, 2011 (3).

65 Xiaodan Guo, Weijia Song. The timing of entering strategic emerging industries: leading or following up. *China Industrial Economics*, 2011 (5).

66 Jun Wan, Xiaoqi Feng. Discussion on the development model of China's strategic emerging industries from a global perspective. *Jiangxi Social Sciences*, 2012 (5).

often observed in emerging industries supported by the government. They argued that misguided decisions made at the national level were frequently amplified, driven by distorted incentives, and encouraged enterprises to overinvest. As a result, this investment ultimately led to significant overproduction and capacity surplus in the targeted industries.[67]

In recent years, when domestic academic circles carried out research on industrial policy and the development of emerging industries, they did not stop at the level of qualitative analysis in terms of the evaluation of the effect of industrial policy, but used new analytical tools to carry out quantitative research. Many domestic scholars tried to establish an index system for industrial policy evaluation. They carried out quantitative analyses to assess the impact of high-tech industry policies across key regions of the country, especially in representative provinces such as Jiangsu, Guangdong, Hubei, and Zhejiang, and found that under the impetus of industrial policies, both the number and output scale of high-tech industries had seen rapid growth. However, this was mainly due to the increase in scale rather than technological progress. Therefore, it was believed that the current industrial policy had improved the resource allocation efficiency of emerging industries, but the incentives for innovation activities were not obvious.[68] Several academics have probed into the recent growth of China's solar power industry, utilizing the production function method to gauge capacity utilization levels across its three major segments. They also evaluated factors such as the extent of government subsidies, land price distortions, and levels of financial, analyzing their impacts on overcapacity. Their findings suggested that inappropriate government intervention in emerging industries had contributed significantly to the problem of overcapacity.

IV. Research on Industrial Policy and Competition Policy

With the ongoing advancement within the socialist market economy system and increasing openness to the outside world, a growing number of scholars have recognized that within this system, the market mechanism and competitive processes

---

67 Weiguo Qiao, Juan Zhou. Research on the causes and countermeasures of policy-induced overcapacity. *Future and Development*, 2012 (9).

68 Mingjie Lu, Song Chen. China's high-tech industry policy performance and its convergence analysis. *Science of Science and Management of S. & T.*, 2011 (2); Zelei Xiao, Shunfa Han. Evaluation of the effect of high-tech industry policy implementation: taking the high-tech industry policy group in Jiangsu Province as an example (1998–2008). *Science & Technology Progress and Policy*, 2011 (14); Ling Ning, Liang Wang, Zefang Liao. Research on high-tech industry policy evaluation based on DEA: taking Guangdong Province as an example. *Journal of Chinese Academy of Governance*, 2011 (2).

are crucial for optimizing resource allocation, driving industrial growth, and fostering the rationalization of industrial and economic structures. Accordingly, the government must shift its role from being the primary driver of economic development to becoming the guardian of fair competition. To successfully expand its opening up and make the most of both domestic and global markets and resources, China must gradually put in place institutional systems and norms that guarantee fair, open, and non-discriminatory competition. As a result, balancing the relationship between industrial policy and competition policy has become an urgent and crucial issue that China needs to tackle promptly.[69] Wu Jinglian underscored the significance of conducting in-depth reflection on more than three decades of China's industrial policy practices, advocating a shift from an industrial policy-oriented framework to one grounded in competition policy—thus enabling the market to assume a pivotal role in resource allocation.[70] Some scholars argued that the global resource allocation driven by economic globalization has inevitably weakened sovereign states' direct control over their resources, increasing the risk of industrial policy failure. For developing countries like China, competition policy, rather than industrial policy, was more effective for promoting industrial development and enhancing enterprise competitiveness, and thus should be prioritized.[71] Other scholars proposed substituting selective industrial policies with functional ones, redirecting the focus from enlarging the scale of specific industries to enhancing the quality of industrial development, and shifting from preferential measures to inclusive competition preservation and innovation encouragement.[72] In the implementation of functional industrial policies, governments should also formulate and improve competition policies, and regulate enterprises' competitive practices to ensure they comply with the principles of voluntariness, fairness, reciprocity, compensation, and good faith—thereby safeguarding the order of fair trade and competition.[73] This required that China should realize the transformation of economic policy that could promote

[69] Donghua Yu, Yinan Lu. Improper government intervention and overcapacity in strategic emerging industries: taking China's photovoltaic industry as an example. *China Industrial Economics*, 2015 (10).

[70] Jinglian Wu. China's industrial policy: not to abolish, but to transform. *China Business and Market*, 2017 (11).

[71] Dongjiang Zhang. *WTO Competition Policy Negotiation and the Choice of Developing Countries*. Beijing: China Social Sciences Press, 2005.

[72] Jun Wang, Zhen Zhou. Seeing the transformation of China's industrial policy from the relevant debates. *Comparative Economic & Social Systems*, 2017 (1).

[73] Bei Jin. *Competition Order and Competition Policy*. Beijing: Social Sciences Academic Press, 2005.

industrial development as soon as possible, from an industrial policy-led to a competition policy-led pattern.

References

Bai, Qinxian. A comparison of inflation between China and foreign countries and the characteristics, causes and countermeasures of current inflation in China. *Studies of International Finance*, 1995 (1).

Chen, Huai. *Research on Japanese Industrial Policy*. Beijing: China Renmin University Press, 1991.

Chen, Qingtai, Shijin Liu, Fei Feng, et al. *Meeting the Chinese Automobile Society: Prospects, Problems, and Policies.* Beijing: China Development Press, 2004.

China National Accounting and Economic Growth Research Center, Peking University. Analysis of China's economic trend from 2003 to 2004—has China's economy overheated? *Economic Science Journal*, 2003 (6).

Decision of the Central Committee of the Communist Party of China on Reform of the Economic Structure. Oct. 20, 1984.

Fan, Conglai. On the effectiveness of monetary policy in the period of deflation. *Economic Research Journal*, 2000 (7).

Fan, Gang. "Soft Constraint Competition" and China's Inflation in Recent Years. *Journal of Financial Research*, 1994 (9).

Fan, Gang. Deflation, effective price reduction and economic fluctuation: an analysis of several characteristics of China's current macro-economy. *Economic Research Journal*, 2003 (7).

Fang, Weizhong. Some views on the current economic situation and macro-control. *Shanghai Enterprise*, 2006 (10); Dong Tao. Be wary of economic overheating without inflation. *Development Herald*, 3rd Edition, August 12, 2003.

Gao, He. Fiscal decentralization, economic structure and local government behavior. *The Journal of World Economy*, 2006 (10).

Gao, Huiqing, Yizhi Xiong, Shaowei Hu. The world financial crisis and its impact on China's economy. *Studies of International Finance*, 2008 (11).

Gao, Peiyong. Tax policy choices under deflation—a discussion on current tax cut propositions. *Economic Research Journal*, 2000 (1).

Genliang Jia. Evolutionary development economics and new structural economics—which theoretical paradigm of industrial policy is more suitable for China's national conditions. *South China Journal of Economics*, 2018 (1).

Guo, Xiaodan, Weijia Song. The timing of entering strategic emerging industries: leading or following up. *China Industrial Economics*, 2011 (5).

Han, Wenxiu. Research on the relationship between economic growth and inflation. *Management World*, 1996 (6).

Hu, Angang. The characteristics, causes and countermeasures of China's deflation. *Management World*, 1999 (3).

Hu, Angang. The characteristics, causes and countermeasures of China's deflation. *Management World*, 1999 (3).

Huang, Peihua, Deepak Bhattasali. *China: National Development and Sub-National Finance.* Beijing: CITIC Press, 2003;

Institute of International Trade and Economic Cooperation, Comprehensive Department of the Ministry of Commerce. Report on China's Foreign Trade Situation (Spring 2009). *Website of the Ministry of Commerce*, May 4, 2009.

Jia, Kang. Macro-control with Chinese characteristics: we must pay attention to rational "supply management." *Contemporary Finance & Economics*, 2010 (1); Wei Liu. China's macro-control under the "new normal." *Economic Science*, 2014 (4).

Jiang, Xiaojuan, et al. *Growth, Performance and Industrial Organization Changes in Institutional Transition—An Empirical Study on Several Industries in China*. Shanghai: Shanghai SDX Joint Publishing Company, 1999.

Jiang, Xiaojuan. *Industrial Policy in the Period of Economic Transition*. Shanghai: Shanghai SDX Joint Publishing Company, 1996.

Jiang, Xiaojuan. The problem of public choice in the implementation of industrial policy in China. *Economic Research Journal*, 1993 (6).

Jin, Bei. *Competition Order and Competition Policy*. Beijing: Social Sciences Academic Press, 2005.

Ju, Jinwen. "Variables" in the development of strategic emerging industries: the division of labor between the government and the market. *Reform*, 2011 (3).

Li, Boxi, Zhishen Qian. *Industrial Policy and National Economies*. Shanghai: Shanghai Scientific and Technological Literature Press, 1990.

Li, Xianpei, Lijun Hu. *China's Industrial Policy in the Early 21st Century*. Beijing: Economy & Management Publishing House, 2005.

Li, Xiaoping, Feitao Jiang. To intervene the market or to enhance and expand the market: issues, debates and theoretical reconstructions in industrial policy. *Comparative Studies*, 2012 (3).

Li, Xiaoxi. Structural inflation in the transition process. *Economic Research Journal*, 1994 (10).

Lin, Yifu. *New Structural Economics.* Beijing: Peking University Press, 2012.

Lin, Yifu, Fang Cai, Zhou Li. The connotation of modern enterprise system and the reform direction of state-owned enterprises. *Economic Research Journal*, 1997 (3).

Liu, Guoguang, et al. Economic system reform and macroeconomic management—review of "International Symposium on Macroeconomic Management." *Economic Research Journal*, 1985 (12).
Liu, Guoguang. Double prudent macro-control policies. *Chinese Cadres Tribune*, 2005 (1).
Liu, Guoguang. Miscellaneous talks about macro-control. *Economic Perspectives*, 2004 (10).
Liu, Shucheng. Deflation: neither underestimation nor overestimation. *Economic Research Journal*, 1999 (10).
Lu, Feng, Kaidong Feng. *Policy Choices for Developing China's Auto Industry with Independent Intellectual Property Rights*. Major National Science and Technology Innovation Policy Commissioned Research Project, February 2004.
Lu, Mingjie, Song Chen. China's high-tech industry policy performance and its convergence analysis. *Science of Science and Management of S. & T.*, 2011 (2).
Ma, Jiantang, Haiping Mu, Xiaoguang Wang. Major innovations in China's macro-control ideas and methods under the new normal. *Journal of Chinese Academy of Governance*, 2015 (5).
Macroeconomic Group, China Economic Research Center, Peking University. Facing up to the pressure of deflation, and speeding up the reform of micro-mechanism. *Economic Research Journal*, 1999 (7).
Macroeconomic Research Center, Comprehensive Development Research Institute (Shenzhen, China). The Phillips model and China's inflation: a theoretical analysis of the causes, trends and policy choices of China's comprehensive inflation. *Economic Research Journal*, 1996 (2).
Macroeconomic Research Group of Chinese Academy of Governance. Research on the impact of the international financial crisis on China's economy and its countermeasures. *Review of Economic Research*, 2009 (13).
National Bureau of Statistics. *Bulletin of the main data of the third national industrial census*. National Bureau of Statistics website.
National Bureau of Statistics. Reform and opening up creates a new chapter of brilliant economic development—the great changes in China's economic and social development since 1978. *Website of the National Bureau of Statistics*, Nob. 6, 2013.
Ning, Ling, Wang, Liang, Zefang Liao. Research on high-tech industry policy evaluation based on DEA: taking Guangdong Province as an example. *Journal of Chinese Academy of Governance*, 2011 (2).
Pei, Ping, Qian Zhang, Zhifeng Hu. The impact of the international financial crisis on China's export trade: an empirical study based on monthly data from 2007 to 2008. *Journal of Financial Research*, 2009 (8).

Qian, Xiaoan. The causes, hazards and countermeasures of deflation. *Journal of Financial Research*, 1999 (9).

Qiao, Weiguo, Juan Zhou. Research on the causes and countermeasures of policy-induced overcapacity. *Future and Development*, 2012 (9).

The research group of the Development Research Center of the State Council. China: Seeking new breakthroughs in responding to the crisis. *Management World*, 2009 (6).

Wan, Jun, Xiaoqi Feng. Discussion on the development model of China's strategic emerging industries from a global perspective. *Jiangxi Social Sciences*, 2012 (5).

Wang, Jun, Zhen Zhou. Seeing the transformation of China's industrial policy from the relevant debates. *Comparative Economic & Social Systems*, 2017 (1).

Wang, Tongsan, Tao Li. The deep-seated causes of China's deflation. *Social Sciences in China*, 2001 (6).

Wang, Yijiang. The behavioral mechanism of investment expansion and inflation in economic reform. *Economic Research Journal*, 1994 (6).

Wei Liu, Zhizhou Cai. China's macro-control mode faces challenges and reforms. *Economic Herald*, 2006 (6).

Wei, Houkai. *From Repetitive Construction to Orderly Competition*. Beijing: People's Publishing House, 2001.

Wei, Houkai. *Market Competition, Economic Performance and Industrial Concentration: An Empirical Analysis of China's Manufacturing Concentration and Market Structure*. Beijing: Economy & Management Publishing House, 2003.

Wen Jiabao's government work report at the 2nd Session of the 11th National People's Congress. *Chinese Government Website*, March 5, 2009.

Wu, Jinglian. China's economic "soft landing" is possible. *Chinese Cadres Tribune*, 2004 (6).

Wu, Jinglian. China's industrial policy: not to abolish, but to transform. *China Business and Market*, 2017 (11).

Xi Jinping made four latest judgments on the world economic situation. *People's Daily Online*, Nov. 16, 2015.

Xi, Jinping. Seeking sustainable development and building the Asia-Pacific dream together. *People's Daily Online*, Nov. 10, 2014.

Xiao, Zelei, Shunfa Han. Evaluation of the effect of high-tech industry policy implementation: taking the high-tech industry policy group in Jiangsu Province as an example (1998–2008). *Science & Technology Progress and Policy*, 2011 (14).

Xie, Ping, Bingxi Shen. Deflation and monetary policy. *Economic Research Journal*, 1999 (8).

Xie, Ping. Inflation and currency control in China's transition economy. *Journal of Financial Research*, 1994 (10).

Yang, Mu. *Industrial Policy Research*. Shanghai: Shanghai SDX Joint Publishing Company, 1989.

Yang, Zhi. *Introduction to Industrial Economics*. Beijing: China Renmin University Press, 1985.

Yin, Shijie. Several issues of China's current expansion of consumer demand. *China Business and Market*, 2009 (7).

Yu, Bin, Changsheng Chen. Expanding consumer demand and promoting substantial transformation of development mode. *Journal of the Party School of the Central Committee of the CPC*, 2010 (6).

Yu, Donghua, Yinan Lu. Improper government intervention and overcapacity in strategic emerging industries: taking China's photovoltaic industry as an example. *China Industrial Economics*, 2015 (10).

Yu, Yang, Wei Lu, Xingzhi Xiao, et al. *China's Economic Reform and Development: Policy and Performance*. Dalian: Dongbei University of Finance and Economics Press, 2005.

Yu, Yongding. Breaking the vicious circle of deflation: a new challenge for China's economic development. *Economic Research Journal*, 1999 (7).

Yu, Zuyao. The assertion that "China is currently in a deflationary predicament" is groundless. *Journal of Shenyang Party Institute of CPC*, 1999 (2).

Zeng, Guoan. The causes of China's deflation in the 1990s and anti-deflation policies. *Contemporary Economic Research*, 2001 (2).

Zhang, Chewei. The impact of the global financial crisis on the employment of migrant workers: impact analysis and countermeasures. *Chinese Journal of Population Science*, 2009 (2).

Zhang, Dongjiang. *WTO Competition Policy Negotiation and the Choice of Developing Countries*. Beijing: China Social Sciences Press, 2005.

Zhang, Xuying. Game analysis of the reasons for the failure of industrial policy. *Economic Survey*, 2004 (1).

Zhang, Zhuoyuan. Research and innovation of macroeconomic management theory with Chinese characteristics. *30 Years of Chinese Economics (1978–2008)*. Beijing: China Social Sciences Press, 2008: 167.

Zhao, Renwei. Retrospect and reflection on the "Bashan" Cruise Conference in 1985. *Economic Research Journal*, 2008 (12).

Zhao, Xiao. China's high return on investment does not mean that the economy is overheating. *China Logistics & Purchasing*, 2006 (21).

Zhao, Ying. *Empirical Analysis of China's Industrial Policy*. Beijing: Social Science Academic Press, 2000.

Zhao, Ying. *Empirical Analysis of China's Industrial Policy*. Beijing: Social Sciences Academic Press, 2000.

Zhou, Shulian, et al. *Exploration of industrial policy issues*. Beijing: Economy & Management Publishing House, 1987.

Zhou, Zhenhua. *A Systematic Analysis of the Economic Theory of Industrial Policy*. Beijing: China Renmin University Press, 1991.

Zhu, Shaohong, Yi Quan. The conditions for effective implementation of industrial policy and the practice of industrial policy in China. *Asia-Pacific Journal of Economics*, 2002 (4).

Zuo, Dapei. Macroeconomic overheating essentially stems from the economic predicament. *China Opening Journal*, 2004 (5).

The Evolution of the Theory of Opening up

Wider and deeper opening up is China's basic state policy. Since the Third Plenary Session of the 11th Central Committee of the Communist Party of China, China has continuously improved the level of opening up, realizing a major transition from a closed and semi-closed state to all-round opening. In the course of deepening its integration with the global economy, China has effectively leveraged both domestic and international markets and resources, organically combined "bringing in" and "going global," optimized the regional layout of opening up, promoted the implementation of the *Belt and Road Initiative*, and actively participated in the governance of the global economy. A fresh framework characterized by comprehensive, multi-tiered, and extensive openness has been formed. To more effectively respond to emerging shifts in the international political and economic environment, China has been establishing a renewed framework for an open economy "to accelerate the cultivation of new advantages in international cooperation and competition, and more actively promote the balance between domestic demand and external demand, imports and exports, and foreign capital introduction and outbound investment. China is committed to achieving the basic balance of payments gradually, forming a new pattern of all-round opening up, and realizing the modernization of an open economic governance system and governance capacity."[1] As China's overall national economy steadily grows, China is set to take on a progressively greater role in driving global economic growth and advancing the reform and enhancement of international governance structures.

As the principal architect behind China's reform, opening up, and socialist modernization, Deng Xiaoping was instrumental in the formation and

1 Several opinions of the Central Committee of the Communist Party of China and the State Council on building a new system of open economy. *Xinhuanet*, Sept. 17, 2015.

improvement of China's opening-up system. Deng Xiaoping once made a thorough exposition on the general idea of China's opening to the outside world. First, the reason why China implemented the policy of external engagement was not only a summary of historical experience and lessons, but also to satisfy the demands of new changes in the world economy. "The present world is open. One important reason for China's backwardness after the industrial revolution in Western countries was its closed-door policy. After the founding of the People's Republic, we were blockaded by others, so the country remained virtually closed, which created difficulties for us. The experience of the past 30 or so years has demonstrated that a closed-door policy would hinder construction and inhibit development. There could be two kinds of exclusion: one would be directed against other countries; the other would be directed against China itself, with one region or department closing its doors to the others. Both kinds of exclusion would be harmful. We are suggesting that we should develop rapidly, but not too rapidly because that would be unrealistic. To do this, we have to invigorate the domestic economy and open to the outside world."[2] Second, he clarified the principles and paths of opening up. "It goes without saying that a large country like China cannot depend on others for its development; it must depend mainly on itself, on its own efforts. Nevertheless, while holding to self-reliance, we should open our country to the outside world to obtain such aid as foreign investment capital and technology."[3] "We have opened 14 large and medium-sized coastal cities. We welcome foreign investment and advanced techniques. Management is also a technique."[4] Third, China should expand the areas of opening up to more countries. We should expand opening up, which has not been enough. Given the current economic challenges facing Western European nations, it is imperative that we seize the opportunity to pursue cooperation with them to accelerate our technological upgrading. Similar efforts should be made with Eastern European countries, as some of their technologies are more advanced than ours, while they also have a demand for certain technologies we possess. As China represents a vast market, many countries are eager to collaborate or engage in trade with us. We must grasp this opportunity without delay, as it holds significant strategic value.[5] Fourth, opening to the outside world was not a pragmatic solution, but a long-term national policy. "Invigorating our domestic economy and opening

---

2 Xiaoping Deng. *Selected Works of Deng Xiaoping, Vol. 3.* Beijing: People's Publishing House, 1993, pp. 64–65.

3 Ibid., pp. 78–79.

4 Ibid., p. 65.

5 Ibid., p. 32.

to the outside world are long-term, not short-term, policies that will remain unchanged for at least 50 or 70 years. Why? Because quadrupling the GNP, which will take 20 years, is only our first step and will be followed by a second, approaching the level of developed countries, which will take 30 or 50, let's say 50, years. The two steps together will take 50 or 70 years. By then it will be even less likely that the policies will change. If anything, we shall open up still more. Our people would not allow anything else."[6] Fifth, as China's economy became increasingly integrated with the global economic system, China would actively contribute to global economic development. "China's foreign trade makes up a very small portion of the world's total. If we succeed in quadrupling the GNP, the volume of our foreign trade will increase considerably, promoting economic relations with other countries and expanding the Chinese market. Therefore, judged from the international perspective, China's development will benefit world peace and the world economy." Deng Xiaoping's thought on opening to the outside world has become a key component of the theory of socialism with Chinese characteristics, and has provided strategic guidance in China's opening to the outside world.

Economists have taken an active part in the ongoing advancement of China's external openness. Domestic academic circles have focused on developing foreign trade, "bringing in" and "going global," optimizing the layout of open areas, promoting the *Belt and Road Initiative*, engaging in international economic governance, etc., and have achieved fruitful results, which have provided important theoretical support for the continuous upgrading of China's opening to the outside world.

1. Research on Foreign Trade

Since reform and opening up, especially after joining the WTO, China's foreign trade has achieved tremendous development. In 1978, the total value of China's imports and exports amounted to just US$20.6 billion, ranking 32nd in the world. In 2004, China's total foreign trade volume exceeded the US$1 trillion mark; it doubled in just three years, and exceeded US$2 trillion in 2007. In 2011, when the impact of the global financial crisis had not yet dissipated, China's total import and export volume exceeded US$3 trillion. In 2013, the total import and export volume reached US$4.16 trillion, surpassing the United States in one fell swoop and becoming the world's largest trader of goods. In 2017, the total

[6] Ibid., p. 79.

import and export value of China's trade in goods reached 27.79 trillion yuan, continuing to uphold its position as the world's leading goods trader. The swift expansion of foreign trade has generated numerous issues and rich materials for theoretical research. Researchers have conducted thorough investigations into important issues in foreign trade theory and practice, which have promoted the evolution and flourishing of China's foreign trade theory. Since China's foreign trade scale, structure, major problems, and foreign trade development strategies were different prior to and following China's accession to the WTO, the research hotspots in academia also showed certain differences. This section will discuss them separately.

I. Research on foreign trade before joining the WTO

(1) The important status and role of foreign trade

For a long period of time after the founding of the People's Republic of China, the domestic understanding of the role and significance of foreign trade in building a socialist economy was very limited. It was believed that the role of foreign trade was only to "exchange what is needed and adjust what is left and what is missing," and it was only to adjust the economic structure within a local scope and make up for the shortage of materials. At the outset of reform and opening up, while embracing openness to the outside world had become a fundamental national strategy, in the field of foreign trade, there were still views that advocated the expansion of foreign economic relations but opposed the international division of labor as the guiding principle. Wang Linsheng pointed out that holders of such contradictory views might think that the global division of labor conflicts with the goal of building an independent and relatively comprehensive national economic system.[7] In fact, what was opposed to the international division of labor was not an independent and complete economic system, but a closed-off, self-sufficient system. In foreign economic and trade relations, the principle of "enhancing strengths and avoiding weaknesses, and giving full play to advantages" should be implemented, and the global division of labor should be actively utilized. Yuan Wenqi and Wang Jianmin also advocated that the importance and position of foreign trade in the development of China's national economy should be re-understood and evaluated.[8] They believed that, as a country with highly socialized mass production, China should engage in the global division of labor

7 Linsheng Wang. On the status and role of socialist foreign trade. *Intertrade*, 1982 (2).

8 Wenqi Yuan, Jianmin Wang. Re-understanding and evaluating the role and status of foreign trade in the development of China's national economy. *Intertrade*, 1982(1).

and establish diverse economic connections, including commodity exchange, with other countries. Participation in international commodity exchange should be aimed at saving social labor by utilizing the international division of labor, rather than just realizing the transformation of physical forms. Foreign trade helped boost labor productivity and could act as a catalyst to drive the growth of the national economy. If foreign trade were to be fully utilized as a lever to promote the advancement of the national economy, the proportion of China's export trade in the GNP and the share in global export trade ought to be suitably raised. He Xinhao analyzed the role of foreign trade in detail. Firstly, it could communicate with other countries; secondly, through engaging in the global division of labor, it could fully utilize the country's most advantageous resource endowment to save social labor and improve economic efficiency; thirdly, it could accelerate the realization of social expansion of reproduction; fourthly, it could bring in advanced foreign technologies to drive economic growth; fifthly, it could help establish a favorable external environment for the growth of the national economy through foreign trade.[9] Zheng Tuobin, then Minister of Foreign Trade, further concluded: "We must understand the importance of developing foreign trade from a strategic perspective, and we must recognize our economic work has two forces and two resources. The two forces mean that we should rely on our own force, make it as the mainstay, and take external forces as the supplements. For the two resources, we must make full use of domestic resources, but do not ignore external resources." "We must make full use of our strengths, make up for our weaknesses through exchanges in the international market, and do a good job in foreign trade."[10]

(2) Foreign trade development strategy

During the 1980s and 1990s, the prevailing view was that advancing foreign trade development was essential for it to serve as a key driver of economic growth; it was necessary to formulate a foreign trade development strategy suited to China's national conditions. Both import substitution strategies and export substitution strategies were once popular in developing countries. Could they be applied to China? One view advocated the implementation of an import substitution strategy as the main method. In the article "Import substitution is China's long-term strategy to catch up with the world's industrial powers," Liu

9 Xinhao He. Correctly play the role of foreign trade and accelerate the development of China's economy. *Intertrade*, 1982 (5).

10 Tuobin Zheng. Emancipate the mind, raise awareness, and strive to speed up the development of foreign trade. *Intertrade*, 1982 (1).

Changli demonstrated the inevitability of China's sustained application of the import substitution strategy over an extended period from eight aspects.[11] Zhang Peiji also believed that when formulating import and export strategies, building upon fully leveraging the strengths of the socialist system, we should absorb the advantages and disadvantages of the import substitution strategy and the export substitution strategy, implement import substitution as the mainstay, and realize the combination of the two at the same time.[12] An alternative perspective held that the export-oriented substitution strategy should take precedence. Huang Fangyi pointed out that from the perspective of the product's target market, import substitution was obviously aimed at the domestic market, and it was actually an inward-looking strategy. Although China's long-term strategy with an import tendency helped to establish a relatively complete and independent industrial system, it might also lead to a sharp increase in imports and a decrease in exports, which might lead to a shortage of foreign exchange and even turn into a debt crisis. Therefore, it was necessary to facilitate the shift in foreign economic strategy from import substitution toward an export-oriented approach as soon as possible.[13] Another point of view was that a balanced development strategy that incorporated the basic elements of both strategies should be implemented. Tang Haiyan believed that neither the import substitution strategy nor the export substitution strategy could adapt to the changed contemporary international economic environment, nor was it aligned with China's fundamental national realities. A strategy of balanced growth emerged as an unavoidable path for advancing China's foreign trade.[14]

In addition to the disputes between inward-focused import substitution and outward-oriented export-led approaches, many foreign trade development strategies with Chinese characteristics were proposed at that time, mainly including the comprehensive economic and trade blueprint, market diversification strategy, the strategy of revitalizing trade through science and technology, international circulation strategy, foreign trade self-driving development strategy, international competitiveness-oriented strategy, etc.[15] Certain strategies once exerted significant

---

[11] Changli Liu. Import substitution is China's long-term strategy to catch up with the world's industrial powers. *Economic Research Journal*, 1987 (8).

[12] Peiji Zhang. Discussion on China's foreign trade development strategy. *Intertrade*, 1984 (1).

[13] Fangyi Huang. At present, the restrictive factors and improvement ideas of my country's import and foreign economic and trade. *Economic Research Journal*, 1985 (12).

[14] Haiyan Tang. On the choice of China's foreign trade development strategy. *Journal of International Trade*, 1994 (2).

[15] Yaqing Wei. Theoretical analysis of the evolution of foreign trade strategy. *Economic Perspectives*, 2001 (7).

influence on China's institutional reforms and foreign trade policies. In the late 1980s, Wang Jian, a research associate at the Investment Research Institute of the State Planning Commission, proposed an economic development strategy based on international circulation, advocating for fully utilizing the rich resource endowment of China's rural labor force and vigorously developing labor-intensive industries.[16] Specifically, it was to encourage coastal areas to vigorously develop processing trade, import raw materials, process them for added value, and then sell them back to the international market, so as to form an export-oriented economy in which both raw materials and sales markets were external, and there were large inflows and large outflows. While vigorously developing the labor-intensive processing industry, we should also develop the export farming according to the same model. Through this model, the rural labor force could participate in the international economic circulation, and support for agriculture and foundational industries would be bolstered by promoting exports in labor-intensive sectors to earn foreign exchange. This strategic concept was affirmed by the central leadership at that time, and it also contributed, to some degree, to China's shift toward an export-driven economic development model. However, as some researchers had pointed out, this development strategy had many drawbacks. It applied the economic development model typically used by small countries to a large nation such as China.[17] It was only suitable for developing the labor-intensive low-end product market,[18] making China stuck in a low-end dependent role within the global division of labor.[19] At present, although the various foreign trade development strategies proposed at that time had various degrees of limitations, they had distinct characteristics of the times, reflecting the practical demands of economic growth for reforms in the foreign trade system and its development. It also reflected the unremitting exploration and pursuit of China's evolving strategy for advancing foreign trade by the theoretical circle.

---

16 Jian Wang. Choosing the right long-term development strategy—concept of the "international great circulation" economic development strategy. *Economic Daily*, Janu. 5, 1988.

17 Guiquan Liang. The concept of "international great circulation" that is not in line with national conditions—also on the sub-step promotion strategy of opening up with multiple advantages. *Academic Research*, 1988(4).

18 Jianshu Min. My opinion on the theory of the international great circulation—Professor Min Jianshu, Dean of the School of Business Administration of the Chinese University of Hong Kong, talks about the Great International Circulation. *Business Management Journal*, 1988 (7).

19 Genliang Jia. The fatal drawbacks of the international great circulation of the economic development strategy. *Studies on Marxism*, 2010 (12).

(3) Reform of the foreign trade system

As China's openness to the global market keeps expanding, China's foreign trade management system is becoming less and less suitable for the actual needs of foreign trade development. During the era of a planned economy's foreign trade system, the acquisition system and the transfer system were implemented for exports and imports, respectively. The scale and commodity structure of imports and exports were carried out entirely by state-owned foreign trade enterprises in strict accordance with national planning, and profits and losses were borne by the state rather than enterprises. Zheng Tuobin wrote in *Economic Research Journal* that the traditional foreign trade system had many drawbacks: first, the exclusive monopoly management system of the foreign trade department was ineffective in encouraging the active participation of all skate-holders; second, the production of industrial enterprises was out of touch with the demand of the international market, and industrial enterprises lacked the right to operate independently, hindering their ability to adapt to the needs of the international market in a timely manner; third, there was no separation between the government and enterprises. When solving economic problems, it was not to follow economic laws, but to prefer administrative intervention, and manage too much and too rigidly; fourth, the various procedures required for foreign trade activities were cumbersome, resulting in low efficiency and inability to address the demands of opening up and invigorating the domestic market.[20] Even though certain adjustments were introduced to the foreign trade framework at the onset of reform and opening up, problems such as the failure of separating the government from enterprises, the egalitarian approach of "sharing from the same big pot," and the disconnection between production and sales had not been effectively resolved, and further reform of the foreign trade system was needed. From the Third Plenary Session of the 11th CPC Central Committee to the end of the twentieth century, the reform of China's foreign trade system had gone through four stages: exploration, overall advancement, tackling, and deepening.[21] Significant advancements were achieved in restructuring the foreign trade system, which was mainly reflected in the following aspects[22]: a clear distinction was made between governmental functions and enterprise operations;

[20] Tuobin Zheng. The reform of China's foreign trade system. *Economic Research Journal*, 1984 (11).

[21] Zhongdi Zhu. Review and prospect of the reform of foreign trade system in new China. *Journal of Finance and Economics*, 1999 (10).

[22] Rongjiu Xue. Fifty years of exploration: a review and reflection on China's foreign trade theories since the founding of the People's Republic of China. *Intertrade*, 1999 (10).

streamlining administration and delegating power had been implemented; the highly centralized external trade administration framework had been broken; the power of foreign trade management had been gradually devolved; the import and export agency system had been gradually implemented; trading companies and manufacturing firms began to explore the way of combining industry and trade; efforts were made to reform the planning system, simplify the planning content, greatly reduce the scope of mandatory planning management of import and export goods, and gradually turn to the combination of mandatory planning, guidance planning and production adjustment; efforts were made to restructure the financial framework supporting foreign trade, strengthen the means of economic adjustment, and begin to use exchange rate, foreign exchange retention, incentive policies and tax rebates for some export commodities to promote the development of foreign trade exports. After over two decades of reform, China's foreign trade system had undergone a fundamental transformation, from an administratively-based, state-monopoly foreign trade system to a foreign trade system under a market economy. A framework for international trade aligned with socialist market economy principles had been formed, and the reforms in macro and micro aspects had mobilized the enthusiasm of foreign trade enterprises and greatly promoted the significant growth of foreign trade. However, the division between government and business functions in foreign trade remained partially unresolved, and the solution to reforming the foreign trade system depended on aligning and advancing further structural changes.[23]

(4) China's WTO accession significantly influenced its economic development

On November 10, 2001, the Fourth Ministerial Conference of the World Trade Organization (WTO) adopted the legal documents for China's accession to the WTO. Joining the WTO was not only a need for China to deeply engage in global economic integration, but also an inherent need for the WTO to reflect the universality and fairness of the international trade framework. In July 1986, China formally requested to reinstate its position as a contracting party within the General Agreement on Tariffs and Trade (GATT), China finally became the 143rd member of the WTO after 16 years of difficult negotiations. Joining the WTO was a historic event during China's economic transformation and market liberalization. This significantly accelerated China's integration into the global economy. Prior to joining the World Trade Organization, the domestic academic

---

[23] Jiadong Tong. Discussion on the reform of China's foreign trade system. *Nankai Journal*, 1998 (1).

circles conducted extensive discussions on the significance and role of joining the WTO, major obstacles, industrial impact, system reform, legal improvement, etc., which provided full theoretical support for China's WTO accession negotiation and post-WTO system and policy adjustment.

At that time, the mainstream domestic view held that China needed the WTO, and the WTO also needed China.[24] Joining the WTO would help improve China's external economic environment, strengthen China's economic ties with global markets, and enhance its participation in worldwide trade and diplomatic relations. This would enable China to expand its influence within global economic governance, and China could rely on the WTO's dispute mediation mechanism to resolve trade frictions with other members; it would help China play a greater role in the international economic arena; it would help strengthen the regulatory framework for a market-based economy, and China could learn from WTO members to implement contemporary corporate governance structures; it would be beneficial for Chinese enterprises to improve their competitiveness; it would help China to introduce foreign direct investment and advanced technology. Scholars did not deny that, in addition to opportunities, joining the WTO would bring challenges to China's economic development. WTO members must achieve a balance between rights and obligations, which means that when China enjoys treatment, it must also gradually open its market to other members in accordance with its commitments. This might have an impact on some domestic industries.[25] However, scholars generally believed that the overall advantages of joining the WTO outweighed the disadvantages.

At that time, most of the domestic literature on the impact of accession to the WTO on China's economy was qualitative analysis, but some literature carried out quantitative analysis and reached some enlightening conclusions. Li Shantong et al. (2000) used the computable general equilibrium model to analyze the impact of China's accession to the WTO on China's economy, and believed that China's accession to the WTO would make China obtain a large efficiency gain, resulting in a significant increase in GDP. The gain was mainly due to the efficiency improvement caused by the reallocation of resources according to comparative advantages. This efficiency gain, however, was not evenly distributed across sectors. On the contrary, the output level of more protected industrial sectors such as agriculture and automobiles was likely to decline to a greater extent, while labor-intensive sectors such as textiles and clothing would be the main

---

[24] Xueming Chen. An overview of the process and advantages and disadvantages of China's entry into the WTO. *Economic Perspectives*, 2000 (3).

[25] Bingxi Zhen. China's entry into WTO and its impact. *China International Studies*, 2000 (1).

beneficiaries. Therefore, while China's accession to the WTO would improve China's efficiency gains, it would also lead to a major adjustment in the economic structure.[26] At that time, China was worried about the potential impact on the industries that might be caused by its entry into the WTO. Many scholars had studied the impact of China's entry into the WTO on industries that were more vulnerable to influence, such as agriculture, the automobile industry, the banking industry, etc., and put forward many countermeasures and suggestions.[27] In fact, China's accession significantly enhanced the competitiveness of its domestic market and the enhancement of corporate competitiveness. Chinese enterprises did not go bankrupt on a large scale due to the impact of WTO entry; on the contrary, they fought more and more bravely in the fierce competition in domestic and foreign markets. In 1999, just nine Chinese mainland firms appeared on the Fortune Global 500 ranking, which grew exponentially to 109 enterprises by 2017, and one out of every five Fortune 500 companies was a mainland Chinese company. In China's auto industry, which was generally considered to be at risk before China's accession to the WTO, six Chinese auto companies were among Fortune 500 companies in 2017, accounting for a quarter of the 23 global auto companies on the list.

II. Research on China's post-WTO accession international trade

China's WTO accession significantly transformed its economic landscape. "China has expanded its opening to the outside world in the fields of industry, agriculture, and services, and accelerated trade liberalization as well as trade and investment facilitation. In the process of fulfilling its commitments, China has deepened reform of the foreign trade system, improved the foreign trade laws and regulations system, reduced trade barriers and administrative intervention, straightened the government's responsibilities in foreign trade management,

---

26 Shantong Li. The impact of China's entry into WTO on China's economy: a dynamic general equilibrium analysis. *The Journal of World Economy*, 2000 (2).

27 Hong Song. The impact of China's entry into WTO on China's industrial development and its countermeasures. *World Economics and Politics*, 2000 (3); Dexiu Zhang. Analysis of the positive and negative impact of WTO on some industries in China's economy. *Journal of Peking University (Philosophy and Social Sciences)*, 2000 (3); The Research Group of the School of Economics and Management, China Agricultural University. The impact of China's entry into WTO on China's agricultural product trade. *The Journal of World Economy*, 1999 (9); Kesha Guo. The impact faced by China's auto industry after entering the WTO and its countermeasures. *China's Industrial Economics*, 2001 (10). Xiaoan Qian. The impact and countermeasures of China's entry into WTO on China's banking industry and financial regulation. *Journal of Financial Research*, 2000 (2).

promoted more open, fair and transparent government behavior, and pushed the open economy into a new stage of development."[28] China's WTO membership triggered significant transformations in its international trade landscape, creating both developmental prospects and complex challenges, while simultaneously advancing theoretical research in trade economics.

(1) Changing the way of foreign trade development

China's international trade has expanded dramatically following its economic liberalization, particularly after gaining WTO membership in 2001. China's import-export volume has experienced sustained growth, accompanied by notable upgrades in its trade commodity composition, and trading partners have become more diversified. However, China's foreign trade also faces many problems. Numerous researchers argue that China's trade expansion remains predominantly quantity-driven rather than efficiency-based.[29] Jian Xinhua and Zhang Hao observed that global trade competitiveness historically stemmed primarily from comparative advantages in production costs and continuous technology introduction. This foreign trade growth mode, characterized by quantitative expansion, labor-intensive and low-price competition, could certainly promote trade expansion. However, it had also led to problems such as constant trade frictions, excessive foreign trade surplus, excessive resource consumption, increased environmental pressure, and low economic benefits, and changes in the expansion pattern of international trade were urgently required.[30] Wang Shouwen also believed that China primarily engaged in labor-intensive, low-value segments of global production chains, which were positioned at the bottom tiers of global production networks with limited indigenous innovation capabilities and brand ownership. Foreign trade was large but not strong.[31] The unbalanced foreign trade structure had also led to the expansion of the surplus and the imbalance of international payments, which had caused great pressure on macro-control. The global financial crisis severely disrupted China's trade dynamics, accelerating the

---

28 State Council Information Office. *White Paper on "China's Foreign Trade" (2011)*. State Council Information Office Website, Dec. 7, 2011.

29 Wanling Chen, Xueyan Shao. Rapid growth of China's foreign trade: problems, dilemmas and solutions: a summary of the academic seminar on "International Economic and Trade Trends and Transformation of Foreign Economic and Trade Growth Modes." *Reform*, 2006 (11).

30 Xinhua Jian, Hao Zhang. On the transformation of China's foreign trade growth mode. *China Industrial Economics*, 2007 (8).

31 Shouwen Wang. Change the development mode of foreign trade and promote the stable and balanced development of foreign trade. *Intertrade*, 2007 (7).

imperative to transform its export-led growth model. Zhang Yansheng observed that in the post-crisis era, China's foreign trade evolution faced pressure from six types of transformation: the transformation of low-cost competitive advantages, the modernization of export-processing industrial frameworks, the transformation of imitation and innovation models, the transformation of foreign trade growth patterns, the strategic adjustment of intra-East Asian trade patterns, and the transformation of foreign trade incentive mechanisms.[32] Pei Changhong et al.(2011) believed that revamping China's trade growth model requires going beyond mere export basket diversification and value-chain upgrading. It included four economic implications: changing the way and pattern of national income distribution, changing the way of competition, reforming market expansion strategies, and optimizing resource allocation mechanisms.[33]

Promoting the optimization of export structure while maintaining the steady growth of export scale is a crucial component in transforming international trade growth strategies. Since 2000, China's export portfolio has undergone significant qualitative upgrading. At present, manufactured goods now constitute over 95% of China's export volume, and the proportion of capital goods and innovation-driven export items in manufactured products has also increased. However, Long Guoqiang pointed out that China's high-tech product exports were still labor-intensive value-added activities. For a long time, China's comparative advantage had been mainly concentrated in labor-intensive industries, and the most internationally competitive products were also concentrated in products with medium technical content.[34] Qi Junyan also believed that traditional classification methods to measure trade structure overestimated the degree of enhancement of China's trade composition. If we analyzed by the classification method of technical content and added value, we would find that China's export products were still mainly concentrated in low-tech and low-value-added production links, while medium-tech products that could best reflect a country's technical depth, especially those that required more high-tech and scale-intensive automation products, including technology-intensive exports demanding proprietary innovation capabilities and high R&D investment, not only remained underrepresented in

---

32 Yansheng Zhang. Post-crisis era: the most important thing is to change the growth mode of China's foreign trade. *International Economic Review*, 2010 (1).

33 Changhong Pei, Lei Peng, Wen Zheng. Experience and theoretical analysis of changing the development mode of foreign trade: a summary of China's response to the impact of the international financial crisis. *Social Sciences in China*, 2011 (1).

34 Guoqiang Long. The current opportunity is not the expansion of scale but the upgrading of export structure. *Practice in Foreign Economic Relations and Trade*, 2014 (7).

China's export composition but also had a relatively low share of international competition. If we wanted to change the export growth mode, we should optimize the export structure while maintaining the steady growth of export scale.[35] Jin Bei et al.(2013) suggested attaching great importance to the outstanding problems of low competitiveness and low product density of medium-tech manufactured products; objectively viewing the dual role of labor-intensive manufactured products during the export portfolio modernization process; strategically refining innovation-driven sector policies, and making value chain climbing a top policy priority.[36] There were also scholars who advocated actively playing the key role of research and development advancement to realize a new foreign trade pattern of "importing and exporting to our best advantage"; exploring the establishment of autonomous global value network leadership, and realizing the optimization of trade composition aligned with contemporary global benchmarks; focusing on optimizing workforce deployment strategies; Harnessing human capital's pivotal role in driving technological advancement and trade modernization.[37]

(2) Actively developing service trade

The contemporary services sector has emerged as a vital component of numerous nations' economic systems and a key driver of expansion. Correspondingly, services' share of global commerce has also been increasing. Service globalization has been the most distinctive phase feature amidst contemporary global economic integration, and sustained rapid expansion is projected for the foreseeable future. It has promoted world economic growth and welfare improvement, and also provided China with a chance to take advantage of the opportunities of service globalization to promote its own development.[38] In recent years, China's service trade sector has experienced significant growth acceleration. In 2017, services trade volume was 4,699.11 billion yuan, of which exports were 1,540.68 billion yuan, imports were 3,158.43 billion yuan, and the service deficit

[35] Junyan Qi. Whether China has exported more high-tech products—based on technical content and added value. *World Economy Studies*, 2008 (9).

[36] Bei Jin, Pengfei Li, Jianhui Liao. The status quo and evolution trend of China's industrial international competitiveness—based on the analysis of export commodities. *China Industrial Economics*, 2013 (5).

[37] Xiuzhen Li, Fangna Xu. Technological innovation and the transformation of China's foreign trade development mode. *Journal of East China Normal University (Philosophy and Social Sciences)*, 2015 (4).

[38] Xiaojuan Jiang. The development trend and theoretical analysis of service globalization. *Economic Research Journal*, 2008 (2).

was 1,617.75 billion yuan. The scale of service imports and exports was expected to maintain the second place worldwide across four consecutive years.[39] As China's services trade volume expands, its compositional mix has undergone continuous transformation. Zhao Jingfeng and Chen Ce found through empirical analysis that since the 1980s, China's services trade balance shifted from positive to negative territory, and the scale of the deficit in service trade had continued to expand after China's accession to the WTO. Within services trade subsectors, conventional labor-driven industries like tourism and transport maintained stronger comparative advantages, while the supply of the capital, technology, and knowledge-intensive modern service sectors, including finance, insurance, computer and information, and consulting, was insufficient, making it difficult to meet domestic and foreign market demand.[40] Some scholars reached similar conclusions by using different methods and from different perspectives. Sheng Bin and Ma Yingying conducted a value-added analysis of China's services export composition and global competitive positioning. Their analysis revealed that between 2000 and 2014, China's services export composition underwent marked improvement, with knowledge-intensive sectors accounting for a growing portion of value-added exports, though their share remained below global levels.[41] The main reasons for the change of the value-added export structure of service trade are: the service-orientation of the manufacturing industry, the substitution of domestic services for foreign services, and transformations in manufactured export composition. While China's services trade has gained global competitiveness over time, China's services trade competitiveness remains substantially behind both advanced and developing economies overall, such as Brazil, India, and Russia.[42] Scholars suggested that to strengthen services trade competitiveness, strategic development of knowledge-based and tech-driven service sectors should be prioritized, coupled with continuous enhancement of supportive policy

[39] The person in charge of the Department of Trade in Services of the Ministry of Commerce talked about the situation of China's trade in services in 2017. *Chinese Government Network*, Feb. 6, 2018.

[40] Jingfeng Zhao, Ce Chen. China's trade in services: total volume and structure analysis. *The Journal of World Economy*, 2006 (8).

[41] Nanyang Cheng, Hongqiang Yang, Ying Nie. An empirical analysis of the structural changes of China's service trade exports. *Journal of International Trade*, 2006 (8); Hong Chen, Guorong Zhang. An empirical study on the international competitiveness of China's trade in services. *Management World*, 2010 (10).

[42] Bin Sheng, Yingying Ma. An Analysis of China's service trade export structure and international competitiveness: based on the perspective of trade added-value. *Journal of Southeast University (Philosophy and Social Sciences)*, 2018 (1).

frameworks; we must pay attention to education and training, and enhance both the stock and caliber of skilled workforce. Additionally, phased deregulation of service industries must integrate foreign capital deployment, tech absorption, and best practice adoption to enhance sectoral efficiency.[43] On the premise of maintaining the trade in goods and current account surplus, the deficit in trade in services can be treated as a normal condition, and the import of services such as patents, brands, technical training, knowledge, and information purchases can be regarded as a key mechanism for upgrading domestic factor endowments so as to improve the domestic factor productivity.

(3) Preventing and responding to trade frictions

As China's economic expansion and export volumes maintain steady growth, Chinese products have been subject to trade remedy investigations by some countries in the name of anti-dumping and countervailing duties. China's global trade expansion has increasingly faced commercial disputes, reflecting its dual status as both the world's top merchandise trader and the most frequent subject of trade defense actions. Annual data reveals persistent challenges—during 2017, Chinese exporters confronted 75 trade remedy cases across 21 jurisdictions, maintaining the nation's unenviable position as the primary target of anti-dumping and countervailing duty measures globally. This trend underscores how China's export dominance has made it particularly vulnerable to protective trade policies, even as its trade volumes continue growing. And one China-related case occurred in less than four days on average.[44] Through extensive literature research, Yin Xiangshuo et al.(2007) summarized the main trends of trade frictions under the WTO-based multilateral trade system: under the constraints of WTO rules, the use of traditional trade remedy measures such as tariffs and quotas has been decreasing, and anti-dumping, countervailing, and safeguard measures have become the main policy tool. In addition, intellectual property protection, technical standards, health inspection and quarantine standards, labor conditions, environmental protection, etc., are being used by many countries as new trade remedy tools.[45] Mao Yanqiong summarized the characteristics and development

---

43 Changhong Pei and Ying Fan. Continue to enhance the function of foreign trade to promote China's economic development. *Intertrade*, 2014 (6).

44 The fourteenth year-end summary of business work in 2017: actively carry out trade remedy work, and effectively maintain trade order and industrial security. *Website of the Ministry of Commerce of the People's Republic of China*, Jan. 19, 2018.

45 Xiangshuo Yin, Chunding Li, Lei Sun. The types, causes, effects and solutions of international trade frictions. *The Journal of World Economy*, 2007 (7).

trend of China-related trade frictions in the past more than 10 years since China joined the WTO: the forms of foreign trade frictions with China are increasingly diversified and complicated, and trade defense mechanisms are increasingly transitioning from traditional anti-dumping cases to more frequent application of countervailing duties, general safeguards, and China-specific transitional safeguards; the trade friction with China implemented by foreign countries has changed from specific commodities from individual enterprises to entire industrial sectors, and even involves the RMB exchange rate, market opening, intellectual property protection and other macroeconomics levels; the intensity and impact of trade frictions have increased significantly; trade frictions have become increasingly politicized; in addition to developed countries, trade frictions between developing countries and China are also increasing.[46] After the global financial crisis, foreign trade frictions with China have emerged with new features: the steel industry has become the industry that has encountered the most trade frictions in China, and trade frictions against high-tech industries are also increasing day by day. The main ways China encounters trade frictions are still anti-dumping and countervailing investigations.[47]

Some scholars have investigated the underlying drivers of escalating trade disputes involving China, and they usually attribute them to the following reasons: First, as the global leader in merchandise trade, China's massive trade volumes naturally generate more commercial tensions through sheer economic gravity; Second, the financial crisis triggered lasting defensive trade policies worldwide, particularly targeting major exporting nations. Third, persistent concentration in labor-intensive manufacturing leaves Chinese exports vulnerable to trade remedies aimed at lower-value segments. Low value-added primary processed products are overcapacity, and high value-added products are in short supply, resulting in foreign trade exports competing on quantity, and further triggering trade frictions.[48] However, some researchers believe that the trade friction cannot simply be blamed on China's large export of low-tech products with low added value, or the high concentration of export markets. Zhang Yu and Dai Xiang found through empirical analysis that China's export product upgrade and export

---

46 Yanqiong Mao. Review and prospect of international trade friction with China in 10 Years of WTO Accession. *World Economic Study*, 2011 (11).

47 Yuwen Gong, Xiaohong Hua. Research on China's countermeasures to deal with trade disputes under the new international economic situation. *Intertrade*, 2017 (11).

48 Yanqiong Mao, Yuwen Gong and other aforementioned documents. Anlei Zuo. The characteristics, trends and countermeasures of China's international trade friction in the post-financial crisis era. *Journal of Shanghai institute of Foreign Trade—World Trade Organization Focus*, 2012 (9).

market diversification did not reduce China-related trade friction, but increased it.[49] Therefore, as China's export scale expands and its position in global trade improves, the trade frictions China faces may continue to increase. Scholars suggest actively using the multilateral trading system and regional dispute settlement mechanisms; establishing a new concept of cooperative international trade friction settlement mechanism, and actively exploring China's cooperative dispute settlement methods that are of equal consultation and mutual benefit; building a working mechanism and social service system for dealing with trade frictions; establishing and improving an early warning mechanism for trade frictions and industrial safety, as well as industrial damage investigation rules; regulating the export competition order of enterprises, and guiding and assisting enterprises in responding to anti-dumping lawsuits.[50]

2. Research on Foreign Investment

Since initiating economic reforms in 1978, China has maintained consistent growth in inbound foreign direct investment, establishing itself as the top foreign investment destination among developing economies for a quarter-century. By December 2016, China's cumulative foreign direct investment inflows reached US$1,354.404 billion, representing 5.07% of global foreign investment stocks.[51] Foreign direct investment has significantly contributed to China's development by closing domestic capital gaps through external financing, facilitating technology and knowledge transfers of advanced production methods, boosting export-generated forex reserves via integrated global supply chains, and analyzing multidimensional progress across macroeconomic expansion, industrial value-chain upgrading, trade volume growth, and labor market development. During China's progressive enhancement of foreign investment absorption capabilities, domestic academic circles have conducted a lot of research on foreign investment-related issues, and their understanding of how to better attract and utilize foreign investment is also deepening.

---

49 Yu Zhang, Xiang Dai. Can export product upgrades and market diversification ease China's trade frictions? *World Economic Study*, 2013 (6).

50 Changhong Pei. China's foreign trade development: challenges, opportunities and countermeasures. *Economic Research Journal*, 2005 (9); Yabin Wu, Yong Wang. The Chinese concept of establishing a cooperative international trade friction settlement mechanism. *Intertrade*, 2017 (3).

51 Ministry of Commerce. China Foreign Investment Report 2017. *Ministry of Commerce website*.

I. Theoretical foundations of capital utilization

Foreign capital utilization constitutes a core component of China's economic liberalization strategy. However, due to the long-term influence of the "Left" ideology, during the initial phase of economic liberalization, significant societal debates about the necessity of introducing foreign capital persisted regarding this transformative policy direction. This concern was mainly manifested in five aspects: first, the use of foreign capital might affect self-reliance and make China's economy dependent on foreign countries; second, the utilization of foreign investment raised concerns about potential ideological influences from market-oriented economies, which in turn affected the operation of the planned economy; third, it was believed that China's low level of economic management made it difficult to effectively utilize, digest and absorb the introduced foreign capital, potentially triggering debt service defaults and systemic financial instability; fourth, it was believed that the introduction of foreign capital would make foreign equipment and commodities flood into the domestic market, which would impact national industry and commerce; fifth, it was believed that the bourgeois ideology and rotten way of life brought by the utilization of foreign capital would corrode the officials and the masses and hinder the promotion of socialist cultural and ethical standards.[52] Under the circumstances at that time, if there were ideological issues, it would be difficult to facilitate the effective implementation of foreign investment initiatives. Therefore, in the early 1980s, academic researchers extensively analyzed both the rationale and practical viability of foreign capital absorption.

Scholars initially looked for the theoretical basis for introducing foreign capital from the works of classic Marxist-Leninist writers. According to Lenin's thoughts on introducing technology and utilizing foreign capital after the October Revolution, Xiao Zhuoji believed that acquiring cutting-edge technologies and imported machinery formed a cornerstone of China's modernization strategy during its economic transition period.[53] Jiang Jianping analyzed the relevant expositions of Marx and Engels in the *Manifesto of the* Communist Party and Lenin's thoughts on foreign capital utilization, and discussed the fundamental distinction between foreign capital utilization in socialist China and imperialist investment in pre-revolutionary China.[54] In addition to citing classics, more

---

52 Ke Peng. We must raise awareness of the use of foreign capital. *Journal of International Trade*, 1982 (4).

53 Zhuoji Xiao. Actively and steadily introduce technology and utilize foreign capital. *Dongyue Tribune*, 1982 (5).

54 Jianping Jiang. The essential difference between the introduction of foreign capital in socialist China and the investment of imperialism in old China. *Economic Science*, 1986 (5).

scholars have studied the experience of Japan, Eastern European countries, and developing nations in Southeast Asia and Latin America in attracting foreign investment from the perspective of international comparison, and believed that introducing foreign investment was an important means commonly used by countries in the world to develop their economies. It was conducive to supplementing the shortage of domestic funds and accelerating national economic advancement. This facilitated the creation of novel industrial segments. It was conducive to expanding and driving exports, and promoting changes in the export structure; it was conducive to expanding employment and increasing residents' income.[55] Researchers acknowledged that although the use of foreign capital also had various disadvantages, in general, the advantages outweighed the disadvantages. Foreign capital utilization significantly contributed to advancing China's Four Modernizations initiative, encompassing agricultural, industrial, defense, and technological upgrading. Therefore, "we open up to the outside world and introduce foreign capital, technology, and scientific management experience in order to make them serve as a supplement to the socialist economy, accelerate the construction and development of socialism, and strengthen rather than weaken the ability to be independent and self-reliant"[56].

II. Foreign direct investment's economic effects in China

China's economic expansion has been fueled by its market liberalization policies, while its thriving consumer base and growth prospects have increasingly drawn foreign capital inflows. China has maintained consistent growth in foreign direct investment since initiating economic reforms in 1978, remaining the top FDI destination among developing economies for a quarter-century through 2018. China's industrial integration into global value chains, facilitated by foreign direct investment, has cemented its role as the global manufacturing hub. Many scholars have studied the impact of foreign direct investment on China's economy. Guo Xibao and Luo Zhi believed that in simulating economic expansion, the promotion effect of foreign direct investment was significantly greater than that of domestic fixed capital investment. Larger scale of individual foreign direct

---

[55] Chongwei Ji. The relationship between the utilization of foreign capital and China's economic development. *Social Science*, 1982 (2); Jizu Wang. Learn from foreign experience and do a good job in utilizing foreign capital. *Journal of International Trade*, 1982 (4); Yinfang Chen, Yangui Zhang. China's strategic issues of utilizing foreign capital. *Social Science Front*, 1985(3).

[56] Chongwei Ji. The theory and practice of China's opening-up policy. *Economic Research Journal*, 1984 (11).

investment and larger share of foreign capital within China's manufacturing industries compared to other sectors would be more conducive to promoting economic growth. However, a higher export proportion of foreign-funded enterprises would be less conducive to economic growth.[57] After developing a theoretical framework grounded in endogenous growth models and empirically validating it with China's economic metrics, Sang Xiuguo found that foreign direct investment was positively correlated with China's economic growth. Foreign direct investment primarily stimulated economic expansion via technology-driven productivity enhancements. This was especially true in the long run.[58] He Jie and Xu Luodan found that a 1% rise in foreign direct investment-driven technological advancement generated a 2.3% amplification in knowledge spillovers to China's domestic industrial firms.[59] Yao Yang's comparative analysis revealed that "three types of foreign-funded" enterprises demonstrated 39% greater technical efficiency than state-owned enterprises, with Hong Kong, Macao, and Taiwan-invested firms showing 33% higher productivity. A one percentage point rise in the industry share of "three types of foreign-funded" enterprises correlated with a 1.1 percentage point efficiency gain per firm.[60]

Foreign direct investment not only expanded China's export scale but also simultaneously accelerated the transformation of China's industrial framework toward higher-value activities. Zhang Fan and Zheng Jingping studied the impact of multinational corporations on economic efficiency and economic structure employing official sectoral and firm-level datasets from the National Bureau of Statistics' Third Industrial Census Database. They found that compared with small and medium-sized investments in Hong Kong, Macao, and Taiwan, multinational enterprises predominantly channeled investments into capital—and technology-concentrated industries, facilitating China's industrial transformation from labor-dependent production toward knowledge—and skill-intensive activities. In general, it would facilitate China's economic restructuring toward enhanced resource allocation productivity, but it would also make the income distribution

---

57 Xibao Guo, Zhi Luo. Adverse effects on China's economic growth. *Economic Research Journal*, 2009 (5).

58 Xiuguo Sang. Harnessing economic growth: a model based on new economic growth theory and validation on Chinese Data. *Journal of Management World*, 2002 (9).

59 Jie He, Luodan Xu. An empirical study on the spillover effects of introducing FDI in China's industrial sector. *World Economic Papers*, 1999 (2).

60 Yang Yao. The influence of non-state-owned economic components on ensuring the technical efficiency of industrial enterprises. *Economic Research Journal*, 1998 (12).

within and between industries more unequal.[61] Studies by Li Jian (1996) and Xin Chengyue (2005) showed that under the leadership of overseas-funded ventures, China's export of mechanical and electrical products had grown rapidly, high-technology export volume had also continued to expand, and the structure of export commodities had continued to improve.[62] Zhan Xiaoning, Chen Jianguo, Ge Shunqi et al.(2002) believed that multinational corporations intensified competition within the industry, which not only had a positive demonstration effect of competition on domestic companies, but also forced companies that were previously dominant in the domestic market to increase efforts in technological innovation and product research and development.[63] Therefore, Jiang Xiaojuan pointed out that, in general, foreign direct investment had significantly enhanced the sophistication of China's export portfolio, facilitating industrial upgrading while strengthening the global competitiveness of both manufactured goods and advanced technology exports.[64]

However, some scholars have come to different key findings about the impact of foreign direct investment on China's economy. Wang Chunfa and Jiang Jiang analyzed the results of enterprise questionnaires in Beijing, Shanghai, Dongguan, and Suzhou, and found that empirical evidence suggests limited technological diffusion from foreign-invested enterprises within China's domestic economy.[65] Song Hong and Chai Yu found through empirical analysis that Foreign-funded enterprises of these three categories demonstrated stronger investment preferences for downstream processing sectors such as electronic appliances and transportation tools, rather than in upstream industries such as ferrous metal smelting, coal mining, oil and natural gas mining, etc. Judging from the industrial distribution of the three types of foreign-funded enterprises, we could find that these foreign-invested enterprises were more likely to compete fiercely with domestic enterprises in the downstream industries, but had little interest in the

---

[61] Fan Zhang, Jingping Zheng. The impact of multinational corporations on the structure and efficiency of the Chinese economy. *Economic Research Journal*, 1999 (1).

[62] Jian Li. Foreign-funded enterprises: a new source of growth for China's foreign trade exports. *Intertrade*, 1996 (10); Chengyue Xin. *Economic Globalization and China's Business Development*. Beijing: People's Publishing House, 2005.

[63] Xiaoning Zhan, Jianguo Chen. Export competitiveness and the role of multinational Corporations' FDI. *The Journal of World Economy*, 2002 (11); Jianguo Chen, Shunqi Ge. Export competitiveness and the role of foreign direct investment. *Nankai Economic Studies*, 2002 (1).

[64] Xiaojuan Jiang. Contribution of China's foreign-invested economy to growth, structural upgrading and competitiveness. *Social Sciences in China*, 2002 (6).

[65] Chunfa Wang, Jiang Jiang. FDI and the cultivation of endogenous technological capabilities: a case study in China. *High-technology & Industrialization*, 2005 (2).

upstream industries that were in urgent need of development in China. They believed that, compared with all industrial enterprises in China, or compared with domestic enterprises after excluding three types of foreign-funded enterprises, these foreign-invested enterprises had not only failed to significantly enhance the systemic efficiency of China's industrial framework, instead the effect had dropped significantly.[66]

III. The interplay between foreign investment absorption and domestic enterprise growth

Although government agencies and theoretical circles have formed a basic consensus on the "greenfield investment" of foreign capital and its role, there are different opinions on foreign direct investment through mergers and acquisitions and its role. In the mid-1990s, China Strategic Holdings Limited (in Chinese, Zhongce Group), a Hong Kong company, took advantage of the opportunities in various regions to proactively facilitate strategic partnerships between domestic SOEs and foreign investors to drive enterprise modernization, and in just two years, through joint ventures, acquisitions and other methods, it controlled hundreds of state-owned enterprises in the mainland.[67] The "Zhongce Phenomenon" not only caused a great shock in society, but also prompted the academic circle to think deeply about the advantages and disadvantages of foreign mergers and acquisitions. Li Shuguang, after analyzing the "Zhongce Phenomenon" in the context within China's economic transition framework concluded that for Chinese state-owned enterprises lacking new sources of capital injection, the "Zhongce Phenomenon" should not be rejected, but instead should be taken as an opportunity, which could facilitate market-based resource distribution, optimize both existing asset allocation and the efficient circulation of production inputs and societal capital.[68] Huang Sujian identified state-owned enterprises' adoption of joint ventures and asset divestment strategies as pragmatic responses to existential, restructuring, and expansion challenges. Equity partnerships and state asset restructuring served as vital channels for foreign capital integration, and should not be opposed in a general way. The key was how to carry out joint ventures and transfer enterprise property rights without damaging the legitimate rights

---

[66] Hong Song, Yu Chai. An empirical study on the impact of foreign-funded enterprises on China's industrial structure and benefits. *Economic Research Journal*, 1998 (1).

[67] Shuli Hu. Analysis and Reflection of the "Zhongce Phenomenon" on the Transformation of Capital Introduction. *Reform*, 1994 (3).

[68] Shuguang Li. Look at the "Zhongce Phenomenon" with an open mind. *Reform*, 1994 (5).

of state-owned property and ensuring national economic security.[69] Qin Hai believed that the various controversies caused by the "Zhongce Phenomenon" were actually indirect reflections of China's lack of theoretical preparation during China's economic liberalization process.[70] Wang Zhenzhong believed that international direct investment could not be regarded as an ordinary currency flow. The core of direct investment behavior was the control of enterprises. Therefore, capital had a banner. China should implement appropriate regulatory oversight on foreign merger and acquisition activities involving domestic firms, drawing insights from advanced economies' frameworks.[71]

During the initial phase of economic liberalization, Chinese firms faced significant technological gaps compared to advanced economies. China's "market-for-technology" strategy emerged as a pivotal mechanism for acquiring advanced know-how during foreign capital absorption. Article 5 of the "Notice on Further Improving the Production and Operation Conditions of Foreign-invested Enterprises" ([1986] No. 76) issued by the State Council in 1986 emphasized: "We must resolutely implement the policy of exchanging technology with the market, implement the import substitution measures, and encourage foreign investors to provide advanced technology." By the 1990s, "exchanging technology with the market" had become popular in many industries. How to evaluate the "exchanging technology with the market" strategy? There was considerable disagreement among different researchers on this issue. Li Yining believed that "exchanging technology with the market" was a good strategy, because it would not only attract more foreign investment in China, but also simultaneously elevate domestic firms' collective technological capabilities and strengthen their global market competitiveness, thereby creating conditions for domestic enterprises to develop international markets.[72] After establishing and analyzing a capital asset appreciation model, Li's research proposed that accelerated accumulation of domestic capital capabilities required temporary relinquishment of corporate control rights. By giving up the control rights of enterprises, introducing and developing technology mainly with foreign capital, improving the technical capability of national capital with the help of the technology of foreign enterprises, and then looking for an appropriate time and method to acquire foreign equity

---

69 Sujian Huang. Think of it from the so-called "Zhongce Phenomenon." *Reform*, 1994 (5).
70 Hai Qin. The "Zhongce Phenomenon" needs to be more fully analyzed. *Reform*, 1994 (4).
71 Zhenzhong Wang. Does capital really have no banners? *Reform*, 1994 (5).
72 Yining Li. *Economic Talks*. Beijing: Peking University Press, 1998.

with capital, this might be an effective strategy to realize the rapid development of national enterprises.[73]

However, there had been constant voices of criticism for the strategy of "exchanging technology with the market." Zhang Ping analyzed the case of Beijing Jeep Company, China's inaugural automotive joint venture, and discussed that multinational corporations used their monopoly advantages in automobile production technology to achieve industrial control over Chinese enterprises. It was found that even if the American company did not hold a controlling stake, it could control the joint venture by virtue of market expectations, technological advantages, brand, intellectual property rights, and production system, and its income also came from the non-dividend part. Therefore, for domestic auto companies, if they wanted to get rid of the industrial control of multinational companies, they must take the road of independent innovation.[74] Lu Feng and Feng Kaidong conducted interviews and case studies with several Chinese auto companies and believed that the original intention of the "exchanging technology with the market" policy was to introduce technology and acquire its spillover effects among Chinese companies, thereby boosting the technical capabilities of China's automotive sector. However, instead of technology diffusion, the joint ventures showed increased dependence on foreign technology. Therefore, strengthening independent development was the only way to revitalize China's auto industry.[75] Xia Liang conducted a historical review of the establishment and evolution of the "exchanging technology with the market" policy and believed that the proposal of this policy had historical inevitability and significantly contributed to China's technological catch-up in a specific historical period. However, there were also many negative factors, especially an inherent inhibitory effect on China's independent innovation. As China's technological capabilities converged with global leaders, "exchanging technology with the market" should give way to independent innovation.[76]

From the beginning of the twenty-first century to the global financial crisis, multinational corporations were very active in the "decapitation" acquisition and consolidation of industry frontrunners in several industries in China, especially

---

73 Li Li. The development model of national industrial enterprises under the condition of foreign capital competition. *Economic Research Journal*, 1997 (12).

74 Ping Zhang. Technological superiority and industrial control of multinational corporations: An analysis of the case of Beijing Jeep. *Economic Research Journal*, 1995 (11).

75 Feng Lu, Kaidong Feng. Policy choices for developing China's auto industry with independent intellectual property rights. *Business Weekly*, 2004 03 20.

76 Liang Xia. How was "exchanging technology with the market" proposed (1978–1988). *Researches in Chinese Economic History*, 2015 (4).

in the equipment manufacturing industry. The Carlyle Group's takeover bid for Xuzhou Construction Machinery Group, Citigroup's acquisition of Guangdong Development Bank (now known as China Guangfa Bank), Goldman Sachs's acquisition of Shineway Group, Schaeffler's acquisition of LYC Bearing Corporation, Coca-Cola's proposed takeover of Huiyuan Juice Group Limited, and other foreign acquisitions of large domestic enterprises had attracted widespread attention in domestic public opinion, and once again triggered a fierce debates on the advantages and disadvantages of foreign mergers and acquisitions. Wang Zhile's analysis positioned foreign-invested enterprises as integral components of China's corporate ecosystem, arguing that cross-ownership transactions between domestic and foreign entities represent standard commercial activities rather than national security concerns. China was in a period of the highest economic security in a century and a half, and there was no industry that was truly monopolized by foreign-invested companies.[77] After analyzing the influence of foreign capital in 189 industries from seven aspects, Ge Shunqi believed that some industries had been controlled by foreign capital, but these industries were not national strategic or sensitive industries, and there were hundreds of foreign-invested enterprises in each sub-sector. From the perspective of market form, it was not a complete monopoly structure. Foreign capital's sectoral impact in China largely remained within moderate bounds, and foreign capital was not a threat to national economic security. Nevertheless, he also advocated that while encouraging foreign mergers and acquisitions, China should establish appropriate regulatory frameworks for cross-border mergers and acquisitions, drawing on advanced economies' governance models.[78]

IV. Adjustment of foreign direct investment management system and policies

Since the 1990s, with the increasing scale of foreign capital introduced to China, foreign investment has significantly contributed to China's economic expansion and industrial transformation, but many problems have also arisen. On the issue of whether it was necessary to continue to expand foreign capital inflows, differences of opinion also began to emerge in domestic academic circles. Wang Xi's economic growth model determined China's optimal FDI thresholds, revealing that current inflows exceed efficient levels, and direct management of FDI (foreign direct

---

[77] Zhile Wang. Also talk on foreign mergers and acquisitions and China's economic security. *Economic Herald*, 2006 (9).

[78] Shunqi Ge. Cross-border mergers and acquisitions and their impact on China's economic security. *International Economic Review*, 2007 (1112).

investment) should be implemented to appropriately reduce the scale of foreign investment.[79] While affirming the important contribution of foreign capital, Zhao Beiwen also pointed out that since local governments unilaterally pursued quantitative expansion in the process of utilizing foreign capital, this growth mode of foreign capital expansion had led to negative effects such as foreign capital's industrial monopoly, dominance over exports, weak technological spillovers, and loss of tax revenue sources.[80] Although some scholars advocated limiting the scale of foreign investment, more researchers believed that during the current phase of economic transformation, the purpose of introducing foreign capital was not only to use foreign capital to supplement the shortage of domestic construction funds, but also to use foreign capital to facilitate the transition of China's economic development model. Jiang Xiaojuan believed that domestic capital and foreign capital were not completely substitutes. Due to the huge amount of financing for infrastructure construction, the imperative for innovative state-owned enterprises restructuring frameworks and accelerated indigenous technological advancement, strategic foreign capital utilization remains essential. Enhanced strategic direction of foreign capital inflows remained imperative, and encouraged foreign capital to introduce processing and manufacturing links and R&D institutions with a higher technical level and greater value-added content into China, thereby enhancing the efficacy of foreign capital deployment.[81] Academic discussions had also promoted policy adjustments within measured parameters. From 1995 onward, China's policymakers promulgated the "Interim Provisions on Guiding Foreign Investment Direction" and "Catalogue for the Guidance of Foreign Investment Industries," which had been revised several times since then and clearly stipulated the areas where foreign investment was incentivized, permitted, controlled, and barred. China's strategy for utilizing foreign investment had shifted from focusing on the quantity and scale of foreign investment to putting more emphasis on the caliber and tier of foreign capital inflows.

In recent years, the international investment landscape has undergone transformative shifts. The global financial crisis has compelled advanced economies to actively promote the "re-industrialization" strategy and the "industrial re-shoring" policy. More and more developing countries have also been actively

---

79 Xi Wang. On the scale management of foreign direct investment in China. *Economic Research Journal*, 1998 (5).

80 Beiwen Zhao. The negative effects of the expansionary growth model of foreign capital. *World Economy Studies*, 2007 (1).

81 Xiaojuan Jiang. The utilization of foreign capital and the transformation of economic growth mode. *Management World*, 1999 (2).

undertaking global industry relocation, leveraging comparative wage advantages. The new international investment rules promoted by advanced industrial nations, including the US and EU member states, which are oriented toward investment liberalization and combined with pre-entry national treatment with negative list regulation, have gained increasing global adoption. Amid evolving global investment norms, China faces the dual challenge of modernizing its foreign investment governance framework while sustaining capital inflow momentum. Academic research proposes several strategic pathways, and this research mainly focuses on the following areas: the first focus is on how to unify domestic and foreign legal systems and establish a more equitable and transparent investment environment. Hao Hongmei believed that, amid evolving global and domestic economic dynamics, the three foreign investment laws had been falling short of contemporary standards for deepened economic liberalization across multiple dimensions, and the conditions for the integration of the three laws had become mature.[82] Liu Junhai analyzed multiple substantive inconsistencies between the foreign-invested enterprise regulations and corporate governance statutes, and argued that bifurcating corporate legislation based solely on investor nationality—into domestic and foreign-invested enterprise laws—introduced systemic inconsistencies into China's legal framework. It was suggested that legislators should unify the legislation of domestic and foreign-invested enterprises in alignment with the governance principle of equality and national treatment.[83] The secondary research priority examines institutional design for integrating pre-entry national treatment with negative list regulation in FDI governance. Sang Baichuan proposed to take the opportunity of the negotiation of the Sino-American Bilateral Investment Treaty (BIT) to adjust the long-implemented foreign capital access system characterized by access restrictions and preferential measures, implement a management system mainly based on competition policy and environmental and technical standards, and strive to implement the foreign investment registration system as soon as possible.[84] Sheng Bin and Duan Ran conducted a comparative analysis between China's free trade zones negative lists and the United States commitments in the *Trans-Pacific Partnership* (TPP). Scholars advocated that China should strategically liberalize FDI access in manufacturing and services,

---

[82] Hongmei Hao. Explore the foreign investment management model of pre-establishment national treatment plus a negative list. *China Economic and Trade Herald*, 2014 (10).

[83] Junhai Liu. Thoughts and suggestions on unifying the legislation of domestic and foreign-funded enterprises. *Jianghan Tribune*, 2014 (1).

[84] Baichuan Sang. Coping strategies for a new round of global investment rule changes: From the perspective of Sino-US investment agreement negotiation. *Frontiers*, 2014 (1).

balancing national security imperatives with technology collaboration incentives, while phasing out contentious regulatory barriers.[85] The third is how to standardize the management of foreign capital and strengthen the operational and post-operational oversight. Once the pre-establishment national treatment is implemented, it means that the government's jurisdiction over foreign investment will be greatly weakened in the policy space allowed by international economic rules and international investment agreements. Faced with this situation, Yang Liyan and Li Tingting carefully studied the development direction of international laws regarding national security reviews. They examined the specialized legal framework of the United States and studied how other countries have created and implemented their laws. Based on this research, they made suggestions to help China build and improve its own system for reviewing foreign investments that might affect national security.[86] Yang Zhen proposed strategically applying the *Anti-Monopoly Law of the People's Republic of China* to mitigate foreign capital's anti-competitive practices while fostering balanced domestic-foreign enterprise dynamics.[87] While scholars held divergent opinions on specific aspects of foreign investment regulatory reform, they largely agreed on the fundamental objectives: liberalizing market entry requirements and modernizing oversight frameworks to foster a more accessible, clear, and stable investment climate—leveraging improved commercial conditions to enhance global investor appeal.

3. Optimizing the Regional Layout of Opening Up

Since the landmark Third Plenary Session of the 11th CPC Central Committee, China has achieved substantial advancements in geographically-targeted economic liberalization. China's regional economic liberalization began with the establishment of Special Economic Zones. On July 15, 1979, the Central Committee of the Communist Party of China and China's State Council jointly approved and endorsed policy proposals from Guangdong and Fujian provincial authorities regarding external economic activities. These approvals granted enhanced decision-making authority to both provinces in conducting international commerce and implementing flexible economic measures. Concurrently,

85 Bin Sheng, Ran Duan. New rules for TPP investment and Sino-US bilateral investment treaty negotiation. *International Economic Review*, 2016 (5).

86 Liyan Yang, Tingting Li. Research on the legal issues of China's foreign direct investment national security review. *International Law Review of Wuhan University*, 2017 (2).

87 Zhen Yang. The dilemma, challenges and strategies of opening foreign capital supervision. *Theoretical Horizon*, 2016 (11).

authorities designated pilot export processing zones in Shenzhen and Zhuhai, with plans to expand to Shantou and Xiamen pending operational evaluation. In late August 1980, China's National People's Congress reviewed and approved the "Regulations on Special Economic Zones in Guangdong Province." Article 1 of the regulations declares that "certain areas shall be delineated respectively in the three cities of Shenzhen, Zhuhai, and Shantou in Guangdong Province for the establishment of special economic zones," which formally initiates China's special economic zone development program. In early 1984, Deng Xiaoping officially recognized the accomplishments of the special economic zones after inspecting Shenzhen and other special economic zones. Subsequently, the CPC Central Committee endorsed and circulated the key conclusions from the coastal development strategy meeting, authorizing expanded economic openness for 14 major port cities along China's coastline, including Tianjin, Shanghai, and Dalian. In 1988, Hainan Island attained special economic zone status. In the subsequent decade through the early 2000s, China had successively established Shanghai Pudong New Area, and implemented geographically-targeted growth initiatives including "large-scale development of the northwest," "revitalizing the northeast," and "rising in the central region." China's economic openness evolved from coastal-centric to comprehensive spatial integration, extending from eastern seaboard development to riverine, borderland, and inland expansion—establishing a multidimensional, tiered globalization framework. To advance economic liberalization under evolving global conditions, China has strategically expanded its experimental reforms through 12 pilot free trade zones since 2013, with Shanghai as the inaugural site, while pioneering a bold free trade port initiative in Hainan. This phased regional openness approach has generated significant academic analysis regarding special economic zones and free trade zones development models.

I. Discussions on China's Special Economic Zones (SEZs)

The creation of SEZs represents a strategic national initiative by China's leadership to advance economic liberalization and socialist modernization through targeted policy experimentation. As a new thing during the initial phase of China's economic liberalization, SEZs had gained widespread attention, but the fundamental characteristics of SEZs had also caused heated debates. At that time, there was a view against the establishment of SEZs in society, holding that the SEZs were a capitalist enclave, and even believing that the SEZs were the same in nature as the concessions of the old society. In response to the vague understanding of SEZs at that time, many scholars expressed their opinions on the nature of SEZs. Fang Zhuofen admitted that the economic component of state capitalism in the special economic zone occupied a relatively large proportion. The ways of utilizing foreign capital within special economic zone jurisdictions included processing trade, compensation trade, China-foreign cooperative operation, China-foreign joint venture, wholly foreign-owned operation, etc., leading to the coexistence of internal socialist elements and private capital elements, which was a typical form of state capitalism. However, it was state capitalism under the leadership of the socialist regime, a kind of state capitalism "capable of restricting, and capable of defining the scope of its activities" in Lenin's words. It was conducive to attracting foreign capital, introducing new technologies and equipment, and learning advanced management methods. At the same time, its field of activity could only be limited within a specified range, and it was a restricted capitalism, which could be used to serve socialism.[88] But Xu Dixin believed that wholly foreign-funded or internationally-capitalized ventures operating within SEZs were basically not state capitalist economies, but capitalist enterprises. He further pointed out that there was exploitation in China-foreign joint ventures or wholly foreign-funded enterprises in the SEZs. But the reason why they were allowed to make profits was also a kind of redemption policy in a sense, which was conducive to the introduction of new technologies in the SEZs and attracting more foreign capital to establish new enterprises, so that the foreign exchange income of the SEZs could increase year by year. The fundamental purpose of establishing SEZs was to strategically harness foreign investment as a catalyst for advancing socialist modernization under Chinese conditions.[89] Yu Guangyuan believed that the nature of SEZs should be understood from two aspects. The existence of state capitalism was only one aspect of the problem. These state capitalist economic forms also included China's socialist economic activities, the labor of socialist workers and socialist funds, as well as the organizational strength of China's socialism, etc., which were the main aspects of the problem. In this respect, its nature was not state capitalist, but socialist.[90]

During the 1980s, the economy in China's mainland was still in the transitional phase from centralized planning to a planned commodity market framework, and the SEZ economy had already shown new characteristics such as a diversified economic structure, market-oriented economic operation, and export-oriented economy. Scholars discussed how to comprehend the position and function of special economic zones in China's economic system, and how to better enhance

---

88 Zhuofen Fang. On the nature of special economic zones. *Economic Research Journal*, 1981 (8).
89 Dixin Xu. Actively and steadily run the special economic zones. *Fujian Tribune*, 1981 (4).
90 Guangyuan Yu. Talking about the understanding of several issues in Shenzhen Special Economic Zone. *Economic Research Journal*, 1983 (2).

the coordination between the SEZ economy and the mainland economy. They widely agreed that SEZs should not only play a role as a "window" to extend their impact beyond merely advancing coastal export-driven economic growth, introduce capital and technology, provide information, and open up export channels for the national modern economic construction, but also facilitate a greater impact on becoming an "experimental field" for the marketization of economic operation and an explorer and forerunner of economic system reform.[91] The establishment of SEZs had experienced accelerated growth within a brief timeframe, though certain observers argued that their progress primarily stemmed from preferential policies, adaptive strategies, and financial support originating from inland regions, thus crowding out the development funds of the mainland. At the same time, the high wages, high consumption, and high prices in the special zones would be transmitted to the mainland through various channels, which would have an adverse impact on the mainland. Regarding the previous question, Zheng Liangyu pointed out that in the total investment of the Shenzhen Special Economic Zone in the first ten years, the state investment was less than 2%, and the direct utilization of foreign capital and intranet investment only accounted for 20.95% and 11.23%, respectively. However, the investment accumulated by the local finance and enterprises in Shenzhen by means of "snowballing" was as high as 51.19%. Therefore, the rapid development of Shenzhen not only benefited from the full use of foreign investment and foreign capital, but also relied on self-accumulation and rolling development.[92] Regarding the latter question, Zhu Tiezhen and Zhou Tianyong believed that due to the different positioning of the economy between the SEZs and the mainland, the mainland predominantly adopted an import-substituting industrialization approach during this period, while the export-oriented economic development strategy was implemented in the SEZs. Therefore, the economy of the SEZs and the mainland economy not only reinforced each other, but also had many frictions. Simultaneously, the SEZs' external economic interactions revealed systemic institutional shortcomings across multiple dimensions. To maximize their strategic function, granting these zones greater economic independence and decision-making authority became

---

91 Weiwu Gao. A summary of the arguments of the "Theoretical Seminar on the 10th Anniversary of the Establishment of Special Economic Zones." *Economic Research Journal*, 1991 (1).

92 Liangyu Zheng. Review and Prospect of Shenzhen Special Economic Zone's 10-year Development. *Economic Research Journal*, 1991 (1).

imperative—enabling them to pioneer innovative economic frameworks aligned with both socialist market economy tenets and global trade norms.[93]

As a designated administrative area with unique economic mandates, the special economic zone has evolved over 40 years since its birth, and almost every stage of its development and growth has been accompanied by doubts and debates. However, the practice of the special economic zone has fully proved that the special economic zone "has the courage to break through the constraints of the traditional economic system, takes the lead in carrying out market-oriented economic system reform, and has played an important role in the historical process of China's realization from a highly centralized planned economic system to a vigorous socialist market economic system," and "has explored and accumulated successful experience in achieving rapid development and becoming prosperous; adheres to opening up, effectively implements 'bringing in' and 'going global,' actively utilizes both international and domestic markets and resources, and successfully uses foreign and overseas funds, technology, talents and management experience. It has carried out pioneering explorations for China to achieve a transition from seclusion and semi-seclusion to all-round openness. Adhering to serving the overall situation of national development, the whole country supports the development of SEZs, while the SEZs reward the whole country in turn. The SEZs have promoted the coordinated development of the eastern, central and Western regions, and played an important radiating and driving role in the development of the whole country."[94]

II. About the Pilot Free Trade Zone

Since initiating economic reforms and opening its markets, China has not only created five pioneering SEZs but also developed an extensive network of export processing zones, bonded logistics hubs, free trade ports, and diversified economic development zones. These specialized economic zones have significantly facilitated China's seamless integration into the global economic system. To deepen alignment with international investment standards and trade norms while elevating the country's openness, China has adopted progressively more proactive policies for external engagement in recent years. Advancing the free trade zone initiative constitutes a pivotal element of China's latest phase of economic liberalization. Launched in September 2013, the China (Shanghai)

---

[93] Tiezhen Zhu, Tianyong Zhou. Analysis and thinking on the dilemma of the two-way operation of the special economic zone and its way out. *Economic Research Journal*, 1989 (8).

[94] Jintao Hu. Speech at the celebration of the 30th anniversary of the establishment of the Shenzhen Special Economic Zone. *People's Daily Online*, Sept. 6, 2010.

Pilot Free Trade Zone (hereafter "Shanghai FTZ") bears the critical responsibility of pioneering regulatory reforms aligned with advanced global investment and trade standards, serving as a strategic platform for China's deeper participation in global economic integration.

The academic community has conducted a relatively comprehensive study on the establishment background, important mission, and management mode of the pilot free trade zone. Zhang Hanlin and Gai Xinzhe conducted a comprehensive analysis of pilot free trade zones (FTZ), examining their distinctive features, strategic positioning, and economic roles within the framework of functional economic zone development: facilitating balanced regional development by addressing disparities in openness across different areas of China; upgrading China's global value chain participation to better capitalize on globalization benefits; accelerating service sector advancement through trade expansion and industrial structure optimization; strengthening domestic market integration to enhance factor allocation efficiency; pioneering autonomous liberalization approaches to increase China's influence in shaping new international trade norms.[95] Zhang Youwen believed that the strategic positioning of the pilot free trade zone was to force reform through opening up rather than simply expanding opening up. The driving force for development depended on institutional innovation rather than special policies. The theme of opening up was to promote investment liberalization rather than pure trade liberalization. The institutional positioning was a pilot park rather than a special economic zone. Therefore, the opening mode of the pilot free trade zone was to formulate a negative list instead of expanding a positive list. The government's function was to explore regulatory reform rather than weaken its management. The industrial orientation was to focus on the modern service industry rather than the expansion of the processing and manufacturing industry. The development theme was to focus on improving trade functions rather than reducing tariffs to increase trade volume. This required pilot free trade zones to make bold explorations in financial innovation, negative list management, proper handling of first—and second-line relationships, reform of the administrative governance framework, optimization of fiscal policies, and safeguarding of national economic security.[96]

Different from the free trade zones commonly implemented in foreign countries, the functional orientation of the Shanghai Free Trade Zone is not

---

95 Hanlin Zhang, Xinzhe Gai. The ins and outs, functional positioning and contingent strategies of free trade zones. *Reform*, 2013 (9).

96 Youwen Zhang. Pilot free trade zone and the construction of an open economic system. *Academic Monthly*, 2014 (1).

limited to promoting regional economic development, but also to proactively align with cutting-edge international trade and investment standards through experimental policy implementations, accumulate experience for further expansion of reform and opening up, and lead the country's opening up and innovation. Since its establishment, the Shanghai Free Trade Zone has made a lot of explorations in the aspects of establishing a foreign investment management system centered on negative list management, a trade supervision system focusing on trade facilitation, a financial innovation framework focusing on capital account liberalization and financial services sector deregulation, coupled with a comprehensive supervision mechanism centered on governmental role transformation. In terms of establishing a basic institutional framework linked to the internationally accepted investment and trade rules, a number of replicable and scalable reform and innovation achievements have been formed. In order to better promote the implementation of a new round of high-level opening up across the country, the State Council decided to promote the pilot experience of the Shanghai Free Trade Zone on a larger scale, and successively established 11 pilot free trade zones in Tianjin, Fujian, Guangdong, Liaoning, Hubei, and other places. The 19th CPC National Congress report additionally emphasized: "We will grant more powers to pilot free trade zones to conduct reform, and explore the opening of free trade ports." In April 2018, Xi Jinping announced in Hainan: "The Central Committee of the Communist Party of China has decided to build a pilot free trade zone on the whole island of Hainan, and support Hainan in gradually exploring and steadily advancing the construction of a free trade port with Chinese characteristics."[97] The development of pilot free trade zones and free trade ports will pioneer innovative approaches and consolidate practical insights for advancing comprehensive reforms and broadening market liberalization, significantly shaping China's next phase of economic openness.

4. Research on Direct Investment in Foreign Countries

In the 1980s, China's primary focus in its opening-up strategy was attracting foreign capital and generating foreign exchange through exports. At the time, Chinese enterprises' overseas investments were minimal, with most international operations being handled by a few large foreign trade companies that also established branches abroad. The "Opinions on Strengthening the

[97] Jinping Xi. Speech at the celebration of the 30th anniversary of Hainan's establishment of a special economic zone. *People's Daily Online*, April 14, 2018.

Management of Overseas Investment Projects" presented to the State Council by the former State Planning Commission in 1991 still held that "China did not yet have the conditions for large-scale overseas investment." As China's economic power grew, the conditions for outbound direct investment began to improve. The "Outline of the Tenth Five-Year Plan for National Economic and Social Development," approved at the Fourth Session of the Ninth National People's Congress in 2001, marked the first time that the government advocated for enterprises to pursue the "going global" strategy. Since then, the importance of pursuing a "going global" strategy has been consistently highlighted in the reports of all the CPC National Congresses. The "Decision" of the Third Plenary Session of the 18th CPC Central Committee explicitly stated: "We will expand both enterprise and individual investment overseas, establish themselves as foreign-investment entities, allow them to exploit their advantages in overseas investment cooperation, allow them to freely undertake engineering contracts and labor cooperation projects at their own risk in any country or region, and allow them to go global in an innovative way for greenfield investment, mergers and acquisitions, securities investment, joint investment, etc." The document of the 19th CPC National Congress once again emphasized the need to "give equal emphasis to 'bringing in' and 'going global,'" and "develop new ways of making outbound investments, and promote international cooperation on production capacity," which had defined the specific orientation for Chinese businesses to conduct overseas investment.

Since the beginning of the twenty-first century, the outbound direct investment (ODI) by Chinese enterprises has begun to accelerate significantly. In most years before 2003, China's outbound direct investment hovered around US$2 billion, but exceeded US$10 billion in 2005 and US$100 billion in 2013, with outbound non-financial direct investment reaching US$196.15 billion in 2016, which held the second spot globally for two straight years. By 2016, China's overseas direct investment stock had hit US$1,357.39 billion, ranking sixth worldwide. Since 2015, China's outbound direct investment has exceeded the amount of imported foreign investment for two consecutive years, which indicates that China has basically realized the transformation from a capital-importing country to a capital-exporting country.

As early as the mid-1980s, some scholars began to discuss the issue of China's outbound investment. However, due to the small scale of China's outbound investment at that time, relevant research mainly focused on the significance of China's cross-border investment, the difference between China's overseas investment and the capital export of Western multinational companies, the experience and lessons of developing countries' outbound investment, and what strategies China should adopt for outbound investment.[98] Since the beginning of the twenty-first century, with the increasingly active outbound investment of Chinese enterprises, the domestic academic literature on outbound direct investment has increased significantly. Researchers have conducted extensive studies on the driving factors, location selections, economic effects, and risk assessments related to China's overseas direct investment.

I. The motivation of China's outbound direct investment.

Western international investment theories believe that multinational companies will only carry out outbound investment when they have specific advantages. Despite the continuous strengthening of China's overall capabilities since the economic reform, the country remains, at its core, a developing country, and many Chinese enterprises still lack ownership advantages (especially technological advantages and management skills) emphasized by mainstream international theories when carrying out the outbound investment. What factors are driving Chinese companies to invest abroad? Wei Dong and Wang Jingmin attributed the motivations of Chinese enterprises' outbound direct investment to five types: natural resource-based, market-focused, efficiency-prioritized, strategic asset-driven, and politics-guided.[99] Chen En and Yuan Qunhua attributed the motivation of Chinese enterprises' outbound investment to three aspects: avoiding tariff and non-tariff barriers to achieve market expansion; developing and utilizing local resources to alleviate the shortage of domestic resources; learning foreign advanced technologies and improving technological innovation capabilities.[100] Chen Yan et al.(2012) believed that China was an emerging economy with a relatively high degree of government regulation. Examining the motivations behind enterprises' outbound investments solely from the standpoint of their resources and capabilities was insufficient. The authorities' impact on enterprises' outbound investment should be analyzed from an institutional perspective. Employing

---

98 Shalian Liu. On China's foreign investment. *World Economy Studies*, 1984 (3); Liping He. Discussion on the development strategy of China's foreign investment. *Finance & Economics*, 1985 (5); Ninggeng Wu. Discussion on China's foreign investment. *Journal of Peking University (Philosophy and Social Sciences)*, 1986 (3); Hou Xinbing. The development of foreign direct investment is an effective way to promote the introduction of foreign capital in China. *Foreign Economics & Management*, 1986 (4).

99 Dong Wei, Jingmin Wang. Analysis on the motivation of China's foreign direct investment. *Dongyue Tribune*, 2005 (5).

100 En Chen, Qunhua Yuan. The motivation and strategic choice of Chinese enterprises' foreign investment. *International Business—Journal of University of International Business and Economics*, 2004 (3).

provincial-level panel data on China's overseas investment spanning 2003 to 2009, they conducted an empirical analysis and found that the government's resource allocation indeed played an important role in regulating enterprises' outbound investment.[101] The findings of Huang Jingbo and Zhang Anmin do not support the above conclusion.[102] After executing a factual examination rooted in the movement of cross-border investment between 1982 and 2007, they believed that changes in institutional factors, such as avoiding trade barriers and economic freedom, had no significant impact on China's outbound investment. There was a significant positive correlation between China's outbound direct investment and exports, energy demand, GDP, and manufacturing, which unveiled a comparative advantage (RCA) metric. Among the elements exerting the strongest influence on China's overseas direct investment, shifts in exports and energy demand stood out.

Some scholars also used new analytical tools to analyze this issue from a new theoretical perspective. Li Junjiang and Sun Li used the Heterogeneous-firm Trade Theory in the New-New Trade Theory as an analytical tool to investigate the determinants of overseas direct investment by Chinese natural resource-based firms, and believed that the fundamental factors affecting the "going global" of Chinese resource enterprises were the level of productivity.[103] Tan Yanzhi elucidated the determinants behind the international expansion of Chinese business entities from the perspective of the dynamic accumulation of technical capabilities within the enterprises, and believed that the motivation of Chinese enterprises to become internationalized was not to take advantage of their own ownership like Western multinational companies, but to overcome their own competitive disadvantages. The primary incentive for Chinese firms to invest overseas was to seek and absorb the tacit knowledge of foreign enterprises, and at the same time, to further develop domestically formed technological capabilities to enhance the technological capabilities of enterprises.[104]

Although many scholars have different views on the motives of Chinese enterprises' outbound investment, in general, as Jiang Xiaojuan sums up, the foreign

---

101 Yan Chen, Huan Yang, Bin Zhang. Motivation of China's foreign investment: Institutional adjustment and regional differences. *Journal of Management Science*, 2012 (3).

102 Jingbo Huang, Anmin Zhang. An empirical study on the main drivers of China's outbound foreign direct investment—based on the analysis of outbound investment flow from 1982 to 2007. *International Economics and Trade Research*, 2009 (7).

103 Junjiang Li, Li Sun. Chinese resource enterprises "go global": an analysis based on the trade theory of heterogeneous enterprises. *Jianghan Tribune*, 2012 (1).

104 Yanzhi Tan. Foreign direct investment of Chinese enterprises: characteristics, new theoretical exploration and enlightenment. *Teaching and Research*, 2009 (3).

investment and the establishment of China's multinational companies are urgent requirements for further reform, opening up, and structural adjustment. China's engagement in outbound investment is a proactive response to the global economic trend, as it allows the country to better utilize foreign natural and technological resources, boost exports of Chinese goods, better meet local market demands, and position Chinese manufacturing advantageously within the global division of labor. At the same time, carrying out outbound investment is also an urgent requirement for domestic structural adjustment, because outbound investment allows for the optimal use of existing production capacities, fostering the growth of high-tech industries, and launch world famous brand products and globally famous enterprises.[105]

II. The location selection of China's outbound investment

Based on dominant transnational investment theory, when enterprises choose the host country for outbound direct investment, the main factors to consider include resource endowment, market size, and political stability. So, do the elements that affect the site choice of Chinese enterprises' outbound direct investment conform to mainstream theories, or are they unique? This question has stimulated the research interest of many scholars. Some researchers used theoretical models and econometric analysis to discuss the factors that affected the location selection of Chinese enterprises' overseas investment. Cheng Huifang and Ruan Xiang used the gravitational space model to explain the location selection of outbound direct investment. By incorporating variables such as the economic scale of the two countries, per capita national income, bilateral trade volume, and geographic distance between countries into the gravitational model and testing, they found that the outbound direct investment flow had a strong positive correlation with the economic aggregate of the host country, and a negative correlation with the distance.[106] On this basis, they divided the optional locations of China's outbound direct investment into four categories: huge gravitational type, gravitational type, general gravitational type, and insufficient gravitational type. It was believed that China's outbound direct investment should be concentrated in the Asian region first, followed by the American and European countries. Investment in the African region could also be appropriately increased. Jiang Guanhong and Jiang Dianchun additionally employed the investment gravity model to analyze the location

[105] Xiaojuan Jiang. "Tenth Five-Year Plan" China's foreign investment trend research: global background, investment scale and key selection. *Management World*, 2001(1).

[106] Huifang Cheng, Xiang Ruan. Using gravity model to analyze the location choice of China's foreign direct investment. *The Journal of World Economy*, 2004 (11).

choices of China's overseas direct investment.[107] By analyzing China's investment in 95 countries between 2003 and 2009, they found that market size, resource availability, and technological development were key factors affecting China's outbound direct investment. This resulted in a clear pattern of location selection driven by market-pursuing, resource-acquiring, and strategic asset-procuring objectives. China had different motives for choosing developing countries and developed countries to carry out direct investment. Investing in developing countries was mainly motivated by market-seeking and resource-seeking, and the motive of technology export was obvious, while investment in developed countries was mainly based on strategic assets-seeking motivation.

In the process of outbound investment by Chinese enterprises, government-owned entities initially took the lead as the main players. Yet, in the past few years, privately held businesses have grown more prominent in their pursuit of global expansion. Some researchers have studied the location selection and influencing factors of the outbound investment of enterprises of different ownership types. Xue Yanru et al.(2016) believed that because state-owned enterprises had a government background and could easily obtain resources such as funds and policies, their motives for outbound investment were different from general motives. They examined the data on outbound direct investment by China's mineral resource-based state-owned enterprises from 2000 to 2014, and identified that among the elements influencing the site choice of government-owned entities' overseas investment, the host country's resource endowment, political environment, market size, and geographic distance were not the key factors. The motivations for ownership and timing arbitrage significantly influenced the location choices of state-owned enterprises, leading them to favor countries or regions with high market entry barriers and lower regulatory standards.[108] Qiu Licheng et al. (2015) believed that the nature of state-owned enterprises determined their dual motives for outbound direct investment, while private enterprises and state-owned enterprises were significantly different in terms of ownership, enterprise scale, and policy support. Therefore, there were also significant differences in the motives and location selection of outbound investment.[109]

---

107 Guanhong Jiang, Dianchun Jiang. The Location selection of China's foreign investment: panel data test based on investment gravity model. *The Journal of World Economy*, 2012 (9).

108 Yanru Xue, Hailiang Zhang, Ping Zou. Ownership differences, arbitrage motives and the location decision of foreign direct investment: an analysis based on mineral resource-based state-owned enterprises. *Economic Review*, 2016 (2).

109 Licheng Qiu, Debin Yang. The location choice of Chinese enterprises' OFDI: a comparative analysis of state-owned enterprises and private enterprises. *Journal of International Trade*, 2015 (6).

Employing the figures of China's publicly traded firms' overseas direct investment from 2005 to 2013, they conducted an empirical analysis and found that the main motive for the outbound investment of state-owned enterprises was resource-seeking. This type of investment showed limited sensitivity to the political risks of host nations, with state-owned enterprises often focusing on countries abundant in natural resources, particularly in developing countries; while private enterprises invested abroad in order to obtain markets and strategic assets, and were more willing to invest in politically stable countries. For private enterprises, the main influencing factor for investment in developing countries was market motives, while the motivation for investing in developed countries was to obtain strategic assets.

III. The home country economic effect of outbound direct investment

(1) Trade effects

Will outbound direct investment lead to trade substitution or trade complementarity? In other words, will it increase the foreign trade of the home country or reduce it? As the scale of China's overseas direct investment expands continuously, homegrown studies on this matter have grown gradually. The research methods used by domestic scholars are basically based on empirical research, where they use econometric models and related data to test trade effects. Xiang Benwu maintained that China's overseas direct investment exerted a trade-boosting function.[110] From a short-term perspective, outbound direct investment does not have a crowding-out effect on imports and exports, but from a long-term perspective, outbound direct investment has a very obvious effect of driving China's imports and exports. For every 1% rise in China's overseas direct investment, its foreign trade volume grows by 0.9 percentage points. Numerous studies have highlighted that the "export effect" of China's overseas direct investment is notably pronounced. According to the research by Lang Lihua and Liu Xinyu, every 1% increase in China's outbound direct investment would boost exports by 0.435%.[111] Jiang Guanhong and Jiang Dianchun investigated the "export effect" of China's outward foreign direct investment from the micro-level perspective of individual firms. Their findings indicated that such overseas expansion generally facilitated firms' export performance. In terms of geographical distribution, the

110 Benwu Xiang. A study on the trade effect of China's foreign direct investment—co-integration analysis based on panel data. *Finance & Trade Economics*, 2009 (4).

111 Lihua Lang, Xinyu Liu. The impact of China's foreign direct investment on export scale: based on a panel data model of 143 countries from 2003 to 2014. *Research on Economics and Management*, 2016 (9).

enhancement in exports was more noticeable when targeting affluent economies, whereas the boost was comparatively limited in developing nations, along with regions such as Hong Kong, Macao, and offshore financial centers; in terms of investment industries, the "export effect" of outbound direct investment in business services was the most obvious.[112] Fan Hongzhong and Chen Pan argued that while China's outward foreign direct investment had a notable impact on boosting trade, the degree of this trade-enhancing effect varied considerably across different host regions. The trade promotion effect for low-income countries was significantly stronger than that for middle—and high-income countries. The trade promotion effect on Asian countries was stronger than that on European and African countries.[113] Further research showed that China's outbound direct investment was not only conducive to the expansion of export scale, but also to the upgrading of export commodity structure. In Sui Yuehong and Zhao Zhenhua's view, China's overseas direct investment was characterized by the coexistence of both forward and reverse gradients. It not only transferred domestic industries without comparative advantages through forward gradient outbound investment, but also accumulated strategic assets and expanded the market through reverse gradient outbound investment. This kind of outbound investment, with the coexistence of forward and reverse gradients, had a significant positive effect on the shipment of advanced technology goods.[114] Chen Juncong and Huang Fanhua's study revealed a clear positive relationship between the growth of China's outward direct investment scale and the rising technological sophistication of its manufactured exports. Their findings indicate that overseas investment has played a key role in enhancing the technological content of China's export-oriented manufacturing sector.[115]

(2) The effect of technological progress

Since the 1990s, Chinese researchers have extensively explored the technological spillovers associated with Foreign Direct Investment (FDI). However, most of these

---

[112] Guanhong Jiang, Dianchun Jiang. The "export effect" of Chinese enterprises' foreign direct investment. *Economic Research Journal*, 2014 (5).

[113] Hongzhong Fan, Pan Chen. Analysis of the relationship between China's OFDI and export trade and its temporal and spatial differences. *International Business (Journal of University of International Business and Economics)*, 2017 (2).

[114] Yuehong Sui, Zhenhua Zhao. The mechanism and evidence of the impact of China's OFDI on trade structure—and on the expansion of China's OFDI motivation. *Finance & Trade Economics*, 2012 (4).

[115] Juncong Chen, Fanhua Huang. The technical complexity of foreign direct investment and export. *World Economy Studies*, 2013 (11).

studies have concentrated on how inbound FDI has contributed to advancements in China's domestic technology. As China's overseas investment activities have expanded steadily, growing academic interest has turned toward examining whether outward FDI generates reverse technology spillovers that benefit the investing country, marking a new and increasingly important area of investigation. More and more studies have shown that foreign direct investment not only has technological spillover effects on the host country receiving the investment, but also has a reverse technological spillover effect on the home country of the investment to varying degrees. Scholars such as Zhao Wei had studied this issue earlier and believed that the impact of outbound direct investment on China's technological progress had begun to appear, and direct investment in countries and regions with abundant R&D factors, in particular, had a relatively obvious reverse technology spillover effect.[116] Chen Hao and Wu Wen studied the different effects of country differences in outbound direct investment on China's technological progress, and held that investments in advanced nations exerted a reverse technological spillover impact, while investments in transitional countries and developing countries would produce positive technology output rather than reverse technology spillover.[117] Ye Hongyu et al.(2017) further studied the influence of the host country's characteristic elements affecting the reverse technological spillover impact of China's overseas investment from the aspects of the host country's technological innovation level, human capital level, cultural differences, and financial development level.[118] Scholars had found that although China's outbound direct investment generally had a reverse technology spillover effect, there were regional differences and industry differences in this effect. Li Mei and Yang Shichang believed that the reverse technology spillover effects of outbound direct investment in different regions of the country were not the same.[119] The eastern region experienced a markedly greater boost in total factor productivity, innovation, and technical efficiency compared to the central and Western parts

---

116 Wei Zhao, Guangdong Gu, Yuanqing He. Outbound foreign direct investment and China's technological progress: mechanism analysis and tentative empirical evidence. *Management World*, 2006 (7).

117 Hao Chen, Wen Wu. Country differences of China's outbound foreign direct investment and the technological progress of the home country. *Studies in Science of science*, 2016 (1).

118 Hongyu Ye, Dong Han, Shenghao Wang. A quantile regression study on the influencing factors of China's OFDI reverse technology spillovers—from the perspective of host country characteristics. *Review of Economy and Management*, 2017 (5).

119 Mei Li, Shichang Liu. Regional differences and threshold effect of reverse technological spillover of foreign direct investment—through regression analysis based on China's interprovincial panel data. *Management World*, 2012 (1).

of the country. This disparity primarily stemmed from regional variations in their ability to absorb and utilize advanced technologies. Chai Qingchun and Zhang Nannan studied the industry differences of reverse technology spillover effects and believed that outbound direct investment in manufacturing, scientific research, and technical services had a strong reverse technology spillover effect, but this effect was not obvious in mining and construction industries.[120]

(3) The effect of industrial upgrading

The relationship between China's outbound direct investment and the effect of domestic industrial upgrading has been a topic that domestic scholars have discussed a lot in recent years. Some scholars conducted research from a more macroscopic perspective. Bu Wei and Yi Qian believed that China's outbound direct investment could promote China's industrial upgrading through the industrial relocation effect, technological progress effect, and resource filling effect.[121] Empirical research indicated a positive association between overseas direct investment and industrial upgrading in typical regions of China, but its regression coefficient was small, indicating that its promoting effect on industrial upgrading was not outstanding. Ouyang Yanyan et al.(2016) and Zhao Yunpeng et al.(2018) conducted tests with different data samples and believed that outbound direct investment could promote China's industrial structure upgrade, but this industrial structure upgrade had a significant lag effect. Although the impact of outbound direct investment on domestic industrial upgrading was not significant in the short term, it had a more obvious promoting effect in the long run.[122] There were also significant spatial interactions between the industrial structures of different regions. The optimization of the industrial structure of some provinces could drive the technological progress and industrial upgrading of neighboring and economically connected provinces. There were also some scholars who carried out research at the mesoscopic or microscopic level. The research of Chen Lin and Zhu Mingrui showed that outbound direct investment could significantly promote the upgrading of industries, but it failed to

---

[120] Qingchun Chai, Nannan Zhang. The reverse technology spillover effect of China's foreign direct investment: a test analysis based on industry differences. *Journal of Central University of Finance & Economics*, 2016 (8).

[121] Wei Bu, Qian Yi. Research on the impact of OFDI on China's industrial upgrading. *Macroeconomics*, 2015 (10).

[122] Yanyan Ouyang, Li Liu, Yanyi Chen. Research on the industrial effect of China's outbound foreign direct investment. *Review of Industrial Economics*, 2016 (1); Yunpeng Zhao, Jiao Ye. A study on the impact of outbound foreign direct investment on China's industrial structure. *The Journal of Quantitative & Technical Economics*, 2018 (3).

notably boost the productivity of the second and third economic sectors, and the effect of intra-industry upgrading was not obvious.[123] Jia Nisha and Shen Chen examined the enterprise-level data and found that outbound direct investment by enterprises had promoted the upgrading of the manufacturing industry, yet discrepancies existed in the industrial advancement impact of investments across various regions. Investing in developed countries was conducive to promoting the manufacturing industry upgrading, but the effect of investing in developing countries on manufacturing upgrading was not obvious.[124]

5. Research on the *Belt and Road Initiative*

The *Initiative* refers to the proposal for jointly developing the *Silk Road Economic Belt* (BRI) and the *21st Century Maritime Silk Road*. Advancing this initiative has become a key strategic move in China's efforts to establish a more open and globally integrated economic framework. In September and October 2013, during visits to Central Asia and ASEAN, President Xi introduced these two major proposals. Speaking at Nazarbayev University in Kazakhstan in September, Xi emphasized the importance of closer economic cooperation across Eurasia and called for innovative collaborative models to build the *Silk Road Economic Belt*. The following month, during his trip to ASEAN nations, he expressed China's willingness to enhance maritime collaboration and work with ASEAN countries to construct the *21st Century Maritime Silk Road*. These proposals quickly attracted considerable international attention. In November 2013, the "Decision of the Central Committee of the Communist Party of China on Some Major Issues Concerning Comprehensively Deepening the Reform" adopted by the Third Plenary Session of the 18th CPC Central Committee further clearly stated: "Accelerate the construction of infrastructure connecting China with neighboring countries and regions, and work hard to build a *Silk Road Economic Belt* and a *Maritime Silk Road*, so as to form a new pattern of all-round opening." Following its initial proposal, China moved swiftly to shift the BRI from a strategic vision to practical implementation. At the Bo'ao Forum for Asia in late March 2015, the National Development and Reform Commission, along with the Ministries of Foreign Affairs and Commerce, jointly released a policy document titled "Joining

---

123 Lin Chen, Mingrui Zhu. An empirical study on the upgrading of China's industrial structure by outbound foreign direct investment: based on the test of inter-industry and intra-industry upgrading. *Modern Economic Science*, 2015 (6).

124 Nisha Jia, Chen Shen. Research on the upgrading effect of China's outbound foreign direct investment in the manufacturing industry. *Journal of International Trade*, 2016 (8).

Hands to Build a *Silk Road Economic Belt* and a *21st-Century Maritime Silk Road*—Vision and Actions." This marked the first comprehensive articulation of the BRI's overall framework, key areas of cooperation, and operational mechanisms. Later, during the 19th CPC National Congress in 2018, it was emphasized that advancing the BRI should remain a high priority. Equal importance was placed on attracting foreign investment and encouraging Chinese enterprises to expand abroad. The guiding principle of shared development through consultation and partnership was reaffirmed, alongside a stronger push for openness, cross-border collaboration, and innovation-driven development. These efforts aim to broaden China's integration with the global economy via enhanced land and maritime connectivity in all directions. This shows that accelerating the construction of the *Belt and Road Initiative* will become a key area for China to build a new pattern of an open economy. The *Belt and Road Initiative* (BRI) not only brings new historical opportunities to China's foreign trade and outbound investment, but also deepens the economic and trade cooperation between China and countries along the BRI routes, which has received positive responses and participation from more than 140 countries and regions. The volume of trade between China and the nations along the routes has kept growing, the investment field has continued to expand, and major projects have been steadily advanced. To date, China's total direct investment in related countries has exceeded 60 billion US dollars, accompanied by the establishment of 75 overseas economic and trade cooperation zones and parks. By 2017, the combined trade volume between China and these partner nations had reached an impressive 1.1 trillion US dollars.[125] In recent years, with the gradual transformation of the *Belt and Road Initiative* from a vision to a reality, the "Belt and Road" research has become a hot field in the theory of opening up.

I. The significance, strategic connotation, and implementation path of the *Belt and Road Initiative*

The *Initiative* represents China's innovative strategy for expanding openness in response to the global economic restructuring that followed the financial crisis, as well as the shift toward a "new normal" in its domestic economy. A number of researchers have examined the *Initiative*'s broader implications for both China and the global economy, analyzing its influence from a macroeconomic standpoint amid evolving internal and international economic dynamics. Lu Feng et al.(2015) analyzed the multiple strategic orientations of the *Belt and Road Initiative* from

[125] Ministry of Commerce: China's investment in the "Belt and Road" has exceeded 60 billion US dollars. *Ministry of Commerce website*, March 12, 2018.

the perspectives of economic diplomacy strategy, global economic growth, and domestic structural adjustment. It was considered that the *Initiative* constitutes a key part of China's strategy to advance all-round opening up in the new era, and has created a positive interaction between the national policy of opening up, diplomatic strategy, structural adjustment, and the goal of promoting growth.[126] Shen Xianjie and Xiao Jincheng held the view that the *Initiative* helps China cope with the external pressures generated by the US-led *Trans-Pacific Partnership Agreement* (TPPA) and *Trans-Atlantic Trade and Investment Partnership* (TTIP). The initiative has the potential to enhance China's participation in both international and regional collaborations, thereby contributing to the advancement of a higher-standard open economy.[127] Researchers have also explored the *Silk Road Economic Belt* and the *Maritime Silk Road*, respectively. In an in-depth analysis of the geopolitical and economic dynamics shaping the *Silk Road Economic Belt*, Hu Angang et al.(2014) emphasized that while its core aim lies in promoting trade and economic ties, the initiative carries profound strategic weight, as it is closely linked to safeguarding China's economic interests, maintaining regional stability, and fostering regional development.[128] Compared with the ancient *Silk Road*, the modern *Silk Road Economic Belt* integrates political economy, internal affairs, diplomacy, and time and space in nature, and integrates westward opening and the development of Western China in content. In terms of formation, it is a contemporary update of the national security and economic strategies that have been collectively planned by generations of leaders. He Fan et al.(2017) examined the economic conditions of regions situated along the *Maritime Silk Road* and their collaborative engagement with China. Their study explored the potential for deepened partnerships between China and these nations across five key dimensions: industrial investment, infrastructure investment, resource development and cooperation, foreign commercial and trade zones, and marine economy.[129] Scholars have not only studied the important connotation of the *Belt and Road Initiative*, but also proposed specific policy recommendations regarding the "Belt

126 Feng Lu, Xin Li, Shuangshuang Li, Zhixiao Jiang, Jieping Zhang, Yewei Yang. Why is it China? The economic logic of the "Belt and Road." *International Economic Review*, 2015 (3).

127 Xianjie Shen, Jincheng Xiao. The new situation of international regional economic cooperation and China's "Belt and Road" cooperation strategy. *Macroeconomics*, 2014 (11).

128 Angang Hu, Wei Ma, Yilong Yan. "Silk Road Economic Belt": strategic connotation, positioning and realization path. *Journal of Xinjiang Normal University (Philosophy and Social Sciences)*, 2014 (2).

129 Fan He, He Zhu, Qian Zhang. Construction of the Maritime Silk Road in the 21st Century: Status Quo, Opportunities, Problems and Countermeasures. *International Economic Review*, 2017(5).

and Road" international cooperation mechanism. There is a broad consensus that the *Initiative* should prioritize infrastructure development, trade facilitation, and investment cooperation. At the same time, it is also important to foster stronger economic and commercial engagement, public diplomacy, social culture, and other aspects between China and participating countries along the routes. Moreover, sustained efforts are needed to enhance policy alignment, improve transport links, facilitate smooth trade flows, promote currency exchange, and strengthen cultural and people-to-people connections, thereby elevating bilateral cooperation to a higher stage.

II. The *Belt and Road Initiative* and the structural facilities building of nations along the paths

For both China and the countries situated along the routes, developing infrastructure plays a crucial role in improving the investment climate and accelerating economic growth. As a result, it has emerged as a central focus of the "Belt and Road." Luo Yuze believed that promoting the "Belt and Road" facility connectivity was conducive to breaking through development bottlenecks, accelerating the economic growth of nations within the area, and improving people's livelihood. This helped create a more favorable setting for regional economic and trade collaboration, encouraged the leveraging of comparative strengths, and supported mutually beneficial growth. It was conducive to obtaining early harvests as soon as possible and strengthening confidence in the *Initiative*.[130] Numerous empirical analyses have demonstrated that the "Belt and Road" has contributed to enhancing infrastructure development in participating countries. Huang Liangxiong et al.(2018), using unbalanced panel data from 64 nations along the BRI corridors spanning 2003 to 2013, examined how China's outbound investment influenced local infrastructure. Their findings indicate a statistically significant positive effect: a 1% rise in China's investment in these countries corresponded to a 0.006% improvement in their infrastructure performance. During the sample period from 2003 to 2013, the contribution rate of China's investment to the improvement of the infrastructure level in the countries along the routes was about 12%.[131] According to Sui Guangjun et al. (2017), China's outward direct investment plays a notable role in boosting per capita real GDP

---

[130] F Yuze Luo. Ideas and policies to promote the "Belt and Road" facility connectivity. *Journal of Chongqing University of Technology (Social Sciences)*, 2017 (7).

[131] Liangxiong Huang, Xinbei Qian, Guangjun Sui. Has Chinese OFDI improved the infrastructure of the countries along the "Belt and Road"? *Management Review*, 2018 (3).

in partner countries.[132] Their analysis suggests that approximately 30% of this growth effect is attributed to improvements in infrastructure driven by Chinese investment. Other researchers have pointed out that the *Initiative* has not only spurred development in host countries but has also generated favorable outcomes for China's own economy. Using the Global Trade Analysis Project (GTAP) model, Huang Xianhai and Chen Hangyu explored the reciprocal impact of improved connectivity between China and states along the trails.[133] The simulation outcomes indicated that the advancement of the "Belt and Road" facility connectivity was conducive to promoting unimpeded trade, and the combined effect of the two would not only raise the well-being standard and GDP of the regions along the routes to varying degrees, but also increase China's GDP and improve China's welfare level, import and export level and terms of trade. Scholars not only studied the overall economic effect of facility connectivity on China and countries along the routes, but also further discussed the impact of infrastructure construction on different regions or nations within the framework of the *Belt and Road Initiative*. Pan Zhiping(2016), Xie Wenze(2018), Li Lingqiu(2017), and Liu Shuang, et al. (2017), respectively studied the cooperation fields, project progress, development prospects, and major issues in the infrastructure sector in the China-Central Asia-West Asia Economic Corridor, China-Latin America, China-Myanmar, China-Russia, and other regions or countries, and put forward policy suggestions for further expanding two-party collaboration in the realm of structural facilities building.[134]

---

[132] Guangjun Sui, Liangxiong Huang, Xing Huang. China's outbound foreign direct investment, infrastructure construction and economic growth of the countries along the "Belt and Road." *Journal of Guangdong University of Finance and Economics*, 2017 (1).

[133] Xianhai Huang, Hangyu Chen. A study on the implementation effect of the "Belt and Road"—simulation analysis based on GTAP. *Social Science Front*, 2016 (5).

[134] Zhiping Pan. The connection point of facility connectivity under the "Belt and Road" vision: taking the "China-Central Asia-West Asia" economic corridor as an example. *Journal of Xinjiang Normal University (Philosophy and Social Sciences)*, 2016 (3); Wenze Xie. Analysis on the joint construction of the "Belt and Road" in China and Latin America. *Pacific Journal*, 2018 (2); Lingqiu Li. Investment cooperation in infrastructure construction between China and Myanmar under the background of the "Belt and Road." *Northeast Asia Economic Research*, 2017 (3); Shuang Liu, Youjun Ma, Jianping Zhong. Investigation and analysis on the status of infrastructure construction in Sino-Russian border areas. *Journal of Eurasian Economy*, 2017 (1).

III. Global manufacturing capacity collaboration within the structure of the *Belt and Road Initiative*

Cross-border industrial capacity collaboration forms a core component of the *Initiative*. Against the backdrop of expanding infrastructure and promoting industrial diversification in partner countries, China has engaged in such cooperation by integrating multiple tools, including foreign trade, investment, and other economic instruments. Qu Fengjie believed that advancing the *Initiative*, along with international industrial capacity cooperation, would support the formation of a China-centered regional production network and foster a new version of the Flying Geese model to drive regional economic development.[135] Li Xiaoyu compared two different modes of foreign capacity collaboration between the US and Japan from the aspects of industry selection and subject transfer, and proposed that the international capacity cooperation under the *Initiative* had two modes of cooperation, namely one model of capacity cooperation between China and developing countries, and another model of collaboration between China and advanced economies.[136] More literature combined the specific situation of China and related countries or regions, and deeply studied the fields, mechanisms, problems, and prospects of international production capacity cooperation. The production capacity cooperation between China and Kazakhstan could be regarded as a model of global manufacturing capacity collaboration. Wang Zhimin explored the purpose, progress, and implications of China-Kazakhstan industrial capacity cooperation, asserting that this new model offers a foundational framework for broader collaboration on production capacity across countries and regions involved in the "Belt and Road." He further noted that as cooperation between China and Kazakhstan deepens, it is likely to generate spillover effects, encouraging other BRI participants to transition from primarily bilateral arrangements to more extensive multilateral partnerships.[137] Separately, Shen Minghui and Zhang Zhongyuan analyzed Indonesia's national development strategies, policy frameworks, and legal provisions. They emphasized that for China-Indonesia industrial capacity cooperation to succeed, it must be aligned with Indonesia's development goals and planning priorities, and selectively establish cooperation mechanisms

---

135 Fengjie Qu. Breaking out of the horses group pattern and constructing a new flying geese group pattern—building a China-led regional industrial division system through international production capacity cooperation. *Intertrade*, 2017 (2).

136 Xiaoyu Li. The development and deepening strategy of international production capacity cooperation in the "Belt and Road" initiative. *Review of Economic Research*, 2016 (67).

137 Zhimin Wang. China-Kazakhstan production capacity cooperation and its spillover effect under the background of the "Belt and Road." *Northeast Asia Forum*, 2017 (1).

in Indonesia's priority development industries.[138] Through the calculation of the Sino-Russian trade complementarity index and industrial complementarity index, Sun Xuemeng found that China and Russia had high industrial complementarity indexes in the fields of manufactured products, mechanical devices and transport apparatus, miscellaneous products, mineral fuels, and primary materials, indicating high production capacity cooperation potential.[139] Yao Guimei believed that Africa was a key component of the westward advancement of the "Belt and Road," and China-Africa production capacity cooperation centered on connectivity and industrialization was being piloted in some African countries. However, due to the "fragmented" market characteristics of Africa, China-Africa production capacity cooperation should be carried out in an orderly manner rather than a large-scale comprehensive promotion.[140] Wan Jun examined the driving forces, current status, and difficulties associated with industrial capacity cooperation between China and Latin America. He argued that deepening this collaboration would enable Latin American countries to better leverage China's equipment, technology, and capital to advance infrastructure development and accelerate industrialization. At the same time, such cooperation would support China's efforts to restructure its economy and foster a new model of openness. Despite steady progress, China-Latin America production capacity partnerships still face limitations, particularly in terms of their scope and depth.[141]

As part of its efforts to advance international industrial capacity cooperation, China has been proactively experimenting with innovative cooperation models centered around cross-border economic cooperation zones with some countries along the routes. Liu Dong advocated that the industrial park model could be selected for manufacturing capacity collaboration between China and Arab countries. The initial approach involved identifying priority partner countries for capacity collaboration by assessing their comparative strengths. Subsequently, industrial parks were established in these regions to cultivate a favorable business climate, encourage the development of industrial clusters, and facilitate

---

138 Minghui Shen, Zhongyuan Zhang. International production capacity cooperation under the background of the "Belt and Road" —taking China-Indonesia cooperation as an example. *International Economic Cooperation*, 2017 (3).

139 Xuemeng Sun. Research on Sino-Russian production capacity cooperation under the background of the "Belt and Road." *Foreign Economic Relations & Trade*, 2017 (6).

140 Guimei Yao. China-Africa production capacity cooperation: achievements, problems and prospects. *International Economic Cooperation*, 2017 (6).

141 Jun Wan. The motivation, progress and challenges of China-Latin America production capacity cooperation. *Journal of Latin American Studies*, 2016 (3).

the relocation of China's competitive industries to Arab nations.[142] From the perspective of investment and establishment of foreign commercial and trade collaboration zones, the research group of China Development Bank screened potential key areas of production capacity cooperation from two aspects: surplus production capacity output and medium-to-high-grade manufacturing capacity collaboration.[143] At present, China has set up dozens of foreign commercial and trade collaboration zones, and the construction and operation of some of them have achieved initial results. Some literature has summarized the operation mode and successful experience of foreign commercial and trade collaboration zones by analyzing relatively successful cases. Ma Xia and Song Caicen recapitulated the evolution history of the Suez Commercial and Trade Collaboration Zone and concluded that the park had formed an operation model based on asset-heavy operation and using asset-light operation to create value through land sales and lease of operating assets, which not only provided a key platform for Chinese businesses to go to Africa, but also achieved sustainable profitability.[144]

IV. Risks and prevention of the "Belt and Road" construction

The countries involved in the *Initiative* differ widely in terms of political structures, economic models, legal frameworks, and historical and cultural backgrounds. These disparities have introduced a range of risks and complexities to the advancement of the initiative. Numerous Chinese researchers have explored the origins, classifications, manifestations, and potential responses to these risks from various analytical viewpoints. Zhang Ming listed six potential risks faced by the development of the "Belt and Road."[145] First, the rate of return on relevant investments is relatively low; second, investment security faces greater challenges; third, the private sector and foreign entities have limited capital contributions, thus the Chinese authorities have to act as the primary investor; fourth, it may hinder rather than accelerate the structural adjustment of the Chinese economy; fifth, it may deepen rather than ease the doubts and resistance of the countries

---

[142] Dong Liu. Construction of overseas industrial parks and Sino-Arab production capacity cooperation. *West Asia and Africa*, 2017 (6).

[143] The research group of China Development Bank's "Research on the Development Model of Cross-border Development Zone and Its Investment and Financing." From the perspective of investment and construction of overseas economic and trade cooperation zones the "Belt and Road" focuses on regional analysis. *Port Economy*, 2017 (1).

[144] Xia Ma, Caicen Song. China-Egypt Suez Economic and Trade Cooperation Zone—a new oasis on the "Belt and Road." *West Asia and Africa*, 2016 (2).

[145] Ming Zhang. Facing the six major risks of the "Belt and Road." *International Economic Review*, 2015 (4).

along the routes to China's rise; sixth, it may intensify the confrontation with the United States. In terms of the project implementation cycle, Zhou Fangyin discussed respectively the risks in the start-up stage; the risks with a smooth start but partial reversal in the middle; the risks with an effective start and normal progress, and the ability to overcome various risks and obstacles in the middle, but followed by a failure of the strategic return to match the strategic investment, or the strategic return which was not very obvious for a fairly lengthy time span.[146] Wang Yongzhong and Li Xichen examined the risks associated with China's investment in "Belt and Road" countries by considering factors such as geographic distribution, industrial composition, and the nature of investing firms. They recommended that the Chinese government actively renegotiate and sign updated bilateral investment treaties with partner nations. At the same time, they emphasized that Chinese enterprises should refine their investment approaches, mitigate political sensitivities and project-related risks, and strengthen their understanding of regulatory compliance. Additionally, they proposed establishing a national system for outbound investment risk assessment, early warning, and governance.[147] Wang Yiwei and Zheng Dong studied the moral hazard in the advancement of the "Belt and Road." Through the analysis of the three levels of national reputation, corporate credit, and personal trust, they believed that the construction of the "Belt and Road" would not only face political, economic, legal, and other risks, but also needed to deal with the moral hazard from the economic agents of nations along the corridors, and they proposed coping strategies from three aspects: concept, mechanism, and practice.[148]

6. Vigorously Engaging in Worldwide Economic Governance

Over the past four decades of economic restructuring, China has emerged as the world's second-largest economy. As its economic strength continues to expand, China's engagement with the international community has grown significantly. Its prominence and influence in global affairs have steadily risen, along with its ability to shape discussions in the international economic governance arena.

146 Fangyin Zhou. Risks and challenges faced by the "Belt and Road" and its countermeasures. *International Survey*, 2015 (4).

147 Yongzhong Wang, Xichen Li. China's investment risk assessment in the countries along the "Belt and Road." *China Opening Journal*, 2015 (4).

148 Yiwei Wang, Dong Zheng. Moral hazard and countermeasures of the "Belt and Road" initiative. *Northeast Asia Forum*, 2015 (4).

Meanwhile, the global financial crisis triggered profound shifts in the structure of the world economy and the architecture of global governance, presenting China with a strategic window to take a more active role in shaping global economic rules and institutions. In the "Several Opinions of the Central Committee of the Communist Party of China and the State Council on Building a New Open Economic System" promulgated in 2015, it clearly pointed out: "we must actively participate in global economic governance, promote the reform of the global economic governance system, support the United Nations and the G20 to play the role of the major platform for global economic governance, and promote the role of the BRICS cooperation mechanism. It is also necessary to jointly improve the voice and representation of emerging markets and the developing countries in the field of global economic governance, fully participate in the reform of the international economic system and the formulation of rules, and take the initiative to propose new propositions, new initiatives and new action plans on global issues to enhance China's right to speak in the formulation of international economic and trade rules and standards." The "Outline of the 13th Five-Year Plan for National Economic and Social Development of the People's Republic of China" also proposed "to promote the improvement of the international economic governance system. We will actively participate in cooperation on global economic governance mechanisms, support the major platforms for global governance and those for regional cooperation in better playing their respective roles, and help make the global governance system more equal and sounder." Establishing a comprehensive and multidimensional opening-up framework was a key objective for China during the "13th Five-Year Plan" period.

I. The reform of the worldwide economic governance regime and China's function

Economic globalization has not only delivered opening-up dividends to all nations worldwide, but also made it possible for economic fluctuations and financial crises to spill over national borders and spread among more countries. The financial crisis sweeping across the world showed that the traditional global economic governance system based on the Bretton Woods system could not effectively coordinate and deal with the complex world economic problems in the context of globalization, and a major reform of the global economic governance system was needed. This required all economies to collaboratively handle and address challenges in the global economy and international finance by continuously enhancing the standard of global economic collaboration, improving the representativeness and legitimacy of the current governance framework, and improving governance institutions, systems, and rules in different fields. Researchers have examined the shortcomings of the current global economic governance framework, explored potential pathways for its reform, and analyzed how China can contribute to driving these changes forward.

Prior to the global financial crisis, the architecture of global economic governance was largely shaped by developed nations and centered around institutions such as the G8, the World Trade Organization, the International Monetary Fund, and the World Bank. However, some scholars have highlighted the inherent weaknesses and limitations of these, for instance, arguing. Zhang Yuyan, for instance, argued that many existing international rules and systems were far from impartial, often serving as instruments to protect and expand the interests of a small group of powerful countries. As a result, traditional governance structures have struggled to keep pace with evolving global economic dynamics.[149] He Fan et al.(2013) held that worldwide governance was not only showing a trend of "fragmentation," but was also facing a series of new challenges, such as dealing with significant shifts in the global economic landscape and a large number of problems caused by the financial crisis. It was imperative to revise the current worldwide governance regime.[150] So, how should China engage in the reform of the global governance mechanism and play a greater role in it? From the perspective of functional positioning and practical role, the G20 is undoubtedly the most important international cooperation platform within the present worldwide economic administration, coordinating and leading other economic governance mechanisms. According to researchers at the Guangdong Institute for International Strategy, China's involvement in worldwide economic administration ought to prioritize three key strategic platforms: the G20 mechanism, international economic organizations, and regional economic organizations, and China's participation strategy should be implemented for different areas of global economic governance.[151] He Fan et al.(2013) discussed three basic principles that China should adhere to in engaging in worldwide economic administration: "compliance with powers and responsibilities," "inclusive interests," and "differentiated shared responsibilities," and believed that China ought to emphasize the function of G20 as the primary forum for worldwide governance in equal consultation between major developed countries and major emerging

---

[149] Yuyan Zhang. A Chinese perspective on global governance. *World Economics and Politics*, 2016 (9).

[150] Fan He, Weijiang Feng, Jin Xu. Challenges faced by the global governance mechanism and China's countermeasures. *World Economics and Politics*, 2013 (4).

[151] Research group of Guangdong Institute of International Strategy. China's strategy for participating in global economic governance: the next 10–15 years. *Reform*, 2014 (5).

countries, and should play a more active and constructive role. Sang Baichuan and Wang Wei measured the G20 from three aspects: member representation, decision-making effectiveness, and institutional synergy, and believed that the G20 was a global economic governance mechanism with strong representation and sustainability. They advocated that China should adopt a strategy centered on multilateral cooperation and regional integration. This includes backing the G20's central role in global economic governance, upholding the WTO's authority in regulating international trade, advancing reforms within the governance frameworks of the IMF and the World Bank, and actively supporting negotiations toward establishing the Free Trade Area of the Asia-Pacific (FTAAP).[152] China has exerted a proactive function in promoting the continuous improvement of the G20 mechanism. The G20 is the first global economic governance mechanism that China has participated in as an original member and a central one. The G20 serves as a vital platform for China to showcase its influence on the world stage. During the G20 Summit in Hangzhou in September 2016, China played a key role in helping member countries reach an agreement on several critical matters related to global economic growth, and promoted the formulation of relevant action programs. The summit issued the "G20 Hangzhou Summit Communiqué" and 28 specific outcome documents. China's effective organization of the G20 Summit in Hangzhou strengthened its influence within global economic governance and underscored its prominent leadership in international economic matters.

The emergence of developing economies is significantly reshaping the global economic landscape and influencing international governance structures. Gao Zugui et al.(2009) noted that this rise has challenged the traditional dominance of developed nations in the world economy and spurred reforms in governance systems historically controlled by Western powers, and weakened the influence of Western countries in many international affairs.[153] Shen Minghui and Ge Wei believed that the strength equilibrium between rising economies and advanced economies led to changes in their power in the world economic structure, which has compelled developed nations to pay greater attention to the interests and demands of developing countries within global economic governance.[154] The BRICS, consisting of Brazil, Russia, India, China, and South Africa, is often

---

[152] Baichuan Sang, Wei Wang. Reform of global economic governance system and prevention of fragmentation risks. *Intertrade*, 2017 (12).

[153] Zugui Gao, Zonglei Wei, Yu Liu. The rise of emerging economies and their impact. *International Data Information*, 2009 (8).

[154] Minghui Shen, Wei Ge. The collective rise of emerging economies and their external risks. *Asia-Pacific Economic Review*, 2012 (5).

regarded as a representative body of emerging economies. He Fan et al. (2013) argued that China should actively engage with the BRICS countries to foster strategic collaboration, using the bloc not only as a platform for economic partnerships but also for political coordination.[155] According to Xu Xiujun, the BRICS cooperation framework, as an emerging influence in global governance, has become a significant venue for dialogue and negotiation among its members on international issues, wielding substantial impact.[156] Through addressing global challenges, the BRICS countries have the potential to serve as a cooperative for emerging nations, a negotiation forum for interregional economic governance, and a communication bridge linking developing and developed countries within the global governance process.

In recent years, China has taken an active role in reshaping global economic governance across various sectors. In the reform of the international monetary and financial governance mechanism, China has promoted the quota adjustment and voting rights reform of the International Monetary Fund and the World Bank, and improved the representation and voice of developing countries in international financial institutions. Following persistent efforts, China succeeded in having RNB incorporated into the International Monetary Fund's Special Drawing Rights (SDR) currency basket. This was the first time that a currency of an emerging economy had joined the SDR and had become an international reserve currency. This development not only advanced the global use of RNB but also disrupted the longstanding dominance of developed countries' currencies as reserves, thereby enhancing the stability of the international monetary system the stability of the international monetary system. Regarding global trade governance, China has consistently advocated for the liberalization and simplification of international trade and investment within the framework of the multilateral trading system, actively promoting multilateral trade negotiations under the WTO framework, and enhancing the global commerce and investment governance system. China has cooperated with the international community to tackle the pressing issue of climate change and has actively embraced its shared yet distinct responsibilities. It has made notable contributions to the adoption and implementation of the *Paris Agreement*. In shaping a sustainable and low-emission framework for global climate and energy governance. China has taken on a constructive and influential role. A key voice among developing nations and emerging markets, the country

[155] Fan He, Weijiang Feng, Jin Xu. Challenges faced by the global governance mechanism and China's countermeasures. *World Economics and Politics*, 2013 (4).

[156] Xiujun Xu. Institutional non-neutrality and BRICS cooperation. *World Economics and Politics*, 2013 (6).

is increasingly recognized as both a driving force and a pivotal participant in reshaping the global economic governance landscape.

II. China's function in regional economic administration

Currently, economic globalization is experiencing deep transformations, with the aftermath of the global financial crisis leading to a period of stagnation in its momentum. Despite these setbacks, the multilateral trade framework established under the WTO has played a vital role in advancing international trade and supporting global economic growth, but due to the very different interests and demands of developed and developing countries, the WTO Doha Round of trade negotiations has not achieved substantial progress for a long time since its launch in 2001. This has also affected some countries' confidence in the multilateral trading system to a certain extent. Britain's withdrawal from the European Union and Donald Trump's trade protectionism have made the noise of "de-globalization" rampant for a time. However, economic globalization has not been fundamentally reversed, but faced new adjustments in form and content. While the multilateral trading system is stagnant, more and more countries are actively developing bilateral and regional free trade arrangements. "Regional economic cooperation is booming, and various free trade agreements have emerged in large numbers, which have become an important driving force for economic globalization."[157]

As the most vibrant engine of the world economy, the Asia-Pacific region has long drawn significant attention in discussions on regional economic integration. Efforts to shape this integration have taken various forms, with the United States and ASEAN each advancing distinct frameworks, such as the *Trans-Pacific Partnership* (TPP) and the *Regional Comprehensive Economic Partnership* (RCEP). The US, in particular, took an active role in spearheading negotiations for both the TPP and the *Transatlantic Trade and Investment Partnership* (TTIP), aiming to reassert its influence in the global investment and trade landscape after the financial crisis. Through the establishment of elevated benchmarks for international trade norms, it sought to preserve its dominant position in the evolving global economic architecture. Scholars have conducted in-depth analyses of the basic framework of TPP and its impact on China. Since China was excluded from the TPP negotiations, domestic research mainly focused on China's countermeasures.[158] With Trump's announcement that the United States would withdraw from

---

[157] Yang Wang. Building a new system of open economy. *People's Daily*, Nov. 22, 2013.

[158] International Trade Research Office, Institute of World Economics and Politics, Chinese Academy of Social Sciences. *Interpretation of the Text of the Trans-Pacific Partnership Agreement.*

the TPP, how to further promote the RCEP has attracted more attention from scholars. Liu Junsheng believed that the Obama administration's promotion of the TPP negotiation had posed a real challenge to both China and ASEAN, and had also given birth to the RCEP.[159] With the withdrawal of the United States, the challenge by TPP to China had also been greatly weakened. But China still had to continue to support the RCEP negotiation. The formation of the RCEP is set to create the largest free trade zone globally, significantly enhancing the efficiency and integration of the production and supply chains across the Asia-Pacific region. The experience accumulated by participating in high-standard free trade areas would assist China in acquiring a stronger voice in the crafting of future regional and global economic rules. Zhang Bin and Zhang Fei reviewed the progress and main contents of the RCEP negotiation, analyzed the practical obstacles faced in the process of RCEP promotion, and believed that China should accelerate the execution of the enhanced version of the ASEAN-China Free Trade Area, improve the level of regional economic collaboration, and steadily advance free trade zone negotiations between China, Japan, and South Korea. China, while backing ASEAN's central role, should also contribute positively by engaging in the rule-making process of the RCEP.[160] Quan Yi et al.(2017) believed that RCEP presents a valuable opportunity for China to take an active part in shaping the regulatory framework for regional economic integration and to participate in leading the direction of future economic cooperation. China should fully coordinate the RCEP negotiation with its own free trade zone construction process, adhere to the combination of domestic reform and international rule building, and comply with the requirements of RCEP to sort out production networks in East Asia and promote sustainable development in Asia. It was also necessary to accept a higher level of commitment consciously and boldly to openness.[161]

Beijing: China Social Sciences Press, 2016; Maoxing Huang, et al. *TPP's China Policy*. Beijing: Peking University Press, 2016; Xiangyang Li. Trans-Pacific Partnership Agreement: a major challenge in the process of China's rise. *International Economic Review*, 2012 (2).

159 Junsheng Liu. RCEP negotiation process and challenges: an assessment from a regional perspective. *Journal of International Economic Cooperation*, 2017 (8).

160 Bin Zhang, Fei Zhang. RCEP's progress, obstacles and China's strategic choices. *Nankai Journal (Philosophy and Social Sciences)*, 2016 (6).

161 Yi Quan, Minghui Shen, Lina Qiu. How to build a Regional Comprehensive Economic Partnership (RCEP): a Chinese perspective. *Peace and Development*, 2017 (5).

References

Bu, Wei, Qian Yi. Research on the impact of OFDI on China's industrial upgrading. *Macroeconomics*, 2015 (10).

Chai, Qingchun, Nannan Zhang. The reverse technology spillover effect of China's foreign direct investment: a test analysis based on industry differences. *Journal of Central University of Finance & Economics*, 2016 (8).

Chen, En, Qunhua Yuan. The motivation and strategic choice of Chinese enterprises' foreign investment. *International Business—Journal of University of International Business and Economics*, 2004 (3).

Chen, Hao, Wen Wu. Country differences of China's outbound foreign direct investment and the technological progress of the home country. *Studies in Science of science*, 2016 (1).

Chen, Hong, Guorong Zhang. An empirical study on the international competitiveness of China's trade in services. *Management World*, 2010 (10).

Chen, Juncong, Fanhua Huang. The technical complexity of foreign direct investment and export. *World Economy Studies*, 2013 (11).

Chen, Lin, Mingrui Zhu. An empirical study on the upgrading of China's industrial structure by outbound foreign direct investment: based on the test of inter-industry and intra-industry upgrading. *Modern Economic Science*, 2015 (6).

Chen, Wanling, Xueyan Shao. Rapid growth of China's foreign trade: problems, dilemmas and solutions: a summary of the academic seminar on "International Economic and Trade Trends and Transformation of Foreign Economic and Trade Growth Modes." *Reform*, 2006 (11).

Chen, Xueming. An overview of the process and advantages and disadvantages of China's entry into the WTO. *Economic Perspectives*, 2000 (3).

Chen, Yan, Huan Yang, Bin Zhang. Motivation of China's foreign investment: Institutional adjustment and regional differences. *Journal of Management Science*, 2012 (3).

Chen, Yinfang, Yangui Zhang. China's strategic issues of utilizing foreign capital. *Social Science Front*, 1985(3).

Cheng, Huifang, Xiang Ruan. Using gravity model to analyze the location choice of China's foreign direct investment. *The Journal of World Economy*, 2004 (11).

Cheng, Nanyang, Hongqiang Yang, Ying Nie. An empirical analysis of the structural changes of China's service trade exports. *Journal of International Trade*, 2006 (8).

Deng, Xiaoping. *Selected Works of Deng Xiaoping, Vol. 3.* Beijing: People's Publishing House, 1993, pp. 64–65.

Fan, Hongzhong, Pan Chen. Analysis of the relationship between China's OFDI and export trade and its temporal and spatial differences. *International Business (Journal of University of International Business and Economics)*, 2017 (2).

Fang, Zhuofen. On the nature of SEZs. *Economic Research Journal*, 1981 (8).

Gao, Weiwu. A summary of the arguments of the "Theoretical Seminar on the 10th Anniversary of the Establishment of SEZs." *Economic Research Journal*, 1991 (1).

Gao, Zugui, Zonglei Wei, Yu Liu. The rise of emerging economies and their impact. *International Data Information*, 2009 (8).

Ge, Shunqi. Cross-border mergers and acquisitions and their impact on China's economic security. *International Economic Review*, 2007 (1112).

Gong, Yuwen, Xiaohong Hua. Research on China's countermeasures to deal with trade disputes under the new international economic situation. *Intertrade*, 2017 (11).

Guo, Kesha. The impact faced by China's auto industry after entering the WTO and its countermeasures. *China's Industrial Economics*, 2001 (10).

Guo, Xibao, Zhi Luo. Adverse effects on China's economic growth. *Economic Research Journal*, 2009 (5).

Hao, Hongmei. Explore the foreign investment management model of pre-establishment national treatment plus a negative list. *China Economic and Trade Herald*, 2014 (10).

He, Fan, He Zhu, Qian Zhang. Construction of the Maritime Silk Road in the 21st Century: Status Quo, Opportunities, Problems and Countermeasures. *International Economic Review*, 2017(5).

He, Fan, Weijiang Feng, Jin Xu. Challenges faced by the global governance mechanism and China's countermeasures. *World Economics and Politics*, 2013 (4).

He, Jie, Luodan Xu. An empirical study on the spillover effects of introducing FDI in China's industrial sector. *World Economic Papers*, 1999 (2).

He, Liping. Discussion on the development strategy of China's foreign investment. *Finance & Economics*, 1985 (5).

He, Xinhao. Correctly play the role of foreign trade and accelerate the development of China's economy. *Intertrade*, 1982 (5).

Hou, Xinbing. The development of foreign direct investment is an effective way to promote the introduction of foreign capital in China. *Foreign Economics & Management*, 1986 (4).

Hu, Angang, Wei Ma, Yilong Yan. "Silk Road Economic Belt": strategic connotation, positioning and realization path. *Journal of Xinjiang Normal University (Philosophy and Social Sciences)*, 2014 (2).

Hu, Jintao. Speech at the celebration of the 30th anniversary of the establishment of the Shenzhen Special Economic Zone. *People's Daily Online*, Sept. 6, 2010.

Hu, Shuli. Analysis and Reflection of the "Zhongce Phenomenon" on the Transformation of Capital Introduction. *Reform*, 1994 (3).

Huang, Fangyi. At present, the restrictive factors and improvement ideas of my country's import and foreign economic and trade. *Economic Research Journal*, 1985 (12).
Huang, Jingbo, Anmin Zhang. An empirical study on the main drivers of China's outbound foreign direct investment—based on the analysis of outbound investment flow from 1982 to 2007. *International Economics and Trade Research*, 2009 (7).
Huang, Liangxiong, Xinbei Qian, Guangjun Sui. Has Chinese OFDI improved the infrastructure of the countries along the "Belt and Road"? *Management Review*, 2018 (3).
Huang, Maoxing, et al. *TPP's China Policy*. Beijing: Peking University Press, 2016.
Huang, Sujian. Think of it from the so-called "Zhongce Phenomenon." *Reform*, 1994 (5).
Huang, Xianhai, Hangyu Chen. A study on the implementation effect of the "Belt and Road" —simulation analysis based on GTAP. *Social Science Front*, 2016 (5).
International Trade Research Office, Institute of World Economics and Politics, Chinese Academy of Social Sciences. *Interpretation of the Text of the Trans-Pacific Partnership Agreement.* Beijing: China Social Sciences Press, 2016.
Ji, Chongwei. The relationship between the utilization of foreign capital and China's economic development. *Social Science*, 1982 (2).
Ji, Chongwei. The theory and practice of China's opening-up policy. *Economic Research Journal*, 1984 (11).
Jia, Genliang. The fatal drawbacks of the international great circulation of the economic development strategy. *Studies on Marxism*, 2010 (12).
Jia, Nisha, Chen Shen. Research on the upgrading effect of China's outbound foreign direct investment in the manufacturing industry. *Journal of International Trade*, 2016 (8).
Jian, Xinhua, Hao Zhang. On the transformation of China's foreign trade growth mode. *China Industrial Economics*, 2007 (8).
Jiang, Guanhong, Dianchun Jiang. The "export effect" of Chinese enterprises' foreign direct investment. *Economic Research Journal*, 2014 (5).
Jiang, Guanhong, Dianchun Jiang. The Location selection of China's foreign investment: panel data test based on investment gravity model. *The Journal of World Economy*, 2012 (9).
Jiang, Jianping. The essential difference between the introduction of foreign capital in socialist China and the investment of imperialism in old China. *Economic Science*, 1986 (5).
Jiang, Xiaojuan. "Tenth Five-Year Plan" China's foreign investment trend research: global background, investment scale and key selection. *Management World*, 2001(1).

Jiang, Xiaojuan. Contribution of China's foreign-invested economy to growth, structural upgrading and competitiveness. *Social Sciences in China*, 2002 (6).
Jiang, Xiaojuan. The development trend and theoretical analysis of service globalization. *Economic Research Journal*, 2008 (2).
Jiang, Xiaojuan. The utilization of foreign capital and the transformation of economic growth mode. *Management World*, 1999 (2).
Jin, Bei, Pengfei Li, Jianhui Liao. The status quo and evolution trend of China's industrial international competitiveness—based on the analysis of export commodities. *China Industrial Economics*, 2013 (5).
Lang, Lihua, Xinyu Liu. The impact of China's foreign direct investment on export scale: based on a panel data model of 143 countries from 2003 to 2014. *Research on Economics and Management*, 2016 (9).
Li, Jian. Foreign-funded enterprises: a new source of growth for China's foreign trade exports. *Intertrade*, 1996 (10).
Li, Junjiang, Li Sun. Chinese resource enterprises "go global": an analysis based on the trade theory of heterogeneous enterprises. *Jianghan Tribune*, 2012 (1).
Li, Li. The development model of national industrial enterprises under the condition of foreign capital competition. *Economic Research Journal*, 1997 (12).
Li, Lingqiu. Investment cooperation in infrastructure construction between China and Myanmar under the background of the "Belt and Road." *Northeast Asia Economic Research*, 2017 (3).
Li, Mei, Shichang Liu. Regional differences and threshold effect of reverse technological spillover of foreign direct investment—through regression analysis based on China's interprovincial panel data. *Management World*, 2012 (1).
Li, Shantong. The impact of China's entry into WTO on China's economy: a dynamic general equilibrium analysis. *The Journal of World Economy*, 2000 (2).
Li, Shuguang. Look at the "Zhongce Phenomenon" with an open mind. *Reform*, 1994 (5).
Li, Xiangyang. Trans-Pacific Partnership Agreement: a major challenge in the process of China's rise. *International Economic Review*, 2012 (2).
Li, Xiaoyu. The development and deepening strategy of international production capacity cooperation in the "Belt and Road" initiative. *Review of Economic Research*, 2016 (67).
Li, Xiuzhen, Fangna Xu. Technological innovation and the transformation of China's foreign trade development mode. *Journal of East China Normal University (Philosophy and Social Sciences)*, 2015 (4).
Li, Yining. *Economic Talks*. Beijing: Peking University Press, 1998.
Liang, Guiquan. The concept of "international great circulation" that is not in line with national conditions—also on the sub-step promotion

strategy of opening up with multiple advantages. *Academic Research*, 1988(4).
Liu, Changli. Import substitution is China's long-term strategy to catch up with the world's industrial powers. *Economic Research Journal*, 1987 (8).
Liu, Dong. Construction of overseas industrial parks and Sino-Arab production capacity cooperation. *West Asia and Africa*, 2017 (6).
Liu, Junhai. Thoughts and suggestions on unifying the legislation of domestic and foreign-funded enterprises. *Jianghan Tribune*, 2014 (1).
Liu, Junsheng. RCEP negotiation process and challenges: an assessment from a regional perspective. *Journal of International Economic Cooperation*, 2017 (8).
Liu, Shalian. On China's foreign investment. *World Economy Studies*, 1984 (3).
Liu, Shuang, Youjun Ma, Jianping Zhong. Investigation and analysis on the status of infrastructure construction in Sino-Russian border areas. *Journal of Eurasian Economy*, 2017 (1).
Long, Guoqiang. The current opportunity is not the expansion of scale but the upgrading of export structure. *Practice in Foreign Economic Relations and Trade*, 2014 (7).
Lu, Feng, Kaidong Feng. Policy choices for developing China's auto industry with independent intellectual property rights. *Business Weekly*, 2004 03 20.
Lu, Feng, Xin Li, Shuangshuang Li, Zhixiao Jiang, Jieping Zhang, Yewei Yang. Why is it China? The economic logic of the "Belt and Road." *International Economic Review*, 2015 (3).
Luo, Yuze. Ideas and policies to promote the "Belt and Road" facility connectivity. *Journal of Chongqing University of Technology (Social Sciences)*, 2017 (7).
Ma, Xia, Caicen Song. China-Egypt Suez Economic and Trade Cooperation Zone—a new oasis on the "Belt and Road." *West Asia and Africa*, 2016 (2).
Mao, Yanqiong. Review and prospect of international trade friction with China in 10 Years of WTO Accession. *World Economic Study*, 2011 (11).
Min, Jianshu. My opinion on the theory of the international great circulation—Professor Min Jianshu, Dean of the School of Business Administration of the Chinese University of Hong Kong, talks about the Great International Circulation. *Business Management Journal*, 1988 (7).
Ministry of Commerce: China's investment in the "Belt and Road" has exceeded 60 billion US dollars. *Ministry of Commerce website*, March 12, 2018.
Ministry of Commerce. China Foreign Investment Report 2017. *Ministry of Commerce website*.
Ouyang, Yanyan, Li Liu, Yanyi Chen. Research on the industrial effect of China's outbound foreign direct investment. *Review of Industrial Economics*, 2016 (1).
Pan, Zhiping. The connection point of facility connectivity under the "Belt and Road" vision: taking the "China-Central Asia-West Asia" economic

corridor as an example. *Journal of Xinjiang Normal University (Philosophy and Social Sciences)*, 2016 (3).
Pei, Changhong and Ying Fan. Continue to enhance the function of foreign trade to promote China's economic development. *Intertrade*, 2014 (6).
Pei, Changhong, Lei Peng, Wen Zheng. Experience and theoretical analysis of changing the development mode of foreign trade: a summary of China's response to the impact of the international financial crisis. *Social Sciences in China*, 2011 (1).
Pei, Changhong. China's foreign trade development: challenges, opportunities and countermeasures. *Economic Research Journal*, 2005 (9).
Peng, Ke. We must raise awareness of the use of foreign capital. *Journal of International Trade*, 1982 (4).
Qi, Junyan. Whether China has exported more high-tech products—based on technical content and added value. *World Economy Studies*, 2008 (9).
Qian, Xiaoan. The impact and countermeasures of China's entry into WTO on China's banking industry and financial regulation. *Journal of Financial Research*, 2000 (2).
Qin, Hai. The "Zhongce Phenomenon" needs to be more fully analyzed. *Reform*, 1994 (4).
Qiu, Licheng, Debin Yang. The location choice of Chinese enterprises' OFDI: a comparative analysis of state-owned enterprises and private enterprises. *Journal of International Trade*, 2015 (6).
Qu, Fengjie. Breaking out of the horses group pattern and constructing a new flying geese group pattern—building a China-led regional industrial division system through international production capacity cooperation. *Intertrade*, 2017 (2).
Quan, Yi, Minghui Shen, Lina Qiu. How to build a Regional Comprehensive Economic Partnership (RCEP): a Chinese perspective. *Peace and Development*, 2017 (5).
Research group of Guangdong Institute of International Strategy. China's strategy for participating in global economic governance: the next 10–15 years. *Reform*, 2014 (5).
Sang, Baichuan, Wei Wang. Reform of global economic governance system and prevention of fragmentation risks. *Intertrade*, 2017 (12).
Sang, Baichuan. Coping strategies for a new round of global investment rule changes: From the perspective of Sino-US investment agreement negotiation. *Frontiers*, 2014 (1).
Sang, Xiuguo. Harnessing economic growth: a model based on new economic growth theory and validation on Chinese Data. *Journal of Management World*, 2002 (9).
Several opinions of the Central Committee of the Communist Party of China and the State Council on building a new system of open economy. *Xinhuanet*, Sept. 17, 2015.

Shen, Minghui, Zhongyuan Zhang. International production capacity cooperation under the background of the "Belt and Road"—taking China-Indonesia cooperation as an example. *International Economic Cooperation*, 2017 (3).

Shen, Xianjie, Jincheng Xiao. The new situation of international regional economic cooperation and China's "Belt and Road" cooperation strategy. *Macroeconomics*, 2014 (11).

Sheng, Bin, Ran Duan. New rules for TPP investment and Sino-US bilateral investment treaty negotiation. *International Economic Review*, 2016 (5).

Sheng, Bin, Yingying Ma. An Analysis of China's service trade export structure and international competitiveness: based on the perspective of trade added-value. *Journal of Southeast University (Philosophy and Social Sciences)*, 2018 (1).

Song, Hong, Yu Chai. An empirical study on the impact of foreign-funded enterprises on China's industrial structure and benefits. *Economic Research Journal*, 1998 (1).

Song, Hong. The impact of China's entry into WTO on China's industrial development and its countermeasures. *World Economics and Politics*, 2000 (3).

State Council Information Office. *White Paper on "China's Foreign Trade" (2011)*. State Council Information Office Website, Dec. 7, 2011.

Sui, Guangjun, Liangxiong Huang, Xing Huang. China's outbound foreign direct investment, infrastructure construction and economic growth of the countries along the "Belt and Road." *Journal of Guangdong University of Finance and Economics*, 2017 (1).

Sui, Yuehong, Zhenhua Zhao. The mechanism and evidence of the impact of China's OFDI on trade structure—and on the expansion of China's OFDI motivation. *Finance & Trade Economics*, 2012 (4).

Sun, Xuemeng. Research on Sino-Russian production capacity cooperation under the background of the "Belt and Road." *Foreign Economic Relations & Trade*, 2017 (6).

Tan, Yanzhi. Foreign direct investment of Chinese enterprises: characteristics, new theoretical exploration and enlightenment. *Teaching and Research*, 2009 (3).

Tang, Haiyan. On the choice of China's foreign trade development strategy. *Journal of International Trade*, 1994 (2).

The fourteenth year-end summary of business work in 2017: actively carry out trade remedy work, and effectively maintain trade order and industrial security. *Website of the Ministry of Commerce of the People's Republic of China*, Janu. 19, 2018.

The person in charge of the Department of Trade in Services of the Ministry of Commerce talked about the situation of China's trade in services in 2017. *Chinese Government Network*, Feb. 6, 2018.

The research group of China Development Bank's "Research on the Development Model of Cross-border Development Zone and Its Investment and Financing." From the perspective of investment and construction of overseas economic and trade cooperation zones the "Belt and Road" focuses on regional analysis. *Port Economy*, 2017 (1).
The Research Group of the School of Economics and Management, China Agricultural University. The impact of China's entry into WTO on China's agricultural product trade. *The Journal of World Economy*, 1999 (9).
Tong, Jiadong. Discussion on the reform of China's foreign trade system. *Nankai Journal*, 1998 (1).
Wan, Jun. The motivation, progress and challenges of China-Latin America production capacity cooperation. *Journal of Latin American Studies*, 2016 (3).
Wang, Chunfa, Jiang Jiang. FDI and the cultivation of endogenous technological capabilities: a case study in China. *High-technology & Industrialization*, 2005 (2).
Wang, Jian. Choosing the right long-term development strategy—concept of the "international great circulation" economic development strategy. *Economic Daily*, Jan. 5, 1988.
Wang, Jizu. Learn from foreign experience and do a good job in utilizing foreign capital. *Journal of International Trade*, 1982 (4).
Wang, Linsheng. On the status and role of socialist foreign trade. *Intertrade*, 1982 (2).
Wang, Shouwen. Change the development mode of foreign trade and promote the stable and balanced development of foreign trade. *Intertrade*, 2007 (7).
Wang, Xi. On the scale management of foreign direct investment in China. *Economic Research Journal*, 1998 (5).
Wang, Yang. Building a new system of open economy. *People's Daily*, Nov. 22, 2013.
Wang, Yiwei, Dong Zheng. Moral hazard and countermeasures of the "Belt and Road" initiative. *Northeast Asia Forum*, 2015 (4).
Wang, Yongzhong, Xichen Li. China's investment risk assessment in the countries along the "Belt and Road." *China Opening Journal*, 2015 (4).
Wang, Zhenzhong. Does capital really have no banners? *Reform*, 1994 (5).
Wang, Zhile. Also talk on foreign mergers and acquisitions and China's economic security. *Economic Herald*, 2006 (9).
Wang, Zhimin. China-Kazakhstan production capacity cooperation and its spillover effect under the background of the "Belt and Road." *Northeast Asia Forum*, 2017 (1).
Wei, Dong, Jingmin Wang. Analysis on the motivation of China's foreign direct investment. *Dongyue Tribune*, 2005 (5).
Wei, Yaqing. Theoretical analysis of the evolution of foreign trade strategy. *Economic Perspectives*, 2001 (7).

Wu, Ninggeng. Discussion on China's foreign investment. *Journal of Peking University (Philosophy and Social Sciences)*, 1986 (3).
Wu, Yabin, Yong Wang. The Chinese concept of establishing a cooperative international trade friction settlement mechanism. *Intertrade*, 2017 (3).
Xi, Jinping. Speech at the celebration of the 30th anniversary of Hainan's establishment of a special economic zone. *People's Daily Online*, April 14, 2018.
Xia, Liang. How was "exchanging technology with the market" proposed (1978–1988). *Researches in Chinese Economic History*, 2015 (4).
Xiang, Benwu. A study on the trade effect of China's foreign direct investment—co-integration analysis based on panel data. *Finance & Trade Economics*, 2009 (4).
Xiao, Zhuoji. Actively and steadily introduce technology and utilize foreign capital. *Dongyue Tribune*, 1982 (5).
Xie, Wenze. Analysis on the joint construction of the "Belt and Road" in China and Latin America. *Pacific Journal*, 2018 (2).
Xin, Chengyue. *Economic Globalization and China's Business Development*. Beijing: People's Publishing House, 2005.
Xu, Dixin. Actively and steadily run the SEZs. *Fujian Tribune*, 1981 (4).
Xue, Rongjiu. Fifty years of exploration: a review and reflection on China's foreign trade theories since the founding of the People's Republic of China. *Intertrade*, 1999 (10).
Xue, Yanru, Hailiang Zhang, Ping Zou. Ownership differences, arbitrage motives and the location decision of foreign direct investment: an analysis based on mineral resource-based state-owned enterprises. *Economic Review*, 2016 (2).
Yang, Liyan, Tingting Li. Research on the legal issues of China's foreign direct investment national security review. *International Law Review of Wuhan University*, 2017 (2).
Yang, Zhen. The dilemma, challenges and strategies of opening foreign capital supervision. *Theoretical Horizon*, 2016 (11).
Yao, Guimei. China-Africa production capacity cooperation: achievements, problems and prospects. *International Economic Cooperation*, 2017 (6).
Yao, Yang. The influence of non-state-owned economic components on ensuring the technical efficiency of industrial enterprises. *Economic Research Journal*, 1998 (12).
Ye, Hongyu, Dong Han, Shenghao Wang. A quantile regression study on the influencing factors of China's OFDI reverse technology spillovers—from the perspective of host country characteristics. *Review of Economy and Management*, 2017 (5).
Yin, Xiangshuo, Chunding Li, Lei Sun. The types, causes, effects and solutions of international trade frictions. *The Journal of World Economy*, 2007 (7).

Yu, Guangyuan. Talking about the understanding of several issues in Shenzhen Special Economic Zone. *Economic Research Journal*, 1983 (2).
Yuan, Wenqi, Jianmin Wang. Re-understanding and evaluating the role and status of foreign trade in the development of China's national economy. *Intertrade*, 1982(1).
Zhan, Xiaoning, Jianguo Chen. Export competitiveness and the role of multinational Corporations' FDI. *The Journal of World Economy*, 2002 (11); Jianguo Chen, Shunqi Ge. Export competitiveness and the role of foreign direct investment. *Nankai Economic Studies*, 2002 (1).
Zhang, Bin, Fei Zhang. RCEP's progress, obstacles and China's strategic choices. *Nankai Journal (Philosophy and Social Sciences)*, 2016 (6).
Zhang, Dexiu. Analysis of the positive and negative impact of WTO on some industries in China's economy. *Journal of Peking University (Philosophy and Social Sciences)*, 2000 (3).
Zhang, Fan, Jingping Zheng. The impact of multinational corporations on the structure and efficiency of the Chinese economy. *Economic Research Journal*, 1999 (1).
Zhang, Hanlin, Xinzhe Gai. The ins and outs, functional positioning and contingent strategies of free trade zones. *Reform*, 2013 (9).
Zhang, Ming. Facing the six major risks of the "Belt and Road." *International Economic Review*, 2015 (4).
Zhang, Peiji. Discussion on China's foreign trade development strategy. *Intertrade*, 1984 (1).
Zhang, Ping. Technological superiority and industrial control of multinational corporations: An analysis of the case of Beijing Jeep. *Economic Research Journal*, 1995 (11).
Zhang, Yansheng. Post-crisis era: the most important thing is to change the growth mode of China's foreign trade. *International Economic Review*, 2010 (1).
Zhang, Youwen. Pilot free trade zone and the construction of an open economic system. *Academic Monthly*, 2014 (1).
Zhang, Yu, Xiang Dai. Can export product upgrades and market diversification ease China's trade frictions? *World Economic Study*, 2013 (6).
Zhang, Yuyan. A Chinese perspective on global governance. *World Economics and Politics*, 2016 (9).
Zhao, Beiwen. The negative effects of the expansionary growth model of foreign capital. *World Economy Studies*, 2007 (1).
Zhao, Jingfeng, Ce Chen. China's trade in services: total volume and structure analysis. *The Journal of World Economy*, 2006 (8).
Zhao, Wei, Guangdong Gu, Yuanqing He. Outbound foreign direct investment and China's technological progress: mechanism analysis and tentative empirical evidence. *Management World*, 2006 (7).

Zhao, Yunpeng, Jiao Ye. A study on the impact of outbound foreign direct investment on China's industrial structure. *The Journal of Quantitative & Technical Economics*, 2018 (3).
Zhen, Bingxi. China's entry into WTO and its impact. *China International Studies*, 2000 (1).
Zheng, Liangyu. Review and Prospect of Shenzhen Special Economic Zone's 10-year Development. *Economic Research Journal*, 1991 (1).
Zheng, Tuobin. Emancipate the mind, raise awareness, and strive to speed up the development of foreign trade. *Intertrade*, 1982 (1).
Zheng, Tuobin. The reform of China's foreign trade system. *Economic Research Journal*, 1984 (11).
Zhou, Fangyin. Risks and challenges faced by the "Belt and Road" and its countermeasures. *International Survey*, 2015 (4).
Zhu, Tiezhen, Tianyong Zhou. Analysis and thinking on the dilemma of the two-way operation of the special economic zone and its way out. *Economic Research Journal*, 1989 (8).
Zhu, Zhongdi. Review and prospect of the reform of foreign trade system in new China. *Journal of Finance and Economics*, 1999 (10).
Zuo, Anlei. The characteristics, trends and countermeasures of China's international trade friction in the post-financial crisis era. *Journal of Shanghai institute of Foreign Trade—World Trade Organization Focus*, 2012 (9).

Theory of Economic Development[1]

Over the past four decades, China has undergone a monumental transformation, marked by two major shifts: first, a transition from a centrally controlled economy to one driven by market forces within a socialist framework; and second, a shift from an agrarian-based society to an industrialized one, ultimately evolving into a modern socialist nation. These dual changes have been remarkably successful. From an economic standpoint, China has achieved extraordinary growth that has garnered global attention. The country has charted its own distinct course for development, offering a model for other nations striving for modernization. This journey has also led to the formulation of a unique theoretical framework for socialist economic progress with Chinese insights, contributing solutions to global development challenges.

1. Building Development Consensus and Transforming Development Strategy

The Third Plenary Session of the 11th Central Committee marked the beginning of a new chapter in China's economic reform. This pivotal moment was a direct outcome of the evolving contradictions within the early phase of socialism in China and aligned with the fundamental principles of socialism itself. As the openness progressed, a broad societal accord emerged, recognizing "development as the foremost priority." Economic scholars began to delve into how best to foster growth and explore strategies for advancing the nation's economic progress.

1 The research in this chapter was assisted by Dr. Wu Peng, and I would like to express my thanks!

I. "Development is the absolute principle"

After the Third Plenary Session of the 8th CPC Central Committee in 1957, "taking class struggle as the key link" gradually took root as the guiding thought for all tasks of the whole nation. According to the definition of China's principal contradiction made by the Party, "the contradiction between the people's demand for the establishment of an advanced industrial country and the reality of a backward agricultural country" and "the contradiction between the people's needs for rapid economic and cultural development and the current situation that the economy and culture cannot meet the needs of the people" put forward by the Eighth CPC National Congress had been transformed into "the contradiction between the proletariat and the bourgeoisie and the contradiction between the socialist road and the capitalist road." At the same time, the "Gang of Four" also provoked criticism of the so-called theory in which "only productive forces matter." Due to delayed economic development, China's progress was held back by two decades. By the time the reform and opening-up period began in 1978, China's GDP per capita was just 7.9% of the global average. Between 1956 and 1978, the country's real per capita GDP grew at an average annual rate of only 3.4%, which put China far behind its neighboring nations like Japan, South Korea, Singapore, Malaysia, Thailand, and even Hong Kong and Taiwan. The policy that focused heavily on heavy industry development contributed to a slower improvement in living standards compared to the growth of real per capita GDP. For example, the proportion of people's consumption expenditures relative to GDP per capita decreased from 56.0% in 1957 to 39.2% in 1978. This shift was visible in both metropolitan and rural regions. In 1978, the general population faced significant housing shortages, with the average residential space per person being only 6.7 square meters in cities and 8.1 square meters in the countryside. Furthermore, 30.7% of the rural population (roughly 250 million) still struggled with basic necessities like food and clothing, and an overwhelming 97.5% of people in rural areas (around 770 million) lived in poverty (as shown in Table 1).

In response to the challenging national economic conditions and the hardships faced by the population, following the downfall of the "Gang of Four," the Party's leadership and economic scholars began to emphasize the importance of productive forces. They made it clear that the development of social productive forces needed to be accelerated, aiming to overcome poverty and stagnation, and redirect the Party and the country's priorities toward economic development. In August 1977, the report of the 11th Congress stressed that "productive forces are the most revolutionary factor"; from September 13 to 20, 1978, Deng Xiaoping delivered a speech (which is also referred to as "Northern Talks") when he inspected the three northeastern provinces as well as Tangshan and Tianjin. He emphatically called for a swift and determined shift in the Party's priorities toward economic

Table 1: National Economy and People's Living Standard in 1978

GDP per capita (yuan)	GDP per capita and the world average ratio (%)	1957–1978 Real GDP per capita average annual growth rate (%)	National residents' average living consumption expenditure (yuan)	National residents' average living consumption expenditure / GDP per capita (%)	National residents' average living consumption expenditure in 1957 / GDP per capita (%)
385	7.9	3.4	151	39.2	56

Urban residents per capita living consumption expenditure (yuan)	Urban residents per capita living consumption expenditure / GDP per capita (%)	Urban residents per capita living consumption expenditure in 1957 / GDP per capita (%)	Rural residents per capita living consumption expenditure (yuan)	Rural residents per capita living consumption expenditure / GDP per capita (%)	Rural residents per capita living consumption expenditure in 1957 / GDP per capita (%)
311.2	80.8	132.1	116.1	30.1	42.2

Residential buildings per capita in urban area (square meters)	Residential buildings per capita in rural area (square meters)	Number of rural population unresolved food and clothing (100 million people)	Proportion of the population unresolved food and clothing in the rural population (%)	Number of poor people in rural areas (100 million people)	Proportion of poor people in the rural population (%)
6.7	8.1	2.5	30.7	7.7	97.5

Sources: Based on the relevant data from the Sixty Years of New China Statistical Data Compilation, China Statistical Yearbook 2017, and the World Bank database.

development and provided a thorough explanation of the reform and opening-up agenda. In December 1978, during the Third Plenary Session of the 11th CPC Central Committee, the formal decision was made to redirect the Party's efforts and the nation's focus toward the goal of socialist modernization[2]. This marked

2 The Literature Research Office of the Central Committee of the Communist Party of China. Selection of Important Documents since the 3rd Plenary Session, I. Beijing: Central Literature Publishing House, 2011, pp. 3–4.

the beginning of China's economic reform. It can be said that, from the outset of these reforms, "prioritizing development and focusing on construction" became the core agreement within both the Party and society. In October 1987, the 13th Congress outlined the fundamental principles of socialism's primary stage, emphasizing "one central task, two basic points." It moved the focus of the Party and state's work from being a secondary concern to the core priority. Additionally, it provided a comprehensive analysis of the economic development strategy and the objectives for reforming the economic system during this stage of socialism. This document addressed critical questions related to the stage of development, growth trajectory, goals, phases, and strategies, marking the beginning of the formation of economic advancement doctrines with Chinese characteristics.

However, there are differences in people's thinking and understanding, and they cannot change their ideas at the same time. At a major historical turning point, it takes enormous effort to unify everyone's thoughts and actions on the issue of development. Throughout this procedure, Chairman Deng, as the chief architect of the economic reform, played a key historical role. His series of incisive analyses and judgments built the theoretical and ideological foundation for the development of a socialist economy with Chinese characteristics, and concentrated the energy of the whole Party and all of society on development-related matters.

To begin with, by reflecting on the successes and failures of socialist modernization, Chairman Deng addressed the core issue of "what socialism is and how to construct it." He deeply emphasized that the essence of socialism lies in "the liberation and advancement of productive forces." In April 1985, Deng Xiaoping highlighted this perspective during his meeting with foreign guests: "The fundamental principle of Marxism is that the productive forces must be developed ... Our experience in the 20 years from 1958 to 1978 teaches us that poverty is not socialism, that socialism means eliminating poverty. Unless you are developing the productive forces and raising people's living standards, you cannot say that you are building socialism."[3] In 1992, Chairman Deng noted in his "Southern Talks": "The essence of socialism is liberation and development of the productive forces, elimination of exploitation and polarization, and the ultimate achievement of prosperity for all."[4]

Secondly, to further stimulate open-mindedness, break free from outdated ideologies, and motivate both officials and the public to experiment with innovative approaches, methods, and policies that could effectively foster economic

---

3 Xiaoping Deng. *Selected Works of Deng Xiaoping: Volume 3*. Beijing: People's Publishing House, 1993, p. 116.

4 Ibid., p. 373.

growth, the "three favorable" criteria were introduced. These criteria (which assess whether actions contribute to the growth of productive forces in a socialist society, enhance the overall strength of the socialist state, and elevate people's quality of life) provided a framework for evaluating and guiding actions. Chairman Deng outlined these "three favorable" standards during his "Southern Talks" in 1992: "The reason some people hesitate to carry out the reform and the open policy and dare not break new ground is, in essence, that they're afraid it would mean introducing too many elements of capitalism and, indeed, taking the capitalist road. The crux of the matter is whether the road is capitalist or socialist. The chief criterion for making that judgement should be whether it promotes the growth of the productive forces in a socialist society, increases the overall strength of the socialist state and raises living standards."[5]

Chairman Deng's firm and significant statements emphasized that "the key to addressing all of China's challenges lies in its own development."[6] He declared that "Development is the fundamental principle,"[7] immediately drawing the full attention of both the Party and the nation to the overarching theme of development as the central focus for progress.

II. Heated discussion on "the law of priority growth of means of production" and the dialectical negation of traditional development strategies

After development had become the focus of all the work of the Party and the country, the next problem was to choose a development strategy that suited the national conditions. In the early stages of economic reform, the debate over "the principle of prioritizing the growth of production resources" was directly linked to the selection of the economic growth strategy.

In the initial phase of the economic restructuring, economic research within China's circles largely followed the approach established since the founding of the People's Republic, mainly focusing on Marx's theory of expanded reproduction. However, some scholars began to openly question the theory of "law of priority growth of means of production," which was rooted in Marx's theory of scaled-up reproduction, as outlined in the Soviet *Political Economics Textbook*, and was complemented by the strategy that prioritized the development of heavy industry, derived from this "principle," thus setting off a heated discussion on the "law of priority growth of means of production." This heated discussion was

---

5 Xiaoping Deng. *Selected Works of Deng Xiaoping: Volume 3*. Beijing: People's Publishing House, 1993, p. 372.

6 Ibid., p. 265.

7 Ibid., p. 377.

conducted against the backdrop that the line of thought of "emancipating the mind and seeking the truth from facts" gradually became entrenched and widely accepted by the population. The discussion directly pointed to whether "the law of priority growth of means of production" itself existed, and whether major adjustments should be made to the traditional socialist economic development strategy. An important consensus was formed on the issue, which contributed to the liberation of China's economic growth mindset.

First, scholars widely agreed that the goal of socialist development was to satisfy rising popular cravings for material and cultural advancement. However, under the strategy that prioritized heavy industry, people's living conditions had failed to see consistent and reasonable improvements over a prolonged period. Ouyang Sheng noted that, while the average wages of Chinese workers and the urban-rural consumption standards had risen within a limited scope over the past two decades, many workers' wages had remained at the same level as they were during the "first five years"; the supply of many consumables in the market was insufficient, and more and more invoice certificates were used to limit purchasing power; the shortage of workers' housing had become a serious problem, etc.[8] Liu Guoguang and Wang Xiangming pointed out that in the 30 years before 1980, China's production development did not seem to be slow, but the people's living standard only grew annually in the first eight years; In 1979, the average wage of workers was 705 yuan. After adjusted by the price index, the actual wage level was even lower than that in 1957.[9] Certain scholars argued that prioritizing the growth of the production sector for a period of time could establish the essential groundwork for the more rapid expansion of the consumer goods sector in the future. In the long run, this roundabout strategic arrangement did not violate but contributed to more effectively achieving the objectives of socialist production. In practice, however, the overemphasis on directing economic assets toward productive resources, particularly the heavy industry sector, did not yield the anticipated outcomes. Not only had the people's consumption demand been suppressed, but the national economy had not achieved the expected rapid development, and the final result was not "win-win"

---

8 Sheng Ouyang. On the balance of means of production and means of consumption. *Economic Research Journal*, 1979 (6).

9 Guoguang Liu & Xiangming Wang. A discussion on the relationship between the development speed and proportion of China's national economy. *Social Sciences in China*, 1980 (4). The serious disconnection between production and consumption is manifested as follows: on the one hand, due to the large consumption and waste in production, there are many intermediate products, and there are few final products available for consumption by residents; on the other hand, many products are produced due to poor quality and wrong varieties, and the situation of sluggishness and backlog is very serious.

but "lose-lose." Liu Guoguang and Wang Xiangming, analyzing statistical data since the establishment of the People's Republic of China, highlighted that the three decades of focusing predominantly on heavy industry development had led to several economic issues, including fluctuations, a slight decrease in the mean growth rate, and a significant gap between production and consumption. The disproportion eventually "resulted in a general decline in economic effectiveness, and more haste, less speed."[10] Theoretically speaking, even as a roundabout development tactic, the strategy of developing the means of production as a priority should not be implemented disproportionately. A large amount of literature has clarified from the level of logic and mathematical analysis that the prioritized expansion of productive assets must be constrained by the law of balanced development of the two major sectors. In general, the vast majority of participants in this discussion believed that in the face of the disconnection between means and goals, it was necessary to make major adjustments to the traditional strategy of prioritizing heavy industry development. In crafting future economic policies, it is essential to respect the objective principles of economic development, while ensuring that economic growth and the enhancement of people's living conditions progress together through a thoughtful allocation of resources across diverse spheres of the national economy.

Secondly, the discussion led to the consensus that technological advancement was the key to driving both national economic growth and improvements in quality of life. As we all know, the realization of expanded reproduction includes two types: extensional expanded reproduction and connotative expanded reproduction. During the discussion, whether those "proposing the extinction of laws," those "proposing the variation of laws" or those "proposing the ontologism of laws" clearly opposed the view that economic development could ultimately only be achieved through extensional expanded reproduction. Advocates of abolishing restrictive laws argued that technological advancements could drive growth in both output and spending realms. Therefore, rapid economic development did not have to be achieved by sacrificing the consumption sector. Moreover, with the overall improvement of social production efficiency, the trend of organic composition improvement would slow down, the growth rate of the two major sectors would gradually approach, and the development of the means of consumption sector would be even faster. Those advocating for changes in the laws argued that technological advancement was a necessary foundation for favoring the expansion of productive resources. They believed that as long as technological progress occurred, the principle of emphasizing productive assets would remain

10 Guoguang Liu & Xiangming Wang. A discussion on the relationship between the development speed and proportion of China's national economy. *Social Sciences in China*, 1980 (4).

unchanged. However, over time, as technology advanced, the growth rate of the consumption sector would catch up with that of the production sector. While proponents of the ontological view of these laws did not define specific conditions for the principle of prioritizing production, most agreed on the crucial role of technological progress in enabling sustained, qualitative growth and viewed it as an inevitable aspect of human societal development. This positive impact extended beyond the production sector, influencing the expansion of the consumption sector as well. In essence, during this intense debate, technological progress was given greater emphasis than the accumulation of resources in driving economic development. It was not only highly consistent with the idea of "science and technology are the primary productive forces," but also consistent with the policy orientation of modern economic development theory.

III. Introduction and application of foreign modern and contemporary economic development theories

Affected by the "decade of turmoil," China's economic development theory had been stagnant for a long time. This was not only manifested in the fact that the study of Marxist economic development theory was bound by a series of so-called orthodox, mechanical, and dogmatic viewpoints, but also prominently manifested that the main achievements of the foreign modern economic growth doctrines had not been learned and absorbed in a timely and discriminating manner. In the initial phase of the economic restructuring, amidst the wave of ideological liberation, Chinese economic scholars undertook extensive translation and introduction of foreign economic development theories. By critically engaging with and adapting these ideas, they applied them to analyze the economic progress of the nation. It must be pointed out that the introduction of foreign economic development theories during this period was carried out against the background of backward technical means of knowledge dissemination, single knowledge acquisition channels, and the forced interruption of knowledge accumulation for many years. It was vital for advancing the study of China's economic growth doctrine and for training personnel. Since 1981, Chinese translations of foreign works on modern economic development theory have been published successively, covering representative works of many famous economists such as Roy Forbes Harold, Evsey David Domar, Simon Smith Kuznets, Walter Whitman Rostow, William Arthur Lewis, Michal Kalecki, Robert M. Solow, Dale W. Jorgensen, etc. The translators included not only Tan Chongtai, Gao Hongye, Huang Fanzhang, Li Jingwen, and other well-known economists at the time, but also young and middle-aged economists and policy think tanks such as Li Yang, Jin Bei, Ping

Xinqiao, Chen Jiyong, Guo Xibao, Lu Zhongyuan, Chen Dongqi, Hu Heli, etc. Late 1980s to early 1990s, translations of foreign works on modern economic development theories showed an explosive increase, and the publication interval between Chinese and foreign editions was significantly shortened. The publication interval between domestic and foreign editions of works such as *Industrialization and Growth: A Comparative Study*, *Productivity and U.S. Economic Growth*, and *Alternative Strategies for Economic Development*, etc., was shortened to two or three years. Through the rendering and importation of important foreign books on development economics, China's accumulation of knowledge in economic development theory has been accelerating.

Building on foreign economic growth theories, scholars have attempted to apply these frameworks to analyze China's economic progress. In general, the localization of foreign economic development theories shows two trends: firstly, formalized theories such as the Harrod-Domar model, the Kalecki model, and the neoclassical model have been adopted to study specific practical problems. This is in line with the trend that modern economics uses more and more mathematical and statistical tools; secondly, since the 1990s, the theories and methods used in economic development research have gradually tended to modern mainstream economics. The Harrod-Domar model, the Cambridge growth model, the Kalecki model, etc., have gradually withdrawn from the field of application. The rise of these two trends has driven a shift in domestic research approaches to economic progress theories. The study and application of modern economic advancement frameworks have progressively followed a path of healthy growth, offering a wider international perspective to advance the development of economic theories with distinct Chinese features.

2. Explaining the Miracle of China's Economic Growth and its Theory

With the Party and the state shifting their focus to economic development and the progress of China's market-oriented reforms, the country's economy has generally followed a pattern of sustained, rapid growth over the past 40 years of reform, with only a few exceptions. China has transformed from an economically backward nation into an upper-tier income country, significantly boosting its national strength and global stature. This transformation has not only improved living standards but also resulted in the creation of the "China Miracle," which has garnered global attention. From the mid-1990s to the present, the Chinese economic circle has launched extensive and in-depth discussions around the "China Miracle."

I. "China Miracle"

In 1993, the World Bank published a 500-page research report, *The East Asian Miracle: Economic Growth and Public Policy*,[11] which elaborated the economic achievements and the reasons for success in five East Asian countries, including Japan, Singapore, South Korea, Indonesia, Malaysia, and Thailand, and two East Asian regions, including Hong Kong, China, and Taiwan, China. Subsequently, in 1994, Lin Yifu, Cai Fang, and Li Zhou released *The China Miracle: Development Strategy and Economic Reform*, and proposed the "China Miracle."[12] Figure 1 illustrates China's remarkable economic advance through the per capita GDP ratio. As shown in the figure, China's per capita GDP has experienced a sharp and substantial rise compared to the global average, high-income nations, upper-tier income countries, the East Asia and Pacific region, and transitional economies such as Russia and Nations of Central and Eastern Europe. This growth became particularly evident after the socialist market economy reform was established in 1992. At the start of the reform era, China's per capita GDP was just 7.85% of the global average, positioning it among the poorest nations at the time. By 2016, it had surged to 79.70%, a tenfold increase, surpassing the average of upper-tier income countries. At the beginning of the upheaval in Eastern Europe, China's per capita GDP was only 9.12% of Russia's and 13.73% of Central and Eastern Europe's; in 2016, it reached 92.85% and 63.76%, respectively. This indicates that, in terms of growth outcomes, China's market reforms have yielded far superior results compared to former socialist nations like Russia and countries in Eastern Europe.

The "East Asian Miracle" and the "China Miracle" have a large degree of similarities, but also have significant and even fundamental differences. In one aspect, both exhibit similar characteristics in terms of rapid economic expansion, such as high accumulation rate, rapid human capital formation, effective government, and full utilization of international markets; In another, unlike the "Asian Tigers" and other economies that simply transitioned to industrialization, the "China miracle" emerged during the shift of the economic structure. As it moved toward becoming an industrialized nation, it also shifted from a centrally controlled economic system to one driven by market forces. That is to say, the "China miracle" occurred in the "double transformation." Therefore, the factors related to the "China Miracle" not only have something in common with the

---

11 World Bank. *The East Asian Miracle: Economic Growth and Public Policy.* Beijing: China Financial and Economic Publishing House, 1995.

12 Yifu Lin, Fang Cai, Zhou Li. *The China Miracle: Development Strategy and Economic Reform.* Shanghai: Shanghai SDX Joint Publishing Company, Shanghai People's Publishing House, 1994.

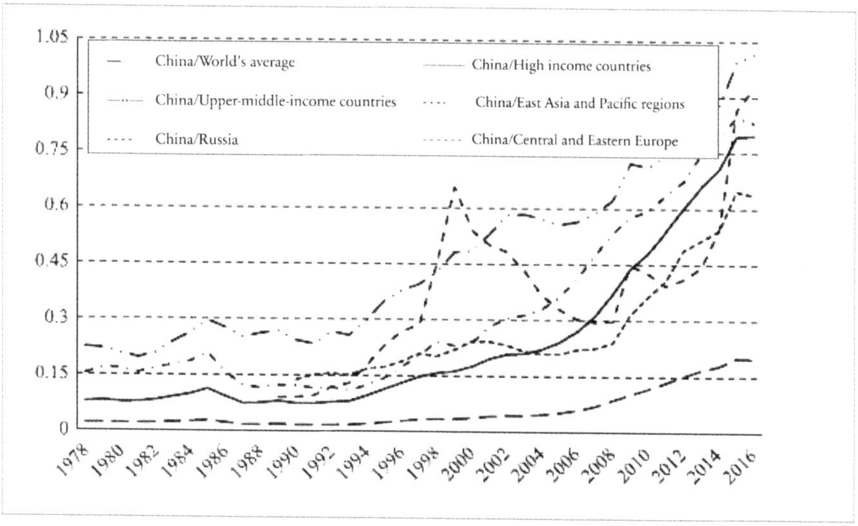

Figure 1: The catch-up growth of China's economy since the reform and opening up

Source: World Bank database.

"East Asian Miracle," but also involve factors such as institutional reform and economic transformation.

The "China miracle" has been questioned, and the question is also twofold, which corresponds to the "double transformation." First, after the "East Asian Miracle" was proposed, Paul R. Krugman argued in the prominent journal *Foreign Affairs* in 1994 that the economic progress in East Asia could be solely attributed to expanded factor inputs, with no significant role played by technological advancement. Therefore, there was no so-called "East Asian Miracle," and the growth of East Asian economies was unsustainable.[13] This view is supported by empirical literature such as Young (1995)[14]. At the same time, faced with the stark contrast between the chaos brought about by radical reform and the results achieved by phased reform of the nation, some economists attributed the success of China's incremental reform to some special objective conditions. It was argued that China's level of economic advancement at the start of its transition was much lower compared to Eastern European nations. Based on the convergence hypothesis of neoclassical growth theory, China faced fewer limitations from tapering

13 P. Krugman. Myth of Asia's Miracle. *Foreign Affairs*, 1994, Vol. 73, No. 6, pp. 62–78.

14 A. Young. The Tyranny of Numbers: Confronting the Statistical Realities of the East Asian Growth Experience. *Quarterly Journal of Economics*, 1995, Vol. 110, No. 3, pp. 641–680.

returns and had a greater potential to benefit from technological spillovers from leading economies. Therefore, it was natural that China's economy was growing faster than most Eastern European countries that had adopted a radical approach to reform. Second, unlike Eastern European countries, the initial conditions for China's reforms included typical urban-rural divisions. After the system reform, the repositioning of labor between urban and rural sectors would significantly improve social productivity, thereby promoting economic growth. This kind of growth was the economic growth under the dual economic structure that development economics had expounded long ago. With the emergence of the J-Curve effect after shock therapy and the hidden dangers left by the incomplete reform of the incremental reform, the long-term performance of the Chinese economy was bound to lag behind that of the Eastern European countries that adopted the radical reform. "Double questioning" had provided theoretical support for the "Badmouth China" for a long time.

Chinese economists disagree with the arguments put forward by those who badmouth China. First of all, according to the modern economic growth theory, a nation's economy cannot sustain high growth over an extended period without adequate support from advancements in overall productivity. Conversely, if the economy achieves long-term rapid growth, it must be supported by corresponding total factor productivity improvements. Robert Merton Solow regarded the applicable period of the neoclassical economic growth model as 30–50 years. China's economy has sustained rapid expansion for four decades, which is in line with Solow's definition of "long-term." As a result, the previous conclusion holds theoretical validity. Additionally, after World War II, rather than narrowing, the gap between wealthy and impoverished nations became a persistent feature of the global economy and the growth trajectories of many countries. Research by several Western scholars indicated that the disparity in quality of life between the poorest and wealthiest nations increased fivefold from 1870 to 1990[15]. Furthermore, from 1950 to 1998, the difference in per capita income between the richest and the poorest nations grew by 1.75 times[16]. Even if there was evidence of convergence, it mainly existed in developed countries or between the regions within them, which meant that convergence in practice was conditional, showing the characteristics of a "rich country club." Solow once pointed out that there might be economic convergence among US states and among OECD countries,

---

15 L. Pritchett. Divergence, Big Time. *Journal of Economic Perspectives*, 1997, Vol. 11, No. 3, pp. 3–17.

16 A. Maddison. The World Economy: A Millennial Perspective. Development Research Center, OECD, Paris, 2001.

but there was no trend of convergence on a larger scale.[17] Therefore, the "China miracle" cannot be effectively explained by a low base alone. Finally, a dual economic structure typifies the majority of developing nations, not unique to China, but only a few developing countries, such as China, have jumped out of the "poverty trap" and achieved economic catch-up development. It shows at least two problems: First, the dual economic structure is not a sufficient condition for developing countries to achieve catch-up development, and even in many cases it may only be a result of economic underdevelopment rather than a driver of economic growth; Second, the dual economic structure can only explain the level of economic growth that developing countries can generally achieve, but cannot explain the high-speed growth. In other words, the transformation of the dual economic structure can only partially explain the "China miracle."

Therefore, it is very meaningful and challenging to explore and explain the causes of the "China Miracle," whether from both a practical and theoretical perspective, we can better understand the underlying principles and progression of the nation's economic development.

II. General drivers of the "China Miracle"

The analysis of the "China Miracle" can be framed within the context of contemporary economic theory, beginning with fundamental elements such as investment, workforce, and technological advancement. This approach offers a useful reference for understanding China's economic progress.

(1) Elevated accumulation and savings rates

From the standpoint of growth analysis, China's economic expansion primarily results from the buildup of capital inputs. Researchers at the CASS Institute of Economics noted that the swift rise in investment has been closely linked with China's rapid economic advancement. The average level of China's fixed asset investment rate rose from 28.6% in 1978–1991 to 37.5% in 1993 when the economy was overheated. After several years of adjustment, in 1997, it dropped to 33.8%, and then rose sharply again to 43.6% in 2004.[18] During the period of rapid expansion, China's capital input rate exceeded that of the United States, OECD nations, and also outpaced countries like Japan, South Korea, Malaysia,

---

17 R. M. Solow. Neoclassical Growth Theory. In J. B. Taylor and M. Woodford (eds.), *Handbook of Macroeconomics, Vol. 1 a*. Amsterdam: Elsevier Science Publishers, 1999, pp. 637–667.

18 Frontier Research Group of China's Economic Growth, Institute of Economics, Chinese Academy of Social Sciences. High investment, macro costs and sustainability of economic growth. *Economic Research Journal*, 2005 (10).

Singapore, Thailand, and other Southeast Asian economies. As far as empirical literature containing specific measurement results was concerned, Dong Minjie and Liang Yongmei used a nonparametric analysis framework to calculate provincial samples and found that from 1978 to 2010, the contribution share of capital investment in China's economic growth was as high as 85.4%. Before the 1990s, it was generally in a downward trend and fluctuated greatly. After 1992, it basically showed an upward trend, and after 2005, it was close to 90%.[19] Using provincial panel datasets from China between 1978 and 2010, Wu Peng applied the Stochastic Frontier Analysis (SFA) and Data Envelopment Analysis (DEA) methods. He discovered that capital investment accounted for a mean of 92% of China's economic expansion, making it the primary driver of the country's continuous and steady growth. The investment-driven nature of China's growth was clearly evident, marked by a protracted, fluctuating upward trend. In the twenty-first century, this upward movement became especially prominent, with the contribution value increasing by nearly 1% yearly on average. At the same time, thanks to the rapid progress of reification, high accumulation did not lead to the rapid decline in China's return on capital and the consequent decline in economic growth.[20] Zhao Zhiyun et al.(2007) pointed out that China's economic growth was defined by a dynamic combination of physical capital growth and technological advancement. From 1990 to 2005, the reification progress rate reflected in equipment capital was between 5.1% and 6.0%.[21]

China's economic growth stands apart from certain export-driven economies that heavily rely on foreign capital and transition countries that have embraced privatization and open foreign investment. Its distinctive feature is the high level of accumulation, primarily fueled by a robust savings rate. This savings rate is shaped by three major factors. First, during the transformation from a dual economic structure, a significant migration of surplus rural labor into urban areas has been a key driver, demanding complementary capital investments. This migration has also helped mitigate the diminishing returns on capital, with labor costs remaining highly flexible due to the dual economic framework, thereby sustaining capital's return rate and encouraging investment. Consequently, the process of labor migration has had a direct link to the persistence of high savings and investment rates. Second, from the government's standpoint, China's

[19] Minjie Dong, Yongmei Liang. Sources of China's economic growth from 1978 to 2010: A nonparametric decomposition framework. *Economic Research Journal*, 2013 (5).

[20] Wu Peng. The power conversion of China's economic growth since the reform. *China Industrial Economics*, 2013 (2).

[21] Zhiyun Zhao, Bingyang Lu, Qingwang Guo, Junxue Jia. Dynamic fusion of capital accumulation and technological progress: a typical fact of China's economic growth. *Economic Research Journal*, 2007 (11).

authorities have frequently backed production-oriented industries with a range of supportive, and at times distorting, policies, alongside the national banking system's guarantees. These efforts come with high macroeconomic costs, aiming to channel savings and resources into industrial growth. Additionally, the fiscal decentralization and local governments' incentive structures foster strong investment impulses and a deep desire for economic expansion. Finally, Chinese cultural values contribute to this pattern. The tradition of thriftiness, deeply ingrained in Chinese culture, further reinforces the propensity to save. Thirdly, Chinese culture plays a role. Chinese culture advocates frugality.

(2) Dual-structure evolution and population dividend

The dual economic framework is a defining characteristic of China's economy, and the nation's swift economic growth can be viewed as a transition from this dual system to a more integrated economic framework. Although the "Lewis–Ranis–Fei" dual economic development model cannot fully explain the "China Miracle," it cannot be disputed that it still pinpoints a major impetus for China's economic expansion. Regarding this point, Chinese academic communities have formed an extensive agreement, and on the basis of the original model, improvements and innovations have been made to explain China's problems. By incorporating insights from in-built growth theory, Chen Zongsheng and Li Defu modified the assumption of external agricultural technological advancements in the original model. They introduced a dual economic advancement framework based on internal agricultural innovation to examine the "East Asian Miracle" and China's economic progress, with a focus on the shift in its dual economic structure. They believed that the "East Asian Miracle" was the result of the continuous transfer of traditional agricultural labor to the modern non-agricultural sector: on the one hand, the modern sector channeled capital back into the traditional sector, driving progress in agricultural technologies and labor mobility; on the other hand, its expansion absorbed surplus labor, speeding up structural shifts. While total factor productivity growth in non-agricultural industries remained modest, changes in the labor force structure still sustained rapid economic expansion.[22] Additionally, through empirical analysis, Li Defu and Chen Zongsheng found that the transformation of the dual structure accounted for 26.32% of China's improved economic efficiency between 1978 and 2004. This contribution peaked at 48.46% during 1978–1990 before dropping to 13.39% in 1990–2004. When

[22] Zongsheng Chen, Defu Li. High savings, high investment and China's economic growth in the process of labor transfer. *Economic Research Journal*, 2005 (2).

recalculated, the dual structure transformation's overall contribution to China's economic growth from 1978 to 2004 stood at 17.83%.[23]

Some economists have examined the economic growth driven by surplus labor during the transformation of the dual economic structure, particularly through the lens of the demographic dividend. A notable study by Cai Fang and his team provides valuable insights. Their empirical research revealed that the demographic dividend accounted for 26.8% of China's per capita GDP growth from 1982 to 2000. Moreover, their analysis showed that every one percentage point decline in the ratio of dependents to the working-age population corresponded to a 0.115 percentage point uptick in the growth rate of per capita GDP.[24]

(3) Assimilation of technologies and self-reliant innovation

China's economic catch-up can also be viewed as a process of closing the gap with the global technological frontier, essentially representing a phase of technological advancement. Growth accounting results indicate that most of China's economic expansion has been driven by capital investment. However, while the movement of surplus agricultural workforce to urban areas and high capital stock buildup occur concurrently, they tend to slow down the increase of per capita capital, thereby mitigating the diminishing returns on capital input. Additionally, alongside technological progress, a significant portion of capital stock buildup manifests as a dynamic transfer, which ultimately stems from advancements in technology. Particularly, as the transfer of surplus labor slows and the population bonus fades, China's economic catch-up has become increasingly dependent on technological innovation to drive further growth.

Technological advancement can be analyzed from two perspectives based on its different formation mechanisms: the adoption of external technology and homegrown innovation. The adoption of external technology primarily occurs through channels such as international trade, foreign direct investment (FDI), and other means, where countries absorb global technological spillovers and replicate or adapt foreign innovations. Independent innovation is mainly realized through the R&D investment of domestic enterprises. Whether technology absorption or independent innovation plays an important role in promoting China's technological progress (or total factor efficiency enhancement) and economic expansion.

---

23 Defu Li, Zongsheng Chen. Has there been rapid efficiency improvement in the Chinese economy since the reform? *Economics (Quarterly)*, 2006 (1).

24 Fang Cai and Dewen Wang. China's demographic transition: implications for growth. In Garnaut and Song (eds.), *The China Boom and Its Discontents*. Canberra: Asia Pacific Press, 2005.

Moreover, in contrast to the adoption of external technologies, homegrown innovation has played a more crucial role in driving China's economic advancement and technological breakthroughs. Research by Jiang Ren'ai and Feng Genfu highlighted that investment in domestic R&D was the primary catalyst for China's technological development, contributing more significantly to improvements in overall productivity than both international trade and non-physical technology transfers.[25] Research by Chen Jiyong and Sheng Yangyi, based on provincial panel data, indicated that regional investment in technology was the key driver of local advancements in innovation. Without the enhancement of local scientific and technological capabilities, it would be challenging to fully leverage the impact of foreign R&D capital channeled through FDI on boosting regional innovation.[26] Both theoretical and empirical studies suggest that for China's future technological advancements and economic growth, a greater emphasis will need to be placed on strengthening its domestic innovation capacity.

(4) Steady promotion of market-oriented reforms

Market-oriented reforms have unleashed social productivity, forming the bedrock of the "China miracle" and a lasting source of its sustained growth. The transition to a market-based economy encourages competition, expands market scale, improves factor markets and resource allocation, builds robust incentive mechanisms, promotes innovation, and reinforces the non-public sector, all of which drive China's economic progress. Most studies recognize the pivotal role of marketization in fueling economic expansion. Research by Wang Wenju and Fan Hejun, using provincial panel data from 2001 to 2005, showed that China's market reforms significantly spurred economic growth, with its contribution standing at 14.22%.[27] Fan Gang and his colleagues analyzed the impact of market-oriented reforms on overall productivity and economic expansion. Their findings revealed that between 1997 and 2007, market reforms contributed an average of 1.45% to economic growth per year, while their impact on overall productivity was as high as 39.2%.[28]

---

25 Ren'ai Jiang, Genfu Feng. Has there been rapid efficiency improvement in the Chinese economy since the reform? *Economics (Quarterly)*, 2006 (1).

26 Jiyong Chen, Yangyi Sheng. Knowledge spillovers of foreign direct investment and China's regional economic growth. *Economic Research Journal*, 2008 (12).

27 Wenju Wang, Hejun Fan. An empirical analysis of the contribution of China's market reform to economic growth. *China Industrial Economics*, 2007 (9).

28 Gang Fan, Xiaolu Wang, Guangrong Ma. The contribution of China's marketization process to economic growth. *Economic Research Journal*, 2011 (9).

It is important to note that highlighting the beneficial effects of marketization does not negate the importance of the government. While recognizing the market's central role, it is equally essential to leverage the government's proactive guiding influence, ensuring a harmonious integration of a dynamic market and effective governance. This has been a fundamental lesson from China's economic development over the past four decades. It is, to a large extent, in common with the successful experience of East Asia drawn from the World Bank report, *The East Asian Miracle: Economic Growth and Public Policy*. It is also crucial to recognize that the active role of the Chinese government extends beyond the central level. As a large nation, China inevitably faces challenges related to regional governance. Therefore, the market system must be effectively integrated with the actions of local authorities to ensure balanced and coordinated development across different areas. Zhou Ye'an and Zhang Quan found through empirical analysis that both local fiscal decentralization and marketization were important forces driving China's economic development, and the impact of the marketization process on economic growth depended on the level of fiscal decentralization.[29] Looking ahead, further research is needed on how market-driven reforms can be aligned with the restructuring of local government roles and responsibilities, in order to foster steady and enduring economic growth.

III. The Singular Determinants of the "China Miracle"

It is uncommon in the course of worldwide economic growth for an economy as large as China to experience rapid expansion over a span of 40 years, suggesting that there are distinctive elements driving this success. In contrast to the general drivers of growth, these unique factors are largely non-replicable, or their applicability is very limited. More importantly, it is unlikely that any country could replicate all of these distinctive elements simultaneously.

(1) Chinese culture

After World War II, economics has quickly moved toward the path of mathematics and instrumentalism, and culture as a factor that is difficult to be formally analyzed and captured by variables has long been ignored by mainstream economic theories. Beginning in the 1980s, the role of culture in economic progress has gained increasing recognition among scholars, and efforts have been made to integrate it into the core analysis of prevailing economic growth theories. Philip Aghion and Peter W. Howitt's *The Economics of Growth* put culture in the last

29 Ye'an Zhou, Quan Zhang. Marketization, fiscal decentralization and China's economic growth. *Journal of Renmin University of China*, 2008 (1).

chapter, "Looking Ahead: Culture and Development," which regarded culture as an important direction for future economic development research. They argued that culture, representing a third layer of growth, could be the most essential factor at its core.[30] Much of this resurgence of Weberian ideas stems from the economic successes of East Asia and China. While Christian ethics were once used to explain the rapid rise of the modern capitalist economy in Western Europe, Confucian culture now offers an explanation for why late-developing nations and areas are largely centered in East Asia. Furthermore, as the "East Asian Miracle" becomes more concentrated within the Confucian cultural sphere,[31] the role of culture in shaping economic growth has become a focal point in global scholarly debates. Research in this area was introduced to China in the 1990s and has been developed and used by Chinese scholars. Justin Yifu Lin questions this cultural attribution theory,[32] but most scholars still agree with it. For instance, a number of academics argue that the primary factor behind China's achievements lies in the diligence, intelligence, and perseverance of its people. "As long as they can see hope for tomorrow, they can endure huge hardships today." No country could muster such optimism amid such harsh circumstances.[33] China's achievements stem, first and foremost, from the diligence and ingenuity of its people, followed by the emphasis on thrift in Chinese culture, along with a strong focus on tech innovation, cultural progress, and educational cause.[34]

In 2016, Zhu Tian published *The Chinese Growth Puzzle*, where he thoroughly explored the critical role of Chinese culture in driving the country's economic progress. Through a detailed analysis, he argued that typical explanations for the

---

30 Philip Aghion and Peter W. Howitt regard the process of economic growth and the design of growth policies to be composed of several levels. In addition to the third level of culture, the first level is the direct incentive for innovation and capital, and the second level is institutional and structural reforms. Philip Aghion and Peter W. Howitt. *The Economics of Growth*. Beijing: China Renmin University Press, 2011, pp. 344 345.

31 After the publication of the World Bank's East Asian Miracle: Economic Growth and Public Policy, Thailand, Indonesia, Malaysia and other Southeast Asian countries with Buddhist and Islamic civilizations gradually faded from the halo of growth miracle, and the crown of the fastest economic growth in East Asia has been won by Vietnam within the Confucian cultural circle. At the same time, the "Asian Four Little Dragons" located in the Confucian cultural circle were successfully promoted to high-income economies, and China, as the center of Confucian civilization, continued to show a growth myth.

32 Justin Yifu Lin. Economic Development and Chinese Culture. *Strategy and Management*, 2003 (1).

33 Wuchang Zhang. *China's Economic System*. Beijing: CITIC Press, 2009.

34 Shujie Yao. China's economic development and theoretical innovation under the "new normal." *Economic Research Journal*, 2015 (12).

"China miracle," such as a low starting point, the demographic dividend, and the economic restructuring, fail to offer adequate answers. He posited that the true explanation lies in cultural factors. Regarding why Chinese culture only became influential in the past 30 years, Zhu Tian explained that culture alone was a necessary but insufficient condition for the "China miracle." It needed to be coupled with institutional factors, such as the reforms, to create the right conditions for the phenomenon to occur. From the perspective of the market system, China does not hold a particular edge over other nations; rather, its cultural heritage provides a unique advantage.[35] The history of global economic development suggests that cultural strengths, rather than institutional ones, are the key drivers of a nation's exceptional economic success. So, what makes Chinese culture advantageous? In essence, there are two key aspects: one is a strong emphasis on hard work and frugality, and the other is a deep value placed on education and learning. The former influences the buildup of tangible capital, while the latter impacts the growth of human capital and the pace of technological advancement.

(2) Merits of large states

As one of the important endowment conditions of a country, country size has many influences on its economic development. Simon Kuznets's *Economic Growth of Nations: Total Output and Production Structure*, Hollis Chenery and Moises Syrquin's *Patterns of Development, 1950–1970*, and *Industrialization and Growth: A Comparative Study* by Hollis Chenery et al.(1989) have made special discussions on this. Hollis Chenery et al. (1989) observed that large countries had obvious advantages in industrial take-off—the per capita income of large nations at the brink of the quasi-industrial stage was roughly around US$250, compared to around US$400 for standard-sized countries and around US$600 for a small primary product exporter. China has the largest population in the world and the third largest territorial area in the world. This set of natural endowments can only be matched by a handful of nations like the United States, Russia, Brazil, and India. Consequently, the diverse strengths stemming from it are equally distinctive.

In China, during the early 1990s, some scholars began to focus on the economic growth of large nations, providing a comprehensive analysis of the unique advantages such countries possess. These advantages are primarily reflected in several areas: they can better safeguard national security while keeping defense costs relatively low; they can build international prestige and influence more easily; their vast domestic markets allow for effective regional cooperation, where

[35] Tian Zhu. *The Mystery of China's Growth*. Beijing: CITIC Press, 2016.

different regions can collaborate, exchange ideas, learn from each other, and reduce reliance on external sources. Additionally, large countries can concentrate resources, both financial and technical, to invest in large-scale modernization projects that are urgently needed. Once these projects and sectors begin to develop, they generate a network effect, where each component influences and drives the others, creating a momentum for continuous development.[36] Li Daokui, Hai Wen, and others emphasized that China's economic progress must strategically leverage the benefits of being a large nation. These inherent advantages, they argued, are crucial to sustaining and accelerating China's economic growth in the long run.[37] Ouyang Yao conducted a systematic analysis of the connection between the comprehensive strengths of large nations and China's economic development.[38] He argued that, in contrast to "comparative advantage" and "late-mover advantage," the concept of "large country advantage" offers a more comprehensive explanation for China's economic growth. The foundation of the "comprehensive advantages of a large country" lies in the "multi-structure" characteristic of a large developing nation, encompassing diverse regions, economies, and technologies. This diversity allows a large developing country like China to create a well-rounded and coordinated industrial framework. Additionally, it enables the maximization of traditional and labor-intensive industries while fostering the development of high-tech sectors with competitive strengths through the integration of domestic resources. Backed by the all-round strengths of a large nation, China is able to pursue a "multiple development strategy of utilizing comparative advantages and cultivating competitive advantages," which is quite different from the industrialization path represented by the "Asian Tigers" that rely on the strategy of comparative advantages.[39]

Justin Yifu Lin, Cai Fang, and Li Zhou also highlighted that the size of China provides significant advantages, which serve as a crucial factor in ensuring its continuous and rapid economic expansion. They specifically pointed out the regional comparative advantages within China, emphasizing how its large

---

36 Zhongmin Wu. Comprehensive advantages of great powers and great power syndrome. *Science and Technology Review*, 1992 (8).

37 Daokui Li. The advantages of great powers give birth to the creation of China. *21st Century Business Review*, 2005 (7); Wen Hai. China's economy has the advantage of being a big country and can grow strongly for another 20 years. *Beijing Morning News*, June 1, 2007.

38 Yao Ouyang. *Comprehensive Advantages of Large Countries*. Shanghai: Truth & Wisdom Press, Shanghai SDX Joint Publishing Company, Shanghai People's Publishing House, 2011.

39 Yao Ouyang. Comprehensive advantages of large countries: a new interpretation of China's economic competitiveness—also discuss with Professor Justin Yifu Lin. *Economic Theory and Business Management*, 2009 (11).

population contributes to technological diversity and progress.[40] In recent years, India, whose rate of capital accumulation and the level of human capital are not as good as those of China, has obvious technological diversification characteristics and has gradually shown a development trend of catching up and surpassing, offering support for the theory of large nations' all-round strengths to a certain extent.

(3) Competitive dynamics in growth among local administrations

The rivalry among local governments has been a key driver of China's economic growth. Fan Gang and Zhang Shuguang were among the early scholars to examine this competition, referring to it as "brotherly competition."[41] G. Montinola and Qian Yingyi sought to account for China's economic growth miracle through an analysis of its government system, proposing the "Chinese-style federalism" hypothesis. They argued that the administrative and fiscal decentralization implemented early in the reform era granted local governments strong economic motivations. This, in turn, spurred local authorities to actively leverage their relatively independent economic decision-making powers to sustain market operations and boost regional economic expansion, all with the aim of securing greater fiscal gains.[42] Zhou Li' an argued that economic incentives were not the "fundamental and enduring source" driving the competition among local governments.[43] He noted that since the mid-1990s, administrative powers shifted from "block management" to "strip management." Following changes in the tax distribution system, local fiscal and tax revenues sharply declined, and fiscal lump sum contracts were frequently adjusted by the central government, leading to a scenario of "rewarding the fast and hardworking, penalizing unfairly." Despite this, local governments' drive to promote economic growth remained strong. This suggests that, in addition to economic incentives, there are deeper motivations, particularly promotion incentives tied to GDP performance. Although promotion incentives may not fully support the functioning of the market under the "federalism with Chinese characteristics" framework, they can serve as a partial

---

40 Justin Yifu Lin, Fang Cai, Zhou Li. *China's Miracle: Development Strategy and Economic Reform (Updated Edition)*. Shanghai: Shanghai SDX Joint Publishing Company, Shanghai People's Publishing House, 1999, p. 18.

41 Gang Fan, Shuguang Zhang. *Outline of Public Ownership Macroeconomic Theory*. Shanghai: Shanghai SDX Joint Publishing Company, 1990, pp. 32–44.

42 G. Montinola, Yingyi Qian and B. Weingast. Federalism, Chinese style: the political basis for economic success in China. *World Politics*, 1995, Vol. 48, No. 1, pp. 50–81.

43 Li'an Zhou. Research on the promotion tournament mode of local officials in China. *Economic Research Journal*, 2007 (7).

substitute for formal property rights protection and the judicial system, enabling local governments to act as "helpers" rather than "grabbers." Some scholars have proposed the theory of regional competition, arguing that such competition fuels local economic development. The ability for regional competition largely stems from China's public land ownership system, where the distribution rights are concentrated at the regional level. This enables local governments to effectively utilize land resources in their competition.

To put it briefly, China's pattern of regional rivalry is highly distinctive and stands as a singular element behind the "China miracle." That said, the current institutional framework has brought about certain adverse impacts on regional competition. Examples include an "insatiable appetite for investment," the use of GDP as the exclusive yardstick for assessing performance and determining promotions, and the consequent disregard by local governments for ecological preservation and enhancements to people's well-being. As a result, figuring out how to refine regional competition—amplifying its beneficial aspects while curbing its harmful ones—will become a key area of focus in future research on economic development theories and policy formulation.

3. The New Development Philosophy

As China's economy keeps growing at a rapid pace and ascending to new heights, a host of contradictions and issues are gradually piling up. Since the start of the twenty-first century, these contradictions and problems have become more and more conspicuous, imposing increasingly evident constraints on the sustainable, stable, and healthy development of China's economy. Meanwhile, the internal conditions and external environment for economic development are constantly evolving. As the saying goes, "As time passes and the situation changes, everything follows suit." With the alterations in the conditions and contradictions encountered in economic development, the concept of economic development is continuously updated and advanced. In the first decade of the twenty-first century, the Party Central Committee, with Comrade Jiang Zemin at its core, put forward the significant Theory of Three Represents. Subsequently, the Party Central Committee, with Comrade Hu Jintao as General Secretary, put forward the Scientific Outlook on Development. After the 18th CPC National Congress, the CPC Central Committee, with Comrade Xi Jinping at its core, put forward the new development philosophy featuring "innovative, coordinated, green, open, and shared" development, which has given shape to *Xi Jinping Thought on the Economic Development of Socialism with Chinese Characteristics for a New Era*.

I. The Scientific Outlook on Development

Over the four decades of reform and opening up, China's GDP has achieved an average annual growth rate of approximately 9.5% when calculated at comparable prices. In 2009, it overtook Japan to become the world's second-largest economy. Since World War II, numerous countries and regions have gone through short phases of rapid growth, yet only 25 economies have managed to sustain an average annual growth rate of 7% or higher for 25 years or longer.[44] The rapid economic growth has brought profound changes to China's economic and social life, and we have also paid a high price for it. The most obvious is the cost of resources and the environment. According to preliminary estimates, from 2003 to 2012, the cost of environmental degradation and resource depletion in China was close to 10% of GDP, of which air pollution accounted for 6.5%, water pollution made up 2.1%, and soil degradation constituted 1.1%. The increasing medical expenses and the deterioration in the quality of life resulting from diseases induced by environmental pollution are growing ever more severe. The World Bank and the Development Research Center of the State Council pointed out in a report: "China's current growth model has put great pressure on environmental factors such as land, air and water, and the pressure on the supply of natural resources is increasing. The challenge ahead is to turn these pressures into a source of economic growth by adopting a green growth model."[45]

In 2003, China's per capita GDP crossed the $1,000 threshold, marking an important leap forward and pushing its economy and society into a pivotal phase of development. Drawing on global experience, once a nation reaches this stage, profound shifts unfold across multiple dimensions of its economic and social landscape. Household consumption undergoes a rapid upgrade, shifting from mere subsistence spending to meet basic needs toward development-focused consumption aimed at enhancing quality of life and personal capabilities. Industrial and agricultural production sees a notable rise in technological input, moving away from the high-pollution, high-energy-consumption, high-emission extensive model toward an intensive, sustainable path. Meanwhile, urbanization accelerates dramatically, becoming deeply intertwined with industrialization, agricultural modernization, the conversion of farmers to urban residents, and the expansion

---

44 The 25 economies include Botswana, Brazil, China, Indonesia, Japan, South Korea, Malaysia, Malta, Oman, Thailand and other countries, as well as Hong Kong, China and Taiwan, China.

45 A joint research group of the World Bank and the Development Research Center of the State Council. *China in 2030: Building A Modern, Harmonious and Creative Society*. Beijing: China Financial & Economic Publishing House, 2013, p. 9.

and upgrading of the service sector, among other areas. Yet, looking at China's actual circumstances, the extensive pattern of economic growth remains largely unaltered, with an intensive development model still far from being established. Pressures from population, resources, and the environment are mounting, and issues related to people's livelihoods have become increasingly prominent. All these problems are becoming increasingly urgent.

Problems in development must be solved by means of development. Jiang Zemin pointed out: "The Marxist ruling party must attach great importance to the emancipation and development of productive forces"; "development must be the first priority for the Party to govern and rejuvenate the country"; "on the basis of economic development, we should promote all-round social progress, continuously improve people's living standards, and ensure that the people share the fruits of development."[46] Meanwhile, against the historical backdrop of profound shifts in the nation's economic and social progress, the Party has introduced significant adjustments to its philosophy of economic development. In line with the inherent laws governing economic growth, it has put forward the Scientific Outlook on Development. The Third Plenary Session of the 16th CPC Central Committee held in 2003 passed the "Decision of the Central Committee of the Communist Party of China on Several Issues Concerning the Improvement of the Socialist Market Economic System," which pointed out: "We should uphold the principle of 'man first' and form the concept of overall, coordinated and sustainable development so as to promote the overall economic, social and human development."[47] At this gathering, Hu Jintao explicitly put forward "establishing and implementing the *Scientific Outlook on Development*," and pointed out: "The relationship between quantity and quality, speed and efficiency of growth must be properly handled … Growth is not simply equal to development. If we simply expand quantity and pursue speed, we do not pay attention to quality and efficiency, do not pay attention to the coordinated development of economy, politics, and culture, and do not pay attention to the harmony between man and nature, there will be growth disorders that will ultimately constrain development."[48]

To steer economic development onto the path of scientific growth, the primary task is to effectively shift the economic development model and adjust the economic structure. As far back as 1995, the "Proposal of the Central Committee

---

46 The Literature Research Office of the Central Committee of the Communist Party of China. *Selection of Important Documents since the 16th National Congress of the Communist Party of China, I.* Beijing: Central Party Literature Press, 2005, pp. 6–10.

47 Ibid., p. 465.

48 Ibid., p. 484.

of the Communist Party of China on Formulating the Ninth Five-Year Plan for National Economic and Social Development and the Long-Term Objectives for 2010," which was adopted at the Fifth Plenary Session of the 14th CPC Central Committee, explicitly put forward the initiative "to vigorously advance the transformation of the economic growth pattern and place economic efficiency at the core of economic work." In 2005, the "Proposal of the Central Committee of the Communist Party of China on Formulating the 11th Five-Year Plan for National Economic and Social Development" adopted by the Fifth Plenary Session of the 16th CPC Central Committee re-emphasized the importance of changing the mode of economic growth, pointing out: "China's land, fresh water, energy, mineral resources and environmental conditions have posed serious constraints on economic development."[49] On June 25, 2007, Hu Jintao gave a speech at the Central Party School's training program for provincial and ministerial-level officials. In this address, he replaced the earlier phrasing "shifting the mode of economic growth" with "transforming the mode of economic development." He pointed out, "From the transformation of the economic growth mode to the transformation of the economic development mode, although it is only a one-word change, it has a very profound connotation. The transformation of economic development mode, in addition to covering the entire content of the transformation of economic growth mode, also puts forward new and higher requirements for the concept, purpose, strategy and approach of economic development."[50] To be specific, economic growth is primarily centered on quantitative expansion, whereas economic development places greater emphasis on qualitative enhancement and structural optimization. Economic growth focuses on means, while economic development is oriented toward goals—namely, adhering to people-centered development and ultimately achieving the all-round development of individuals. Economic growth mainly targets the production sector, while economic development encompasses all aspects of national economic activities, including production, distribution, exchange, and consumption. As a result, formulating development strategies requires a more comprehensive and systematic approach. Economic growth is mainly achieved through input and scale expansion, while economic development must rely on efficiency-driven

---

49 The Literature Research Office of the Central Committee of the Communist Party of China. *Selection of Important Documents since the 16th National Congress of the Communist Party of China, II*. Beijing: Central Party Literature Press, 2005, p. 1064.

50 The Literature Research Office of the Central Committee of the Communist Party of China. *Summary of Important Expositions on the Scientific Outlook on Development*. Beijing: Central Party Literature Press, Party Building Books Publishing House, 2008, pp. 24–25.

and sustainable development. To meet these "new and higher requirements," the central government has successively launched a series of strategic measures, such as building an innovative country and taking a new path of industrialization with Chinese characteristics.

Since the inception of the *Scientific Outlook on Development*, the field of economics has engaged in extensive and profound discussions. A key focus of these discussions, both theoretically and practically, has been exploring the institutional mechanisms necessary to realize scientific development. Zhang Zhuoyuan argues that deepening fiscal and taxation reforms and refining fiscal and taxation policies are of vital importance for transforming the economic growth model and enhancing the quality and efficiency of economic activities. To this end, he suggests several measures: improving budgetary oversight of government revenue and establishing and perfecting a tax system that supports resource conservation, environmental protection, and economic growth. It is also crucial to prioritize deepening price reforms, ensuring that the prices of production factors and resource products accurately reflect resource scarcity. Additionally, reforms in other areas should be advanced to create a synergistic effect in promoting the transformation of the economic growth model. These include shifting government functions from being a key player in economic activities to serving as a public service-oriented government, reforming the performance evaluation and promotion systems for officials, and deepening enterprise reforms—particularly those of state-owned enterprises—to lay a micro-level foundation for changing the economic growth model.[51] Liu Wei argues that the transformation of the economic growth pattern first hinges on technological innovation, and the root of technological innovation lies in institutional innovation. The core lies in making efficiency enhancement the primary driver of growth, while a significant contradiction that needs to be addressed is the expanding income distribution gap.[52] Regarding China's growth model characterized by high input, Justin Yifu Lin and Su Jian note that this is mainly a result of the long-standing policy-driven factor price system in China, which features low interest rates, low land prices, low energy prices, and low raw material prices. Therefore, to shift the economic growth pattern, it is essential to push forward reforms in areas such as the factor price system. This will ensure that the factor price framework encountered by enterprises aligns with China's factor endowment structure and that the

---

51 Zhuoyuan Zhang. To deepen reform and promote the transformation of extensive economic growth mode. *Economic Research Journal*, 2005 (11).

52 Wei Liu. Historical changes in economic development and reform and fundamental transformation of growth patterns. *Economic Research Journal*, 2006 (1).

optimization efforts of individual enterprises are brought as close as possible to the overall optimization of the national economy.[53] In addressing the issues of high consumption, high emissions, and high pollution in China's economic development, Cai Fang and his colleagues argue that passively awaiting the emergence of the Kuznets turning point is no longer sufficient to tackle the mounting environmental pressures. Instead, proactive measures must be taken. This requires leveraging the central government's resolve, stimulating local governments' and enterprises' motivation to transform the growth model, and strengthening incentive mechanisms to achieve sustainable economic growth.[54] Li Lingling and Zhang Yaohui, after conducting a comprehensive index-based assessment of the shifts in China's economic development model between 2000 and 2009, suggest that to speed up the transformation of the economic development mode, efforts should start with addressing weak links. This includes optimizing the income distribution structure, enhancing the level of marketization and the input-output ratio of scientific research, as well as transforming the production mode, among other approaches.

II. Economic development's new normal and supply-side structural reform

Since the 18th CPC National Congress, the Party Central Committee with Comrade Xi Jinping as the core has made new important judgments on the stage of China's economic development based on the new characteristics of China's economic development. In May 2014, when inspecting work in Henan, Comrade Xi Jinping proposed: "We must strengthen our confidence, proceed from the current stage characteristics of China's economic development, adapt to the new normal, and maintain a normal mentality in strategy."[55] This marks the first occasion on which the new normal of economic development was formally put forward. Since then, Xi Jinping has expounded on the new normal on numerous significant occasions, thereby giving shape to an economic development concept and policy framework that adapts to and guides the new normal.

China's economic development is entering a new normal, marked by four distinct features. First, the growth pace has shifted from high speed to a medium-high

53 Justin Yifu Lin, Jian Su. On the transformation of China's economic growth mode. *Journal of Management World*, 2007 (11).

54 Fang Cai, Yang Du, Meiyan Wang. The transformation of economic development mode and the internal driving force of energy saving and emission reduction. *Economic Research Journal*, 2008 (6).

55 Jinping Xi. Xi Jinping's speech during his inspection tour in Henan. *People's Daily*, May 11, 2014.

speed. Second, the development model has transformed—from prioritizing scale and speed to emphasizing quality and efficiency. Third, the economic structure has undergone a change: whereas growth once relied primarily on expanding increments and boosting industrial capacity, it now centers on adjusting existing capacity and maximizing the utility of new additions. Fourth, the engine of development has shifted—from depending on inputs of resources, low-cost labor, and other factors to being driven by innovation.[56] In the realm of economic theory, fruitful explorations have been made regarding the new stage of economic development. A notable contribution emerged in 2012, when Yuan Fuhua, through an analysis of the economic evolution of modern and contemporary developed nations, introduced the notion of "structural slowdown" and provided a corresponding theoretical account.[57]

He noted that as the economic structure matures, employment tends to cluster in the service sector. The expansion of this sector—characterized by a high employment share yet slow growth in labor productivity—exerts a downward pull on the overall labor productivity growth of society as a whole. China, at the time, was undergoing a service-oriented shift in its industrial structure alongside changes in its population makeup, with these transformations converging within a relatively brief historical window. Scholars like Jin Pei and Guo Kesha, drawing on historical and cross-country comparisons, argued that the shift toward slower economic growth is not only an objective law independent of human will but also an inevitable phase that China's economy must traverse after a prolonged period of rapid expansion. This perspective underscored the systemic nature of growth deceleration, framing it as a natural progression tied to structural evolution rather than a temporary or avoidable setback.[58]

As the economy steps into the new normal, the essence of economic development is set to see major shifts in trends. First, the phase of consumption that followed imitation and trends has largely ended. Consumption is now expanding, with personalized and diverse demands gradually becoming the dominant pattern. In this context, ensuring product quality and safety, as well as boosting

---

[56] Jinping Xi. Speech at the seminar on the study and implementation of the spirit of the 5th Plenary Session of the 18th CPC Central Committee by leading cadres at the provincial and ministerial level. Beijing: People's Publishing House, 2016.

[57] Fuhua Yuan. "Structural acceleration" and "structural deceleration" in the long-run growth process: An explanation. *Economic Research Journal*, 2012 (3).

[58] Bei Jin. Research on the new normal of China's economic development. *China Industrial Economics*, 2015 (1); Kesha Guo. The theoretical basis of China's economic development entering a new normal—the analytical perspective of socialist political economics with Chinese characteristics. *Economic Research Journal*, 2016 (9).

demand through innovative supply, have grown far more significant. Second, traditional industries and real estate investment are reaching a state of relative saturation. On the flip side, a host of investment opportunities are popping up in areas like interconnected infrastructure, along with new technologies, products, business forms, and models. This has raised fresh demands for innovative ways of investing and financing. Third, as global market demands change and China's once strong low-cost edge fades, there's an urgent need to speed up the building of new comparative advantages. It is also crucial to play a positive role in reshaping international rules for trade and investment. Fourth, against the backdrop of overcapacity, the industrial structure must be upgraded and optimized. At the same time, with the rapid progress of internet technology and the rise of new innovation approaches, production is becoming more small-scale, intelligent, and specialized—these are emerging as new traits of industrial organization. Fifth, as the population ages and key technologies face international restrictions, the growth impetus from sheer factor scale is weakening. Economic growth will instead depend more on the quality of human capital and advances in technology. Sixth, competition is gradually moving toward a focus on quality and differentiation. Consumers are paying more attention to product quality and unique features. In the past, companies relied on preferential policies like tax breaks and land benefits to gain a competitive edge, and foreign capital enjoyed better-than-national treatment. But such practices are no longer viable. Unifying the national market and improving the efficiency of resource allocation have become endogenous requirements for economic development. Seventh, the environment's capacity to sustain development has hit or is approaching its limit, making it hard to support high-consumption and extensive growth models. People's desire for ecological amenities—like fresh air, clean drinking water, and a pollution-free environment—is growing stronger by the day, elevating the value of a sound ecological setting. Eighth, as economic growth slows, various long-hidden risks are gradually coming to the surface. Issues are emerging in areas such as local government debt, shadow banking, and real estate, while structural problems in employment are also becoming more apparent. Ninth, on the demand side, the marginal effectiveness of large-scale stimulus policies has noticeably weakened. On the supply side, it is essential to tackle overcapacity comprehensively and, at the same time, rely on market mechanisms to explore the future direction of industrial development.[59]

[59] The Literature Research Office of the Central Committee of the Communist Party of China. *Selection of Important Documents since the 18th National Congress of the Communist Party of China, II.* Beijing: Central Party Literature Press, 2016, pp. 241–245.

The key to adapting to these trend—changes is to expedite the transformation of the economic development pattern, with the strategic adjustment of the economic structure as the main focus, so as to fundamentally address a series of imbalance issues. The previous approach of short-term demand-side adjustment is no longer applicable to the new normal, as it can only postpone the emergence of problems and contradictions at best, and cannot prevent a more severe and concentrated outburst in the long run. For a long time, short-term and contingency macro-management has led to path dependence. On one hand, when facing economic risks and growth slowdowns, the government tends to implement over-expansionary policies. This not only undermines the quality of development, but also imposes constraints on subsequent macro-policy formulation, such as financial risks, debt traps, and overcapacity, making it hard to reverse these expansionary policies. On the other hand, it is challenging to essentially control the investment impulse in some regions. The practice of regarding GDP as the sole performance evaluation criterion still persists, and people's development concept can hardly shift from quantity to quality in a short time, especially in the context of regional competition. The absence of an interest-coordination mechanism further fuels the blind pursuit of growth rates. Therefore, it is essential to break away from the previous economic development and policy-making mindset, carry out supply-side reforms, and guide China's economic development onto a new path. This is crucial for adapting to the new normal of economic development, resolving various hidden risks, and promoting the sustainable and high-quality development of the economy: "Promoting supply-side structural reform is an inevitable choice for China's economic development to enter the new normal, and it is a strategic idea that must be established for China's macroeconomic management under the new normal of economic development."[60] To promote supply-side structural reform, we must "pay more attention to meeting the needs of the people, to the analysis of market and consumption psychology, to guiding social expectations, to strengthening the protection of property rights and intellectual property rights, to giving full play to the talents of entrepreneurs, to strengthening education and improving the quality of human capital, to building ecological civilization, and to scientific and technological progress and comprehensive innovation."[61]

---

[60] Jinping Xi. Speech at the 38th collective study of the Political Bureau of the 18th Central Committee. *People's Daily*, January 23, 2017.

[61] The Literature Research Office of the Central Committee of the Communist Party of China. *Selection of Important Documents since the 18th National Congress of the Communist Party of China, II*. Beijing: Central Party Literature Press, 2016, p. 246.

III. New development philosophy

At the Fifth Plenary Session of the 18th CPC Central Committee held in October 2015, the Party Central Committee with Comrade Xi Jinping at its core, by profoundly summarizing the experiences and lessons from both domestic and foreign development and conducting in-depth analyses of the overall trends in domestic and foreign development, put forward the new development philosophy characterized by "innovative, coordinated, green, open, and shared development" in response to the prominent contradictions and problems that emerged after China's economic development entered the new normal.[62] The new development philosophy embodies the Communist Party of China's ever-deepening grasp of the laws governing China's economic and social development. It stands as the most recent accomplishment in the theory of socialism with Chinese characteristics for economic development, a theoretical distillation of the Party-led practice of socialist economic development with Chinese characteristics over the 40 years of reform and opening up. Moreover, it represents both a continuation and an innovation of Marxist development concepts, serving as the fundamental theoretical principle and practical roadmap for China's economic advancement in the days ahead. General Secretary Xi Jinping pointed out: "Concepts are the forerunners of actions, and certain development practices are guided by certain development concepts. Whether the development concepts are right or not fundamentally determines the development effectiveness and even success or failure."[63]

The new development philosophy embodies the dialectical connection between individual elements and the entire system. On one aspect, it sets clear, targeted priorities for tackling urgent development issues: innovation is centered on boosting the momentum of growth, coordination focuses on addressing lopsided development, green development zeros in on humans coexisting harmoniously with nature, openness emphasizes linking internal and external development dynamics, and sharing is directed at enhancing social equity and justice. Each of these aspects targets specific, pressing problems in the development process, forming distinct yet vital parts of the overall framework. On the other hand, the new development philosophy is an unbreakable whole. Its various components are interlinked, interwoven, and mutually supportive. They must be upheld and put into practice as a complete set—none can be overlooked, nor can anyone take the place of another. This integrated nature reflects the understanding that

---

62 Ibid., p. 824.

63 Jinping Xi. Xi Jinping's speech during his investigation in Chongqing. *People's Daily*, January 7, 2016.

development is a multifaceted process where each part relies on and reinforces the others, making holistic implementation essential.

First, innovation acts as the foremost propellant for development. It represents the foundational means to adapt to shifts in the development landscape, boost the underlying potential for growth, gain the upper hand in development efforts, and more effectively guide the new normal. In addition to scientific and technological innovation, it also includes innovation in theory, system, culture, and other aspects.

Upholding innovation-driven development means placing innovation at the heart of the country's overall development strategy, integrating it into all aspects of the Party and government's work, and turning it into a widespread practice across society. Currently, insufficient innovation capacity has become a critical bottleneck hindering China's economic growth. For instance, in the 2012 ranking of the world's top 100 innovative companies—with patents as the main evaluation criterion—not a single Chinese enterprise made the list. When it comes to the world's top 100 brands, measured primarily by well-known trademarks, only four were from China. Data on 25 typical innovative enterprises revealed that their intangible assets accounted for a mere 0.65% of total assets on average, and within those intangibles, intellectual property assets made up just 16.98%. These figures show a clear gap between China and the average levels of developed nations.[64] A lack of robust innovation capacity has hampered the upgrading of China's industries. This has made it challenging to move up from the low-end segments of the global value chain to the higher-value upstream links. Consequently, it has become difficult to drive an overall leap in China's economy by building a large number of international brands that possess independent intellectual property rights.[65]

The need for innovation-driven development is pressing in practical terms. For one thing, as the phase of updating and replacing old capital equipment comes to an end, the once-fast advancement of technology embedded in physical assets is set to slow to a normal rate. For another, as the demographic dividend fades away bit by bit, the restrictive effect of diminishing marginal returns to capital is becoming increasingly pronounced. The conditions that once fueled the sustained "China miracle" through high levels of accumulation are gradually vanishing.

---

64 Yang Li, Xiaojing Zhang. "New normal": the logic and prospect of economic development. *Economic Research Journal*, 2015 (5).

65 Zhibiao Liu. The path and brand strategy of China's manufacturing industry upgrading under the background of globalization. *Research on Financial and Economic Issues*, 2005 (5).

This situation indicates that China's long-standing economic growth model—one that has relied heavily on massive capital input while contributing little to total factor productivity—must urgently shift to an efficiency-centered path driven by innovation. Thus, pursuing innovative development has become an unavoidable option for boosting China's economic transformation and upgrading, as well as for changing its development model in the new era.

Second, coordination is an inherent need for sustainable and healthy development. It serves not just as a method to drive development, but also as a development target, and even acts as a standard and gauge for assessing development. To achieve coordinated development, we must maintain the unity of the "two-point theory" and the "focal-point theory," balance the relationship between balanced and unbalanced development, and integrate efforts to address development weaknesses by tapping into development potentials. Priority should be given to advancing the coordinated growth of urban and rural areas, as well as the balanced progress of the economy and society. Meanwhile, we need to push for the synchronous advancement of new industrialization, informatization, urbanization, and agricultural modernization, strengthen both the country's hard power and soft power, and keep enhancing the comprehensiveness of development. This emphasis on coordination ensures that development does not lean excessively toward one side but forms an interconnected whole, where different aspects support and promote each other, thus laying a solid foundation for long-term stability and vitality. It should be noted that the large differences in development between urban and rural areas, as well as regions, and the unreasonable industrial structure are a significant feature of China's long-term economic and social development. On one side, this stems from objective factors like the country's vast size, uneven geographic distribution of natural resources, and the relatively late start of industrialization and urbanization. On the other side, there are also institutional and policy-related causes, such as the urban-rural dual structure and distortions in regional competition mechanisms. To advance coordinated development in the new era, the crux lies in properly balancing the roles of the market and the government. For one thing, letting the market mechanism operate without any constraints will inevitably widen development gaps excessively. This calls for the government to step in appropriately—through means like fiscal transfer payments and the equalization of public services—to rectify the overly large urban-rural and regional disparities created by market forces. For another, it is vital to strictly curb improper government interference, which can lead to a host of issues such as redundant construction, excessive investment, and overcapacity. Efforts should also be made to reform deep-seated systemic issues: these include the "ambiguity of property rights" concerning land and the environment, the "soft budget constraints" in the financial system, and the failure to fully separate state-owned enterprises from government control. Only by addressing these can the market be enabled to play a decisive role in resource allocation.

Third, Green development is an essential prerequisite for sustainable growth. It represents the direction of today's technological revolution and industrial transformation, as well as the most promising field for development, embodying people's aspiration for a better life. We must firmly embrace the modern development concept that "lucid waters and lush mountains are invaluable assets," recognizing that protecting the environment is protecting productivity, and improving the environment is developing productivity. The goal is to foster green modes of production and lifestyles, strike a proper balance between economic growth, improved living standards, resource conservation, and ecological protection, and ultimately build a beautiful China with blue skies, green lands, and clean waters. For a long time, China's economic growth has come at a high environmental cost. The extensive growth model—characterized by high pollution, high energy consumption, and high emissions—has not been fundamentally transformed, undermining the capacity for sustainable development. Estimates show that from the start of reform and opening up to 2008, China's average potential economic growth rate stood at 9.5%, with approximately 1.3 percentage points driven by environmental consumption. Since the twenty-first century, environmental consumption has contributed an average of two percentage points to economic growth each year;[66] from 1998 to 2010, the cost of environmental pollution in China accounted for 8% to 10% of the actual GDP, and the cost in economically developed areas was significantly higher than that in less developed areas. The long-term elasticity of household health spending relative to economic growth came in at 1.66. Meanwhile, the marked slowdown in the country's high-speed economic expansion has been significantly worsened by a decline in public health status.[67] The historical experiences of developed nations demonstrate that the outdated path of "pursuing development first, then addressing its consequences" is unfeasible. This approach brings about economic, social, and human costs that are impossible to bear—and some of these costs can never be undone. For this reason, green development is the sole path forward for China's future, whether measured by the long-term, fundamental interests of the people or by practical economic results.

---

66 Fuhua Yuan. China's potential economic growth under the constraints of low-carbon economy. *Economic Research Journal*, 2010 (8).

67 Jisheng Yang, Juan Xu, Xiangjun Wu. Historical changes in economic development and reform and fundamental changes in growth patterns. *Economic Research Journal*, 2006 (1).

Fourth, opening up stands as the indispensable path for a nation's prosperity and growth. It fuels innovation, spurs reform, and boosts development—serving as a key driver behind China's remarkable achievements over time. To uphold open development, we must keep advancing the strategy of integrating "bringing in" and "going global," adopt a more proactive opening-up approach, work to establish a new open economic system, and foster a higher-standard open economy. It is important to note that, on one hand, the global economy's overall growth momentum remains weak, with conflicts and frictions between nations and regions rising notably. In response, there's a need to explore new external growth drivers, develop new models of win-win cooperation, and build extensive communities of shared interests. Initiatives like the Belt and Road and the founding of the Asian Infrastructure Investment Bank (AIIB) are proactive steps China has taken to adapt to new international circumstances. On the other hand, as China's economy has expanded rapidly, it has become a significant "internal factor" in the global economy. Whether from the standpoint of safeguarding national interests or shaping a fair and rational international economic order, China is called to play an increasingly vital role and integrate more deeply into the global economic system. The internationalization of the RMB, the creation of a petroleum RMB settlement market, and the expansion of free trade zones are all major moves to actively build a new open economic framework and advance a higher-level open economy. At the same time, it is crucial to recognize that the global economic landscape is growing more complex, with policy outcomes becoming far more uncertain. Thus, pursuing open development should not be misinterpreted as mindlessly chasing speed or expansion; instead, it should be advanced flexibly and steadily, drawing on accumulated experiences and lessons as circumstances evolve.

Fifth, sharing constitutes a core demand of socialism with Chinese characteristics and stands as a vivid embodiment of the strengths inherent in the socialist system. Adhering to shared development, the essence is to adhere to the people-centered development idea, and the key is to make more effective institutional arrangements, and do a good job from top-level design to the "last mile" implementation. In practical terms, efforts should be made to expand the middle-income bracket, strengthen support for vulnerable groups, and firmly secure victory in the fight against poverty. For a long time, China has seen a persistently wide income gap among its residents, meaning the fruits of economic growth have not been fully shared by all. This has also dampened the role of domestic demand in driving economic expansion. Data from China's National Bureau of Statistics—including the Gini coefficient—and research findings by

Hu Jiayong, Wu Peng,[68] and others indicate that since the reform and opening-up era, both urban-rural disparities and overall income gaps among residents have grown notably. When excluding the influence of the Northeast's sharp relative economic decline, the development gap between coastal and inland regions has also widened considerably. Various forms of inequality have lessened in recent years, yet the degree of narrowing remains quite slight. Numerous theoretical and practical studies have demonstrated that such wide gaps constrain economic development from the demand side. Thus, shared development is not only an essential part of governing to serve the people's interests but also the key approach to advance the integration of distribution and development, thereby achieving shared economic and social progress.

4. Embarking on a Fresh Voyage Toward the Comprehensive Advancement of Socialist Modernization

Xi Jinping pointed out at the 2018 Bo'ao Forum for Asia Annual Conference: "Over the last four decades, the Chinese people have significantly unleashed and enhanced productive forces in China through hard work with an unyielding spirit ... Over the last four decades, the Chinese people have blazed a path of socialism with Chinese characteristics through determined exploration with a pioneering spirit."[69] After enduring years of painstaking work, socialism with Chinese characteristics has stepped into a new epoch. Having accomplished the building of a moderately prosperous society in all aspects and met the first centenary target, China is on the verge of setting out on a fresh path toward comprehensively constructing a modern socialist nation. Accomplishing socialist modernization represents a long-term strategic endeavor and arrangement by the Party and the nation. As far back as the Third National People's Congress in 1964, Zhou Enlai proposed the ambitious objective of achieving the "Four Modernizations" (modernizing agriculture, industry, national defense, and science and technology) by the close of the twentieth century in his government work report. In 1978, the Third Plenary Session of the 11th CPC Central Committee clearly proposed "to shift the focus of the whole Party's work and the attention

68 Jiayong Hu, Peng Wu. Promoting the phased transition from "rich first" to "shared wealth." *Economic Perspectives*, 2012 (12).

69 Jinping Xi. Keynote speech at the opening ceremony of the Boao Forum for Asia Annual Conference 2018. *People's Daily Online*, April 10, 2018.

of the whole nation to the socialist modernization drive." In October 1984, Deng Xiaoping summed up China's medium- and long-term development strategy with a "two-step approach" when meeting with Chinese and foreign representatives attending a seminar on Sino-foreign economic cooperation. He proposed "to quadruple economic production by the end of the century, achieving a per capita gross national product of US$800 and a better standard of living for our people … with that achievement as a foundation we can strive to approach the level of the developed countries within 30 to 50 years."[70] In August 1987, just before the 13th National Congress of the Communist Party of China, Deng Xiaoping articulated the "three-step" strategy in explicit terms during a meeting with leaders of the Italian Communist Party: "China is developing its economy in three steps. Two steps will be taken in this century, to reach the point where our people have adequate food and clothing and lead a fairly comfortable life. The third step, which will take us 30 to 50 years into the next century, is to reach the level of the moderately developed countries."[71] The 13th National Congress of the Communist Party of China incorporated the "three-step" strategy into its agenda. The first phase, spanning from 1981 to 1990, aimed to double the 1980 gross national product (GNP) and ensure people's basic needs for food and clothing were met. The second step, from 1991 to the end of the twentieth century, sought to double the GNP again, lifting people's living standards to a moderately prosperous level. The third stage targeted the mid-twenty-first century, by which time per capita GNP was expected to reach that of moderately developed countries, people's lives would be relatively affluent, and basic modernization would be achieved. In 1997, the 15th National Congress of the CPC put forward a new "three-step" strategy for the new century. The first decade aimed to double the 2000 GDP, enhance people's moderately prosperous lives, and establish a relatively complete socialist market economic system. After another decade of efforts, by the centenary of the Party's founding, the national economy would be more developed and various systems more refined. By the mid-twenty-first century, when New China marks its centenary, basic modernization would be realized, and a prosperous, strong, democratic, and culturally advanced socialist country would take shape. At the Sixth Plenary Session of the 16th CPC Central Committee in 2006, the term "harmonious" was added to the modernization goals. Then, at the 19th National Congress of the CPC in 2017, "beautiful" was

---

[70] Xiaoping Deng. *Selected Works of Deng Xiaoping, Vol. 3*. Beijing: People's Publishing House, 1993, p. 77.

[71] Ibid., p. 251.

included, with the vision of building a great modern socialist country that is prosperous, strong, democratic, culturally advanced, harmonious, and beautiful.

Data from the National Bureau of Statistics shows that China's per capita national income stood at $3,650 in 2009. Based on the World Bank's 2008 criteria, this placed the country among lower-middle-income nations. By 2010, per capita income had risen to $4,260, and under the World Bank's 2010 standards, China moved into the category of upper-middle-income countries. In 2016, China's per capita national income was US$8,260. The pace of China's march toward socialist modernization has been significantly faster than expected.

Scholars in the academic circle are generally quite positive about China's medium- and long-term economic growth prospects. Drawing on both domestic and international historical experiences as well as statistical patterns of medium- and long-term economic growth, the China Economic Growth Frontier Research Group, affiliated with the Institute of Economics, Chinese Academy of Social Sciences, carried out projections for China's future economic growth. They did this by conducting parameter estimations and simulating the production function. The findings indicated that China's potential growth rate would range from 5.7% to 6.6% between 2016 and 2020, and from 5.4% to 6.3% during the 2021–2030 period. Overall, China's economic growth is set to undergo a shift in driving forces—moving away from factor accumulation and toward technological advancement—with the quality of economic growth seeing a marked improvement.[72] Using a global growth framework, the research team from Tsinghua University's Institute for Contemporary China Studies made projections about China's future economic growth rates. Their analysis yielded the following results: between 2020 and 2035, China's GDP is expected to grow at an average annual rate of 4.84% to 5.59%; and from 2035 to 2050, the average annual GDP growth rate is projected to be 3.20% to 3.95%.[73] A collaborative research team from the World Bank and the Development Research Center of the State Council made projections indicating that China's potential GDP growth rate would stand at 5.9% between 2012 and 2025, and then ease to 5.0% from 2026 to 2030.[74] The core

---

72 Frontier Research Group of China's Economic Growth, Institute of Economics, Chinese Academy of Social Sciences. China's long-term economic growth path, efficiency and potential growth level. *Economic Research Journal*, 2012 (11).

73 Research Group of the Institute of National Conditions of Tsinghua University. Analysis of China's economic growth prospects and driving forces from 2015 to 2050. *Governance*, 2017 (45).

74 Joint Research Group of the World Bank and the Development Research Center of the State Council. *China in 2030: Building a Modern, Harmonious and Creative Society*. Beijing: China Financial and Economic Publishing House, 2013, p. 10.

of China's future economic development lies in prioritizing the enhancement of growth quality and efficiency while sustaining medium-to-high growth rates. This entails boosting total factor productivity, making green development a driver of economic expansion, and establishing a modern economic system. By doing so, China can successfully navigate the "middle-income trap" and steadily join the ranks of high-income nations.2020 marked a pivotal moment. China completed the building of a moderately prosperous society in all aspects, with a system that is comprehensive, scientifically sound, standardized, and efficiently operational, seeing all institutional facets grow more mature and well-established. This achievement laid the groundwork for embarking on a fresh phase of comprehensively constructing a modern socialist nation. As outlined in the strategic blueprint of the 19th National Congress of the Communist Party of China, the period from 2020 to the mid-twenty-first century is divided into two phases. The first, spanning 2020 to 2035, aims to basically achieve socialist modernization, building on the foundation of a moderately prosperous society. The second phase, from 2035 to the mid-twenty-first century, seeks to develop China into a great modern socialist country that is prosperous, strong, democratic, culturally advanced, harmonious, and beautiful, building on the progress of basic modernization. It is foreseeable that as the new journey of socialist modernization unfolds in full, both the practice and theory of socialist economic development with Chinese characteristics will enter an entirely new era. This transition will reflect deeper integration of institutional strengths, developmental quality, and people-centered progress, driving forward a more mature and dynamic model of growth.

References

Cai, Fang, Du Yang & Wang Meiyan. The transformation of economic development mode and the internal driving force of energy saving and emission reduction. *Economic Research Journal*, 2008 (6).

Chen, Jiyong, Sheng Yangyi. Knowledge spillovers of foreign direct investment and China's regional economic growth. *Economic Research Journal*, 2008 (12).

Chen, Zongsheng, Li Defu. High savings, high investment, and China's economic growth in the process of labor transfer. *Economic Research Journal*, 2005 (2).

Deng, Xiaoping. *Selected Works of Deng Xiaoping, Volume 3*. Beijing: People's Publishing House, 1993.

Dong, Minjie, Liang Yongmei. Sources of China's economic growth from 1978 to 2010: a nonparametric decomposition framework. *Economic Research Journal*, 2013 (5).

Fan, Gang, Wang Xiaolu, Ma Guangrong. The contribution of China's marketization process to economic growth. *Economic Research Journal*, 2011 (9).
Fan, Gang, Zhang Shuguang. *Outline of Public Ownership Macroeconomic Theory*. Shanghai: Shanghai Sanlian Bookstore, 1990.
Frontier Research Group of China's Economic Growth, Institute of Economics, Chinese Academy of Social Sciences. China's long-term economic growth path and efficiency and potential growth. *Economic Research Journal*, 2012 (11).
Frontier Research Group of China's Economic Growth, Institute of Economics, Chinese Academy of Social Sciences. High investment, macro costs and sustainability of Economic Growth. *Economic Research Journal*, 2005 (10).
Guo, Kesha. Theoretical basis for China's economic development entering the new normal—the analysis perspective of socialist political economics with Chinese Characteristics. *Economic Research Journal*, 2016 (9).
Hu, Jiayong, Wu Peng. Promoting the phased transition from "rich first" to "shared wealth." *Economic Perspectives*, 2012 (12).
Jiang, Ren'ai, Feng Genfu. Has there been rapid efficiency improvement in the Chinese economy since the reform? *Economics* (Quarterly), 2006 (1).
Jin, Bei. Research on the new normal of China's economic development. *China Industrial Economics*, 2015 (1).
Joint research group of the World Bank and the Development Research Center of the State Council. *China in 2030: Building a Modern, Harmonious and Creative Society*. Beijing: China Financial and Economic Publishing House, 2013.
Li, Yang, Zhang Xiaojing. "New normal": the logic and prospect of economic development. *Economic Research Journal*, 2015 (5).
Lin, Justin Yifu, Cai Fang, Li Zhou. *China's Miracle: Development Strategy and Economic Reform (Updated Edition)*. Shanghai: Shanghai SDX Joint Publishing Company, Shanghai People's Publishing House, 1999.
Lin, Justin Yifu, Su Jian. On the transformation of China's economic growth mode. *Journal of Management World*, 2007 (11).
Lin, Justin Yifu. Economic Development and Chinese Culture. *Strategy and Management*, 2003 (1).
Liu, Guoguang, Wang Xiangming. A discussion on the relationship between the development speed and proportion of China's national economy. *Social Sciences in China*, 1980(4).
Liu, Wei. Historical changes in economic development and reform and fundamental changes in growth patterns. *Economic Research Journal*, 2006 (1).

Liu, Zhibiao. The path and brand strategy of China's manufacturing industry upgrading under the background of globalization. *Research on Financial and Economic Issues*, 2005 (5).
Ouyang, Sheng. On the balance of means of production and means of consumption. *Economic Research Journal*, 1979 (6).
Ouyang, Yao. *Comprehensive Advantages of Large Countries*. Shanghai: Truth & Wisdom Press, Shanghai SDX Joint Publishing Company, Shanghai People's Publishing House, 2011.
World Bank. *The East Asian Miracle: Economic Growth and Public Policy*. Beijing: China Financial and Economic Publishing House, 1995.
Wang, Wenju, Fan Hejun. An empirical analysis of the contribution of China's market reform to economic growth. *China Industrial Economics*, 2007(9).
Wu, Zhongmin. Comprehensive advantages of large countries and large country syndrome. *Science and Technology Review*, 1992 (8).
Wu, Peng. The power conversion of China's economic growth since the reform. *China Industrial Economics*, 2013 (2).
Yang, Jisheng, Xu Juan, Wu Xiangjun. Historical changes in economic development and reform and fundamental changes in growth patterns. *Economic Research Journal*, 2006 (1).
Yao, Shujie. China's economic development and theoretical innovation under the "new normal." *Economic Research Journal*, 2015 (12).
Yuan, Fuhua. China's potential economic growth under the constraints of low-carbon economy. *Economic Research Journal*, 2010 (8).
Yuan, Fuhua. "Structural acceleration" and "structural deceleration" in the long-run growth process: an explanation. *Economic Research Journal*, 2012 (3).
Zhang, Zhuoyuan. To deepen reform and promote the transformation of extensive economic growth mode. *Economic Research Journal*, 2005 (11).
Zhao, Zhiyun, Lu Bingyang, Guo Qingwang, Jia Junxue. The dynamic fusion of capital accumulation and technological progress: a typical fact of China's economic growth. *Economic Research Journal*, 2007 (11).
Zhou, Ye'an, Zhang Quan. Marketization, fiscal decentralization and China's economic growth. *Journal of Renmin University of China*, 2008 (1).
Zhu, Tian. *The Mystery of China's Growth*. Beijing: CITIC Press, 2016.

Theory of Developing a Modernized Economy

The 19th CPC National Congress report identifies the development of a modernized economy as a new long-term strategic imperative. It stands out as the most dazzling bright spot in the economic field, indicating that the Chinese people have solved the problem of food and clothing after reform and opening up, and after becoming a moderately prosperous society, China will enter a new period of directly building a great modern country. Building a modernized economy is a very inspiring and arduous task with strong theoretical and practical guidance. It also marks that the socialist economic theoretical system with Chinese characteristics has added an element. Marxist historical materialism tells us that the economy is the foundation of society. To lay a solid foundation for building a powerful nation, it is essential to establish a modern economic system, which is a prerequisite for realizing the vision of a prosperous, strong, democratic, culturally vibrant, harmonious, and beautiful socialist China by the mid-twenty-first century. It is our belief that, with the firm leadership of the Communist Party of China, the Chinese people will steadily advance toward the realization of this grand vision with unwavering confidence.

1. New Tasks Proposed in the New Era

In the report of the 19th CPC National Congress of the Communist Party of China, General Secretary Xi Jinping emphasized the following point: "With decades of hard work, socialism with Chinese characteristics has crossed the threshold into a new era. This is a new historic juncture in China's development." "The period between the 19th and the 20th National Congress is the period in which the timeframes of the two centenary goals converge. In this period, not only must we finish building a moderately prosperous society in all respects and achieve the first centenary goal; we must also build on this achievement to embark on a new journey toward the second centenary goal of fully building a modern socialist country." "China's economy has been transitioning from a phase of rapid growth to a stage of high-quality development. This is a pivotal stage for transforming our growth model, improving our economic structure, and fostering new drivers of growth. It is imperative that we develop a modernized economy. This is both an urgent requirement for getting us smoothly through this critical transition and a strategic goal for China's development. We must put quality first and give priority to performance. We should pursue supply-side structural reform as our main task, and work hard for better quality, higher efficiency, and more robust drivers of economic growth through reform. We need to raise total factor productivity and accelerate the building of an industrial system that promotes coordinated development of the real economy with technological innovation, modern finance, and human resources. We should endeavor to develop an economy with more effective market mechanisms, dynamic micro-entities, and sound macro-regulation. This will steadily strengthen the innovation capacity and competitiveness of China's economy."

The assertion that socialism with Chinese characteristics has entered a new era is grounded in the transformation of the principal contradiction in Chinese society—from one between the people's increasing material and cultural demands and underdeveloped production, to one between uneven and insufficient development and their growing aspirations for a better quality of life. First of all, from the perspective of social needs, when people's life has reached a moderately prosperous level, their needs for a better life are no longer limited to the needs of general material and cultural life. Instead, they will have higher and broader needs with diversified, multi-faceted, and multi-level features. People all look forward to more stable employment, more income, better education, more comfortable living conditions, better ecological environment, higher level of medical and health services, and better social security. Their demands for democracy, rule of law, security, fairness, and justice are also increasing. From the perspective of social production, after 40 years of development since reform and opening up, China's social productive forces have reached a great level. In 2017, China's economic aggregate reached 82 trillion yuan, equivalent to about US$12 trillion, ranking second in the world. China's overall production capacity has reached a globally advanced stage, with the production levels of more than 220 major categories in the industrial and agricultural sectors topping global rankings. The situation of shortage economy and insufficient product supply that has plagued the common people for a long time has undergone a fundamental change, so "backward social production" is no longer in line with the objective reality. China's development increasingly falls short of meeting the people's rising expectations for a better life. Many deficiencies need to be remedied, and the quality of development needs to be greatly improved. The economic and social structure should be optimized and advanced.

It can be seen that the construction of a modern economic system proposed at the 19th CPC National Congress is a high-level strategic goal, which can be comparable with the three-step strategic goal proposed by Deng Xiaoping and the goal of building a moderately prosperous society in all respects in the first 20 years of the twenty-first century proposed at the 16th CPC National Congress. However, the time span of building a modern economic system is longer than that of building a moderately prosperous society in all respects. The former spans more than 30 years, while the latter spans 20 years. Moreover, the former is based on the latter to achieve a more ambitious development goal with greater global influence. During the drafting of the report to the 16th CPC National Congress, some people advocated that after entering the twenty-first century, we could make the acceleration of socialist modernization as the development goal of the first 20 years, while the mainstream opinion held that considering China's national conditions, it was more in line with objective laws and prudent to regard building a moderately prosperous society in all respects as the development goal of the first 20 years of the twenty-first century. Practice has proved that this choice is correct, and building a moderately prosperous society in all respects is a necessary stage for China to achieve modernization. Modernization has been the dream of the Chinese people for more than 100 years, and it is the fundamental symbol of the great rejuvenation of the Chinese nation. After 40 years of tireless efforts since the launch of reform and opening up, and with the goal of building a moderately prosperous society in all respects now within reach, China is well-positioned and fully capable of turning this dream into reality. As stated in the report of the 19th CPC National Congress, "today, we are closer, more confident, and more capable than ever before of making the goal of national rejuvenation a reality."

In the 1960s, the First Session of the Third National People's Congress put forward the grand vision of building China into a great modern socialist country for the first time. In the 1980s, the CPC Central Committee put forward a three-step strategic goal of China's socialist modernization drive. The first step is to solve the problem of food and clothing for the people, which was achieved at the end of the 1980s; the second step is to make people's lives reach a moderately prosperous level, which was also achieved at the end of the twentieth century; the third step is to basically achieve modernization by the 100th anniversary of the founding of the People's Republic of China. In this regard, in 1987, the

13th CPC National Congress once stated: "Ever since the Third Plenary Session of the 11th CPC Central Committee, we have been carrying out a strategic plan for economic development. This plan involves three steps. The first step is to double the GNP of 1980 and solve the problem of food and clothing for our people. This task has been largely fulfilled. The second step is to double it again by the end of this century, thus enabling our people to lead a fairly comfortable life. The third step is to reach the per capita GNP level of moderately developed countries. This will mean that modernization has been basically accomplished and that our people have begun to enjoy a relatively affluent life." The report of the 16th CPC National Congress further emphasized: "In accordance with the development objectives up to 2010, the centenary of the Party and that of New China, as proposed at the 15th National Congress, we need to concentrate on building a well-off society of a higher standard in an all-round way to the benefit of well over one billion people in this period. We will further develop the economy, improve democracy, advance science, and education, enrich culture, foster social harmony, and upgrade the texture of life for the people. The two decades of development will serve as an inevitable connecting link for attaining the third-step strategic objectives for our modernization drive as well as a key stage for improving the socialist market economy and opening wider to the outside world. Building on what is achieved at this stage and continuing to work for several more decades, we will have in the main accomplished the modernization program and turned China into a strong, prosperous, democratic and culturally advanced socialist country by the middle of this century." After the 17th CPC National Congress, it was further proposed to build China into a prosperous, strong, democratic, culturally advanced, and harmonious socialist country by the middle of the twenty-first century.

It can be seen from the above discussions that the second centenary goal proposed by the 19th CPC National Congress has higher requirements than the previous discussions of the Party. First, the second centenary goal discussed in the previous Party documents was to basically achieve modernization by the middle of the twenty-first century, but the 19th National Congress of the Party advanced this goal to 2035, 15 years earlier. Second, while earlier goals emphasized building a modern socialist nation that is prosperous, strong, democratic, culturally advanced, and harmonious by the mid-twenty-first century, the 19th CPC National Congress further refined this vision by adding "beautiful" to the list—calling for the creation of a great modern socialist country that is prosperous, strong, democratic, culturally advanced, harmonious, and beautiful. In addition to adding the content of "a beautiful country," it also proposed the goal of building a great country for the first time, so as to achieve a great transformation of China from standing up to getting rich and then becoming strong.

2. Taking a Two-Step Approach Practically

The report of the 19th CPC National Congress articulated a phased, two-stage plan aimed at fulfilling the second centenary goal. The report stated: "Based on a comprehensive analysis of the international and domestic environments and the conditions for China's development, we have drawn up a two-stage development plan for the period from 2020 to the middle of this century. In the first stage from 2020 to 2035, we will build on the foundation created by the moderately prosperous society with a further 15 years of hard work to see that socialist modernization is basically realized. The vision is that by the end of this stage, the following goals will have been met: China's economic and technological strength has increased significantly. China has become a global leader in innovation. The rights of the people to participate and to develop as equals are adequately protected. The rule of law for the country, the government, and society is basically in place. Institutions in all fields are further improved; the modernization of China's system and capacity for governance is basically achieved. Social etiquette and civility are significantly enhanced. China's cultural soft power has grown much stronger; Chinese culture has greater appeal. People are leading more comfortable lives, and the size of the middle-income group has grown considerably. Disparities in urban-rural development, in development between regions, and in living standards are significantly reduced; equitable access to basic public services is basically ensured; and solid progress has been made toward prosperity for everyone. A modern social governance system has basically taken shape, and society is full of vitality, harmonious, and orderly. There is a fundamental improvement in the environment; the goal of building a Beautiful China is basically attained. In the second stage from 2035 to the middle of the twenty-first century, we will, building on having basically achieved modernization, work hard for a further 15 years and develop China into a great modern socialist country that is prosperous, strong, democratic, culturally advanced, harmonious, and beautiful. By the end of this stage, the following goals will have been met: new heights are reached in every dimension of material, political, cultural, and ethical, social, and ecological advancement. Modernization of China's system and capacity for governance is achieved. China has become a global leader in terms of composite national strength and international influence. Common prosperity for everyone is basically achieved. The Chinese people enjoy happier, safer, and healthier lives. The Chinese nation will become a proud and active member of the community of nations."

It is very necessary to divide the 30-year socialist modernization drive into two stages, so that the overarching of the first stage can be designed in a more specific and clear way under the premise of clear general goals, and even a road map and timetable can be devised, which will help to implement the grand task.

We believe that after China attains a moderately prosperous society in all respects, the first major challenge in the initial stage of basically realizing socialist modernization will be to ensure that the country steadily enters the ranks of high-income nations by 2030, thereby avoiding the "middle-income trap." According to the classification standard of the World Bank in 2014, low-income countries are those whose per capita Gross National Income (GNI per capita, roughly equivalent to GDP per capita) is less than US$1,035 (2014 US dollars, the same below). A country with a per capita GNI between US$1,035 and US$4,086 is classified as a lower-middle-income country, between US$4,087 and US$12,616 as an upper-middle-income country, and above US$12,616 as a high-income country. By the time China built a moderately prosperous society in all respects in 2020, its per capita GDP had risen from around US$9,000 in 2017 to US$10,500. According to our calculations, after 2020, as long as there is no serious world economic crisis, no Korean nuclear war, and no serious work mistakes, China's economy can maintain an average annual growth rate of about 5%, and can achieve the basic stability of the exchange rate of RMB against the US dollar. In this way, China will be able to reach the threshold of a high-income country set by the World Bank in 2014 after five, six, or seven years of hard work. After another three or four years of hard work, by 2030, it can be said that China will have steadily entered the ranks of high-income countries and have truly crossed the "middle-income trap." By then, China's industries will have reached the mid-to-high-end level, industrialization, informatization, and urbanization will have been basically realized, the economic structure will have basically been modernized, the proportion of middle-income earners will increase to about half, and the Gini coefficient, which reflects the income gap between residents, will drop to about 0.4. The socialist market economic system will be more mature and finalized, and the socialist market-based economy theory will be more fully confirmed and firmly stand at the peak of economic theory. In 2017 or even earlier, some economists believed that China would enter the ranks of high-income countries in 2020, asserting that the "middle-income trap" would not pose a challenge. It now appears that their forecasts are too optimistic and unrealistic.

To establish a modern economic system, whether in pursuit of the two-stepgoal of socialist modernization or in overcoming the "middle-income trap" to join the ranks of high-income countries, the most important thing is to change the concept of development, change the way of development, insist on quality first and efficiency first, and take the supply-side structural reform as the main line, so that economic growth can truly shift from increasing factor input to innovation-driven development. In 2005, the Fifth Plenary Session of the 16th CPC Central Committee put forward the task of transforming the mode of economic growth. In 2007, the 17th CPC National Congress further emphasized the need to change the mode of economic development, although implementation remained insufficient. Since the 18th CPC National Congress, the CPC Central Committee has recognized that China's economy has transitioned into a new normal phase and called for a focus on advancing supply-side structural reforms. Following this, improving the quality of economic development has gradually gained widespread attention, and concrete steps toward economic transformation have been initiated. The industry structure has transformed from a focus on middle- and low-end industries to an endeavor in mid-to-high-end industries. Significant progress has been achieved in the industrialization of key scientific and technological innovations, such as high-speed railways, hydropower equipment, UHV power transmission and transformation, hybrid rice, earth observation satellites, Beidou navigation, electric vehicles, etc. Some industries are at the forefront of the world, continuously improving the quality and efficiency of China's economic development, and opening up new space for China's development.

The report of the 19th CPC National Congress did not propose a GDP growth rate requirement for building a modern economic system in two steps, mainly to allow everyone to concentrate on improving the quality and efficiency of economic development, dilute the economic growth rate indicators, and change the inertial thinking that people have been pursuing GDP growth for a long time. Of course, it does not mean that the GDP growth rate should not be calculated in the future. On the contrary, while upholding the principles of prioritizing quality and efficiency, the economy must maintain a medium speed or medium-to-high-speed growth, and the economic aggregate must continue to grow. When the 13th CPC National Congress proposed that China should realize socialist modernization by the middle of the twenty-first century, it also indicated that the economy should reach the level of medium developed countries by then. At that time, there was an article explaining that the grand target referred to the level of the medium developed countries in the late 1980s, which was, the per capita GDP was about US$30,000. It seems that this standard is low now, and to reach the level of medium developed countries in the middle of the twenty-first century, it is estimated to reach the level of per capita GDP of US$35,000 to US$45,000 in 2015 US dollars.[1] It requires that, in the next 30 years, on the premise that the exchange rate of RMB against the US dollar remains stable, the average annual GDP growth rate should be maintained at about 5%. Therefore, in the actual economic work in the future, it is still necessary to make the economy grow at a certain speed, but it is necessary to seek fast growth while maintaining quality, and not to pursue rapid economic growth one-sidedly, regardless of the consequences.

The series of discussions on establishing a contemporary economic framework in the report of the 19th CPC National Congress has significantly enriched the field of development economics with many new insights, especially about how a large developing country can successfully build a modern and great country through reform and opening up within a comparatively brief timeframe, which is a major contribution and improvement to development economics.

3. A Modernized Economy: A Necessary Condition for High-Quality Development

To establish a modernized economy, we must implement high-quality development, which is different from extensive development. First, extensive development mainly relies on increasing factor input and extension expansion, while high-quality development is mainly driven by innovation, and by improving total factor productivity, that is, by improving efficiency. Second, extensive development is difficult to optimize and upgrade the industry, and it is difficult to improve the quality and grade of products and services, even for several years, which cannot satisfy people's pursuit of a better life, while high-quality development requires continuous optimization and upgrading of the industry, often at the mid-to-high-end level, and constantly improving the technical content and quality of products and services, which can satisfy people's yearning and pursuit for a better life. Third, extensive development depletes limited resources, destroys ecology, and harms the environment, while high-quality development promotes resource conservation and reuse, which is conducive to protecting the ecological environment and thereby contributing to the creation of a resource-conserving and environmentally friendly society. Fourth, extensive development is not conducive to driving technological progress or stimulating innovation, which affects the improvement of competitiveness, while high-quality development encourages technological progress and innovation, thereby enhancing competitiveness in

1 Qinchuan Du, et al. Quantitative research on the income standard of "moderately developed countries in 2050"— an estimation based on the principle of long-term trend extrapolation and random sampling. *Prices in China*, 2017 (6).

order to remain invincible in the market competition. Developed countries all over the world rely on long-term high-quality development to become developed countries, and they attach great importance to technological progress as well. This is an objective law of social and economic development. In order to modernize and become an economically developed country, China must be determined to take the road of high-quality development. The report of the 19th CPC National Congress sounded the clarion call for building a modernized economy, and at the same time, clearly pointed out that China's economy had shifted to a stage of high-quality development, which is very logical.

To achieve high-quality development, it is essential to prioritize supply-side structural reform. The report of the 19th CPC National Congress placed deepening such reform at the forefront of the strategic agenda for implementing the new development philosophy and advancing the construction of a modernized economy. In the past, economic growth was often driven by stimulating demand, which also led to extensive expansion and development. Since the beginning of the twenty-first century, people have gradually realized that the promotion of economic growth by stimulating demand, especially investment demand and export demand, for so many years, has led to more and more prominent bottleneck constraints on resources and the environment, and the efficiency of investment has been declining and unsustainable. In terms of output structure, the majority of China's production capacity can only meet the requirements of mid-low-end, low-quality, and low-price products, and there is a large amount of overcapacity. The supply structure does not adapt to changes in demand, and the effective high-end supply is seriously insufficient. As a result, the phenomenon of overseas shopping continues to emerge. At the same time, many key technologies are controlled by other countries and regions. Some important raw materials, key components, high-end equipment, and high-quality agricultural products rely on imports. The supply of tourism, sports, health care services, elderly care services, and housekeeping cannot meet the needs of residents as well. This represents a significant structural imbalance in China's current economy. To address this situation, the Party Central Committee emphasized the importance of moderately expanding overall social demand while placing greater focus on structural reforms on the supply side. The goal is to improve the quality of supply, significantly boost mid-to-high-end output, better align with shifting demand patterns, and ultimately reach a new equilibrium between supply and demand. At present, a new round of scientific and technological revolution and industrial transformation is emerging around the world. Information technology, biotechnology, new material technology, and new energy technology have become deeply integrated across various sectors. Major technological innovations continue to emerge, and various new technologies and new formats, such as intelligent manufacturing and the sharing economy, keep appearing. The reindustrialization of the United States and the strategy of Industry 4.0 of Germany have emerged one after another to cope with the world's technological and industrial changes. We must seize this historical opportunity, turn it into a driving force for development, accelerate the transformation of economic development, and win the initiative.

In order to promote the supply-side structural reform, the central government has put forward major measures of scaling down overcapacity, cutting excess inventory, deleveraging, reducing costs, and making up for deficiencies. This is a major decision based on the actual situation. The priority among them is to cut overcapacity. Years of extensive expansion have accumulated a lot of backward production capacity, occupied a lot of resources, destroyed the ecology, and polluted the environment. Under the vigorous promotion of the Party Central Committee and the State Council, China has made progress in cutting overcapacity in the past two or three years, improving the supply-demand relationship in some industries. In 2016, more than 65 million tons of steel production capacity was cut, and more than 290 million tons of coal production capacity were cut as well. In 2017, the production capacity of steel and coal was cut by 50 million tons and 150 million tons, respectively, and the capacity of coal power was cut by 50 million kilowatts. An important aspect of cutting overcapacity is to resolutely deal with "zombie companies" that have long been losing money and have no hope of turning around, especially the state-owned ones that are often protected by local governments. Progress has also been made in this area, and could allow for a combination of cutting overcapacity and advancing SOE reform. The results achieved in cutting overcapacity are mainly reflected in the fact that the Producer Price Index (PPI) has turned positive since the third quarter of 2016 after 54 months of negative growth, thus creating favorable conditions for the development of industrial production. The profits of industrial enterprises have also ended ten months of negative growth. In 2017, the total profits of industrial enterprises above designated size in China increased by 21% year-on-year, 12.5 percentage points higher than the previous year.

Reducing excess inventory mainly refers to destocking real estate, especially in third- and fourth-tier cities. There has also been some progress in this regard, but it is not enough, and efforts must be continued. At the end of 2017, the area of commercial housing for sale across the country decreased by 106.16 million square meters compared with the end of 2016, and housing prices in 70 large and medium-sized cities remained stable. We must adhere to the position that housing is for living in, not for speculation, and we should implement classified regulation and city-specific policies. Centering on the goal of promoting the urbanization of 100 million agricultural migrants, China is advancing reform of the household registration system, aligning efforts to reduce excess inventory with the promotion of population urbanization. It is also necessary to strengthen the interconnection between megacities, large cities, and small and medium-sized cities, continuously improve the equalization level of basic public services such as education and medical care in small and medium-sized cities, enhance the attractiveness of small and medium-sized cities to the population, and promote the destocking of real estate in small and medium-sized cities.

Deleveraging is also a hard part, and China's overall leverage ratio has remained high in recent years. At the end of 2016, China's macro leverage ratio was 247%, of which the corporate sector leverage ratio reached 165%, much higher than the international warning line of 90%. Overcapacity industries are highly leveraged. Some state-owned enterprises have outstanding debt risks, and some "zombie companies" are reluctant to withdraw from the market and rely on increased debt to survive, which increases corporate leverage. Some local governments have also violated regulations by borrowing money for projects in various ways or by increasing leverage by purchasing services. On December 18–20, 2017, the Central Economic Work Conference put preventing and defusing major risks, especially financial risks, as the top priority of three tough battles to be focused on in the next three years for the decisive victory in building a moderately prosperous society in all respects. "The conference declares that, in accordance with the requirements of the 19th CPC National Congress, in the next three years, we will focus on the three tough battles of preventing and defusing major risks, targeted poverty alleviation, and tackling pollution for the decisive victory in building a moderately prosperous society in all respects. To fight the tough battle of preventing and defusing major risks, the key is to prevent and control financial risks. We must serve the main line of supply-side structural reform, promote the formation of a virtuous circle within the financial and real economy, finance and real estate, and financial systems, do a good job in risk prevention and disposal in key areas, resolutely crack down on illegal financial activities, and strengthen the construction of supervision system for weak links."[2]

Lowering costs refers to reducing the costs of enterprises. The state should make efforts to lower the costs of enterprises to reduce the burden on enterprises. On February 8, 2017, the executive meeting of the State Council decided to further clean up and standardize enterprise-related charges and continue to reduce the burden on the real economy. From 2013 to 2016, more than 2 trillion yuan of

---

2 Hongxia Liu. The central government has made it clear that in the next three years, it will focus on three tough battles. *Xinhuanet*, December 20, 2017.

burden has been reduced for enterprises. In 2017, the burden would continue to be reduced by 1 trillion yuan. In 2017, the government maintained its focus on alleviating the tax burden on enterprises by implementing and refining the pilot policy of "replacing business tax with value-added tax," introducing measures such as simplifying the value-added tax rate, and further cleaned up and standardized government funds and enterprise-related charges, reducing the burden on enterprises by more than 1 trillion yuan throughout the year. From January to November 2017, the cost per 100 yuan of the main business income of industrial enterprises above a designated size in China decreased by 0.28 yuan year-on-year. The Ministry of Finance proposed that, on the basis of the tax reduction and fee reduction in 2017, which had reached a scale of one trillion yuan, the policy of tax reduction and fee reduction would continue to be implemented in 2018 to further reduce the burden on enterprises. In addition, efforts should be made to reduce various transaction costs, especially institutional transaction costs, such as reducing the approval procedures, reducing the evaluation and appraisal fees of various intermediary organizations, and strengthening the supervision of charges in violation of regulations in monopoly industries and natural monopoly links. It would also continue to reduce the cost of electricity and logistics for enterprises.

It is also important to make up for deficiencies. Due to a large number of deficiencies, it is necessary to prioritize and implement the tasks gradually. In 2017, the investment in ecological protection and environmental governance, water conservancy management, and agriculture investment increased by 23.9%, 16.4%, and 16.4%, respectively, over the previous year, which was faster than the total investment growth of 16.7%, 9.2%, and 9.2%, respectively. Looking ahead, we should focus on resolving critical obstacles that impede economic and social progress, while responding to the most pressing public concerns through thoughtful planning and strong implementation. At present, the greatest shortfall lies in public welfare. Poverty alleviation remains a decisive battle: every citizen must be lifted out of poverty by the time we complete the building of a moderately prosperous society in all respects in 2020. State capital should expand its investment, while private capital should also be encouraged to enter sectors such as healthcare, education, elder care, health services, environmental protection, ecological restoration, etc. This is the most strongly reflected demand of the people. It is necessary to increase investment in research and development, strengthen education and training, continuously improve human capital, and improve weak links in infrastructure, including upgrading the grade of rural roads, so as to create favorable conditions for improving the quality of development.

The Party Central Committee and General Secretary Xi Jinping attach great importance to building a modernized economy. On January 30, 2018, shortly after the conclusion of the 19th CPC National Congress, the Political Bureau of the CPC Central Committee held a collective study session focused on the development of a modernized economy. General Secretary Xi Jinping made an important speech. He said: "The modern economy is an organic whole composed of the interrelations and internal connections of all links, levels, and fields of social and economic activities." He also proposed to build the following systems and institutions. The first priority should be given to building an innovation-led industrial structure that promotes synergy across sectors—ensuring alignment among the real economy, scientific advancement, modern financial system, and talent development. This will enable technological innovation to play an increasingly central role in driving real economic growth, enhance the capacity of finance to support industrial activities, and optimize the strategic value of human capital in economic development. The second is to build a unified and open market system with orderly competition, to achieve smooth market access, orderly market opening, sufficient market competition, and standardized market order, and to accelerate the formation of the modern market system which allows for fair competition and independent operating for enterprises, free choices and consumption for consumers, and free flow and equal exchanges for commodities and factors. The third priority is the development of an income distribution system that ensures both efficiency and fairness. The objective is to achieve a more equitable allocation of income, uphold social justice, promote shared prosperity, advance the equal provision of basic public services, and progressively reduce disparities in income distribution. The fourth is to build an urban-rural regional development system that highlights advantages, coordination, and linkage, to achieve positive regional interaction, integrated urban-rural development, and overall optimization of land and sea coordination, to cultivate and give play to regional comparative advantages, and to strengthen the complementarity of regional advantages, and shape a new pattern of regional coordinated development. The fifth is to develop an eco-friendly system grounded in resource efficiency and green growth. This entails advancing circular and low-carbon development, internalizing the view that ecological health equates to economic wealth, and fostering sustainable modernization through harmony between humanity and the natural world. The sixth is to build a diversified, balanced, safe, and efficient comprehensive opening system, develop a higher-level open economy, and promote the transformation of opening up in the direction of optimizing structure, expanding depth, and improving efficiency. The seventh is to build an economic system that gives full play to the role of the market and better plays the role of the government, so as to realize the effective market mechanism, the dynamic micro-entities, and sound macro-regulation. General Secretary Xi Jinping pointed out, "The above systems are a unified whole, and they should be built and promoted as a whole. To build a modernized economy, we must learn from the useful practices of developed countries, and more importantly, it must conform to China's national conditions and have Chinese characteristics."

4. Six Major Tasks for Building a Modernized Economy

The report of the 19th CPC National Congress not only pointed out the important significance and scientific connotation of building a modernized economy, but also clearly and systematically expounded six major tasks.

I. Deepening supply-side structural reforms

This is a strategic move to build a modernized economy. Firstly, to advance the modernization of the economy, it is essential to prioritize the real economy, concentrate on upgrading the supply system, and strengthen the economy by improving quality and efficiency. In the new era, due to the evolution of the principal contradiction, improving the quality of development and supply has become the main task of sustainable and healthy economic development. It requires vigorously developing the real economy and reversing the trend of deviating from the real to the virtual for a period of time. The virtual economy, such as finance, should really serve the real economy and continuously transfuse blood for the real economy, so that the real economy has more R&D funds, technological transformation funds, employee training funds, etc., which can help facilitate the transformation of the development mode of the real economy, and turn to innovation-driven development.

Secondly, accelerating the transformation of China into a high-quality manufacturing powerhouse is essential. This includes advancing cutting-edge manufacturing capabilities, deepening the integration of the internet, big data, and artificial intelligence with the real economy, and cultivating new engines of growth in areas such as premium consumption, innovation-led progress, green and low-carbon industries, the sharing economy, modern logistics networks, and talent-based services. Manufacturing is the backbone of the real economy. Whether a country's manufacturing industry is advanced is an important indicator of whether the country's economic strength is strong. If we want to focus on developing the real economy, we must focus on developing manufacturing, especially advanced manufacturing. In 2016, the added value of China's manufacturing industry sector accounted for approximately 21% of the country's GDP, compared with 35% to 40% in developed countries; the per capita added value was US$3,000, ranking 54th in the world, only 16.5% of the United States.

In the era of the industrial revolution led by a new generation of information technology, it is necessary to promote the integration of information technology with the real economy, and promote the development of Chinese manufacturing to Chinese innovation. Efforts should be made to accelerate the construction of an industrial system with coordinated development of the real economy, technological innovation, modern finance, and human resources. Meanwhile, we will promote the transformation and upgrading of traditional sectors, while speeding up the growth of modern service industries to align them with global benchmarks. Our goal is to push China's industrial system toward the mid-to-high tiers of the global value chain and to cultivate several world-leading clusters in advanced manufacturing. It means that the service industry, especially the modern service industry, is in a dominant position in the economic structure, which is an objective requirement for industrial transformation and upgrading, and becoming a strong manufacturing country. In 2016, the contribution rate of China's tertiary industry to GDP growth had increased to 58.2%, but it was still at a low level. At that time, the per capita output of China's manufacturing industry was only one-third of that of developed countries, mainly because the producer services of R&D, design, and branding were not developed enough. Therefore, accelerating the development of the modern service industry is precisely an important condition for the manufacturing industry to improve its technological content, and transform and upgrade.

Thirdly, it is essential to enhance foundational infrastructure systems, including those related to water resources, rail transport, road networks, waterways, aviation, pipelines, power grids, information, and logistics. Infrastructure construction is also an important aspect of developing the real economy. Some infrastructure construction, such as high-speed railways, highways, power grids, etc., is China's strength and is at the forefront of the world. At the same time, the construction of water conservancy, rural roads, etc., needs to be strengthened. In particular, the network construction of various infrastructures must be accelerated to better play the role of infrastructure in supporting the high-quality and efficient development of the economy.

Fourthly, continued actions are needed to address overcapacity, trim excess inventories, reduce financial leverage, bring down operational costs, and reinforce weak links. This goal is to achieve a flexible equilibrium between supply and demand by optimizing resource distribution and boosting the availability of quality supply. Since this topic has been covered earlier, it will not be reiterated here.

Finally, it is essential to cultivate and safeguard the spirit of entrepreneurship, motivating more market participants to pursue innovation and engage in business creation. We aim to develop a workforce that is well-educated, highly skilled, and driven by innovation. At the same time, we will promote the social value of labor by honoring exemplary workers, advocating craftsmanship excellence, and fostering a culture where diligence and pursuit of quality are widely embraced and respected. The Apple mobile phone launched by Steve Jobs in the United States has brought hundreds of billions of dollars in demand for smartphones and brought revolutionary changes to the lives of countless people, fully demonstrating the important role of entrepreneurs in social and economic development. In the era of high-quality development, the role of human capital is prominent, and higher requirements are placed on workers. It requires workers to have knowledge, understand technology, be good at innovation, have a high level of craftsmanship and professionalism, and become skilled craftsmen.

II. Making China a country of innovators

It is not only the key to building a modernized economy, but also the fundamental support for high-quality development. Firstly, innovation serves as the core engine of progress and is a critical foundation for establishing a modern economy. We must actively pursue advancements at the forefront of global science and technology, enhance investment in fundamental research, and strive for significant progress in original and pioneering innovations. Emphasis will be placed on strengthening applied basic research, initiating major national-level scientific and technological programs, and promoting breakthroughs in general-purpose technologies, frontier innovation, advanced engineering techniques, and disruptive technological fields. These actions will reinforce efforts to build China into a powerhouse in science and technology, high-quality manufacturing, aerospace, cyberspace, and transportation. They will also advance the development of a digitalized nation and an intelligent society. Additionally, we will further refine the national innovation system and increase our capacity for strategic scientific and technological advancement. Since the 18th CPC National Congress, China has intensified its pursuit of becoming an innovative-driven economy. The contribution of scientific and technological progress to GDP growth increased from 52.2% in 2012 to 56.2% in 2016 and reached 57.5% in 2017, effectively promoting industrial transformation and upgrading. In 2016, the added value of high-tech industries accounted for 12.4% of the added value of industrial enterprises above designated size, an increase of three percentage points from 2012. In 2017, the added value of the high-tech industry and the equipment manufacturing industry increased by 13.4% and 11.3% respectively over the previous year, and the growth rate was 6.8 and 4.7 percentage points faster than that of industries above a designated size. Breakthroughs have been made in the industrialization of major scientific and technological achievements such as high-speed railways, hydroelectric equipment, UHV power transmission and transformation, hybrid rice, and Beidou navigation, which continue to improve the quality and efficiency of China's economic development.

Secondly, it is essential to deepen reforms in the science and technology governance framework and establish an innovation system driven by the market, with enterprises playing a central role. This system should promote close collaboration among businesses, academic institutions, and research organizations to enhance coordinated innovation. Targeted support will be provided to encourage small and medium-sized enterprises to pursue technological innovation, while also fostering the practical application and commercialization of scientific research outcomes. To fully harness the driving force of scientific and technological innovation, it is essential to deepen reform of the science and technology management system, and to move away from a government-dominated, policy-driven model in which enterprises, universities, and research institutes operate in isolation from one another. At the same time, efforts should be made to refine the policy framework that encourages innovation within enterprises. This includes expanding the application of measures such as extra tax deductions for research and development expenditures, preferential tax treatment for high-tech firms, and faster depreciation schedules for fixed assets.

Finally, it is essential to promote an innovation-oriented culture and enhance efforts in intellectual property creation, protection, and utilization. We should focus on training a robust pool of globally competitive scientists and technologists in key strategic areas, develop leading figures in science and technology, support young scientific talents, and build high-efficiency teams dedicated to innovation. Ultimately, the competition among nations in science, technology, and economic strength is a competition for talent. China is rich in scientific and technological talents, but lacks world-class, highly talented professionals. In the future, the focus will be on strengthening the cultivation of high-end scientific and technological innovation talents. We must enhance the protection of intellectual property rights, as it serves as the most effective incentive for attracting and motivating scientific and technological talent. It is also necessary to cultivate a large number of entrepreneurial talents with global vision, innovation ability, and social responsibility, and protect the innovation income and property rights of entrepreneurs through sound legal mechanisms. We should continue to expand efforts to attract top international talent, introducing globally renowned experts such as chief scientists. It is necessary to vigorously enhance the innovation consciousness and innovation ability of the whole society, so that the whole society is full of an innovative spirit.

III. Pursuing a rural vitalization strategy

Vitalizing the countryside can be considered the most prominent practice to strengthen the areas of weakness. Firstly, agriculture is the foundation of the development of the national economy. Agriculture, rural development, and the well-being of rural populations are the bedrock of national stability and the livelihood of the people in China. These concerns must remain a top priority on the Party's agenda. Advancing agriculture and rural development should be given precedence. To realize rural revitalization characterized by prosperous industries, livable environments, cultural advancement, strong governance, and shared prosperity, it is essential to establish robust systems, mechanisms, and policy frameworks that support the integrated development of urban and rural areas, and to accelerate the modernization of agriculture and rural communities. The large gap between workers and farmers and between urban and rural areas is an important manifestation of China's long-standing unbalanced economic and social development. For over two decades, the issue of "agriculture, rural areas and rural people" has been regarded as a top priority for the Party. Following the 18th CPC National Congress, numerous supportive policies have been steadily implemented to enhance the agriculture sector. The grain production capacity has reached the level of 1.2 trillion jin (600 million metric tons). The income of farmers has grown rapidly, and the disposable income of rural residents has exceeded 1.2 trillion yuan. The gap between workers and farmers and between urban and rural areas has narrowed slightly. However, it is still necessary to continue to make efforts and adhere to the priority development of agriculture and rural areas. In 2005, the Fifth Plenary Session of the 16th CPC Central Committee put forward the strategy of building a new socialist countryside. In accordance with the will of the farmers, rural revitalization should be advanced steadily by adhering to the goal of economic development, improved livelihoods, social civility, environmental cleanliness, and domestic village governance. However, it is a pity that the results of the construction of a new socialist countryside have not been significant enough since then. The requirements for rural revitalization this time cover five items, including thriving businesses, which are higher and more comprehensive than the requirements for building a new socialist countryside before. It represents an upgraded approach to building a new socialist countryside. In actual work, to promote rural revitalization, we must give top priority to vigorously developing agricultural productive forces and improving quality and efficiency; we must uphold the integrated development of urban and rural areas, while ensuring that priority is given to agriculture and rural development; we must pay attention to follow the laws of rural development, and retain the characteristics of remote townships.

Secondly, we should strengthen and refine the fundamental operational framework in non-urban regions, push forward reforms of land-use policies in these zones, and enhance the mechanism that distinguishes between land ownership, contractual rights, usage rights, and management rights for contracted rural land. Rural land contracting practices will remain stable and unchanged on a long-term basis; the current round of contracts will be extended for another 30 years upon expiration. We will press ahead with reform of the rural collective property rights system, safeguard the property rights and interests of rural people, and strengthen the collective economy. Two reforms are particularly important here: the first is to make it clear that the second round of land contracts will be extended for another 30 years. This major decision has made the rural land contracting relationship stable for 75 years from the first round of contracting, showing the central government's firm determination to protect farmers' land rights and interests and giving farmers a "reassurance." The second is to implement the "three rights separations" of land ownership rights, contract rights, and management rights. This is a major innovation in China's rural reform, which stabilizes farmers' contract rights and activates management rights. It is also conducive to land circulation and efficient use, thereby contributing to the realization of agricultural modernization.

Thirdly, safeguarding national food security remains a top priority to ensure firm control over our food supply. We will build modern agricultural systems that encompass industry, production, and business operations, and enhance the frameworks that support and protect agricultural development. Various forms of appropriately scaled farming operations will be encouraged, alongside the cultivation of new agricultural business entities and the enhancement of specialized farming services. Small household farmers will be guided to participate in modern agricultural practices. Additionally, we will promote the integration of agriculture with secondary and tertiary sectors in rural regions, foster job creation and entrepreneurship, and expand income-generating opportunities for rural populations. Ensuring the food supply for nearly 1.4 billion people in the country has always been the top priority for national security. The tragedy of the nation's lack of food in the late 1950s and early 1960s must never happen again. Therefore, it is necessary to consolidate and improve grain production capacity, implement the strategy of ensuring food security by protecting arable land and improving technology, insist on protecting arable land, build high-standard farmland, improve the quality of grain seeds, and continuously produce more high-quality grain to meet the people's growing demand for high-quality grain. The industrial system, production system, and management system are the three pillars of modern agriculture. To gradually make these three pillars modernized, we must vigorously promote the innovation and application of agricultural science and technology, so that agriculture can achieve high-quality development. To adjust the agricultural structure, at present, we must focus on corn to promote the structural adjustment of the planting industry, focus on pig and grass-fed animal husbandry to promote the structural adjustment of the animal husbandry, and focus on the agricultural product processing industry and rural "entrepreneurship and innovation" to promote the integrated development of primary, secondary, and tertiary industries. It is also necessary to develop new industries and new formats, such as characteristic industries, leisure agriculture, green agriculture, rural tourism, rural e-commerce, etc., to increase farmers' income through multiple channels.

Finally, we must strengthen services in rural communities and improve the rural governance model, which combines self-governance, rule of law, and rule of virtue. We will train professional rural service personnel who have a good knowledge of agriculture, love our rural areas, and care about rural people. Social etiquette and civility are very important. To make people keep nostalgia in mind, effective rural governance is essential, as it plays a vital role in encouraging people to remain in the countryside and engage in agricultural activities. Modern agriculture needs people with knowledge and professionalism. Many farmers in the United States are college students who graduated from agricultural colleges. They master modern agricultural knowledge and can use modern agricultural equipment. This is an important reason why their labor productivity is dozens of times higher than that of Chinese farmers. If we want to realize agricultural modernization, we must cultivate a large number of new-type farmers with professional knowledge and understanding of modern agricultural technology.

IV. Implementing the coordinated regional development strategy

China is a big country with a vast territory, and the economic gap between different regions is relatively large. The economic development of the eastern region is relatively fast, and the western region is relatively backward. Until 2016, the per capita regional GDP of Gansu Province was less than a quarter of that of Beijing and Shanghai. The lower the level of comparison is, the greater the gap it shows. Therefore, first of all, narrowing the regional economic gap and promoting the coordinated development of the regional economy are important aspects to solve the unbalanced economic development of China. The report of the 19th CPC National Congress emphasized the need to intensify efforts to accelerate development in old revolutionary base areas, ethnic minority regions, border zones, and poverty-stricken areas. It called for strengthened initiatives to advance the large-scale development of the western region, deeper reforms to revitalize the northeast and other traditional industrial bases, support for the central region to rise by leveraging its unique strengths, and encouragement for the eastern region to lead high-quality development through innovation. To achieve these goals, new and effective mechanisms must be established to promote harmonized development across regions. Since 1999, following the CPC Central Committee's proposal to launch the strategy for the large-scale development of the western region, China gradually established a comprehensive regional development framework that includes advancing the western region, revitalizing the northeast, promoting the rise of the central region, and giving priority to the development of the eastern region. Progress has since been made in the regional coordination, especially in advancing development in the western region. For example, the regional GDP of Chongqing and Guizhou remained the country's pace-setter with double-digit growth for seven consecutive years from 2010 to 2016; since 2010, the annual growth rate of the regional GDP of other western provinces and regions has been higher than that of the national GDP. Nevertheless, former revolutionary bases, minority-inhabited areas, frontier areas, and poverty-stricken areas, mainly in the West, are still relatively poor areas in China, and they are also key areas for poverty alleviation. In the future, former revolutionary bases, minority-inhabited areas, frontier areas and impoverished areas should be given priority in the regional coordinated development strategy, and greater efforts should be made to support these areas to improve infrastructure conditions, continuously improve basic public service capabilities, cultivate and develop an economy with advantageous industries and characteristic economies, and further restore the ecology and improve the environment, so as to accelerate the advancement of former revolutionary bases, minority-inhabited regions, frontier zones and underdeveloped areas. This challenge is more prominent in the three northeastern provinces. From 2014 to 2017, the regional GDP growth rate of the three northeastern provinces was lower than the national average growth rate, and Liaoning Province even experienced negative growth in 2016, which was called the Northeast phenomenon. The main reason why the three northeastern provinces have become economically depressed is that their economic reform is lagging behind; the reform of the state-owned economy, which accounts for a large proportion, is not in place, the development of non-public economies, such as individual and private ownership, is insufficient, and the overall economic vitality is not strong. Revitalizing the old industrial bases in Northeast China has become an important task for the coordinated regional development at present.

Secondly, it is essential to establish urban and town systems centered around city clusters, promoting the integrated development of large, medium, and small cities along with small towns, while accelerating efforts to provide permanent urban residency for rural migrants. Urban agglomerations serve as key engines driving China's economic expansion. We should further advance the development of urban agglomerations in key regions, including the Yangtze River Delta, the Pearl River Delta, the Beijing-Tianjin-Hebei region, the Chengdu-Chongqing area, the middle reaches of the Yangtze River, the Central Plains, the Harbin-Changchun corridor, and the Beibu Gulf region. A central task in promoting new urbanization is to grant permanent urban residency to rural migrants. Since the 18th CPC National Congress, the CPC Central Committee had proposed that by 2020, about 100 million agricultural migrants would have been settled in cities and towns. At the end of 2016, the urbanization rate of the national houschold registration population and the permanent resident population reached 41.2% and 57.4%, respectively, an increase of 5.9 and 4.8 percentage points over the end of 2012. The urbanization rate of China's household registration population increased to 45.4% in 2020. Moving forward, we will further advance reform of the household registration system and gradually ease residency requirements

Thirdly, it is necessary to shift non-capital functions away from Beijing to better define its role as the national capital and use this effort to drive the coordinated development of the Beijing-Tianjin-Hebei region; and we will develop forward-looking plans and adopt high standards for building the Xiong'an New Area. The coordinated development of the Beijing-Tianjin-Hebei region is a major regional strategy proposed by the Party Central Committee after the 18th CPC National Congress. The core is to relieve Beijing's non-capital functions and find a way to deal with "big city disease" with Chinese characteristics. To this end, it is necessary to speed up the construction of Beijing's urban sub-center, build an integrated modern transportation network, effectively improve the environment, step up ecological conservation endeavors, optimize the industrial layout, and build a Beijing-Tianjin-Hebei coordinated development community. In spring 2017, the Party Central Committee, with Comrade Xi Jinping as the core, made the strategic decision to establish the Xiong'an New Area, aiming to promote the coordinated development across Beijing, while transferring non-essential functions away from Beijing. It is essential to uphold the principles of "world vision, international standards, Chinese characteristics, and high-point positioning." Formulate visionary planning and implement high-level standards to steadily advance the development of the Xiong'an New Area.

Fourthly, we should promote the sustainable development of the Yangtze Economic Belt through coordinated environmental measures and avoiding restrained development. This is another major regional development strategy proposed by the Party Central Committee after the 18th CPC National Congress. The Yangtze River Economic Belt is the most densely populated, industrial, and relatively developed area in China. The development of the Yangtze River Economic Belt plays an important role in China. With China transitioning to high-quality development, it is imperative that the Yangtze River Economic Belt advances without compromising ecological integrity. Rather, it is necessary to restore the ecological environment along the Yangtze River as the primary task, implement ecological restoration projects such as the Yangtze River shelterbelt system, and build ecological corridors. On the basis of the golden road, we will build a comprehensive transportation network, promote industrial upgrading and new urbanization construction, and make the upper, middle, and lower reaches of the Yangtze River develop in a coordinated manner.

Finally, Assistance will be provided to help resource-exhausted regions shift toward new economic pathways. Development in the border regions will be sped up to reinforce both stability and security. Land and ocean development will proceed in a coordinated manner, advancing China's goal of becoming a maritime power.

V. Speeding up the enhancement of the socialist market system

Firstly, in advancing our economic reforms, the focus should be on enhancing the property rights framework and guaranteeing that factors are allocated through market mechanisms, allowing property rights to serve as strong motivators. It is essential to promote the unrestricted movement of factors, maintain flexible pricing, uphold fair and orderly competition, and ensure that businesses thrive based on competitive performance. This time, particular emphasis is placed on property rights, marking a progression beyond the 2013 "Decision" of the Third Plenary Session of the 18th CPC Central Committee. The "Decision" emphasizes the improvement of the property rights protection system, while this report emphasizes the improvement of the entire property rights system, that is, to improve the modern property rights system with clear-cut ascription, clearly defined rights and responsibilities, strict protection, and smooth transfer. A well-established modern system of property rights is the cornerstone underpinning the socialist market economic framework. To improve the socialist market economic system, we must first improve the modern property rights system in order to achieve effective incentives for property rights. The concept of market-based factor allocation underscores the market's decisive function in allocating resources. This is consistent with the 2013 "Decision" of the Third Plenary Session of the 18th CPC Central Committee, which calls for advancing economic reforms centered on the market's dominant role in resource allocation.

Secondly, we need to enhance the management frameworks for various types of state-owned assets and reform the authorized operation system of state capital. Within the state-owned sector, efforts will be intensified to improve distribution, adjust structures, and carry out strategic reorganization. Our goal is to preserve and increase the value of state assets; to strengthen, improve, and expand state capital; and to implement effective measures to prevent asset loss. Further reforms of state-owned enterprises will be promoted, mixed-ownership economic entities will be developed, and Chinese companies will be transformed into world-class, globally competitive firms. Reforming state-owned enterprises remains the paramount and most demanding undertaking within China's reform agenda. After the 18th CPC National Congress, there has been considerable progress in the reform of state-owned enterprises, such as the development of a mixed-ownership economy, the development of employee stock ownership in mixed-ownership enterprises, the promotion of the reform of the management remuneration system of state-owned enterprises, the acceleration of the pace of asset restructuring, the initiation of the pilot program for state-owned capital investment and operation companies, and the completion of the corporate reform of central SOEs by the end of 2017, etc. Of course, everyone still hopes that the reform of state-owned enterprises will be faster and more effective. The report of the 19th CPC National Congress proposes that it is very important and innovative to promote state-owned capital to become stronger, better, and bigger. In 1999, when the Party Central Committee drafted the "Decision of the Central Committee of the Communist Party of China on Several Major Issues Concerning the Reform and Development of State-owned Enterprises" at the Fourth Plenary Session of the 15th CPC Central Committee, it was discussed and realized that since there were hundreds of thousands of state-owned enterprises, it was impossible to make every state-owned enterprise do everything well, and we must focus on improving the entire state-owned economy. State-owned enterprises are expected to operate according to the survival-of-the fittest principle. Only a small number of "zombie companies" that have been losing money for a long time and have no hope of turning around are going to withdraw from the market. At the same time, there are some public welfare and welfare units in the state-owned economy, and their main task is to provide good services. They are not necessarily required to become stronger, better, and bigger. It is a great progress to replace the development of the state-owned economy as a whole with developing stronger, better, and bigger state-owned capital.

Thirdly, it is essential to implement a nationwide list for market access, thoroughly review, and eliminate rules and practices that hinder the development of a unified and competitive market. Efforts should be made to foster the development of the private sector and energize all types of market entities. Reforms in the business environment must be deepened, administrative monopolies dismantled, and market monopolies effectively prevented. We should accelerate the reform of factor pricing through market mechanisms, further open up the service industry, and enhance regulatory systems to ensure fair, transparent, and efficient market supervision. In the Party's documents, "private business" is a new term, and the "Decision" of the Third Plenary Session of the 18th Central Committee of the Party still used the term of non-public economy. The formulation of private businesses is relatively straightforward and practical. Many of the above measures are conducive to encouraging and facilitating the growth of private enterprises, among which precluding the formation of market monopolies was first proposed in an important document of the Party. These measures were introduced in response to a significant slowdown in private fixed asset investment in 2016, which grew by only 3.2% over the previous year, while the annual growth rate of general private investment reached double digits or nearly double digits (10.1% in 2015). The proportion of Capital input by private enterprises into fixed assets (excluding rural households) in the whole society in 2016 also dropped from 64.2% in the previous year to 61.2%. In 2017, the growth rate of private investment was 6%, showing an increase in the growth rate, but the proportion further dropped to 60.4%. The report of the 19th CPC National Congress proposed that "we will inspire and protect entrepreneurship, and encourage more entities to make innovations and start businesses." The entrepreneurs mentioned here, of course, include private entrepreneurs. Since the launch of reform and opening up, practice has proved that the development of private enterprises has been indispensable in sustaining economic growth, fostering innovation, expanding employment, and enhancing fiscal revenues. The private economy and the state-owned economy have their own advantages, and each has its own broad space for development. The advancement of the country does not necessarily mean that the people will fall behind, and the advancement of the people does not necessarily mean that the country will lag behind. We must strive to achieve common development of the country and the people.

Fourthly, we should modernize macro-regulation by strengthening the strategic alignment of national development plans and improving the coordination of financial, industrial, regional, and other macroeconomic policies for synergy. We will improve systems and mechanisms for stimulating consumer spending and leverage the fundamental role of consumption in promoting economic growth. We will deepen reform of the investment and financing systems, and enable investment to play a crucial role in improving the supply structure. Contrasted with the "Decision" of the Third Plenary Session of the 18th CPC Central Committee, in the coordination of fiscal and monetary policy measures in the macro-control system, the report of the 19th CPC National Congress no longer mentions the price policy, and at the same time adds the regional policy. We believe it is for this reason that price reforms have progressed rapidly in recent years. By the end of 2016, Market forces were setting the prices for more than 97% of goods and services. Government-set prices accounted for less than 3%, primarily covering key public utilities, essential public services, and segments of natural monopolies involving network-based infrastructure. Consequently, the use of price-based policy instruments in macro-control has become increasingly limited. It is necessary to add regional policies. Given China's vast size, advancing the coordinated growth of regional economies is integral to optimizing broader structural frameworks. One of the key objectives of macroeconomic regulation is to improve the alignment of major economic structures and enhance the spatial distribution of productive forces. The proposition of the system and mechanism to improve and promote consumption this time is a highlight. Over the years, an important aspect of China's economic structural imbalance has been the low consumption rate, especially the proportion of household consumption expenditure in GDP, which is seriously low. The proportion of household consumption expenditure in GDP in 2008–2011was 36.1%, 36.2%, 35.6%, and 36.3% respectively. After the 18th CPC National Congress, this proportion has gradually increased, reaching 36.7% in 2012, 36.8% in 2013, 37.5% in 2014, 38% 2015, and 39.2% in 2016. The proportion of GDP growth has also driven by final consumption spending, from 44.2% in 2008 to 58.8% in 2017. The total retail sales of consumer goods increased from 21.4 trillion yuan in 2012 to 33.2 trillion yuan in 2016 and 37 trillion yuan in 2017. Consumption has been the primary driver of economic growth for four consecutive years. The rapid increase in household consumption expenditure is closely linked to the fact that, in recent years, household income has slightly outpaced GDP growth. It reflects a striking feature of China's economy entering a new normal. General Secretary Xi Jinping said in the report of the 19th CPC National Congress that the Party would always take the people's yearning for a better life as its goal. Therefore, continuously improving the people's consumption level and quality is the goal of China's development of the socialist market economy. Starting from this requirement, we must see that the current proportion of consumption expenditure is still relatively low, and the proportion of consumption expenditure to GDP in many countries in the world is above 70%. The report of the 19th CPC National Congress proposed to "foster new growth areas and drivers of growth in medium-high end consumption, innovation-driven development, the green and low-carbon economy, the sharing economy, modern supply chains, and human capital services." It seems that in the future, medium-high-end consumption will become a new economic growth point to be cultivated. Specifically, brand consumption, information consumption, service consumption, and cultural consumption will receive more policy support, which will lead to rapid development. Supply-side structural reform emphasizes the quality and efficiency of economic development and advancing toward the medium-high end of the value chain. This is aimed at better meeting the growing demands of consumers and fully reflects the new development philosophy of shared prosperity.

Fifthly, efforts must be accelerated to build an advanced fiscal framework. This entails building a fiscal framework between central and local authorities characterized by clearly delineated duties, a balanced distribution of financial resources, and enhanced fairness across regions. A comprehensive, rule-based, and transparent budget management system should be developed, guided by well-designed standards and reinforced by effective constraints. Nationwide implementation of performance-based budgeting will be promoted. In addition, tax system reforms will be deepened, with a particular focus on improving the structure and effectiveness of local taxation. Public finance can and should play a more important role in adjusting the structure and changing the way. Constructing a contemporary economic framework to advance sustainable and quality-driven growth requires strong financial support and active guidance of fiscal policies. Therefore, establishing a modern fiscal and taxation system is both very important and arduous. For example, these are all challenging tasks, including improving the central fiscal transfer payment system, developing a unified and prudent system for managing debt and monitoring financial risks across central and local authorities, enhancing the local tax system, increasing the share of direct taxes, introducing a hybrid personal income tax framework that integrates overall income sources and category-based approaches, and advancing real estate tax reform, etc.

Sixthly, further institutional reforms in finance are needed to enhance support for the real economy, increase direct-financing channels, and nurture a robust multi-tier capital market. A policy mix centered on momentary tools and macro-prudential measures will be improved, with interest and exchange rates increasingly determined by the market. A stronger regulatory architecture is required to prevent system risks, making the introduction of the two-pillar approach especially significant. Monetary policy has traditionally prioritized price stability, and there has long been debate over whether it should also address fluctuations within the valuation of assets. Ahead of the eruption of the 2008 worldwide financial turmoil, consumer prices in the United States remained relatively stable. However, financial stability was not maintained, as asset prices, particularly in the financial sector-soared dramatically. After the outbreak of the crisis, everyone has reflected that: to promote a stable and resilient financial infrastructure, the monetary policy, which only focuses on prices, is not enough, and macro-prudential policies are also required. During the National Financial Work Conference convened on July 14–15, 2017, policymakers proposed the adoption of a two-pillar regulatory framework to strengthen financial governance. According to the official of the relevant department, the so-called macro-prudential framework mainly includes three aspects: First, in 2011, the dynamic reserve requirement adjustment mechanism was officially implemented, mandating that financial institutions align the scale of their business operations with the level of available funding.; in 2016, the mechanism for dynamically adjusting differentiated reserve requirements was further developed into a comprehensive macro-prudential assessment framework, which expanded regulatory coverage to a broader range offinancial activities and institutions, enhancing the system's counter-cyclical capabilities. Additionally, cross-border capital movements were included under the scope of macro-prudential supervision to help maintain the stability of international capital flows. Furthermore, oversight of the real estate sector was intensified through macro-prudential tools, focusing on building a regulatory framework for housing finance that emphasizes city-specific measures and targeted credit policies based on local housing market conditions.

By doing well in the above-mentioned reforms, this will enable us to establish an economic framework that features efficient market mechanisms, vibrant micro-level actors, and appropriate macro-level regulation, thereby steadily boosting the innovation capacity and overall competitiveness of China's economy.

VI. Breaking new ground in advancing comprehensive opening up.

A very important point put forward in the report of the 19th CPC National Congress is to insist on promoting the building of a community with a shared future for mankind. China's opening up to the outside world should be guided by this, and China will always be a builder of world peace, a contributor to global development, and a defender of the international order. First of all, openness leads to progress, while isolation results in falling behind. China will never shut itself off from the world; instead, it will continue to deepen its openness. Prioritizing the Belt and Road Initiative, China aims to balance attracting foreign investment and expanding overseas presence, adhering to the principle of mutual growth through dialogue and cooperation. Efforts will focus on enhancing openness and collaboration to boost innovation capacity. Through these measures, China seeks to pioneer new paths in connecting east and west, by land and sea, further advancing its openness. Since the 18th CPC National Congress, the Party Central Committee, led by Comrade Xi Jinping, has formulated a comprehensive strategic blueprint, promoted the theoretical and practical innovation of opening up, implemented the Belt and Road Initiative, expedited the building of a new open economic system, promoted the growth of a globally integrated economy, and taken an active role in international economic governance, resulting in significant new accomplishments in opening up. We must adhere to a better combination of "bringing in" and "going global." It can effectively expand the space for national economic development. Balancing the development of coastal openness with inland border opening can enhance the regional opening-up strategy and optimize its spatial arrangement. The degree of opening up of the inland and borders to the outside world is relatively low. As of 2016, the western region had 72% of China's land area, 27% of the population, and 20% of the country's economic aggregate, while foreign trade accounted for only 7% of the country's total, and the utilization of foreign capital and outbound investment accounted for 7.6% and 7.7% of the country's total. With the advancement of the *Belt and Road Initiative*, the pace of opening up in the western region to the outside world should be accelerated, from an open depression to a highland. We must aim toward a better combination of opening up in the manufacturing sector and opening up in the service sector, and promote deep-level structural adjustment with high-level opening up. While further deepening the openness of the manufacturing industry, it is also essential to intensify efforts to promote the gradual and well-regulated opening of service sectors such as finance, education, culture, and healthcare. Limitations on foreign investment should be eased in sectors including childcare and elderly care, architectural design, accounting, and auditing, as well as trade and logistics. It is also necessary to adhere to a better combination of opening to developed economies and opening to developing economies, and expand the convergence of interests with other countries. Developed economies are China's main economic and trade partners. In 2016, the trade with the United States, the European Union, and Japan accounted for 36.4% of China's total foreign trade. At the same time, China's economic and trade relations with developing economies have become increasingly close. From 2014 to 2016, China's import and export volume to countries along the "Belt and Road" reached US$3.1 trillion, accounting for more than a quarter of the total foreign trade in the same period; direct investment in countries along the routes was nearly US$50 billion, accounting for about one tenth of the total outbound direct investment during the same period. Looking ahead, in accordance with the requirements of the report of the 19th CPC National Congress, we will insist on opening up to developed countries and developing countries equally, and realize the diversification of export markets, import sources, and investment partners. We must adhere to a better combination of multilateral opening and regional opening, and become the builder and contributor of an open world economy.

Secondly, we need to broaden foreign trade, foster innovative trade models and formats, and transform China into a high-quality trading nation. Politics will be enacted to advance high-standard trade and investment liberalization and facilitation. The pre-establishment national treatment system, combined with a negative list, will be fully implemented, greatly easing market access, further opening up the service sector, and safeguarding the legitimate rights and interests of foreign investors. Equal treatment will be guaranteed for enterprises registered in China. It is also necessary to speed up the transformation of the development mode of foreign trade, from focusing on trade in goods to the coordinated development of trade in goods and services, from relying on imitation and following to relying on innovation and creation, and from large imports and large exports to high-quality and high-price imports and exports. To this end, it is necessary to speed up the optimization and upgrading of trade in goods, promote the innovative development of trade in services, foster new forms and models of trade, support the healthy development of cross-border e-commerce, market procurement trade, and comprehensive foreign trade services, and implement more active import policies. We should improve the foreign investment environment. To cultivate a competitive advantage in attracting investment, the most important thing is to create a business environment that shows stability, fairness, transparency, the rule of law, and predictability, in particular, to improve the foreign investment management system. The trial implementation of the pre-establishment national treatment, plus a negative list management system in 11 free trade zones in China, has achieved remarkable results. The time required to set up a foreign-funded enterprise has been reduced from the past one month to about three days. The Chinese government will give equal treatment to domestic and foreign-funded enterprises following the law in terms of qualification licensing, standard setting, government procurement, and enjoyment of the "Made in China 2025" policy.

Thirdly, we need to enhance the equilibrium of opening across various regions and further broaden the openness of the western region. It is essential to promote development through opening up, improve infrastructure for opening up, such as harbors and international transit, implement more flexible policies, and build open platforms like free trade zones, national development zones, border economic cooperation zones, and cross-border economic cooperation zones. We will create a number of regional hub cities, support the opening up of characteristic industries, and form a number of new growth poles of an open economy in the western region. Greater authority should be granted to pilot free trade zones to carry out reforms, alongside efforts to explore the establishment of free trade ports like Hong Kong, Singapore, Rotterdam, and Dubai.

Finally, we need to explore innovative approaches to outbound investment, enhance international collaboration in production capacity, establish global networks spanning trade, investment, financing, production, and services, and strengthen our capabilities for global economic cooperation and competition. From 2007 to 2016, the average annual growth rate of China's outbound investment was 27.2%. China has emerged as a leading nation in outbound investment. In 2016, China recorded outbound direct investment totaling US$170.1 billion, while its actual utilization of foreign capital amounted to US$126 billion. China has thus become a net capital outflow country. However, China's outbound investment is still in its primary stage, and the ability to utilize two markets (domestic and foreign markets) and two resources (domestic and foreign resources) is not strong. Problems such as irrational investment and non-standard operation are relatively prominent, and some of them still harbor considerable risks. It is necessary to encourage global collaboration in production capacity development and promote the global expansion of China's equipment, technology, standards, and services. It is crucial to enhance supervision and guidance over overseas mergers and acquisitions, standardize overseas business operations, guide enterprises to abide by the laws and regulations of host countries, protect the environment, fulfill social responsibilities, and curb vicious competition. It is also necessary to improve service guarantees, strengthen and improve information, legal, consular protection, and other services to ensure personnel safety and safeguard overseas interests.

References

Communist Party of China Central Committee. *Decision of the Central Committee of the Communist Party of China on several major issues concerning comprehensively deepening the Reform*. November 12, 2013.

Communist Party of China Central Committee. *Suggestions of the Central Committee of the Communist Party of China on formulating the eleventh Five-Year Plan for national economic and social development.* October 11, 2005.

Deng, Xiaoping. *Selected Works of Deng Xiaoping.* Volume 3. Beijing: People's Publishing House, 1993.

Jiang, Zemin. Building a moderately prosperous society in all respects and creating a new situation for the cause of socialism with Chinese characteristics. November 8, 2002.

The writing team of this book. *The guidebook for the report of the 19th National Congress of the Communist Party of China.* Beijing: People's Publishing House, 2017.

Xi, Jinping. Decisive victory in building a moderately prosperous society in all respects and win the great victory of socialism with Chinese characteristics in the new era. October 18, 2017.

Xi, Jinping. Deeply understand the importance of building a modern economic system, and promote China's economic development to rejuvenate and enter a new stage. *People's Daily*, February 1, 2018.

Efforts to Construct a Political Economy of Socialism with Chinese Characteristics

Since the convening of the 18th National Congress of the Communist Party of China in 2012, General Secretary Xi Jinping has put forward the historic mission of developing a political economy in the Chinese context. In a sequence of significant addresses, he has offered profound insights into the establishment and refinement of such a theoretical system. As a result, the development of socialist political economics suited to China's national circumstances has become a central topic of research and discussion within Chinese academic and policy circles. A wide range of valuable ideas and perspectives have been proposed, along with a number of important issues that warrant further exploration. This book aims to contribute to this ongoing dialogue by offering several reflections on how to further improve the construction of socialist political economy with Chinese characteristics, and to invite further engagement from scholars and practitioners in the field of economics.

1. The Political Economy of Socialism with Chinese Characteristics: A Significant Component and Deepening Development of the Theoretical System of Socialism with Chinese Characteristics

On November 25, 2015, during the 28th collective study session of the Political Bureau of the CPC Central Committee, General Secretary Xi Jinping stressed that the development of contemporary Chinese Marxist political economy must be rooted in China's national realities and informed by its development practice. Subsequently, on July 8, 2016, while presiding over a symposium with economic experts on the national economic situation, he further stressed that in order to maintain and advance the development of socialist political economy with

Chinese characteristics, it is essential to take Marxist political economy as the guiding framework. At the same time, it is imperative to systematically synthesize and polish the valuable experiences accumulated in the course of China's reform and opening up and socialist modernization, while also selectively drawing on relevant elements of Western economics. A political economy with Chinese characteristics must not only be enriched and developed through practice, but also withstand the test of practice in order to effectively guide it. It is necessary to strengthen research and exploration, strengthen the summary of understanding of regularity, constantly improve the theoretical system of socialist political economics with Chinese characteristics, and promote the construction of economic disciplines that fully reflect Chinese characteristics, Chinese style, and Chinese manner.

Contemporary Chinese Marxist political economy is a socialist political economy with Chinese characteristics. Following Deng Xiaoping's first formulation of socialism with Chinese characteristics at the 12th CPC National Congress (1982), the project has flourished under the leadership of the Party, achieving remarkable and transformative results. As reform and opening up continue to deepen, alongside the rapid advancement of economic and social development, the understanding we hold toward socialism with Chinese characteristics—particularly its political economy—has continued to evolve and expand. Notably, the process of China's reform and opening up was set in motion by implementing economic system reforms, with its opening to the outside world starting with the setting up of special economic zones and the introduction of foreign investment. The initiatives have consistently prioritized economic reform, leading to the most practical and rich experiences. As a result, within the theoretical edifice of socialism with Chinese characteristics, economic theory stands out as the most conspicuous and systematic component. The economic theory of socialism with Chinese characteristics is considered the "pearl" of the whole theoretical system.

The Third Plenary Session of the 12th CPC Central Committee, convened in October 1984, approved the "Decision on Reform of the Economic Structure," which first put forward the idea that China's socialist economy was a planned commodity economy centered on public ownership. This marked the first significant theoretical leap following reform and opening up. Shortly after, Deng Xiaoping addressed the Third Plenary Session of the Central Advisory Commission of the CPC, where he further elaborated on these ideas. "Take, for example, the 'Decision on Reform of the Economic Structure.' When the decision was adopted by the Central Committee the day before yesterday, I made a few remarks. I said I thought it read like the draft of a textbook on political economy that integrated the fundamental tenets of Marxism with the practice of socialism in China.

That was my assessment of it."[1] In 1997, General Secretary Jiang Zemin, in his report to the 15th CPC National Congress, stated that *Deng Xiaoping Theory* had developed the theoretical system of socialism with Chinese characteristics: "To sum up, *Deng Xiaoping Theory* constitutes a new, scientific system of the theory of building socialism with Chinese characteristics." "For the first time, it has given preliminary but systematic answers to a series of basic questions concerning the road to socialism in China, the stages of development, the fundamental tasks, the motive force, the external conditions, the political guarantee, the strategic steps, Party leadership, the forces to be relied on, and the reunification of the motherland. It has guided our Party in formulating the basic line for the primary stage of socialism. It is a fairly complete scientific system which embraces philosophy, political economics and scientific socialism and covers, among other things, the economy, politics, science and technology, education, culture, military and foreign affairs, the united front and Party building. It is also a scientific system which needs to be further enriched and developed in all aspects." The year 2007 witnessed Hu Jintao highlighting in the report to the 17th CPC National Congress that, "To sum up, the fundamental reason behind all our achievements and progress since reform and opening-up policy was introduced is that we have blazed a path of socialism with Chinese characteristics and established a system of theories of socialism with Chinese characteristics. Essentially, to hold high the great banner of socialism with Chinese characteristics means to keep to this path and uphold this system." The report provided a reliable explanation of both the course of socialism with Chinese characteristics and its theoretical structure. In 2011, Hu Jintao incorporated the idea of the "socialist system with Chinese characteristics" into his address at the commemoration of the 90th anniversary of the establishment of the Communist Party of China, saying: "We have embarked on the path of socialism with Chinese characteristics, formed a system of theories of socialism with Chinese characteristics and established a socialist system with Chinese characteristics. These achievements made over 90 years of endeavors, innovation, and enrichment, should be valued, upheld on a long-term basis and continuously built upon by our Party and people." Since then, a unified framework encompassing the banner, the path, and the theoretical system has been established.

Since the convening of the 18th CPC National Congress, as reform and opening up were further deepened and advanced, socialism with Chinese characteristics achieved significant new progress in both theory and practice. A sequence of new

---

1 Xiaoping Deng. *Selected Works of Deng Xiaoping. Volume 3.* Beijing: People's Publishing House, 1993, p. 83.

ideas, plans, and strategies was introduced, including the "five-sphere integrated plan," "four-pronged comprehensive strategy," the "three Initiatives," the shift of China's economy toward a new normal, the five development concepts, as well as supply-side structural reform, among others. Apart from the banner, path, institution, and theoretical system of socialism with Chinese characteristics, socialist culture with Chinese characteristics has been incorporated. Moreover, China has been actively engaged in and contributed to the improvement of global economic and financial governance, advocated the building of a community with a shared future for mankind, and has been playing an ever more influential international role.

On May 17, 2017, in the complimentary letter marking the 40th anniversary of the Chinese Academy of Social Sciences, General Secretary Xi Jinping reiterated his hope that the academy's comrades and the broader community of philosophy and social science workers would make fresh and greater contributions to the development of the disciplinary, academic, and discourse systems of philosophy and social sciences with Chinese characteristics, thereby enhancing the international influence of China's philosophy and social sciences. This also includes the task of constructing contemporary Chinese Marxist political economics, specifically, socialist political economics with Chinese characteristics. This is not only a crucial step in enriching and developing the theoretical system of socialism with Chinese characteristics, but also a significant responsibility assigned to Chinese scholars in the field of economics. And it is playing a vital role in promoting the study of the Marxist political economics of contemporary China. To conduct research on the political economics of socialism with Chinese characteristics, it is essential to thoroughly understand the actual situation of China's socialist modernization, the progress of its reform and opening up, and the growth of China's socialist market economy. This involves exploring their underlying patterns and summarizing them theoretically, with the aim of facilitating the smooth and healthy advancement of China's socialist modernization efforts.

2. The Mature Political Economy of Socialism with Chinese Characteristics: A Derivation from the Mature Economic Institutions and Systems of Socialism with Chinese Characteristics

Up to now, there has not emerged a piece of work on socialist political economy or socialist market economics with Chinese characteristics that has gained wide recognition. However, we think that this situation is not primarily because Chinese economists have not made enough efforts. The crucial factor lies in the fact that under China's socialist economic system with Chinese characteristics, the level of productive forces remains insufficiently high. Modernization has yet to be completely achieved, and the economic system has not reached a state of full maturity and finalization. It is well known that when Marx wrote *Capital*, he exposed the regularities of capitalist production and its inevitable transition to socialism. A major reason he chose to write in London was that the United Kingdom had a relatively advanced level of capitalist economic development and a mature economic system during that period. It has been over 40 years since China launched the reform and opening up at the end of 1978. The socialist market economy has witnessed rapid growth. It has not only addressed the basic food and clothing needs of the people but also enabled the achievement of a moderately prosperous society by the end of the twentieth century. By 2020, China successfully built a moderately prosperous society in all respects and has been continuously moving forward toward modernization. Nevertheless, as of 2017, China has not yet joined the ranks of high-income countries, and the full realization of modernization still awaits in the future.

Meanwhile, the socialist market economic system has been firmly established and is undergoing continuous improvement. The basic framework of this system, which is supported by the five pillars outlined by the Third Plenary Session of the 14th CPC Central Committee in 1993, has been set up. However, it is not yet fully mature or finalized. In 1992, Deng Xiaoping, in his Southern Talks, predicted that, "It will probably take another thirty years for us to develop a more mature and well-defined system in every field. The principles and policies to be applied under each system will also be more firmly established." Thirty years have passed since Deng Xiaoping made this prediction. In 2013, the "Decision" of the Third Plenary Session of the 18th CPC Central Committee also stipulated: "By 2020, decisive results will have been achieved in the reform of important areas and crucial segments. The reform tasks put forward in this 'Decision' are to be completed within this period, and institutions and systems that are structurally complete, scientifically standardized and effective in operation are to be formed, to ensure that institutions in all areas become more mature and complete." Pursuant to the principles enshrined in the "Decision" of the Third Plenary Session of the 18th CPC Central Committee, the critical domains and pivotal junctures in economic reform demanding decisive outcomes are systematically articulated below, organized to highlight policy priorities and structural transformations: State-owned assets regulatory bodies must affect a functional pivot to prioritize capital management, transitioning from operational oversight to strategic asset governance. Central SOEs, particularly group holding companies, are mandated to establish and refine modern corporate governance frameworks, aligning with international standards of enterprise management. Boards of directors in state-owned holding companies shall exercise decision-making power over major affairs as stipulated by *the Company Law*, enhancing corporate autonomy and accountability. We must eradicate ownership-based discrimination to foster the healthy development of the non-public economy, ensuring equitable market access for all entities. It is necessary to implement an investment and market access negative list system, dismantle administrative barriers, combat monopolistic practices, and cultivate a level playing field for fair competition. Key initiatives include: Separating farmers' land contractual rights from management rights to develop a standardized land use rights transfer market. Strengthening macroeconomic control mechanisms to preempt systemic risks, integrating fiscal, monetary, and industrial policy tools. Progressively institute a comprehensive tiered individual income tax system. Expedite legislation on real estate taxes, promote legal reforms, and increase the proportion of direct taxes to optimize fiscal structure. Expand private banking initiatives and enhance financial market infrastructure. Advance market-driven exchange rate formation and ensure RMB capital account convertibility, aligning with global financial norms. Furthermore, we must work to expand the middle-income group, reduce the Gini coefficient, and address wealth disparity through targeted policy adjustments. Optimize social insurance relationship, transfer mechanisms, and strengthen the basic pension insurance personal account system to enhance social security sustainability. Construct a new open economic system by expanding institutional opening up, integrating domestic and international markets, and fostering global competitiveness. These "deep-water zone" reforms are inherently arduous, requiring sustained commitment. Given that China has not yet achieved full modernization and the socialist economic system with Chinese characteristics remains incomplete and immature, it is difficult to generalize and discuss the development and operational laws of the socialist economy with Chinese characteristics comprehensively and systematically.

However, passivity and inaction are not viable options. Over the four decades since the launch of reform and opening up, alongside rapid economic growth and overall social advancement, a series of theoretical achievements have emerged that integrate Marxist economic principles with the practice of reform and opening up. These include the theory of socialist market economy; the theory of primary stage of socialism; the theory of the basic economic system in the primary stage of socialism; the distribution theory, which emphasizes that distribution according to work is dominant, with multiple forms of distribution coexisting; theory of incremental reform from the start of rural reform to the comprehensive deepening of reforms; the tripartite separation of rural land ownership, farmers' land contract rights, and farmland management rights; the theory of promoting social fairness and justice to gradually achieve common prosperity for all people; the evolutionary trajectory of development theories, from the absolute primacy of development to the *Scientific Outlook on Development,* and further to the new development philosophy of innovation, coordination, green development, openness, and sharing; the theory of economic transformation and the shift from traditional growth models to quality oriented development patterns; the theory of China's economy entering a new normal; the theory of coordinating new-type industrialization, informatization, urbanization, and agricultural modernization; and the theory of opening up to the outside world, including the strategy of leveraging both domestic and international markets and resources to foster dual circulation. We must carefully and thoroughly conduct meticulous and in-depth studies of these theoretical systems to clarify their scientific connotations and practical significance. It is essential to continuously sum up new experiences from tackling tough reform challenges, building a moderately prosperous society in all respects, and constructing a modern economic system. We should undertake fresh theoretical generalizations to shape a mature economic theory system that aligns with China's fundamentally modernized economic institutions. Going forward, we must proactively advance systematic and profound research on the political economy of socialism with Chinese characteristics, striving for continuous breakthroughs in theoretical innovation to underpin national development strategies.

In the discourse on accelerating the development of socialist political economy with Chinese characteristics, some economists have proposed a disciplinary orientation: in terms of production relations, it belongs to the political economy of the primary stage of socialism; in terms of productive forces development, China has transcended the low-income stage and entered the middle-income stage based on per capita GDP. Thus, they argue that the political economy of socialism with Chinese characteristics can be classified as the political economy of socialism in the middle-income development stage.[2] This formulation, however, warrants further deliberation. As is well-known, China embarked on the path of socialism with Chinese characteristics following the reform and opening-up policy in 1978. At that time, China's per capita GNI stood at merely US$190, placing the country in a low-income bracket. The reform and opening-up drive significantly liberated social productive forces, unleashing rapid economic growth. According to World Bank standards, China entered the lower-middle-income category in 1999, with its per capita GDP nearing US$800 (in 1999, the World Bank defined

[2] Yinxing Hong. Promoting the construction of the theoretical system of socialist political economics with Chinese characteristics. *Chinese Social Sciences Today*, May 5, 2017.

the lower-middle-income threshold as a per capita GNP exceeding US$756, and China's per capita GNP that year was US$780). In 2009, China advanced to the upper-middle-income group. In 2017, China's per capita GDP approached US$9,000, but it was still a long way from the ranks of high-income countries (As per the World Bank's 2014 criteria, a country is classified as high-income when its per capita GDP reaches US$12,616). Since China began its journey along the path of socialism with Chinese characteristics in 1978—at a time when the country was still in the low-income stage—the stage-based understanding of socialist political economy with Chinese characteristics should have a lineage dating to the launch of reform and opening up, rather than being confined to 1999, the year China officially entered the middle-income category. Furthermore, the middle-income stage is merely a transitional phase. By 2020, China had successfully established a moderately prosperous society in all respects. Based on current projections, with another five to six years of sustained effort, China is expected to join the ranks of high-income countries. However, this milestone alone is insufficient. The ultimate target of China's socialist development is to achieve full socialist modernization and transform the country into a great modern socialist nation that is prosperous, strong, democratic, culturally advanced, harmonious, and beautiful.

From the 14th to the 19th CPC National Congress, China has proposed and continually refined the "two centenaries goals" —a foundational strategic framework for national development. Specifically: the first, to build a moderately prosperous society in all respects by the 100th anniversary of the CPC's founding (2021); and the second, to achieve full socialist modernization by the 100th anniversary of the People's Republic of China's founding (2049). The report of the 19th CPC National Congress (2017) points out: "The period between the 19th and the 20th National Congress is the period in which the timeframes of the two centenary goals converge. In this period, not only must we finish building a moderately prosperous society in all respects and achieve the first centenary goal; we must also build on this achievement to embark on a new journey toward the second centenary goal of fully building a modern socialist country. Based on a comprehensive analysis of the international and domestic environments and the conditions for China's development, we have drawn up a two-stage development plan for the period from 2020 to the middle of this century. In the first stage from 2020 to 2035, we will build on the foundation created by the moderately prosperous society with a further 15 years of hard work to see that socialist modernization is basically realized … In the second stage from 2035 to the middle of the twenty-first century, we will, building on having basically achieved modernization, work hard for a further 15 years and develop China into a great modern socialist country that is prosperous, strong, democratic, culturally advanced, harmonious, and beautiful." The report of the 19th CPC National Congress, in turn, outlines the strategic task of constructing a modern economic system, emphasizing that "China's economy has been transitioning from a phase of rapid growth to a stage of high-quality development. This is a pivotal stage for transforming our growth model, improving our economic structure, and fostering new drivers of growth. It is imperative that we develop a modernized economy. This is both an urgent requirement for getting us smoothly through this critical transition and a strategic goal for China's development." Therefore, the political economy of socialism with Chinese characteristics is fundamentally oriented toward studying and addressing a series of epoch-making questions: How has China transitioned from a low-income nation to a socialist society with distinct Chinese characteristics through reform and opening up? How can it continuously overcome the "low-income trap" and "middle-income trap," join the ranks of high-income countries, and gradually realize modernization? The ultimate goal is to build a great modern socialist country that is prosperous, strong, democratic, culturally advanced, harmonious, and beautiful, thus achieving the great rejuvenation of the Chinese nation. Understanding the inherent regularities and inevitability of this process can also provide valuable references for many developing countries. As a result, the stage-oriented positioning of this discipline should span a long historical period—encompassing at least the timeline from the launch of reform and opening up in 1978 to the establishment of a great modern socialist country—endowing it with extremely rich content.

Based on this, we believe that a "mature economy" should not only involve a finalized and mature socialist market economic system, but also reflect certain achievements in the maturity degree of productive forces. The strategic trajectory includes: Successfully surmounting the "middle-income trap," steadily joining the ranks of high-income economies, and then gradually achieving socialist modernization. This necessitates the full success of comprehensive economic transformation, encompassing both the reform of the economic system and the shift of the economic development model. Without a comprehensive and systematic accumulation of successful experiences in economic transformation, it would be arduous to fully summarize the laws governing socialist construction with Chinese characteristics. Once China completes its economic transformation, avoids the "middle-income trap," and realizes socialist modernization, its economic might will reach new heights, and its capacity to engage in global governance will be significantly enhanced.

However, it does not mean that efforts to build the political economy of socialism with Chinese characteristics are currently absent. Over the 40 years since the launch of reform and opening up, China's economy has ascended to become the world's second largest, amassing a profound reservoir of successful experiences in building a socialist economy with Chinese characteristics. On this foundation, a sequence of significant theoretical achievements has been developed. As General Secretary Xi Jinping stressed during the 28th collective study session of the Political Bureau of the CPC Central Committee, "Since the Third Plenary Session of the 11th Central Committee of the Communist Party of China, our Party has combined the basic principles of Marxist political economics with the new practice of reform and opening up, constantly enriched and developed Marxist political economics, and formed many important theoretical achievements of contemporary Chinese Marxist political economics, such as the theory about the nature of socialism, the theory of the basic economic system in the primary stage of socialism, the theory of establishing and implementing the development philosophy featuring innovative, coordinated, green, open and shared development, the theory of developing the socialist market economy, the theory of making the market play a decisive role in resource allocation and better playing the role of the government, the theory of China's economic development entering a new normal, the theory of promoting the coordination of new industrialization, informatization, urbanization and agricultural modernization, the theory of making good use of both domestic and international markets and resources, the theory of promoting social fairness and justice, and the gradual realization of common prosperity for all people, etc. These theoretical achievements are political economics adapted to contemporary China's national conditions and the characteristics of the times. They have not only effectively guided the practice of China's economic development, but also opened up a new realm of Marxist political economics."[3] It is evident that we are now in a critical phase of establishing the foundational framework of socialist political economy with Chinese characteristics. The mission is both glorious and weighty, demanding our utmost dedication and rigorous effort.

3. Identifying the Central Thread of the Political Economy of Socialism with Chinese Characteristics

Socialist political economy with Chinese characteristics represents both a new academic discipline and a distinct theoretical framework. What are the central thread or foundational pillars of this new framework? This is the fundamental

---

3 Jinping Xi. To develop contemporary Chinese Marxist political economics based on China's national conditions and development practice. *People's Daily Online*, November 25, 2015.

task we have to solve and identify when researching and building this new framework. The central thread generally refers to the core clue that weaves through the entire theoretical structure. It defines the system's key categories and underlying principles, thereby shaping its unique identity and elevating it beyond existing theoretical paradigms. In *Capital*, Karl Marx established the main line of classical political economy as the analysis of how capital exploits labor and appropriates surplus value. In the early 1960s, Sun Yefang, a prominent economist of his generation, spearheaded the writing of *On Socialist Economics* and proposed adopting the structure used by Marx in *Capital*. This involved analyzing economic relations through the interconnected process of direct production, circulation, and the overall reproduction of the capitalist system. He also suggested using the principle of "minimum and maximum" — that is, "achieving the maximum useful effect with the minimum labor consumption" —as the central thread of the book. Moreover, he advocated for fully utilizing the labor-based value principle to regulate both production and distribution. At the time, Sun Yefang's ideas represented a forward-thinking and valuable attempt to innovate within the limitations inherent in the traditional planned economy. Today, as we work to develop a political economy framework for socialism with Chinese characteristics, determining its central theme or guiding principle remains a critical issue that demands collective reflection and rigorous academic discussion. Here, we offer our preliminary thoughts.

We believe the theory of socialist market economy serves as the cornerstone of socialist political economy with Chinese characteristics. Its central theme should be the integration of socialism with the market-based economy—specifically, the integration of public ownership with market mechanisms. Since the initiation of reform and opening up, market forces have been gradually introduced into China's economic framework. In 1984, the theoretical framework of a socialist commodity-based economy was established. The year 1992 marked the formal adoption of the socialist market economy as the guiding target of China's economic reform. As market-oriented reforms steadily progressed, China's economy experienced fast-paced development. From 1979 to 2016, the average rate of growth per year reached 9.6%, setting a new global benchmark for sustained rapid economic growth. Practice has proven that developing a socialist market economy tailored to China's specific national circumstances is both correct and effective. In this framework, the theory of socialist market economy has emerged as the fundamental pillar underpinning socialist political economy with Chinese characteristics. At its core, this theory emphasizes the integration of socialism with a market-based economy. Consequently, the fusion of socialist principles with market mechanisms—particularly the integration of public ownership and the market economy—has naturally become the main thread running through socialist political economy with Chinese characteristics.

Our perspective is grounded in historical context. On December 7, 2008, Zhang Zhuoyuan, one of the co-authors of this book, contributed a comprehensive analysis for *Guangming Daily*, titled "On the socialist market economy: the main theoretical pillar of China's reform and opening up." He said, "China's development of a market economy under socialist conditions is an unprecedented great initiative and a brand-new project. The theory of socialist market economy, summarized on the basis of successful practice, is a major theoretical innovation of scientific socialism by Chinese Communists and Marxist economists, and it is also an epoch-making contribution to economic science." The establishment of a socialist economy with Chinese characteristics fundamentally centers on the development of a socialist market economy. Consequently, the theory of the socialist market economy naturally holds the most important critical position within socialist political economy with Chinese characteristics.

The meaning and scope of socialist market economy theory have continuously evolved alongside the deepening of reform. At the 1992 14th CPC National Congress, the goal was established to reform the socialist market economic system. It emphasized "allowing the market to play a fundamental role in resource allocation under the macro-control of socialist countries." A decade later, in 2002, the 16th CPC National Congress called for giving fuller play to the market's basic role in resource allocation and building a unified, open, competitive, and orderly modern market system. By 2012, the 18th CPC National Congress further stressed expanding and deepening the market's basic role in resource allocation. Then, in 2013, the Third Plenary Session of the 18th CPC Central Committee elevated the market's function from a fundamental to a pivotal role, underscoring that the market should decisively guide allocating resources while the government enhances its regulatory oversight. Zhang Zhuoyuan, one of the authors of this book, argued in a book published in 2014 (*A New Journey of Economic Reform*, published by Social Sciences Academic Press, China) that the pivotal role of the market in allocating resources builds upon and advances the basic function that has been practiced for over two decades. It involves three key aspects: first, addressing the issue of excessive state interference in resource allocation; second, rectifying the imperfections in the market framework to establish a just and competitive market environment; and third, eliminating discriminatory regulations against the non-state-owned economy, including removing invisible barriers and other related obstacles.

A central challenge in the theoretical discussion of the viability of the socialist market economy hinges on the possibility of reconciling public ownership with market principles. Capitalist economic theory traditionally argues that under socialist conditions, the development of a market economy faces significant obstacles. However, China's experience since the launch of reform and opening up has disproved this claim. Through reform, China has developed sustainable public ownership structures—such as joint-stock and mixed ownership systems—that enable the integration of public ownership, including state-owned assets, into the framework of the market economy. State-owned enterprises, transformed into modern corporations through state holdings or equity participation, now operate under independent management and self-financing, becoming genuine market players. They actively compete both domestically and internationally, continuously striving to grow and strengthen through equitable market competition. Since the launch of reform and opening up, China has witnessed remarkable economic growth, driven by the simultaneous development of both state-owned and non-public sectors. This practical success has provided a strong response to the theoretical question of whether socialism can coexist with a market economy.

In a socialist market economy, the integration of public ownership with market mechanisms is both contingent upon specific institutional conditions and characterized by a process of mutual adaptation. On one hand, public ownership must adopt realizable forms—such as the shareholding system—that make it compatible with the market economy. Because the system is based on shareholding, the market economy cannot be dominated solely by public ownership; rather, it should feature the coexistence and coordinated development of diverse ownership forms, including individual, private, and foreign-invested sectors. At the same time, the market economy development must align with the socialist goal of promoting common prosperity in a gradual and inclusive manner, avoiding the extreme wealth gaps and polarization typical of capitalist economies. The government's policies aim to leverage socialism's strengths in ensuring fairness and justice while harnessing the market economy's ability to improve the efficiency of resource allocation. Of course, it is a very difficult task. For example, how to properly handle the relationship between the government and the market, so that the market can serve a pivotal function in allocating resources, and at the same time the government can better perform its responsibilities, is a difficult project. Another example can be found in 1993, when the Third Plenary Session of the 14th CPC Central Committee set the goal of transforming SOEs by building a modern corporate structure. Over the following two decades, significant progress was made in corporatizing SOEs and introducing shareholding mechanisms. However, efforts to fully implement the modern enterprise system remained incomplete. As of 2017, many centrally administered SOEs still faced the task of deepening reforms in ownership structure and governance frameworks.

In certain state-controlled corporations, boards of directors had yet to fully carry out their responsibilities in accordance with the Company Law. Meanwhile, a fair, competitive environment between public and non-public entities remained underdeveloped. Furthermore, guiding the socialist market economy toward the long-term objective of common prosperity poses an even greater institutional challenge. Addressing this requires continuous improvement of the fundamental economic structure, in which public ownership retains a leading position while various ownership types coexist and evolve in parallel. Simultaneously, it is crucial to optimize the distribution mechanism—anchored in labor-based allocation and supplemented by multiple complementary modes. Redistributive fiscal and taxation policies should also be strengthened to promote more inclusive sharing of development benefits. In addition, foundational social policy functions, such as targeted and integrated poverty reduction strategies, must continue to be refined and expanded.

It can be seen from the above that the integration of socialist principles with market-oriented mechanisms—particularly the alignment of public ownership with market operations—constitutes the central axis of the development of the socialist market economy and permeates every dimension of its structure and function. This dynamic integration has played a vital role in driving the progressive refinement and institutional maturation of China's market system with socialist characteristics. Simultaneously, it has served as a catalyst for sustained socioeconomic advancement. Consequently, in the theoretical construction of socialist political economy with Chinese characteristics, it is imperative to regard this dual integration—as both ideological foundation and structural mechanism—as a guiding thread. Doing so enables the formation of a coherent and logically consistent theoretical framework, characterized by systematic organization and internal unity.

Recently, a number of economists have contributed scholarly articles asserting that the core orientation of research in China's socialist political economy lies in the effective integration and coherence between the foundational socialist economic system and market-based mechanisms. According to their view, adhering to the reform trajectory of the socialist market economy not only constitutes a key principle in shaping China's broader reform and development agenda but also serves as a central pillar in defining the theoretical identity of this economic discipline with Chinese characteristics. These perspectives align closely with our own understanding.

At the same time, differing opinions have also emerged in academic discussions. Some scholars argue that the primary concern of China's socialist political economy should be the liberation, advancement, and safeguarding of productive capacity. From this perspective, constructing a theoretical framework entails formulating an economic system that prioritizes the continuous enhancement of productive potential.[4] However, we contend that this viewpoint does not fully reflect the distinctive nature of China's socialist political economy, especially in contrast to the classical socialist model. Historically, the traditional socialist system—characterized by public ownership, centralized planning, and distribution based on labor—proved effective, particularly in its early stages, at mobilizing resources to meet strategic national goals and spurring economic progress. As a result, conventional socialist economic thought has long underscored the role of socialism in unleashing and expanding productive capabilities. Yet it is important to recognize that earlier social formations—including slavery, feudalism, and capitalism—also fostered productivity growth during their respective ascendancies. This explains why many Western mainstream economists continue to argue that capitalism promotes productive development. What truly differentiates China's approach is its effort to advance a market-oriented economy within a socialist institutional framework—anchored by public ownership—while leveraging the advantages of both systems to support long-term economic vitality. This model uniquely integrates reform, openness, and market principles under the broader umbrella of socialism. Indeed, as Jiang Zemin emphasized in his address to the 15th CPC National Congress, the construction of a socialist economy with Chinese characteristics involves developing a market economy compatible with socialism and persistently unlocking productive forces. Thus, the most salient feature that distinguishes this model from earlier socialist paradigms is its embrace of the socialist market economy as a dynamic and evolving mechanism. In conclusion, identifying a coherent and persuasive main thread, central theme, and core categories of socialist political economics with Chinese characteristics remains a significant subject requiring further in-depth exploration and academic dialogue. The perspectives presented above merely reflect our preliminary thoughts on the matter.

4. Exploring the Fundamental Economic Laws Underlying Socialism with Chinese Characteristics

In the 1950s, the foundational economic laws of traditional socialist political economics were articulated by Joseph Stalin in his book *Economic Problems of Socialism in the USSR*, that is, "the essential features and requirements of the

4 Yinxing Hong. Promoting the construction of the theoretical system of socialist political economy with Chinese characteristics. *Chinese Social Sciences Today*, May 5, 2017.

basic law of socialism might be formulated roughly in this way: the securing of the maximum satisfaction of the constantly rising material and cultural requirements of the whole society through the continuous expansion and perfection of socialist production on the basis of higher techniques"[5]. One of the major shortcomings of the economic model that prevailed in socialist countries for decades was its inability to evolve the underlying structures of production relations and institutional arrangements. This rigid paradigm, heavily influenced by ideological orthodoxy, led many nations—most notably the Soviet Union—to develop an excessive confidence in the assumed superiority of the socialist framework. Consequently, they overlooked the necessity of systemic reform and failed to make timely adjustments to economic mechanisms and production structures in response to changing technological and productive conditions. This lack of adaptability hampered long-term innovation and scientific advancement. As a result, strategies aimed at fostering continuous economic growth through technological modernization proved ineffective. Additionally, these economic systems struggled to satisfy the population's rising material and cultural expectations, thereby preventing socialism from realizing its full potential. Beginning in the late 1950s, economic momentum across the Soviet bloc slowed markedly, marked by declining efficiency and stagnating innovation. These persistent structural issues played a central role in the eventual disintegration of the Soviet Union in 1991 and the far-reaching political transformations across Eastern Europe between 1989 and 1992.

What, then, constitutes the fundamental laws governing the socialist market economy with Chinese characteristics? This question represents a novel challenge in economic theory. From our perspective, since the socialist market economy fundamentally operates as a variant of the broader market economy, its underlying principles must correspond with the general laws that regulate market-based systems. Among these, the law of value is widely recognized as the foundational law, as Friedrich Engels stated in *Anti-Dühring*: "The law of value is the basic law of commodity production."[6] Commodity production, commodity economy, and market economy can all be classified within the same broad category. Within the context of socialized production, a commodity economy fundamentally operates as a form of market economy. Consequently, the law of value—which governs commodity-based economies—constitutes the central regulatory principle of the market economy. In this framework, the law of value functions as the essential

5 Stalin. *Selected Works of Stalin (1934–1952)*. Beijing: People's Publishing House, 1962, p. 602.

6 Marx and Engels. *The Complete Works of Marx and Engels: Volume 20*. Beijing: People's Publishing House, 1971, p. 337.

mechanism overseeing social production and exchange, while the market assumes a decisive role in the distribution of resources. Marx's comprehensive examination of the law of value in Capital continues to serve as the foundational basis for understanding this concept. We interpret the law of value to mean that a commodity's value is determined by the socially necessary labor time embedded within it, and that its market price is governed by this value, fluctuating around it accordingly. Producers with a high technical level and high quality of laborers will consume less labor than socially necessary labor for the production of commodities, so they will enjoy a favorable position within the competitive marketplace. Conversely, without meeting these conditions, market participants will find themselves at a disadvantage—or may even be forced out of the market altogether. The mechanism of the law of value operates as follows: when a particular commodity is in short supply, its price rises. This price increase incentivizes producers and sellers to expand supply while discouraging demand. Over time, this leads to an oversupply, causing prices to fall. The lower prices then prompt producers to cut back on supply while encouraging greater consumption. As a result, prices rise again, and the cycle repeats itself. This continuous adjustment ensures equilibrium between supply and demand, as well as between production and consumption. The operation of the law of value is intrinsically linked to the broader market mechanism, encompassing price signals, supply-demand interactions, and competitive forces. It exerts both pressure and motivation on all market participants, compelling them to optimize their actions—seeking advantages and avoiding disadvantages. In this way, scarce resources are naturally directed toward the most efficient uses, thereby driving production and contributing to overall economic growth and wealth creation.

It is worth noting that the idea that "the law of value is the basic law of the socialist economy" was proposed in the 1950s and 1960s by the esteemed Chinese economist Sun Yefang. In 1956, he published an article titled "Placing planning and statistical work on the basis of the law of value" in the sixth issue of *Economic Research Journal*. Later, in a 1964 theoretical symposium, he explicitly stated: "There may be a thousand laws, ten thousand laws, but the first is the law of value."[7] After the launch of reform and opening up, this viewpoint continued to gain traction. In 1979, Deng Liqun also echoed this idea, stating: "Some comrades believe that the formulation of doing things according to the laws of economy should be concrete, mainly in accordance with the laws of commodity economy and the law of value. Management system, economic policies and planning work

---

7 Yefang Sun. The law of value always comes first no matter how many laws there are. *Some Theoretical Issues of the Socialist Economy*. Beijing: People's Publishing House, 1979.

should be done in accordance with the laws of commodity economy … I agree with this opinion."[8] Whether one states that the law of value holds a primary position or emphasizes the necessity of acting in accordance with it, both perspectives essentially regard the law of value as the fundamental economic principle.

However, it is equally important to acknowledge that the law of value can have adverse effects on economic and social development. Its inherent "survival of the fittest" dynamic tends to exacerbate income inequality and social polarization, whereby wealth accumulates with the rich while the poor become increasingly marginalized. Such disparities generate social tensions and conflicts that may undermine societal stability. When Marx and Engels discussed the operation of the law of value within capitalist systems, they notably referenced the classical bourgeois economist Adam Smith to articulate its effects: "A relation which hovers over the earth like the fate of the ancients, and with invisible hand allots fortune and misfortune to men."[9] Driven by the law of value, manufacturers engage in intense competition to increase production and secure greater market share. However, when market demand and purchasing power fail to keep pace with the rising supply, it can trigger recurring cycles of economic crisis. The competitive forces propelled by the law of value may give rise to monopolistic structures, which subsequently stifle competition, hinder technological progress, and diminish overall economic dynamism. Additionally, the law of value does not adequately account for externalities generated by economic activities. Consequently, even highly developed capitalist nations implement a range of fiscal, monetary, and social interventions to varying degrees, seeking to counterbalance the adverse impacts of the law of value's "invisible hand" on both the economy and society. However, these measures have yet not been able to fundamentally resolve the persistent issues, including recurring economic and financial crises that challenge nations worldwide.

Fundamental economic principles must also align with the underlying objectives of social production. Capitalism has never been able to escape recurring economic crises largely because its market economy is driven by the pursuit of maximum profit. This relentless profit-seeking often leads to production capacity outstripping the purchasing power of society, while under capitalism, a significant portion of the working population continues to experience poverty as a result of capital's exploitative dynamics. The socialist market economy adopts a

---

[8] Liqun Deng. *The Laws and Plans of Commodity Economy*. Beijing: People's Publishing House, 1979, p. 25.

[9] Marx and Engels. *The Complete Works of Marx and Engels: Volume 3*. Beijing: People's Publishing House, 1960, p. 39.

fundamentally different orientation—one that centers on serving the people. Its aim is to ensure that the fruits of production, reform, and progress are equitably distributed among all members of society. This people-oriented development philosophy was underscored by Hu Jintao in his report to the 17th CPC National Congress, where he put forward the concept of "shared development": "Serving the people wholeheartedly is the fundamental purpose of the Party, and its every endeavor is for the well-being of the people. We must always make sure that the aim and outcome of all the work of the Party and the state is to realize, safeguard and expand the fundamental interests of the overwhelming majority of the people. We must respect the principal position of the people in the country's political life, give play to their creativity, protect their rights and interests, take the path of prosperity for all and promote their all-round development, to ensure that development is for the people, by the people and with the people sharing in its fruits." General Secretary Xi Jinping further elevated the notion of sharing by including it as one of the five major development concepts. In his report to the 19th CPC National Congress, he reaffirmed, "The wellbeing of the people is the fundamental goal of development. We must do more to improve the lives and address the concerns of the people, and use development to strengthen areas of weakness and promote social fairness and justice. We should make steady progress in ensuring people's access to childcare, education, employment, medical services, elderly care, housing, and social assistance. We will intensify poverty alleviation, see that all our people have a greater sense of fulfillment as they contribute to and gain from development, and continue to promote well-rounded human development and common prosperity for everyone."

The above shows that under the conditions of the socialist market economy, both the law of value and the principle of equitable benefit distribution play central roles. In addition to market-driven dynamics, the law governing the fair sharing of development outcomes—rooted in socialist ideals of equity and justice—also holds significant influence. This principle can be viewed as a fundamental economic law of the socialist market economy: the law of sharing the fruits of development. It underscores the notion that the gains from economic and social progress should be broadly distributed among all citizens, with the ultimate objective of gradually realizing common prosperity. By aligning production with the well-being of the people, it fundamentally avoids the capitalist dilemma of overproduction and its resulting crises. In practice, the sharing of development outcomes operates on two levels. First, in terms of primary distribution, income should be allocated based on labor and additional factors of production, balancing both efficiency and social justice. Second, redistribution should be enhanced through fiscal transfer payments, progressive taxation, poverty alleviation programs, an improved social security system, and targeted social assistance. Greater attention should be directed toward ensuring equity in the redistribution process, aiming to reduce income and wealth disparities and gradually lower the Gini coefficient to approximately 0.3. Stronger government intervention in redistribution is required—using the "visible hand" to address the limitations of the "invisible hand" of the market. In the context of the socialist market economy, the "visible hand," which embodies the principle of shared development, is not an arbitrary intervention but rather an inherent requirement arising from the socialist system and the dominance of public ownership. As such, economic policymaking in socialist countries must simultaneously uphold both the law of value and the law of shared development.

The proposition that these two laws are foundational to the socialist market economy aligns logically with the central tenet of socialist political economy with Chinese characteristics—that is, the integration of socialism with the market economy. The principle of sharing development outcomes embodies the socialist nature of the economy, while the law of value reflects its market-oriented aspect. Together, these two guiding principles work in tandem to shape the direction and dynamics of the socialist market economy.

Within this system, the law of value and the principle of sharing development outcomes do not operate as isolated or parallel mechanisms; Instead, they are closely interconnected and mutually reinforcing. Neither holds a superior position—both jointly govern the functioning and evolution of the socialist market economy. When government policies and the actions of market participants align with these fundamental economic laws, the socialist market economy can function effectively, allowing its distinctive advantages to be fully leveraged. Conversely, when behavior deviates from these objective laws, setbacks and failures are likely to occur. That said, understanding and adapting to these laws—like all aspects of economic development—is a process that involves ongoing exploration and, at times, trial and error. Constantly accumulating practical experience and deepening understanding of objective economic laws, especially basic economic laws, will enable people to gradually move to a better place with ease.

References

Deng, Xiaoping. *Selected Works of Deng Xiaoping: Volume 3*. Beijing: People's Publishing House, 1993.

Hu, Jintao. To hold high the great banner of socialism with Chinese characteristics and strive for a new victory in building a moderately prosperous society in all respects. October 15, 2007.

Hu, Jintao. Speech at the celebration of the 90th anniversary of the founding of the Communist Party of China. *People's Daily*, July 1, 2011.

Jiang, Zemin. To hold high the great banner of Deng Xiaoping Theory, and comprehensively push the cause of building socialism with Chinese characteristics to the twenty-first century. September 12, 1997.

Liu, Wei. Constructing socialist political economy with Chinese characteristics in new practice. *People's Daily*, August 1, 2016.

Marx & Engels. *The Complete Works of Marx and Engels: Volume 23.* Beijing: People's Publishing House, 1972.

Marx & Engels. *The Complete Works of Marx and Engels: Volume 20.* Beijing: People's Publishing House, 1971.

Xi, Jinping. To win a decisive victory in building a moderately prosperous society in all respects and win the great victory of socialism with Chinese characteristics in the new era. October 18, 2017.

Zhang, Zhuoyuan, et al. *Outline of the History of Economics in New China (1949–2011).* Beijing: China Social Sciences Press, 2011.

Zhang, Zhuoyuan. Realizing the Organic Combination of Socialism and Market Economy—Constructing the main line of Socialist Political Economics with Chinese Characteristics. *People's Daily*, November 21, 2016.

Afterword

This book is written to commemorate the 40-year journey of China's reform and opening up. Over the past four decades, the policy has brought earth-shaking changes to China's social and economic development, making China leap from a poor and backward country to the second-largest economy in the world. It marks one of the most remarkable chapters in the history of the Chinese nation's 5,000-year civilization. At present, China is making rapid progress toward a great modern country and making more and more outstanding contributions to world economic growth!

The writing of this book has been encouraged and supported by Liu Jing, President of the Economic Branch of China Renmin University Press, and editor Wang Hanxia. Special thanks go to them!

The authors of each chapter in this book are: Zhang Zhuoyuan, Chapters 1, 2, 9, and 10; Hu Jiayong, Chapters 4, 5, and 8; Wan Jun, Chapters 3, 6, and 7.

Due to the deficiencies and incomplete places in this book, criticism is welcome!

—Zhang Zhuoyuan
June 2018

Translators' Postscript

This translation work is supported by the National Social Science Fund of China (Grant No. 21WJLB003).

My acknowledgment and gratitude go to Gao Yan and Liu Yehua for encouragement and support to apply this project. I would also thank my colleagues Prof. Ye Linxiang, Prof. Zhang Li, Associate Prof. Yao Qingtie from School of Economics, Dr. Hu Yang, Dr. Zhang Xiaotian from School of Foreign Languages, Ms. Qu Xiaobing, Ms. Zhai Xiaoting, Ms. Zhu Shanshan from Office of International Cooperation and Exchanges, and Mr. Zhang Jie from College of International Education for their help in preparing the translation samples.

Special thanks go to Qu Xiaobing for proofreading the whole book, and Dr. James Felicity from the University of Leicester for helping polish the language.

—Sun Yongbin
October 2022

www.ingramcontent.com/pod-product-compliance
Ingram Content Group UK Ltd.
Pitfield, Milton Keynes, MK11 3LW, UK
UKHW021835100926
8556IPUK00004B/359

9 783034 359757